THE SECRET DOCTRINE.

THE
SECRET DOCTRINE:

THE SYNTHESIS

OF

SCIENCE RELIGION, AND PHILOSOPHY

BY

H. P. BLAVATSKY,

AUTHOR OF "ISIS UNVEILED."

SATYÂT NÂSTI PARO DHARMAH.

"There is no Religion higher than Truth."

VOLUME III.

LONDON & BENARES:
THE THEOSOPHICAL PUBLISHING SOCIETY.

CHICAGO:
THEOSOPHICAL BOOK CONCERN, 26, VAN BUREN STREET

1897.

Reprinted 1910.

As for what thou hearest others say, who persuade the many that the soul when once freed from the body neither suffers . . . evil nor is conscious, I know that thou art better grounded in the doctrines received by us from our ancestors and in the sacred orgies of Dionysus than to believe them; for the mystic symbols are well known to us who belong to the Brotherhood.

PLUTARCH.

The problem of life is man. Magic, or rather Wisdom, is the evolved knowledge of the potencies of man's interior being, which forces are divine emanations, as intuition is the perception of their origin, and initiation our induction into that knowledge. . . . We begin with instinct; the end is omniscience.

A. WILDER.

TABLE OF CONTENTS.

SECTION I.

SECTION II.

SECTION III.

SECTION IV.

SECTION V.

SECTION VI.

SECTION VII.

SECTION VIII.

SECTION IX.

SECTION X.

SECTION XI.

SECTION XII.

SECTION XIII.

SECTION XIV.

SECTION XV.

SECTION XVI.

SECTION XVII.

SECTION XVIII.

SECTION XIX.

SECTION XX.

SECTION XXI.

SECTION XXII.

SECTION XXIII.

SECTION XXIV.

SECTION XXV.

SECTION XXVI.

SECTION XXVII.

SECTION XXVIII.

SECTION XXIX.

SECTION XXX.

SECTION XXXI.

SECTION XXXII.

SECTION XXXIII.

SECTION XXXIV.

SECTION XXXV.

SECTION XXXVI.

SECTION XXXVII.

SECTION XXXVIII.

SECTION XXXIX.

SECTION XL.

SECTION XLI.

SECTION XLII.

SECTION XLIII.

SECTION XLIV.

SECTION XLV.

SECTION XLVI.

SECTION XLVII.

SECTION XLVIII.

SECTION XLIX.

SECTION L.

SECTION LI.

SOME PAPERS ON THE BEARING OF OCCULT PHILOSOPHY ON LIFE.

PREFACE.

The task of preparing this volume for the press has been a difficult and anxious one, and it is necessary to state clearly what has been done. The papers given to me by H. P. B. were quite unarranged, and had no obvious order: I have, therefore, taken each paper as a separate Section, and have arranged them as sequentially as possible. With the exception of the correction of grammatical errors and the elimination of obviously un-English idioms, the papers are as H. P. B. left them, save as otherwise marked. In a few cases I have filled in a gap, but any such addition is enclosed within square brackets, so as to be distinguished from the text. In "The Mystery of Buddha" a further difficulty arose; some of the Sections had been written four or five times over, each version containing some sentences that were not in the others; I have pieced these versions together, taking the fullest as basis, and inserting therein everything added in any other versions. It is, however, with some hesitation that I have included these Sections in the *Secret Doctrine*. Together with some most suggestive thought, they contain very numerous errors of fact, and many statements based on exoteric writings, not on esoteric knowledge. They were given into my hands to publish, as part of the Third Volume of the *Secret Doctrine*, and I therefore do not feel justified in coming between the author and the public, either by altering the statements, to make them consistent with fact, or by suppressing the Sections. She says she is acting entirely on her own authority, and it will be obvious to any instructed reader that she makes—possibly deliberately—many statements so confused that they are mere blinds, and other statements—probably inadvertently—that are nothing more than the exoteric misunderstandings of esoteric truths. The reader must here, as everywhere, use his own judgment, but feeling bound to publish these Sections, I cannot let them go to the public without a warning that much in them is certainly erroneous. Doubtless, had the author herself issued this book, she would have entirely re-written the whole of this division; as it was, it seemed best to give all she had said in the different copies, and to leave it in its rather unfinished state, for students will best like to have what she said as she said it, even though they may have to study it more closely than would have been the case had she remained to finish her work.

The quotations made have been as far as possible found, and correct references given; in this most laborious work a whole band of earnest and painstaking students, under the guidance of Mrs. Cooper-Oakley, have been my willing assistants. Without their aid it would not have been possible to give the references, as often a whole book had to be searched through, in order to find a paragraph of a few lines.

This volume completes the papers left by H. P. B., with the exception of a few scattered articles that yet remain and that will be published in her own magazine *Lucifer*. Her pupils are well aware that few will be found in the present generation to do justice to the occult knowledge of H. P. B. and to her magnificent sweep of thought, but as she can wait to future generations for the justification of her greatness as a teacher, so can her pupils afford to wait for the justification of their trust.

ANNIE BESANT.

INTRODUCTORY.

"POWER belongs to him who knows;" this is a very old axiom. Knowledge—the first step to which is the power of comprehending the truth, of discerning the real from the false—is for those only who, having freed themselves from every prejudice and conquered their human conceit and selfishness, are ready to accept every and any truth, once it is demonstrated to them. Of such there are very few. The majority judge of a work according to the respective prejudices of its critics, who are guided in their turn by the popularity or unpopularity of the author, rather than by its own faults or merits. Outside the Theosophical circle, therefore, the present volume is certain to receive at the hands of the general public a still colder welcome than its two predecessors have met with. In our day no statement can hope for a fair trial, or even hearing, unless its arguments run on the line of legitimate and accepted enquiry, remaining strictly within the boundaries of official Science or orthodox Theology.

Our age is a paradoxical anomaly. It is preëminently materialistic and as preëminently pietistic. Our literature, our modern thought and progress, so called, both run on these two parallel lines, so incongruously dissimilar and yet both so popular and so very orthodox, each in its own way. He who presumes to draw a third line, as a hyphen of reconciliation between the two, has to be fully prepared for the worst. He will have his work mangled by reviewers, mocked by the sycophants of Science and Church, misquoted by his opponents, and rejected even by the pious lending libraries. The absurd misconceptions, in so-called cultured circles of society, of the ancient Wisdom-Religion (Bodhism) after the admirably clear and scientifically-presented explanations in *Esoteric Buddhism*, are a good proof in point. They might have served as a caution even to those Theosophists who, hardened in an almost life-long struggle in the service of their Cause, are neither timid with their pen, nor in the least appalled by dogmatic assumption and scientific authority. Yet, do what Theosophical writers may, neither Materialism nor doctrinal pietism will ever give their Philosophy a fair hearing. Their doctrines will be systematically rejected, and their theories denied a place even in the ranks of those scientific ephemera, the ever-shifting "working hypotheses" of our day. To the advocate of the "animalistic" theory, our cosmogenetical and anthropogenetical teachings are "fairy-tales" at best. For to those who would shirk any moral responsibility, it seems certainly more convenient to accept descent from a common simian ancestor and see a brother in a dumb, tailless baboon, than to acknowledge the fatherhood of Pitris, the "Sons of God," and to have to recognise as a brother a starveling from the slums.

"Hold back!" shout in their turn the pietists. "You will never make of respectable church-going Christians Esoteric Buddhists!"

Nor are we, in truth, in any way anxious to attempt the metamorphosis. But this cannot, nor shall it, prevent Theosophists from saying what they have to say, especially to those who, in opposing to our doctrine Modern Science, do so not for her own fair sake, but only to ensure the success of their private hobbies and personal glorification. If we cannot prove many of our points, no more can they; yet we may show how, instead of giving historical and scientific facts—for the edification of those who, knowing less than they, look to Scientists to do their thinking and form their opinions—the efforts of most of our scholars seem solely directed to killing ancient facts, or distorting them into props to support their own special views. This will be done in no spirit of malice or even criticism, as the writer readily admits that most of those she finds fault with stand immeasurably higher in learning than herself. But great scholarship does not preclude bias and prejudice, nor is it a safeguard against self-conceit, but rather the reverse. Moreover, it is but in the legitimate defence of our own statements, *i.e.*, the vindication of Ancient Wisdom and its great truths, that we mean to take our "great authorities" to task.

Indeed, unless the precaution of answering beforehand certain objections to the fundamental propositions in the present work be adopted—objections which are certain to be made on the authority of this, that, or another scholar concerning the Esoteric character of all the archaic and ancient works on Philosophy—our statements will be once more contradicted and even discredited. One of the main points in this Volume is to indicate in the works of the old Âryan, Greek, and other Philosophers of note, as well as in all the world-scriptures, the presence of a strong Esoteric allegory and symbolism. Another of the objects is to prove that the key of interpretation, as furnished by the Eastern Hindu-Buddhistic canon of Occultism—fitting as well the Christian Gospels as it does archaic Egyptian, Greek, Chaldæan, Persian, and even Hebrew-Mosaic Books—must have been one common to all the nations, however divergent may have been their respective methods and exoteric "blinds." These claims are vehemently denied by some of the foremost scholars of our day. In his Edinburgh Lectures, Prof. Max Müller discarded this fundamental statement of the Theosophists by pointing to the Hindu Shâstras and Pandits, who know nothing of such Esotericism.* The learned Sanskrit scholar stated in so many words that there was no hidden meaning, no Esoteric element or "blinds," either in the *Purânas* or the *Upanishads*. Considering that the word "Upanishad" means, when translated, the "Secret Doctrine," the assertion is, to say the least, extraordinary. Sir M. Monier Williams again holds the same view with regard to Buddhism. To hear him is to regard Gautama, the Buddha, as an enemy of every pretence to Esoteric teachings. He himself never taught them! All such "pretences" to Occult learning and "magic powers" are due to the later Arhats, the subsequent followers of the "Light of Asia"! Prof. B. Jowett, again, as contemptuously passes the sponge over the "absurd" interpretations of Plato's *Timæus* and the Mosaic Books by the Neoplatonists. There is not a breath of the Oriental (Gnostic) spirit of Mysticism in Plato's *Dialogues*, the Regius Professor of Greek tells us, nor any approach to Science, either. Finally, to cap the climax, Prof. Sayce, the Assyriologist, although he does not deny the actual presence, in the Assyrian tablets and cuneiform literature, of a hidden meaning—

> Many of the sacred texts . . . so written as to be intelligible only to the initiated—

yet insists that the "keys and glosses" thereof are now in the hands of the Assyriologists. The modern scholars, he affirms, have in their possession clues to the interpretation of the Esoteric Records,

> Which even the initiated priests [of Chaldæa] did not possess.

* The majority of the Pandits know nothing of the Esoteric Philosophy now, because they have lost the key to it; yet not one of these, if honest, would deny that the *Upanishads*, and especially the *Purânas*, are allegorical and symbolical; nor that there still remain in India a few great scholars who could, if they would, give them the key to such interpretations. Nor do they reject the actual existence of Mahâtmâs—initiated Yogis and Adepts—even in this age of Kali Yuga.

Thus, in the scholarly appreciation of our modern Orientalists and Professors, Science was in its infancy in the days of the Egyptian and Chaldæan Astronomers. Pânini, the greatest Grammarian in the world, was unacquainted with the art of writing. So was the Lord Buddha, and everyone else in India until 300 B.C. The grossest ignorance reigned in the days of the Indian Rishis, and even in those of Thales, Pythagoras, and Plato. Theosophists must indeed be superstitious ignoramuses to speak as they do, in the face of such learned evidence to the contrary!

Truly it looks as if, since the world's creation, there has been but one age of real knowledge on earth—the present age. In the misty twilight, in the grey dawn of history, stand the pale shadows of the old Sages of world renown. They were hopelessly groping for the correct meaning of their own Mysteries, the spirit whereof has departed without revealing itself to the Hierophants, and has remained latent in space until the advent of the initiates of Modern Science and Research. The noontide brightness of knowledge has only now arrived at the "Know-All," who, basking in the dazzling sun of induction, busies himself with his Penelopeian task of "working hypotheses," and loudly asserts his rights to universal knowledge. Can anyone wonder, then, that according to present views the learning of the ancient Philosopher, and even sometimes that of his direct successors in the past centuries, has ever been useless to the world and valueless to himself? For, as explained repeatedly in so many words, while the Rishis and the Sages of old have walked far over the arid fields of myth and superstition, the mediæval Scholar, and even the average eighteenth century Scientist, have always been more or less cramped by their "supernatural" religion and beliefs. True, it is generally conceded that some ancient and also mediæval Scholars, such as Pythagoras, Plato, Paracelsus, and Roger Bacon, followed by a host of glorious names, had indeed left not a few landmarks over precious mines of Philosophy and unexplored lodes of Physical Science. But then the actual excavation of these, the smelting of the gold and silver, and the cutting of the precious jewels they contain, are all due to the patient labours of the modern man of Science. And is it not to the unparalleled genius of the latter that the ignorant and hitherto-deluded world owes a correct knowledge of the real nature of the Kosmos, of the true origin of the universe and man, as revealed in the automatic and mechanical theories of the Physicists, in accordance with strictly scientific Philosophy?" Before our cultured era, Science was but a name; Philosophy a delusion and a snare. According to the modest claims of contemporary authority on genuine Science and Philosophy, the Tree of Knowledge has only now sprung from the dead weeds of superstition, as a beautiful butterfly emerges from an ugly grub. We have, therefore, nothing for which to thank our forefathers. The Ancients have at best prepared and fertilised the soil; it is the Moderns who have planted the seeds of knowledge and reared the lovely plants called blank negation and sterile agnosticism.

Such, however, is not the view taken by Theosophists. They repeat what was stated twenty years ago. It is not sufficient to speak of the "untenable conceptions of an uncultured past" (Tyndall); of the "*parler enfantin*" of the Vaidic poets (Max Müller); of the "absurdities" of the Neoplatonists (Jowett); and of the ignorance of the Chaldæo-Assyrian initiated Priests with regard to their own symbols, when compared with the knowledge thereon of the British Orientalist (Sayce). Such assumptions have to be proven by something more solid than the mere word of these scholars. For no amount of boastful arrogance can hide the intellectual quarries out of which the representations of so many modern Philosophers and Scholars have been carved. How many of the most distinguished European Scientists have derived honour and credit for the mere dressing-up of the ideas of these old Philosophers, whom they are ever ready to disparage, is left to an impartial posterity to say. Thus it does seem not altogether untrue as stated in *Isis Unveiled*, to say of certain Orientalists and Scholars of dead languages, that they will allow their boundless conceit and self-opinionatedness to run away with their logic and reasoning powers, rather than concede to the ancient Philosophers the knowledge of anything the modern do not know.

As part of this work treats of the Initiates and the secret knowledge imparted during the Mysteries, the statements of those who, in spite of the fact that Plato was an Initiate, maintain that no hidden Mysticism is to be discovered in his works, have to be first examined. Too many of the present scholars, Greek and Sanskrit, are but too apt to forego facts in favour of their own preconceived theories based on personal prejudice. They conveniently forget, at every opportunity, not only the numerous changes in language, but also that the allegorical style in the writings of old Philosophers and the secretiveness of the Mystics had their *raison d'être;* that both the pre-Christian and the post-

Christian classical writers—the great majority at all events—were under the sacred obligation never to divulge the solemn secrets communicated to them in the sanctuaries; and that this alone is sufficient to sadly mislead their translators and profane critics. But these critics will admit nothing of the kind, as will presently be seen.

For over twenty-two centuries everyone who has read Plato has been aware that, like most of the other Greek Philosophers of note, he had been initiated; that therefore, being tied down by the Sodalian Oath, he could speak of certain things only in veiled allegories. His reverence for the Mysteries is unbounded; he openly confesses that he writes "enigmatically," and we see him take the greatest precautions to conceal the true meaning of his words. Every time the subject touches the greater secrets of Oriental Wisdom—the cosmogony of the universe, or the ideal preëxisting world—Plato shrouds his Philosophy in the profoundest darkness. His *Timæus* is so confused that no one but an Initiate can understand the hidden meaning. As already said in *Isis Unveiled*:

> The speculations of Plato in the *Banquet* on the creation, or rather the evolution, of primordial men, and the essay on cosmogony in the *Timæus*, must be taken allegorically if we accept them at all. It is this hidden Pythagorean meaning in *Timæus*, *Cratylus*, and *Parmenides*, and a few other trilogies and dialogues, that the Neoplatonists ventured to expound, as far as the theurgical vow of secresy would allow them. The Pythagorean doctrine that God is the Universal Mind diffused through all things, and the dogma of the soul's immortality, are the leading features in these apparently incongruous teachings. His piety and the great veneration he felt for the Mysteries are sufficient warrant that Plato would not allow his indiscretion to get the better of that deep sense of responsibility which is felt by every Adept. "Constantly perfecting himself in perfect Mysteries a man in them alone becomes truly perfect," says he in the *Phædrus*.
>
> He took no pains to conceal his displeasure that the Mysteries had become less secret than formerly. Instead of profaning them by putting them within the reach of the multitude, he would have guarded them with jealous care against all but the most earnest and worthy of his disciples.* While mentioning the Gods on every page, his monotheism is unquestionable, for the whole thread of his discourse indicates that by the term "Gods" he means a class of beings lower in the scale than Deities, and but one grade higher than men. Even Josephus perceived and acknowledged this fact, despite the natural prejudice of his race. In his

* This assertion is clearly corroborated by Plato himself, who writes: "You say that in my former discourse I have not sufficiently explained to you the nature of the First. I purposely spoke enigmatically, that in case the tablet should have happened with any accident, either by sea or land, a person without some previous knowledge of the subject might not be able to understand its contents." (Plato, *Ep.*, ii. 312; Cory, *Ancient Fragments*, p. 304.)

famous onslaught upon Apion, this historian says: "Those, however, among the Greeks who philosophized in accordance with truth were not ignorant of anything, . . . nor did they fail to perceive the chilling superficialities of the mythical allegories, on which account they justly despised them. . . . By which thing Plato being moved, says it is not necessary to admit any one of the other poets into 'the Commonwealth,' and he dismisses Homer blandly, after having crowned him and pouring unguent upon him, in order that indeed he should not destroy by his myths, the orthodox belief respecting one God." *

And this is the "God" of every Philosopher, God infinite and impersonal. All this and much more, which there is no room here to quote, leads one to the undeniable certitude that (*a*), as all the Sciences and Philosophies were in the hands of the temple Hierophants, Plato, as initiated by them, must have known them; and (*b*), that logical inference alone is amply sufficient to justify anyone in regarding Plato's writings as allegories and "dark sayings," veiling truths which he had no right to divulge.

This established, how comes it that one of the best Greek scholars in England, Prof. Jowett, the modern translator of Plato's works, seeks to demonstrate that none of the Dialogues—including even the *Timæus*—have any element of Oriental Mysticism about them? Those who can discern the true spirit of Plato's Philosophy will hardly be convinced by the arguments which the Master of Balliol College lays before his readers. "Obscure and repulsive" to him, the *Timæus* may certainly be; but it is as certain that this obscurity does not arise, as the Professor tells his public, "in the infancy of physical science," but rather in its days of secresy; not "out of the confusion of theological, mathematical, and physiological notions," or "out of the desire to conceive the whole of Nature without any adequate knowledge of the parts." † For Mathematics and Geometry were the backbone of Occult cosmogony, hence of "Theology," and the physiological notions of the ancient Sages are being daily verified by Science in our age; at least, to those who know how to read and understand ancient Esoteric works. The "knowledge of the parts" avails us little, if this knowledge only leads us the more to ignorance of the Whole, or the "nature and reason of the Universal," as Plato called Deity, and causes us to blunder most egregiously because of our boasted inductive methods. Plato may have

* *Isis Unveiled*, i. 287, 288.

† *The Dialogues of Plato*, translated by B. Jowett, Regius Professor of Greek at the University of Oxford, iii. 523.

been, "incapable of induction, or generalization in the modern sense;"* he may have been ignorant also, of the circulation of the blood, which, we are told, "was absolutely unknown to him,"† but then, there is naught to disprove that he knew what blood *is*—and this is more than any modern Physiologist or Biologist can claim nowadays.

Though a wider and far more generous margin for knowledge is allowed the "physical philosopher" by Prof. Jowett than by nearly any other modern commentator and critic, nevertheless, his criticism so considerably outweighs his laudation, that it may be as well to quote his own words, to show clearly his bias. Thus he says:

> To bring sense under the control of reason; to find some way through the labyrinth or chaos of appearances, either the highway of mathematics, or more devious paths suggested by the analogy of man with the world and of the world with man; to see that all things have a cause and are tending towards an end—this is the spirit of the ancient physical philosopher.‡ But we neither appreciate the conditions of knowledge to which he was subjected, nor have the ideas which fastened upon his imagination the same hold upon us. For he is hovering between matter and mind; he is under the dominion of abstractions; his impressions are taken almost at random from the outside of nature; he sees the light, but not the objects which are revealed by the light; and he brings into juxtaposition things which to us appear wide as the poles asunder, because he finds nothing between them.

The last proposition but one must evidently be distasteful to the modern "physical philosopher," who sees the "objects" before him, but fails to see the light of the Universal Mind, which reveals them, *i.e.*, who proceeds in a diametrically opposite way. Therefore the learned Professor comes to the conclusion that the ancient Philosopher, whom he now judges from Plato's *Timæus*, must have acted in a decidedly unphilosophical and even irrational way. For:

> He passes abruptly from persons to ideas and numbers, and *from ideas and numbers to persons*,§ he confuses subject and object, *first* and *final* causes, and in

* *Op. cit.*, p. 561.

† *Op. cit.*, p. 591.

‡ This definition places (unwittingly, of course), the ancient "physical philosopher" many cubits higher than his modern "physical" *confrère*, since the *ultima thule* of the latter is to lead mankind to believe that neither universe nor man have any cause at all—not an intelligent one at all events—and that they have sprung into existence owing to blind chance and a senseless whirling of atoms. Which of the two hypotheses is the more rational and logical is left to the impartial reader to decide.

§ Italics are mine. Every tyro in Eastern Philosophy, every Kabalist, will see the reason for such an association of persons with ideas, numbers, and geometrical figures. For number, says Philolaus, "is the dominant and self-produced bond of the eternal continuance of things." Alone the modern Scholar remains blind to the grand truth.

drawing of geometrical figures* is lost in a flux of sense. And now an effort of mind is required on our parts *in order to understand his double language*, or to apprehend *the twilight character of the knowledge* and the genius of ancient philosophers which, under such conditions [?], seems by a divine power in many instances to have anticipated the truth.†

Whether "such conditions" imply those of ignorance and mental stolidity in "the genius of ancient philosophers" or something else, we do not know. But what we do know is that the meaning of the sentences we have italicized is perfectly clear. Whether the Regius Professor of Greek believes or disbelieves in a hidden sense of geometrical figures and of the Esoteric "jargon," he nevertheless admits the presence of a "double language" in the writings of these Philosophers. Thence he admits a hidden meaning, which must have had an interpretation. Why, then, does he flatly contradict his own statement on the very next page? And why should he deny to the *Timæus*—that preëminently Pythagorean (mystic) Dialogue—any Occult meaning and take such pains to convince his readers that

The influence which the *Timæus* has exercised upon posterity is partly due to a misunderstanding.

The following quotation from his Introduction is in direct contradiction with the paragraph which precedes it, as above quoted:

In the supposed depths of this dialogue the Neo-Platonists found hidden meanings and connections with the Jewish and Christian Scriptures, and out of them they dictated doctrines quite at variance with the spirit of Plato. Believing that he was inspired by the Holy Ghost, or had received his wisdom from Moses,‡

---

* Here again the ancient Philosopher seems to be ahead of the modern. For he only "confuses ... first and final causes" (which confusion is denied by those who know the spirit of ancient scholarship), whereas his modern successor is confessedly and absolutely ignorant of both. Mr. Tyndall shows Science "powerless" to solve a single one of the final problems of Nature and "disciplined [read, modern materialistic], imagination retiring in bewilderment from the contemplation of the problems" of the world of matter. He even doubts whether the men of present Science possess "the intellectual elements which would enable them to grapple with the ultimate structural energies of Nature." But for Plato and his disciples, the lower types were but the concrete images of the higher abstract ones; the immortal Soul has an arithmetical, as the body has a geometrical, beginning. This beginning, as the reflection of the great universal Archæus (*Anima Mundi*), is self-moving, and from the centre diffuses itself over the whole body of the Macrocosm.

† *Op. cit.*, p. 523.

‡ Nowhere are the Neoplatonists guilty of such an absurdity. The learned Professor of Greek must have been thinking of two spurious works attributed by Eusebius and St. Jerome to Ammonius Saccas, who wrote nothing; or must have confused the Neoplatonists with Philo Judæus. But then Philo lived over 130 years before the birth of the founder of Neoplatonism. He belonged to the School of Aristobulus the Jew, who lived under Ptolemy Philometer (150 years B.C.), and is credited with having inaugurated the movement which tended to prove that Plato and even the Peripatetic Philosophy were derived from the "revealed" Mosaic Books. Valckenaer tries to show that the author of the *Commentaries on the Books of Moses*, was not Aristobulus, the sycophant of Ptolemy. But whatever he was, he was not a Neoplatonist, but lived before, or during the days of Philo Judæus, since the latter seems to know his works and follow his methods.

they seemed to find in his writings the Christian Trinity, the Word, the Church . . . and the Neo-Platonists had a method of interpretation which could elicit any meaning out of any words. They were really incapable of distinguishing between the opinions of one philosopher and another, or between the serious thoughts of Plato and his passing fancies.* . . . [But] there is no danger of the modern commentators on the *Timæus* falling into the absurdity of the Neo-Platonists.

No danger whatever, of course, for the simple reason that the modern commentators have never had the key to Occult interpretations. And before another word is said in defence of Plato and the Neoplatonists, the learned master of Balliol College ought to be respectfully asked: What does, or can he know of the Esoteric canon of interpretation? By the term "canon" is here meant that key which was communicated orally from "mouth to ear" by the Master to the disciple, or by the Hierophant to the candidate for initiation; this from time immemorial throughout a long series of ages, during which the inner—not public—Mysteries were the most sacred institution of every land. Without such a key no correct interpretation of either the *Dialogues* of Plato or any Scripture, from the *Vedas* to Homer, from the *Zend Avesta* to the Mosaic Books, is possible. How then can the Rev. Dr. Jowett know that the interpretations made by the Neoplatonists of the various sacred books of the nations were "absurdities?" Where, again, has he found an opportunity of studying these "interpretations"? History shows that all such works were destroyed by the Christian Church Fathers and their fanatical catechumens, wherever they were found. To say that such men as Ammonius, a genius and a saint, whose learning and holy life earned for him the title of Theodidaktos ("God-taught"), such men as Plotinus, Porphyry, and Proclus, were "incapable of distinguishing between the opinions of one philosopher and another, or between the serious thoughts of Plato and his fancies," is to assume an untenable position for a Scholar. It amounts to saying that, (*a*) scores of the most famous Philosophers, the greatest Scholars and Sages of Greece and of the Roman Empire were dull fools, and (*b*) that all the other commentators, lovers of Greek Philosophy, some of them the acutest intellects of the age—who do not agree with Dr. Jowett—are also fools and no better than those whom they admire. The patronising tone of the last above-quoted passage is modulated with the most *naïve* conceit, remarkable even in our age of self-glorification and mutual-

* Only Clemens Alexandrinus, a Christian Neoplatonist and a very fantastic writer.

admiration cliques. We have to compare the Professor's views with those of some other scholars.

Says Prof. Alexander Wilder of New York, one of the best Platonists of the day, speaking of Ammonius, the founder of the Neoplatonic School:

> His deep spiritual intuition, his extensive learning, his familiarity with the Christian Fathers, Pantænus, Clement, and Athenagoras, and with the most erudite philosophers of the time, all fitted him for the labour which he performed so thoroughly.* He was successful in drawing to his views the greatest scholars and public men of the Roman Empire, who had little taste for wasting time in dialectic pursuits or superstitious observances. The results of his ministration are perceptible at the present day in every country of the Christian world; every prominent system of doctrine now bearing the marks of his plastic hand. Every ancient philosophy has had its votaries among the moderns; and even Judaism . . . has taken upon itself changes which were suggested by the "God-taught" Alexandrian. . . . He was a man of rare learning and endowments, of blameless life and amiable disposition. His almost superhuman ken and many excellencies won for him the title of Theodidaktos; but he followed the modest example of Pythagoras, and only assumed the title of Philalethian, or lover of truth.†

It would be happy for truth and fact were our modern scholars to follow as modestly in the steps of their great predecessors. But not they—Philalethians!

Moreover, we know that:

> Like Orpheus, Pythagoras, Confucius, Socrates, and Jesus himself,‡ Ammonius committed nothing to writing.§ Instead he . . . communicated his most

---

* The labour of reconciling the different systems of religion.

† *New Platonism and Alchemy*, by Alex. Wilder, M.D. pp. 7, 4.

‡ It is well known that, though born of Christian parents, Ammonius had renounced the tenets of the Church,—Eusebius and Jerome notwithstanding. Porphyry, the disciple of Plotinus, who had lived with Ammonius for eleven years together, and who had no interest for stating an untruth, positively declares that he had renounced Christianity entirely. On the other hand, we know that Ammonius believed in the bright Gods, Protectors, and that the Neoplatonic Philosophy was as "pagan" as it was mystical. But Eusebius, the most unscrupulous forger and falsifier of old texts, and St. Jerome, an out-and-out fanatic, who had both an interest in denying the fact, contradict Porphyry. We prefer to believe the latter, who has left to posterity an unblemished name and a great reputation for honesty.

§ Two works are falsely attributed to Ammonius. One, now lost, called *De Consensu Moysis et Jesu*, is mentioned by the same "trustworthy" Eusebius, the Bishop of Cæsarea, and the friend of the Christian Emperor Constantine, who died, however, a heathen. All that is known of this pseudo-work is that Jerome bestows great praise upon it (*Vir. Illust.*, 55; and Euseb., *H. E.*, vi. 19). The other spurious production is called the *Diatessaron* (or the "Harmony of the Gospels"). This is partially extant. But then, again, it exists only in the Latin version of Victor, Bishop of Capua (sixth century), who attributed it himself to Tatian, and as wrongly, probably, as later scholars attributed the *Diatessaron* to Ammonius. Therefore no great reliance can be placed upon it, nor on its "esoteric" interpretation of the Gospels. Is it this work, we wonder, which led Prof. Jowett to regard the Neoplatonic interpretations as "absurdities"?

important doctrines to persons duly instructed and disciplined, imposing on them the obligations of secresy, as was done before him by Zoroaster and Pythagoras, and in the Mysteries. Except a few treatises of his disciples we have only the declarations of his adversaries from which to ascertain what he actually taught.

It is from the biassed statements of such "adversaries," probably, that the learned Oxford translator of Plato's Dialogues came to the conclusion that:

That which was truly great and truly characteristic of him [Plato], his effort to realise and connect abstractions, *was not understood* by them [the Neoplatonists] at all [?].*

He states, contemptuously enough for the ancient methods of intellectual analysis, that:

In the present day . . . an ancient philosopher is to be interpreted from himself and by the contemporary history of thought.†

This is like saying that the ancient Greek canon of proportion (if ever found), and the Athena Promachus of Phidias, have to be interpreted in the present day from the contemporary history of architecture and sculpture, from the Albert Hall and Memorial Monument, and the hideous Madonnas in crinolines sprinkled over the fair face of Italy. Prof. Jowett remarks that "mysticism is not criticism." No; but neither is criticism always fair and sound judgment.

La critique est aisée, mais l'art est difficile.

And such "art" our critic of the Neoplatonists—his Greek scholarship notwithstanding—lacks from *a* to *z*. Nor has he, very evidently, the key to the true spirit of the Mysticism of Pythagoras and Plato, since he denies even in the *Timæus* an element of Oriental Mysticism, and seeks to show Greek Philosophy reäcting upon the East, forgetting that the truth is the exact reverse; that it is "the deeper and more pervading spirit of Orientalism" that had—through Pythagoras and his own initiation into the Mysteries—penetrated into the very depths of Plato's soul.

But Dr. Jowett does not see this. Nor is he prepared to admit that anything good or rational—in accordance with the "contemporary history of thought"—could ever come out of that Nazareth of the Pagan Mysteries; nor even that there is anything to interpret of a hidden nature in the *Timæus* or any other Dialogue. For him,

The so-called mysticism of Plato is purely Greek, arising out of his imperfect

* *Op. cit.*, p. 7. † *Op. cit.*, iii, 524.

knowledge* and high aspirations, and is the growth of an age in which philosophy is not wholly separated from poetry and mythology.†

Among several other equally erroneous propositions, it is especially the assumptions (*a*) that Plato was entirely free from any element of Eastern Philosophy in his writings, and (*b*) that every modern scholar, without being a Mystic and a Kabalist himself, can pretend to judge of ancient Esotericism—which we mean to combat. To do this we have to produce more authoritative statements than our own would be, and bring the evidence of other scholars as great as Dr. Jowett; if not greater, specialists in their subjects, moreover, to bear on and destroy the arguments of the Oxford Regius Professor of Greek. That Plato was undeniably an ardent admirer and follower of Pythagoras no one will deny. And it is equally undeniable, as Matter has it, that Plato had inherited on the one hand his doctrines, and on the other had drawn his wisdom, from the same sources as the Samian Philosopher.‡ And the doctrines of Pythagoras are Oriental to the backbone, and even Brâhmanical; for this great Philosopher ever pointed to the far East as the source whence he derived his information and his Philosophy, and Colebrooke shows that Plato makes the same profession in his Epistles, and says that he has taken his teachings "from ancient and sacred doctrines."§ Furthermore, the ideas of both Pythagoras and Plato coincide too well with the systems of India and with Zoroastrianism to admit any doubt of their origin by anyone who has some acquaintance with these systems. Again:

> Pantænus, Athenagoras, and Clement were thoroughly instructed in the Platonic philosophy, and *comprehended* its essential unity with the Oriental systems.‖

The history of Pantænus and his contemporaries may give the key to the Platonic, and at the same time Oriental, elements that predominate so strikingly in the Gospels over the Jewish Scriptures.

---

* "Imperfect knowledge" of what? That Plato was ignorant of many of the modern "working hypotheses"—as ignorant as our immediate posterity is sure to be of the said hypotheses when they in their turn after exploding join the "great majority"—is perhaps a blessing in disguise.

† *Op. cit.*, p. 524.

‡ *Histoire Critique du Gnosticisme*, by M. J. Matter, Professor of the Royal Academy of Strasburg. "It is in Pythagoras and Plato that we find, in Greece, the first elements of [Oriental] Gnosticism," he says. (Vol. i, pp. 48 and 50.)

§ *Asiat. Trans.*, i, 579.

‖ *New Platonism and Alchemy*, p. 4.

SECTION I.

PRELIMINARY SURVEY.

INITIATES who have acquired powers and transcendental knowledge can be traced back to the Fourth Root Race from our own age. As the multiplicity of the subjects to be dealt with prohibits the introduction of such a historical chapter, which, however historical in fact and truth, would be rejected *à priori* as blasphemy and fable by both Church and Science—we shall only touch on the subject. Science strikes out, at its own sweet will and fancy, dozens of names of ancient heroes, simply because there is too great an element of myth in their histories; the Church insists that biblical patriarchs shall be regarded as historical personages, and terms her seven "Star-angels" the "historical channels and agents of the Creator." Both are right, since each finds a strong party to side with it. Mankind is at best a sorry herd of Panurgian sheep, following blindly the leader that happens to suit it at the moment. Mankind—the majority at any rate—hates to think for itself. It resents as an insult the humblest invitation to step for a moment outside the old well-beaten tracks, and, judging for itself, to enter into a new path in some fresh direction. Give it an unfamiliar problem to solve, and if its mathematicians, not liking its looks, refuse to deal with it, the crowd, unfamiliar with mathematics, will stare at the unknown quantity, and getting hopelessly entangled in sundry *x*'s and *y*'s, will turn round, trying to rend to pieces the uninvited disturber of its intellectual Nirvâna. This may, perhaps, account for the ease and extraordinary success enjoyed by the Roman Church in her conversions of nominal Protestants and Free-thinkers, whose name is legion, but who have never gone to the trouble of thinking for themselves on these most important and tremendous problems of man's inner nature.

And yet, if the evidence of facts, the records preserved in History, and the uninterrupted anathemas of the Church against "Black Magic" and Magicians of the accursed race of Cain, are not to be heeded, our efforts will prove very puny indeed. When, for nearly two millenniums, a body of men has never ceased to lift its voice against *Black* Magic, the inference ought to be irrefutable that if Black Magic exists as a real fact, there must be somewhere its counterpart—*White* Magic. False silver coins could have no existence if there were no genuine silver money. Nature is dual in whatever she attempts, and this ecclesiastical persecution ought alone to have opened the eyes of the public long ago. However much travellers may be ready to pervert every fact with regard to abnormal powers with which certain men are gifted in "heathen" countries; however eager they may be to put false constructions on such facts, and—to use an old proverb—"to call white swan black goose," and to kill it, yet the evidence of even Roman Catholic missionaries ought to be taken into consideration, once they swear in a body to certain facts. Nor is it because they choose to see Satanic agency in manifestations of a certain kind, that their evidence as to the existence of such powers can be disregarded. For what do they say of China? Those missionaries who have lived in the country for long years, and have seriously studied every fact and belief that may prove an obstacle to their success in making conversions, and who have become familiar with every exoteric rite of both the official religion and sectarian creeds—all swear to the existence of a certain body of men, whom no one can reach but the Emperor and a select body of high officials. A few years ago, before the war in Tonkin, the archbishop in Pekin, on the report of some hundreds of missionaries and Christians, wrote to Rome the identical story that had been reported twenty-five years before, and had been widely circulated in clerical papers. They had fathomed, it was said, the mystery of certain official deputations, sent at times of danger by the Emperor and ruling powers to their Sheu and Kiuay, as they are called among the people. These Sheu and Kiuay, they explained, were the Genii of the mountains, endowed with the most miraculous powers. They are regarded as the protectors of China, by the "ignorant" masses; as the incarnation of Satanic power by the good and "learned" missionaries.

The Shen and Kiuay are men belonging to another state of being to that of the ordinary man, or to the state they enjoyed while they were clad in their bodies. They are disembodied spirits, ghosts and larvæ, living, nevertheless, in objective form on earth, and dwelling in the fastnesses of mountains, inaccessible to all but those whom they permit to visit them.*

---

* This fact and others may be found in Chinese Missionary Reports, and in a work by Monseigneur Delaplace, a Bishop in China. *Annales de la Propagation de la Foi.*

In Tibet certain ascetics are also called Lha, Spirits, by those with whom they do not choose to communicate. The Shen and Kitiay, who enjoy the highest consideration of the Emperor and Philosophers, and of Confucianists who believe in no "Spirits," are simply Lohans—Adepts who live in the greatest solitude in their unknown retreats.

But both Chinese exclusiveness and Nature seem to have allied themselves against European curiosity and—as it is sincerely regarded in Tibet—desecration. Marco Polo, the famous traveller, was perhaps the European who ventured farthest into the interior of these countries. What was said of him in 1876 may now be repeated.

The district of the Gobi wilderness, and, in fact, the whole area of Independent Tartary and Tibet is carefully guarded against foreign intrusion. Those who are permitted to traverse it are under the particular care and pilotage of certain agents of the chief authority, and are in duty bound to convey no intelligence respecting places and persons to the outside world. But for this restriction, many might contribute to these pages accounts of exploration, adventure, and discovery that would be read with interest. The time will come, sooner or later, when the dreadful sand of the desert will yield up its long-buried secrets, and then there will indeed be unlooked-for mortifications for our modern vanity.

"The people of Pashai,"* says Marco Polo, the daring traveller of the thirteenth century, "are great adepts in sorceries and the diabolic arts." And his learned editor adds: "This Paschai, or Udyana, was the native country of Padma Sambhava, one of the chief apostles of Lamaism, *i.e.*, of Tibetan Buddhism, and a great master of enchantments. The doctrines of Sakya, as they prevailed in Udyana *in old times*, were probably strongly tinged with Sivaïtic magic, and the Tibetans still regard the locality as the classic ground of sorcery and witchcraft."

The "old times" are just like the "modern times"; nothing is changed as to magical practices except that they have become still more esoteric and arcane, and that the caution of the adepts increases in proportion to the traveller's curiosity. Hiouen-Thsang says of the inhabitants: "The men . . . are fond of study, but pursue it with no ardour. *The science of magical formulæ has become a regular professional business with them.*"† We will not contradict the venerable Chinese pilgrim on this point, and are willing to admit that in the seventh century *some* people made "a professional business" of magic; so, also, do *some* people now, but certainly not the true adepts. Moreover, in that century, Buddhism had hardly penetrated into Tibet, and its races were steeped in the sorceries of the Bhon,—the pre-lamaic religion. It is not Hiouen-Thsang, the pious, courageous man who risked his life a hundred times to have the bliss of perceiving Buddha's shadow in the cave of Peshawur, who would have accused the good lamas and monkish thaumaturgists of "making a professional business" of showing it to travellers.

---

* The regions somewhere about Udyana and Kashmir, as the translator and editor of Marco Polo (Colonel Yule) believes (i. 175).

† *Voyage des Pèlerins Bouddhistes*, Vol. I.; *Histoire de la Vie de Hiouen-Thsang*, etc., traduit du chinois en français, par Stanislas Julien.

The injunction of Gautama, contained in his answer to King Prasenajit, his protector, who called on him to perform miracles, must have been ever-present to the mind of Hiouen-Thsang. "Great king," said Gautama, "I do not teach the law to my pupils, telling them, 'Go, ye saints, and before the eyes of the Brâhmans and householders perform, by means of your supernatural powers, miracles greater than any man can perform.' I tell them when I teach them the law, 'Live ye saints, *hiding your good works, and showing your sins.*'"

Struck with the accounts of magical exhibitions witnessed and recorded by travellers of every age who had visited Tartary and Tibet, Colonel Yule comes to the conclusion that the natives must have had "at their command the whole encyclopædia of modern Spiritualists." Duhalde mentions among their sorceries the art of producing by their invocations the figures of Laotseu* and their divinities *in the air*, and *of making a pencil write answers to questions without anybody touching it.*"†

The former invocations pertain to the religious mysteries of their sanctuaries; if done otherwise, or for the sake of *gain*, they are considered *sorcery*, necromancy, and strictly forbidden. The latter art, that of making a pencil write without contact, was known and practised in China and other countries before the Christian era. It is the A B C of magic in those countries.

When Hiouen-Thsang desired to adore the shadow of Buddha, it was not to "professional magicians" that he resorted, but to the power of his own soul-invocation; the power of prayer, faith, and contemplation. All was dark and dreary near the cavern in which the miracle was alleged to sometimes take place. Hiouen-Thsang entered and began his devotions. He made one hundred salutations, but neither saw nor heard anything. Then, thinking himself too sinful, he cried bitterly and despaired. But as he was about to give up all hope, he perceived on the eastern wall a feeble light, but it disappeared. He renewed his prayers, full of hope this time, and again he saw the light, which flashed and disappeared again. After this he made a solemn vow: he would not leave the cave till he had the rapture to at last see the shadow of the "Venerable of the Age." He had to wait longer after this, for only after two hundred prayers was the dark cave suddenly "bathed in light, and the shadow of Buddha, of a brilliant white colour, rose majestically on the wall, as when the clouds suddenly open, and all at once display the marvellous image of the 'Mountain of Light.' A dazzling splendour lighted up the features of the divine countenance. Hiouen-Thsang was lost in contemplation and wonder, and would not turn his eyes away from the sublime and incomparable object." Hiouen-Thsang adds in his own diary, *See-yu-kee*, that it is only when man prays with sincere faith, and if he has received from above a hidden impression, that he sees the shadow clearly, but he cannot enjoy the sight for any length of time. (Max Müller, *Buddhist Pilgrims*.)

From one end to the other the country is full of mystics, religious philosophers, Buddhist saints and magicians. Belief in a spiritual world, full of invisible beings who, on certain occasions, appear to mortals objectively, is universal. "According

---

* Lao-tse, the Chinese philosopher.

† *The Book of Ser Marco Polo*, i. 318.

to the belief of the nations of Central Asia," remarks I. J. Schmidt, "the earth and its interior, as well as the encompassing atmosphere, are filled with spiritual beings, which exercise an influence, partly beneficent, partly malignant, on the whole of organic and inorganic nature. . . . Especially are deserts, and other wild and uninhabited tracts, or regions in which the influences of nature are displayed on a gigantic and terrible scale, regarded as the chief abode or rendez-vous of evil spirits. And hence the steppes of Turan, and in particular the great sandy desert of Gobi, have been looked on as the dwelling place of malignant beings, from days of hoary antiquity."

The treasures exhumed by Dr. Schliemann at Mycenæ, have awakened popular cupidity, and the eyes of adventurous speculators are being turned toward the localities where the wealth of ancient peoples is supposed to be buried, in crypt or cave, or beneath sand or alluvial deposit. Around no other locality, not even Peru, hang so many traditions as around the Gobi Desert. In independent Tartary this howling waste of shifting sand was once, if report speaks correctly, the seat of one of the richest empires the world ever saw. Beneath the surface is said to lie such wealth in gold, jewels, statuary, arms, utensils, and all that indicates civilization, luxury, and fine arts, as no existing capital of Christendom can show to-day. The Gobi sand moves regularly from east to west before terrific gales that blow continually. Occasionally some of the hidden treasures are uncovered, but not a native dare touch them, for the whole district is under the ban of a mighty spell. Death would be the penalty. Bahti—hideous, but faithful gnomes—guard the hidden treasures of this prehistoric people, awaiting the day when the revolution of cyclic periods shall again cause their story to be known for the instruction of mankind.*

The above is purposely quoted from *Isis Unveiled* to refresh the reader's memory. One of the cyclic periods has just been passed, and we may not have to wait to the end of Mahâ Kalpa to have revealed something of the history of the mysterious desert, in spite of the Bahti, and even the Râkshasas of India, not less "hideous." No tales or fictions were given in our earlier volumes, their chaotic state notwithstanding, to which chaos the writer, entirely free from vanity, confesses publicly and with many apologies.

It is now generally admitted that, from time immemorial, the distant East, India especially, was the land of knowledge and of every kind of learning. Yet there is none to whom the origin of all her Arts and Sciences has been so much denied as to the land of the primitive Âryas. From Architecture down to the Zodiac, every Science worthy of the name was imported by the Greeks, the mysterious Yavanas—agreeably with the decision of the Orientalists! Therefore, it is but logical that even the knowledge of Occult Science should be refused

---

* *Isis Unveiled*, i. 599-601, 603, 598.

in India, since of its general practice in that country less is known than in the case of any other ancient people. It is so, simply because:

With the Hindus it was, and is, more esoteric, if possible, than it was even among the Egyptian priests. So sacred was it deemed that its existence was only half admitted, and it was only practised in public emergencies. *It was more than a religious matter, for it was* [*and is still*] *considered divine*. The Egyptian hierophants, notwithstanding the practice of a stern and pure morality, could not be compared for one moment with the ascetical Gymnosophists, either in holiness of life or miraculous powers developed in them by the supernatural abjuration of everything earthly. By those who knew them well they were held in still greater reverence than the magians of Chaldæa. "Denying themselves the simplest comforts of life, they dwelt in woods, and led the life of the most secluded hermits,"* while their Egyptian brothers at least congregated together. Notwithstanding the slur thrown on all who practised magic and divination, history has proclaimed them as possessing the greatest secrets in medical knowledge and unsurpassed skill in its practice. Numerous are the volumes preserved in Hindu Mathams, in which are recorded the proofs of their learning. To attempt to say whether these Gymnosophists were the real founders of magic in India, or whether they only practised what had passed to them as an inheritance from the earliest Rishis†—the seven primeval sages—would be regarded as mere speculation by exact scholars.‡

Nevertheless, this must be attempted. In *Isis Unveiled*, all that could be stated about Magic was set down in the guise of hints; and thus, owing to the great amount of material scattered over two large volumes, much of its importance was lost upon the reader, while it still more failed to draw his attention on account of the faulty arrangement. But hints may now grow into explanations. One can never repeat it too often—*Magic is as old as man*. It cannot any longer be called charlatanry or hallucination, when its lesser branches—such as mesmerism, now miscalled "hypnotism," "thought reading," "action by suggestion," and what not else, only to avoid calling it by its right and legitimate name—are being so seriously investigated by the most famous Biologists and Physiologists of both Europe and America. Magic is indissolubly blended with the Religion of every country and is

---

* Ammianus Marcellinus, xxiii. 6.

† The Rishis—the first group of seven in number—lived in days preceding the Vedic period. They are now known as Sages and held in reverence like demigods. But they may now be shown as something more than merely mortal Philosophers. There are other groups of ten, twelve and even twenty-one in number. Haug shows that they occupy in the Brâhmanical religion a position answering to that of the twelve sons of Jacob in the Jewish *Bible*. The Brâhmans claim to descend directly from the Rishis.

‡ *Isis Unveiled*, i. 90.

inseparable from its origin. It is as impossible for History to find the time when it was not, as that of the epoch when it sprang into existence, unless the doctrines preserved by the Initiates are taken into consideration. Nor can Science ever solve the problem of the origin of man if it rejects the evidence of the oldest records in the world, and refuses from the hand of the legitimate Guardians of the mysteries of Nature the key to Universal Symbology. Whenever a writer has tried to connect the first foundation of Magic with a particular country or some historical event or character, further research has shown his hypothesis to be groundless. There is a most lamentable contradiction among the Symbologists on this point. Some would have it that Odin, the Scandinavian priest and monarch, originated the practice of Magic some 70 years B.C., although it is spoken of repeatedly in the *Bible*. But as it was proven that the mysterious rites of the priestesses Valas (Voilers) were greatly anterior to Odin's age*, then Zoroaster came in for an attempt, on the ground that he was the founder of Magian rites; but Ammianus Marcellinus, Pliny and Arnobius, with other ancient Historians, have shown that Zoroaster was but a reformer of Magic as practised by the Chaldæans and Egyptians, and not at all its founder. †

Who, then, of those who have consistently turned their faces away from Occultism and even Spiritualism, as being "unphilosophical" and therefore unworthy of scientific thought, has a right to say that he has studied the Ancients; or that, if he has studied them, he has understood all they have said? Only those who claim to be wiser than their generation, who think that they know all that the Ancients knew, and thus, knowing far more to-day, fancy that they are entitled to laugh at their ancient simple-mindedness and superstition; those, who imagine they have discovered a great secret by declaring the ancient royal sarcophagus, now empty of its King Initiate, to be a "corn-bin," and the Pyramid that contained it, a granary, perhaps a wine-cellar! ‡

---

* See Münter "On the most Ancient Religions of the North before Odin." *Mémoires de la Société des Antiquaires de France*, ii. 230.

† Ammianus Marcellinus, xxvi. 6.

‡ "The date of the hundreds of pyramids in the Valley of the Nile is impossible to fix by any of the rules of modern science; Herodotus informs us that each successive king erected one to commemorate his reign, and serve as his sepulchre. But, Herodotus did not tell all, although he knew that the real purpose of the pyramid was very different from that which he assigns to it. Were it not for his religious scruples, he might have added that, externally, it symbolized the creative principle of Nature, and illustrated also the principles of geometry, mathematics, astrology and astronomy.

Modern society, on the authority of some men of Science, calls Magic charlatantry. But there are eight hundred millions on the face of the globe who believe in it to this day; there are said to be twenty millions of perfectly sane and often very intellectual men and women, members of that same society, who believe in its phenomena under the name of Spiritualism. The whole ancient world, with its Scholars and Philosophers, its Sages and Prophets, believed in it. Where is the country in which it was not practised? At what age was it banished, even from our own country? In the New World as in the Old Country (the latter far younger than the former), the Science of Sciences was known and practised from the remotest antiquity. The Mexicans had their Initiates, their Priest-Hierophants and Magicians, and their crypts of Initiation. Of the two statues exhumed in the Pacific States, one represents a Mexican Adept, in the posture prescribed for the Hindu ascetic, and the other an Aztec Priestess, in a head-gear which might be taken from the head of an Indian Goddess; while the "Guatemalan Medal" exhibits the "Tree of Knowledge"—with its hundreds of eyes and ears, symbolical of seeing and hearing—encircled by the "Serpent of Wisdom" whispering into the ear of the sacred bird. Bernard Diaz de Castilla, a follower of Cortez, gives some idea of the extraordinary refinement, intelligence and civilization, and also of the magic arts of the people whom the Spaniards conquered by brute force. Their pyramids are those of Egypt, built according to the same secret canon of proportion as those of the Pharaohs, and the Aztecs appear to have derived their civilization and religion in more than one way from the same source as the Egyptians and, before these, the Indians. Among all these three peoples arcane Natural Philosophy, or Magic, was cultivated to the highest degree.

That it was natural, not supernatural, and that the Ancients so regarded it, is shown by what Lucian says of the "laughing Philosopher," Democritus, who, he tells his readers,

> Believed in no [miracles] . . . but applied himself to discover the method by which the theurgists could produce them; in a word, his philosophy brought him to the conclusion that magic was entirely confined to the application and the imitation of the laws and the works of nature.

Internally, it was a majestic fane, in whose sombre recesses were performed the Mysteries, and whose walls had often witnessed the initiation scenes of members of the royal family. The porphyry sarcophagus, which Professor Piazzi Smyth, Astronomer Royal of Scotland, degrades into a corn-bin, was the baptismal font, upon emerging from which, the neophyte was 'born again,' and became an adept." (*Isis Unveiled*, i. 518, 519.)

Who then can still call the Magic of the Ancients "superstition"?

"In this respect the opinion of Democritus is of the greatest importance to us; since the Magi left by Xerxes, at Abdera, were his instructors, and he had studied magic, moreover, for a considerable time with the Egyptian priests.* For nearly ninety years of the one hundred and nine of his life, this great philosopher had made experiments, and noted them down in a book, which, according to Petronius,† treated of nature—facts that he had verified himself. And we find him not only disbelieving in and utterly rejecting miracles, but asserting that every one of those that were authenticated by eye-witnesses, had, and could have taken place; for all, even the most *incredible*, were produced according to *the "hidden laws of nature."*‡ . . . Add to this that Greece, the "later cradle of the arts and sciences," and India, cradle of religions, were, and one of them still is, devoted to its study and practice—and who shall venture to discredit its dignity as a study, and its profundity as a science?"§

No true Theosophist will ever do so. For, as a member of our great Oriental body, he knows indubitably that the Secret Doctrine of the East contains the Alpha and the Omega of Universal Science; that in its obscure texts, under the luxuriant, though perhaps too exuberant, growth of allegorical Symbolism, lie concealed the corner- and the key-stones of all ancient and modern knowledge. That Stone, brought down by the Divine Builder, is now rejected by the too-human workman, and this because, in his lethal materiality, man has lost every recollection, not only of his holy childhood, but of his very adolescence, when he was one of the Builders himself; when "the morning stars sang together, and the Sons of God shouted for joy," after they had laid the measures for the foundations of the earth—to use the deeply significant and poetical language of Job, the Arabian Initiate. But those who are still able to make room in their innermost selves for the Divine Ray, and who accept, therefore, the data of the Secret Sciences in good faith and humility, they know well that it is in this Stone that remains buried the absolute in Philosophy, which is the key to all those dark problems of Life and Death, some of which, at any rate, may find an explanation in these volumes.

The writer is vividly alive to the tremendous difficulties that present themselves in the handling of such abstruse questions, and to all the dangers of the task. Insulting as it is to human nature to brand truth

---

* Diog. Laërt., in "Democrit. Vit."

† *Satyric*, ix. 3.

‡ Pliny, *Hist. Nat.*

§ *Isis Unveiled*, i. 512.

with the name of imposture, nevertheless we see this done daily and accept it. For every occult truth has to pass through such denial and its supporters through martyrdom, before it is finally accepted; though even then it remains but too often—

> A crown
> Golden in show, yet but a wreath of thorns.

Truths that rest on Occult mysteries will have, for one reader who may appreciate them, a thousand who will brand them as impostures. This is only natural, and the only means to avoid it would be for an Occultist to pledge himself to the Pythagorean "vow of silence," and renew it every five years. Otherwise, cultured society—two-thirds of which think themselves in duty bound to believe that, since the first appearance of the first Adept, one half of mankind practised deception and fraud on the other half—cultured society will undeniably assert its hereditary and traditional right to stone the intruder. Those benevolent critics, who most readily promulgate the now famous axiom of Carlyle with regard to his countrymen, of being "mostly fools," having taken preliminary care to include themselves safely in the only fortunate exceptions to this rule, will in this work gain strength and derive additional conviction of the sad fact, that the human race is simply composed of knaves and congenital idiots. But this matters very little. The vindication of the Occultists and their Archaic Science is working itself slowly but steadily into the very heart of society, hourly, daily, and yearly, in the shape of two monster branches, two stray off-shoots of the trunk of Magic—Spiritualism and the Roman Church. Fact works its way very often through fiction. Like an immense boa-constrictor, Error, in every shape, encircles mankind, trying to smother in her deadly coils every aspiration towards truth and light. But Error is powerful only on the surface, prevented as she is by Occult Nature from going any deeper; for the same Occult Nature encircles the whole globe, in every direction, leaving not even the darkest corner unvisited. And, whether by phenomenon or miracle, by spirit-hook or bishop's crook, Occultism must win the day, before the present era reaches "Shani's (Saturn's) triple septenary" of the Western Cycle in Europe, in other words—before the end of the twenty-first century "A.D."

Truly the soil of the long by-gone past is not dead, for it has only rested. The skeletons of the sacred oaks of the ancient Druids may still send shoots from their dried-up boughs and be reborn to a new life, like that handful of corn, in the sarcophagus of a mummy 3,000 years old, which, when planted, sprouted, grew, and "gave a fine harvest." Why not? Truth is stranger than fiction. It may any day, and most unexpectedly, vindicate its wisdom and demonstrate the conceit of our age, by proving that the Secret Brotherhood did not, indeed, die out with the Philalethians of the last Eclectic School, that the Gnosis flourishes still on earth, and its votaries are many, albeit unknown. All this may be done by one, or more, of the great Masters visiting Europe, and exposing in their turn the alleged exposers and traducers of Magic. Such secret Brotherhoods have been mentioned by several well-known authors, and are spoken of in Mackenzie's *Royal Masonic Cyclopædia*. The writer now, in the face of the millions who deny, repeats boldly, that which was said in *Isis Unveiled*.

> If they [the Initiates] have been regarded as mere fictions of the novelist, that fact has only helped the "brother-adepts" to keep their incognito the more easily. . . .
>
> The St. Germains and Cagliostros of this century, having learned bitter lessons from the vilifications and persecutions of the past, pursue different tactics nowadays.*

These prophetic words were written in 1876, and verified in 1886. Nevertheless, we say again,

> There are numbers of these mystic Brotherhoods which have naught to do with "civilized" countries; and it is in their unknown communities that are concealed the skeletons of the past. These "adepts" could, if they chose, lay claim to strange ancestry, and exhibit verifiable documents that would explain many a mysterious page in both sacred and profane history.† Had the keys to the hieratic writings and the secret of Egyptian and Hindu symbolism been known to the Christian Fathers, they would not have allowed a single monument of old to stand unmutilated.‡

But there exists in the world another class of adepts, belonging to a brotherhood also, and mightier than any other of those known to the profane. Many among these are personally good and benevolent, even pure and holy occasionally, as individuals. Pursuing collectively, however, and as a body, a selfish, one-sided object, with relentless vigour and determination, they have to be ranked with the adepts

---

* *Op. cit.*, ii. 403.

† This is precisely what some of them are preparing to do, and many a "mysterious page" in sacred and profane history are touched on in these pages. Whether or not their explanations will be accepted—is another question.

‡ *Ibid.*

of the Black Art. These are our modern Roman Catholic "fathers" and clergy. Most of the hieratic writings and symbols have been deciphered by them since the Middle Ages. A hundred times more learned in secret Symbology and the old Religions than our Orientalists will ever be, the personification of astuteness and cleverness, every such adept in the art holds the keys tightly in his firmly clenched hand, and will take care the secret shall not be easily divulged, if he can help it. There are more profoundly learned Kabalists in Rome and throughout Europe and America, than is generally suspected. Thus are the professedly public "brotherhoods" of "black" adepts more powerful and dangerous for Protestant countries than any host of Eastern Occultists. People laugh at Magic! Men of Science, Physiologists and Biologists, deride the potency and even the belief in the existence of what is called in vulgar parlance "Sorcery" and "Black Magic"! The Archæologists have their Stonehenge in England with its thousands of secrets, and its twin-brother Karnac of Brittany, and yet there is not one of them who even suspects what has been going on in its crypts, and its mysterious nooks and corners, for the last century. More than that, they do not even know of the existence of such "magic halls" in their Stonehenge, where curious scenes are taking place, whenever there is a new convert in view. Hundreds of experiments have been, and are being made daily at the Salpêtrière, and also by learned hypnotisers at their private houses. It is now proved that certain sensitives—both men and women—when commanded in trance, by the practitioner, who operates on them, to do a certain thing—from drinking a glass of water up to simulated murder—on recovering their normal state lose all remembrance of the order inspired—"suggested" it is now called by Science. Nevertheless, at the appointed hour and moment, the subject, though conscious and perfectly awake, is compelled by an irresistible power within himself to do that action which has been suggested to him by his mesmeriser; and that too, whatever it may be, and whatever the period fixed by him who controls the subject, that is to say, holds the latter under the power of his will, as a snake holds a bird under its fascination, and finally forces it to jump into its open jaws. Worse than this: for the bird is conscious of the peril; it resists, however helpless in its final efforts, while the hypnotized subject does not rebel, but seems to follow the suggestions and voice of his own free-will and soul. Who of our European men of Science, who believe in such *scientific* experiments—and very few are they who still doubt them now-a-days, and who do not feel convinced of their actual reality—who of them, it is asked, is ready to admit this as being Black Magic? Yet it is the genuine, undeniable and actual *fascination* and *sorcery* of old. The Mula Kurumbas of Nilgiri do not proceed otherwise in their *enchantments* when they seek to destroy an enemy, nor do the Dugpas of Sikkim and Bhûtân know of any more potential agent than their *will*. Only in them that will does not proceed by jumps and starts, but acts with certainty; it does not depend on the amount of receptivity or nervous impressibility of the "subject." Having chosen his victim and placed himself *en rapport* with him, the Dugpa's "fluid" is sure to find its way, for his will is immeasurably more strongly developed than the will of the European experimenter—the self-made, untutored, and *unconscious* Sorcerer for the sake of Science—who has no idea (or belief either) of the variety and potency of the world-old methods used to develop this power, by the *conscious* sorcerer, the "Black Magician" of the East and West.

And now the question is openly and squarely asked: Why should not the fanatical and zealous priest, thirsting to convert some selected rich and influential member of society, use the same means to accomplish his end as the French Physician and experimenter uses in his case with his subject? The conscience of the Roman Catholic priest is most likely at peace. He works *personally* for no selfish purpose, but with the object of "saving a soul" from "eternal damnation." In his view, if Magic there be in it, it is holy, meritorious and divine Magic. Such is the power of blind faith.

Hence, when we are assured by trustworthy and respectable persons of high social standing, and unimpeachable character, that there are many well-organised societies among the Roman Catholic priests which, under the pretext and cover of Modern Spiritualism and mediumship, hold *séances* for the purposes of conversion by suggestion, directly and at a distance—we answer: We know it. And when, moreover, we are told that whenever those priest-hypnotists are desirous of acquiring an influence over some individual or individuals, selected by them for conversion, they retire to an underground place, allotted and consecrated by them for such purposes (*viz.*, ceremonial Magic); and there, forming a circle, throw their combined will-power in the direction of that individual, and thus by repeating the process, gain a complete control over their victim—we again answer: Very likely. In fact we know the practice to be so, whether this kind of ceremonial Magic and *envoûtement* is practised at Stonehenge or elsewhere. We know it, we say, through personal experience; and also because several of the writer's best and most loved friends have been unconsciously drawn into the Romish Church and under her "benign" protection by such means. And, therefore, we can only laugh in pity at the ignorance and stubbornness of those deluded men of Science and cultured experimentalists who, while believing in the power of Dr. Charcot and his disciples to "envoûte" their subjects, find nothing better than a scornful smile whenever Black Magic and its potency are mentioned before them. Éliphas Lévi, the Abbé-Kabalist, died before Science and the Faculté de Medecine of France had accepted hypnotism and influence *par suggestion* among its scientific experiments, but this is what he said twenty-five years ago, in his *Dogme et Rituel de la Haute Magie*, on "Les Envoûtements et les Sorts":

That which sorcerers and necromancers sought above all things in their evocations of the Spirit of Evil, was that magnetic potency which is the lawful property of the true Adept, and which they desired to obtain possession of for evil purposes. . . One of their chief aims was the power of spells or of deleterious influences. . . . That power may be compared to real poisonings by a current of astral light. They exalt their will by means of ceremonies to the degree of rendering it venomous at a distance. . . . We have said in our "Dogma" what we thought of magic spells, and how this power was exceedingly real and dangerous. The true Magus throws a spell without ceremony and by his sole disapproval, upon those with whose conduct he is dissatisfied, and whom he thinks it necessary to punish;* he casts a spell, even by his pardon, over those who do him injury, and the enemies of Initiates never long enjoy impunity for their wrong-doing. We have ourselves seen proofs of this fatal law in numerous instances. The executioners of martyrs always perish miserably; and the Adepts are the martyrs of intelligence. Providence [Karma] seems to despise those who despise them, and puts to death those who would seek to prevent them from living. The legend of the Wandering Jew is the popular poetry of this arcanum. A people had sent a sage to crucifixion; that people had bidden him "Move on!" when he tried to rest for one moment. Well! that people will become subject, henceforth, to a similar condemnation; it will become entirely proscribed, and for long centuries it will be bidden "Move on! move on!" finding neither rest nor pity.†

* This is incorrectly expressed. The true Adept of the "Right Hand" never punishes anyone, not even his bitterest and most dangerous enemy; he simply leaves the latter to his Karma, and Karma never fails to do so, sooner or later.

† *Op. cit.*, ii. 239, 242, 240.

"Fables," and "superstition," will be the answer. Be it so. During the lethal breath of selfishness and indifference every uncomfortable fact is transformed into meaningless fiction, and every branch of the once verdant Tree of Truth has become dried up and stripped of its primeval spiritual significance. Our modern Symbologist is superlatively clever only at detecting phallic worship and sexual emblems even where none were ever meant. But for the true student of Occult Lore, White or Divine Magic could no more exist in Nature without its counterpart Black Magic, than day without night, whether these be of twelve hours or of six months' duration. For him everything in this Nature has an occult—a bright and a night side to it. Pyramids and Druid's oaks, dolmens and Bo-trees, plant and mineral—everything was full of deep significance and of sacred truths of wisdom, when the Arch-Druid performed his magic cures and incantations, and the Egyptian Hierophant evoked and guided Chemnu, the "lovely spectre," the female Frankenstein-creation of old, raised for the torture and test of the soul-power of the candidate for initiation, simultaneously with the last agonising cry of his terrestrial human nature. True, Magic has lost its name, and along with it its rights to recognition. But its practice is in daily use; and its progeny, "magnetic influence," "power of oratory," "irresistible fascination," "whole audiences subdued and held as though under a spell," are terms recognised and used by all, generally meaningless though they now are. Its effects, however, are more determined and definite among religious congregations such as the Shakers, the Negro Methodists, and Salvationists, who call it "the action of the Holy Spirit" and "grace." The real truth is that Magic is still in full sway amidst mankind, however blind the latter to its silent presence and influence on its members, however ignorant society may be, and remain, to its daily and hourly beneficent and maleficent effects. The world is full of such unconscious magicians—in politics as well as in daily life, in the Church as in the strongholds of Free-Thought. Most of those magicians are "sorcerers" unhappily, not metaphorically but in sober reality, by reason of their inherent selfishness, their revengeful natures, their envy and malice. The true student of Magic, well aware of the truth, looks on in pity, and, if he be wise, keeps silent. For every effort made by him to remove the universal cecity is only repaid with ingratitude, slander, and often curses, which, unable to reach him, will react on those who wish him evil. Lies and calumny—the latter a teething lie, adding actual bites to empty harmless falsehoods—become his lot, and thus the well-wisher is soon torn to pieces, as a reward for his benevolent desire to enlighten.

Enough has been given, it is believed, to shew that the existence of a Secret Universal Doctrine, besides its practical methods of Magic, is no wild romance or fiction. The fact was known to the whole ancient world, and the knowledge of it has survived in the East, in India especially. And if there be such a Science, there must be naturally, somewhere, professors of it, or Adepts. In any case it matters little whether the Guardians of the Sacred Lore are regarded as living, actually existing men, or are viewed as myths. It is their Philosophy that will have to stand or fall upon its own merits, apart from, and independent of any Adepts. For in the words of the wise Gamaliel, addressed by him to the Synedrion: "If this doctrine is false it will perish, and fall of itself; but if true, then—*it cannot be destroyed.*"

SECTION II.

Modern Criticism and the Ancients

The Secret Doctrine of the Âryan East is found repeated under Egyptian symbolism and phraseology in the Books of Hermes. At, or near, the beginning of the present century, all the books called Hermetic were, in the opinion of the average man of Science, unworthy of serious attention. They were set down and loudly proclaimed as simply a collection of tales, of fraudulent pretences and most absurd claims. They "never existed before the Christian era," it was said: "they were all written with the triple object of speculation, deceiving and pious fraud;" they were all, even the best of them, silly apocrypha.* In this respect the nineteenth century proved a most worthy scion of the eighteenth, for, in the age of Voltaire as well as in this century, everything, save what emanated direct from the Royal Academy, was false, superstitious, foolish. Belief in the wisdom of the Ancients was laughed to scorn, perhaps more so even than it is now. The very thought of accepting as authentic the works and vagaries of "a false Hermes, a false Orpheus, a false Zoroaster," of false Oracles, false Sibyls, and a thrice false Mesmer and his absurd fluid, was tabooed all along the line. Thus all that had its genesis outside the learned and dogmatic precincts of Oxford and Cambridge,† or the Academy of France, was

---

* See, in this connection, *Pneumatologie des Esprits*, by the Marquis de Mirville, who devotes six enormous volumes to show the absurdity of those who deny the reality of Satan and Magic, or the Occult Sciences—the two being with him synonymous.

† We think we see the sidereal phantom of the old Philosopher and Mystic—once of Cambridge University—Henry More, moving about in the astral mist over the old moss-covered roofs of the ancient town in which he wrote his famous letter to Glanvil about "witches." The "soul" seems restless and indignant, as on that day of May, 1678, when the doctor complained so bitterly to the author of *Sadducismus Triumphatus* of Scot, Adie and Webster. "Our new inspired saints," the soul is heard to mutter, "sworn advocates of the witches . . . who against all sense and reason . . . will have no Samuel but a confederate knave . . . these in-blown buffoons, puffed up with . . . ignorance, vanity and stupid infidelity!" (See "Letter to Glanvil," and *Isis Unveiled*, i. 205, 206.)

denounced in those days as "unscientific," and "ridiculously absurd." This tendency has survived to the present day.

Nothing can be further from the intention of any true Occultist—who stands possessed, by virtue of his higher psychic development, of instruments of research far more penetrating in their power than any as yet in the hands of physical experimentalists—than to look unsympathetically on the efforts that are being made in the area of physical enquiry. The exertions and labours undertaken to solve as many as possible of the problems of Nature have always been holy in his sight. The spirit in which Sir Isaac Newton remarked that at the end of all his astronomical work he felt a mere child picking up shells beside the Ocean of Knowledge, is one of reverence for the boundlessness of Nature which Occult Philosophy itself cannot eclipse. And it may freely be recognised that the attitude of mind which this famous simile describes is one which fairly represents that of the great majority of *genuine* Scientists in regard to all the phenomena of the physical plane of Nature. In dealing with this they are often caution and moderation itself. They observe facts with a patience that cannot be surpassed. They are slow to cast these into theories, with a prudence that cannot be too highly commended. And, subject to the limitations under which they observe Nature, they are beautifully accurate in the record of their observations. Moreover, it may be conceded further that modern Scientists are exceedingly careful not to affirm negations. They may say it is immensely improbable that any discovery will ever conflict with such or such a theory, now supported by such and such an aggregation of recorded facts. But even in reference to the broadest generalizations—which pass into a dogmatic form only in brief popular text books of scientific knowledge—the tone of "Science" itself, if that abstraction may be held to be embodied in the persons of its most distinguished representatives, is one of reserve and often of modesty.

Far, therefore, from being disposed to scoff at the errors into which the limitations of their methods may betray men of Science, the true Occultist will rather appreciate the pathos of a situation in which great industry and thirst for truth are condemned to disappointment, and often to confusion.

That which is to be deplored, however, in respect to Modern Science, is in itself an evil manifestation of the excessive caution which in its most favourable aspect protects Science from over-hasty conclusions:

namely, the tardiness of Scientists to recognise that other instruments of research may be applicable to the mysteries of Nature besides those of the physical plane, and that it may consequently be impossible to appreciate the phenomena of any one plane correctly without observing them as well from the points of view afforded by others. In so far then as they wilfully shut their eyes to evidence which ought to have shown them clearly that Nature is more complex than physical phenomena alone would suggest, that there are means by which the faculties of human perception can pass sometimes from one plane to the other, and that their energy is being misdirected while they turn it exclusively on the minutiæ of physical structure or force, they are less entitled to sympathy than to blame.

One feels dwarfed and humbled in reading what M. Renan, that learned modern "destroyer" of every religious belief, past, present and future, has to say of poor humanity and its powers of discernment. He believes

> Mankind has but a very narrow mind; and the number of men capable of seizing acutely (*finement*) the true analogy of things, is quite imperceptible.*

Upon comparing, however, this statement with another opinion expressed by the same author, namely, that:

> The mind of the critic should yield to facts, hands and feet bound, to be dragged by them wherever they may lead him,†

one feels relieved. When, moreover, these two philosophical statements are strengthened by a third enunciation of the famous Academician, which declares that:

> *Tout parti pris à priori, doit être banni de la science,*‡

there remains little to fear. Unfortunately M. Renan is the first to break this golden rule.

The evidence of Herodotus—called, sarcastically no doubt, the "Father of History," since in every question upon which Modern Thought disagrees with him, his testimony goes for nought—the sober and earnest assurances in the philosophical narratives of Plato and Thucydides, Polybius, and Plutarch, and even certain statements of Aristotle himself, are invariably laid aside whenever they are involved in what modern criticism is pleased to regard as a myth. It is some time since Strauss proclaimed that:

* *Études Religieuses.*
† *Études Historiques.*
‡ *Mémoire* read at the Académie des Inscriptions des Belles Lettres, in 1859.

The presence of a supernatural element or miracle in a narrative is an infallible sign of the presence in it of a myth;

and such is the canon of criticism tacitly adopted by every modern critic. But what is a myth—μῦθος—to begin with? Are we not told distinctly by ancient writers that the word means tradition? Was not the Latin term *fabula*, a fable, synonymous with something told, as having happened in pre-historic times, and not necessarily an invention. With such autocrats of criticism and despotic rulers as are most of the French, English, and German Orientalists, there may, then, be no end of historical, geographical, ethnological and philological surprises in store for the century to come. Travesties in Philosophy have become so common of late, that the public can be startled by nothing in this direction. It has already been stated by one learned speculator that Homer was simply "a mythical personification of the épopée"*; by another, that Hippocrates, son of Esculapius "could only be a chimera"; that the Asclepiades, their seven hundred years of duration notwithstanding, might after all prove simply a "fiction"; that "the city of Troy (Dr. Schliemann to the contrary) existed only on the maps," etc. Why should not the world be invited after this to regard every hitherto historical character of days of old as a myth? Were not Alexander the Great needed by Philology as a sledge-hammer wherewith to break the heads of Brâhmanical chronological pretensions, he would have become long ago simply "a symbol for annexation," or "a genius of conquest," as has been already suggested by some French writer.

Blank denial is the only refuge left to the critics. It is the most secure asylum for some time to come in which to shelter the last of the sceptics. For one who denies unconditionally, the trouble of arguing is unnecessary, and he also thus avoids what is worse, having to yield occasionally a point or two before the irrefutable arguments and facts of his opponent. Creuzer, the greatest of all the modern Symbologists, the most learned among the masses of erudite German Mythologists, must have envied the placid self-confidence of certain sceptics, when he found himself forced in a moment of desperate perplexity to admit that:

> We are compelled to return to the theories of trolls and genii, as they were understood by the ancients; [it is a doctrine] without which it becomes absolutely impossible to explain to oneself anything with regard to the Mysteries†

of the Ancients, which Mysteries are undeniable.

---

* See Alfred Maury's *Histoire des Religions de la Grèce*, i. 248; and the speculations of Holzmann in *Zeitschrift für Vergleichende Sprach forschung*, ann. 1852, p. 487, *sq.*

† Creuzer's *Introduction des Mystères*, iii. 456.

3 D

Roman Catholics, who are guilty of precisely the same worship, and to the very letter—having borrowed it from the later Chaldæans, the Lebanon Nabathæans, and the baptized Sabæans,* and not from the learned Astronomers and Initiates of the days of old—would now, by anathematizing it, hide the source from which it came. Theology and Churchianism would fain trouble the clear fountain that fed them from the first, to prevent posterity from looking into it, and thus seeing their original prototype. The Occultists, however, believe the time has come to give everyone his due. As to our other opponents—the modern sceptic and the Epicurean, the cynic and the Sadducee—they may find an answer to their denials in our earlier volumes. As to many unjust aspersions on the ancient doctrines, the reason for them is given in these words in *Isis Unveiled:*

> The thought of the present-day commentator and critic as to the ancient learning, is limited to and runs round the *exoterism* of the temples; his insight is either unwilling or unable to penetrate into the solemn adyta of old, where the hierophant instructed the neophyte to regard the public worship in its true light. No ancient sage would have taught that man is the king of creation, and that the starry heaven and our mother earth were created for his sake.†

When we find such works as *Phallicism*‡ appearing in our day in print, it is easy to see that the day for concealment and travesty has passed away. Science, in Philology, Symbolism and Comparative Religion, has progressed too far to make wholesale denials any longer, and the Church is too wise and cautious not to be now making the best of the situation. Meanwhile, the "rhombs of Hecate" and the "wheels of Lucifer,"§ daily exhumed on the sites of Babylonia, can no longer be used as clear evidence of a Satan-worship, since the same symbols are shown in the ritual of the Latin Church. The latter is too learned to be ignorant of the fact that even the later Chaldæans, who had gradually fallen into dualism, reducing all things to two primal Principles, never worshipped Satan or idols, any more than did the Zoroastrians, who now lie under the same accusation, but that their Religion was as highly philosophical as any; their dual and exoteric Theosophy became the heirloom of the Jews, who, in their turn, were forced to share it with the Christians. Pârsîs are to this day charged with

* The later Nabathæans adhered to the same belief as the Nazarenes and the Sabeans, honoured John the Baptist, and used Baptism. (See *Isis Unveiled*, ii. 127; Munck, *Palestine*, p. 525; Dunlap, *Sôd, the Son of Man*, etc.)

† i. 535.

‡ By Hargrave Jennings.

§ See De Mirville's *Pneumatologie*, iii. 267 *et seq.*

Heliolatry, and yet in the Chaldæan Oracles, under the "Magical and Philosophical Precepts of Zoroaster" one finds the following:

> Direct not thy mind to the vast measures of the earth;
> For the plant of truth is not upon ground.
> Nor measure the measures of the sun, collecting rules,
> For he is carried by the eternal will of the Father, not for your sake.
> Dismiss the impetuous course of the moon; for she runs always by work of necessity.
> The progression of the stars was not generated for your sake.

There was a vast difference between the true worship taught to those who showed themselves worthy, and the state religions. The Magians are accused of all kinds of superstition, but this is what the same Chaldæan Oracle says:

> The wide aerial flight of birds is not true,
> Nor the dissections of the entrails of victims; they are all mere toys,
> The basis of mercenary fraud; flee from these
> If you would open the sacred paradise of piety,
> Where virtue, wisdom, and equity are assembled. *

As we say in our former work:

> Surely it is not those who warn people against "mercenary fraud" who can be accused of it; and if they accomplished acts which seem miraculous, who can with fairness presume to deny that it was done merely because they possessed a knowledge of natural philosophy and psychological science to a degree unknown to our schools? †

The above quoted stanzas are a rather strange teaching to come from those who are universally believed to have worshipped the sun, and moon, and the starry hosts, as Gods. The sublime profundity of the Magian precepts being beyond the reach of modern materialistic thought, the Chaldæan Philosophers are accused of Sabæanism and Sun-worship, which was the religion only of the uneducated masses.

* Psellus, 4; in Cory's *Ancient Fragments*, 269. † *Isis Unveiled*, i, 535, 536.

SECTION III.

THE ORIGIN OF MAGIC.

THINGS of late have changed, true enough. The field of investigation has widened; old religions are a little better understood; and since that miserable day when the Committee of the French Academy, headed by Benjamin Franklin, investigated Mesmer's phenomena only to proclaim them charlatanry and clever knavery, both heathen Philosophy and Mesmerism have acquired certain rights and privileges, and are now viewed from quite a different standpoint. Is full justice rendered them, however, and are they any better appreciated? We are afraid not. Human nature is the same now, as when Pope said of the force of prejudice that:

> The difference is as great between
> The optics seeing, as the objects seen.
> All manners take a tincture from our own,
> Or some discolour'd through our passions shown,
> Or fancy's beam enlarges, multiplies,
> Contracts, inverts, and gives ten thousand dyes.

Thus in the first decades of our century Hermetic Philosophy was regarded by both Churchmen and men of Science from two quite opposite points of view. The former called it sinful and devilish; the latter denied point-blank its authenticity, notwithstanding the evidence brought forward by the most erudite men of every age, including our own. The learned Father Kircher, for instance, was not even noticed; and his assertion that all the fragments known under titles of works by Mercury Trismegistus, Berosus, Pherecydes of Syros, etc., were rolls that had escaped the fire which devoured 100,000 volumes of the great Alexandrian Library—was simply laughed at. Nevertheless the educated classes of Europe knew then, as they do now, that the famous Alexandrian Library, the "marvel of the ages," was founded by Ptolemy Philadelphus; that numbers of its MSS. had been carefully copied from hieratic texts and the oldest parchments, Chaldean, Phœnician, Persian, etc.; and that these transliterations and copies amounted, in their turn, to another 100,000 rolls, as Josephus and Strabo assert.

There is also the additional evidence of Clemens Alexandrinus, that ought to be credited to some extent.* Clemens testified to the existence of an additional 30,000 volumes of the Books of Thoth, placed in the library of the Tomb of Osymandias, over the entrance of which were inscribed the words, "A Cure for the Soul."

Since then, as all know, entire texts of the "apocryphal" works of the "false" Pymander, and the no less "false" Asclepias, have been found by Champollion in the most ancient monuments of Egypt.† As said in *Isis Unveiled*:

> After having devoted their whole lives to the study of the records of the old Egyptian wisdom, both Champollion-Figéac and Champollion Junior publicly declared, notwithstanding many biassed judgments hazarded by certain hasty and unwise critics, that the *Books of Hermes* "truly contain a mass of Egyptian traditions which are constantly corroborated by the most authentic records and monuments of Egypt of the hoariest antiquity."‡

The merit of Champollion as an Egyptologist none will question, and if he declare that everything demonstrates the accuracy of the writings of the mysterious Hermes Trismegistus, and if the assertion that their antiquity runs back into the night of time be corroborated by him in

* The forty-two Sacred Books of the Egyptians, mentioned by Clement of Alexandria as having existed in his time, were but a portion of the Books of Hermes. Iamblichus, on the authority of the Egyptian priest Abammon, attributes 1,200 of such books to Hermes, and Manetho 36,000. But the testimony of Iamblichus as a Neoplatonist and Theurgist is of course rejected by modern critics. Manetho, who is held by Bunsen in the highest consideration as a "purely historical personage," with whom "none of the later native historians can be compared" (see *Égypte*, i. 97), suddenly becomes a Pseudo-Manetho, as soon as the ideas propounded by him clash with the scientific prejudices against Magic and the Occult knowledge claimed by the ancient priests. However, none of the Archæologists doubt for a moment the almost incredible antiquity of the Hermetic books. Champollion shows the greatest regard for their authenticity and truthfulness, corroborated as it is by many of the oldest monuments. And Bunsen brings irrefutable proofs of their age. From his researches, for instance, we learn that there was a line of sixty-one kings before the days of Moses, who preceded the Mosaic period by a clearly-traceable civilisation of several thousand years. Thus we are warranted in believing that the works of Hermes Trismegistus were extant many ages before the birth of the Jewish law-giver. "Styli and inkstands were found on monuments of the fourth Dynasty, the oldest in the world," says Bunsen. If the eminent Egyptologist rejects the period of 48,863 years before Alexander, to which Diogenes Laërtius carries back the records of the priests, he is evidently more embarrassed with the ten thousand of astronomical observations, and remarks that "if they were actual observations, they *must have* extended over 10,000 years" (p. 14). "We learn, however," he adds, "from one of their own old chronological works . . . that the genuine Egyptian traditions concerning the mythological period treated of *myriads* of years." (*Égypte*, i. 15; *Isis Unveiled*, i. 33.)

† These details are taken from *Pneumatologie*, iii. pp. 204, 205.

‡ *Égypte*, p. 143; *Isis Unveiled*, i. 625.

minutest details, then indeed criticism ought to be fully satisfied." Says Champollion:

> These inscriptions are only the faithful echo and expression of the most ancient verities.

Since these words were written, some of the "apocryphal" verses by the "mythical" Orpheus have also been found copied word for word, in hieroglyphics, in certain inscriptions of the Fourth Dynasty, addressed to various Deities. Finally, Creuzer discovered and immediately pointed out the very significant fact that numerous passages found in Homer and Hesiod were undeniably borrowed by the two great poets from the Orphic Hymns, thus proving the latter to be far older than the *Iliad* or the *Odyssey*.

And so gradually the ancient claims come to be vindicated, and modern criticism has to submit to evidence. Many are now the writers who confess that such a type of literature as the Hermetic works of Egypt can never be dated too far back into the prehistoric ages. The texts of many of these ancient works, that of Enoch included, so loudly proclaimed "apocryphal" at the beginning of this century, are now discovered and recognised in the most secret and sacred sanctuaries of Chaldæa, India, Phœnicia, Egypt and Central Asia. But even such proofs have failed to convince the bulk of our Materialists. The reason for this is very simple and evident. All these texts—held in universal veneration in Antiquity, found in the secret libraries of all the great temples, studied (if not always mastered) by the greatest statesmen, classical writers, philosophers, kings and laymen, as much as by renowned Sages—what were they? Treatises on Magic and Occultism, pure and simple; the now derided and tabooed Theosophy—hence the ostracism.

Were people, then, so simple and credulous in the days of Pythagoras and Plato? Were the millions of Babylonia and Egypt, of India and Greece, with their great Sages to lead them, all fools, that during those periods of great learning and civilization which preceded the year *one* of our era—the latter giving birth but to the intellectual darkness of mediæval fanaticism—so many otherwise great men should have devoted their lives to a mere illusion, a superstition called Magic? It would seem so, had one to remain content with the word and conclusions of modern Philosophy.

Every Art and Science, however, whatever its intrinsic merit, has had its discoverer and practitioner, and subsequently its proficients to teach

ii. What is the origin of the Occult Sciences, or Magic? Who were its professors, and what is known of them, whether in history or legend? Clemens Alexandrinus, one of the most intelligent and learned of the early Christian Fathers, answers this question in his *Stromateis*. That ex-pupil of the Neoplatonic School argues:

If there is instruction, you must seek for the master.*

And so he shows Cleanthes taught by Zeno, Theophrastus by Aristotle, Metrodorus by Epicurus, Plato by Socrates, etc. And he adds that when he had looked further back to Pythagoras, Pherecydes, and Thales, he had still to search for their masters. The same for the Egyptians, the Indians, the Babylonians, and the Magi themselves. He would not cease questioning, he says, to learn who it was they all had for their masters. And when he (Clemens) had traced down the enquiry to the very cradle of mankind, to the first generation of men, he would reiterate once more his questioning, and ask, "Who is their teacher?" Surely, he argues, their master could be "no one of men." And even when we should have reached as high as the Angels, the same query would have to be offered to them: "Who were their (meaning the 'divine' and the 'fallen' Angels) masters?"

The aim of the good father's long argument is of course to discover two distinct masters, one the preceptor of biblical patriarchs, the other the teacher of the Gentiles. But the students of the Secret Doctrine need go to no such trouble. Their professors are well aware who were the Masters of their predecessors in Occult Sciences and Wisdom.

The two professors are finally traced out by Clemens, and are, as was to be expected, God, and his eternal and everlasting enemy and opponent, the Devil; the subject of Clemens' enquiry relating to the *dual* aspect of Hermetic Philosophy, as cause and effect. Admitting the moral beauty of the virtues preached in every Occult work with which he was acquainted, Clemens desires to know the cause of the apparent contradiction between the doctrine and the practice, good and evil Magic, and he comes to the conclusion that Magic has two origins—divine and diabolical. He perceives its bifurcation into two channels, hence his deduction and inference.

We perceive it too, without, however, necessarily designating such bifurcation diabolical, for we judge the "left-hand path" as it

* *Strom.*, VI. vii. The following paragraph is paraphrased from the same chapter.

issued from the hands of its founder. Otherwise, judging also by the effects of Clemens' own religion and the walk in life of certain of its professors, since the death of their Master, the Occultists would have a right to come to somewhat the same conclusion as Clemens. They would have a right to say that while Christ, the Master of all true Christians, was in every way godly, those who resorted to the horrors of the Inquisition, to the extermination and torture of heretics, Jews and Alchemists, the Protestant Calvin who burnt Servetus, and his persecuting Protestant successors, down to the whippers and burners of witches in America, must have had for *their* Master, the Devil. But Occultists, not believing in the Devil, are precluded from retaliating in this way.

Clemens' testimony, however, is valuable in so far as it shows (1) the enormous number of works on Occult Sciences in his day; and, (2) the extraordinary powers acquired through those Sciences by certain men.

He devotes, for instance, the whole of the sixth book of his *Stromateis* to this research for the first two "Masters" of the true and the false Philosophy respectively, both preserved, as he says, in the Egyptian sanctuaries. Very pertinently too, he apostrophises the Greeks, asking them why they should not accept the "miracles" of Moses as such, since they claim the very same privileges for their own Philosophers, and he gives a number of instances. It is, as he says, Æachus obtaining through his Occult powers a marvellous rain; it is Aristæus causing the winds to blow; Empedocles quieting the gale, and forcing it to cease, etc.*

The books of Mercurius Trismegistus most attracted his attention.† He is also warm in his praise of Hystaspes (or Gushtasp), of the Sibylline books, and even of the right Astrology.

There have been in all ages use and abuse of Magic, as there are use and abuse of Mesmerism or Hypnotism in our own. The ancient world had its Apollonii and its Pherecydæ, and intellectual people could discriminate then, as they can now. While no classical or pagan writer has ever found one word of blame for Apollonius of Tyana, for instance, it is not so with regard to Pherecydes. Hesychius of Miletia,

---

* See *Pneumatologie*, iii. 107. Therefore Empedocles is called κωλυθάνεμος, the "dominator of the wind." *Strom.*, VI. iii.

† *Ibid.*, iv.

Philo of Byblos and Eusthathius charge the latter unstintingly with having built his Philosophy and Science on demoniacal traditions—*i.e.*, on Sorcery. Cicero declares that Pherecydes is, *potius divinus quam medicus*, "rather a soothsayer than a physician," and Diogenes Laërtius gives a vast number of stories relating to his predictions. One day Pherecydes prophesies the shipwreck of a vessel hundreds of miles away from him; another time he predicts the capture of the Lacedæmonians by the Arcadians; finally, he foresees his own wretched end.*

Bearing in mind the objections that will be made to the teachings of the Esoteric Doctrine as herein propounded, the writer is forced to meet some of them beforehand.

Such imputations as those brought by Clemens against the "heathen" Adepts, only prove the presence of clairvoyant powers and prevision in every age, but are no evidence in favour of a Devil. They are, therefore, of no value except to the Christians, for whom Satan is one of the chief pillars of the faith. Baronius and De Mirville, for instance, find an unanswerable proof of Demonology in the belief in the co-eternity of Matter with Spirit!

De Mirville writes that Pherecydes

> Postulates in principle the primordiality of Zeus or Ether, and then, on the same plane, a principle, coëternal and coäctive, which he calls the fifth element, or Ogenos.†

He then points out that the meaning of Ogenos is given as that which shuts up, which holds captive, and that is Hades, "or in a word, hell."

The synonyms are known to every schoolboy without the Marquis going to the trouble of explaining them to the Academy; as to the deduction, every Occultist will of course deny it and only smile at its folly. And now we come to the theological conclusion.

The *résumé* of the views of the Latin Church—as given by authors of the same character as the Marquis de Mirville—amounts to this: that the Hermetic Books, their wisdom—fully admitted in Rome—notwithstanding, are "the heirloom left by Cain, the accursed, to mankind." It is "generally admitted," says that modern memorialist of Satan in History:

> That immediately after the Flood Cham and his descendants had propagated anew the ancient teachings of the Cainites and of the submerged Race.‡

---

* Summarised from *Pneumatologie*, iii. 209. † *Loc. cit.* ‡ *Op. cit.*, iii. 208.

This proves, at any rate, that Magic, or Sorcery as he calls it, is an antediluvian Art, and thus one point is gained. For, as he says [illegible]

> The evidence of Berosius makes Ham identical with the first Zoroaster, founder of Bactria, the first author of all the magic arts of Babylonia, the *Chemmesenuus* Cham,* the *infamous*† of the faithful Noachians, finally the object of adoration for Egypt, which having received its name χημεία, whence chemistry, built in his honour a town called *Choemnis*, or the "city of fire."‡ Ham adored it, it is said, whence the name *Chammaim* given to the pyramids; which in their turn have been vulgarised into our modern noun "chimney."§

This statement is entirely wrong. Egypt was the cradle of Chemistry and its birth-place—this is pretty well known by this time. Only Kenrick and others show the root of the word to be *chemi* or *chem*, which is not *Cham* or Ham, but *Khem*, the Egyptian phallic God of the Mysteries.

But this is not all. De Mirville is bent upon finding a satanic origin even for the now innocent Tarot.

He goes on to say:

> As to the means for the propagation of this evil Magic, tradition points it out, in certain runic characters traced on metallic plates [or leaves, *des lames*] which have escaped destruction by the Deluge.‖ This might have been regarded as legendary, had not subsequent discoveries shown it far from being so. Plates were found covered with curious and utterly undecipherable characters, characters of undeniable antiquity, to which the Chamites [Sorcerers, with the author] attribute the origin of their marvellous and terrible powers.¶

The pious author may, meanwhile, be left to his own orthodox

---

* The English speaking people who spell the name of Noah's disrespectful son "Ham" have to be reminded that the right spelling is "Kham" or "Cham."

† Black Magic, or Sorcery, is the *evil* result obtained in any shape or way through the practice of Occult Arts; hence it has to be judged only by its effects. The name of neither Ham nor Cain, when pronounced, has ever killed any one; whereas, if we have to believe that same Clemens Alexandrinus who traces the teacher of every Occultist, outside of Christianity, to the Devil, the name of Jehovah (pronounced Jevo and in a peculiar way) had the effect of killing a man at a distance. The mysterious Schemham-phorasch was not always used for holy purposes by the Kabalists, especially since the Sabbath or Saturday, sacred to Saturn or the evil Shani, became—with the Jews—sacred to "Jehovah."

‡ Khoemnis, the pre-historic city, may or may not have been built by Noah's son, but it was not his name that was given to the town, but that of the Mystery Goddess Khoemnu or Khoemnis (Greek form); the deity that was created by the ardent fancy of the neophyte, who was thus tantalised during his "twelve labours" of probation before his final initiation. Her male counterpart is Khem. The city of Choemnis or Khemmis (to-day Akhmem) was the chief seat of the God Khem. The Greeks identifying Khem with Pan, called this city "Panopolis."

§ *Pneumatologie*, iii, 210. This looks more like pious vengeance than philology. The picture, however, seems incomplete, as the author ought to have added to the "chimney" a witch flying out of it on a broomstick.

‖ How could they escape from the Deluge unless God so willed it? This is scarcely logical.

¶ *Loc. cit.*, p. 210.

beliefs. He, at any rate, seems quite sincere in his views. Nevertheless, his able arguments will have to be sapped at their very foundation, for it must be shown on mathematical grounds who, or rather what, Cain and Ham really were. De Mirville is only the faithful son of his Church, interested in keeping Cain in his anthropomorphic character and in his present place in "Holy Writ." The student of Occultism, on the other hand, is solely interested in the truth. But the age has to follow the natural course of its evolution.

SECTION IV.

The Secresy of Initiates.

The false rendering of a number of parables and sayings of Jesus is not to be wondered at in the least. From Orpheus, the first initiated Adept of whom history catches a glimpse in the mists of the pre-Christian era, down through Pythagoras, Confucius, Buddha, Jesus, Apollonius of Tyana, to Ammonius Saccas, no Teacher or Initiate has ever committed anything to writing for public use. Each and all of them have invariably recommended silence and secresy on certain facts and deeds; from Confucius, who refused to explain publicly and satisfactorily what he meant by his "Great Extreme," or to give the key to the divination by "straws," down to Jesus, who charged his disciples to tell no man that he was Christ* (Chrestos), the "man of sorrows" and trials, before his supreme and last Initiation, or that he had produced a "miracle" of resurrection.† The Apostles had to preserve silence, so that the left hand should not know what the right hand did; in plainer words, that the dangerous proficients in the Left Hand Science—the terrible enemies of the Right Hand Adepts, especially before their supreme Initiation—should not profit by the publicity so as to harm both the healer and the patient. And if the above is maintained to be simply an assumption, then what may be the meaning of these awful words:

> Unto you it is given to know the mystery of the Kingdom of God; but unto them that are without all these things are done in parables; that seeing they may see and not perceive; and hearing, they may hear and not understand; lest at any time they should be converted and their sins should be forgiven them. ‡

---

* *Matthew*, xvi. 20. † *Mark*, v. 43. ‡ *Mark*, iv. 11, 12.

Unless interpreted in the sense of the law of silence and Karma, the utter selfishness and uncharitable spirit of this remark are but too evident. These words are directly connected with the terrible dogma of predestination. Will the good and intelligent Christian cast such a slur of cruel selfishness on his Saviour?*

The work of propagating such truths in parables was left to the disciples of the high Initiates. It was their duty to follow the key-note of the Secret Teaching without revealing its mysteries. This is shown in the histories of all the great Adepts. Pythagoras divided his classes into hearers of exoteric and esoteric lectures. The Magians received their instructions and were initiated in the far hidden caves of Bactria. When Josephus declares that Abraham taught Mathematics he meant by it "Magic," for in the Pythagorean code Mathematics mean Esoteric Science, or Gnosis.

Professor Wilder remarks:

> The Essenes of Judæa and Carmel made similar distinctions, dividing their adherents into neophytes, brethren and the perfect. . . . Ammonius obligated his disciples by oath not to divulge his higher doctrines, except to those who had been thoroughly instructed and exercised [prepared for initiation].†

One of the most powerful reasons for the necessity of strict secrecy is given by Jesus Himself, if one may credit Matthew. For there the Master is made to say plainly:

> Give not that which is holy unto the dogs, neither cast ye your pearls before swine, lest they trample them under their feet, and turn again and rend you.‡

Profoundly true and wise words. Many are those in our own age, and even among us, who have been forcibly reminded of them—often when too late.§

---

* Is it not evident that the words: "lest at any time they should be converted (or: "lest haply they should turn again"—as in the revised version) and their sins be forgiven them"—do not at all mean to imply that Jesus feared that through repentance any outsider, or "them that are without," should escape damnation, as the literal dead-letter sense plainly shows—but quite a different thing? Namely, "lest any of the profane should by understanding his preaching, undisguised by parable, get hold of some of the secret teachings and mysteries of Initiation—and even of Occult powers? "Be converted" is, in other words, to obtain a knowledge belonging exclusively to the Initiated; "and their sins be forgiven them," that is, their sins would fall upon the illegal revealer, on those who had helped the unworthy to reap there where they have never laboured to sow, and had given them, thereby, the means of escaping on this earth their deserved Karma, which must thus re-act on the revealer, who, instead of good, did harm and failed.

† "*New Platonism and Alchemy*, 1869, pp. 7, 9.

‡ vii. 6.

§ History is full of proofs of the same. Had not Anaxagoras enunciated the great truth taught in the Mysteries, *viz.*, that the sun was surely larger than the Peloponnesus, he would not have been persecuted and nearly put to death by the fanatical mob. Had that other rabble which was raised

Even Maimonides recommends silence with regard to the true meaning of the *Bible* texts. This injunction destroys the usual affirmation that "Holy Writ" is the only book in the world whose divine oracles contain plain unvarnished truth. It may be so for the learned Kabalists; it is certainly quite the reverse with regard to Christians. For this is what the learned Hebrew Philosopher says:

Whoever shall find out the true sense of the Book of *Genesis* ought to take care not to divulge it. This is a maxim that all our sages repeat to us, and above all respecting the work of the six days. If a person should discover the true meaning of it by himself, or by the aid of another, then he ought to be silent, or if he speaks he ought to speak of it obscurely, in an enigmatical manner, as I do myself, leaving the rest to be guessed by those who can understand me.

The Symbology and Esoterism of the *Old Testament* being thus confessed by one of the greatest Jewish Philosophers, it is only natural to find Christian Fathers making the same confession with regard to the *New Testament*, and the *Bible* in general. Thus we find Clemens Alexandrinus and Origen admitting it as plainly as words can do it. Clemens, who had been initiated into the Eleusinian Mysteries says, that:

The doctrines there taught contained in them *the end of all instructions as they were taken from Moses and the prophets*,

a slight perversion of facts pardonable in the good Father. The words admit, after all, that the Mysteries of the Jews were identical with those of the Pagan Greeks, who took them from the Egyptians, who borrowed them, in their turn, from the Chaldæans, who got them from the Âryans, the Atlanteans and so on—far beyond the days of that Race. The secret meaning of the Gospel is again openly confessed by Clemens when he says that the Mysteries of the Faith are not to be divulged to all.

But since this tradition is not published alone for him who perceives the magnificence of the word; it is requisite, therefore, to hide in a Mystery the wisdom spoken, which the Son of God taught.*

---

against Pythagoras understood what the mysterious Sage of Crotona meant by giving out his remembrance of having been the "Son of Mercury"—God of the Secret Wisdom—he would not have been forced to fly for his life; nor would Socrates have been put to death, had he kept secret the revelations of his divine Daimon. He knew how little his century—save those initiated—would understand his meaning, had he given out all he knew of the moon. Thus he limited his statement to an allegory, which is now proven to have been more scientific than was hitherto believed. He maintained that the moon was inhabited and that the lunar beings lived in profound, vast and dark valleys, our satellite being airless and without any atmosphere outside such profound valleys; this, disregarding the revelation full of meaning for the few only, must be so of necessity, if there is any atmosphere on our bright Selene at all. The facts recorded in the secret annals of the Mysteries had to remain veiled under penalty of death.

* *Stromateis*, xii.

Not less explicit is Origen with regard to the *Bible* and its symbolical fables. He exclaims:

If we hold to the letter, and must understand what stands written in the law after the manner of the Jews and common people, then I should blush to confess aloud that it is God who has given these laws: then the laws of men appear more excellent and reasonable.*

And well he might have "blushed," the sincere and honest Father of early Christianity in its days of relative purity. But the Christians of this highly literary and civilised age of ours do not blush at all; they swallow, on the contrary, the "light" before the formation of the sun, the Garden of Eden, Jonah's whale and all, notwithstanding that the same Origen asks in a very natural fit of indignation:

What man of sense will agree with the statement that the first, second and third days in which the *evening* is named and the *morning*, were without sun, moon, and stars, and the first day without a heaven? What man is found such an idiot as to suppose that God planted trees in Paradise, in Eden, like a husbandman, etc.? I believe that every man must hold these things for images, under which a hidden sense lies concealed?†

Yet millions of "such idiots" are found in our age of enlightenment and not only in the third century. When Paul's unequivocal statement in *Galatians*, iv. 22-25, that the story of Abraham and his two sons is all "an allegory," and that "Agar is Mount Sinai" is added to this, then little blame, indeed, can be attached to either Christian or Heathen who declines to accept the *Bible* in any other light than that of a very ingenious allegory.

Rabbi Simeon Ben-"Jochai," the compiler of the *Zohar*, never imparted the most important points of his doctrine otherwise than orally, and to a very limited number of disciples. Therefore, without the final initiation into the *Mercavah*, the study of the *Kabalah* will be ever incomplete, and the *Mercavah* can be taught only "in darkness, in a deserted place, and after many and terrific trials." Since the death of that great Jewish Initiate this hidden doctrine has remained, for the outside world, an inviolate secret.

Among the venerable sect of the Tanaim, or rather the Tananim, the wise men, there were those who taught the secrets practically and initiated some disciples into the grand and final Mystery. But the *Mishna Hagiga*, 2nd Section, say that the table of contents of the *Mercaba* "must only be delivered to wise old ones." The *Gemara* is still more dogmatic. "The more important secrets of the Mysteries

* See *Homilies* 7, in *Levit.*, quoted in the *Source of Measures*, p. 307.

† Origen: Huet., *Origeniana*, 167; Franck, 121; quoted from Dunlap's *Sôd*, p. 176.

were not even revealed to all priests. Alone the initiates had them divulged." And so we find the same great secresy prevalent in every ancient religion.*

What says the *Kabalah* itself? Its great Rabbis actually threaten him who accepts their sayings *verbatim*. We read in the *Zohar*:—

> Woe to the man who sees in the Thorah, *i.e.*, Law, only simple recitals and ordinary words! Because if in truth it only contained these, we would even to-day be able to compose a Thorah much more worthy of admiration. For if we find only the simple words, we would only have to address ourselves to the legislators of the earth,† to those in whom we most frequently meet with the most grandeur. It would be sufficient to imitate them, and make a Thorah after their words and example. But it is not so; each word of the Thorah contains an elevated meaning and a sublime mystery. . . . The recitals of the Thorah are the vestments of the Thorah. Woe to him who takes this garment for the Thorah itself. . . . The simple take notice only of the garments or recitals of the Thorah, they know no other thing, they see not that which is concealed under the vestment. The more instructed men do not pay attention to the vestment, but to the body which it envelops.‡

Ammonius Saccas taught that the Secret Doctrine of the Wisdom-Religion was found complete in the *Books of Thoth* (Hermes), from which both Pythagoras and Plato derived their knowledge and much of their Philosophy; and these Books were declared by him to be "identical with the teachings of the Sages of the remote East." Professor A. Wilder remarks:

> As the name Thoth means a college or assembly, it is not altogether improbable that the books were so named as being the collected oracles and doctrines of the sacerdotal fraternity of Memphis. Rabbi Wise has suggested the same hypothesis in relation to the divine utterances recorded in the Hebrew Scriptures.§

This is very probable. Only the "divine utterances" have never been, so far, understood by the profane. Philo Judæus, a non-initiate, attempted to give their secret meaning and—failed.

But *Books of Thoth* or *Bible*, *Vedas* or *Kabalah*, all enjoin the same secresy as to certain mysteries of nature symbolised in them. "Woe be to him who divulges *unlawfully* the words whispered into the ear of

---

* *Isis Unveiled*, ii. 350.

† The materialistic "law-givers," the critics and Sadducees who have tried to tear to shreds the doctrines and teachings of the great Asiatic Masters past and present—no scholars in the modern sense of the word—would do well to ponder over these words. No doubt that doctrines and secret teachings had they been invented and written in Oxford and Cambridge would be more brilliant outwardly. Would they equally answer to universal truths and facts, is the next question however.

‡ iii. fol. 152*b*, quoted in Myer's *Qabbalah*, p. 102.

§ *New-Platonism and Alchemy*, p. 6.

Manushi by the *First Initiator*." Who that "Initiator" was is made plain in the *Book of Enoch*:

> From them [the Angels] I heard all things, and understood what I saw; that which will not take place in this generation [Race], but in a generation which is to succeed at a distant period [the 6th and 7th Races] on account of the elect [the Initiates].*

Again, it is said with regard to the judgment of those who, when they have learned "every secret of the angels," reveal them, that:

> They have discovered secrets, and *they are* those who have been judged; but not thou, my son [Noah] . . . thou art pure and good and *free* from the reproach of *discovering* [revealing] secrets.†

But there are those in our century, who, having "discovered secrets" unaided and owing to their own learning and acuteness only, and who being, nevertheless, honest and straightforward men, undismayed by threats or warning since they have never pledged themselves to secresy, feel quite startled at such revelations. One of these is the learned author and discoverer of one "Key to the Hebrew-Egyptian Mystery." As he says, there are "some strange features connected with the promulgation and condition" of the *Bible*.

> Those who compiled this Book were men as we are. They knew, saw, handled and realized, through the key measure,‡ the *law* of the living, ever-active God.§ They needed no faith that He was, that He worked, planned, and accomplished, as a mighty mechanic and architect.|| What was it, then, that reserved to them alone this knowledge, while first as men of God, and second as Apostles of Jesus the Christ, they doled out a blinding ritual service, and an empty teaching of *faith* and no substance as proof, properly coming through the exercise of just those senses which the Deity has given all men as the essential means of obtaining any right understanding? *Mystery* and *parable*, and *dark saying*, and *cloaking* of the true meanings are the burden of the Testaments, Old and New. Take it that the narratives of the *Bible* were purposed inventions to deceive the ignorant masses, even while enforcing a most perfect code of moral obligations: How is it possible to justify so great frauds, as part of a Divine economy, when to that economy, the attribute of simple and perfect *truthfulness* must, in the nature of things, be

---

* i. 2.

† lxiv. 10.

‡ The *key* is shown to be "in the source of measures originating the British inch and the ancient cubit" as the author tries to prove.

§ The word as a plural might have better solved the mystery. God is *ever-present;* if he were [illegible] he could no longer be an infinite God—nor ever-present in his limitation.

|| The author is evidently a Mason of the way of thinking of General Pike. So long as the American and English Masons will reject the "Creative Principle" of the "Grand Orient" of France they will remain in the dark.

ascribed? What has, or what by possibility ought mystery to have, with the promulgation of the truths of God?*

Nothing whatever most certainly, if those mysteries had been given from the first. And so it was with regard to the first, semi-divine, pure and spiritual Races of Humanity. They had the "truths of God," and lived up to them, and their ideals. They preserved them, so long as there was hardly any evil, and hence scarcely a possible abuse of that knowledge and those truths. But evolution and the gradual fall into materiality is also one of the "truths" and also one of the laws of "God." And as mankind progressed, and became with every generation more of the earth, earthly, the individuality of each temporary Ego began to assert itself. It is personal selfishness that develops and urges man on to abuse of his knowledge and power. And selfishness is a human building, whose windows and doors are ever wide open for every kind of iniquity to enter into man's soul. Few were the men during the early adolescence of mankind, and fewer still are they now, who feel disposed to put into practice Pope's forcible declaration that he would tear out his own heart, if it had no better disposition than to love only himself, and laugh at all his neighbours. Hence the necessity of gradually taking away from man the divine knowledge and power, which became with every new human cycle more dangerous as a double-edged weapon, whose evil side was ever threatening one's neighbour, and whose power for good was lavished freely only upon self. Those few "elect" whose inner natures had remained unaffected by their outward physical growth, thus became in time the sole guardians of the mysteries revealed, passing the knowledge to those most fit to receive it, and keeping it inaccessible to others. Reject this explanation from the Secret Teachings, and the very name of Religion will become synonymous with deception and fraud.

Yet the masses could not be allowed to remain without some sort of moral restraint. Man is ever craving for a "beyond" and cannot live without an ideal of some kind, as a beacon and a consolation. At the same time, no average man, even in our age of universal education, could be entrusted with truths too metaphysical, too subtle for his mind to comprehend, without the danger of an imminent reaction setting in, and faith in Gods and Saints making room for an unscientific blank Atheism. No real philanthropist, hence no Occultist, would

* *Source of Measures*, pp. 308, 309.

dream for a moment of a mankind without one tittle of Religion. Even the modern day Religion in Europe, confined to Sundays, is better than none. But if, as Bunyan put it, "Religion is the best armour that a man can have," it certainly is the "worst cloak"; and it is that "cloak" and false pretence which the Occultists and the Theosophists fight against. The true ideal Deity, the one living God in Nature, can never suffer in man's worship if that outward cloak, woven by man's fancy, and thrown upon the Deity by the crafty hand of the priest greedy of power and domination, is drawn aside. The hour has struck with the commencement of this century to dethrone the "highest God" of every nation in favour of One Universal Deity—the God of Immutable Law, not charity; the God of Just Retribution, not mercy, which is merely an incentive to evil-doing and to a repetition of it. The greatest crime that was ever perpetrated upon mankind was committed on that day when the first priest invented the first prayer with a selfish object in view. A God who may be propitiated by iniquitous prayers to "bless the arms" of the worshipper, and send defeat and death to thousands of his enemies—his brethren; a Deity that can be supposed not to turn a deaf ear to chants of laudation mixed with entreaties for a "fair propitious wind" for self, and as naturally disastrous to the selves of other navigators who come from an opposite direction—it is this idea of God that has fostered selfishness in man, and deprived him of his self-reliance. Prayer is an ennobling action when it is an intense feeling, an ardent desire rushing forth from our very heart, for the good of other people, and when entirely detached from any selfish personal object; the craving for a beyond is natural and holy in man, but on the condition of sharing that bliss with others. One can understand and well appreciate the words of the "heathen" Socrates, who declared in his profound though untaught wisdom, that:

> Our prayers should be for blessings on all, in general, for the Gods know best what is good for us.

But official prayer—in favour of a public calamity, or for the benefit of one individual irrespective of losses to thousands—is the most ignoble of crimes, besides being an impertinent conceit and a superstition. This is the direct inheritance by spoliation from the Jehovites—the Jews of the Wilderness and of the Golden Calf.

It is "Jehovah," as will be presently shown, that suggested the necessity of veiling and screening this substitute for the unpronounceable name, and that led to all this "mystery, parables, dark sayings and cloaking." Moses had, at any rate, initiated his seventy Elders into the hidden truths, and thus the writers of the *Old Testament* stand to a degree justified. Those of the *New Testament* have failed to do even so much, or so little. They have disfigured the grand central figure of Christ by their dogmas, and have led people ever since into millions of errors and the darkest crimes, in His holy name.

It is evident that with the exception of Paul and Clement of Alexandria, who had been both initiated into the Mysteries, none of the Fathers knew much of the truth themselves. They were mostly uneducated, ignorant people; and if such as Augustine and Lactantius, or again the Venerable Bede and others, were so painfully ignorant until the time of Galileo* of the most vital truths taught in the Pagan temples—of the rotundity of the earth, for example, leaving the heliocentric system out of question—how great must have been the ignorance of the rest! Learning and sin were synonymous with the early Christians. Hence the accusations of dealing with the Devil lavished on the Pagan Philosophers.

But truth must out. The Occultists, referred to as "the followers of the accursed Cain," by such writers as De Mirville, are now in a position to reverse the tables. That which was hitherto known only to the ancient and modern Kabalists in Europe and Asia, is now published and shown as being mathematically true. The author of the *Key to the Hebrew-Egyptian Mystery or the Source of Measures* has now proved to general satisfaction, it is to be hoped, that the two great God-names, Jehovah and Elohim, stood, in one meaning of their numerical values, for a diameter and a circumference value, respectively; in other words, that they are numerical indices of geometrical relations; and finally that *Jehovah is Cain* and *vice versâ*.

This view, says the author,

Helps also to take the horrid blemish off from the name of Cain, as a put-up job to destroy his character; for even without these showings, by the very text, *he* [Cain] *was Jehovah*. So the theological schools had better be alive to making the

---

* In his *Pneumatologie*, in Vol. iv., pp. 105-112, the Marquis de Mirville claims the knowledge of the heliocentric system—earlier than Galileo—for Pope Urban VIII. The author goes further. He tries to show that famous Pope, not as the persecutor but as one persecuted by Galileo, and calumniated by the Florentine Astronomer into the bargain. If so, so much the worse for the Latin Church, since her Popes, knowing of it, still preserved silence upon this most important fact, either to screen Joshua or their own infallibility. One can understand well that the *Bible* having been so exalted over all the other systems, and its alleged monotheism depending upon the silence preserved, nothing remained of course but to keep quiet over its symbolism, thus allowing all its blunders to be fathered on its God.

amend honorable, if such a thing is possible, to the good name and fame of the God they worship.*

This is not the first warning received by the "theological schools," which, however, no doubt knew it from the beginning, as did Clemens of Alexandria and others. But if it be so they will profit still less by it, as the admission would involve more for them than the mere sacredness and dignity of the established faith.

But, it may also be asked, why is it that the Asiatic religions, which have nothing of this sort to conceal and which proclaim quite openly the Esoterism of their doctrines, follow the same course? It is simply this: While the present, and no doubt enforced silence of the Church on this subject relates merely to the external or theoretical form of the *Bible*—the unveiling of the secrets of which would have involved no practical harm, had they been explained from the first—it is an entirely different question with Eastern Esoterism and Symbology. The grand central figure of the Gospels would have remained as unaffected by the symbolism of the *Old Testament* being revealed, as would that of the Founder of Buddhism had the Brâhmanical writings of the *Purânas*, that preceded his birth, all been shown to be allegorical. Jesus of Nazareth, moreover, would have gained more than he would have lost had he been presented as a simple mortal left to be judged on his own precepts and merits, instead of being fathered on Christendom as a God whose many utterances and acts are now so open to criticism. On the other hand the symbols and allegorical sayings that veil the grand truths of Nature in the *Vedas*, the *Brâhmanas*, the *Upanishads* and especially in the Lamaist *Chagpa Thogmed* and other works, are quite of a different nature, and far more complicated in their secret meaning. While the Biblical glyphs have nearly all a triune foundation, those of the Eastern books are worked on the septenary principle. They are

---

* *Op. cit.*, App. vii. p. 296. The writer feels happy to find this fact now mathematically demonstrated. When it was stated in *Isis Unveiled* that Jehovah and Saturn were one and the same with Adam Kadmon, Cain, Adam and Eve, Abel, Seth, etc., and that all were convertible symbols in the Secret Doctrine (see Vol. ii. pp. 446, 448, 464 *et seq.*); that they answered, in short, to secret numerals and stood for more than one meaning in the *Bible* as in other doctrines—the author's statements remained unnoticed. *Isis* had failed to appear under a scientific form, and by giving too much, in fact, gave very little to satisfy the enquirer. But now, if mathematics and geometry, besides the evidence of the *Bible* and *Kabalah* are good for anything, the public must find itself satisfied. No fuller, more scientifically given proof can be found to show that Cain is the transformation of an Elohim (the Sephira Binah) into Jah-veh (or God-Eve) androgyne, and that Seth is the Jehovah male, than in the combined discoveries of Seyffarth, Knight, etc., and finally in Mr. Ralston Skinner's most erudite work. The further relations of these personifications of the first human races, in their gradual development, will be given later on in the text.

as closely related to the mysteries of Physics and Physiology, as to Psychism and the transcendental nature of cosmic elements and Theogony; unriddled they would prove more than injurious to the uninitiated; delivered into the hands of the present generations in their actual state of physical and intellectual development, in the absence of spirituality and even of practical morality, they would become absolutely disastrous.

Nevertheless the secret teachings of the sanctuaries have not remained without witness; they have been made immortal in various ways. They have burst upon the world in hundreds of volumes full of the quaint, head-breaking phraseology of the Alchemist; they have flashed like irrepressible cataracts of Occult mystic lore from the pens of poets and bards. Genius alone had certain privileges in those dark ages when no dreamer could offer the world even a fiction without suiting his heaven and his earth to biblical text. To genius alone it was permitted in those centuries of mental blindness, when the fear of the "Holy Office" threw a thick veil over every cosmic and psychic truth, to reveal unimpeded some of the grandest truths of Initiation. Whence did Ariosto, in his *Orlando Furioso*, obtain his conception of that valley in the Moon, where after our death we can find the ideas and images of all that exists on earth? How came Dante to imagine the many descriptions given in his *Inferno*—a new Johannine Apocalypse, a true Occult Revelation in verse—his visit and communion with the Souls of the Seven Spheres? In poetry and satire every Occult truth has been welcomed—none has been recognised as serious. The Comte de Gabalis is better known and appreciated than Porphyry and Iamblichus. Plato's mysterious Atlantis is proclaimed a fiction, while Noah's Deluge is to this day on the brain of certain Archæologists, who scoff at the archetypal world of Marcel Palingenius' *Zodiac*, and would resent as a personal injury being asked to discuss the four worlds of Mercury Trismegistus—the Archetypal, the Spiritual, the Astral and the Elementary, with three others behind the opened scene. Evidently civilised society is still but half prepared for the revelation. Hence, the Initiates will never give out the whole secret, until the bulk of mankind has changed its actual nature and is better prepared for truth. Clemens Alexandrinus was positively right in saying, "It is requisite to hide in a mystery the wisdom spoken"—which the "Sons of God" teach.

That Wisdom, as will be seen, relates to all the primeval truths delivered to the first Races, the "Mind-born," by the "Builders" of the Universe Themselves.

> There was in every ancient country having claims to civilisation, an Esoteric Doctrine, a system which was designated WISDOM,* and those who were devoted to its prosecution were first denominated sages, or wise men. . . . Pythagoras termed this system ἡ γνῶσις τῶν ὄντων, the Gnosis or Knowledge of things that are. Under the noble designation of WISDOM, the ancient teachers, the sages of India, the magians of Persia and Babylon, the seers and prophets of Israel, the hierophants of Egypt and Arabia, and the philosophers of Greece and the West, included all knowledge which they considered as essentially divine; classifying a part as esoteric and the remainder as exterior. The Rabbis called the exterior and secular series the *Mercavah*, as being the body or vehicle which contained the higher knowledge.†

Later on, we shall speak of the law of the silence imposed on Eastern chelas.

---

* The writings extant in olden times often personified Wisdom as an emanation and associate of the Creator. Thus we have the Hindu Buddha, the Babylonian Nebo, the Thoth of Memphis, the Hermes of Greece; also the female divinities, Neitha, Metis, Athena, and the Gnostic potency Achamoth or Sophia. The Samaritan *Pentateuch* denominated the *Book of Genesis*, Akamouth, or Wisdom, and two remnants of old treatises, the *Wisdom of Solomon* and the *Wisdom of Jesus*, relate to the same matters. The *Book of Mashalim*—the *Discourses* or *Proverbs* of Solomon—thus personifies Wisdom as the auxiliary of the Creator. In the Secret Wisdom of the East that auxiliary is found collectively in the first emanations of Primeval Light, the Seven Dhyani-Chohans, who have been shown to be identical with the "Seven Spirits of the Presence" of the Roman Catholics.

† *New Platonism and Alchemy*, p. 6.

SECTION V.

SOME REASONS FOR SECRESY.

THE fact that the Occult Sciences have been withheld from the world at large, and denied by the Initiates to Humanity, has often been made matter of complaint. It has been alleged that the Guardians of the Secret Lore were selfish in withholding the "treasures" of Archaic Wisdom; that it was positively criminal to keep back such knowledge—"if any"—from the men of Science, etc.

Yet there must have been some very good reasons for it, since from the very dawn of History such has been the policy of every Hierophant and "Master." Pythagoras, the first Adept and real Scientist in pre-Christian Europe, is accused of having taught in public the immobility of the earth, and the rotatory motion of the stars around it, while he was declaring to his privileged Adepts his belief in the motion of the Earth as a planet, and in the heliocentric system. The reasons for such secresy, however, are many and were never made a mystery of. The chief cause was given in *Isis Unveiled*. It may now be repeated.

From the very day when the first mystic, taught by the first Instructor of the "divine Dynasties" of the early races, was taught the means of communication between this world and the worlds of the invisible host, between the sphere of matter and that of pure spirit, he concluded that to abandon this mysterious science to the desecration, willing or unwilling, of the profane rabble—was to lose it. An abuse of it might lead mankind to speedy destruction; it was like surrounding a group of children with explosive substances, and furnishing them with matches. The first divine Instructor initiated but a select few, and these kept silence with the multitudes. They recognised *their* "God" and each Adept felt the great "SELF" within himself. The Âtman, the Self, the mighty Lord and Protector, once that man knew him as the "I am," the "Ego Sum," the "Asmi," showed his full power to him who could recognise the "still small voice." From the days of the primitive man described by the first Vedic poet, down to our modern age, there has not been a philosopher worthy of that name, who did not carry in the silent sanctuary of his heart the grand and mysterious truth. If initiated, he learnt it as a

> sacred science; if otherwise, then, like Socrates, repeating to himself as well as his fellow-men, the noble injunction, "O man, know thyself," he succeeded in recognising his God within himself. "Ye are Gods," the king-psalmist tells us, and we find Jesus reminding the scribes that this expression was addressed to other mortal men, claiming for themselves the same privilege without any blasphemy. And as a faithful echo, Paul, while asserting that we are all "the temple of the living God," cautiously remarked elsewhere that after all these things are only for the "wise," and it is "unlawful" to speak of them.*

Some of the reasons for this secresy may here be given.

The fundamental law and master-key of practical Theurgy, in its chief applications to the serious study of cosmic and sidereal, of psychic and spiritual, mysteries was, and still is, that which was called by the Greek Neoplatonists "Theophania." In its generally-accepted meaning this is "communication between the Gods (or God) and those initiated mortals who are spiritually fit to enjoy such an intercourse." Esoterically, however, it signifies more than this. For it is not only the presence of a God, but an actual—howbeit temporary—incarnation, the blending, so to say, of the personal Deity, the Higher Self, with man—its representative or agent on earth. As a general law, the Highest God, the Over-soul of the human being (Âtma-Buddhi), only overshadows the individual during his life, for purposes of instruction and revelation; or as Roman Catholics—who erroneously call that Over-soul the "Guardian Angel"—would say, "It stands outside and watches." But in the case of the theophanic mystery, it incarnates itself in the Theurgist for purposes of revelation. When the incarnation is temporary, during those mysterious trances or "ecstasy," which Plotinus defined as

> The liberation of the mind from its finite consciousness, becoming one and identified with the Infinite,

this sublime condition is very short. The human soul, being the offspring or emanation of its God, the "Father and the Son" become one, "the divine fountain flowing like a stream into its human bed."† In exceptional cases, however, the mystery becomes complete; the

* ii. 317, 318. Many verbal alterations from the original text of *Isis Unveiled* were made by H. P. B. in her quotations therefrom, and these are followed throughout.

† Proclus claims to have experienced this sublime ecstasy six times during his mystic life; Porphyry asserts that Apollonius of Tyana was thus united four times to his deity—a statement which we believe to be a mistake, since Apollonius was a Nirmânakâya (divine incarnation—not Avatâra)—and he (Porphyry) only once, when over sixty years of age. Theophany (or the actual appearance of a God to man), Theopathy (or "assimilation of divine nature"), and Theopneusty (inspiration, or rather the mysterious power to hear orally the teachings of a God) have never been rightly understood.

Word is made Flesh in real fact, the individual becoming divine in the full sense of the term, since his personal God has made of him his permanent life-long tabernacle—"the temple of God," as Paul says.

Now that which is meant here by the *personal* God of Man is, of course, not his seventh Principle alone, as *per se* and in essence that is merely a beam of the infinite Ocean of Light. In conjunction with our Divine Soul, the Buddhi, it cannot be called a Duad, as it otherwise might, since, though formed from Âtmâ and Buddhi (the two higher Principles), the former is no entity but an emanation from the Absolute, and indivisible in reality from it. The personal God is not the Monad, but indeed the prototype of the latter, what for want of a better term we call the *manifested* Kâranâtmâ* (Causal Soul), one of the "seven" and chief reservoirs of the human Monads or Egos. The latter are gradually formed and strengthened during their incarnation-cycle by constant additions of individuality from the personalities in which incarnates that androgynous, half-spiritual, half-terrestrial principle, partaking of both heaven and earth, called by the Vedântins Jîva and Vijñânamaya Kosha, and by the Occultists the Manas (mind); that, in short, which uniting itself partially with the Monad, incarnates in each new birth. In perfect unity with its (seventh) Principle, the Spirit unalloyed, it is the divine Higher Self, as every student of Theosophy knows. After every new incarnation Buddhi-Manas culls, so to say, the aroma of the flower called personality, the purely earthly residue of which—its dregs—is left to fade out as a shadow. This is the most difficult—because so transcendentally metaphysical—portion of the doctrine.

As is repeated many a time in this and other works, it is not the Philosophers, Sages, and Adepts of antiquity who can ever be charged with idolatry. It is they in fact, who, recognising divine unity, were the only ones, owing to their initiation into the mysteries of Esotericism, to understand correctly the ὑπόνοια (hyponéa), or under-meaning of the anthropomorphism of the so-called Angels, Gods, and spiritual Beings of every kind. Each, worshipping the one Divine Essence that pervades the whole world of Nature, reverenced, but never worshipped or idolised, any of these "Gods," whether high or low—not even his own personal Deity, of which he was a Ray, and to whom he appealed.†

* Kârana Sharîra is the "causal" body and is sometimes said to be the "personal God." And so it is, in one sense.

† This would be in one sense Self-worship.

"The holy Triad emanates from the One, and is the Tetraktys; the gods, dæmons, and souls are an emanation of the Triad. Heroes and men repeat the hierarchy in themselves.

Thus said Metrodorus of Chios, the Pythagorean, the latter part of the sentence meaning that man has within himself the seven pale reflections of the seven divine Hierarchies; his Higher Self is, therefore, in itself but the refracted beam of the direct Ray. He who regards the latter as an Entity, in the usual sense of the term, is one of the "infidels and atheists," spoken of by Epicurus, for he fastens on that God "the opinions of the multitude"—an anthropomorphism of the grossest kind.* The Adept and the Occultist know that "what are styled the Gods are only the first principles" (Aristotle). None the less they are intelligent, conscious, and *living* "Principles," the Primary Seven Lights *manifested* from Light *unmanifested*—which to us is Darkness. They are the Seven—exoterically four—Kumâras or "Mind-Born Sons" of Brahmâ. And it is they again, the Dhyân Chohans, who are the prototypes in the æonic eternity of lower Gods and hierarchies of divine Beings, at the lowest end of which ladder of being are we—men.

Thus perchance Polytheism, when philosophically understood, may be a degree higher than even the Monotheism of the Protestant, say, who limits and conditions the Deity in whom he persists in seeing the Infinite, but whose supposed actions make of that "Absolute and Infinite" the most absurd paradox in Philosophy. From this standpoint Roman Catholicism itself is immeasurably higher and more logical than Protestantism, though the Roman Church has been pleased to adopt the exotericism of the heathen "multitude" and to reject the Philosophy of pure Esotericism.

Thus every mortal has his immortal counterpart, or rather his Archetype, in heaven. This means that the former is indissolubly united to the latter, in each of his incarnations, and for the duration of the cycle of births; only it is by the spiritual and intellectual Principle in him, entirely distinct from the lower *self*, never through the earthly personality. Some of these are even liable to break the union altogether, in case of absence in the moral individual of binding, *viz.*, of spiritual ties. Truly, as Paracelsus puts it in his quaint, tortured

* "The Gods exist," said Epicurus, "but they are not what the *hoi polloi* [the multitude] suppose them to be. He is not an infidel or atheist who denies the existence of Gods whom the multitude worship, but he is such who fastens on the Gods the opinions of the multitude."

phraseology, man with his three (compound) Spirits is suspended like a fœtus by all three to the matrix of the Macrocosm; the thread which holds him united being the "Thread-Soul," Sûtrâtmâ, and Taijasa (the "Shining") of the Vedântins. And it is through this spiritual and intellectual Principle in man, through Taijasa—the Shining, "because it has the luminous internal organ as its associate"—that man is thus united to his heavenly prototype, never through his lower inner self or Astral Body, for which there remains in most cases nothing but to fade out.

Occultism, or Theurgy, teaches the means of producing such union. But it is the actions of man—his personal merit alone—that can produce it on earth, or determine its duration. This lasts from a few seconds—a flash—to several hours, during which time the Theurgist or Theophanist is that overshadowing "God" himself; hence he becomes endowed for the time being with relative omniscience and omnipotence. With such perfect (divine) Adepts as Buddha* and others such a hypostatical state of avatâric condition may last during the whole life; whereas in the case of full Initiates, who have not yet reached the perfect state of Jîvanmukta,† Theopneusty, when in full sway, results for the high Adept in a full recollection of everything seen, heard, or sensed.

Taijasa has fruition of the supersensible.‡

For one less perfect it will end only in a partial, indistinct remembrance; while the beginner has to face in the first period of his psychic experiences a mere confusion, followed by a rapid and finally complete oblivion of the mysteries seen during this super-hypnotic condition. The degree of recollection, when one returns to his waking state and physical senses, depends on his spiritual and psychic purification, the greatest enemy of spiritual memory being man's physical brain, the organ of his sensuous nature.

The above states are described for a clearer comprehension of terms used in this work. There are so many and such various conditions and states that even a Seer is liable to confound one with the other.

---

* Esoteric, as exoteric, Buddhism rejects the theory that Gautama was an incarnation or Avatâra of Vishnu, but teaches the doctrine as herein explained. Every man has in him the materials, if not the conditions, for theophanic intercourse and Theopneusty, the inspiring "God" being, however, in every case, his own Higher Self, or divine prototype.

† One entirely and absolutely purified, and having nothing in common with earth except his body.

‡ *Mândâkyopanishad*, 4.

To repeat: the Greek, rarely-used word, "Theophania," meant more with the Neoplatonists than it does with the modern maker of dictionaries. The compound word, "Theophania" (from "theos," "God," and "phainomai," "to appear"), does not simply mean "a manifestation of God to man by *actual* appearance"—an absurdity, by the way—but the actual presence of a God in man, a *divine* incarnation. When Simon the Magician claimed to be "God the Father," what he wanted to convey was just that which has been explained, namely, that he was a *divine* incarnation of his own Father, whether we see in the latter an Angel, a God, or a Spirit; therefore he was called "that power of God which is called great,"* or that power which causes the Divine Self to enshrine itself in its lower self—man.

This is one of the several mysteries of being and incarnation. Another is that when an Adept reaches during his lifetime that state of holiness and purity that makes him "equal to the Angels," then at death his apparitional or astral body becomes as solid and tangible as was the late body, and is transformed into the real man.† The old physical body, falling off like the cast-off serpent's skin, the body of the "new" man remains either visible or, at the option of the Adept, disappears from view, surrounded as it is by the Âkâshic shell that screens it. In the latter case there are three ways open to the Adept:

(1.) He may remain in the earth's sphere (Vâyu or Kâma-loka), in that ethereal locality concealed from human sight save during flashes of clairvoyance. In this case his astral body, owing to its great purity and spirituality, having lost the conditions required for Âkâshic light (the nether or terrestrial ether) to absorb its semi-material particles, the Adept will have to remain in the company of disintegrating shells—doing no good or useful work. This, of course, cannot be.

(2.) He can by a supreme effort of will merge entirely into, and get united with, his Monad. By doing so, however, he would (*a*) deprive his Higher Self of posthumous Samâdhi—a bliss which is not real Nirvâna—the astral, however pure, being too earthly for such state; and (*b*) he would thereby open himself to Karmic law; the action being, in fact, the outcome of personal selfishness—of reaping the fruits produced by and for oneself—alone.

(3.) The Adept has the option of renouncing conscious Nirvâna and

---

* *Acts*, viii. 10 (Revised Version).

† See the explanations given on the subject in "The Elixir of Life," by G. M (From a Chelâ's Diary), *Five Years of Theosophy*.

rest, to work on earth for the good of mankind. This he can do in a two-fold way; either, as above said, by consolidating his astral body into physical appearance, he can reässume the self-same personality; or he can avail himself of an entirely new physical body, whether that of a newly-born infant or—as Shankarâchârya is reported to have done with the body of a dead Râjah—by "entering a deserted sheath," and living in it as long as he chooses. This is what is called "continuous existence." The Section entitled "The Mystery about Buddha" will throw additional light on this theory, to the profane incomprehensible, or to the generality simply *absurd*. Such is the doctrine taught, every one having the choice of either fathoming it still deeper, or of leaving it unnoticed.

The above is simply a small portion of what might have been given in *Isis Unveiled*, had the time come then, as it has now. One cannot study and profit by Occult Science, unless one gives himself up to it —heart, soul, and body. Some of its truths are too awful, too dangerous, for the average mind. None can toy and play with such terrible weapons with impunity. Therefore it is, as St. Paul has it, "unlawful" to speak of them. Let us accept the reminder and talk only of that which is "lawful."

The quotation on p. 56 relates, moreover, only to psychic or spiritual Magic. The practical teachings of Occult Science are entirely different, and few are the strong minds fitted for them. As to ecstasy, and such like kinds of self-illumination, this may be obtained by oneself and without any teacher or initiation, for ecstacy is reached by an inward command and control of Self over the physical Ego; as to obtaining mastery over the forces of Nature, this requires a long training, or the capacity of one born a "natural Magician." Meanwhile, those who possess neither of the requisite qualifications are strongly advised to limit themselves to purely spiritual development. But even this is difficult, as the first necessary qualification is an unshakable belief in one's own powers and the Deity within oneself; otherwise a man would simply develop into an irresponsible medium. Throughout the whole mystic literature of the ancient world we detect the same idea of spiritual Esoterism, that the personal God exists within, nowhere outside, the worshipper. That personal Deity is no vain breath, or a fiction, but an immortal Entity, the Initiator of the Initiates, now that the heavenly or Celestial Initiators of primitive humanity—the Shishta of the preceding cycles—are no more among us. Like an undercurrent, rapid and clear, it runs, without mixing its crystalline purity with the muddy and troubled waters of dogmatism, an enforced anthropomorphic Deity and religious intolerance. We find this idea in the tortured and barbarous phraseology of the *Codex Nazaræus*, and in the superb Neoplatonic language of the Fourth Gospel of the later Religion, in the oldest *Veda* and in the *Avesta*, in the *Abhidharma*, in Kapila's *Sânkhya*, and the *Bhagavad Gîtâ*. We cannot attain Adeptship and Nirvâna, Bliss and the "Kingdom of Heaven," unless we link ourselves indissolubly with our Rex Lux, the Lord of Splendour and of Light, our immortal God within us. "Aham eva param Brahman"—"I am verily the Supreme Brahman"—has ever been the one living truth in the heart and mind of the Adepts, and it is this which helps the Mystic to become one. One must first of all recognise one's own immortal Principle, and then only can one conquer, or take the Kingdom of Heaven by violence. Only this has to be achieved by the higher—not the middle, nor the third—man, the last one being of dust. Nor can the second man, the "Son"—on this plane, as his "Father" is the Son on a still higher plane—do anything without the assistance of the first, the "Father." But to succeed one has to identify oneself with one's divine Parent.

> The first man is of the earth, earthy; the second [inner, our higher] man is the Lord from heaven. . . . . Behold, I show you a mystery.*

Thus says Paul, mentioning but the dual and trinitarian man for the better comprehension of the non-initiated. But this is not all, for the Delphic injunction has to be fulfilled: man must know himself in order to become a perfect Adept. How few can acquire the knowledge, however, not merely in its inner mystical, but even in its literal sense, for there are two meanings in this command of the Oracle. This is the doctrine of Buddha and the Bodhisattvas pure and simple.

Such is also the mystical sense of what was said by Paul to the Corinthians about their being the "temple of God," for this meant Esoterically:

> Ye are the temple of [the, or your] God, and the Spirit of [a, or your] God dwelleth in you.†

---

* I. *Cor.*, xv. 47, 50.

† I. *Cor.*, iii. 16. Has the reader ever meditated upon the suggestive words, often pronounced by Jesus and his Apostles? "Be ye therefore perfect as your Father . . is perfect" (*Matt.*, v. 48), says the Great Master. The words are, "as perfect as your Father which is in heaven," being interpreted as meaning God. Now the utter absurdity of any man becoming as perfect as the infinite, all-perfect omniscient and omnipresent Deity, is too apparent. If you accept it in such a sense, Jesus is made

This carries precisely the same meaning as the "I am verily Brahman" of the Vedântin. Nor is the latter assertion more blasphemous than the Pauline—if there were any blasphemy in either, which is denied. Only the Vedântin, who never refers to his body as being himself, or even a part of himself, or aught else but an illusory form for others to see him in, constructs his assertion more openly and sincerely than was done by Paul.

The Delphic command "Know thyself" was perfectly comprehensible to every nation of old. So it is now, save to the Christians, since, with the exception of the Mussulmans, it is part and parcel of every Eastern religion, including the Kabalistically instructed Jews. To understand its full meaning, however, necessitates, first of all, belief in Reincarnation and all its mysteries; not as laid down in the doctrine of the French Reincarnationists of the Allan Kardec school, but as they are expounded and taught by Esoteric Philosophy. Man must, in short, know who he was, before he arrives at knowing what he is. And how many are there among Europeans who are capable of developing within themselves an absolute belief in their past and future reincarnations, in general, even as a law, let alone mystic knowledge of one's immediately precedent life? Early education, tradition and training of thought, everything is opposing itself during their whole lives to such a belief. Cultured people have been brought up in that most pernicious idea that the wide difference found between the units of one and the same mankind, or even race, is the result of chance; that the gulf between man and man in their respective social positions, birth, intellect, physical and mental capacities—every one of which qualifications has a direct influence on every human life—that all this is simply due to blind hazard, only the most pious among them finding equivocal consolation in the idea that it is "the will of God." They have never analysed, never stopped to think of the depth of the opprobrium that is thrown upon their God, once the grand and most equitable law of the manifold re-births of man upon this earth is foolishly rejected. Men and women anxious to be regarded as Christians, often

---

to utter the greatest fallacy. What was Esoterically meant is, "Your Father who is above the material and astral man, the highest Principle (save the Monad) within man, his own personal God, or the God of his own personality, of whom he is the 'prison' and the temple.'" "*If thou wilt be perfect* (*i.e.*, an Adept and Initiate) *go and sell that thou hast*" (*Matt.*, xix. 21). Every man who desired to become a neophyte, a chelâ, then, as now, had to take the vow of poverty. The "Perfect," was the name given to the Initiates of every denomination. Plato calls them by that term. The Essenes had their "Perfect," and Paul plainly states that they, the Initiates, can only speak before other Adepts. "We speak wisdom among them (only) that are perfect" (I. *Cor.* ii. 6.)

truly and sincerely trying to lead a Christ-like life, have never paused to reflect over the words of their own *Bible*. "Art thou Elias?" the Jewish priests and Levites asked the Baptist.* Their Saviour taught His disciples this grand truth of the Esoteric Philosophy, but verily, if His Apostles comprehended it, no one else seems to have realised its true meaning. No; not even Nicodemus, who, to the assertion: "Except a man be born again† he cannot see the Kingdom of God," answers: "How can a man be born when he is old?" and is forthwith reproved by the remark: "Art thou a master in Israel and knowest not these things?"—as no one had a right to call himself a "Master" and Teacher, without having been initiated into the mysteries (*a*) of a spiritual re-birth through water, fire and spirit, and (*b*) of the re-birth from flesh.‡ Then again what can be a clearer expression as to the doctrine of manifold re-births than the answer given by Jesus to the Sadducees, "who deny that there is any resurrection," *i.e.*, any re-birth, since the dogma of the resurrection in the flesh is now regarded as an absurdity even by the intelligent clergy;

> They who shall be accounted worthy to obtain that world (Nirvâna)‖ . . . neither marry . . . neither can they die any more,

which shows that they had already died, and more than once. And again;

> Now that the dead are raised even Moses shewed . . . he calleth the Lord the God of Abraham, and the God of Isaac, and the God of Jacob, for he is not a God of the dead but of the living.¶

The sentence "now that the dead *are raised*" evidently applied to the then actual re-births of the Jacobs and the Isaacs, and not to their

---

* *John*, i. 21.

† *John*, iii. "Born" from above, *viz.*, from his Monad or divine EGO, the seventh Principle, which remains till the end of the Kalpa, the nucleus of, and at the same time the overshadowing Principle, as the Kâranâtmâ (Causal Soul) of the personality in every rebirth. In this sense, the sentence "born anew" means "descends from above," the last two words having no reference to heaven or space, neither of which can be limited or located, since one is a state and the other infinite, hence having no cardinal points. (See *New Testament, Revised Version, loc. cit.*)

‡ This can have no reference to Christian Baptism, since there was none in the days of Nicodemus and he could not therefore know anything of it, even though a "Master."

‖ This word, translated in the *New Testament* "world" to suit the official interpretation, means rather an "age" (as shown in the *Revised Version*) or one of the periods during the Manvantara, a Kalpa, or Æon. Esoterically the sentence would read: "He who shall reach, through a series of births and Karmic law, that state in which Humanity shall find itself after the Seventh Round and the Seventh Race, when comes Nirvâna, Moksha, and when man becomes 'equal unto the Angels' or Dhyân Chohans, is a 'son of the resurrection' and 'can die no more': then there will be no marriage, as there will be no difference of sexes"—a result of our present materiality and animalism.

¶ *Luke*, xx. 37-38.

future resurrection; for in such case they would have been still dead in the interim, and could not be referred to as "the living."

But the most suggestive of Christ's parables and "dark sayings" is found in the explanation given by him to his Apostles about the blind man:

Master, who did sin, this man or his parents, that he was born blind? Jesus answered, Neither hath this [blind, physical] man sinned nor his parents; but that the works of [his] God should be made manifest in him.*

Man is the "tabernacle," the "building" only, of his God; and of course it is not the temple but its inmate—the vehicle of "God"†—that had sinned in a previous incarnation, and had thus brought the Karma of cecity upon the new building. Thus Jesus spoke truly; but to this day his followers have refused to understand the words of wisdom spoken. The Saviour is shown by his followers as though he were paving, by his words and explanation, the way to a preconceived programme that had to lead to an intended miracle. Verily the Grand Martyr has remained thenceforward, and for eighteen centuries, the Victim crucified daily far more cruelly by his clerical disciples and lay followers than he ever could have been by his allegorical enemies. For such is the true sense of the words "that the works of God should be made manifest in him," in the light of theological interpretation, and a very undignified one it is, if the Esoteric explanation is rejected.

Doubtless the above will be regarded as fresh blasphemy. Nevertheless there are a number of Christians whom we know—whose hearts go out as strongly to their ideal of Jesus, as their souls are repelled from the theological picture of the official Saviour—who will reflect over our explanation and find in it no offence, but perchance a relief.

* *John*, ix. 2, 3.

† The conscious Ego, or Fifth Principle Manas, the vehicle of the divine Monad or "God."

SECTION VI.

THE DANGERS OF PRACTICAL MAGIC.

MAGIC is a dual power: nothing is easier than to turn it into Sorcery; *an evil thought suffices for it.* Therefore while theoretical Occultism is harmless, and may do good, practical Magic, or the fruits of the Tree of Life and Knowledge,* or otherwise the "Science of Good and Evil," is fraught with dangers and perils. For the study of theoretical Occultism there are, no doubt, a number of works that may be read with profit, besides such books as the *Finer Forces of Nature*, etc., the *Zohar*, *Sepher Jetzirah*, *The Book of Enoch*, Franck's *Kabalah*, and many Hermetic treatises. These are scarce in European languages, but works in Latin by the mediæval Philosophers, generally known as Alchemists and Rosicrucians, are plentiful. But even the perusal of these may prove dangerous for the unguided student. If approached without the right key to them, and if the student is unfit, owing to mental incapacity, for Magic, and is thus unable to discern the Right from the Left Path, let him take our advice and leave this study alone; he will only bring on himself and on his family unexpected woes and sorrows, never suspecting whence they come, nor what are the powers awakened by his mind being bent on them. Works for advanced students are many, but these can be placed at the disposal of only sworn or "pledged" chelâs (disciples), those who have pronounced the ever-binding oath, and who are, therefore, helped and protected. For all other purposes, well-intentioned as such works may

---

* Some Symbologists, relying on the correspondence of numbers and the symbols of certain things and personages, refer these "secrets" to the mystery of generation. But it is more than this. The glyph of the "Tree of Knowledge of Good and Evil" has no doubt a phallic and sexual element in it, as has the "Woman and the Serpent"; but it has also a psychical and spiritual significance. Symbols are meant to yield more than one meaning.

be, they can only mislead the unwary and guide him imperceptibly to Black Magic or Sorcery—if to nothing worse.

The mystic characters, alphabets and numerals found in the divisions and sub-divisions of the *Great Kabalah*, are, perhaps, the most dangerous portions in it, and especially the numerals. We say dangerous, because they are the most prompt to produce effects and results, and this with or without the experimenter's will, even without his knowledge. Some students are apt to doubt this statement, simply because after manipulating these numerals they have failed to notice any dire physical manifestation or result. Such results would be found the least dangerous: it is the moral causes produced and the various events developed and brought to an unforeseen crisis, that would testify to the truth of what is now stated had the lay students only the power of discernment.

The point of departure of that special branch of the Occult teaching known as the "Science of Correspondences," numerical or literal or alphabetical, has for its epigraph with the Jewish and Christian Kabalists, the two mis-interpreted verses which say that God

> ordered all things in number, measure and weight;*

and:

> He created her in the Holy Ghost, and saw her, and numbered her, and measured her.†

But the Eastern Occultists have another epigraph: "*Absolute Unity*, x, within number and plurality." Both the Western and the Eastern students of the Hidden Wisdom hold to this axiomatic truth. Only the latter are perhaps more sincere in their confessions. Instead of putting a mask on their Science, they show her face openly, even if they do veil carefully her heart and soul before the inappreciative public and the profane, who are ever ready to abuse the most sacred truths for their own selfish ends. But Unity is the real basis of the Occult Sciences—physical and metaphysical. This is shown even by Éliphas Lévi, the learned Western Kabalist, inclined as he is to be rather jesuitical. He says:

> Absolute Unity is the supreme and final reason of things. Therefore, that reason can be neither one person, nor three persons; it is Reason, and pre-eminently Reason (*raison par excellence*).‡

* *Wisdom*, xi. 21. Douay version.

† *Ecclesiasticus*, i. 9. Douay version.

‡ *Dogme et Rituel de la Haute Magie*, i. 361.

The meaning of this Unity in Plurality in "God" or Nature, can be solved only by the means of transcendental methods, by numerals, as by the correspondences between soul and the Soul. Names, in the *Kabalah* as in the *Bible*, such as Jehovah, Adam Kadmon, Eve, Cain, Abel, Enoch, are all of them more intimately connected, by geometrical and astronomical relations, with Physiology (or Phallicism) than with Theology or Religion. Little as people are as yet prepared to admit it, this will be shown to be a fact. If all those names are symbols for things hidden, as well as for those manifested, in the *Bible* as in the *Vedas*, their respective mysteries differ greatly. Plato's motto "God geometrises" was accepted by both Âryans and Jews; but while the former applied their Science of Correspondences to veil the most spiritual and sublime truths of Nature, the latter used their acumen to conceal only one—to them the most divine—of the mysteries of Evolution, namely, that of birth and generation, and then they deified the organs of the latter.

Apart from this, every cosmogony, from the earliest to the latest, is based upon, interlinked with, and most closely related to, numerals and geometric figures. Questioned by an Initiate, these figures and numbers will yield numerical values based on the integral values of the Circle—"the secret habitat of the ever-invisible Deity" as the Alchemists have it—as they will yield every other Occult particular connected with such mysteries, whether anthropographical, anthropological, cosmic, or psychical. "In reuniting Ideas to Numbers, we can operate upon Ideas in the same way as upon Numbers, and arrive at the Mathematics of Truth," writes an Occultist, who shows his great wisdom in desiring to remain unknown.

Any Kabalist well acquainted with the Pythagorean system of numerals and geometry can demonstrate that the metaphysical views of Plato were based upon the strictest mathematical principles. "True mathematics," says the *Magicon*, "is something with which all higher sciences are connected; common mathematics is but a deceitful phantasmagoria, whose much praised infallibility only arises from this—that materials, conditions and references are made to foundations."

The cosmological theory of numerals which Pythagoras learned in India, and from the Egyptian Hierophants, is alone able to reconcile the two units, matter and spirit, and cause each to demonstrate the other mathematically. The sacred numbers of the universe in their esoteric combination can alone solve the great problem, and explain the theory of radiation and the cycle of the emanations. The lower orders, before they develop into higher ones, must emanate from the higher spiritual ones, and when arrived at the turning-point, be reabsorbed into the infinite.*

It is upon these true Mathematics that the knowledge of the Kosmos and of all mysteries rests, and to one acquainted with them, it is the easiest thing possible to prove that both Vaidic and Biblical structures are based upon "God-in-Nature" and "Nature-in-God," as the radical law. Therefore, this law—as everything else immutable and fixed in eternity—could find a correct expression only in those purest transcendental Mathematics referred to by Plato, especially in Geometry as transcendentally applied. *Revealed* to men—we fear not and will not retract the expression—in this geometrical and symbolical garb, Truth has grown and developed into additional symbology, invented by man for the wants and better comprehension of the masses of mankind that came too late in their cyclic development and evolution to have shared in the primitive knowledge, and would never have grasped it otherwise. If later on, the clergy—crafty and ambitious of power in every age—anthropomorphised and degraded abstract ideals, as well as the real and divine Beings who do exist in Nature, and are the Guardians and Protectors of our manvantaric world and period, the fault and guilt rests with those would-be leaders, not with the masses.

But the day has come when the gross conceptions of our forefathers during the Middle Ages can no longer satisfy the thoughtful religionist. The mediæval Alchemist and Mystic are now transformed into the sceptical Chemist and Physicist; and most of them are found to have turned away from truth, on account of the purely anthropomorphic ideas, the gross Materialism, of the forms in which it is presented to them. Therefore, future generations have either to be gradually initiated into the truths underlying Exoteric Religions, including their own, or be left to break the feet of clay of the last of the gilded idols. No educated man or woman would turn away from any of the now called "superstitions" which they believe to be based on nursery tales and ignorance, if they could only see the basis of fact that underlies every "superstition." But let them once learn for a certainty that there is hardly a claim in the Occult Sciences that is not founded on philosophical and scientific facts in Nature, and they will pursue the study of those Sciences with the same, if not with greater, ardour than that they have expended in shunning them. This cannot be achieved at

* *Isis Unveiled*, i. 6, 7.

rance, for to benefit mankind such truths have to be revealed gradually and with great caution, the public mind not being prepared for them. However much the Agnostics of our age may find themselves in the mental attitude demanded by Modern Science, people are always apt to cling to their old hobbies so long as the remembrance of them lasts. They are like the Emperor Julian—called the Apostate, because he loved truth too well to accept aught else—who, though in his last Theophany he beheld his beloved Gods as pale, worn-out, and hardly discernible shadows, nevertheless clung to them. Let, then, the world cling to its Gods, to whatever plane or realm they may belong. The true Occultist would be guilty of high treason to mankind, were he to break for ever the old deities before he could replace them with the whole and unadulterated truth—and this he cannot do as yet. Nevertheless, the reader may be allowed to learn at least the alphabet of that truth. He may be shown, at any rate, what the Gods and Goddesses of the Pagans, denounced as demons by the Church, are not, if he cannot learn the whole and final truth as to what they are. Let him assure himself that the Hermetic "Tres Matres," and the "Three Mothers" of the *Sepher Jetzirah* are one and the same thing; that they are no Demon-Goddesses, but Light, Heat, and Electricity, and then, perchance, the learned classes will spurn them no longer. After this, the Rosicrucian Illuminati may find followers even in the Royal Academies, which will be more prepared, perhaps, than they are now, to admit the grand truths of archaic Natural Philosophy, especially when their learned members shall have assured themselves that, in the dialect of Hermes, the "Three Mothers" stand as symbols for the whole of the forces or agencies which have a place assigned to them in the modern system of the "correlation of forces." * Even the polytheism of the "superstitious" Brâhman and idolater shows its *raison d'être*, since the three Shaktis of the three great Gods, Brahmâ, Vishnu, and Shiva, are identical with the "Three Mothers" of the monotheistic Jew.

The whole of the ancient religious and mystical literature is symbolical. The *Books of Hermes*, the *Zohar*, the *Ya-Yakav*, the Egyptian *Book*

---

* "Synesius mentions books of stone which he found in the temple of Memphis, on one of which was engraved the following sentence: 'One *nature* delights in another, one nature overcomes another, one nature overrules another, and the whole of them are *one*'."

"The inherent restlessness of matter is embodied in the saying of Hermes: 'Action is the life of Phta'; and Orpheus calls nature πολυμήχανος μάτηρ, 'the mother that makes many things,' or the ingenious, the contriving, the inventive mother."—*Isis Unveiled*, i. 257.

of the Dead, the *Vedas*, the *Upanishads*, and the *Bible*, are as full of symbolism as are the Nabathean revelations of the Chaldean Qû-tamy. It is a loss of time to ask which is the earliest; all are simply different versions of the one primeval Record of prehistoric knowledge and revelation.

The first four chapters of *Genesis* contain the synopsis of all the rest of the *Pentateuch*, being only the various versions of the same thing in different allegorical and symbolical applications. Having discovered that the Pyramid of Cheops with all its measurements is to be found contained in its minutest details in the structure of Solomon's Temple; and having ascertained that the biblical names Shem, Ham and Japhet are determinative

> of pyramid measures, in connection with the 600-year period of Noah and the 500-year period of Shem, Ham and Japhet; . . . the term "Sons of Elohim" and "Daughters" of H-Adam, [are] for one thing astronomical terms,*

the author of the very curious work already mentioned—a book very little known in Europe, we regret to say—seems to see nothing in his discovery beyond the presence of Mathematics and Metrology in the *Bible*. He also arrives at most unexpected and extraordinary conclusions, such as are very little warranted by the facts discovered. His impression seems to be that because the Jewish biblical names are all astronomical, therefore the Scriptures of all the other nations can be "only this and nothing more." But this is a great mistake of the erudite and wonderfully acute author of *The Source of Measures*, if he really thinks so. The "Key to the Hebrew-Egyptian Mystery" unlocks but a certain portion of the hieratic writings of these two nations, and leaves those of other peoples untouched. His idea is that the *Kabalah* "is only that sublime Science upon which Masonry is based"; in fact he regards Masonry as the substance of the *Kabalah*, and the latter as the "rational basis of the Hebrew text of Holy Writ." About this we will not argue with the author. But why should all those who may have found in the *Kabalah* something beyond "the sublime Science" upon which Masonry is alleged to have been built, be held up to public contempt?

In its exclusiveness and one-sidedness such a conclusion is pregnant with future misconceptions and is absolutely wrong. In its uncharitable criticism it throws a slur upon the "Divine Science" itself.

* *Source of Measures*, p. x.

The *Kabalah* is indeed "of the essence of Masonry," but it is dependent on Metrology only in one of its aspects, the less Esoteric, as even Plato made no secret that the Deity was ever geometrising. For the uninitiated, however learned and endowed with genius they may be, the *Kabalah*, which treats only of "the garment of God," or the *veil* and *cloak* of truth,

is built from the ground upward with a practical application to present uses.*

Or in other words represents an exact Science only on the terrestrial plane. To the initiated, the Kabalistic Lord descends from the primeval Race, generated spiritually from the "Mind-born Seven." Having reached the Earth the Divine Mathematics—a synonym for Magic in his day, as we are told by Josephus—veiled her face. Hence the most important secret yet yielded by her in our modern day is the identity of the old Roman measures and the present British measures, of the Hebrew-Egyptian cubit and the Masonic inch.†

The discovery is most wonderful, and has led to further and minor unveilings of various riddles in reference to Symbology and biblical names. It is thoroughly understood and proven, as shown by Nachanides, that in the days of Moses the initial sentence in *Genesis* was made to read *B'rash ithbara Elohim*, or "In the head-source [or Mûlaprakiti—the Rootless Root] developed [or evolved] the Gods [Elohim], the heavens and the earth;" whereas it is now, owing to the Massora and theological cunning, transformed into *B'rashith bara Elohim*, or, "In the beginning God created the heavens and the earth;"—which word juggling alone has led to materialistic anthropomorphism and dualism. How many more similar instances may not be found in the *Bible*, the last and latest of the Occult works of antiquity? There is no longer any doubt in the mind of the Occultist, that, notwithstanding its form and outward meaning, the *Bible*—as explained by the *Zohar* or *Midrash*, the *Yetzirah* (Book of Creation) and the *Commentary on the Ten Sephiroth* (by Azariel Ben Manachem of the XIIth century)—is part and parcel of the Secret Doctrine of the Âryans, which explains in the same manner the *Vedas* and all other allegorical books. The *Zohar*, in teaching that the Impersonal One Cause manifests in the Universe through Its Emanations, the Sephiroth—that Universe being in its

* *Masonic Review*, July, 1886.

† See *Source of Measures*, pp. 47—50, *et pass.*

totality simply the veil woven from the Deity's own substance—is undeniably the copy and faithful echo of the earliest *Vedas*. Taken by itself, without the additional help of the Vaidic and of Brahmanical literature in general, the *Bible* will never yield the universal secrets of Occult Nature. The cubits, inches, and measures of this physical plane will never solve the problems of the world on the spiritual plane—for Spirit can neither be weighed nor measured. The working out of these problems is reserved for the "mystics and the dreamers" who alone are capable of accomplishing it.

Moses was an initiated priest, versed in all the mysteries and the Occult knowledge of the Egyptian temples—hence thoroughly acquainted with primitive Wisdom. It is in the latter that the symbolical and astronomical meaning of that "Mystery of Mysteries," the Great Pyramid, has to be sought. And having been so familiar with the geometrical secrets that lay concealed for long æons in her stony bosom—the measurements and proportions of the Kosmos, our little Earth included—what wonder that he should have made use of his knowledge? The Esoterism of Egypt was that of the whole world at one time. During the long ages of the Third Race it had been the heirloom, in common, of the whole of mankind, received from their Instructors, the "Sons of Light," the primeval Seven. There was a time also when the Wisdom-Religion was not symbolical, for it became Esoteric only gradually, the change being necessitated by misuse and by the Sorcery of the Atlanteans. For it was the "misuse" only, and not the use, of the divine gift that led the men of the Fourth Race to Black Magic and Sorcery, and finally to become "forgetful of Wisdom"; while those of the Fifth Race, the inheritors of the Rishis of the Treta Yuga, used their powers to atrophise such gifts in mankind in general, and then, as the "Elect Root," dispersed. Those who escaped the "Great Flood" preserved only its memory, and a belief founded on the knowledge of their direct fathers of one remove, that such a Science existed, and was now jealously guarded by the "Elect Root" exalted by Enoch. But there must again come a time when man shall once more become what he was during the second Yuga (age), when his probationary cycle shall be over and he shall gradually become what he was—semi-corporeal and pure. Does not Plato, the Initiate, tell us in the *Phædrus* all that man once was, and that which he may yet again become:

Before man's spirit sank into sensuality and became embodied through the loss of his wings, he lived among the Gods in the airy spiritual world where everything is true and pure.*

Elsewhere he speaks of the time when men did not perpetuate themselves, but lived as pure spirits.

Let those men of Science who feel inclined to laugh at this, themselves unravel the mystery of the origin of the first man.

Unwilling that his chosen people—chosen by him—should remain as grossly idolatrous as the profane masses that surrounded them, Moses utilised his knowledge of the cosmogonical mysteries of the Pyramid, to build upon it the Genesiacal Cosmogony in symbols and glyphs. This was more accessible to the minds of the *hoi polloi* than the abstruse truths taught to the educated in the sanctuaries. He invented nothing but the outward garb, added not one iota; but in this he merely followed the example of older nations and Initiates. If he clothed the grand truths revealed to him by his Hierophant under the most ingenious imagery, he did it to meet the requirements of the Israelites; that stiff-necked race would accept of no God unless He were as anthropomorphic as those of the Olympus; and he himself failed to foresee the times when highly educated statesmen would be defending the husks of the fruit of wisdom that grew and developed in him on Mount Sinai, when communing with his own personal God—his divine Self. Moses understood the great danger of delivering such truths to the selfish, for he understood the fable of Prometheus and remembered the past. Hence, he veiled them from the profanation of public gaze and gave them out allegorically. And this is why his biographer says of him, that when he descended from Sinai,

> Moses wist not that the skin of his face shone . . . and he put a veil upon his face.†

And so he "put a veil" upon the face of his *Pentateuch;* and to such an extent that, using orthodox chronology, only 3376 years after the event people begin to acquire a conviction that it is "a veil indeed." It is not the face of God or even of a Jehovah shining through; not even the face of Moses, but verily the faces of the later Rabbis.

No wonder if Clemens wrote in the *Stromateis* that:

> Similar, then, to the Hebrew enigmas in respect to concealment are those of the Egyptians also.‡

---

* See Cary's translation, pp. 322, 323.

† *Exodus*, xxxiv. 29, 33.

‡ *Op. cit.*, V. vii.

SECTION VII.

OLD WINE IN NEW BOTTLES.

IT is more than likely, that the Protestants in the days of the Reformation knew nothing of the true origin of Christianity, or, to be more explicit and correct, of Latin Ecclesiasticism. Nor is it probable that the Greek Church knew much of it, the separation between the two having occurred at a time when, in the struggle for political power the Latin Church was securing, at any cost, the alliance of the highly educated, the ambitious and influential Pagans, while these were willing to assume the outward appearance of the new worship, provided they were themselves kept in power. There is no need to remind the reader here of the details of that struggle, well-known to every educated man. It is certain that the highly cultured Gnostics and their leaders—such men as Saturnilus, an uncompromising ascetic, as Marcion, Valentinus, Basilides, Menander and Cerinthus—were not stigmatised by the (new) Latin Church because they were heretics, nor because their tenets and practices were indeed "*ob turpitudinem portentosam nimium et horribilem*," "monstrous, revolting abominations," as Baronius says of those of Carpocrates; but simply because they knew too much of fact and truth. Kenneth R. H. Mackenzie correctly remarks:

> They were stigmatised by the later Roman Church because they came into conflict with the purer Church of Christianity—the possession of which was usurped by the Bishops of Rome, but which original continues in its docility towards the founder, in the Primitive Orthodox Greek Church.*

Unwilling to accept the responsibility of gratuitous assumptions, the writer deems it best to prove this inference by more than one personal and defiant admission of an ardent Roman Catholic writer, evidently entrusted with the delicate task by the Vatican. The Marquis de Mirville

---

* *The Royal Masonic Cyclopædia*, under "Gnosticism."

makes desperate efforts to explain in the Catholic interest certain remarkable discoveries in Archæology and Palæography, though the Church is cleverly made to remain outside of the quarrel and defence. This is undeniably shown by his ponderous volumes addressed to the Academy of France between 1803 and 1865. Seizing the pretext of drawing the attention of the materialistic "Immortals" to the "epidemic of Spiritualism," the invasion of Europe and America by a numberless host of Satanic forces, he directs his efforts towards proving the same, by giving the full Genealogies and the Theogony of the Christian and Pagan Deities, and by drawing parallels between the two. All such wonderful likenesses and identities are only "seeming and superficial," he assures the reader. Christian symbols, and even characters, Christ, the Virgin, Angels and Saints, he tells them, were all personated centuries beforehand by the fiends of hell, in order to discredit eternal truth by their ungodly copies. By their knowledge of futurity the devils anticipated events, having "discovered the secrets of the Angels." Heathen Deities, all the Sun-Gods named Soters—Saviours—born of immaculate mothers and dying a violent death, were only Ferouers*—as they were called by the Zoroastrians—the demon-ante-dated copies *(copies anticipées)* of the Messiah to come.

The danger of recognition of such *facsimiles* had indeed lately become dangerously great. It had lingered threateningly in the air, hanging like a sword of Damocles over the Church, since the days of Voltaire, Dupuis and other writers on similar lines. The discoveries

* In the *Ferouers* and *Devs* of Jacobi (Letters F. and D.) the word "ferouer" is explained in the following manner: The Ferouer is a part of the creature (whether man or animal) of which it is the type and which it survives. It is the Nous of the Greeks, therefore divine and immortal, and thus can hardly be the Devil or the satanic copy De Mirville would represent it (see *Mémoires de l'Academie des Inscriptions*, Vol. XXXVII. p. 623, and chap. xxxix. p. 749). Foucher contradicts him entirely. The Ferouer was never the "principle of sensations," but always referred to the most divine and pure portion of Man's Ego—the spiritual principle. Anquetil says that the Ferouer is the purest portion of man's soul. The Persian Dev is the antithesis of the Ferouer, for the Dev has been transformed by Zoroaster into the Genius of Evil (whence the Christian Devil), but even the Dev is only finite; for having become possessed of the soul of man by *usurpation*, it will have to leave it at the great day of Retribution. The Dev obsesses the soul of the defunct for three days, during which the soul wanders about the spot at which it was forcibly separated from its body; the Ferouer ascends to the region of Eternal Light. It was an unfortunate idea that made the noble Marquis de Mirville imagine the Ferouer to be a "satanic copy" of a *divine* original. By calling all the Gods of the Pagans—Apollo, Osiris, Brahmâ, Ormazd, Bel, etc., the "Ferouers of Christ and of the chief Angels," he merely exhibits the God and the Angels he would honour as inferior to the Pagan Gods, as man is inferior to his Soul and Spirit; since the Ferouer is the immortal part of the mortal being of which it is the type and which it survives. Perchance the poor author is unconsciously prophetic; and Apollo, Brahmâ, Ormazd, Osiris, etc., are destined to survive and replace—as eternal cosmic verities—the evanescent fictions about the God, Christ and Angels of the Latin Church!

of the Egyptologists, the finding of Assyrian and Babylonian pre-Mosaic relics bearing the legend of Moses* and especially the many rationalistic works published in England, such as *Supernatural Religion*, made recognition unavoidable. Hence the appearance of Protestant and Roman Catholic writers deputed to explain the inexplicable; to reconcile the fact of Divine Revelation with the mystery that the divine personages, rites, dogmas and symbols of Christianity were so often identical with those of the several great heathen religions. The former—the Protestant defenders—tried to explain it, on the ground of "prophetic, precursory ideas"; the Latinists, such as De Mirville, by inventing a double set of Angels and Gods, the one divine and true, the other—the earlier—"copies ante-dating the originals" and due to a clever plagiarism by the Evil One. The Protestant stratagem is an old one, that of the Roman Catholics is so old that it has been forgotten, and is as good as new. Dr. Lundy's *Monumental Christianity* and *A Miracle in Stone* belong to the first attempts. De Mirville's *Pneumatologie* to the second. In India and China, every such effort on the part of the Scotch and other missionaries ends in laughter, and does no harm; the plan devised by the Jesuits is more serious. De Mirville's volumes are thus very important, as they proceed from a source which has undeniably the greatest learning of the age at its service, and this coupled with all the craft and casuistry that the sons of Loyola can furnish. The Marquis de Mirville was evidently helped by the acutest minds in the service of Rome.

He begins by not only admitting the justice of every imputation and charge made against the Latin Church as to the originality of her dogmas, but by taking a seeming delight in anticipating such charges; for he points to every dogma of Christianity as having existed in Pagan rituals in Antiquity. The whole Pantheon of Heathen Deities is passed in review by him, and each is shown to have had some point of resemblance with the Trinitarian personages and Mary. There is hardly a mystery, a dogma, or a rite in the Latin Church that is not shown by the author as having been "parodied by the Curvati"—the "Curved," the Devils. All this being admitted and explained, the Symbologists ought to be silenced. And so they would be, if there were no materialistic critics to reject such omnipotency of the Devil in this world. For, if Rome admits the likenesses, she also claims the right of judgment between

* See George Smith's *Babylon* and other works.

the true and the false Avatâra, the real and the unreal God, between the original and the copy—though the copy precedes the original by millenniums.

Our author proceeds to argue that whenever the missionaries try to convert an idolater, they are invariably answered:

> We had our Crucified before yours. What do you come to show us?* Again, what should we gain by denying the mysterious side of this copy, under the plea that according to Weber all the present *Purânas* are remade from older ones, since here we have in the same order of personages a positive precedence which no one would ever think of contesting.†

And the author instances Buddha, Krishna, Apollo, etc. Having admitted all this he escapes the difficulty in this wise:

> The Church Fathers, however, who recognized their own property under all such sheep's clothing . . . knowing by means of the Gospel . . . all the ruses of the pretended spirits of light; the Fathers, we say, meditating upon the decisive words, "all that ever came before me are robbers" (*John*, x. 8), did not hesitate in recognizing the Occult agency at work, the general and superhuman direction given beforehand to falsehood, the universal attribute and environment of all these false Gods of the nations; "*omnes dii gentium dæmonia (elilim)*." (*Psalm* xcv.)‡

With such a policy everything is made easy. There is not one glaring resemblance, not one fully proven identity, that could not thus be made away with. The above-quoted cruel, selfish, self-glorifying words, placed by John in the mouth of Him who was meekness and charity personified, could never have been pronounced by Jesus. The Occultists reject the imputation indignantly, and are prepared to defend the man as against the God, by showing whence come the words plagiarised by the author of the Fourth Gospel. They are taken bodily from the "Prophecies" in the *Book of Enoch*. The evidence on this head of the learned biblical scholar, Archbishop Laurence, and of the author of the *Evolution of Christianity*, who edited the translation, may be brought forward to prove the fact. On the last page of the Introduction to the *Book of Enoch* is found the following passage:

> The parable of the sheep rescued by the good Shepherd from hireling guardians and ferocious wolves, is obviously borrowed by the fourth Evangelist from

---

* This is as fanciful as it is arbitrary. Where is the Hindu or Buddhist who would speak of his "Crucified"?

† *Op. cit.*, iv. 237.

‡ *Loc. cit.*, 250.

Enoch, lxxxix, in which the author depicts the shepherds as killing and destroying the sheep before the advent of their Lord, and thus discloses the true meaning of that hitherto mysterious passage in the Johannine parable—"All that ever came before me are thieves and robbers"—language in which we now detect an obvious reference to the allegorical shepherds of Enoch.

"Obvious" truly, and something else besides. For, if Jesus pronounced the words in the sense attributed to him, then he must have read the *Book of Enoch*—a purely Kabalistic, Occult work, and he therefore recognised the worth and value of a treatise now declared apocryphal by his Churches. Moreover, he could not have been ignorant that these words belonged to the oldest ritual of Initiation.* And if he had not read it, and the sentence belongs to John, or whoever wrote the Fourth Gospel, then what reliance can be placed on the authenticity of other sayings and parables attributed to the Christian Saviour?

Thus, De Mirville's illustration is an unfortunate one. Every other proof brought by the Church to show the infernal character of the ante-and-anti-Christian copyists may be as easily disposed of. This is perhaps unfortunate, but it is a fact, nevertheless—*Magna est veritas et prevalebit.*

The above is the answer of the Occultists to the two parties who charge them incessantly, the one with "Superstition," and the other with "Sorcery." To those of our Brothers who are Christians, and twit us with the secresy imposed upon the Eastern Chelâs, adding invariably that their own "Book of God" is "an open volume" for all "to read, understand, and *be saved*," we would reply by asking them to study what we have just said in this Section, and then to refute it—if they can. There are very few in our days who are still prepared to assure their readers that the *Bible* had

* "*Q.*: Who knocks at the door?
A.: The good cowherd.
Q.: Who preceded thee?
A.: The three robbers.
Q.: Who follows thee?
A.: The three murderers," etc., etc.

Now this is the conversation that took place between the priest-initiators and the candidates for initiation during the mysteries enacted in the oldest sanctuaries of the Himâlayan fastnesses. The ceremony is still performed to this day in one of the most ancient temples in a secluded spot of Nepaul. It originated with the Mysteries of the first Krishna, passed to the First Tirthankara and ended with Buddha, and is called the Kurukshetra rite, being enacted as a memorial of the great battle and death of the divine Adept. It is not Masonry, but an initiation into the Occult teachings of that Hero—Occultism, pure and simple.

God for its author, salvation for its end, and truth without any mixture of error for its matter.

Could Locke be asked the question now, he would perhaps be unwilling to repeat again that the *Bible* is

all pure, all sincere, nothing too much, nothing wanting.

The *Bible*, if it is not to be shown to be the very reverse of all this, sadly needs an interpreter acquainted with the doctrines of the East, as they are to be found in its secret volumes; nor is it safe now, after Archbishop Laurence's translation of the *Book of Enoch*, to cite Cowper and assure us that the *Bible*

> . . . gives a light to every age,
> It gives, but borrows none.

for it does borrow, and that very considerably; especially in the opinion of those who, ignorant of its symbolical meaning and of the universality of the truths underlying and concealed in it, are able to judge only from its dead-letter appearance. It is a grand volume, a master-piece composed of clever, ingenious fables containing great verities; but it reveals the latter only to those who, like the Initiates, have a key to its inner meaning; a tale sublime in its morality and didactics truly—still a tale and an allegory; a repertory of invented personages in its older Jewish portions, and of dark sayings and parables in its later additions, and thus quite misleading to anyone ignorant of its Esotericism. Moreover it is Astrolatry and Sabæan worship, pure and simple, that is to be found in the *Pentateuch* when it is read exoterically, and Archaic Science and Astronomy to a most wonderful degree, when interpreted—Esoterically.

SECTION VIII.

THE BOOK OF ENOCH THE ORIGIN AND THE FOUNDATION OF CHRISTIANITY.

WHILE making a good deal of the *Mercavah*, the Jews, or rather their synagogues, rejected the *Book of Enoch*, either because it was not included from the first in the Hebrew Canon, or else, as Tertullian thought, it was

> Disavowed by the Jews like all other Scripture which speaks of Christ.*

But neither of these reasons was the real one. The Synedrion would have nothing to do with it, simply because it was more of a magic than a purely kabalistic work. The present day Theologians of both Latin and Protestant Churches class it among apocryphal productions. Nevertheless the *New Testament*, especially in the *Acts* and *Epistles*, teems with ideas and doctrines, now accepted and established as dogmas by the infallible Roman and other Churches, and even with whole sentences taken bodily from Enoch, or the "pseudo-Enoch," who wrote under that name in Aramaic or Syro-Chaldaic, as asserted by Bishop Laurence, the translator of the Ethiopian text.

The plagiarisms are so glaring that the author of *The Evolution of Christianity*, who edited Bishop Laurence's translation, was compelled to make some suggestive remarks in his Introduction. On internal evidence† this book is found to have been written before the Christian period (whether two or twenty centuries does not matter). As correctly argued by the Editor, it is

> Either the inspired forecast of a great Hebrew prophet, predicting with miraculous accuracy the future teaching of Jesus of Nazareth, or the Semitic romance

---

* *Book of Enoch*, Archbishop Laurence's translation. Introduction, p. v.

† *The Book of Enoch* was unknown to Europe for a thousand years, when Bruce found in Abyssinia some copies of it in Ethiopic; it was translated by Archbishop Laurence in 1821, from the text in the Bodleian Library, Oxford.

from which the latter borrowed His conceptions of the triumphant return of the Son of man, to occupy a judicial throne in the midst of rejoicing saints and trembling sinners, expectant of everlasting happiness or eternal fire; and whether these celestial visions be accepted as human or Divine, they have exercised so vast an influence on the destinies of mankind for nearly two thousand years that candid and impartial seekers after religious truth can no longer delay enquiry into the relationship of the *Book of Enoch* with the revelation, or the evolution, of Christianity.*

The *Book of Enoch*

Also records the supernatural control of the elements, through the action of individual angels presiding over the winds, the sea, hail, frost, dew, the lightning's flash, and reverberating thunder. The names of the principal fallen angels are also given, among whom we recognize some of the invisible powers named in the incantations [magical] inscribed on the terra-cotta cups of Hebrew-Chaldee conjurations.†

We also find on these cups the word "Halleluiah," showing that

A word with which ancient Syro-Chaldæans conjured has become, through the vicissitudes of language, the Shibboleth of modern Revivalists.‡

The Editor proceeds after this to give fifty-seven verses from various parts of the *Gospels* and *Acts*, with parallel passages from the *Book of Enoch*, and says:

The attention of theologians has been concentrated on the passage in the *Epistle of Jude*, because the author specifically names the prophet; but the cumulative coincidence of language and ideas in Enoch and the authors of the *New Testament Scripture*, as disclosed in the parallel passages which we have collated, clearly indicates that the work of the Semitic Milton was the inexhaustible source from which Evangelists and Apostles, or the men who wrote in their names, borrowed their conceptions of the resurrection, judgment, immortality, perdition, and of the universal reign of righteousness, under the eternal dominion of the Son of man. This evangelical plagiarism culminates in the Revelation of John, which adapts the visions of Enoch to Christianity, with modifications in which we miss the sublime simplicity of the great master of apocalyptic prediction, who prophesied in the name of the antediluvian patriarch.§

In fairness to truth, the hypothesis ought at least to have been suggested, that the *Book of Enoch* in its present form is simply a transcript—with numerous pre-Christian and post-Christian additions and interpolations—from far older texts. Modern research went so far as to point out that Enoch is made, in Chapter lxxi, to divide the day and night into eighteen parts, and to represent the longest day in the year as consisting of twelve out of these eighteen parts, while a day of six-

* *Op. cit.*, p. xx. † *Loc. cit.* ‡ *Op. cit.*, p. xiv., note. § *Op. cit.*, p. xxxv.

teen hours in length could not have occurred in Palestine.* The translator, Archbishop Laurence, remarks thus:

The region in which the author lived must have been situated not lower than forty-five degrees north latitude, where the longest day is fifteen hours and a half, nor higher perhaps than forty-nine degrees, where the longest day is precisely sixteen hours. This will bring the country where he wrote as high up at least as the northern districts of the Caspian and Euxine Seas . . . the author of the *Book of Enoch* was perhaps a member of one of the tribes which Shalmaneser carried away, and placed "in Halah and in Habor by the river Gozan, and in the cities of the Medes."*

Further on, it is confessed that:

It cannot be said that internal evidence attests the superiority of the *Old Testament* to the *Book of Enoch*. . . . The *Book of Enoch* teaches the pre-existence of the Son of man, the Elect One, the Messiah, who "from the beginning existed in secret,† and whose name was invoked in the presence of the Lord of Spirits, before the sun and the signs were created." The author also refers to the "other Power who was upon Earth over the water on that day"—an apparent reference to the language of *Genesis*, i. 2.‡ [We maintain that it applies as well to the Hindu Nârâyana—the "mover on the waters."] We have thus the Lord of Spirits, the Elect One, and a third Power, seemingly foreshadowing this Trinity [as much as the Trimûrti] of futurity; but although Enoch's ideal Messiah doubtless exercised an important influence on primitive conceptions of the Divinity of the Son of man, we fail to identify his obscure reference to another "Power" with the Trinitarianism of the Alexandrine school; more especially as "angels of power" abound in the visions of Enoch.§

An Occultist would hardly fail to identify the said "Power." The Editor concludes his remarkable reflections by adding:

Thus far we learn that the *Book of Enoch* was published before the Christian Era by some great Unknown of Semitic [?] race, who, believing himself to be inspired in a post-prophetic age, borrowed the name of an antediluvian patriarch‖ to authenticate his own enthusiastic forecast of the Messianic kingdom. And as the contents of his marvellous book enter freely into the composition of the *New Testament*, it follows that if the author was not an inspired prophet, who predicted the teachings of Christianity, he was a visionary enthusiast whose illusions were accepted by Evangelists and Apostles as revelation—alternative conclusions which involve the Divine or human origin of Christianity.¶

---

* *Op. cit.*, p. xiii.

† The Seventh Principle, the First Emanation.

‡ *Op. cit.*, pp. xxxvii. and xl.

§ *Op. cit.*, pp. xl. and li.

‖ Who stands for the "Solar" or Manvantaric Year.

¶ *Op. cit.*, pp. xli., xlii.

The outcome of all of which is, in the words of the same Editor:

> The discovery that the language and ideas of alleged revelation are found in a pre-existent work, accepted by Evangelists and Apostles as inspired, but classed by modern theologians among apocryphal productions.*

This accounts also for the unwillingness of the reverend librarians of the Bodleian Library to publish the Ethiopian text of the *Book of Enoch*.

The prophecies of the *Book of Enoch* are indeed prophetic, but they were intended for, and cover the records of, the five Races out of the seven—everything relating to the last two being kept secret. Thus the remark made by the Editor of the English translation, that:

> Chapter xcii. records a series of prophecies extending from Enoch's own time to about one thousand years beyond the present generation,†

is faulty. The prophecies extend to the end of our present Race, not merely to a "thousand years" hence. Very true that:

> In the system of [Christian] chronology adopted, a day stands [occasionally] for a hundred, and a week for seven hundred years.‡

But this is an arbitrary and fanciful system adopted by Christians to make Biblical chronology fit with facts or theories, and does not represent the original thought. The "days" stand for the undetermined periods of the Side-Races, and the "weeks" for the Sub-Races, the Root-Races being referred to by an expression that is not even found in the English translation. Moreover the sentence at the bottom of page 150:

> Subsequently, in the fourth week . . . the visions of the holy and the righteous shall be seen, the order of generation after generation shall take place,§

is quite wrong. It stands in the original: "the order of generation after generation had taken place on the earth," etc.; that is, after the first human race procreated in the truly human way had sprung up in the Third Root-Race; a change which entirely alters the meaning. Then all that is given in the translation—as very likely also in the Ethiopic text, since the copies have been sorely tampered with—as about things which were to happen in the future, is, we are informed, in the past tense in the original Chaldæan MSS., and is not prophecy, but a narrative of what had already come to pass. When Enoch begins "to speak from a book" ‖ he is reading the account

* *Op. cit.*, p. xlviii. † *Op. cit.*, p. xxiii. ‡ *Loc. cit.* § xcii. 9. ‖ *Op. cit.*, xcii. 4.

given by a great Seer, and the prophecies are not his own, but are from the Seer. Enoch or Enoichion means "internal eye" or Seer. Thus every Prophet and Adept may be called "Enoichion," without becoming a pseudo-Enoch. But here, the Seer who compiled the present *Book of Enoch* is distinctly shown as reading out from a book.

I have been born the seventh in the first week [the seventh branch, or side-race, of the first Sub-Race, after physical generation had begun, namely, in the Third Root-Race] . . . But after me, in the second week [second Sub-Race], great wickedness shall arise [arose, rather] and in that week the end of the first shall take place, in which mankind shall be safe. But when the first is completed iniquity shall grow up.*

As translated it has no sense. As it stands in the Esoteric text, it simply means, that the First Root-Race shall come to an end during the second Sub-Race of the Third Root-Race, in the period of which time mankind will be safe; all this having no reference whatever to the biblical Deluge. Verse 10th speaks of the sixth week [sixth Sub-Race of the Third Root-Race] when

All those who are in it shall be darkened, the hearts of all of them shall be forgetful of wisdom [the divine knowledge will be dying out] and in it shall a man ascend.

This "man" is taken by the interpreters, for some mysterious reasons of their own, to mean Nebuchadnezzar; he is in reality the first Hierophant of the purely human Race (after the allegorical Fall into generation) selected to perpetuate the dying Wisdom of the Devas (Angels or Elohim). He is the first "Son of Man"—the mysterious appellation given to the divine Initiates of the first human school of the Mânushi (men), at the very close of the Third Root-Race. He is also called the "Saviour," as it was He, with the other Hierophants, who saved the Elect and the Perfect from the geological conflagration, leaving to perish in the cataclysm of the Close† those who forgot the primeval wisdom in sexual sensuality.

And during its completion [of the "sixth week," or the sixth Sub-Race] he shall burn the house of dominion [the half of the globe or the then inhabited continent] with fire, and all the race of the elect root shall be dispersed.‡

---

* *Op. cit.*, xcii, 4-7.

† At the close of every Root-Race there comes a cataclysm, in turn by fire or water. Immediately after the "Fall into generation" the dross of the third Root-Race—those who fell into sensuality by falling off from the teaching of the Divine Instructors—were destroyed, after which the Fourth Root-Race originated, at the end of which took place the last Deluge. (See the "Sons of God" mentioned in *Isis Unveiled*, 593 *et seq.*)

‡ *Op. cit.*, xcii, 11.

The above applies to the Elect Initiates, and not at all to the Jews, the supposed chosen people, or to the Babylonian captivity, as interpreted by the Christian theologians. Considering that we find Enoch, or his perpetuator, mentioning the execution of the "decree upon sinners", in several different weeks,* saying that "every work of the ungodly shall disappear from the whole earth" during this fourth time (the Fourth Race), it surely can hardly apply to the one solitary Deluge of the *Bible*, still less to the Captivity.

It follows, therefore, that as the *Book of Enoch* covers the five Races of the Manvantara, with a few allusions to the last two, it does not contain "Biblical prophecies," but simply facts taken out of the Secret Books of the East. The editor, moreover, confesses that:

> The preceding six verses, *viz.*, 13th, 14th, 15th, 16th, 17th, and 18th, are taken from between the 14th and 15th verses of the nineteenth chapter, where they are to be found in the MSS.†

By this arbitrary transposition, he has made confusion still more confused. Yet he is quite right in saying that the doctrines of the *Gospels*, and even of the *Old Testament*, have been taken bodily from the *Book of Enoch*, for this is as evident as the sun in heaven. The whole of the *Pentateuch* was adapted to fit in with the facts given, and this accounts for the Hebrews refusing to give the book a place in their Canon, just as the Christians have subsequently refused to admit it among their canonical works. The fact that the Apostle Jude and many of the Christian Fathers referred to it as a revelation and a sacred volume, is, however, an excellent proof that the early Christians accepted it; among these the most learned—as, for instance, Clement of Alexandria—understood Christianity and its doctrines in quite a different light from their modern successors, and viewed Christ under an aspect that Occultists only can appreciate. The early Nazarenes and Chrestians, as Justin Martyr calls them, were the followers of Jesus, of the true Chrestos and Christos of Initiation; whereas, the modern Christians, especially those of the West, may be Papists, Greeks, Calvinists, or Lutherans, but can hardly be called Christians, *i.e.*, the followers of Jesus, the Christ.

Thus the *Book of Enoch* is entirely symbolical. It relates to the history of the human Races and of their early relation to Theogony, the symbols being interblended with astronomical and cosmic mysteries.

---

* *Op. cit.*, xcii. 7, 11, 13, 15.

† *Op. cit.*, note, p. 152.

One chapter is missing, however, in the Noachian records (from both the Paris and the Bodleian MSS.), namely, Chapter lviii. in Sect. XI.; this could not be remodelled, and therefore it had to disappear, disfigured fragments alone having been left of it. The dream about the cows, the black, red and white heifers, relates to the first Races, their division and disappearance. Chapter lxxxviii, in which one of the four Angels "went to the white cows and taught them a mystery," after which, the mystery being born "became a man," refers to (a) the first group evolved of primitive Âryans, and (b) to the "mystery of the Hermaphrodite" so called, having reference to the birth of the first human Races as they are now. The well-known rite in India, one that has survived in that patriarchal country to this day, known as the passage, or rebirth through the cow—a ceremony to which those of lower castes who are desirous of becoming Brâhmans have to submit—has originated in this mystery. Let any Eastern Occultist read with careful attention the above-named chapter in the *Book of Enoch*, and he will find that the "Lord of the Sheep," in whom Christians and European Mystics see Christ, is the Hierophant Victim whose name in Sanskrit we dare not give. Again, that while the Western Churchmen see Egyptians and Israelites in the "sheep and wolves," all these animals relate in truth to the trials of the Neophyte and the mysteries of initiation, whether in India or Egypt, and to that most terrible penalty incurred by the "wolves"—those who reveal indiscriminately that which is only for the knowledge of the Elect and the "Perfect."

The Christians who, thanks to later interpolations,* have made out in that chapter a triple prophecy relating to the Deluge, Moses, and Jesus, are mistaken, as in reality it bears directly on the punishment and loss of Atlantis and the penalty of indiscretion. The "Lord of the sheep" is Karma and the "Head of the Hierophants" also, the Supreme Initiator on earth. He says to Enoch, who implores him to save the leaders of the sheep from being devoured by the beasts of prey:

> I will cause a recital to be made before me . . . how many they have

---

* Those interpolations and alterations are found almost in every case where figures are given—especially whenever the numbers eleven and twelve come in—as these are all made (by the Christians) to relate to the numbers of Apostles, and Tribes, and Patriarchs. The translator of the Æthiopic text—Archbishop Laurence—attributes them generally to "mistakes of the transcriber" whenever the two texts, the Paris and the Bodleian MSS., differ. We fear it is no mistake, in most cases.

delivered up to destruction, and . . . what they will do; whether they will act as I have commanded them or not.

Of this, however, they shall be ignorant; neither shalt thou make any explanation to them, neither shalt thou reprove them; but there shall be an account of all the destruction done by them in their respective seasons.*

. . . He looked in silence, rejoicing they were devoured, swallowed up, and carried off, and leaving them in the power of every beast for food. . . .†

Those who labour under the impression that the Occultists of any nation reject the *Bible*, in its original text and meaning, are wrong. As well reject the *Books of Thoth*, the Chaldæan *Kabalah* or the *Book of Dzyan* itself. Occultists only reject the one-sided interpretations and the human element in the *Bible*, which is an Occult, and therefore a sacred, volume as much as the others. And terrible indeed is the punishment of all those who transgress the permitted limits of secret revelations. From Prometheus to Jesus, and from Him to the highest Adept as to the lowest disciple, every revealer of mysteries has had to become a Chrestos, a "man of sorrow" and a martyr. "Beware," said one of the greatest Masters, "of revealing the Mystery to those without"—to the profane, the Sadducee and the unbeliever. All the great Hierophants in history are shown ending their lives by violent deaths—Buddha,‡ Pythagoras, Zoroaster, most of the great Gnostics, the founders of their respective schools; and in our own more modern epoch a number of Fire-Philosophers, of Rosicrucians and Adepts. All of these are shown—whether plainly or under the veil of allegory—as paying the penalty for the revelations they had made. This may seem to the profane reader only coincidence.

* *Op. cit.*, lxxxviii. 99, 100.

† *Loc. cit.*, 94. This passage, as will be presently shown, has led to a very curious discovery.

‡ In the profane history of Gautama Buddha he dies at the good old age of eighty, and passes off from life to death peacefully with all the serenity of a great saint, as Barthélemy St. Hilaire has it. Not so in the Esoteric and true interpretation which reveals the real sense of the profane and allegorical statement that makes Gautama, the Buddha, die very unpoetically from the effects of too much pork, prepared for him by Tsonda. How one who preached that the killing of animals was the greatest sin, and who was a perfect vegetarian, could die from eating pork, is a question that is never asked by our Orientalists, some of whom made (as now do many charitable missionaries in Ceylon) great fun at the alleged occurrence. The simple truth is that the said rice and pork are purely allegorical. Rice stands for "forbidden fruit," like Eve's "apple," and means Occult knowledge with the Chinese and Tibetans; and "pork" for Brâhmanical teachings—Vishnu having assumed in his first Avatâra the form of a boar, in order to raise the earth on the surface of the waters of space. It is not, therefore, from "pork" that Buddha died, but for having divulged some of the Brâhmanical mysteries, after which, seeing the bad effects brought on some unworthy people by the revelation, he preferred, instead of availing himself of Nirvâna, to leave his earthly form, remaining still in the sphere of the living, in order to help humanity to progress. Hence his constant reincarnations in the hierarchy of the Dalai and Teshu Lamas, among other bounties. Such is the Esoteric explanation. The life of Gautama will be more fully discussed later on.

To the Occultist, the death of every "Master" is significant, and appears pregnant with meaning. Where do we find in history that "Messenger" grand or humble, an Initiate or a Neophyte, who, when he was made the bearer of some hitherto concealed truth or truths, was not crucified and rent to shreds by the "dogs" of envy, malice and ignorance? Such is the terrible Occult law; and he who does not feel in himself the heart of a lion to scorn the savage barking, and the soul of a dove to forgive the poor ignorant fools, let him give up the Sacred Science. To succeed, the Occultist must be fearless; he has to brave dangers, dishonour and death, to be forgiving, and to be silent on that which cannot be given. Those who have vainly laboured in that direction must wait in these days—as the *Book of Enoch* teaches—"until the evil-doers be consumed" and the power of the wicked annihilated. It is not lawful for the Occultist to seek or even to thirst for revenge; let him

> Wait until sin pass away; for their [the sinners'] names shall be blotted out of the holy books [the astral records], their seed shall be destroyed and their spirits slain.*

Esoterically, Enoch is the "Son of man," the first; and symbolically, the first Sub-Race of the *Fifth* Root Race.† And if his name yields for purposes of numerical and astronomical glyphs the meaning of the solar year, or 365, in conformity to the age assigned to him in *Genesis*, it is because, being the seventh, he is, for Occult purposes, the personified period of the two preceding Races with their fourteen Sub-Races. Therefore, he is shown in the Book as the great grandfather of Noah who, in his turn, is the personification of the mankind of the Fifth, struggling with that of the Fourth Root-Race—the great period of the revealed and profaned Mysteries, when the "sons of God" coming down on Earth took for wives the daughters of men, and taught them the secrets of the Angels; in other words, when the "mind-born" men of the Third Race mixed themselves with those of the Fourth, and the divine Science was gradually brought down by men to Sorcery.

---

* *Op. cit.*, cv. 21.

† In the *Bible* (*Genesis*, iv and v) there are three distinct Enochs (Kanoch or Chanoch)—the son of Cain, the son of Seth, and the son of Jared; but they are all identical, and two of them are mentioned for purposes of misleading. The years of only the last two are given, the first one being left without further notice.

SECTION IX.

HERMETIC AND KABALISTIC DOCTRINES.

THE cosmogony of Hermes is as veiled as the Mosaic system, only it is upon its face far more in harmony with the doctrines of the Secret Sciences and even of Modern Science. Says the thrice great Trismegistus, "the hand that shaped the world out of formless pre-existent matter is no hand"; to which *Genesis* is made to reply, "The world was created out of nothing," although the *Kabalah* denies such a meaning in its opening sentences. The Kabalists have never, any more than have the Indian Âryans, admitted such an absurdity. With them, Fire, or Heat, and Motion* were chiefly instrumental in the formation of the world out of preëxisting Matter. The Parabrahman and Mûlaprakriti of the Vedântins are the prototypes of the En Suph and Shekinah of the Kabalists. Aditi is the original of Sephira, and the Prajâpatis are the elder brothers of the Sephiroth. The nebular theory of Modern Science, with all its mysteries, is solved in the cosmogony of the Archaic Doctrine; and the paradoxical though very scientific enunciation, that "cooling causes contraction and contraction causes heat; therefore cooling causes heat," is shown as the chief agency in the formation of the worlds, and especially of our sun and solar system.

All this is contained within the small compass of *Sepher Jetsirah* in its thirty-two wonderful Ways of Wisdom, signed "Jah Jehovah Sabaoth," for whomsoever has the key to its hidden meaning. As to the dogmatic or theological interpretation of the first verses in *Genesis* it is pertinently answered in the same book, where speaking of the

* The eternal and incessant "in-breathing and out-breathing of Parabrahman" or Nature, the Universe in Space, whether during Manvantara or Pralaya.

Three Mothers, Air, Water and Fire, the writer describes them as a balance with

> The good in one scale, the evil in the other, and the oscillating tongue of the Balance between them.*

One of the secret names of the One Eternal and Ever-Present Deity, was in every country the same, and it has preserved to this day a phonetic likeness in the various languages. The Aum of the Hindus, the sacred syllable, had become the Αἰὼν with the Greeks, and the Ævum with the Romans—the Pan or All. The "thirtieth way" is called in the *Sepher Jetzirah* the "gathering understanding," because

> Thereby gather the celestial adepts judgments of the stars and celestial signs, and their observations of the orbits are the perfection of science.†

The thirty-second and last is called therein the "serving understanding," and it is so-called because it is

> A disposer of all those that are serving in the work of the Seven Planets according to their Hosts.‡

The "work" was Initiation, during which all the mysteries connected with the "Seven Planets" were divulged, and also the mystery of the "Sun-Initiate" with his seven radiances or beams cut off—the glory and triumph of the anointed, the Christos; a mystery that makes plain the rather puzzling expression of Clemens:

> For we shall find that very many of the dogmas that are held by such sects [of Barbarian and Hellenic Philosophy] as have not become utterly senseless, and are not cut out from the order of nature ["by cutting off Christ,"§ or rather Christos] . . . correspond in their origin and with the truth as a whole.‖

In *Isis Unveiled*,¶ the reader will find fuller information than can be given here on the *Zohar* and its author, the great Kabalist, Simeon Ben Jochai. It is said there that on account of his being known to be in possession of the secret knowledge and of the Mercaba, which insured the reception of the "Word," his very life was endangered,

---

* *Op. cit.*, iii. 1.

† *Op. cit.*, 30.

‡ *Op. cit.*, 32.

§ Those who are aware that the term Christos was applied by the Gnostics to the Higher Ego (the ancient Pagan Greek Initiates doing the same), will readily understand the allusion. Christos was said to be cut off from the lower Ego, Chrestos, after the final and supreme Initiation, when the two became blended in one; Chrestos being conquered and resurrected in the glorified Christos.—Franck, *Die Kabbala*, 75; Dunlap, *Sôd*, Vol. II.

‖ *Stromateis*, I. xiii.

¶ *Op. cit.*, II. viii.

and he had to fly to the wilderness, where he lived in a cave for twelve years surrounded by faithful disciples, and finally died there amid signs and wonders.* His teachings on the origin of the Secret Doctrine, or, as he also calls it, the Secret Wisdom, are the same as those found in the East, with the exception that in place of the Chief of a Host of Planetary Spirits he puts "God," saying that this Wisdom was first taught by God himself to a certain number of Elect Angels; whereas in the Eastern Doctrine the saying is different, as will be seen.

Some synthetic and kabalistic studies on the sacred *Book of Enoch* and the Taro (Rota) are before us. We quote from the MS. copy of a Western Occultist, which is prefaced by these words:

> There is but one Law, one Principle, one Agent, one Truth and one Word. That which is above is analogically as that which is below. All that which is, is the result of quantities and of equilibriums.

The axiom of Éliphas Lévi and this triple epigraph show the identity of thought between the East and the West with regard to the Secret Science which, as the same MS. tells us, is:

> The key of things concealed, the key of the sanctuary. This is the Sacred Word which gives to the Adept the supreme reason of Occultism and its Mysteries. It is the Quintessence of Philosophies and of Dogmas; it is the Alpha and Omega; it is the Light, Life and Wisdom Universal.

The Taro of the sacred *Book of Enoch*, or Rota, is prefaced, moreover, with this explanation:

> The antiquity of this Book is lost in the night of time. It is *of Indian origin*, and goes back to an epoch long before Moses. . . . It is written upon detached leaves, which at the first were of fine gold and precious metals. . . . It is symbolical, and its combinations adapt themselves to all the wonders of the Spirit. Altered by its passage across the Ages, it is nevertheless preserved—thanks to the ignorance of the curious—in its types and its most important primitive figures.

This is the Rota of Enoch, now called Taro of Enoch, to which De Mirville alludes, as we saw, as the means used for "evil Magic," the

* Many are the marvels recorded as having taken place at his death, or we should rather say his translation; for he did not die as others do, but having suddenly disappeared, while a dazzling light filled the cavern with glory, his body was again seen upon its subsidence. When this heavenly light gave place to the habitual semi-darkness of the gloomy cave—then only, says Ginsburg, "the disciples of Israel perceived that the lamp of Israel was extinguished." His biographers tell us that there were voices heard from Heaven during the preparation for his funeral, and at his interment, when the coffin was lowered into the deep cave prepared for it, a flame broke forth and a voice mighty and majestic pronounced these words: "This is he who caused the earth to quake, and the kingdoms to shake!"

"metallic plates [or leaves] escaped from destruction during the Deluge," and which are attributed by him to Cain. They have escaped the Deluge for the simple reason that this Flood was not "Universal." And it is said to be "of Indian origin," because its origin is with the Indian Âryans of the first Sub-Race of the Fifth Root-Race, before the final destruction of the last stronghold of Atlantis. But, if it originated with the forefathers of the primitive Hindus, it was not in India that it was first used. Its origin is still more ancient and must be traced beyond and into the Himaleh,* the Snowy Range. It was born in that mysterious locality which no one is able to locate, and which is the despair of both Geographers and Christian Theologians—the region in which the Brâhman places his Kailâsa, the Mount Sumeru, and the Pârvatî Pamir, transformed by the Greeks into Paropamisus.

Round this locality, which still exists, the traditions of the Garden of Eden were built. From these regions the Greeks obtained their Parnassus†; and thence proceeded most of the biblical personages, some of them in their day men, some demi-gods and heroes, some—though very few—myths, the astronomical doubles of the former. Abram was one of them—a Chaldæan Brâhman,‡ says the legend, transformed later, after he had repudiated his Gods and left his Ur (*pur*, "town") in Chaldæa, into A-brahm§ (or A-braham) "no-brâhman" who emigrated. Abram becoming the "father of many nations" is thus explained. The student of Occultism has to bear in mind that every God and hero in ancient Pantheons (that of the *Bible* included), has three biographies in the narrative, so to say, running parallel with each other and each connected with one of the aspects of the hero—historical, astronomical and perfectly mythical, the last serving to connect the other two together and smooth away the asperities and discordances in the narrative, and gathering into one or more symbols the verities of the first two. Localities are made to correspond with astronomical

* Pockocke, may be, was not altogether wrong in deriving the German Heaven, Himmel, from Himâlaya; nor can it be denied that it is the Hindu Kailâsa (Heaven) that is the father of the Greek Heaven (Koilon), and of the Latin Cœlum.

† See Pockocke's *India in Greece*, and his derivation of Mount Parnassus from Parnasa, the leaf and branch huts of the Hindu ascetics, half shrine and half habitation. "Part of the Par-o-Pamisus (the hill of Bamian), is called Parnassus. 'These mountains are called Devanica, because they are so full of Devas or Gods, called "Gods of the Earth," Bhu Devas. They lived, according to the Purânas, in bowers or huts, called Parnasas, because they were made of leaves' (Parnas)," p. 302.

‡ Rawlinson is justly very confident of an Âryan and Vedic influence on the early mythology and history of Babylon and Chaldæa.

§ This is a Secret Doctrine affirmation, and may or may not be accepted. Only Abraham, Isaac and Judah resemble terribly the Hindu Brahmâ, Ikshvâku and Yadu.

and even with psychic events. History was thus made captive by ancient Mystery, to become later on the great Sphynx of the nineteenth century. Only, instead of devouring her too dull querists who will unriddle her whether she acknowledges it or not, she is desecrated and mangled by the modern Œdipus, before he forces her into the sea of speculations in which the Sphynx is drowned and perishes. This has now become self-evident, not only through the Secret Teachings, parsimoniously as they may be given, but by earnest and learned Symbologists and even Geometricians. The *Key to the Hebrew Egyptian Mystery*, in which a learned Mason of Cincinnati, Mr. Ralston Skinner, unveils the riddle of a God, with such ungodly ways about him as the Biblical Jah-ve, is followed by the establishment of a learned society under the presidentship of a gentleman from Ohio and four vice-presidents, one of whom is Piazzi Smyth, the well-known Astronomer and Egyptologist. The Director of the Royal Observatory in Scotland and author of *The Great Pyramid, Pharaonic by name, Humanitarian by fact, its Marvels, Mysteries, and its Teachings*, is seeking to prove the same problem as the American author and Mason: namely, that the English system of measurement is the same as that used by the ancient Egyptians in the construction of their Pyramid, or in Mr. Skinner's own words that the Pharaonic "source of measures" originated the "British inch and the ancient cubit." It "originated" much more than this, as will be fully demonstrated before the end of the next century. Not only is everything in Western religion related to measures, geometrical figures, and time-calculations, the principal period-durations being founded on most of the historical personages,* but the latter are also connected with heaven and earth truly, only with the Indo-Aryan heaven and earth, not with those of Palestine.

The prototypes of nearly all the biblical personages are to be sought

---

* It is said in *The Gnostics and their Remains*, by C. W. King (p. 13), with regard to the names of Brahmâ and Abram; "This figure of the *man*, Seir Anpin, consists of 243 numbers, being the numerical value of the letters in the name 'Abram' signifying the different orders in the celestial Hierarchies. In fact the names Abram and Brahmâ are equivalent in numerical value." Thus to one acquainted with Esoteric Symbolism, it does not seem at all strange to find in the Loka-pâlas (the four cardinal and intermediate points of the compass personified by eight Hindu Gods) Indra's elephant, named Abhra—(mâtanga) and his wife Abhramu. Abhra is in a way a Wisdom Deity, since it is this elephant's head that replaced that of Ganesha (Ganapati) the God of Wisdom, cut off by Shiva. Now Abhra means "cloud," and it is also the name of the city where Abram is supposed to have resided—when read backwards—"Arba (Kirjath) the city of four. . . . Abram is Abra with an appended *m* final, and Abra read backward is Arba" (*Key to the Hebrew Egyptian Mystery*). The author might have added that Abra meaning in Sanskrit "in, or of, the clouds," the cosmo-astronomical symbol of Abram becomes still plainer. All of these ought to be read in their originals, in Sanskrit.

for in the early Pantheon of India. It is the "Mind-born" Sons of Brahmâ, or rather of the Dhyâni-Pitara (the "Father-Gods"), the "Sons of Light," who have given birth to the "Sons of Earth," or the Patriarchs. For if the *Rig Veda* and its three sister *Vedas* have been "milked out from fire, air and sun," or Agni, Indra, and Sûrya, as *Manu Smriti* tells us, the *Old Testament* was most undeniably "milked out" of the most ingenious brains of Hebrew Kabalists, partly in Egypt and partly in Babylonia—"the seat of Sanskrit literature and Brâhman learning from her origin," as Colonel Vans Kennedy truly declared. One of such copies was Abram or Abraham, into whose bosom every orthodox Jew hopes to be gathered after death, that bosom being localised as "heaven in the clouds" or Abhra.*

From Abraham to Enoch's Taro there seems to be a considerable distance, yet the two are closely related by more than one link. Gaffarel has shown that the four symbolical animals on the twenty-first key of the Taro, at the third septenary, are the Teraphim of the Jews invented and worshipped by Abram's father Terah, and used in the oracles of the Urim and Thummim. Moreover, astronomically Abraham is the sun-measure and a portion of the sun, while Enoch is the solar year, as much as are Hermes or Thot; and Thot, numerically, "was the equivalent of Moses, or Hermes," "the lord of the lower realms, also esteemed as a teacher of wisdom," the same Mason-mathematician tells us; and the Taro being, according to one of the latest bulls of the Pope, "an invention of Hell," the same "as Masonry and Occultism," the relation is evident. The Taro contains indeed the mystery of all such transmutations of personages into sidereal bodies and *vice versâ*. The "wheel of Enoch" is an archaic invention, the most ancient of all, for it is found in China. Éliphas Lévi says there was not a nation but had it, its real meaning being preserved in the greatest secresy. It was a universal heirloom.

As we see, neither the *Book of Enoch* (his "Wheel"), nor the *Zohar*, nor any other kabalistic volume, contains merely Jewish wisdom.

---

* Before these theories and speculations—we are willing to admit they are such—are rejected, the following few points ought to be explained. (1) Why, after leaving Egypt, was the patriarch's name changed by Jehovah from Abram to Abraham. (2) Why Sarai becomes on the same principle Sarah (*Gen.*, xvii.). (3) Whence the strange coincidence of names? (4) Why should Alexander Polyhistor say that Abraham was born at Kamarina or Uria, a city of soothsayers, and invented Astronomy? (5) "The Abrahamic recollections go back at least three millenniums beyond the grandfather of Jacob," says Bunsen (*Egypt's Place in History*, v. 35.)

The doctrine itself being the result of whole millenniums of thought, is therefore the joint property of Adepts of every nation under the sun. Nevertheless, the *Zohar* teaches practical Occultism more than any other work on that subject; not as it is translated and commented upon by its various critics though, but with the secret signs on its margins. These signs contain the hidden instructions, apart from the metaphysical interpretations and apparent absurdities so fully credited by Josephus, who was never initiated and gave out the *dead letter* as he had received it.*

* *Isis Unveiled*, ii. 25.

SECTION X.

Various Occult Systems of Interpretations of Alphabets and Numerals.

The transcendental methods of the *Kabalah* must not be mentioned in a public work; but its various systems of arithmetical and geometrical ways of unriddling certain symbols may be described. The *Zohar* methods of calculation, with their three sections, the Gematria, Notaricon and Temura, also the Albath and Algath, are extremely difficult to practise. We refer those who would learn more to Cornelius Agrippa's works.* But none of those systems can ever be understood unless a Kabalist becomes a real Master in his Science. The Symbolism of Pythagoras requires still more arduous labour. His symbols are very numerous, and to comprehend even the general gist of his abstruse doctrines from his Symbology would necessitate years of study. His chief figures are the square (the Tetraktys), the equilateral triangle, the point within a circle, the cube, the triple triangle, and finally the forty-seventh proposition of Euclid's Elements, of which proposition Pythagoras was the inventor. But with this exception, none of the foregoing symbols originated with him, as some believe. Millenniums before his day, they were well known in India, whence the Samian Sage brought them, not as a speculation, but as a demonstrated Science, says Porphyry, quoting from the Pythagorean Moderatus.

> The numerals of Pythagoras were hieroglyphical symbols by means whereof he explained *all* ideas concerning the nature of things.†

---

* See *Isis Unveiled*, ii. 218-300. Gematria is formed by a metathesis from the Greek word γραμματεία; Notaricon may be compared to stenography; Temura is permutation—a way of dividing the alphabet and shifting letters.

† *De Vita Pythag.*

The fundamental geometrical figure of the *Kabalah*, as given in the *Book of Numbers*,* that figure which tradition and the Esoteric Doctrines tell us was given by the Deity Itself to Moses on Mount Sinai,† contains the key to the universal problem in its grandiose, because simple, combinations. This figure contains in itself all the others.

The Symbolism of numbers and their mathematical inter-relations is also one of the branches of Magic, especially of mental Magic, divination and correct perception in clairvoyance. Systems differ, but the root idea is everywhere the same. As shown in the *Royal Masonic Cyclopædia*, by Kenneth R. H. Mackenzie:

One system adopts unity, another trinity, a third quinquinity; again we have sexagons, heptagons, novems, and so on, until the mind is lost in the survey of the materials alone of a science of numbers.‡

The Devanâgarî characters in which Sanskrit is generally written, have all that the Hermetic, Chaldæan and Hebrew alphabets have, and in addition the Occult significance of the "eternal sound," and the meaning given to every letter in its relation to spiritual as well as terrestrial things. As there are only twenty-two letters in the Hebrew alphabet and ten fundamental numbers, while in the Devanâgarî there are thirty-five consonants and sixteen vowels, making altogether fifty-one simple letters, with numberless combinations in addition, the margin for speculation and knowledge is in proportion considerably wider. Every letter has its equivalent in other languages, and its equivalent in a figure or figures of the calculation table. It has also numerous other significations, which depend upon the special idiosyncrasies and characteristics of the person, object, or subject to be studied. As the Hindus claim to have received the Devanâgarî characters from Sarasvatî, the inventress of Sanskrit, the "language of the Devas" or Gods (in their exoteric pantheon), so most of the ancient nations claimed the same privilege for the origin of their letters and tongue. The *Kabalah*

---

* We are not aware that a copy of this ancient work is embraced in the catalogue of any European library; but it is one of the "Books of Hermes," and it is referred to and quotations are made from it in the works of a number of ancient and mediæval philosophical authors. Among these authorities are Arnoldo di Villanova's *Rosarium Philosoph.*, Francesco Arnuphi's *Opus de Lapide*, Hermes Trismegistus' *Tractatus de Transmutatione Metallorum* and *Tabula Smaragdina*, and above all the treatise of Raymond Lully, *Ab Angelis Opus Divinum de Quinta Essentia*.

† *Exodus*, xxv. 40.

‡ *Sub voce* "Numbers."

calls the Hebrew alphabet the "letters of the Angels," which were communicated to the Patriarchs, just as the Devanâgarî was to the Rishis by the Devas. The Chaldæans found their letters traced in the sky by the "yet unsettled stars and comets," says the *Book of Numbers*; while the Phœnicians had a sacred alphabet formed by the twistings of the sacred serpents. The Natar Khari (hieratic alphabet) and secret (sacerdotal) speech of the Egyptians is closely related to the oldest "Secret Doctrine Speech." It is a Devanâgarî with mystical combinations and additions, into which the Senzar largely enters.

The power and potency of numbers and characters are well known to many Western Occultists as being compounded from all these systems, but are still unknown to Hindu students, if not to their Occultists. In their turn European Kabalists are generally ignorant of the alphabetical secrets of Indian Esoterism. At the same time the general reader in the West knows nothing of either; least of all how deep are the traces left by the Esoteric numeral systems of the world in the Christian Churches.

Nevertheless this system of numerals solves the problem of cosmogony for whomsoever studies it, while the system of geometrical figures represents the numbers objectively.

To realise the full comprehension of the Deific and the Abstruse enjoyed by the Ancients, one has to study the origin of the figurative representations of their primitive Philosophers. The *Books of Hermes* are the oldest repositories of numerical Symbology in Western Occultism. In them we find that the number *ten** is the Mother of the Soul, Life and Light being therein united. For as the sacred anagram Teruph shows in the *Book of the Keys* (Numbers), the number 1 (one) is born from Spirit, and the number 10 (ten) from Matter; "the unity has made the ten, the ten, the unity"; and this is only the Pantheistic axiom, in other words "God in Nature and Nature in God."

The kabalistic Gematria is arithmetical, not geometrical. It is one of the methods for extracting the hidden meaning from letters, words, and sentences. It consists in applying to the letters of a word the sense they bear as numbers, in outward shape as well as in their individual sense. As illustrated by Ragon:

> The figure I signified the living man (a body erect), man being the only living being enjoying this faculty. A head being added to it, the glyph (or letter) P was

* See Johannes Meursius, *Denarius Pythagoricus*.

obtained, meaning paternity, creative potency; the R signifying the walking man (with his foot forward) going, *iens, iturus*.*

The characters were also made supplementary to speech, every letter being at once a figure representing a sound for the ear, an idea to the mind; as, for instance, the letter F, which is a cutting sound like that of air rushing quickly through space; fury, fusee, fugue, all words expressive of, and depicting what they signify.†

But the above pertains to another system, that of the primitive and philosophical formation of the letters and their outward glyphic form—not to Gematria. The Temura is another kabalistic method, by which any word could be made to yield its mystery out of its anagram. So in *Sepher Jetsirah* we read "One—the Spirit of the Alahim of Lives." In the oldest kabalistic diagrams the Sephiroth (the seven and the three) are represented as wheels or circles, and Adam Kadmon, the primitive Man, as an upright pillar. "Wheels and seraphim and the holy creatures" (Chioth) says Rabbi Akiba. In still another system of the symbolical *Kabalah* called Albath—which arranges the letters of the alphabet by pairs in three rows—all the couples in the first row bear the numerical value ten; and in the system of Simeon Ben Shetah (an Alexandrian Neoplatonist under the first Ptolemy) the uppermost couple—the most sacred of all—is preceded by the Pythagorean cypher: one, and a nought—10.

All beings, from the first divine emanation, or "God manifested," down to the lowest atomic existence, "have their particular number which distinguishes each of them and becomes the source of their attributes and qualities as of their destiny." Chance, as taught by Cornelius Agrippa, is in reality only an unknown progression; and time but a succession of numbers. Hence, futurity being a compound of chance and time, these are made to serve Occult calculations in order to find the result of an event, or the future of one's destiny. Said Pythagoras:

> There is a mysterious connection between the Gods and numbers, on which the science of arithmancy is based. The soul is a world that is self-moving; the soul contains in itself, and is, the quaternary, the tetraktys [the perfect cube].

There are lucky and unlucky, or beneficent and maleficent numbers. Thus while the ternary—the first of the odd numbers (the one being the perfect and standing by itself in Occultism)—is the divine figure or the triangle; the duad was disgraced by the Pythagoreans from the

* Ragon, *Maçonnerie Occulte*, p. 426, note.

† *Ibid*., p. 412, note.

first. It represented Matter, the passive and evil principle—the number of Mâyâ, illusion.

While the number *one* symbolized harmony, order or the good principle (the one God expressed in Latin by Solus, from which the word Sol, the Sun, the symbol of the Deity), number *two* expressed a contrary idea. The science of good and evil began with it. All that is double, false, opposed to the only reality, was depicted by the binary. It also expressed the contrasts in Nature which are always double: night and day, light and darkness, cold and heat, dampness and dryness, health and sickness, error and truth, male and female, etc. . . . The Romans dedicated to Pluto the second month of the year, and the second day of that month to expiations in honour of the Manes. Hence the same rite established by the Latin Church, and faithfully copied. Pope John XIX. instituted in 1003 the Festival of the Dead, which had to be celebrated on the 2nd of November, the second month of autumn.*

On the other hand the triangle, a purely geometrical figure, had great honour shewn it by every nation, and for this reason:

In geometry a straight line cannot represent an absolutely perfect figure, any more than two straight lines. Three straight lines, on the other hand, produce by their junction a triangle, or the first absolutely perfect figure. Therefore, it symbolized from the first and to this day the Eternal—the first perfection. The word for deity in Latin, as in French, begins with D, in Greek the delta or triangle, Δ, whose three sides symbolize the trinity, or the three kingdoms, or, again, divine nature. In the middle is the Hebrew Yod, the initial of Jehovah [see Éliphas Lévi's *Dogme et Rituel*, i. 154], the animating spirit or fire, the generating principle represented by the letter G, the initial of "God" in the northern languages, whose philosophical significance is generation.†

As stated correctly by the famous Mason Ragon, the Hindu Trimûrti is personified in the world of ideas by Creation, Preservation and Destruction, or Brahmâ, Vishnu and Shiva; in the world of matter by Earth, Water and Fire, or the Sun, and symbolised by the Lotus, a flower that lives by earth, water, and the sun.‡ The Lotus, sacred to

---

* Extracted from Ragon, *Maçonnerie Occulte*, p. 427, note.

† Summarised from Ragon, *ibid.*, p. 428, note.

‡ Ragon mentions the curious fact that the first four numbers in German are named after the elements.

"Ein, or one, means the air, the element which, ever in motion, penetrates matter throughout, and whose continual ebb and tide is the universal vehicle of life.

"Zwei, two, is derived from the old German Zweig, signifying germ, fecundity; it stands for earth the fecund mother of all.

"Drei, three, is the *trienos* of the Greeks, standing for water, whence the Sea-gods, Tritons; and trident, the emblem of Neptune—the water, or sea, in general being called Amphitrite (surrounding-water).

"Vier, four, a number meaning in Belgian fire. . . It is in the quaternary that the first solid figure is found, the universal symbol of immortality, the Pyramid, 'whose first syllable means fire.' Lysis and Timæus of Locris claimed that there was not a thing one could name that had not the

Isis, had the same significance in Egypt, whereas in the Christian symbol, the Lotus, not being found in either Judæa or Europe, was replaced by the water-lily. In every Greek and Latin Church, in all the pictures of the Annunciation, the Archangel Gabriel is depicted with this trinitarian symbol in his hand standing before Mary, while above the chief altar or under the dome, the Eye of the Eternal is painted within a triangle, made to replace the Hebrew Yod or God.

Truly, says Ragon, there was a time when numbers and alphabetical characters meant something more they do now—the images of a mere insignificant sound.

> Their mission was nobler then. Each of them represented by its form a complete sense, which, besides the meaning of the word, had a double* interpretation adapted to a dual doctrine. Thus when the sages desired to write something to be understood only by the savants, they confabulated a story, a dream, or some other fictitious subject with personal names of men and localities, that revealed by their lettered characters the true meaning of the author by that narrative. Such were all their religious creations.†

Every appellation and term had its *raison d'être*. The name of a plant or mineral denoted its nature to the Initiate at the first glance. The essence of everything was easily perceived by him once that it was figured by such characters. The Chinese characters have preserved much of this graphic and pictorial character to this day, though the secret of the full system is lost. Nevertheless, even now, there are those among that nation who can write a long narrative, a volume, on one page; and the symbols that are explained historically, allegorically and astronomically, have survived until now.

Moreover, there exists a universal language among the Initiates, which an Adept, and even a disciple, of any nation may understand by reading it in his own language. We Europeans, on the contrary, possess only one graphic sign common to all, & (and); there is a language richer in metaphysical terms than any on earth, whose every

---

quaternary for its root. . . The ingenious and mystical idea which led to the veneration of the ternary and the triangle was applied to number four and its figure: it was said to express a living being, 1, the vehicle of the triangle 4, vehicle of God, or man carrying in him the divine principle."

Finally, "the Ancients represented the world by the number five. Diodorus explains it by saying that this number represents earth, fire, water, air and ether or spiritus. Hence, the origin of Pente [five] and of Pan (the God) meaning in Greek all." (Compare Ragon, *op. cit.*, pp. 428-430.) It is left with the Hindu Occultists to explain the relation this Sanskrit word Pancha (five) has to the elements, the Greek Pente having for its root the Sanskrit term.

* The system of the so-called Senzar characters is still more wonderful and difficult, since each letter is made to yield several meanings, a sign placed at the commencement showing the true meaning.

† Ragon, *op. cit.*, p. 431, note.

word is expressed by like common signs. The Litera Pythagoræ, so called, the Greek Y (the English capital Y) if traced alone in a message, was as explicit as a whole page filled with sentences, for it stood as a symbol for a number of things—for white and black Magic, for instance.* Suppose one man enquired of another: To what School of Magic does so and so belong? and the answer came back with the letter traced with the right branch thicker than the left, then it meant "to right hand or divine Magic;" but if the letter were traced in the usual way, with the left branch thicker than the right, then it meant the reverse, the right or left branch being the whole biography of a man. In Asia, especially in the Devanâgarî characters, every letter had several secret meanings.

Interpretations of the hidden sense of such apocalyptic writings are found in the keys given in the *Kabalah*, and they are among its most sacred lore. St. Hieronymus assures us that they were known to the School of the Prophets and taught therein, which is very likely. Molitor, the learned Hebraist, in his work on tradition says that:

> The two and twenty letters of the Hebrew alphabet were regarded as an emanation, or the visible expression of the divine forces inherent in the ineffable name.

These letters find their equivalent in, and are replaced by numbers, in the same way as in the other systems. For instance, the twelfth and the sixth letter of the alphabet yield eighteen in a name; the other letters of that name added being always exchanged for that figure which corresponds to the alphabetical letter; then all those figures are subjected to an algebraical process which transforms them again into letters; after which the latter yield to the enquirer "the most hidden secrets of divine Permanency (eternity in its immutability), in the Futurity."

---

* The Y exoterically signifies only the two paths of virtue or vice, and stands also for the numeral 150 and with a dash over the letter Y for 150,000.

SECTION XI.

The Hexagon with the Central Point, or the Seventh Key.

Arguing upon the virtue in names (Baalshem), Molitor thinks it impossible to deny that the *Kabalah*—its present abuses notwithstanding—has some very profound and scientific basis to stand upon. And if it is claimed, he argues,

> That before the Name of Jesus every other Name must bend, why should not the Tetragrammaton have the same power? *

This is good sense and logic. For if Pythagoras viewed the hexagon formed of two crossed triangles as the symbol of creation, and the Egyptians as that of the union of fire and water (or of generation), the Essenes saw in it the Seal of Solomon, the Jews the Shield of David, the Hindus the Sign of Vishnu (to this day); and if even in Russia and Poland the double triangle is regarded as a powerful talisman—then so widespread a use argues that there is something in it. It stands to reason, indeed, that such an ancient and universally revered symbol should not be merely laid aside to be laughed at by those who know nothing of its virtues or real Occult significance. To begin with, even the known sign is merely a substitute for the one used by the Initiates. In a Tântrika work in the British Museum, a terrible curse is called down upon the head of him who shall ever divulge to the profane the real Occult hexagon known as the "Sign of Vishnu," "Solomon's Seal," etc.

The great power of the hexagon—with its central mystic sign the T, or the Svastika, a septenary—is well explained in the seventh key of *Things Concealed*, for it says:

---

* *Tradition*, chap. on "Numbers."

The seventh key is the hieroglyph of the sacred septenary, of royalty, of the priesthood [the Initiate], of triumph and true result by struggle. It is magic power in all its force, the true "Holy Kingdom." In the Hermetic Philosophy it is the quintessence resulting from the union of the two forces of the great Magic Agent [Âkâsha, Astral Light.] . . . It is equally Jakin and Boaz bound by the will of the Adept and overcome by his omnipotence.

The force of this key is absolute in Magic. All religions have consecrated this sign in their rites.

We can only glance hurriedly at present at the long series of antediluvian works in their postdiluvian and fragmentary, often disfigured, form. Although all of these are the inheritance from the Fourth Race—now lying buried in the unfathomed depths of the ocean—still they are not to be rejected. As we have shown, there was but one Science at the dawn of mankind, and it was entirely divine. If humanity on reaching its adult period has abused it—especially the last Sub-Races of the Fourth Root-Race—it has been the fault and sin of the practitioners who desecrated the divine knowledge, not of those who remained true to its pristine dogmas. It is not because the modern Roman Catholic Church, faithful to her traditional intolerance, is now pleased to see in the Occultist, and even in the innocent Spiritualist and Mason, the descendants of "the Kischuph, the Hamite, the Kasdim, the Cephene, the Ophite and the Khartumim"—all these being "the followers of Satan," that they are such indeed. The State or National Religion of every country has ever and at all times very easily disposed of rival schools by professing to believe they were dangerous heresies—the old Roman Catholic State Religion as much as the modern one.

The anathema, however, has not made the public any the wiser in the Mysteries of the Occult Sciences. In some respects the world is all the better for such ignorance. The secrets of Nature generally cut both ways, and in the hands of the undeserving they are more than likely to become murderous. Who in our modern day knows anything of the real significance of, and the powers contained in, certain characters and signs—talismans—whether for beneficent or evil purposes? Fragments of the Runes and the writing of the Kischuph, found scattered in old mediæval libraries; copies from the Ephesian and Milesian letters or characters; the thrice famous *Book of Thoth*, and the terrible treatises (still preserved) of Targes, the Chaldæan, and his disciple Tarchon, the Etruscan—who flourished long before the Trojan War—are so many names and appellations void of sense (though met with in classical literature) for the educated modern scholar. Who, in the nineteenth century, believes in the art, described in such treatises as those of Targes, of evoking and directing thunder-bolts? Yet the same is described in the Brâhmanical literature, and Targes copied his "thunder-bolts" from the Astra,* those terrible engines of destruction known to the Mahâbhâratan Âryans. A whole arsenal of dynamite bombs would pale before this art—if it ever becomes understood by the Westerns. It is from an old fragment that was translated to him, that the late Lord Bulwer Lytton got his idea of Vril. It is a lucky thing, indeed, that, in the face of the virtues and philanthropy that grace our age of iniquitous wars, of anarchists and dynamiters, the secrets contained in the books discovered in Numa's tomb should have been burnt. But the science of Circe and Medea is not lost. One can discover it in the apparent gibberish of the Tântrika Sûtras, the *Kuku-ma* of the Bhûtânî and the Sikhim Dugpas and "Red-caps" of Tibet, and even in the sorcery of the Nîlgiri Mula Kurumbas. Very luckily few outside the high practitioners of the Left Path and of the Adepts of the Right—in whose hands the weird secrets of the real meaning are safe—understand the "black" evocations. Otherwise the Western as much as the Eastern Dugpas might make short work of their enemies. The name of the latter is legion, for the direct descendants of the antediluvian sorcerers hate all those who are not with them, arguing that, therefore, they are against them.

As for the "Little Albert"—though even this small half-esoteric volume has become a literary relic—and the "Great Albert" or the "Red Dragon," together with the numberless old copies still in existence, the sorry remains of the mythical Mother Shiptons and the Merlins—we mean the false ones—all these are vulgarised imitations of the original works of the same names. Thus the "Petit Albert" is the disfigured imitation of the great work written in Latin by Bishop Adalbert, an Occultist of the eighth century, sentenced by the second Roman Concilium. His work was reprinted several centuries later and named *Alberti Parvi Lucii Libellus de Mirabilibus Naturæ Arcanis*. The severities of the Roman Church have ever been spasmodic. While one learns of this condemnation, which placed the Church, as will be shown, in relation to the Seven Archangels, the Virtues or Thrones of God, in the most embarrassing position for long centuries, it remains a

* This is a kind of magical bow and arrow calculated to destroy in one moment whole armies; it is mentioned in the *Râmâyana*, the *Purânas* and elsewhere.

wonder indeed, to find that the Jesuits have not destroyed the archives, with all their countless chronicles and annals, of the History of France and those of the Spanish Escurial, along with them. Both history and the chronicles of the former speak at length of the priceless talisman received by Charles the Great from a Pope. It was a little volume on Magic—or Sorcery, rather—all full of kabalistic figures, signs, mysterious sentences and invocations to the stars and planets. These were talismans against the enemies of the King (*les ennemis de Charlemagne*), which talismans, the chronicler tells us, proved of great help, as "every one of them [the enemies] died a violent death." The small volume, *Enchiridium Leonis Papæ*, has disappeared and is very luckily out of print. Again the Alphabet of Thoth can be dimly traced in the modern Tarot which can be had at almost every bookseller's in Paris. As for its being understood or utilised, the many fortune-tellers in Paris, who make a professional living by it, are sad specimens of failures of attempts at reading, let alone correctly interpreting, the symbolism of the Tarot without a preliminary philosophical study of the Science. The real Tarot, in its complete symbology, can be found only in the Babylonian cylinders, that any one can inspect and study in the British Museum and elsewhere. Any one can see these Chaldæan, antediluvian rhombs, or revolving cylinders, covered with sacred signs; but the secrets of these divining "wheels," or, as de Mirville calls them, "the rotating globes of Hecate," have to be left untold for some time to come. Meanwhile there are the "turning-tables" of the modern medium for the babes, and the *Kabalah* for the strong. This may afford some consolation.

People are very apt to use terms which they do not understand, and to pass judgments on *primâ facie* evidence. The difference between White and Black Magic is very difficult to realise fully, as both have to be judged by their motive, upon which their ultimate though not their immediate effects depend, even though these may not come for years. Between the "right and the left hand [Magic] there is but a cobweb thread," says an Eastern proverb. Let us abide by its wisdom and wait till we have learned more.

We shall have to return at greater length to the relation of the *Kabalah* to Gupta Vidyâ, and to deal further with esoteric and numerical systems, but we must first follow the line of Adepts in post-Christian times.

SECTION XII.

THE DUTY OF THE TRUE OCCULTIST TOWARD RELIGIONS.

HAVING disposed of pre-Christian Initiates and their Mysteries—though more has to be said about the latter—a few words must be given to the earliest post-Christian Adepts, irrespective of their personal beliefs and doctrines, or their subsequent places in History, whether sacred or profane. Our task is to analyse this adeptship with its abnormal thaumaturgical, or, as now called, psychological powers; to give each of such Adepts his due, by considering, firstly, what are the historical records about them that have reached us at this late day, and secondly, to examine the laws of probability with regard to the said powers.

And at the outset the writer must be allowed a few words in justification of what has to be said. It would be most unfair to see in these pages any defiance to, or disrespect for, the Christian religion—least of all, a desire to wound anyone's feelings. The Theosophist believes in neither Divine nor Satanic miracles. At such a distance of time he can only obtain *primâ facie* evidence and judge of it by the results claimed. There is neither Saint nor Sorcerer, Prophet nor Soothsayer for him; only Adepts, or proficients in the production of feats of a phenomenal character, to be judged by their words and deeds. The only distinction he is now able to trace depends on the results achieved—on the evidence whether they were beneficent or maleficent in their character as affecting those for or against whom the powers of the Adept were used. With the division so arbitrarily made between proficients in "miraculous" doings of this or that Religion by their respective followers and advocates, the Occultist cannot and *must not* be concerned. The Christian whose Religion commands him to regard Peter and Paul as Saints, and divinely inspired and glorified Apostles, and to view Simon and Apollonius as Wizards and Necromancers, helped by, and serving the ends of, supposed Evil Powers—is quite justified in thus doing if he be a sincere orthodox Christian. But so also is the Occultist justified, if he would serve truth and only truth, in rejecting such a one-sided view. The student of Occultism must belong to no special creed or sect, yet he is bound to show outward respect to every creed and faith, if he would become an Adept of the Good Law. He must not be bound by the pre-judged and sectarian opinions of anyone, and he has to form his own opinions and to come to his own conclusions in accordance with the rules of evidence furnished to him by the Science to which he is devoted. Thus, if the Occultist is, by way of illustration, a Buddhist, then, while regarding Gautama Buddha as the grandest of all the Adepts that lived, and the incarnation of unselfish love, boundless charity, and moral goodness, he will regard in the same light Jesus—proclaiming Him another such incarnation of every divine virtue. He will reverence the memory of the great Martyr, even while refusing to recognise in Him the incarnation on earth of the One Supreme Deity, and the "Very God of Gods," in Heaven. He will cherish the ideal man for his personal virtues, not for the claims made on his behalf by fanatical dreamers of the early ages, or by a shrewd calculating Church and Theology. He will even believe in most of the "asserted miracles," only explaining them in accordance with the rules of his own Science and by his psychic discernment. Refusing them the term "miracle"—in the theological sense of an event "contrary to the established laws of nature"—he will nevertheless view them as a deviation from the laws known (so far) to Science, quite another thing. Moreover the Occultist will, on the *primâ facie* evidence of the *Gospels*—whether proven or not—class most of such works as beneficent, divine Magic, though he will be justified in regarding such events as casting out devils into a herd of swine* as allegorical, and as pernicious to true faith in their dead-letter sense. This is the view a genuine, impartial Occultist would take. And in this respect even the fanatical Mussulmans who regard Jesus of Nazareth as a great Prophet, and show respect to Him, are giving a wholesome lesson in charity to Christians, who teach and accept that "religious tolerance is impious and absurd,"† and who will

* *Matthew*, viii. 30-34. † *Dogmatic Theology*, iii. 345.

never refer to the prophet of Islam by any other term but that of a "false prophet." It is on the principles of Occultism, then, that Peter and Simon, Paul and Apollonius, will now be examined.

These four Adepts are chosen to appear in these pages with good reason. They are the first in post-Christian Adeptship—as recorded in profane and sacred writings—to strike the key-note of "miracles," that is of psychic and physical phenomena. It is only theological bigotry and intolerance that could so maliciously and arbitrarily separate the two harmonious parts into two distinct manifestations of Divine and Satanic Magic, into "godly" and "ungodly" works.

SECTION XIII.

POST-CHRISTIAN ADEPTS AND THEIR DOCTRINES.

WHAT does the world at large know of Peter and Simon, for example? Profane history has no record of these two, while that which the so-called sacred literature tells us of them is scattered about, contained in a few sentences in the *Acts*. As to the *Apocrypha*, their very name forbids critics to trust to them for information. The Occultists, however, claim that, one-sided and prejudiced as they may be, the apocryphal *Gospels* contain far more historically true events and facts than does the *New Testament*, the *Acts* included. The former are crude tradition, the latter (the official *Gospels*) are an elaborately made up legend. The sacredness of the *New Testament* is a question of private belief and of blind faith, and while one is bound to respect the private opinion of one's neighbour, no one is forced to share it.

Who was Simon Magus, and what is known of him? One learns in the *Acts* simply that on account of his remarkable magical Arts he was called "the Great Power of God." Philip is said to have baptised this Samaritan; and subsequently he is accused of having offered money to Peter and John to teach him the power of working true "miracles," false ones, it is asserted, being of the Devil.* This is all, if we omit the words of abuse freely used against him for working "miracles" of the latter kind. Origen mentions him as having visited Rome during the reign of Nero,† and Mosheim places him among the open enemies of Christianity;‡ but Occult tradition accuses him of nothing worse than refusing to recognise "Simeon" as a Vicegerent of God, whether that "Simeon" was Peter or anyone else being still left an open question with the critic.

* viii. 9, 10. † *Adv. Celsum*. ‡ *Eccles. Hist.*, i. 140.

That which Irenæus[*] and Epiphanius[†] say of Simon Magus—namely, that he represented himself as the incarnated trinity; that in Samaria he was the Father, in Judæa the Son, and had given himself out to the Gentiles as the Holy Spirit—is simply backbiting. Times and events change; human nature remains the same and unaltered under every sky and in every age. The charge is the result and product of the traditional and now classical *odium theologicum*. No Occultists—all of whom have experienced personally, more or less, the effects of theological rancour—will ever believe such things merely on the word of an Irenæus, if, indeed, he ever wrote the words himself. Further on it is narrated of Simon that he took about with him a woman whom he introduced as Helen of Troy, who had passed through a hundred reincarnations, and who, still earlier, in the beginning of æons, was Sophia, Divine Wisdom, an emanation of his own (Simon's) Eternal Mind, when he (Simon) was the "Father"; and finally, that by her he had "begotten the Archangels and Angels, by whom this world was created," etc.

Now we all know to what a degree of transformation and luxuriant growth any bare statement can be subjected and forced, after passing through only half a dozen hands. Moreover, all these claims may be explained and even shown to be true at bottom. Simon Magus was a Kabalist and a Mystic, who, like so many other reformers, endeavoured to found a new Religion based on the fundamental teachings of the Secret Doctrine, yet without divulging more than necessary of its mysteries. Why then should not Simon, a Mystic, deeply imbued with the fact of serial incarnations (we may leave out the number "one hundred," as a very probable exaggeration of his disciples), speak of any one whom he knew psychically as an incarnation of some heroine of that name, and in the way he did—if he ever did so? Do we not find in our own century some ladies and gentlemen, not charlatans but intellectual persons highly honoured in society, whose inner conviction assures them that they were—one Queen Cleopatra, another one Alexander the Great, a third Joan of Arc, and who or what not? This is a matter of inner conviction, and is based on more or less familiarity with Occultism and belief in the modern theory of reincarnation. The latter differs from the one genuine doctrine of old, as will be shown, but there is no rule without its exception.

---

* *Contra Hæreses*, I. xxiii. 1-4.   † *Contra Hæreses*, ii. 1-6.

As to the Magus being "one with God the Father, God the Son, and God the Holy Ghost," this again is quite reasonable, if we admit that a Mystic and Seer has a right to use allegorical language; and in this case, moreover, it is quite justified by the doctrine of Universal Unity taught in Esoteric Philosophy. Every Occultist will say the same, on (to him) scientific and logical grounds, in full accordance with the doctrine he professes. Not a Vedântin but says the same thing daily: he is, of course, Brahman, and he is Parabrahman, once that he rejects the individuality of his personal spirit, and recognises the Divine Ray which dwells in his Higher Self as only a reflection of the Universal Spirit. This is the echo in all times and ages of the primitive doctrine of Emanations. The first Emanation from the Unknown is the "Father," the second the "Son," and all and everything proceeds from the One, or that Divine Spirit which is "unknowable." Hence, the assertion that by her (Sophia, or Minerva, the Divine Wisdom) he (Simon), while yet in the bosom of the Father, himself the Father (or the first collective Emanation), begot the Archangels—the "Son"—who were the creators of this world.

The Roman Catholics themselves, driven to the wall by the irrefutable arguments of their opponents—the learned Philologists and Symbologists who pick to shreds Church dogmas and their authorities, and point out the plurality of the Elohim in the *Bible*—admit to-day that the first "creation" of God, the Tsaba, or Archangels, must have participated in the creation of the Universe. Might not we suppose:

> Although "God alone created the heaven and the earth" . . . that however unconnected they [the Angels] may have been with the primodial creation, they may have received a mission to achieve, to continue, and to sustain it?*

exclaims De Mirville, in answer to Renan, Lacour, Maury and the *tutti quanti* of the French Institute. With certain alterations it is precisely this which is claimed by the Secret Doctrine. In truth there is not a single doctrine preached by the many Reformers of the first and the subsequent centuries of our era, that did not base its initial teachings on this universal cosmogony. Consult Mosheim and see what he has to say of the many "heresies" he describes. Cerinthus, the Jew,

> Taught that the Creator of this world . . . the Sovereign God of the Jewish people, was a Being . . . who derived his birth from the Supreme God;

that this Being, moreover,

> Fell by degrees from his native virtue and primitive dignity.

* *Op. cit.*, ii. 337.

Basilides, Carpocrates and Valentinus, the Egyptian Gnostics of the second century, held the same ideas with a few variations. Basilides preached seven Æons (Hosts or Archangels), who issued from the substance of the Supreme. Two of them, Power and Wisdom, begot the heavenly hierarchy of the first class and dignity; this emanated a second; the latter a third, and so on; each subsequent evolution being of a nature less exalted than the precedent, and each creating for itself a Heaven as a dwelling, the nature of each of these respective Heavens decreasing in splendour and purity as it approached nearer to the earth. Thus the number of these Dwellings amounted to 365; and over all presided the Supreme Unknown called Abraxas, a name which in the Greek method of numeration yields the number 365, which in its mystic and numerical meaning contains the number 355, or the man value.* This was a Gnostic Mystery based upon that of primitive Evolution, which ended with "man."

Saturnilus of Antioch promulgated the same doctrine slightly modified. He taught two eternal principles, Good and Evil, which are simply Spirit and Matter. The seven Angels who preside over the seven Planets are the Builders of our Universe—a purely Eastern doctrine, as Saturnilus was an Asiatic Gnostic. These Angels are the natural Guardians of the seven Regions of our Planetary System, one of the most powerful among these seven creating Angels of the *third* order being "Saturn," the presiding genius of the Planet, and the God of the Hebrew people: namely, Jehovah, who was venerated among the Jews, and to whom they dedicated the seventh day or Sabbath, Saturday—"Saturn's day" among the Scandinavians and also among the Hindus.

Marcion, who also held the doctrine of the two opposed principles of Good and Evil, asserted that there was a third Deity between the two—one of a "mixed nature"—the God of the Jews, the Creator (with his Host) of the lower, or our, World. Though ever at war with the Evil

* Ten is the perfect number of the Supreme God among the "manifested" deities, for number I is the symbol of the Universal Unit, or male principle in Nature, and number O the feminine symbol Chaos, the Deep, the two forming thus the symbol of Androgyne nature as well as the full value of the solar year, which was also the value of Jehovah and Enoch. Ten, with Pythagoras, was the symbol of the Universe; also of Enos, the Son of Seth, or the "Son of Man" who stands as the symbol of the solar year of 365 days, and whose years are therefore given as 365 also. In the Egyptian Symbology Abraxas was the Sun, the "Lord of the Heavens."

The circle is the symbol of the one Unmanifesting Principle, the plane of whose figure is infinitude eternally, and this is crossed by a diameter only during Manvantaras.

Principle, this intermediate Being was nevertheless also opposed to the Good Principle, whose place and title he coveted.

Thus Simon was only the son of his time, a religious Reformer like so many others, and an Adept among the Kabalists. The Church, to which a belief in his actual existence and great powers is a necessity—in order the better to set off the "miracle" performed by Peter and his triumph over Simon—extols unstintingly his wonderful magic feats. On the other hand, Scepticism, represented by scholars and learned critics, tries to make away with him altogether. Thus, after denying the very existence of Simon, they have finally thought fit to merge his individuality entirely in that of Paul. The anonymous author of *Supernatural Religion* assiduously endeavoured to prove that by Simon Magus we must understand the Apostle Paul, whose *Epistles* were secretly as well as openly calumniated and opposed by Peter, and charged with containing "dysnoëtic learning." Indeed this seems more than probable when we think of the two Apostles and contrast their characters.

The Apostle of the Gentiles was brave, outspoken, sincere, and very learned; the Apostle of Circumcision, cowardly, cautious, insincere, and very ignorant. That Paul had been, partially at least, if not completely, initiated into the theurgic mysteries, admits of little doubt. His language, the phraseology so peculiar to the Greek philosophers, certain expressions used only by the Initiates, are so many sure ear-marks to that supposition. Our suspicion has been strengthened by an able article entitled "Paul and Plato," by Dr. A. Wilder, in which the author puts forward one remarkable and, for us, very precious observation. In the *Epistles to the Corinthians*, he shows Paul abounding with "expressions suggested by the initiations of Sabazius and Eleusis, and the lectures of the (Greek) philosophers. He (Paul) designates himself an *idiotes*—a person unskilful in the Word, but not in the *gnosis* or philosophical learning. 'We speak wisdom among the perfect or initiated,' he writes, *even* the *hidden wisdom*, 'not the wisdom of this world, nor of the Archons of this world, but divine wisdom in a mystery, secret—which *none of the Archons of this world knew*.'"*

What else can the Apostle mean by those unequivocal words, but that he himself, as belonging to the Mystæ (Initiated), spoke of things shown and explained only in the Mysteries? The "divine wisdom in a mystery which none of the *Archons of this world knew*," has evidently some direct reference to the Basileus of the Eleusinian Initiation who did know. The Basileus belonged to the staff of the great Hierophant, and was an Archon of Athens; and as such was one of the chief Mystæ, belonging to the *interior* Mysteries, to which a very select and small number obtained an entrance.† The magistrates supervising the Eleusinia were called Archons.‡

We will deal, however, first with Simon the Magician.

* *I. Cor.*, ii. 6-8. † Compare Taylor's *Eleusinian and Bacchic Mysteries*. ‡ *Isis Unveiled*, ii. 89.

SECTION XIV.

SIMON AND HIS BIOGRAPHER HIPPOLYTUS.

As shown in our earlier volumes, Simon was a pupil of the Tanaim of Samaria, and the reputation he left behind him, together with the title of "the Great Power of God," testify in favour of the ability and learning of his Masters. But the Tanaim were Kabalists of the same secret school as John of the *Apocalypse*, whose careful aim it was to conceal as much as possible the real meaning of the names in the Mosaic Books. Still the calumnies so jealously disseminated against Simon Magus by the unknown authors and compilers of the *Acts* and other writings, could not cripple the truth to such an extent as to conceal the fact that no Christian could rival him in thaumaturgic deeds. The story told about his falling during an aerial flight, breaking both his legs and then committing suicide, is ridiculous. Posterity has heard but one side of the story. Were the disciples of Simon to have a chance, we might perhaps find that it was Peter who broke both his legs. But as against this hypothesis we know that this Apostle was too prudent ever to venture himself in Rome. On the confession of several ecclesiastical writers, no Apostle ever performed such "supernatural wonders," but of course pious people will say this only the more proves that it was the Devil who worked through Simon. He was accused of blasphemy against the Holy Ghost, only because he introduced as the "Holy Spiritus" the Mens (Intelligence) or "the Mother of all." But we find the same expression used in the *Book of Enoch*, in which, in contradistinction to the "Son of Man," he speaks of the "Son of the Woman." In the *Codex* of the Nazarenes, and in the *Zohar*, as well as in the *Books of Hermes*, the same expression is used; and even in the apocryphal *Evangelium of the Hebrews* we read that Jesus admitted the female sex of the Holy Ghost by using the expression "My Mother, the Holy Pneuma."

After long ages of denial, however, the actual existence of Simon Magus has been finally demonstrated, whether he was Saul, Paul or Simon. A manuscript speaking of him under the last name has been discovered in Greece and has put a stop to any further speculation.

In his *Histoire des Trois Premiers Siècles de l'Eglise*,* M. de Pressensé gives his opinion on this additional relic of early Christianity. Owing to the numerous myths with which the history of Simon abounds—he says—many Theologians (among Protestants, he ought to have added) have concluded that it was no better than a clever tissue of legends. But he adds:

> It contains positive facts, it seems, now warranted by the unanimous testimony of the Fathers of the Church and the narrative of Hippolytus recently discovered.†

This MS. is very far from being complimentary to the alleged founder of Western Gnosticism. While recognising great powers in Simon, it brands him as a priest of Satan—which is quite enough to show that it was written by a Christian. It also shows that, like another "servant of the Evil One"—as Manes is called by the Church—Simon was a *baptised* Christian; but that both, being too well versed in the mysteries of true *primitive* Christianity, were persecuted for it. The secret of such persecution was then, as it is now, quite transparent to those who study the question impartially. Seeking to preserve his independence, Simon could not submit to the leadership or authority of any of the Apostles, least of all to that of either Peter or John, the fanatical author of the *Apocalypse*. Hence charges of heresy followed by "anathema maranatha." The persecutions by the Church were never directed against Magic, when it was orthodox; for the new Theurgy, established and regulated by the Fathers, now known to Christendom as "grace" and "miracles," was, and is still, when it does happen, only Magic—whether conscious or unconscious. Such phenomena as have passed to posterity under the name of "divine miracles" were produced through powers acquired by great purity of life and ecstasy. Prayer and contemplation added to asceticism are the best means of discipline in order to become a Theurgist, where there is no regular initiation. For intense prayer for the accomplishment of some object is only intense *will* and desire, resulting in unconscious Magic. In our own day George Müller of Bristol has proved it. But

* *Op. cit.*, ii. 395.

† Quoted by De Mirville, *Op. cit.*, vi. 41 and 42.

"divine miracles" are produced by the same causes that generate effects of Sorcery. The whole difference rests on the good or evil effects aimed at, and on the actor who produces them. The thunders of the Church were directed only against those who dissented from the formulæ and attributed to themselves the production of certain marvellous effects, instead of fathering them on a personal God; and thus, while those Adepts in Magic Arts who acted under her direct instructions and auspices were proclaimed to posterity and history as saints and friends of God, all others were hooted out of the Church and sentenced to eternal calumny and curses from their day to this. Dogma and authority have ever been the curse of humanity, the great extinguishers of light and truth.*

It was perhaps the recognition of a germ of that which, later on, in the then nascent Church, grew into the virus of insatiate power and ambition, culminating finally in the dogma of infallibility, that forced Simon, and so many others, to break away from her at her very birth. Sects and dissensions began with the first century. While Paul rebukes Peter to his face, John slanders under the veil of vision the Nicolaitans, and makes Jesus declare that he hates them.† Therefore we pay little attention to the accusations against Simon in the MS. found in Greece.

It is entitled *Philosophumena*. Its author, regarded as Saint Hippolytus by the Greek Church, is referred to as an "unknown heretic" by the Papists, only because he speaks in it "very slanderously" of Pope Callistus, also a Saint. Nevertheless, Greeks and Latins agree in declaring the *Philosophumena* to be an extraordinary and very erudite work. Its antiquity and genuineness have been vouched for by the best authorities of Tübingen.

Whoever the author may have been, he expresses himself about Simon in this wise:

Simon, a man well versed in magic arts, deceived many persons partly by the

---

* Mr. St. George Lane-Fox has admirably expressed the idea in his eloquent appeal to the many rival schools and societies in India. "I feel sure," he said, "that the prime motive, however dimly perceived, by which you, as the promoters of these movements, were actuated, was a revolt against the tyrannical and almost universal establishment throughout all existing social and so-called religious institutions of a usurped authority in some external form supplanting and obscuring the only real and ultimate authority, the indwelling spirit of truth revealed to each individual soul, true conscience in fact, that supreme source of all human wisdom and power which elevates man above the level of the brute." (*To the Members of the Ârya Samâj, the Theosophical Society, Brahmo and Hindu Samâj and other Religious and Progressive Societies in India.*)

† *Revelation*, ii. 6.

art of Thrasymedes,* and partly *with the help of demons*.† . . . He determined to pass himself off as a god. . . . Aided by his wicked arts, he turned to profit not only the teachings of Moses, but those of the poets. . . . His disciples use to this day his charms. Thanks to incantations, to philtres, to their attractive caresses,‡ and what they call "sleeps," they send demons to influence all those whom they would fascinate. With this object they employ what they call "familiar demons."§

Further on the MS. reads:

"The Magus (Simon) made those who wished to enquire of the demon, write their question was on a leaf of parchment; this, folded in four, was thrown into a burning brazier, in order that the smoke should reveal the contents of the writing to the Spirit (demon) (*Philos.*, IV. iv.) Incense was thrown *by handfuls* on the blazing coals, the Magus adding, on pieces of papyrus, the Hebrew names of the Spirits he was addressing, and the flame devoured all. Very soon the *divine* Spirit seemed to overwhelm the Magician, who uttered unintelligible invocations, and plunged in such a state he answered every question—phantasmal apparitions being often raised over the flaming brazier (*ibid.*, iii.); at other times fire descended from heaven upon objects previously pointed out by the Magician (*ibid.*); or again the deity evoked, crossing the room, would trace fiery orbs in its flight (*ibid.*, ix.)."||

So far the above statements agree with those of Anastasius the Sinaite:

People saw Simon causing statues to walk; precipitating himself into the flames without being burnt; metamorphosing his body into that of various animals [lycanthropy]; raising at banquets phantoms and spectres; *causing the furniture in the rooms to move about*, by invisible *spirits*. He gave out that he was escorted by a number of shades to whom he gave the name of "souls of the dead." Finally, he used to fly in the air . . . (Anast., *Patrol. Grecque*, vol. lxxxix., col. 523, quest. xx.).¶

Suetonius says in his *Nero*,

In those days an Icarus fell at his first ascent near Nero's box and covered it with his blood.**

This sentence, referring evidently to some unfortunate acrobat who

---

* This "art" is not common jugglery, as some define it now: it is a kind of psychological jugglery, if jugglery at all, where fascination and glamour are used as means of producing illusions. It is hypnotism on a large scale.

† The author asserts in this his Christian persuasion.

‡ Magnetic passes, evidently, followed by a trance and sleep.

§ "Elementals" used by the highest Adept to do mechanical, not intellectual work, as a physicist uses gases and other compounds.

|| Quoted from De Mirville, *op. cit.*, vi. 43.

¶ *Ibid.*, vi. 45.

** *Ibid.*, p. 46.

missed his footing and tumbled, is brought forward as a proof that it was Simon who fell.* But the latter's name is surely too famous, if one must credit the Church Fathers, for the historian to have mentioned him simply as "an Icarus." The writer is quite aware that there exists in Rome a locality named Simonium, near the Church of SS. Cosmas and Daimanus (Via Sacra), and the ruins of the ancient temple of Romulus, where the broken pieces of a stone, on which it is alleged the two knees of the Apostle Peter were impressed in thanksgiving after his supposed victory over Simon, are shown to this day. But what does this exhibition amount to? For the broken fragments of one stone, the Buddhists of Ceylon show a whole rock on Adam's Peak with another imprint upon it. A crag stands upon its platform, a terrace of which supports a huge boulder, and on the boulder rests for nearly three thousand years the sacred foot-print, of a foot five feet long. Why not credit the legend of the latter, if we have to accept that of St. Peter? "Prince of Apostles," or "Prince of Reformers," or even the "First-born of Satan," as Simon is called, all are entitled to legends and fictions. One may be allowed to discriminate, however.

That Simon could fly, *i.e.*, raise himself in the air for a few minutes, is no impossibility. Modern mediums have performed the same feat supported by a force that Spiritualists persist in calling "spirits." But if Simon did so, it was with the help of a self-acquired blind power that heeds little the prayers and commands of rival Adepts, let alone Saints. The fact is that logic is against the supposed fall of Simon at the prayer of Peter. For had he been defeated publicly by the Apostle, his disciples would have abandoned him after such an evident sign of inferiority, and would have become orthodox Christians. But we find even the author of *Philosophumena*, just such a Christian, showing otherwise. Simon had lost so little credit with his pupils and the masses, that he went on daily preaching in the Roman Campania after his supposed fall from the clouds "far above the Capitolium," in which fall he broke his legs only! Such a lucky fall is in itself sufficiently miraculous, one would say.

* Amédée Fleury, *Rapports de St. Paul avec Sénèque*, ii. 100. The whole of this is summarised from De Mirville.

SECTION XV.

St. Paul the real Founder of present Christianity.

We may repeat with the author of *Phallicism* :

We are all for *construction*—even for *Christian*, although of course philosophical *construction*. We have nothing to do with reality, in man's limited, mechanical, scientific sense, or with *realism*. We have undertaken to show that mysticism is the very life and soul of religion;* . . . that *the Bible is only misread and misrepresented when rejected as advancing supposed fabulous and contradictory things*; that Moses did not make mistakes, but spoke to the "children of men" in the only way in which *children* in their nonage can be addressed; that the world is, indeed, a very different place from that which it is assumed to be; that what is derided as superstition is the only true and the only scientific *knowledge*, and moreover that modern knowledge and modern science are to a great extent not only superstition, but superstition of a very destructive and deadly kind.†

All this is perfectly true and correct. But it is also true that the *New Testament*, the *Acts* and the *Epistles*—however much the historical figure of Jesus may be true—are all symbolical and allegorical sayings; and that "it was not Jesus but Paul who was the real founder of Christianity;" ‡ but it was not the official Church Christianity, at any rate. "The disciples were called Christians first in Antioch," the *Acts of the Apostles* tell us,§ and they were not so called before, nor for a long time after, but simply Nazarenes.

This view is found in more than one writer of the present and the past centuries. But, hitherto, it has always been laid aside as an un-

---

* But we can never agree with the author "that rites and ritual and formal worship and prayers are of the absolute necessity of things," for the external can develop and grow and receive worship only at the expense of, and to the detriment of, the internal, the only real and true.

† H. Jennings, *op. cit.*, pp. 37, 38.

‡ See *Isis Unveiled*, ii. 574.

§ xi. 26.

proven hypothesis, a blasphemous assumption; though, as the author of *Paul, the Founder of Christianity** truly says:

> Such men as Irenæus, Epiphanius and Eusebius have transmitted to posterity a reputation for such untruth and dishonest practices that the heart sickens at the story of the crimes of that period.

The more so, since the whole Christian scheme rests upon *their* sayings. But we find now another corroboration, and this time on the perfect reading of biblical glyphs. In *The Source of Measures* we find the following:

> It must be borne in mind that our present Christianity is *Pauline*, not *Jesus*. Jesus, in his life, was a Jew, conforming to the law; even more, He says: "The scribes and pharisees sit in Moses' seat; whatsoever therefore they command you to do, that observe and do." And again: "I did not come to destroy but to fulfil the law." Therefore, He was under the law to the day of his death, and could not, while in life, abrogate one jot or tittle of it. He was circumcised and commanded circumcision. But Paul said of circumcision that it availed nothing, and *he* (Paul) abrogated the law. *Saul* and *Paul*—that is, Saul, under the law, and Paul, freed from the obligations of the law—were in one man, but parallelisms *in the flesh*, of Jesus the man under the law as observing it, who thus died in *Chréstos* and arose, freed from its obligations, in the spirit world as *Christos*, or the triumphant Christ. It was the Christ who was freed, but Christ was in the Spirit. Saul in the flesh was the function of, and parallel of Chréstos. Paul in the flesh was the function and parallel of Jesus become Christ in the spirit, as an early reality to answer to and act for the *apotheosis*; and so armed with all authority in the flesh to abrogate human law.†

The real reason why Paul is shown as "abrogating the law" can be found only in India, where to this day the most ancient customs and privileges are preserved in all their purity, notwithstanding the abuse levelled at the same. There is only one class of persons who can disregard the law of Brâhmanical institutions, caste included, with impunity, and that is the *perfect* "Svâmîs," the Yogîs—who have reached, or are supposed to have reached, the first step towards the Jîvanmukta state—or the full Initiates. And Paul was undeniably an Initiate. We will quote a passage or two from *Isis Unveiled*, for we can say now nothing better than what was said then:

> Take Paul, read the little of original that is left of him in the writings attributed to this brave, honest, sincere man, and see whether anyone can find a word therein to show that Paul meant by the word Christ anything more than the abstract ideal of the personal divinity indwelling in man. For Paul, Christ is not a person, but

* Art., by Dr. A. Wilder, in *Evolution*.

† *Op. cit.*, p. 262.

as embodied idea. "If any man is in Christ, he is a new creation," he is reborn, as after initiation, for the Lord is spirit—the spirit of man. Paul was the only one of the apostles who had understood the secret ideas underlying the teachings of Jesus, although he had never met him.

But Paul himself was not infallible or perfect.

Bent upon inaugurating a new and broad reform, one embracing the whole of humanity, he sincerely set his own doctrines far above the wisdom of the ages, above the ancient Mysteries and final revelation to the Epoptæ.

Another proof that Paul belonged to the circle of the "Initiates" lies in the following fact. The apostle had his head shorn at Cenchreæ, where Lucius (*Apuleius*) was initiated, because "he had a vow." The Nazars—or set apart—as we see in the Jewish Scriptures, had to cut their hair, which they wore long, and which "no razor touched" at any other time, and sacrifice it on the altar of initiation. And the Nazars were a class of Chaldæan Theurgists or Initiates.

It is shown in *Isis Unveiled* that Jesus belonged to this class.

Paul declares that: "According to the grace of God which is given unto me, as a wise *master-builder*, I have laid the foundation." (*I. Corinth.*, iii. 10.)

This expression, master-builder, used only *once* in the whole *Bible*, and by Paul, may be considered as a whole revelation. In the Mysteries, the third part of the sacred rites was called Epopteia, or revelation, reception into the secrets. In substance it means the highest stage of clairvoyance—the divine; . . . but the real significance of the word is "overseeing," from ὄπτομαι—"I see myself." In Sanskrit the root *âp* had the same meaning originally, though now it is understood as meaning "to obtain." *

The word *epopteia* is compound, from ἐπί "upon," and ὄπτομαι "to look," or an overseer, an inspector—also used for a master-builder. The title of master-mason, in Freemasonry, is derived from this, in the sense used in the Mysteries. Therefore, when Paul entitles himself a "master-builder," he is using a word pre-eminently kabalistic, theurgic, and masonic, and one which no other apostle uses. He thus declares himself an *adept*, having the right to initiate others.

If we search in this direction, with those sure guides, the Grecian Mysteries and the *Kabalah*, before us, it will be easy to find the secret reason why Paul was so persecuted and hated by Peter, John, and James. The author of the *Revelation* was a Jewish Kabalist, *pur sang*, with all the hatred inherited by him from his forefathers toward the pagan Mysteries.† His jealousy during the life of Jesus extended even to Peter; and it is but after the death of their common master that we see the

---

* In its most extensive meaning, the Sanskrit word has the same literal sense as the Greek term; both imply "revelation," by no human agent, but through the "receiving of the sacred drink." In India the initiated received the "Soma," sacred drink, which helped to liberate his soul from the body; and in the Eleusinian Mysteries it was the sacred drink offered at the Epopteia. The Grecian Mysteries are wholly derived from the Brâhmanical Vaidic rites, and the latter from the Ante-Vaidic religious Mysteries—primitive Wisdom Philosophy.

† It is needless to state that the *Gospel according to John* was not written by John, but by a Platonist or a Gnostic belonging to the Neoplatonic school.

two apostles—the former of whom wore the Mitre and the Petaloon of the Jewish Rabbis—preach so zealously the rite of circumcision. In the eyes of Peter, Paul, who had humiliated him, and whom he felt so much his superior in "Greek learning" and philosophy, must have naturally appeared as a magician, a man polluted with the "Gnosis," with the "wisdom" of the Greek Mysteries—hence, perhaps, "Simon the Magician" as a comparison, not a nickname.*

---

* *Ibid.*, *loc. cit.* The fact that Peter persecuted the "Apostle to the Gentiles" under that name, does not necessarily imply that there was no Simon Magus individually distinct from Paul. It may have become a generic name of abuse. Theodoret and Chrysostom, the earliest and most prolific commentators on the Gnosticism of those days, seem actually to make of Simon a rival of Paul and to state that between them passed frequent messages. The former, as a diligent propagandist of what Paul terms the "antithesis of the Gnosis" (*I. Epistle to Timothy*), must have been a sore thorn in the side of the apostle. There are sufficient proofs of the actual existence of Simon Magus.

SECTION XVI.

PETER A JEWISH KABALIST, NOT AN INITIATE.

As to Peter, biblical criticism has shown that in all probability he had no more to do with the foundation of the Latin Church at Rome than to furnish the pretext, so readily seized upon by the cunning Irenæus, of endowing the Church with a new name for the Apostle—Petra or Kiffa—a name which, by an easy play upon words, could be readily connected with Petroma. The Petroma was a pair of stone tablets used by the Hierophants at the Initiations, during the final Mystery. In this lies concealed the secret of the Vatican claim to the seat of Peter. As already quoted in *Isis Unveiled*, ii. 92:

> In the Oriental countries the designation Peter (in Phœnician and Chaldaic an interpreter), appears to have been the title of this personage.*

So far, and as the "interpreters" of *Neo*-Christianism, the Popes have most undeniably the right to call themselves successors to the title of Peter, but hardly the successors to, least of all the interpreters of, the doctrines of Jesus, the Christ; for there is the Oriental Church, older and far purer than the Roman hierarchy, which, having ever faithfully held to the primitive teachings of the Apostles, is known historically to have refused to follow the Latin seceders from the original Apostolic Church, though, curiously enough, she is still referred to by her Roman sister as the "Schismatic" Church. It is useless to repeat the reasons for the statements above made, as they may all be found in *Isis Unveiled*,† where the words, Peter, Patar, and Pitar, are explained, and the origin of the "Seat of Pitah" is shown. The reader will find upon referring to the above pages that an inscription was found on the coffin of Queen Mentuhept of the Eleventh Dynasty (2250 B.C. according to Bunsen), which in its turn was shown

---

* Taylor's *Eleusinian and Bacchic Mysteries*, Wilder's ed., p. x. † ii. 91-94.

to have been transcribed from the Seventeenth Chapter of the *Book of the Dead*, dating certainly not later than 4500 B.C. or 496 years before the World's Creation, in the Genesiacal chronology. Nevertheless, Baron Bunsen shows the group of the hieroglyphics given (*Peter-ref-su*, the "Mystery Word") and the sacred formulary mixed up with a whole series of glosses and various interpretations on a monument 4,000 years old.

This is identical with saying that the record (the true interpretation) was at that time no longer intelligible. . . . We beg our readers to understand that a sacred text, a hymn, containing the words of a departed spirit, existed in such a state, about 4,000 years ago, as to be all but unintelligible to royal scribes.*

"Unintelligible" to the non-initiated—this is certain; and it is so proved by the confused and contradictory glosses. Yet there can be no doubt that it was—for it *still is*—a mystery word. The Baron further explains:

It appears to me that our PTR is literally the old Aramaic and Hebrew "Patar," which occurs in the history of Joseph as the specific word for *interpreting*, whence also Pitrum is the term for interpretation of a text, a dream.†

This word, PTR, was partially interpreted owing to another word similarly written in another group of hieroglyphics, on a stele, the glyph used for it being an opened eye, interpreted by De Rougé‡ as "to appear," and by Bunsen as "illuminator," which is more correct. However it may be, the word Patar, or Peter, would locate both master and disciple in the circle of initiation, and connect them with the Secret Doctrine; while in the "Seat of Peter" we can hardly help seeing a connection with Petroma, the double set of stone tablets used by the Hierophant at the Supreme Initiation during the final Mystery, as already stated, also with the Pîtha-sthâna (seat, or the place of a seat), a term used in the Mysteries of the Tântriks in India, in which the limbs of Satî are scattered and then united again, as those of Osiris by Isis.§ Pîtha is a Sanskrit word, and is also used to designate the seat of the initiating Lama.

Whether all the above terms are due simply to "coincidences" or otherwise is left to the decision of our learned Symbologists and Philologists. We state facts—and nothing more. Many other writers, far

* Bunsen, *Egypt's Place in History*, v. 90.

† *Ibid.*

‡ *Stele*, p. 44.

§ See Dowson's *Hindu Classical Dict.*, *sub voc.*, "Pîtha-sthânam."

more learned and entitled to be heard than the author has ever claimed to be, have sufficiently demonstrated that Peter never had anything to do with the foundation of the Latin Church; that his supposed name Petra or Kiffa, also the whole story of his Apostleship at Rome, are simply a play on the term, which meant in every country, in one or another form, the Hierophant or Interpreter of the Mysteries; and that finally, far from dying a martyr at Rome, where he had probably never been, he died at a good old age at Babylon. In *Sepher Toldoth Jeshu*, a Hebrew manuscript of great antiquity—evidently an original and very precious document, if one may judge from the care the Jews took to hide it from the Christians—Simon (Peter) is referred to as "a faithful servant of God," who passed his life in austerities and meditation, a Kabalist and a Nazarene who lived at Babylon "at the top of a tower, composed hymns, preached charity," and died there.

SECTION XVII.

Apollonius of Tyana.

It is said in *Isis Unveiled* that the greatest teachers of divinity agree that nearly all ancient books were written symbolically and in a language intelligible only to the Initiated. The biographical sketch of Apollonius of Tyana affords an example. As every Kabalist knows, it embraces the whole of the Hermetic Philosophy, being a counterpart in many respects of the traditions left us of King Solomon. It reads like a fairy story, but, as in the case of the latter, sometimes facts and historical events are presented to the world under the colours of fiction. The journey to India represents in its every stage, though of course allegorically, the trials of a Neophyte, giving at the same time a geographical and topographical idea of a certain country as it is even now, if one knows where to look for it. The long discourses of Apollonius with the Brâhmans, their sage advice, and the dialogues with the Corinthian Menippus would, if interpreted, give the Esoteric Catechism. His visit to the empire of the wise men, his interview with their king Hiarchas, the oracle of Amphiaraus, explain symbolically many of the secret dogmas of Hermes—in the generic sense of the name—and of Occultism. Wonderful is this to relate, and were not the statement supported by numerous calculations already made, and the secret already half revealed, the writer would never have dared to say it. The travels of the great Magus are correctly, though allegorically described—that is to say, all that is related by Damis had actually taken place—but the narrative is based upon the Zodiacal signs. As *transliterated* by Damis under the guidance of Apollonius and *translated* by Philostratus, it is a marvel indeed. At the conclusion of what may now be related of the wonderful Adept of Tyana our meaning will become clearer. Suffice it to say for the present that the dialogues spoken of would disclose, if correctly understood, some of the most important secrets of Nature. Éliphas Lévi points out the great resemblance which exists between King Hiarchus and the fabulous Hiram, from whom Solomon procured the cedars of Lebanon and the gold of Ophir. But he keeps silent as to another resemblance of which, as a learned Kabalist, he could not be ignorant. Moreover, according to his invariable custom, he mystifies the reader more than he teaches him, divulging nothing and leading him off the right track.

Like most of the historical heroes of hoary antiquity, whose lives and works strongly differ from those of commonplace humanity, Apollonius is to this day a riddle, which has, so far, found no Œdipus. His existence is surrounded with such a veil of mystery that he is often mistaken for a myth. But according to every law of logic and reason, it is quite clear that Apollonius should never be regarded in such a light. If the Tyanean Theurgist may be put down as a fabulous character, then history has no right to her Cæsars and Alexanders. It is quite true that this Sage, who stands unrivalled in his thaumaturgical powers to this day—on evidence historically attested—came into the arena of public life no one seems to know whence, and disappeared from it, no one seems to know whither. But the reasons for this are evident. Every means was used—especially during the fourth and fifth centuries of our era—to sweep from people's minds the remembrance of this great and holy man. The circulation of his biographies, which were many and enthusiastic, was prevented by the Christians, and for a very good reason, as we shall see. The diary of Damis survived most miraculously, and remained alone to tell the tale. But it must not be forgotten that Justin Martyr often speaks of Apollonius, and the character and truthfulness of this good man are unimpeachable, the more is that he had good reasons to feel bewildered. Nor can it be denied that there is hardly a Church Father of the first six centuries that left Apollonius unnoticed. Only, according to invariable Christian customs of charity, their pens were dipped as usual in the blackest ink of *odium theologicum*, intolerance and one-sidedness. St. Jerome (Hieronymus) gives at length the story of St. John's alleged contest with the Sage of Tyana—a competition of "miracles"—in which, of course, the truthful saint* describes in glowing colours the defeat of Apollonius, and seeks

* See *Preface to St. Matthew's Gospel*, Baronius, i. 752, quoted in De Mirville, vi. 63. Jerome is the Father who having found the authentic and original *Evangel* (the Hebrew text), by Matthew the Apostle-publican, in the library of Cæsarea, "*written by the hand* of Matthew" (Hieronymus: *De Viris*, Illust. Chap. iii.)—as he himself admits—set it down as heretical, and substituted for it his own Greek text. And it is also he who perverted the text in the *Book of Job* to enforce belief in the resurrection in flesh (see *Isis Unveiled*, Vol. ii. pp. 181 and 182, *et seq.*), quoting in support the most learned authorities.

corroboration in St. John's *Apocrypha* proclaimed doubtful *even* by the Church.*

Therefore it is that nobody can say where or when Apollonius was born, and everyone is equally ignorant of the date at which, and of the place where, he died. Some think he was eighty or ninety years old at the time of his death, others that he was one hundred or even one hundred and seventeen. But, whether he ended his days at Ephesus in the year 96 A.D., as some say, or whether the event took place at Lindus in the temple of Pallas-Athene, or whether again he disappeared from the temple of Dictynna, or whether, as others maintain, he did not die at all, but when a hundred years old renewed his life by Magic, and went on working for the benefit of humanity, no one can tell. The Secret Records alone have noted his birth and subsequent career. But then—"who hath believed in *that* report?"

All that history knows is that Apollonius was the enthusiastic founder of a new school of contemplation. Perhaps less metaphorical and more practical than Jesus, he nevertheless inculcated the same quintessence of spirituality, the same high moral truths. He is accused of having confined them to the higher classes of society instead of doing what Buddha and Jesus did, instead of preaching them to the poor and the afflicted. Of his reasons for acting in such an exclusive way it is impossible to judge at so late a date. But Karmic law seems to be mixed up with it. Born, as we are told, among the aristocracy, it is very likely that he desired to finish the work undone in this particular direction by his predecessor, and sought to offer "peace on earth and good will" to *all* men, and not alone to the outcast and the criminal. Therefore he associated with the kings and the mighty ones of the age. Nevertheless, the three "miracle-workers" exhibited striking similarity of purpose. Like Jesus and like Buddha, Apollonius was the uncompromising enemy of all outward show of piety, all display of useless religious ceremonies, bigotry and hypocrisy. That his "miracles" were more wonderful, more varied, and far better attested in

* De Mirville gives the following thrilling account of the "contest."

"John, pressed, as St. Jerome tells us, by all the churches of Asia to proclaim more solemnly [in the face of the miracles of Apollonius] the divinity of Jesus Christ, after a long prayer with his disciples on the Mount of Patmos and being in ecstasy by the divine Spirit, made heard amid thunder and lightning his famous *In Principio erat Verbum*. When that sublime extasis, that caused him to be named the 'Son of Thunder,' had passed, Apollonius was compelled to retire and to disappear. Such was his defeat, less bloody but as hard as that of Simon, the Magician. ("The Magician Theurgist," vi. 63) For our part we have never heard of extasis producing thunder and lightning and we are at a loss to understand the meaning.

History than any others, is also true. Materialism denies this evidence, and the affirmations of even the Church herself, however much he is branded by her, show this to be the fact.*

The calumnies set afloat against Apollonius were as numerous as they were false. So late as eighteen centuries after his death he was defamed by Bishop Douglas in his work against miracles. In this the Right Reverend bishop crushed himself against historical facts. For it is not in the *miracles*, but in the identity of ideas and doctrines preached that we have to look for a similarity between Buddha, Jesus and Apollonius. If we study the question with a dispassionate mind, we shall soon perceive that the ethics of Gautama, Plato, Apollonius, Jesus, Ammonius Sakkas, and his disciples, were all based on the same mystic philosophy—that all worshipped one divine Ideal, whether they considered it as the "Father" of humanity, who lives in man, as man lives in Him, or as the Incomprehensible Creative Principle. All led God-like lives. Ammonius, speaking of his philosophy, taught that their school dated from the days of Hermes, who brought his wisdom from India. It was the same mystical contemplation throughout as that of the Yogin: the communion of the Brâhman with his own luminous Self—the "Âtman."†

The groundwork of the Eclectic School is thus shown to be identical with the doctrines of the Yogis—the Hindu Mystics; it is proved that it had a common origin, from the same source as the earlier Buddhism of Gautama and of his Arhats.

The *Ineffable Name* in the search for which so many Kabalists—unacquainted with any Oriental or even European Adepts—vainly consume their knowledge and lives, dwells latent in the heart of every man. This mirific name which, according to the most ancient oracles, "rushes into the infinite worlds, ἀφοιτήτῳ στροφάλιγγι," can be obtained in a twofold way: by regular initiation, and through the "small voice" which Elijah heard in the cave of Horeb, the mount of God. And "when Elijah heard it he wrapped his *face in his mantle* and stood in the entering of the cave. And behold there came *the* voice."

When Apollonius of Tyana desired to hear the "small voice," he used to wrap himself up entirely in a mantle of fine wool, on which he placed both his feet, after having performed certain magnetic passes, and pronounced not the "name" but an invocation well known to every adept. Then he drew the mantle over his head and face, and his translucid or astral spirit was free. On ordinary occasions he no more wore wool than the priests of the temples. The possession of the secret combination of the "name" gave the Hierophant supreme power over every being, human or otherwise, inferior to himself in soul-strength.‡

* This is the old, old story. Who of us, Theosophists, but knows by bitter personal experience what clerical hatred, malice and persecution can do in this direction; to what an extent of falsehood, calumny and cruelty these feelings can go, even in our modern day, and what exemplars of Christ-like charity His alleged and self-constituted servants have shown themselves to be!

† *Isis Unveiled*, ii. 342.

‡ *Loc. cit.*, ii. 343, 344.

To whatever school he belonged, this fact is certain, that Apollonius of Tyana left an imperishable name behind him. Hundreds of works were written upon this wonderful man; historians have seriously discussed him; pretentious fools, unable to come to any conclusion about the Sage, have tried to deny his very existence. As to the Church; although she execrates his memory, she has ever tried to present him in the light of a historical character. Her policy now seems to be to direct the impression left by him into another channel—a well known and a very old stratagem. The Jesuits, for instance, while admitting his "miracles," have set going a double current of thought, and they have succeeded, as they succeed in all they undertake. Apollonius is represented by one party as an obedient "medium of Satan," surrounding his theurgical powers by a most wonderful and dazzling light; while the other party professes to regard the whole matter as a clever romance, written with a predetermined object in view.

In his voluminous Memoirs of Satan, the Marquis de Mirville, in the course of his pleading for the recognition of the enemy of God as the producer of spiritual phenomena, devotes a whole chapter to this great Adept. The following translation of passages in his book unveils the whole plot. The reader is asked to bear in mind that the Marquis wrote every one of his works under the auspices and authorisation of the Holy See of Rome.

> It would be to leave the first century incomplete and to offer an insult to the memory of St. John, to pass over in silence the name of one who had the honour of being his special antagonist, as Simon was that of St. Peter, Elymas that of Paul, etc. In the first years of the Christian era, . . . there appeared at Tyana in Cappadocia one of those extraordinary men of whom the Pythagorean School was so very lavish. As great a traveller as was his master, initiated in all the secret doctrines of India, Egypt and Chaldæa, endowed, therefore, with all the theurgic powers of the ancient Magi, he bewildered, each in its turn, all the countries which he visited, and which all—we are obliged to admit—seem to have blessed his memory. We could not doubt this fact without repudiating real historical records. The details of his life are transmitted to us by a historian of the fourth century (Philostratus), himself the translator of a diary that recorded day by day the life of the philosopher, written by Damis, his disciple and intimate friend.*

De Mirville admits the possibility of *some* exaggerations in both recorder and translator; but he "does not believe they hold a very wide space in the narrative." Therefore, he regrets to find the Abbé

* *Pneumatologie*, vi. 62.

Freppel "in his eloquent *Essays*,* calling the diary of Damis a romance." Why?

[Because] the orator bases his opinion on the perfect similitude, calculated as he imagines, of that legend with the life of the Saviour. But in studying the subject more profoundly, he [Abbé Freppel] can convince himself that neither Apollonius, nor Damis, nor again Philostratus ever claimed a greater honour than a likeness to St. John. This programme was in itself sufficiently fascinating, and the travesty as sufficiently scandalous; for owing to magic arts Apollonius had succeeded in counterbalancing, in appearance, several of the miracles at Ephesus [produced by St. John], etc.†

The *anguis in herba* has shown its head. It is the perfect, the wonderful similitude of the life of Apollonius with that of the Saviour that places the Church between Scylla and Charybdis. To deny the life and the "miracles" of the former, would amount to denying the trustworthiness of the same Apostles and patristic writers on whose evidence is built the life of Jesus himself. To father the Adept's beneficent deeds, his raisings of the dead, acts of charity, healing powers, etc., on the "old enemy" would be rather dangerous at this time. Hence the stratagem to confuse the ideas of those who rely upon authorities and criticisms. The Church is far more clear-sighted than any of our great historians. The Church *knows* that to deny the existence of that Adept would lead her to denying the Emperor Vespasian and *his* Historians, the Emperors Alexander Severus and Aurelianus and *their* Historians, and finally to deny Jesus and every evidence about Him, thus preparing the way to her flock for finally denying *herself*. It becomes interesting to learn what she says in this emergency, through her chosen speaker, De Mirville. It is as follows:

What is there so new and so impossible in the narrative of Damis concerning their voyages to the countries of the Chaldees and the Gymnosophists?—he asks. Try to recall, before denying, what were in those days those countries of marvels *par excellence*, as also the testimony of such men as Pythagoras, Empedocles and Democritus, who ought to be allowed to have known what they were writing about. With what have we finally to reproach Apollonius? Is it for having made, as the Oracles did, a series of prophecies and predictions wonderfully verified? No: because, better studied now, we *know what they* are.‡ The Oracles have now become to us, what they were to every

* *Les Apologistes Chrétiens au Second Siècle*, p. 106.

† *Pneumatologie*, vi, 62.

‡ Many are they who *do not know*; hence, they do not believe in them.

one during the past century, from Van Dale to Fontenelle. Is it for having been endowed with second sight, and having had visions at a distance?* No; for such phenomena are at the present day endemical in half Europe. Is it for having boasted of his knowledge of every existing language under the sun, without having ever learned one of them? But who can be ignorant of the fact that this is the best criterion† of the presence and assistance of a spirit of whatever nature it may be? Or is it for having believed in transmigration (reincarnation)? It is still believed in (by millions) in our day. No one has any idea of the number of the men of Science who long for the re-establishment of the Druidical Religion and of the Mysteries of Pythagoras. Or is it for having exorcised the demons and the plague? The Egyptians, the Etruscans and all the Roman Pontiffs had done so long before.‡ For having conversed with the dead? We do the same to-day, or believe we do so—which is all the same. For having believed in the Empuses? Where is the Demonologist that does not know that the Empuse is the "south demon" referred to in David's *Psalms*, and dreaded then as it is feared even now in all Northern Europe?§ For having made himself invisible at will? It is one of the achievements of mesmerism. For having appeared after his (supposed) death to the Emperor Aurelian above the city walls of Tyana, and for having compelled him thereby to raise the siege of that town? Such was the mission of every hero beyond the tomb, and the reason of the worship vowed to the Manes.‖ For having descended into the famous den of Trophonius, and taken from it an old book preserved for years after by the Emperor Adrian in his Antium library? The trustworthy and sober Pausanias had descended into the same den before Apollonius, and came back no less a believer. For having disappeared at his death? Yes, like Romulus, like Votan, like Lycurgus, like Pythag-

* Just so. Apollonius, during a lecture he was delivering at Ephesus before an audience of many thousands, perceived the murder of the Emperor Domitian in Rome and notified it at the very moment it was taking place, to the whole town; and Swedenborg, in the same manner, saw from Gothenburg the great fire at Stockholm and told it to his friends, no telegraph being in use in those days.

† No criterion at all. The Hindu Sâddhus and Adepts acquire the gift by the holiness of their lives. The Yoga-Vidyâ teaches it, and no "spirits" are required.

‡ As to the Pontiffs, the matter is rather doubtful.

§ But this alone is no reason why people should believe in this class of spirits. There are better authorities for such belief.

‖ De Mirville's aim is to show that all such apparitions of the Manes or disembodied Spirits are the work of the Devil, "Satan's simulacra."

osas,* always under the most mysterious circumstances, ever attended by apparitions, revelations, etc. Let us stop here and repeat unceasingly: had the life of Apollonius been simple *romance*, he would never have attained such a celebrity during his lifetime or created such a numerous sect, one so enthusiastic after his death.

And, to add to this, had all this been a romance, never would a Caracalla have raised a heroön to his memory† or Alexander Severus have placed his bust between those of two Demi-Gods and of the true God,‡ or an Empress have corresponded with him. Hardly rested from the hardships of the siege at Jerusalem, Titus would not have hastened to write to Apollonius a letter, asking to meet him at Argos and adding that his father and himself (Titus) owed all to him, the great Apollonius, and that, therefore, his first thought was for their benefactor. Nor would the Emperor Aurelian have built a temple and a shrine to that great Sage, to thank him for his apparition and communication at Tyana. That *posthumous* conversation, as all knew, saved the city, inasmuch as Aurelian had in consequence raised the siege. Furthermore, had it been a romance, History would not have had Vopiscus,§ one of the most trustworthy Pagan Historians, to certify to it. Finally, Apollonius would not have been the object of the admiration of such a noble character as Epictetus, and even of several of the Fathers of the Church; Jerome for instance, in his better moments, writing thus of Apollonius:

> This travelling philosopher found something to learn wherever he went; and profiting everywhere thus improved with every day.‖

---

* He might have added: like the great Shankarâchârya, Tsong-Kha-Pa, and so many other real Adepts—even his own Master, Jesus; for this is indeed a criterion of true Adeptship, though "to disappear" one need not fly up in the clouds.

† See *Dion Cassius*, XXVII. xviii. 2.

‡ Lampridius, *Adrian*, xxix. 2.

§ The passage runs as follows: "Aurelian had determined to destroy Tyana, and the town owed its salvation only to a miracle of Apollonius; this man so famous and so wise, this great friend of the Gods, appeared suddenly before the Emperor, as he was returning to his tent, in his own figure and form, and said to him in the Pannonian language: 'Aurelian, if thou wouldst conquer, abandon those evil designs against my fellow-citizens; if thou wouldst command, abstain from shedding innocent blood; and if thou wouldst live, abstain from injustice.' Aurelian, familiar with the face of Apollonius, whose portraits he had seen in many temples, struck with wonder, immediately vowed to him (Apollonius) statue, portrait and temple, and returned completely to ideas of mercy." And then Vopiscus adds: "If I have believed more and more in the virtues of the *majestic* Apollonius, it is because, after gathering my information from the most serious men, I have found all these facts corroborated in the Books of the Ulpian Library." (See Flavius Vopiscus, *Aurelianus*). Vopiscus wrote in 290 and consequently preceded Philostratus by a century.

‖ *Ep. ad Paulinum*.

As to his prodigies, without wishing to fathom them, Jerome most undeniably admits them as such; which he would assuredly never have done, had he not been compelled to do so by facts. To end the subject, had Apollonius been a simple hero of a romance, dramatised in the fourth century, the Ephesians would not, in their enthusiastic gratitude, have raised to him a golden statue for all the benefits he had conferred upon them.*

* The above is mostly summarised from De Mirville, *loc. cit.*, pp. 66-69.

SECTION XVIII.

FACTS UNDERLYING ADEPT BIOGRAPHIES.

THE tree is known by its fruits; the nature of the Adept by his words and deeds. These words of charity and mercy, the noble advice put into the mouth of Apollonius (or of his sidereal phantom), as given by Vopiscus, show the Occultists who Apollonius was. Why then call him the "Medium of Satan" seventeen centuries later? There must be a reason, and a very potent reason, to justify and explain the secret of such a strong animus of the Church against one of the noblest men of his age. There is a reason for it, and we give it in the words of the author of the *Key to the Hebrew-Egyptian Mystery in the Source of Measures*, and of Professor Seyffarth. The latter analyses and explains the salient dates in the life of Jesus, and thus throws light on the conclusions of the former. We quote both, blending the two.

According to solar months (of thirty days, one of the calendars in use among the Hebrews) all remarkable events of the *Old Testament* happened on the days of the equinoxes and the solstices; for instance, the foundations and dedications of the temples and altars [and consecration of the tabernacle]. On the same cardinal days, the most remarkable events of the *New Testament* happened; for instance, the annunciation, the birth, the resurrection of Christ, and the birth of John the Baptist. And thus we learn that all remarkable epochs of the *New Testament* were typically sanctified a long time before by the *Old Testament*, beginning at the day succeeding the end of the Creation, which was the day of the vernal equinox. During the crucifixion, on the 14th day of Nisan, Dionysius Areopagita saw, in Ethiopia, an eclipse of the sun, and he said, "Now the Lord (Jehovah) is suffering something." Then Christ arose from the dead on the 22d March, 17 *Nisan*, Sunday, the day of the vernal equinox (Seyf., quoting Philo de Septen)—that is, on Easter, or on the day when the sun gives new life to the earth. The words of John the Baptist "He must increase, but I must decrease," serve to prove, as is affirmed by the fathers of the church, that John was born on the longest day of the year, and Christ, who was six months younger, on the shortest, 22d June and 22d December, the solstices.

This only goes to show that, as to another phase, John and Jesus were but epitomisers of the history of the same sun, under differences of aspect or condition; and one condition following another, of necessity, the statement, *Luke*, ix. 7, was not only not an empty one, but it was true, that which "was said of some, that (in Jesus) John was risen from the dead." (And this consideration serves to explain why it has been that the *Life of Apollonius of Tyana*, by Philostratus, has been so persistently kept back from translation and from popular reading. Those who have studied it in the original have been forced to the comment that either the *Life of Apollonius* has been taken from the *New Testament*, or that the *New Testament* narratives have been taken from the *Life of Apollonius*, because of the manifest sameness of the *means of construction* of the narratives. The explanation is simple enough, when it is considered that the names of *Jesus*, Hebrew גי, and Apollonius, or Apollo, are alike names of *the sun in the heavens*; and necessarily the history of the one, as to his travels through *the signs*, with the personifications of his sufferings, triumphs and miracles, could be but the *history of the other*, where there was a widespread, common method of describing those travels by personification.) It seems also that, for long afterward, all this was known to rest upon an astronomical basis; for the secular church, so to speak, was founded by Constantine, and the objective condition of the worship established was that part of his decree, in which it was affirmed that the venerable day of the *sun* should be the day set apart for the worship of Jesus Christ, as *Sun*-day. There is something weird and startling in some other facts about this matter. The prophet Daniel (*true prophet*, as says Graetz),* by use of the pyramid numbers, or astrological numbers, foretold the cutting off of the *Mâshiac*, as it happened (which would go to show the accuracy of his astronomical knowledge, if there was an eclipse of the sun at that time). . . . Now, however, the temple was destroyed in the year 71, in the month Virgo, and 71 is the Dove number, as shown, or 71 × 5 = 355, and with *the fish*, a Jehovah number.

"Is it possible," queries further on the author, thus answering the intimate thought of every Christian and Occultist who reads and studies his work:

Is it possible that the events of humanity do run co-ordinately with these number forms? If so, while Jesus Christ, as an astronomical figure, was true to all that has been advanced, and more, possibly, He may, as a man, have filled up, under the numbers, answers in the sea of life to predestined type. The personality of Jesus does not appear to have been destroyed, because, *as a condition*, he was answering to astronomical forms and relations. The Arabian says, "Your destiny is written in the stars."†

Nor is the "personality" of Apollonius "destroyed" for the same

* A "true prophet" because an Initiate, one perfectly versed in Occult astronomy.

† *Key to Hebrew-Egyptian Mystery*, p. 259 *et seq*. Astronomy and physiology are the bodies, astrology and psychology their informing souls; the former being studied by the eye of sensual perception, the latter by the inner or "soul-eye"; and both are *exact* sciences.

reason. The case of Jesus covers the ground for the same possibility in the cases of all Adepts and Avatâras—such as Buddha, Shankarâchârya, Krishna, etc.—all of these as great and as historical for their respective followers and in their countries, as Jesus of Nazareth is now for Christians and in this land.

But there is something more in the old literature of the early centuries. Iamblichus wrote a biography of the great Pythagoras.

The latter so closely resembles the life of Jesus that it may be taken for a travesty. Diogenes Laërtius and Plutarch relate the history of Plato according to a similar style.*

Why then wonder at the doubts that assail every scholar who studies all these lives? The Church herself knew all these doubts in her early stages; and though only one of her Popes has been known publicly and openly as a Pagan, how many more were there who were too ambitious to reveal the truth?

This "mystery," for mystery indeed it is to those who, not being Initiates, fail to find the key of the perfect similitude between the lives of Pythagoras, Buddha, Apollonius, etc.—is only a natural result for those who know that all these great characters were Initiates of the same School. For them there is neither "travesty" nor "copy" of one from the other; for them they are all "originals," only painted to represent one and the same subject: the mystic, and at the same time the public, life of the Initiates sent into the world to save portions of humanity, if they could not save the whole bulk. Hence, the same programme for all. The assumed "immaculate origin" for each, referring to their "mystic birth" during the Mystery of Initiation, and accepted literally by the multitudes, encouraged in this by the better informed but ambitious clergy. Thus, the mother of each one of them was declared a virgin, conceiving her son directly by the Holy Spirit of God; and the Sons, in consequence, were the "Sons of God," though in truth, none of them was any more entitled to such recognition than were the rest of his brother Initiates, for they were all—so far as their mystic lives were concerned—only "the epitomisers of the history of the same Sun," which epitome is another mystery within the Mystery. The biographies of the external personalities bearing the names of such heroes have nothing to do with, and are quite independent of the private lives of the heroes, being only the mystic records of their public and, parallel therewith, of their *inner* lives, in their characters as

* *New Platonism and Alchemy*, p. 12

Neophytes and Initiates. Hence, the manifest sameness of the means of construction of their respective biographies. From the beginning of Humanity the Cross, or Man, with his arms stretched out horizontally, typifying his kosmic origin, was connected with his psychic nature and with the struggles which lead to Initiation. But, if it is once shown that (*a*) every true Adept had, and still has, to pass through the seven and the twelve trials of Initiation, symbolised by the twelve labours of Hercules; (*b*) that the day of his real birth is regarded as that day when he is born into the world spiritually, his very age being counted from the hour of his second birth, which makes of him a "twice-born," a Dvija or Initiate, on which day he is indeed born of a God and from an immaculate Mother; and (*c*) that the trials of all these personages are made to correspond with the Esoteric significance of initiatory rites—all of which corresponded to the twelve zodiacal signs—then every one will see the meaning of the travels of all those heroes through the signs of the Sun in Heaven; and that they are in each individual case a personification of the "sufferings, triumphs and miracles" of an Adept, before and after his Initiation. When to the world at large all this is explained, then also the mystery of all those lives, so closely resembling each other that the history of one seems to be the history of the other, and *vice versâ*, will, like everything else, become plain.

Take an instance. The legends — for they are *all* legends for exoteric purposes, whatever may be the denials in one case—of the lives of Krishna, Hercules, Pythagoras, Buddha, Jesus, Apollonius, Chaitanya. On the worldly plane, their biographies, if written by one outside the circle, would differ greatly from what we read of them in the narratives that are preserved of their mystic lives. Nevertheless, however much masked and hidden from profane gaze, the chief features of such lives will all be found there in common. Each of those characters is represented as a divinely begotten Sotēr (Saviour), a title bestowed on deities, great kings and heroes; everyone of them, whether at their birth or afterwards, is searched for, and threatened with death (yet never killed) by an opposing power (the world of Matter and Illusion), whether it be called a king Kansa, king Herod, or king Mâra (the Evil Power). They are all tempted, persecuted and finally said to have been murdered at the end of the rite of Initiation, *i.e.*, in their *physical* personalities, of which they are supposed to have been rid for ever after *spiritual* "resurrection" or "birth." And having thus come to an end by this supposed violent death, they all descend into the Nether World, the Pit or Hell—the Kingdom of Temptation, Lust and Matter, therefore of Darkness, whence returning, having overcome the "Chrest-condition," they are glorified and become "Gods."

It is not in the course of their everyday life, then, that the great similarity is to be sought, but in their inner state and in the most important events of their career as religious teachers. All this is connected with, and built upon, an astronomical basis, which serves, at the same time, as a foundation for the representation of the degrees and trials of Initiation: descent into the Kingdom of Darkness and Matter, for the *last time*, to emerge therefrom as "Suns of Righteousness," is the most important of these and, therefore, is found in the history of all the Soters—from Orpheus and Hercules, down to Krishna and Christ. Says Euripides:

> Heracles, who has gone from the chambers of earth,
> Leaving the nether home of Pluto.*

And Virgil writes:

> At Thee the Stygian lakes trembled; Thee the janitor of Orcus
> Feared. . . Thee not even Typhon frightened. . .
> Hail, *true son of Jove*, glory added to the Gods.†

Orpheus seeks, in the kingdom of Pluto, Eurydice, his lost Soul; Krishna goes down into the infernal regions and rescues therefrom his six brothers, he being the seventh Principle; a transparent allegory of his becoming a "perfect Initiate," the whole of the six Principles merging into the seventh. Jesus is made to descend into the kingdom of Satan to save the soul of Adam, or the symbol of material physical humanity.

Have any of our learned Orientalists ever thought of searching for the origin of this allegory, for the parent "Seed" of that "Tree of Life" which bears such verdant boughs since it was first planted on earth by the hand of its "Builders"? We fear not. Yet it is found, as is now shown, even in the exoteric, distorted interpretations of the *Vedas*—of the *Rig Veda*, the oldest, the most trustworthy of all the four—this root and seed of all future Initiate-Saviours being called in it the Visvakarmâ, the "Father" Principle, "beyond the comprehension of mortals;" in the *second* stage Sûrya, the "Son," who offers Himself as a sacrifice to Himself; in the third, the Initiate, who sacrifices His

* *Heracles*, 807.

† *Æneid*, viii., 274, ff.

physical to His *spiritual* Self. It is in Visvakarma, the "omnificent," who becomes (mystically) Vikkartana, the "sun shorn of his beams," who suffers for his too ardent nature, and then becomes glorified (by purification), that the keynote of the Initiation into the greatest Mystery of Nature was struck. Hence the secret of the wonderful "similarity."

All this is allegorical and mystical, and yet perfectly comprehensible and plain to any student of Eastern Occultism, even superficially acquainted with the Mysteries of Initiation. In our objective Universe of Matter and false appearances the Sun is the most fitting emblem of the life-giving, beneficent Deity. In the subjective, boundless World of Spirit and Reality the bright luminary has another and a mystical significance, which cannot be fully given to the public. The so-called "idolatrous" Pârsîs and Hindus are certainly nearer the truth in their religious reverence for the Sun, than the cold, ever-analysing, and as ever-mistaken, public is prepared to believe, at present. The Theosophists, who will be alone able to take in the meaning, may be told that the Sun is the external manifestation of the Seventh Principle of our Planetary System, while the Moon is its Fourth Principle, shining in the borrowed robes of her master, saturated with and reflecting every passionate impulse and evil desire of her grossly material body, Earth. The whole cycle of Adeptship and Initiation and all its mysteries are connected with, and subservient to, these two and the Seven Planets. Spiritual clairvoyance is derived from the Sun; all psychic states, diseases, and even lunacy, proceed from the Moon.

According even to the data of History—her conclusions being remarkably erroneous while her premises are mostly correct—there is an extraordinary agreement between the "legends" of every Founder of a Religion (and also between the rites and dogmas of all) and the names and course of constellations headed by the Sun. It does not follow, however, because of this, that both Founders and their Religions should be, the one myths, and the other superstitions. They are, one and all, the different versions of the same natural primeval Mystery, on which the Wisdom-Religion was based, and the development of its Adepts subsequently framed.

And now once more we have to beg the reader not to lend an ear to the charge—against Theosophy in general and the writer in particular—of disrespect toward one of the greatest and noblest characters in the History of Adeptship—Jesus of Nazareth—nor even of hatred to the Church. The expression of truth and fact can hardly be regarded, with any approximation to justice, as blasphemy or hatred. The whole question hangs upon the solution of that one point: Was Jesus as the "Son of God" and "Saviour" of Mankind, unique in the World's annals? Was His case—among so many similar claims—the only exceptional and unprecedented one; His birth the sole supernaturally immaculate; and were all others, as maintained by the Church, but blasphemous Satanic copies and plagiarisms by anticipation? Or was He only the "son of his deeds," a pre-eminently holy man, and a reformer, one of many, who paid with His life for the presumption of endeavouring, in the face of ignorance and despotic power, to enlighten mankind and make its burden lighter by His Ethics and Philosophy? The first necessitates a blind, all-resisting faith; the latter is suggested to every one by reason and logic. Moreover, has the Church always believed as she does now—or rather, as she pretends she does, in order to be thus justified in directing her anathema against those who disagree with her?—or has she passed through the same throes of doubt, nay, of secret denial and unbelief, suppressed only by the force of ambition and love of power?

The question must be answered in the affirmative as to the second alternative. It is an irrefutable conclusion, and a natural inference based on facts known from historical records. Leaving for the present untouched the lives of many Popes and Saints that loudly belied their claims to infallibility and holiness, let the reader turn to Ecclesiastical History, the records of the growth and progress of the Christian Church (not of Christianity), and he will find the answer on those pages. Says a writer:

> The Church has known too well the suggestions of freethought criticism, enquiry, as also all those doubts that provoke her anger to-day; and the "sacred truths" she would promulgate have been in turn admitted and repudiated, transformed and altered, amplified and curtailed, by the dignitaries of the Church hierarchy, even as regards the most fundamental dogmas.

Where is that God or Hero whose origin, biography, and genealogy were more hazy, or more difficult to define and finally agree upon than those of Jesus? How was the now irrevocable dogma with regard to His true nature settled at last? By His mother, according to the Evangelists, He was a man—a simple mortal man; by His Father He is God! But how? Is He then man or God, or is He both at the same time? asks the perplexed writer. Truly the propositions offered on this point of the doctrine have caused floods of ink and blood to be shed, in turn, on poor Humanity, and still the doubts are not at rest. In this, as in everything else, the wise Church Councils have contradicted themselves" and changed their minds a number of times. Let us recapitulate and throw a glance at the texts offered for our inspection. This is History.

The Bishop Paul of Samosata denied the divinity of Christ at the first Council of Antioch, at the very origin and birth of theological Christianity, He was called "Son of God" merely on account of His holiness and good deeds. His blood was corruptible in the Sacrament of the Eucharist.

At the Council of Nicæa, held A.D. 325, Arius came out with his premisses, which nearly broke asunder the Catholic Union.

Seventeen bishops defended the doctrines of Arius, who was exiled for them. Nevertheless, thirty years after, A.D. 355, at the Council of Milan, three hundred bishops signed a letter of adherence to the Arian views, notwithstanding that ten years earlier, A.D. 345, at a new Council of Antioch, the Eusebians had proclaimed that Jesus Christ was the Son of God and One with His Father.

At the Council of Sirmium, A.D. 357, the "Son" had become no longer consubstantial. The Anomœans, who denied that consubstantiality, and the Arians were triumphant. A year later, at the second Council of Ancyra, it was decreed that the "Son was not consubstantial but only similar to the Father in his substance." Pope Liberius ratified the decision.

During several centuries the Councils fought and quarrelled, supporting the most contradictory and opposite views, the fruit of their laborious travail being the Holy Trinity, which, Minerva-like, issued forth from the theological brain, armed with all the thunders of the Church. The new mystery was ushered into the world amid some terrible strifes, in which murder and other crimes had a high hand. At the Council of Saragossa, A.D. 380, it was proclaimed that the Father, Son and Holy Spirit are one and the same Person, Christ's human nature being merely an "illusion"—an echo of the Avatâric Hindu doctrine. "Once upon this slippery path the Fathers had to slide down *ad absurdum*—which they did not fail of doing." How deny human nature in him who was born of a woman? The only wise remark made during one of the Councils of Constantinople came from Eutyches, who was bold enough to say: "May God preserve me from reasoning on the nature of my God"—for which he was excommunicated by Pope Flavius.

At the Council of Ephesus, A.D. 449, Eutyches had his revenge. As Eusebius, the veracious Bishop of Cæsarea, was forcing him into the admission of *two* distinct natures in Jesus Christ, the Council rose against him and it was proposed that Eusebius should be burned alive. The bishops arose like one man, and with fists clenched, foaming with rage, demanded that Eusebius should be torn into two halves, and be dealt by as he would deal with Jesus, whose nature he divided. Eutyches was re-established in his power and office; Eusebius and Flavius deposed. Then the two parties attacked each other most violently and fought. St. Flavius was so ill-treated by Bishop Dioscoros, who assaulted and kicked him, that he died a few days later from the injuries inflicted.

Every incongruity was courted in these Councils, and the result is the present living paradoxes called Church dogmas. For instance, at the first Council of Ancyra, A.D. 314, it was asked, "In baptizing a woman with child, is the unborn baby also baptized by the fact?" The Council answered in the negative; because, as was alleged, "the person who is receiving baptism must be a consenting party, which is impossible to the child in its mother's womb." Thus then unconsciousness is a canonical obstacle to baptism, and thus no child baptised nowadays is baptised at all in fact. And then what becomes of the tens of thousands of starving heathen babies baptised by the missionaries during famines, and otherwise surreptitiously "saved" by the too zealous Padres? Follow one after another the debates and decisions of the numberless Councils, and behold on what a jumble of contradictions the present infallible and Apostolic Church is built!

And now we can see how greatly paradoxical, when taken literally, is the assertion in *Genesis*: "God created man in his own image." Besides the glaring fact that it is not the Adam of dust (of Chapter ii.), who is thus made in the divine image, but the Divine Androgyne (of Chapter i.), or Adam Kadmon, one can see for oneself that God—the God of the Christians at any rate—was created by man in his own image, amid the kicks, blows and murders of the early Councils.

A curious fact, one that throws a flood of light on the claim that Jesus was an Initiate and a martyred Adept, is given in the work (already so often referred to) which may be called "a mathematical revelation"—*The Source of Measures.*

Attention is called to the part of the 46th verse of the 27th Chapter of Matthew, as follows: "Eli, Eli, Lama Sabachthani?—that is to say, My God, my God, why hast thou forsaken me?" Of course, our versions are taken from the original

Greek manuscripts (the reason why we have no original Hebrew manuscripts concerning these occurrences being because the enigmas in Hebrew would betray themselves on comparison with the sources of their derivation, the *Old Testament*. The Greek manuscripts, without exception, give these words as—

Ἠλί Ἠλί λαμὰ σαβαχθανί

They are *Hebrew words*, rendered into the *Greek*, and in Hebrew are as follows:

אלי אלי לָמה שבחתני

The Scripture of these words says, "that is to say, My God, my God, why hast thou forsaken me?" as their proper translation. Here then are the words, beyond all dispute; and beyond all question, such is the interpretation given of them by Scripture. Now the words will not bear this interpretation, and it is a false rendering. The true meaning is *just the opposite of the one given*, and is—

My God, my God, how thou dost glorify me!

But even more, for while *lama* is *why*, or *how*, as a verbal it connects the idea of *to dazzle*, or adverbially, it could run "*how dazzlingly*," and so on. To the unwary reader this interpretation is enforced, and made to answer, as it were, to the fulfilment of a prophetic utterance, by a marginal reference to the *first* verse of the *twenty-second* Psalm, which reads:

"My God, my God, why hast thou forsaken me?"

The Hebrew of this verse for these words is—

אלי אלי למה עזבתני.

as to which the reference is correct, and the interpretation sound and good, but with an utterly different word. The words are—

Eli, Eli, lamah azabutha-ni?

No wit of man, however scholarly, can save this passage from *falseness of rendering* on its face; and as so, it becomes a most terrible blow upon the proper first-face sacredness of the recital.*

For ten years or more, sat the revisers (?) of the *Bible*, a most imposing and solemn array of the learned of the land, the greatest Hebrew and Greek scholars of England, purporting to correct the mistakes and blunders, the sins of omission and of commission of their less learned predecessors, the translators of the Bible. Are we going to be told that none of them saw the glaring difference between the Hebrew words in *Psalm* xxii., *azabutha-ni*, and *sabachthani* in *Matthew*; that they were not aware of the deliberate falsification?

For "falsification" it was. And if we are asked the reason why the early Church Fathers resorted to it, the answer is plain: Because the *Sacramental* words belonged in their true rendering to Pagan temple

---

* App., vii., p. 301.

rites. They were pronounced after the terrible trials of Initiation, and were still fresh in the memory of some of the "Fathers" when the *Gospel of Matthew* was edited into the Greek language. Finally, many of the Hierophants of the Mysteries, and many more of the Initiates were still living in those days, and the sentence rendered in its true words would class Jesus directly with the simple Initiates. The words "My God, my Sun, thou hast poured thy radiance upon me!" were the final words that concluded the thanksgiving prayer of the Initiate, "the Son and the glorified Elect of the Sun." In Egypt we find to this day carvings and paintings that represent the rite. The candidate is between two divine sponsors; one "Osiris-Sun" with the head of a hawk, representing life, the other Mercury—the ibis-headed, psychopompic genius, who guides the Souls after death to their new abode, Hades—standing for the death of the physical body, figuratively. Both are shown pouring the "stream of life," the water of purification, on the head of the Initiate, the two streams of which, interlacing, form a cross. The better to conceal the truth, this *basso-relievo* has also been explained as a "Pagan presentment of a Christian truth." The Chevalier des Mousseaux calls this Mercury:

> The assessor of Osiris-Sol, as St. Michael is the assessor, Ferouer, of the Word.

The monogram of Chrestos and the Labarum, the standard of Constantine—who, by the by, died a Pagan and was never baptised—is a symbol derived from the above rite and also denotes "life and death." Long before the sign of the Cross was adopted as a Christian symbol, it was employed as a secret sign of recognition among Neophytes and Adepts. Say Éliphas Lévi:

> The sign of the cross adopted by the Christians does not belong exclusively to them. It is kabalistic, and represents the oppositions and quaternary equilibrium of the elements. We see by the occult verse of the *Pater*, to which we have called attention in another work, that there were originally two ways of making it, or, at least, two very different formulas to express its meaning: one reserved for priests and initiates; the other given to neophytes and the profane.*

One can understand now why the *Gospel of Matthew*, the Evangel of the Ebionites, has been for ever excluded in its Hebrew form from the world's curious gaze.

> Jerome found the authentic and original Evangel written in Hebrew, by Matthew the Publican, at the library collected at Cæsarea by the martyr Pamphilius. "*I received permission from the Nazaræans*, who at Berœa of Syria used this (gospel)

* *Dogme et Rituel de la Haute Magie*, ii. 88.

to translate it," he writes toward the end of the fourth century.* "In the Evangel which the *Nazarenes* and *Ebionites use*," said Jerome, "which recently I translated from Hebrew into Greek, and which is called by most persons the *genuine* gospel of Matthew," etc.†

That the apostles had received a "secret doctrine" from Jesus, and that he himself taught one, is evident from the following words of Jerome, who confessed it in an unguarded moment. Writing to the Bishops Chromatius and Heliodorus, he complains that "a difficult work is enjoined, since this (translation) has been commanded me by your Felicities, which *St. Matthew himself*, the Apostle and Evangelist, *did not wish to be openly written*. For if this had not been *secret*, he (Matthew) would have added to the Evangel that what he gave forth *was his*; but he made up this book *sealed up in the Hebrew characters*, which he put forth *even in such a way* that the book, written in Hebrew letters and by the hand of himself, might be possessed *by the men most religious;* who also, in the course of time, received it from those who preceded them. But this very book they never gave to any one to be transcribed, and *its text* they related some one way and some another."‡ And he adds further, on the same page: "And it happened that this book, having been published by a disciple of Manichæus, named Seleucus, who also wrote falsely *The Acts of the Apostles*, exhibited matter not for edification, but for destruction; and that this (book) was *approved in a synod* which the ears of the Church properly refused to listen to."§

Jerome admits, himself, that the book which he authenticates as being written "by the hand of Matthew," was nevertheless a book which, notwithstanding that he translated it twice, was nearly unintelligible to him, for it was arcane. Nevertheless, Jerome coolly sets down every commentary upon it but his own as *heretical*. More than that, Jerome knew that this Gospel was the only *original* one, yet he becomes more zealous than ever in his persecution of the "Heretics." Why? Because to accept it was equivalent to reading the death sentence of the established Church. *The Gospel according to the Hebrews* was well known to have been the

---

* (Hieronymus, *De Viris Illust.*, iii.) "It is remarkable that, while all Church Fathers say that *Matthew* wrote in *Hebrew*, the whole of them use the *Greek* text as the genuine apostolic writing, without mentioning what relation the *Hebrew* Matthew has to our *Greek* one! It had many *peculiar additions* which are wanting in our (Greek) Evangel" (Olshausen, *Nachweis der Echtheit der Sämmtlichen Schriften des Neuen Test.*, p. 32; Dunlap, *Sôd, the Son of the Man*, p. 44.)

† *Commen. to Matthew* (xii. 13) Book II. Jerome adds that it was written in the Chaldaic language, but with Hebrew letters.

‡ "St. Jerome," v. 445; Dunlap, *Sôd, the Son of Man*, p. 46.

§ This accounts also for the rejection of the works of Justin Martyr, who used only this "Gospel according to the Hebrews," as also did most probably Tatian, his disciple. At what a late period the divinity of Christ was fully established we can judge by the mere fact that even in the fourth century Eusebius did not denounce this book as spurious, but only classed it with such as the *Apocalypse* of John; and Credner (*Zur Gesch. des Kan*, p. 120) shows Nicephorus inserting it, together with the *Revelation*, in his *Stichometry*, among the Antilegomena. The Ebionites, the *genuine* primitive Christians, rejecting the rest of the Apostolic writings, make use only of this Gospel (*Adv. Hær.*, i. 26) and the Ebionites, as Epiphanius declares, firmly believed, with the Nazarenes, that Jesus was but a man, "of the seed of a man."

only one accepted for four centuries by the Jewish Christians, the [illegible] the Ebionites. And neither of the latter accepted the *divinity* of Christ.* [illegible]

The Ebionites were the first, the earliest Christians, [illegible] presentative was the Gnostic author of the *Clementine* [illegible] the author of *Supernatural Religion* shows,† Ebionitic [illegible] had once been the purest form of Christianity. They were the [illegible] and followers of the early Nazarenes—the kabalistic Gnostics [illegible] believed in the Æons, as the Cerinthians did, and that "the [illegible] put together by Angels" (Dhyân Chohans), as Epiphanius [illegible] (*Contra Ebionitas*): "Ebion had the opinion of the Nazarenes, [illegible] of Cerinthians." "They decided that Christ was of the seed of a [illegible] he laments.‡ Thus again:

> The badge of Dan-Scorpio is *death-life*, in the symbol ☧, as *cross-bones* [illegible] . . . or *life-death* . . . the standard of Constantine, the Roman [illegible] Abel has been shown to be Jesus, and Cain-Vulcain, or Mars, pierced him. [illegible] tine was the Roman Emperor, whose warlike god was Mars, and a Roman [illegible] pierced Jesus on the cross. . . .
>
> But the piercing of Abel was the consummation of his marriage with Cain, [illegible] this was proper under the form of Mars Generator; hence the double glyph, [illegible] Mars-Generator [Osiris-Sun] and Mars-Destroyer [Mercury the God of Death [illegible] the Egyptian *basso-relievo*] in one; significant, again, of the primal idea of the [illegible] cosmos, or of birth and death, as necessary to the continuation of the stream [illegible] life.§

To quote once more from *Isis Unveiled*:

> A Latin cross of a perfect Christian shape was found hewn upon the granite slabs of the Adytum of the Serapeum; and the monks did not fail to claim that the cross had been hallowed by the Pagans in a "spirit of prophecy." At least, Sozomen, with an air of triumph, records the fact.‖ But archæology and symbolism, those tireless and implacable enemies of clerical false pretences, have found in the hieroglyphics of the legend running round the design at least a partial interpretation of its meaning.
>
> According to King and other numismatists and archæologists, the cross was [illegible]

* *Isis Unveiled*, ii. 182-3.

† *Op. cit.*, ii. 5.

‡ See also *Isis Unveiled*, ii. 180, to end of chapter.

§ *Source of Measures*, p. 299. This "stream of life" being emblematised in the Phallic [illegible] just mentioned, by the water poured in the shape of a Cross on the initiated candidate by [illegible] *Life* and the Sun—and Mercury—*Death*. It was the *finale* of the rite of Initiation after the [illegible] and the *twelve* tortures in the Crypts of Egypt were passed through successfully.

‖ Another untrustworthy, untruthful and ignorant writer, an ecclesiastical historian of the [illegible] century. His alleged history of the strife between the Pagans, Neoplatonists, and the Christians of Alexandria and Constantinople, which extends from the year 324 to 439, dedicated by him to Theodosius, the younger, is full of deliberate falsifications.

placed there as the symbol of eternal life. Such a Tau, or Egyptian cross, was used in the Bacchic and Eleusinian Mysteries. Symbol of the dual generative power, it was laid upon the breast of the Initiate, after his "new birth" was accomplished, and the Mystæ had returned from their baptism in the sea. It was a mystic sign that his spiritual birth had regenerated and united his astral soul with his divine spirit, and that he was ready to ascend in spirit to the blessed abodes of light and glory—the Eleusinia. The Tau was a magic talisman at the same time as a religious emblem. It was adopted by the Christians through the Gnostics and Kabalists, who used it largely, as their numerous gems testify. These in turn had the Tau (or handled cross) from the Egyptians, and the Latin Cross from the Buddhist missionaries, who brought it from India (where it can be found even now) two or three centuries B.C. The Assyrians, Egyptians, ancient Americans, Hindus and Romans had it in various, but very slight modifications of shape. Till very late in the middle ages, it was considered a potent spell against epilepsy and demoniacal possession, and the "signet of the living God" brought down in St. John's vision by the angel ascending from the east to "seal the servants of our God in the foreheads," was but the same mystic Tau—the Egyptian Cross. In the painted glass of St. Denis (France) this angel is represented as stamping this sign on the forehead of the elect; the legend reads, SIGNUM TAY. In King's *Gnostics*, the author reminds us that "this mark is commonly borne by St. Anthony, an *Egyptian* recluse."* What the real meaning of the Tau was, is explained to us by the Christian St. John, the Egyptian Hermes, and the Hindu Brahmans. It is but too evident that, with the Apostle at least, it meant the "Ineffable Name," as he calls this "signet of the living God" a few chapters further on† the "*Father's name written in their foreheads.*"

The Brahmâtmâ, the chief of the Hindu Initiates, had on his head-gear two keys, symbol of the revealed mystery of life and death, placed cross-like; and in some Buddhist pagodas of Tartary and Mongolia, the entrance of a chamber within the temple, generally containing the staircase which leads to the inner dagoba,‡ and the porticos of some *Prachidas*§ are ornamented with a cross formed of two fishes, as found on some of the zodiacs of the Buddhists. We should not wonder at all at learning that the sacred device in the tombs in the catacombs at Rome, the "Vesica Piscis," was derived from the said Buddhist zodiacal sign. How general must have been that geometrical figure in the world-symbols, may be inferred from the fact that there is a Masonic tradition that Solomon's temple was built on three foundations, forming the "triple Tau" or three crosses.

In its mystical sense, the Egyptian cross owes its origin, as an emblem, to the realisation by the earliest philosophy of an *androgynous dualism of every manifestation in nature*, which proceeds from the abstract ideal of a likewise androgynous deity, while the Christian emblem is simply due to chance. Had the Mosaic law

* *Gems of the Orthodox Christians*, vol. i., p. 135.

† *Revelation*, xiv. 1.

‡ A dagoba is a small temple of globular form, in which are preserved the relics of Gautama.

§ Prachidas are buildings of all sizes and forms, like our mausoleums, and are sacred to votive offerings to the dead.

prevailed, Jesus should have been lapidated.* The crucifixion was a mode of torture, and utterly common among Romans as it was unknown among [illegible] nations. It was called the "Tree of Infamy." It is but later that it was adopted as a Christian symbol; but during the first two decades the apostles looked [illegible] with horror.† It is certainly not the Christian Cross that John had in mind [illegible] speaking of the "signet of the living God," but the mystic Tau—the Tetragrammaton, or mighty name, which, on the most ancient Kabalistic talismans, was represented by the four Hebrew letters composing the Holy Word. [illegible]

The famous Lady Ellenborough, known among the Arabs of Damascus [illegible] the desert, after her last marriage, as *Hanoum Medjouye*, had a talisman in her possession, presented to her by a Druse from Mount Lebanon. It was recognized [illegible] certain sign on its left corner as belonging to that class of gems which is known [illegible] Palestine as a "*Messianic*" amulet, of the second or third century B.C. It is a [illegible] stone of a pentagonal form; at the bottom is engraved a fish; higher, Solomon's Seal;‡ and still higher, the four Chaldaic letters—Jod, He, Vau, He, IAHO, which form the name of the Deity. These are arranged in quite an unusual way, [illegible] from below upward, in reversed order, and forming the Egyptian Tau. Around these there is a legend which, as the gem is not our property, we are not at liberty to give. The Tau, in its mystical sense, as well as the *Crux ansata*, is the Tree of *Life*. [illegible]

It is well known that the earliest Christian emblems—before it was ever attempted to represent the bodily appearance of Jesus—were the Lamb, the Good Shepherd, and *The Fish*. The origin of the latter emblem, which has so puzzled the archaeologists, thus becomes comprehensible. The whole secret lies in the [illegible] ascertained fact that, while in the *Kabalah* the King Messiah is called "Interpreter," or Revealer of the Mystery, and shown to be the *fifth* emanation, in the *Talmud*—for reasons we will now explain—the Messiah is very often designated as "[illegible]," or the Fish. This is an inheritance from the Chaldees, and relates—as the very name indicates—to the Babylonian Dagon, the man-fish, who was the instructor and interpreter of the people, to whom he appeared. Abarbanel explains the name, by stating that the sign of his (Messiah's) coming is the conjunction of Saturn and Jupiter in the sign *Pisces*.§ Therefore, as the Christians were intent upon identifying their Christos with the Messiah of the *Old Testament*, they adopted it so readily as to forget that its true origin might be traced still further back than the Babylonian Dagon. How eagerly and closely the ideal of Jesus was united, by the early Christians, with every imaginable kabalistic and pagan tenet, may be inferred from the language of Clemens, of Alexandria, addressed to his co-religionists.

* The Talmudistic records claim that, after having been hanged, he was lapidated and buried under the water at the junction of two streams. *Mishna Sanhedrin*, Vol. VI., p. 4; *Talmud*, of Babylon, same article, 43 a, 67 a.

† *Coptic Legends of the Crucifixion*, MSS. XI.

‡ We are at a loss to understand why King, in his *Gnostic Gems*, represents Solomon's Seal as a five-pointed star, whereas it is six-pointed, and is the signet of Vishnu in India.

§ King (*Gnostics*) gives the figure of a Christian symbol, very common during the middle ages, of three fishes interlaced into a triangle, and having the FIVE letters (a most sacred Pythagorean number) ΙΧΘΥΣ engraved on it. The number five relates to the same kabalistic computation.

When they were debating upon the choice of the most appropriate symbol to remind them of Jesus, Clemens advised them in the following words: "Let the engraving upon the gem of your ring be either *a dove*, or *a ship running before the wind* (the Argha), or *a fish*." Was the good father, when writing this sentence, labouring under the recollection of Joshua, son of Nun (called *Jesus* in the Greek and Slavonian versions); or had he forgotten the real interpretation of these pagan symbols?*

And now, with the help of all these passages scattered hither and thither in *Isis* and other works of this kind, the reader will see and judge for himself which of the two explanations—the Christian or that of the Occultist—is the nearer to truth. If Jesus were not an Initiate, why should all these *allegorical* incidents of his life be given? Why should such extreme trouble be taken, so much time wasted trying to make the above: (*a*) answer and dovetail with purposely picked out sentences in the *Old Testament*, to show them as *prophecies*; and (*b*) to preserve in them the initiatory symbols, the emblems so pregnant with Occult meaning and all of these belonging to Pagan *mystic* Philosophy? The author of the *Source of Measures* gives out that *mystical* intent; but only once now and again, in its one-sided, numerical and kabalistic meaning, without paying any attention to, or having concern with, the primeval and more spiritual origin, and he deals with it only so far as it relates to the *Old Testament*. He attributes the *purposed* change in the sentence "Eli, Eli, lama sabachthani" to the principle already mentioned of the crossed bones and skull in the Labarum,

As an emblem of death, being placed over the door of life and signifying *birth*, or of the intercontainment of two opposite principles in one, just as, mystically, the Saviour was held to be man-woman.†

The author's idea is to show the mystic blending by the Gospel writers of Jehovah, Cain, Abel, etc., with Jesus (in accordance with Jewish kabalistic numeration); the better he succeeds, the more clearly he shows that it was a *forced* blending, and that we have not a record of the real events of the life of Jesus, narrated by eye-witnesses or the Apostles. The narrative is all based on the signs of the Zodiac:

Each a double sign or male-female [in ancient astrological Magic]—viz: it was Taurus-Eve, and Scorpio was Mars-Lupa, or Mars with the female wolf [in relation to

---

* *Op. cit.*, ii., 253-256.

† *Op. cit.*, 300. All this connects Jesus with great Initiates and solar heroes; all this is purely Pagan, under a newly-evolved variation, the Christian scheme.

Romulus). So, as these signs were opposites of each other, yet [illegible] they were connected; and so in fact it was, and in a double sense, [illegible] the year was in Taurus, as the conception of Eve by Mars, [illegible] The birth would be at the winter solstice, or Christmas. On the [illegible] ception in Scorpio—*viz.*, of Lupa by Taurus—birth would be in Leo [illegible] Christos in *humiliation*, while Leo was Christos in *triumph*.—While [illegible] fulfilled astronomical functions, Mars-Lupa fulfilled spiritual ones by type [illegible]

The author bases all this on Egyptian correlations and [illegible] Gods and Goddesses, but ignores the Âryan, which are [illegible]

Mooth or *Mouth*, was the Egyptian cognomen of Venus, (Eve, mother of all [illegible] (as *Vach*, mother of all living, a permutation of *Aditi*, as Eve was one of [illegible] *the moon*. Plutarch (*Isis*, 374) hands it down that Isis was sometimes called [illegible] which word means *mother*. . . (Isha, אשה, woman). (*Isis*, p. 372). [illegible] is that part of Nature, which, as feminine, contains in herself, as [illegible] things to be born. . . "Certainly the moon," speaking astronomically, [illegible] exercises this function in Taurus, Venus being the house (in opposition to [illegible] *generator*, in Scorpio), because the sign is luna, hypsoma. Since . . . Isis [illegible] differs from Isis *Muth* and that in the vocable *Muth* the *notion of bringing forth* [illegible] be concealed, and since fructification must take place, *Sol* being joined with [illegible] *Libra*, it is not improbable that Muth first indeed signifies Venus in Libra [illegible] Luna in Libra." (Beiträge zur Kenntniss, pars. II, S. 9, under *Muth*.)†

Then Fuerst, under *Bohu*, is quoted to show [illegible]

The double play upon the word *Muth* by help of which the real intent [illegible] in the occult way . . . *sin*, *death*, and *woman* are one in the glyph, and [illegible] latively connected with *intercourse* and *death*.‡

All this is applied by the author *only* to the exoteric and [illegible] euhemerised symbols, whereas they were meant, first of all, to conceal cosmogonical mysteries, and then, those of anthropological evolution with reference to the Seven Races, already evoluted and to come, [illegible] especially as regards the last branch races of the third Root-Race. However, the word *void* (primeval Chaos) is shown to be taken [illegible] Eve-Venus-Naamah, agreeably with Fuerst's definition; for [illegible] says:

In this primitive signification [of void] was בהו [bohu] taken in the Biblical cosmogony, and used in establishing the dogma [illegible] *Jes* (us) *m'avin*, [illegible] *from nothing*), respecting creation. [Which shows the writers of the *New Testament* considerably skilled in the *Kabalah* and Occult Sciences, and corroborates [illegible] our assertion.] Hence Aquila translates οὐδὲν vulg. vacua (hence [illegible] (hence also the horns of Isis—Nature, Earth, and the Moon—taken from Vâch, the Hindu "Mother of all that lives," identified with Virâj and called in Atharvaveda the daughter of Kâma, the *first* desires: "That daughter of thine, O Kâma, is called [illegible]

* *Op. cit.*, 290. † Pp. 294, 295. ‡ P. 295.

the cow, she whom Sages name *Vâch-Virâj*," who was *milked* by Brihaspati, the Rishi, which is another mystery] Onkelos and Samarit. [illegible]

The Phœnician cosmogony has connected *Bohu* בהו Baau into a personified expression denoting the *primitive substance*, and as a deity, the *mother of races of the gods* [which is Aditi and Vâch]. The Aramean name [illegible], *Bohû*, *Bohû-ôs*, Buto, for the *mother of the gods*, which passed over to the Gnostics, Babylonians and Egyptians, *is identical then with Mût* ([illegible], our *Muth*) properly, (*Bût*) *originated in Phœnician* from an interchange of *b* with *m*.*

Rather, one would say, go to the origin. The mystic euhemerisation of Wisdom and Intelligence, operating in the work of cosmic evolution, or *Buddhi* under the names of Brahmâ, Purusha, etc., as male power, and Aditi-Vâch, etc., as female, whence Sarasvatî, Goddess of Wisdom, who became under the veils of Esoteric concealment, Butos, *Bythos*-Depth, the grossly material, personal female, called Eve, the "primitive woman" of Irenæus, and the world springing out of *Nothing*.

The workings out of this glyph of 4th *Genesis* help to the comprehension of the division of one character into the forms of two persons; as Adam and Eve, Cain and Abel, Abram and Isaac, Jacob and Esau, and so on [all male and female] . . . Now, as linking together several great salient points in the Biblical structure: (*1*) as to the *Old* and *New Testaments*; with also (*2*) as to the Roman Empire; (*3*) as to confirming the meanings and uses of symbols; and (*4*) as to confirming the entire explanation and reading of the glyphs; as (*5*) recognising and laying down the base of the great pyramid as the *foundation square* of the Bible construction; (*6*) as well as the new Roman adoption under Constantine—the following given:†

Cain has been shown to be . . . the 360 circle of the Zodiac, the perfect and exact standard, by a squared division; hence his name of Melchizadik . . . . [The geometrical and numerical demonstrations here follow.] It has been repeatedly stated that the object of the Great Pyramid construction was to measure the *heavens and the earth* . . . [the objective spheres as evoluting from the subjective, purely spiritual Kosmos, we beg leave to add]; therefore, its measuring containment would indicate all the substance of measure of *the heavens and the earth*, or agreeably to ancient recognition, *Earth*, *Air*, *Water* and *Fire*.‡ (The base side of this pyramid was diameter to a circumference in *feet* of 2400. The characteristic of this is 24 feet, or 6 × 4 = 24, or this very Cain-Adam square.) Now, by the restoration of the encampment of the Israelites, as initiated by Moses, by the great

---

* Pp. 295, 290.

† Had we known the learned author before his book was printed, he might have been perchance prevailed upon to add a seventh link from which all others, far preceding those enumerated in point of time, and surpassing them in universally philosophical meaning, have been derived, aye, even to the great pyramid, whose foundation square was, in its turn, the great Âryan Mysteries.

‡ We would say cosmic Matter, Spirit, Chaos, and Divine Light, for the Egyptian idea was identical in this with the Âryan. However, the author is right with regard to the Occult Symbology of the Jews. They were a remarkably matter of fact, unspiritual people at all times; yet even with them "Ruach" was Divine Spirit, not "air."

scholar, Father Athanasius Kircher, the Jesuit priest, the above is precisely by Biblical record and traditionary sources, the method of laying off this encampment. The *four interior squares* were devoted to (1) Moses and Aaron; (2) Kohath; (3) Gershom; and (4) Merari—the last three being the heads of the Levites. The attributes of these squares were the *primal* attributes of Adam-Man, and were concreted of the elements, *Earth, Air, Fire, Water*, or ים = Iam = *Water*; נור = Nour = *Fire*, רוח = Rouach = *Air*, and יבשה = Iabeshah = *Earth*. The initial letters of these words are INRI—the symbol usually translated as *Iesus Nazarenus Rex Judæorum*—"Jesus of Nazareth, King of the Jews." This square of INRI is the *Adam square*, which was extended from, as a foundation, into four others of 144 × 2 = 288, to the side of the large square of 288 × 4 = 1152, = the whole circumference. But this square is the display of also circular elements and this can denote this. Put *INRI* into a circle, or read it as the letters stand in the Sphinx, as to its values of 1521, and we have  which reads 115-2.

But as seen Cain denotes this as, or in, the 115 of his name: which 115 was the very complement to make up the 360 day year, to agree with the balances of the standard circle, which were Cain. The corner squares of the larger square are A = Leo, and B = Dan Scorpio; and it is seen that Cain pierces Abel at the intersection of the equinoctial with the solstice cross lines, referred to from Dan-Scorpio of the celestial circle. But Dan-Scorpio borders on Libra, the scales, whose sign is ♎ (which sign is that of the ancient *pillow* on which *the back of the head to the neck* rested, the pillow of Jacob), and is represented for one symbol as [illegible]. Also the badge of Dan-Scorpio is death-life, in the symbol ☧.* Now the cross is the emblem of the *origin of measures*, in the *Jehovah* form of a *straight line one of a denomination of 20612, the perfect circumference;* hence Cain was this as Jehovah, for the text says that *he was* Jehovah. But the attachment of a man to this cross was that of 113: 355 to 6561 : 5153 × 4 = 20612, as shown. Now, over the *head* of Jesus crucified was placed the inscription, of which the initial letters of the words have always been retained as symbolic, and handed down and used as a monogram of Jesus Chrestos—*viz.*, INRI or *Jesus Nazarenus Rex Judæorum*; but they are located on the *Cross*, or the cubed *form* of the circular origin of measures which measure the substance of *Earth, Air, Fire* and *Water*, or INRI = 1152 as shown. Here is the *man* on the *cross*, or 113: 355 combined with 6561 : 5153 × 4 = 20612. These are the *pyramid-base* numbers as coming from 113: 355 as the Hebrew source; whence the Adam-square, which *is* the pyramid base, and the centre one to the larger square of the *encampment*. Bend INRI into a circle, and we have 1152, or the circumference of the latter. But Jesus dying (or Abel married) made use of the very words needed to set forth all. He says, *Eli, Eli, Lama Sabachthani* . . . Read them by their power values, in *circular form*, as produced from

---

* Mr. Ralston Skinner shows that the symbol ☧, the crossed bones and skull, has the letters for [illegible] the half of the head behind the ears.

the Adam form is shown) and we have אלי = 113, אלי = 113, or 113–311; למח *al* 345, or Moses in the Cain-Adam pyramid circle; שבחתני = 710, equals Dove, or Jonah and 710 ÷ 2 = 355; or 355–553; and finally, as determinative of all, ני or *ni*, where נ = nun, fish = 565, and י = 1 or 10; together 565 י = יהוה or the Christ value.

[All of the above] throws light on the transfiguration scene on the mount. There were present there Peter and James and John with Jesus; or ים Iami, James, *Water*; שמעון, Peter, *Earth*; יוחנן, John, *Spirit*, *Air*, and ישו Jesus, *Fire*, *Life*—together INRI. But behold Eli and Moses met them there, or אלי and למח or *Eli* and *Lamah*, or 113 and 345. And this shows that the scene of transfiguration was connected with the one above set forth.*

This kabalistical reading of the Gospel narratives—hitherto supposed to record the most important, the most mystically awful, yet most real events of the life of Jesus—must fall with terrible weight upon some Christians. Every honest trusting believer who has shed tears of reverential emotion over the events of the short period of the public life of Jesus of Nazareth, has to choose one of the two ways opening before him after reading the aforesaid: either his faith has to render him quite impervious to any light coming from human reasoning and evident fact; or he must confess that he has lost his Saviour. The One whom he had hitherto considered as the unique incarnation on this earth of the One Living God in heaven, fades into thin air, on the authority of the properly read and correctly interpreted *Bible* itself. Moreover, since on the authority of Jerome himself and his accepted and authentic confession, the book written by the hand of Matthew "exhibits matter not for *edification* but for *destruction*" (of Church and *human* Christianity, and only that) what truth can be expected from his famous *Vulgate*? *Human* mysteries, concocted by generations of Church Fathers bent upon evolving a religion of their own invention, are seen instead of a *divine* Revelation; and that this was so is corroborated by a prelate of the Latin Church. Saint Gregory Nazianzen wrote to his friend and confidant, Saint Jerome:

> Nothing can impose better on a people than verbiage; the less they understand the more they admire. . . . Our fathers and doctors have often said, not what they thought, but that to which circumstances and necessity forced them.

---

* Pp. 296-302. By these numbers, explains the author, "Eli is 113 (by placing the word in a circle); *amah* being 345, is by change of letters to suit the same value משה (in a circle) or Moses, while Sabachtha is John or the dove, or Holy Spirit, because (in a circle) it is 710 (or 355 × 2). The termination *ni*, as *meni* or 5651, becomes Jehovah."

Which then of the two—the clergy, or the Occultists and Theosophists—are the more blasphemous and dangerous? Is it those who would impose upon the world's acceptance a Saviour of their own fashioning, a God with human shortcomings, and who therefore is certainly not a perfect divine Being; or those others who say: Jesus of Nazareth was an Initiate, a holy, grand and noble character, but withal human, though truly "a Son of God"?

If Humanity is to accept a so-called supernatural Religion, how far more logical to the Occultist and the Psychologist seems the transparent allegory given of Jesus by the Gnostics. They, as Occultists, and with Initiates for their Chiefs, differed only in their renderings of the story and in their symbols, and not at all in substance. What say the Ophites, the Nazarenes, and other "heretics"? Sophia, "the Celestial Virgin," is prevailed upon to send Christos, her emanation, to the help of perishing humanity, from whom Ilda-Baoth (the Jehovah of the Jews) and his six Sons of Matter (the lower terrestrial Angels) are shutting out the divine light. Therefore, Christos, the perfect,*

> Uniting himself with Sophia [divine wisdom] descended through the seven planetary regions, assuming in each an analogous form . . . [and] entered into the man Jesus at the moment of his baptism in the Jordan. From this time forth Jesus began to work miracles; before that he had been entirely ignorant of his own mission.

Ilda-Baoth, discovering that Christos was bringing to an end his kingdom of Matter, stirred up the Jews, his own people, against Him, and Jesus was put to death. When Jesus was on the Cross Christos and Sophia left His body, and returned to Their own sphere. The material body of Jesus was abandoned to the earth, but He Himself, the Inner Man, was clothed with a body made up of *æther*.†

> Thenceforth he consisted merely of soul and spirit. . . During his sojourn upon earth of *eighteen* months after he had risen, he received from Sophia that perfect knowledge, that true Gnosis, which he communicated to the small portion of the Apostles who were capable of receiving the same.‡

The above is transparently Eastern and Hindu; it is the Esoteric Doctrine pure and simple, save for the names and the allegory. It is

* The Western personification of that power, which the Hindus call the *Vija*, the "one seed," or *Mahâ Vishnu*—a power, not the God—or that mysterious Principle that contains in Itself the Seed of Avatârism.

† "Arise into Nervi from this decrepit body into which thou hast been sent. Ascend into thy former abode, O blessed Avatâr!"

‡ *The Gnostics and their Remains*, King, pp. 100, 101.

more or less, the history of every Adept who obtains Initiation. The Baptism in the Jordan is the Rite of Initiation, the final purification, whether in sacred pagoda, tank, river, or temple lake in Egypt or Mexico. The perfect Christos and Sophia—divine Wisdom and Intelligence—enter the Initiate at the moment of the mystic rite, by transference from Guru to Chelâ, and leave the physical body, at the moment of the death of the latter, to re-enter the Nirmânakâya, or the astral Ego of the Adept.

> The spirit of Buddha [collectively] overshadows the Bodhisattvas of his Church

says the Buddhist Ritual of Âryâsangha.

Says the Gnostic teaching:

> When he [the spirit of Christos] shall have collected all the Spiritual, all the Light [that exists in matter], out of Ibadaoth's empire, Redemption is accomplished and the end of the world arrived.*

Say the Buddhists:

> When Buddha [the Spirit of the Church] hears the hour strike, he will send Maitreya Buddha—after whom the old world will be destroyed

That which is said of Basilides by King may be applied as truthfully to every innovator, so called, whether of a Buddhist or of a Christian Church. In the eyes of Clemens Alexandrinus, he says, the Gnostics taught very little that was blameable in their mystical transcendental views.

> In his eyes the latter [Basilides], was not a *heretic*, that is an innovator upon the accepted doctrines of the Catholic Church, but only a theosophic speculator who sought to express old truths by new formulæ.†

There was a Secret Doctrine preached by Jesus; and "secresy" in those days meant Secrets, or Mysteries of Initiation, all of which have been either rejected or disfigured by the Church. In the Clementine *Homilies* we read:

> And Peter said: "We remember that our Lord and Teacher, commanding us, said: 'Guard the mysteries for me and the sons of my house.'" Wherefore also he explained to His disciples privately the Mysteries of the Kingdom of the Heavens.‡

* *Loc. cit.* † *Op. cit.*, p. 258. ‡ *Homilies* XIX., xx. 1.

SECTION XIX.

St. Cyprian of Antioch.

The Æons (Stellar Spirits)—emanated from the Unknown of the Gnostics, and identical with the Dhyân Chohans of the Esoteric Doctrine—and their Pleroma, having been transformed into Archangels and the "Spirits of the Presence" by the Greek and Latin Churches, the prototypes have lost caste. The Pleroma* was now called the "Heavenly Host," and therefore the old name had to become identified with Satan and his "Host." Might is right in every age, and History is full of contrasts. Manes had been called the "Paraclete"† by his followers. He was an Occultist, but passed to posterity, owing to the kind exertions of the Church, as a Sorcerer, so a match had to be found for him by way of contrast. We recognise this match in St. Cyprianus of Antioch, a self-confessed if not a real "Black Magician," it seems, whom the Church—as a reward for his contrition and humility—subsequently raised to the high rank of Saint and Bishop.

What history knows of him is not much, and it is mostly based on his own confession, the truthfulness of which is warranted, we are told, by St. Gregory, the Empress Eudoxia, Photius and the Holy Church. This curious document was ferreted out by the Marquis de Mirville,‡ in the Vatican, and by him translated into French for the first time, as he assures the reader. We beg his permission to re-translate a few pages, not for the sake of the penitent Sorcerer, but for that of some students of Occultism, who will thus have an opportunity of comparing the

---

* The Pleroma constituted the synthesis or entirety of all the spiritual entities. St. Paul still used the name in his Epistles.

† The "Comforter," second Messiah, intercessor. "A term applied to the Holy Ghost." Manes was the disciple of Terebinthus, an Egyptian Philosopher, who, according to the Christian Socrates (I. i., cited by Tillemont, iv. 584), "while invoking one day the demons of the air, fell from the roof of his house and was killed."

‡ *Cf. op. cit.*, vi. 169-183.

methods of ancient Magic (or as the Church calls it, Demonism) with those of modern Theurgy and Occultism.

The scenes described took place at Antioch about the middle of the third century, 252 A.D., says the translator. This Confession was written by the penitent Sorcerer after his conversion; therefore, we are not surprised to find how much room he gives in his lamentations to reviling his Initiator "Satan," or the "Serpent Dragon," as he calls him. There are other and more modern instances of the same trait in human nature. Converted Hindus, Pârsîs and other "heathen" of India are apt to denounce their forefathers' religions at every opportunity. Thus runs the Confession:

O all of you who reject the real mysteries of Christ, see my tears! . . . You who wallow in your demoniacal practices, learn by my sad example all the vanity of their [the demons'] baits . . . I am that Cyprianus, who, vowed to Apollo from his infancy, was early initiated into all the arts of the dragon.* Even before the age of seven I had already been introduced into the temple of Mithra: three years later, my parents taking me to Athens to be received as citizen, I was permitted likewise to penetrate the mysteries of Ceres lamenting her daughter,† and I also became the guardian of the Dragon in the Temple of Pallas.

Ascending after that to the summit of Mount Olympus, the Seat of the Gods, as it is called, there too I was initiated into the sense, and the *real* meaning of their [the Gods'] speeches and their clamorous manifestations (*strepitusum*). It is there that I was made to see in imagination (*phantasia*) [or *mâyâ*] those trees and all those herbs that operate such prodigies with the help of demons; . . . and I saw their dances, their warfares, their snares, illusions and promiscuities. I heard their singing.‡ I saw finally, for forty consecutive days, the phalanx of the Gods and Goddesses, sending from Olympus, as though they were Kings, spirits to represent them on earth and act in their name among all the nations.§

At that time I lived entirely on fruit, eaten only after sunset, the virtues of which were explained to me by the seven priests of the sacrifices.‖

When I was fifteen my parents desired that I should be made acquainted, not only with all the natural laws in connection with the generation and corruption of

---

* "The *great serpent* placed to *watch the temple*," comments De Mirville. "How often have we repeated that it was no *symbol*, no personification but really a serpent occupied by a god!"—he exclaims; and we answer that at Cairo in a Mussulman, not a *heathen* temple, we have seen, as thousands of other visitors have also seen, a huge serpent that lived there for centuries, we were told, and was held in great respect. Was it also "occupied by a God," or possessed, in other words?

† The Mysteries of Demeter, or the "afflicted mother."

‡ By the satyrs.

§ This looks rather suspicious and seems interpolated. De Mirville tries to have what he says of Satan and his Court sending their imps on earth to tempt humanity and masquerade at *séances*, corroborated by the ex-sorcerer.

‖ This does not look like sinful food. It is the diet of Chelâs to this day.

bodies on earth, in the air and in the seas, but also with all the other [illegible] (*insitas*) on these by the Prince of the World in order to countenance [illegible] and divine constitution.† At twenty I went to Memphis, where, [illegible] the Sanctuaries, I was taught to discern all that pertains to the [illegible] demons [Daimones or Spirits] with terrestrial matters, their aversion [illegible] places, their sympathy and attraction for others, their expulsion from certain [illegible] certain objects and laws, their persistence in preferring darkness and [illegible] tance to light.‡ There I learned the number of the fallen Princes,§ [illegible] takes place in human souls and the bodies they enter into communication with [illegible]

I learnt the analogy that exists between earthquakes and the rains, [illegible] motion of the earth|| and the motion of the seas; I saw the spirits of the [illegible] plunged in subterranean darkness and seemingly supporting the earth [illegible] carrying a burden on his shoulders.¶

When thirty I travelled to Chaldæa to study there the true power of the [illegible] placed by some in the fire and by the more learned in light [Âkâsha]. I [illegible] to see that the planets were in their variety as dissimilar as the plants [illegible] and the stars were like armies ranged in battle order. I knew the [illegible] division of Ether into 365 parts,** and I perceived that every one of the [illegible] divide it among themselves†† was endowed with that material force [illegible] him to execute the orders of the Prince and guide all the movements [illegible] Ether].‡‡ They [the Chaldees] explained to me how those Princes had [illegible] participants in the Council of Darkness, ever in opposition to the [illegible] Light.

I got acquainted with the Mediatores (surely not mediums as De [illegible] plains!),§§ and upon seeing the covenants they were mutually bound by, I [illegible] struck with wonder upon learning the nature of their oaths and observances [illegible]

---

* "Grafted" is the correct expression. "The seven Builders graft the divine and the [illegible] forces on to the gross material nature of the vegetable and mineral kingdoms every [illegible]" says the *Catechism of Lanoos*.

† Only the Prince of the World is not Satan, as the translator would make us believe, but the [illegible] tive Host of the Planetary. This is a little theological back-biting.

‡ Here the Elemental and Elementary Spirits are evidently meant.

§ The reader has already learned the truth about them in the course of the present work.

|| Pity the penitent *Saint* had not imparted his knowledge of the rotation of the earth and [illegible] centric system earlier to his Church. That might have saved more than one human life—that of [illegible] for one.

¶ Chelâs in their trials of initiation, also see *in trances artificially generated for them*, the [illegible] of the Earth supported by an elephant on the top of a tortoise standing on nothing—and this, to teach them to discern the true from the false.

** Relating to the days of the year, also to 7 × 7 divisions of the earth's sublunary sphere, [illegible] into seven upper and seven lower spheres with their respective Planetary Hosts or "armies."

†† Daimon is not "demon," as translated by De Mirville, but Spirit.

‡‡ All this is to corroborate his dogmatic assertions that Pater Æther or Jupiter is Satan! and that pestilential diseases, cataclysms, and even thunderstorms that prove disastrous, come from the [illegible] Host dwelling in Ether—a good warning to the men of Science!

§§ The translator replaces the word Mediators by mediums, excusing himself in a foot-note by saying that Cyprian *must* have meant modern mediums!

|||| Cyprianus simply meant to hint at the rites and mysteries of Initiation, and the pledge of [illegible] and oaths that bound the Initiates together. His translator, however, has made a Witches' Sabbath of it instead.

Believe me, I saw the Devil; believe me I have embraced him* [like the witches at the Sabbath (?)] when I was yet quite young, and he saluted me by the title of the new Jambres, declaring me worthy of my ministry (initiation). He promised me continual help during life and a principality after death.† Having become in great honour [an Adept] under his tuition, he placed under my orders a phalanx of demons, and when I bid him good-bye, "Courage, good success, excellent Cyprian," he exclaimed, rising up from his seat to see me to the door, plunging thereby those present into a profound admiration.‡

Having bidden farewell to his Chaldæan Initiator, the future Sorcerer and Saint went to Antioch. His tale of "iniquity" and subsequent repentance is long but we will make it short. He became "an accomplished Magician," surrounded by a host of disciples and "candidates to the perilous and sacrilegious art." He shows himself distributing love-philtres and dealing in deathly charms "to rid young wives of old husbands, and to ruin Christian virgins." Unfortunately Cyprianus was not above love himself. He fell in love with the beautiful Justine, a converted maiden, after having vainly tried to make her share the passion one named Aglaides, a profligate, had for her. His "demons failed" he tells us, and he got disgusted with them. This disgust brings on a quarrel between him and his Hierophant, whom he insists on identifying with the Demon; and the dispute is followed by a tournament between the latter and some Christian converts, in which the "Evil One" is, of course, worsted. The Sorcerer is finally baptised and gets rid of his enemy. Having laid at the feet of Anthimus, Bishop of Antioch, all his books on Magic, he became a Saint in company with the beautiful Justine, who had converted him; both suffered martyrdom under the Emperor Diocletian; and both are buried side by side in Rome, in the Basilica of St. John Lateran, near the Baptistery.

* "Twelve centuries later, in full renaissance and reform, the world saw Luther do the same [embrace the Devil he means ?]—according to his own confession and in the same conditions," explains De Mirville in a foot-note, showing thereby the brotherly love that binds Christians. Now Cyprianus meant by the Devil (if the word is really in the original text) his Initiator and Hierophant. No Saint—even a penitent Sorcerer—would be so silly as to speak of his (the Devil's) rising from his seat to see him to the door, were it otherwise.

† Every Adept has "a principality after his death."

‡ Which shows that it was the Hierophant and his disciples. Cyprianus shows himself as grateful as most of the other converts (the modern included) to his Teachers and Instructors.

SECTION XX.

THE EASTERN GUPTA VIDYA & THE KABALAH

WE now return to the consideration of the essential identity between the Eastern Gupta Vidyâ and the Kabalah as a system, while we must also show the dissimilarity in their philosophical interpretations in the Middle Ages.

It must be confessed that the views of the Kabalists—meaning by this word those students of Occultism who study the Jewish *Kabalah* and who know little, if anything, of any other Esoteric literature or of its teachings—are as varied in their synthetic conclusions upon the nature of the mysteries taught even in the *Zohar* alone, and are as wide of the true mark, as are the *dicta* upon it of exact Science itself. Like the mediæval Rosicrucian and the Alchemist—like the Abbot Trithemius, John Reuchlin, Agrippa, Paracelsus, Robert Fludd, Philalethes, etc.—by whom they swear, the continental Occultists see in the Jewish *Kabalah* alone the universal well of wisdom; they find in it the secret lore of nearly all the mysteries of Nature—metaphysical and divine—some of them including herein, as did Reuchlin, those of the Christian *Bible*. For them the *Zohar* is an Esoteric Thesaurus of all the mysteries of the Christian Gospel; and the *Sepher Yetzirah* is the light that shines in every darkness, and the container of the keys to open every secret in Nature. Whether many of our modern followers of the mediæval Kabalists have an idea of the real meaning of the symbology of their chosen Masters is another question. Most of them have probably never given even a passing thought to the fact that the Esoteric language used by the Alchemists was their own, and that it was given out as a blind, necessitated by the dangers of the epoch they lived in, and not as the Mystery-language, used by the Pagan Initiates, which the Alchemists had re-translated and re-veiled once more.

And now the situation stands thus: as the old Alchemists have not left a key to their writings, the latter have become a mystery within an older mystery. The *Kabalah* is interpreted and checked only by the light which mediæval Mystics have thrown upon it, and they, in their forced Christology, had to put a theological dogmatic mask on every ancient teaching, the result being that each Mystic among our modern European and American Kabalists interprets the old symbols in his own way, and each refers his opponents to the Rosicrucian and the Alchemist of three and four hundred years ago. Mystic Christian dogma is the central maëlstrom that engulfs every old Pagan symbol, and Christianity—Anti-Gnostic Christianity, the modern retort that has replaced the alembic of the Alchemists—has distilled out of all recognition the *Kabalah*, *i.e.*, the Hebrew *Zohar* and other rabbinical mystic works. And now it has come to this: The student interested in the Secret Sciences has to believe that the whole cycle of the symbolical "Ancient of Days," every hair of the mighty beard of Macroprosopos, refers only to the history of the earthly career of Jesus of Nazareth! And we are told that the *Kabalah* "was first taught to a select company of angels" by Jehovah himself—who, out of modesty, one must think, made himself only the third Sephiroth in it, and a female one into the bargain. So many Kabalists, so many explanations. Some believe—perchance with more reason than the rest—that the substance of the *Kabalah* is the basis upon which Masonry is built, since modern Masonry is undeniably the dim and hazy reflection of primeval Occult Masonry, of the teaching of those divine Masons who established the Mysteries of the prehistoric and prediluvian Temples of Initiation, raised by truly superhuman Builders. Others declare that the tenets expounded in the *Zohar* relate merely to mysteries terrestrial and profane, having no more concern with metaphysical speculations—such as the soul, or the *post-mortem* life of man—than have the Mosaic books. Others, again—and these are the real, genuine Kabalists, who had their instructions from initiated Jewish Rabbis—affirm that if the two most learned Kabalists of the mediæval period, John Reuchlin and Paracelsus, differed in their religious professions—the former being the Father of the Reformation and the latter a Roman Catholic, at least in appearance—the *Zohar* cannot contain much of Christian dogma or tenet, one way or the other. In other words, they maintain that the numerical language of the Kabalistic works teaches universal truths—and not any one Religion in particular. Those who make this statement are perfectly right in saying that the Mystery-language used in the *Zohar* and in other Kabalistic literature was once, in an unfathomable antiquity, the universal language of Humanity, but they become entirely wrong if to this fact they add the gratuitous theory that *this language was invented by*, or *was the original property of the Hebrews, from whom all the other nations borrowed it.*

They are wrong, because, although the *Zohar* (זהר, ZHR), *The Book of Splendour* of Rabbi Simeon Ben Iochai, did indeed originate with him—his son, Rabbi Eleazar, helped by his secretary, Rabbi Abba, compiling the Kabalistic teachings of his deceased father into a work called the *Zohar*—those teachings were not Rabbi Simeon's, as the Gupta Vidyâ shows. They are as old as the Jewish nation itself, and far older. In short, the writings which pass at present under the title of the *Zohar* of Rabbi Simeon are about as original as were the Egyptian synchronistic Tables after being handled by Eusebius, or St. Paul's *Epistles* after their revision and correction by the Holy Church.*

Let us throw a rapid retrospective glance at the history and the tribulations of that very same *Zohar*, as we know of them from trustworthy tradition and documents. We need not stop to discuss whether it was written in the first century B.C. or in the first century A.D. Suffice it for us to know that there was at all times a Kabalistic literature among the Jews; that though historically it can be traced only from the time of the Captivity, yet from the *Pentateuch* down to the *Talmud* the documents of that literature were ever written in a kind of Mystery-language, were, in fact, a series of symbolical records which the Jews had copied from the Egyptian and the Chaldean Sanctuaries, only adapting them to their own national history—if history it can be called. Now that which we claim—and it is not denied even by the most prejudiced Kabalist, is that although Kabalistic lore had passed orally through long ages down to the latest Pre-Christian Tanaim, and although David and Solomon may have been great Adepts in it, as is claimed, yet no one dared to write it down till the days of Simeon

* This is proved if we take but a single recorded instance. J. Picus de Mirandola, finding that there was more Christianity than Judaism in the *Kabalah*, and discovering in it the doctrines of the Trinity, the Incarnation, the Divinity of Jesus, etc., wound up his proofs of this with a challenge to the world at large from Rome. As Ginsburg shows: "In 1486, when only twenty-four years old, he [Picus] published nine hundred [Kabalistic] *theses*, which were placarded in Rome, and undertook to defend them in the presence of all European scholars whom he invited to the Eternal City, promising to defray their travelling expenses."

Ben Iochai. In short, the lore found in Kabalistic literature was never recorded in writing before the first century of the modern era.

This brings the critic to the following reflection: While in India we find the *Vedas* and the Brâhmanical literature written down and edited ages before the Christian era—the Orientalists themselves being obliged to concede a couple of millenniums of antiquity to the older manuscripts; while the most important allegories in *Genesis* are found recorded on Babylonian tiles centuries B.C.; while the Egyptian sarcophagi yearly yield proofs of the origin of the doctrines borrowed and copied by the Jews; yet the Monotheism of the Jews is exalted and thrown into the teeth of all the Pagan nations, and the so-called Christian Revelation is placed above all others, like the sun above a row of street gas-lamps. Yet it is perfectly well known, having been ascertained beyond doubt or cavil, that no manuscript, whether Kabalistic, Talmudistic, or Christian, which has reached our present generation, is of earlier date than the first centuries of our era, whereas this can certainly never be said of the Egyptian papyri or the Chaldæan tiles, or even of some Eastern writings.

But let us limit our present research to the *Kabalah*, and chiefly to the *Zohar*—called also the *Midrash*. This book, whose teachings were edited for the first time between 70 and 110 A.D., is known to have been lost, and its contents to have been scattered throughout a number of minor manuscripts, until the thirteenth century. The idea that it was the composition of Moses de Leon of Valladolid, in Spain, who passed it off as a pseudograph of Simeon Ben Iochai, is ridiculous, and was well disposed of by Munk—though he does point to more than one modern interpolation in the *Zohar*. At the same time it is more than certain that the present *Book of Zohar* was written by Moses de Leon, and, owing to joint editorship, is more Christian in its colouring than is many a genuine Christian volume. Munk gives the reason why, saying that it appears evident that the author made use of ancient documents, and among these of certain *Midraschim*, or collections of traditions and Biblical expositions, which we do not now possess.

As a proof, also, that the knowledge of the Esoteric system taught in the *Zohar* came to the Jews very late indeed—at any rate, that they had so far forgotten it that the innovations and additions made by de Leon provoked no criticism, but were thankfully received—Munk quotes from Tholuck, a Jewish authority, the following information: Haya Gaon, who died in 1038, is to our knowledge the first author who developed (and perfected) the theory of the Sephiroth, and he gave them names which we find again among the Kabalistic names used by Dr. Jellinek. Moses Ben Schem-Tob de Leon, who held intimate intercourse with the Syrian and Chaldæan Christian learned scribes, was enabled through the latter to acquire a knowledge of some of the Gnostic writings.*

Again, the *Sepher Jetzirah* (*Book of Creation*)—though attributed to Abraham and though very archaic as to its contents—is first mentioned in the eleventh century by Jehuda Ha Levi (Chazzari). And these two, the *Zohar* and *Jetzirah*, are the storehouse of all the subsequent Kabalistic works. Now let us see how far the Hebrew sacred canon itself is to be trusted.

The word "Kabalah" comes from the root "to receive," and has a meaning identical with the Sanskrit "Smriti" ("received by tradition")—a system of oral teaching, passing from one generation of priests to another, as was the case with the Brâhmanical books before they were embodied in manuscript. The Kabalistic tenets came to the Jews from the Chaldæans; and if Moses knew the primitive, universal language of the Initiates, as did every Egyptian priest, and was thus acquainted with the numerical system on which it was based, he may have—and we say he has—written *Genesis* and other "scrolls." The five books that now pass current under his name, the *Pentateuch*, are *not* withal the original Mosaic Records.† Nor were they written in the old Hebrew square letters, nor even in the Samaritan characters, for both alphabets belong to a date later than that of Moses, and Hebrew—as it is now known—did not exist in the days of the great lawgiver, either as a language or as an alphabet.

As no statements contained in the records of the Secret Doctrine of the East are regarded as of any value by the world in general, and since to be understood by and convince the reader one has to quote names familiar to him, and use arguments and proofs out of documents which are accessible to all, the following facts may perhaps demonstrate that our assertions are not merely based on the teachings of Occult Records:

(1) The great Orientalist and scholar, Klaproth, denied positively

---

* This account is summarised from Isaac Myer's *Qabbalah*, p. 10, *et seq.*

† There is not in the decalogue one idea that is not the counterpart, or the paraphrase, of the dogmas and ethics current among the Egyptians long before the time of Moses and Aaron. (The Mosaic Law a transcript from Egyptian Sources; vide *Geometry in Religion*, 1890.)

the antiquity of the so-called Hebrew alphabet, on the ground that the square Hebrew characters in which the Biblical manuscripts are written, and which we use in printing, were probably derived from the Palmyrene writing, or some other Semitic alphabet, so that the Hebrew *Bible* is written merely in the Chaldaic phonographs of Hebrew words.

The late Dr. Kenealy pertinently remarked that the Jews and Christians rely on

> A photograph of a dead and almost unknown language, as abstruse as the cuneiform letters on the mountains of Assyria.*

(2) The attempts made to carry back the square Hebrew character to the time of Esdras (B.C. 458) have all failed.

(3) It is asserted that the Jews took their alphabet from the Babylonians during their captivity. But there are scholars who do not carry the now-known Hebrew square letters beyond the late period of the fourth century, A.D.†

> The Hebrew Bible is precisely as if Homer were printed, not in Greek, but in English letters; or as if Shakespeare's works were phonographed in Burmese.‡

(4) Those who maintain that the ancient Hebrew is the same as the Syriac or Chaldaic have to see what is said in *Jeremiah*, wherein the Lord is made to threaten the house of Israel with bringing against it the mighty and ancient nation of the Chaldæans:

> A nation whose language thou knowest not, neither understandest what they say.§

This is quoted by Bishop Walton‖ against the assumption of the identity of Chaldaic and Hebrew, and ought to settle the question.

(5) The real Hebrew of Moses was lost after the seventy years' captivity, when the Israelites brought back Chaldaic with them and grafted it on their own language, the fusion resulting in a dialectical variety of Chaldaic, the Hebrew tincturing it very slightly and ceasing from that time to be a spoken language.¶

---

* *Book of God.* Kenealy, p. 383. The reference to Klaproth is also from this page.

† See *Asiat. Jour.*, N.S. vii., p. 275, quoted by Kenealy.

‡ *Book of God*, *loc. cit.*

§ *Op. cit.*, v. 15.

‖ *Prolegomena*, iii. 13, quoted by Kenealy, p. 385.

¶ See *Book of God*, p. 385. "Care should be taken," says Butler (quoted by Kenealy, p. 489), "to distinguish between the Pentateuch in the Hebrew language but in the letters of the Samaritan alphabet, and the version of the Pentateuch in the Samaritan language. One of the most important differences between the Samaritan and the Hebrew text respects the duration of the period between

As to our statement that the present *Old Testament* [illegible] the original Books of Moses, this is proven by the facts [illegible]

(1) The Samaritans repudiated the Jewish canonical [illegible] "Law of Moses." They will have neither the *Psalms* of [illegible] the Prophets, nor the *Talmud* and *Mishna*: nothing but the [illegible] of Moses, and in quite a different edition.* The Books of [illegible] of Joshua are disfigured out of recognition by the Talmudists, [illegible]

(2) The "black Jews" of Cochin, Southern India—who [illegible] thing of the Babylonian Captivity or of the *ten* "lost tribes" [illegible] a pure invention of the Rabbis), proving that these Jews [illegible] come to India before the year 600 B.C.—have their Books of [illegible] which they will show to no one. And these Books and Laws [illegible] greatly from the present scrolls. Nor are they written in the [illegible] Hebrew characters (semi-Chaldaic and semi-Palmyrean) but [illegible] archaic letters, as we were assured by one of them—letters [illegible] known to all but themselves and a few Samaritans.

(3) The Karaim Jews of the Crimea—who call themselves the [illegible] dants of the true children of Israel, *i.e.*, of the Sadducees—[illegible] *Torah* and the *Pentateuch* of the Synagogue, reject the Sabbath of [illegible] Jews (keeping Friday), will have neither the Books of the [illegible] nor the *Psalms*—nothing but their own Books of Moses, and [illegible] call his one and real Law.

This makes it plain that the *Kabalah* of the Jews is but the [illegible] echo of the Secret Doctrine of the Chaldæans, and that the real [illegible] is found only in the Chaldæan *Book of Numbers* now in the [illegible] of some Persian Sufis. Every nation in antiquity had its [illegible] based on those of the Âryan Secret Doctrine; and each nation [illegible] to this day to a Sage of its own race who had received the [illegible] revelation from, and had recorded it under the orders of, a more [illegible] divine Being. Thus it was with the Jews, as with all others. [illegible] had received their Occult Cosmogony and Laws from their [illegible] Moses, and they have now entirely mutilated them.

Âdi is the generic name in our Doctrine of all the first men, *i.e.*, the first speaking races, in each of the seven zones—hence probably

---

the deluge and the birth of Abraham. The Samaritan text makes it longer by some [illegible] the Hebrew text; and the Septuagint makes it longer by some centuries than the [illegible] It is observable that in the authentic translation of the Latin Vulgate, the Roman Church [illegible] computation expressed in the Hebrew text; and in her Martyrology follows that of the [illegible] texts being inspired, as she claims.

* See Rev. Joseph Wolff's *Journal*, p. 200.

"Ad-am." And such first men, in every nation, are credited with having been taught the divine mysteries of creation. Thus, the Sabæans (according to a tradition preserved in the Sufi works) say that when the "Third First Man" left the country adjacent to India for Babel, a tree* was given to him, then another and a third tree, whose leaves recorded the history of all the races; the "Third First Man" meant one who belonged to the Third Root-Race, and yet the Sabæans call him Adam. The Arabs of Upper Egypt, and the Mohammedans generally, have recorded a tradition that the Angel Azaz-el brings a message from the Wisdom-Word of God to Adam whenever he is reborn; this the Sufis explain by adding that this book is given to every Seli-Allah ("the chosen one of God") for his wise men. The story narrated by the Kabalists—namely, that the book given to Adam before his Fall (a book full of mysteries and signs and events which either had been, were, or were to be) was taken away by the Angel Rasiel after Adam's Fall, but again restored to him lest men might lose its wisdom and instruction; that this book was delivered by Adam to Seth, who passed it to Enoch, and the latter to Abraham, and so on in succession to the most wise of every generation—relates to all nations, and not to the Jews alone. For Berosus narrates in his turn that Xisuthrus compiled a book, writing it at the command of his deity, which book was buried in Zipara† or Sippara, the City of the Sun, in Ba-bel-on-ya, and was dug up long afterwards and deposited in the temple of Belos; it is from this book that Berosus took his history of the antediluvian dynasties of Gods and Heroes. Ælian (in *Nimrod*) speaks of a Hawk (emblem of the Sun), who in the days of the beginnings brought to the Egyptians a book containing the wisdom of their religion. The *Sam-Sam* of the Sabæans is also a *Kabalah*, as is the Arabic *Zem-Zem* (*Well of Wisdom*).‡

We are told by a very learned Kabalist that Seyffarth asserts that the old Egyptian tongue was only old Hebrew, or a Semitic dialect; and he proves this, our correspondent thinks, by sending him "some 500 words in common" in the two languages. This proves very little to our mind. It only shows that the two nations lived together for centuries, and that before adopting the Chaldæan for their phonetic

* A tree is symbolically a book—as "pillar" is another synonym of the same.

† The wife of Moses, one of the seven daughters of a Midian priest, is called Zipora. It was Jethro, the priest of Midian, who initiated Moses, Zipora, one of the seven daughters, being simply one of the seven Occult powers that the Hierophant was and is supposed to pass to the initiated novice.

‡ See for these details the *Book of God*, pp. 144, 150.

tongue the Jews had adopted the old Coptic or Egyptian. The Semitish Scriptures drew their hidden wisdom from the primeval Wisdom Religion that was the source of other Scriptures, only it was wilfully degraded by being applied to things and mysteries of this Earth, instead of to those in the higher and ever-present, though invisible, spheres. Their national history, if they can claim any autonomy before their return from the Babylonian captivity, cannot be carried back one day earlier than the time of Moses. The language of Abraham—if Zeruan (Saturn, the emblem of time—the "Sar," "Saros," "cycle") can be said to have any language—was not Hebrew, but Chaldaic, perhaps Arabic, and still more likely some old Indian dialect. This is shown by numerous proofs, some of which we give here; and unless, indeed, to please the tenacious and stubborn believers in Bible chronology, we cripple the years of our globe to the Procrustean bed of 7,000 years, it becomes self-evident that the Hebrew cannot be called an old language, merely because Adam is supposed to have spoken it in the Garden of Eden. Bunsen says in *Egypt's Place in Universal History* that in the

> Chaldæan tribe immediately connected with Abraham, we find reminiscences of dates disfigured and misunderstood as genealogies of single men, or symbols of epochs. The Abrahamic recollections go back at least three millennia beyond the grandfather of Jacob.*

The *Bible* of the Jews has ever been an Esoteric Book in its hidden meaning, but this meaning has not remained one and the same throughout since the days of Moses. It is useless, considering the limited space we can give to this subject, to attempt anything like the detailed history of the vicissitudes of the so-called *Pentateuch*, and besides, the history is too well known to need lengthy disquisitions. Whatever was, or was not, the Mosaic *Book of Creation*—from *Genesis* down to the Prophets—the *Pentateuch* of to-day is not the same. It is sufficient to read the criticisms of Erasmus, and even of Sir Isaac Newton, to see clearly that the Hebrew Scriptures had been tampered with and remodelled, had been lost and rewritten, a dozen times before the days of Ezra. This Ezra himself may yet one day turn out to have been Azara, the Chaldæan priest of the Fire and Sun-God, a renegade who, through his desire of becoming a ruler, and in order to create an Ethnarchy, restored the old lost Jewish Books in his own way. It was an

* *Op. cit.*, v. 85.

easy thing for one versed in the secret system of Esoteric numerals, or Symbology, to put together events from the stray books that had been preserved by various tribes, and make of them an apparently harmonious narrative of creation and of the evolution of the Judæan race. But in its hidden meaning, from *Genesis* to the last word of *Deuteronomy*, the Pentateuch is the symbolical narrative of the sexes, and is an apotheosis of Phallicism, under astronomical and physiological personations.* Its coördination, however, is only apparent; and the human hand appears at every moment, is found everywhere in the "Book of God." Hence the Kings of Edom discuss in *Genesis* before any king had reigned in Israel; Moses records his own death, and Aaron dies twice and is buried in two different places, to say nothing of other trifles. For the Kabalist they are trifles, for he knows that all these events are not history, but are simply the cloak designed to envelope and hide various physiological peculiarities; but for the sincere Christian, who accepts all these "dark sayings" in good faith, it matters a good deal. Solomon may very well be regarded as a myth† by the Masons, as they lose nothing by it, for all their secrets are Kabalistic and allegorical—for those few, at any rate, who understand them. For the Christian, however, to give up Solomon, the son of David—from whom Jesus is made to descend—involves a real loss. But how even the Kabalists can claim great antiquity for the Hebrew texts of the old Biblical scrolls now possessed by the scholars is not made at all apparent. For it is certainly a fact of history, based on the confessions of the Jews themselves, and of Christians likewise, that:

> The Scriptures having perished in the captivity of Nabuchodonozar, Esdras, the Levite, the priest, in the times of Artaxerxes, king of the Persians, having become inspired, in the exercise of prophecy restored again the whole of the ancient Scriptures.‡

---

* As is fully shown in the *Source of Measures* and other works.

† Surely even Masons would never claim the *actual* existence of Solomon? As Kenealy shows, he is not noticed by Herodotus, nor by Plato, nor by any writer of standing. It is most extraordinary, he says, "that the Jewish nation, over whom but a few years before the mighty Solomon had reigned in all his glory, with a magnificence scarcely equalled by the greatest monarchs, spending nearly *eight thousand millions* of gold on a temple, was overlooked by the historian Herodotus, writing of Egypt on the one hand, and of Babylon on the other—visiting both places, and of course passing almost necessarily within a few miles of the splendid capital of the national Jerusalem? How can this be accounted for?" he asks (p. 457). Nay, not only are there no proofs of the twelve tribes of Israel having ever existed, but Herodotus, the most accurate of historians, who was in Assyria when Ezra flourished, never mentions the Israelites at all; and Herodotus was born in 484 B.C. How is this?

‡ Clement, *Stromateis*, xxii.

One must have a strong belief in "Esdras," and especially in his good faith, to accept the now-existing copies as genuine Mosaic Books; for:

> Assuming that the copies, or rather phonographs which had been made by Hilkiah and Esdras, and the various anonymous editors, were really thus far genuine, they must have been wholly exterminated by Antiochus; and the books of the Old Testament which now subsist must have been made by Judas, or by some unknown compilers, probably from the Greek of the Seventy, long after the appearance and death of Jesus.*

The *Bible*, therefore, as it is now (the Hebrew texts, that is) depends for its accuracy on the genuineness of the *Septuagint*; this, we are again told, was written miraculously by the Seventy, in Greek, and the original copy having been lost since that time, our books are re-translated back into Hebrew from that language. But in this vicious circle of proofs we once more have to rely upon the good faith of two Jews—Josephus and Philo Judæus of Alexandria; these two Historians being the only witnesses that the Septuagint was written under the circumstances narrated. And yet it is just these circumstances that are very little calculated to inspire one with confidence. For what does Josephus tell us? He says that Ptolemy Philadelphus, desiring to read the Hebrew Law in Greek, wrote to Eleazar, the high-priest of the Jews, begging him *to send him six men from each of the twelve tribes*, who should make a translation for him. Then follows a truly miraculous story, vouchsafed by Aristeas, of these seventy-two men from the twelve tribes of Israel, who, shut up in an island, compiled their translation in exactly seventy-two days, etc.

All this is very edifying, and one might have had very little reason to doubt the story, had not the "ten lost tribes" been made to play their part in it. How could these tribes, lost between 700 and 900 B.C., each send six men some centuries later, to satisfy the whim of Ptolemy, and to disappear once more immediately afterwards from the horizon? A miracle, verily.

We are expected, nevertheless, to regard such documents as the *Septuagint* as containing direct divine revelation: Documents originally written in a tongue about which nobody now knows anything; written by authors that are practically mythical, and at dates as to which no one is able even to make a defensible surmise; documents of the original copies of which there does not now remain a shred. Yet

* *Book of God*, p. 408.

people will persist in talking of the ancient Hebrew, as if there were any man left in the world who now knows one word of it. So little, indeed, was Hebrew known that both the Septuagint and the *New Testament* had to be written in a *heathen* language (the Greek), and no better reasons for it given than what Hutchinson says, namely, that the Holy Ghost chose to write the New Testament in Greek.

The Hebrew language is considered to be very old, and yet there exists no trace of it anywhere on the old monuments, not even in Chaldea. Among the great number of inscriptions of various kinds found in the ruins of that country:

> One in the Hebrew Chaldee letter and language *has never been found*; nor has a single authentic medal or gem in this new-fangled character been ever discovered, which could carry it even to the days of Jesus.*

The original *Book of Daniel* is written in a dialect which is a mixture of Hebrew and Aramaic; it is not even in Chaldaic, with the exception of a few verses interpolated later on. According to Sir W. Jones and other Orientalists, the oldest discoverable languages of Persia are the Chaldaic and Sanskrit, and there is no trace of the "Hebrew" in these. It would be very surprising if there were, since the Hebrew known to the Philologists does not date earlier than 500 B.C., and its characters belong to a far later period still. Thus, while the real Hebrew characters, if not altogether lost are nevertheless so hopelessly transformed—

> A mere inspection of the alphabet showing that it has been shaped and made regular, in doing which the characteristic marks of some of the letters *have been retrenched* in order to make them more square and uniform—†

that no one but an initiated Rabbi of Samaria or a "Jain" could read them, the new system of the masoretic points has made them a sphinx-riddle for all. Punctuation is now to be found everywhere in all the later manuscripts, and by means of it anything can be made of a text; a Hebrew scholar can put on the texts any interpretation he likes. Two instances given by Kenealy will suffice:

> In Genesis, xlix. 21, we read:
>
> Naphtali is a *hind let loose*; he *giveth goodly words*.
>
> By only a slight alteration of the points Bochart changes this into:
>
> Napthali is a *spreading tree, shooting forth beautiful branches*.
>
> So again, in *Psalms* (xxix. 9), instead of:

---

* *Book of God*, p. 453.

† *Asiatic Journal*, vii., p. 275, quoted by Kenealy.

The voice of the Lord *maketh the hind to calve*, and discovereth the forests.

Bishop Lowth gives:

The voice of the Lord *striketh the oak*, and discovereth the forests.

The same word in Hebrew signifies "God" and "nothing," etc.*

With regard to the claim made by some Kabalists that there was in antiquity one knowledge and one language, this claim is also our own, and it is very just. Only it must be added, to make the thing clear, that this knowledge and language have both been esoteric ever since the submersion of the Atlanteans. The Tower of Babel myth relates to that enforced secrecy. Men falling into sin were regarded as no longer trustworthy for the reception of such knowledge, and, from being universal, it became limited to the few. Thus the "one-lip"—or the Mystery-language—being gradually denied to subsequent generations, all the nations became severally restricted to their own national tongue; and forgetting the primeval Wisdom-language, they stated that the Lord—one of the chief Lords or Hierophants of the Mysteries of the Java Aleim—had confounded the language of all the earth, so that the sinners could understand one another's speech no longer. But Initiates remained in every land and nation, and the Israelites, like all others, had their learned Adepts. One of the keys to this Universal Knowledge is a pure geometrical and numerical system, the alphabet of every great nation having a numerical value for every letter,† and, moreover, a system of permutation of syllables and synonyms which is carried to perfection in the Indian Occult methods, and which the Hebrew certainly has not. This one system, containing the elements of Geometry and Numeration, was used by the Jews for the purpose of concealing their Esoteric creed under the mask of a popular and national monotheistic Religion. The last who knew the system to perfection were the learned and "atheistical" Sadducees, the greatest enemies of the pretensions of the Pharisees and of their com-

* *Book of God*, p. 385.

† Speaking of the hidden meaning of the Sanskrit words, Mr. T. Subba Row, in his able article on "The Twelve Signs of the Zodiac," gives some advice as to the way in which one should proceed to find out "the deep significance of ancient Sanskrit nomenclature in the old Âryan myths": "1. Find out the synonyms of the word used which have other meanings. 2. Find out the numerical value of the letters composing the word according to the methods of the ancient Tântrik works [Tântrika *Shâstra*—works on Incantation and Magic]. 3. Examine the ancient myths or allegories, if there are any, which have any special connection with the word in question. 4. Permute the different syllables composing the word and examine the new combinations that will thus be formed and their meanings," etc. But he does not give the principal rule. And no doubt he is quite right. The Tântrika *Shâstras* are as old as Magic itself. Have they also borrowed their Esotericism from the Hebrews?

fused notions brought from Babylon. Yes, the Sadducees, the Illusionists, who maintained that the Soul, the Angels, and all similar Beings, were illusions because they were temporary—thus showing themselves at one with Eastern Esotericism. And since they rejected every book and Scripture, with the exception of the Law of Moses, it seems that the latter must have been very different from what it is now.*

The whole of the foregoing is written with an eye to our Kabalists. Great scholars as some of them undoubtedly are, they are nevertheless wrong to hang the harps of their faith on the willows of Talmudic growth—on the Hebrew scrolls, whether in square or pointed characters, now in our public libraries, museums, or even in the collections of Paleographers. There do not remain half-a-dozen copies from the true Mosaic Hebrew scrolls in the whole world. And those who are in possession of these—as we indicated a few pages back—would not part with them, or even allow them to be examined, on any consideration whatever. How then can any Kabalist claim priority for Hebrew Esotericism, and say, as does one of our correspondents, that "the Hebrew has come down from a far remoter antiquity than any of them [whether Egyptian or even Sanskrit!], and that it was the source, or nearer to the old original source, than any of them"?†

As our correspondent says: "It becomes more convincing to me every day that in a far past time there was *a mighty civilization with*

---

* Their founder, Sadoc, was the pupil, through Antigonus Saccho, of Simon the Just. They had their own secret *Book of the Law* ever since the foundation of their sect (about 400 B.C.) and this volume was unknown to the masses. At the time of the Separation the Samaritans recognised only the *Book of the Law of Moses* and the *Book of Joshua*, and their *Pentateuch* is far older, and is different from the Septuagint. In 168 B.C. Jerusalem had its temple plundered, and its Sacred Books—namely, the *Bible* made up by Ezra and finished by Judas Maccabeus—were lost (see Burder's *Josephus*, vol. ii, pp. 331-335); after which the *Massorah* completed the work of destruction (even of Ezra's once-more adjusted *Bible*) begun by the change into square from horned letters. Therefore the later *Pentateuch* accepted by the Pharisees was rejected and laughed at by the Sadducees. They are generally called atheists; yet, since those learned men, who made no secret of their freethought, furnished from among their number the most eminent of the Jewish high-priests, this seems impossible. How could the Pharisees and the other two believing and pious sects allow notorious atheists to be selected for such posts? The answer is difficult to find for bigotry and for believers in a personal, anthropomorphic God, but very easy for those who accept facts. The Sadducees were called atheists because they believed as the initiated Moses believed, thus differing very widely from the latter made-up Jewish legislator and hero of Mount Sinai.

† The measurements of the Great Pyramid being those of the temple of Solomon, of the Ark of the Covenant, etc., according to Piazzi Smythe and the author of the *Source of Measures*, and the Pyramid of Gizeh being shown on astronomical calculations to have been built 4950 B.C., and Moses having *written* his books—for the sake of argument—not even half that time before our era, how can this be? Surely if any one borrowed from the other, it is not the Pharaohs from Moses. Even philology shows not only the Egyptian, but even the Mongolian, older than the Hebrew.

enormous learning, which had a common language over the earth, as to which its essence can be recovered from the fragments which now exist."

Aye, there existed indeed a mighty civilization, and a still mightier secret learning and knowledge, the entire scope of which can never be discovered by Geometry and the *Kabalah* alone: for there are seven keys to the large entrance-door, and not one, nor even two, keys can ever open it sufficiently to allow more than glimpses of what lies within.

Every scholar must be aware that there are two distinct styles—the *schools*, so to speak—plainly traceable in the Hebrew Scriptures: the Elohistic and the Jehovistic. The portions belonging to these respectively are so blended together, so completely mixed up by later hands, that often all external characteristics are lost. Yet it is also known that the two schools were antagonistic; that the one taught esoteric, the other exoteric, or theological doctrines; that the one, the Elohists, were Seers (Roch), whereas the other, the Jehovists, were prophets (Nabhi),* and that the latter—who later became Rabbis—were generally only nominally prophets by virtue of their official position, as the Pope is called the infallible and inspired vicegerent of God. Then, again, the Elohists meant by "Elohim" "forces," identifying their Deity, as in the Secret Doctrine, with Nature; while the Jehovists made of Jehovah a personal God externally, and used the term simply as a phallic symbol—a number of them secretly disbelieving even in metaphysical, abstract Nature, and synthesizing all on the terrestrial scale. Finally, the Elohists made of man the divine incarnate image of the Elohim, emanated first in all Creation; and the Jehovists show him as the last, the crowning glory of the animal creation, instead of his being the head of all the sensible beings on earth. (This is reversed by some Kabalists, but the reversion is due to the designedly-produced confusion in the texts, especially in the first four chapters of *Genesis*.)

Take the *Zohar* and find in it the description relating to Ain-Suph, the Western or Semitic Parabrahman. What passages have come so nearly up to the Vedântic ideal as the following:

> The creation [the evolved Universe] is the garment of that which has no name, the garment *woven from the Deity's own substance.*†

---

* This alone shows how the Books of Moses were tampered with. In *Samuel* (ix. 9), it is said: "He that is now a prophet [Nabhi] was beforetime called a Seer [Roch]." Now since before *Samuel*, the word "Roch" is met nowhere in the *Pentateuch*, but its place is always taken by that of "Nabhi," this proves clearly that the Mosaic text has been replaced by that of the later Levites. (See for fuller details *Jewish Antiquities*, by the Rev. D. Jennings, D.D.)

† *Zohar*, i, 2a.

Between that which is Ain or "nothing," and the Heavenly Man, there is an Impersonal First Cause, however, of which it is said:

> Before It gave any shape to this world, before It produced any form, It was alone, without form or similitude to anything else. Who, then, can comprehend It, how It was before the creation, since It was formless? Hence it is forbidden to represent It by any form, similitude, or even by Its sacred name, by a single letter or a single point.*

The sentence that follows, however, is an evident later interpolation; for it draws attention to a complete contradiction:

> And to this the words (*Deut.* iv. 15), refer—"Ye saw no manner of similitude on the day the Lord spake unto you."

But this reference to Chapter iv. of *Deuteronomy*, when in Chapter v. God is mentioned as speaking "face to face" with the people, is very clumsy.

Not one of the names given to Jehovah in the *Bible* has any reference whatever to either Ain-Suph or the Impersonal First-Cause (which is the Logos) of the *Kabalah*; but they all refer to the *Emanations*.

It says

> For although to reveal itself to us, the concealed of all the concealed sent forth the Ten Emanations [Sephiroth] called the Form of God, Form of the Heavenly Man, yet since even this luminous form was too dazzling for our vision, it had to assume another form, or had to put on another garment, *which is the Universe*. The Universe, therefore, or the visible world, is a farther expansion of the Divine Substance, and is called in the Kabalah "The Garment of God."†

This is the doctrine of all the Hindu Purânas, especially that of the *Vishnu Purâna*. Vishnu pervades the Universe and is that Universe; Brahmâ enters the Mundane Egg, and issues from it as the Universe; Brahmâ even dies with it and there remains only Brahman, the impersonal, the eternal, the unborn, and the unqualifiable. The Ain-Suph of the Chaldæans and later of the Jews is assuredly a copy of the Vaidic Deity; while the "Heavenly Adam," the Macrocosm which unites in itself the totality of beings and is the *Esse* of the visible Universe, finds his original in the Purânic Brahmâ. In *Sôd*, "the Secret of the Law," one recognizes the expressions used in the oldest fragments of the Gupta Vidyâ, the Secret Knowledge. And it is not venturing too much to say that even a Rabbi quite familiar with his own special Rabbinical *Hebrew* would only comprehend its secrets thoroughly if he added to

* *Zohar*, 42b.

† *Zohar*, i, 2a. See Dr. Ch. Ginsburg's essay on *The Cabbalah, its Doctrines, Developments and Literature*.

his learning a serious knowledge of the Hindu philosophies. Let us turn to Stanza I. of the *Book of Dzyan* for an example.

The *Zohar* premises, as does the Secret Doctrine, a universal, eternal Essence, passive—because absolute—in all that men call attributes. The pregenetic or pre-cosmical Triad is a pure metaphysical abstraction. The notion of a triple hypostasis in one Unknown Divine Essence is as old as speech and thought. Hiranyagarbha, Hari, and Shankara—the Creator, the Preserver, and the Destroyer—are the three manifested attributes of it, appearing and disappearing with Kosmos; the visible Triangle, so to speak, on the plane of the ever-invisible Circle. This is the primeval root-thought of thinking Humanity; the Pythagorean Triangle emanating from the ever-concealed Monad, or the Central Point.

Plato speaks of it and Plotinus calls it an ancient doctrine, on which Cudworth remarks that:

> Since Orpheus, Pythagoras, and Plato, who all of them asserted a Trinity of divine hypostases, unquestionably derived their doctrine from the Egyptians, it may be reasonably suspected that the Egyptians did the like before them.*

The Egyptians certainly derived their Trinity from the Indians. Wilson justly observes:

> As, however, the Grecian accounts and those of the Egyptians are much more perplexed and unsatisfactory than those of the Hindus, it is most probable that we find amongst them the doctrine in its most original, as well as most methodical and significant form.†

This, then, is the meaning:

"*Darkness alone filled the Boundless All, for Father, Mother and Son were once more One.*"‡

Space was, and is ever, as it is between the Manvantaras. The Universe in its pre-kosmic state was once more homogeneous and one—outside its aspects. This was a Kabalistic, and is now a Christian teaching.

As is constantly shown in the *Zohar*, the Infinite Unity, or Ain-Suph, is ever placed outside human thought and appreciation; and in *Sepher Jetzirah* we see the Spirit of God—the Logos, not the Deity itself—called One.

---

* Cudworth, I. iii, quoted by Wilson, *Vishnu Purâna*, i. 14, note.

† *Vishnu Purâna*, i. 14.

‡ Stanza I, 4.

One is the Spirit of the living God, . . who liveth for ever. Voice, Spirit, [of the Spirit], and Word: this is the Holy Spirit.*

—and the Quaternary. From this Cube emanates the whole Kosmos.

Says the Secret Doctrine:

"*It is called to life. The mystic Cube in which rests the Creative Idea, the manifesting Mantra* [or articulate speech—Vâch] *and the holy Purusha* [both radiations of prima materia] *exist in the Eternity in the Divine Substance in their latent state*

—during Pralaya.

And in the *Sepher Jetzirah*, when the Three-in-One are to be called into being—by the manifestation of Shekinah, the first effulgency or radiation in the manifesting Kosmos—the "Spirit of God," or Number One,† fructifies and awakens the dual Potency, Number Two, Air, and Number Three, Water; in these "are darkness and emptiness, slime and dung"—which is Chaos, the Tohu-Vah-Bohu. The Air and Water emanate Number Four, Ether or Fire, the Son. This is the Kabalistic Quaternary. This Fourth Number, which in the manifested Kosmos is the One, or the Creative God, is with the Hindus the "Ancient," Sanat, the Prajâpati of the *Vedas* and the Brahmâ of the Brâhmans—the heavenly Androgyne, as he becomes the male only after separating himself into two bodies, Vâch and Virâj. With the Kabalists, he is at first the Jah-Havah, only later becoming Jehovah, like Virâj, his prototype; after separating himself as Adam-Kadmon into Adam and Eve in the formless, and into Cain-Abel in the semi-objective, world, he became finally the Jah-Havah, or man and woman, in Enoch, the son of Seth.

For, the true meaning of the compound name of Jehovah—of which, unvoweled, you can make almost anything—is: men and women, or humanity composed of its two sexes. From the first chapter to the end of the fourth chapter of *Genesis* every name is a permutation of another name, and every personage is at the same time somebody else. A Kabalist traces Jehovah from the Adam of earth to Seth, the third son—or rather race—of Adam.‡ Thus Seth is Jehovah male; and Enos,

---

* *Mishna*, i. 9.

† In its manifested state it becomes Ten, the Universe. In the Chaldæan *Kabalah* it is sexless. In the Jewish, Shekinah is female, and the early Christians and Gnostics regarded the Holy Ghost as a female potency. In the *Book of Numbers* "Shekina" is made to drop the final "h" that makes it a feminine name. Nârâyana, the Mover on the Waters, is also sexless; but it is our firm belief that Shekinah and Daiviprakriti, the "Light of the Logos," are one and the same thing philosophically.

‡ The Elohim create the Adam of dust, and in him Jehovah-Binah separates himself into Eve, after which the male portion of God becomes the Serpent, tempts himself in Eve, then creates himself

being a permutation of Cain and Abel, is Jehovah male and female of our mankind. The Hindu Brahmâ-Virâj, Virâj-Manu, and Manu-Vaivasvata, with his daughter and wife, Vâch, present the greatest analogy with these personages—for anyone who will take the trouble of studying the subject in both the *Bible* and the *Purânas*. It is said of Brahmâ that he created himself as Manu, and that he was born of, and was identical with, his original self, while he constituted the female portion Shata-rûpâ" (hundred-formed). In this Hindu Eve, "the mother of all living beings," Brahmâ created Virâj, who is himself, but on a lower scale, as Cain is Jehovah on an inferior scale: both are the first males of the Third Race. The same idea is illustrated in the Hebrew name of God (יהוה.) Read from right to left "Jod" (י) is the father, "He" (ה) the mother, "Vau" (ו) the son, and "He" (ה) repeated at the end of the word, is generation, the act of birth, materiality. This is surely a sufficient reason why the God of the Jews and Christians should be personal, as much as the male Brahmâ, Vishnu, or Shiva of the orthodox, exoteric Hindu.

Thus the term of Jhvh alone—now accepted as the name of "One living [male] God"—will yield, if seriously studied, not only the whole mystery of *Being* (in the Biblical sense,) but also that of the Occult Theogony, from the highest divine Being, the third in order, down to man. As shown by the best Hebraists:

> The verbal הוה, or Hâyâh, or E-y-e, means *to be, to exist*, while חוה or Châyâh, or H-y-e, means *to live, as motion of existence.**

Hence Eve stands as the evolution and the never-ceasing "becoming" of Nature. Now if we take the almost untranslatable Sanskrit word Sat, which means the quintessence of absolute immutable Being, or Be-ness—as it has been rendered by an able Hindu Occultist—we shall find no equivalent for it in any language; but it may be regarded as most closely resembling "Ain," or "En-Suph," Boundless Being. Then the term Hâyâh, "to be," as passive, changeless, yet manifested existence may perhaps be rendered by the Sanskrit Jîvâtmâ, universal life or soul, in its secondary and cosmic meaning; while "Châyâh, "to live," as "motion of existence," is simply Prâna, the ever-changing life in its objective sense. It is at the head of this third category that the Occultist finds Jehovah—the Mother, Binah, and the Father, Ain-

in her as Cain, passes into Seth, and scatters from Enoch, the Son of Man, or Humanity, as Jod-heva.

* *The Source of Measures*, p. 8.

Him. This is made plain in the *Zohar*, when the emanation and evolution of the Sephiroth are explained: First, Ain-Suph, then Shekinah, the Garment or Veil of Infinite Light, then Sephira or the Kadmon, and, thus making the fourth, the spiritual Substance sent forth from the Infinite Light. This Sephira is called the Crown, Kether, and has besides, six other names—in all seven. These names are: 1. Kether; 2. the Aged; 3. the Primordial Point; 4. the White Head; 5. the Long Face; 6. the Inscrutable Height; and 7. Ehejeh ("I am".)* This septenary Sephira is said to contain in itself the nine Sephiroth. But before showing how she brought them forth, let us read an explanation about the Sephiroth in the *Talmud*, which gives it as an archaic tradition, or Kabalah.

There are three groups (or orders) of Sephiroth: 1. The Sephiroth called "divine attributes" (the Triad in the Holy Quaternary); 2. the sidereal (personal) Sephiroth; 3. the metaphysical Sephiroth, or a periphrasis of Jehovah, who are the first three Sephiroth (Kether, Chokmah and Binah), the rest of the seven being the personal "Seven Spirits of the Presence" (also of the planets, therefore). Speaking of these, the angels are meant, though not because they are seven, but because they represent the seven Sephiroth which contain in them the universality of the Angels.

This shows (*a*) that, when the first four Sephiroth are separated, as a Triad-Quaternary—Sephira being its synthesis—there remain only seven Sephiroth, as there are seven Rishis; these become ten when the Quaternary, or the first divine Cube, is scattered into units; and (*b*) that while Jehovah might have been viewed as the Deity, if he be included in the three divine groups or orders of the Sephiroth, the collective Elohim, or the quaternary indivisible Kether, once that he becomes a male God, he is no more than one of the Builders of the lower group—a Jewish Brahmâ.† A demonstration is now attempted.

The first Sephira, containing the other nine, brought them forth in

---

* This identifies Sephira, the third potency, with Jehovah the Lord, who says to Moses out of the burning bush: "(Here) I am." (*Exodus*, iii, 4.) At this time the "Lord" had not yet become Jehovah. It was not the one Male God who spoke, but the Elohim manifested, or the Sephiroth in their manifested collectivity of seven, contained in the triple Sephira.

† The Brâhmans were wise in their generation when they gradually, for no other reason than this, abandoned Brahmâ, and paid less attention to him individually than to any other deity. As an abstract synthesis they worshipped him collectively and in every God, each of which represents him. As Brâhma, the male, he is far lower than Shiva, the Lingam, who personates universal generation, or Vishnu, the preserver—both Shiva and Vishnu being the regenerators of life after destruction. The Christians might do worse than follow their example, and worship God in Spirit, and not in the male Creator.

this order: (2) Hokmah (Chokmah, or Wisdom), a masculine active potency represented among the divine names as Jah; and, as a permutation or an evolution into lower forms in this instance—becoming the Auphanim (or the Wheels—cosmic rotation of matter) among the army, or the angelic hosts From this Chokmah emanated a feminine passive potency called (3) Intelligence, Binah, whose divine name is Jehovah, and whose angelic name, among the Builders and Hosts, is *Arelim.** It is from the union of these two potencies, male and female (or Chokmah and Binah) that emanated all the other Sephiroth, the seven orders of the Builders. Now if we call Jehovah by his divine name, then he becomes at best and forthwith "a female passive" potency in Chaos. And if we view him as a male God, he is no more than one of many, an Angel, Arelim. But straining the analysis to its highest point, and if his male name Jah, that of Wisdom, be allowed to him, still he is not the "Highest and the one Living God;" for he is contained with many others within Sephira, and Sephira herself is a third Potency in Occultism, though regarded as the first in the exoteric *Kabalah*—and is one, moreover, of lesser importance than the Vaidic Aditi, or the Primordial Water of Space, which becomes after many a permutation the Astral Light of the Kabalist.

Thus the *Kabalah*, as we have it now, is shown to be of the greatest importance in explaining the allegories and "dark sayings" of the *Bible*. As an Esoteric work upon the mysteries of creation, however, it is almost worthless as it is now disfigured, unless checked by the Chaldæan *Book of Numbers* or by the tenets of the Eastern Secret Science, or Esoteric Wisdom. The Western nations have neither the original *Kabalah*, nor yet the Mosaic *Bible*.

Finally, it is demonstrated by internal as well as by external evidence, on the testimony of the best European Hebraists, and the confessions of the learned Jewish Rabbis themselves, that "an ancient document forms the essential basis of the *Bible*, which received very considerable insertions and supplements;" and that "the Pentateuch arose out of the primitive or older document by means of a supplementary one." Therefore in the absence of the *Book of Numbers*,† the Kabalists of the West are only entitled to come to definite conclusions, when they have at hand some data at least from that "ancient docu-

---

* A plural word, signifying a collective host generically; literally, the "strong lion."

† The writer possesses only a few extracts, some dozen pages in all, verbatim quotations from that priceless work, of which but two or three copies, perhaps, are still extant.

ment"—data now found scattered throughout Egyptian papyri, Assyrian tiles, and the traditions preserved by the descendants of the disciples of the last Nazars. Instead of that, most of them accept as their authorities and infallible guides Sabre d'Olivet—who was a man of immense erudition and of speculative mind, but neither a Kabalist nor an Occultist, either Western or Eastern—and the Mason Ragon, the greatest of the "Widow's sons," who was even less of an Orientalist than d'Olivet, for Sanskrit learning was almost unknown in the days of both these eminent scholars.

SECTION XXI.

HEBREW ALLEGORIES.

How can any Kabalist, acquainted with the foregoing, deduce his conclusions with regard to the true Esoteric beliefs of the primitive Jews from that only which he now finds in the Jewish scrolls? How can any scholar—even though one of the keys to the universal language be now positively discovered, the true key to the numerical reading of a pure geometrical system—give out anything as his *final* conclusion? Modern Kabalistic speculation is on a par now with modern "speculative Masonry;" for as the latter tries vainly to link itself with the ancient—or rather the archaic—Masonry of the Temples, failing to make the link because all its claims have been shown to be inaccurate from an archæological standpoint, so fares it also with Kabalistic speculation. As no mystery of Nature worth running after can be revealed to humanity by settling whether Hiram Abif was a living Sidonian builder, or a solar myth, so no fresh information will be added to Occult Lore by the details of the exoteric privileges conferred on the Collegia Fabrorum by Numa Pompilius. Rather must the symbols used in it be studied in the Âryan light, since all the Symbolism of the ancient Initiations came to the West with the light of the Eastern Sun. Nevertheless, we find the most learned Masons and Symbologists declaring that all these weird symbols and glyphs, that run back to a common origin of immense antiquity, were nothing more than a display of cunning natural phallicism, or emblems of primitive typology. How much nearer the truth is the author of *The Source of Measures*, who declares that the elements of human and numerical construction in the *Bible* do not shut out the spiritual elements in it, albeit so few now understand them. The words we quote are as suggestive as they are true:

How desperately blinding becomes a superstitious use, through ignorance, of such emblems, when they are made to possess the power of bloodshed and torture, through orders of propaganda of any species of religious cultus. When one thinks of the horrors of a *Moloch*, or *Baal*, or *Dagon* worship; of the correlated blood-deluges under the Cross baptized in gore by Constantine, at the initiative of the secular Church; . . . when one thinks of all this and then that the cause of all has been simply ignorance of the real radical reading of the *Moloch*, and *Baal*, and *Dagon*, and the *Cross* and the *T'phillin*, all running back to a common origin, and after all being nothing more than a display of pure and natural mathematics, . . . one is apt to feel like cursing ignorance, and to lose confidence in what are called *intuitions* of religion; one is apt to wish for a return of the day when all the world was of one *lip* and of one *knowledge*. . . . But while these elements [of the construction of the pyramid] are rational and scientific, . . . let no man consider that with this discovery comes a cutting-off of the *spirituality** of the *Bible* intention, or of man's relation to this spiritual foundation. Does one wish to build a house? No house was ever actually built with tangible material *until first the architectural design of building had been accomplished*, no matter whether the structure was palace or hovel. So with these elements and numbers. They are not of man, nor are they of his invention. They have been revealed to him to the extent of his ability to realize a system, which is *the creative system* of the eternal God. . . . But *spiritually*, to man the value of this matter is that he can actually in contemplation, bridge over all material construction of the cosmos, and pass into the very *thought* and *mind* of God, to the extent of recognizing this *system of design* for cosmic creation—yea, even before the words went forth: "*Let there be.*"†

But true as the above words may be, when coming from one who has re-discovered, more completely than anyone else has done during the past centuries, one of the keys to the universal Mystery Language, it is impossible for an Eastern Occultist to agree with the conclusion of the able author of *The Source of Measures*. He "has set out to find the truth," and yet he still believes that:

The best and most authentic vehicle of communication from [the creative] God to man . . . is to be found in the Hebrew Bible.

To this we must and shall demur, giving our reasons for it in a few words. The "Hebrew *Bible*" exists no more, as has been shown in the foregoing pages, and the garbled accounts, the falsified and pale copies we have of the real Mosaic *Bible* of the Initiates, warrant the making of no such sweeping assertion and claim. All that the scholar can fairly claim is that the Jewish *Bible*, as now extant—in its latest and final interpretation, and according to the newly-discovered key—may give

---

* Aye; but that *spirituality* can never be discovered, far less proved, unless we turn to the Âryan Scriptures and Symbology. For the Jews it was lost, save for the Sadducees, from the day that the "chosen people" reached the Promised Land, the national Karma preventing Moses from reaching it.

† *Op. cit.*, pp. 317-319.

a partial presentment of the truths it contained before it was mangled. But how can he tell what the *Pentateuch* contained before it had been re-composed by Esdras; then corrupted still more by the ambitious Rabbis in later times, and otherwise remodelled and interfered with? Leaving aside the opinion of the declared enemies of the Jewish Scriptures, one may quote simply what their most devoted followers say.

Two of these are Horne and Prideaux. The avowals of the former will be sufficient to show how much now remains of the original Mosaic books, unless indeed we accept his sublimely blind faith in the inspiration and editorship of the Holy Ghost. He writes that when a Hebrew scribe found a writing of any author he was entitled, if he thought fit, being "conscious of the aid of the Holy Spirit," to do exactly as he pleased with it—to cut it up, or copy it, or use as much of it as he deemed right, and so to incorporate it with his own manuscript. Dr. Kenealy aptly remarks of Horne, that it is almost impossible to get any admission from him

> That makes against his church, so remarkably guarded is he [Horne] in his phraseology and so wonderfully discreet in the use of words that his language, like a diplomatic letter, perpetually suggests to the mind ideas other than those which he really means; I defy any unlearned person to read his chapter on "Hebrew characters" and to derive *any knowledge* from it whatever on the subject on which he professes to treat.*

And yet this same Horne writes:

> We are persuaded that the things to which reference is made proceeded from the original writers or *compilers* of the books [*Old Testament*]. Sometimes they took other writings, annals, genealogies, and such like, with which they *incorporated additional matter*, or which they put together with greater or less condensation. The *Old Testament* authors used the sources they employed (that is, the writings of other people) with freedom and independence. Conscious of the aid of the Divine Spirit, *they adapted* their own productions, or the productions of others, to the wants of the times. But in these respects they cannot be said to have corrupted the text of Scripture. *They made the text.*†

But of what did they make it? Why, of the writings of other persons, justly observes Kenealy:

> And this is Horne's notion of what the *Old Testament* is—a cento from the writings of unknown persons collected and put together by those who, he says, were divinely inspired. No infidel that I know of has ever made so damaging a charge as this against the authenticity of the *Old Testament*.*

---

* *The Book of God*, pp. 388, 389.

† See Horne's *Introduction* (10th edition), vol. ii, p. 33, as quoted by Dr. Kenealy, p. 389.

This is quite sufficient, we think, to show that no key to the universal language-system can ever open the mysteries of Creation in a work in which, whether through design or carelessness, nearly every sentence has been made to apply to the latest outcome of religious views—to Phallicism, and to nothing else. There are a sufficient number of stray bits in the Elohistic portions of the *Bible* to warrant the inference that the Hebrews who wrote it were Initiates; hence the mathematical coördinations and the perfect harmony between the measures of the Great Pyramid and the numerals of the Biblical glyphs. But surely if one borrowed from the other, it cannot be the architects of the Pyramid who borrowed from Solomon's Temple, if only because the former exists to this day as a stupendous living monument of Esoteric records, while the famous temple has never existed outside of the far later Hebrew scrolls.* Hence there is a great distance between the admission that some Hebrews were Initiates, and the conclusion that because of this the Hebrew *Bible* must be the best standard, as being the highest representative of the archaic Esoteric System.

Nowhere does the *Bible* say, moreover, that the Hebrew is the language of God; of this boast, at any rate, the authors are not guilty. Perhaps because in the days when the *Bible* was last edited the claim would have been too preposterous—hence dangerous. The *compilers* of the *Old Testament*, as it exists in the Hebrew canon, knew well that the language of the Initiates in the days of Moses was identical with that of the Egyptian Hierophants; and that none of the dialects that had sprung from the old Syriac and the pure old Arabic of Yarab—the father and progenitor of the primitive Arabians, long before the time of Abraham, in whose days the ancient Arabic had already become vitiated—that none of those languages was the one sacerdotal universal tongue. Nevertheless all of them included a number of words which could be traced to common roots. And to do this is the business of modern Philology, though to this day, with all the respect due to the labours of the eminent Philologists of Oxford and Berlin, that Science seems to be hopelessly floundering in the Cimmerian darkness of mere hypothesis.

---

* The author says that Parker's *quadrature* is "that identical measure which was used anciently as the perfect measure, by the Egyptians, in the construction of the Great Pyramid, which was built *to monument it and its uses*," and that "from it the *sacred cubit-value was derived*, which was the cubit-value used in the construction of the Temple of Solomon, the Ark of Noah, and the Ark of the Covenant" (p. 22). This is a grand discovery, no doubt, but it only shows that the Jews profited well by their captivity in Egypt, and that Moses was a great Initiate.

Ahrens, when speaking of the letters as arranged in the Hebrew sacred scrolls, and remarking that they were musical notes, had probably never studied Âryan Hindu music. In the Sanskrit language letters are continually arranged in the sacred Ollas so that they may become musical notes. For the whole Sanskrit alphabet and the *Vedas*, from the first word to the last, are musical notations reduced to writing; the two are inseparable.* As Homer distinguished between the "language of Gods" and the "language of men,"† so did the Hindus. The Devanâgarî, the Sanskrit characters, are the "speech of the Gods," and Sanskrit is the divine language.

It is argued in defence of the present version of the Mosaic Books that the mode of language adopted was an "accommodation" to the ignorance of the Jewish people. But the said "mode of language" drags down the "sacred text" of Esdras and his colleagues to the level of the most unspiritual and gross phallic religions. This plainly confirms the suspicions entertained by some Christian Mystics and many philosophical critics, that:

(*a*) Divine Power as an Absolute Unity had never anything more to do with the Biblical Jehovah and the "Lord God" than with any other Sephiroth or Number. The Ain-Suph of the *Kabalah* of Moses is as independent of any relation with the created Gods as is Parabrahman Itself.

(*b*) The teachings veiled in the *Old Testament* under allegorical expressions are all copied from the Magical Texts of Babylonia, by Esdras and others, while the earlier Mosaic Text had its source in Egypt.

A few instances known to almost all Symbologists of note, and especially to the French Egyptologists, may help to prove the statement. Furthermore, no ancient Hebrew Philosopher, Philo no more than the Sadducees, claimed, as do now the ignorant Christians, that

---

* See *Theosophist*, November, 1879, art. "Hindu Music," p. 47.

† The Sanskrit letters are far more numerous than the poor twenty-two letters of the Hebrew alphabet. They are all musical, and they are read—or rather chanted—according to a system given in very old Tântrika works, and are called Devanâgarî, the speech, or language, of the Gods. And since each letter answers to a numeral, the Sanskrit affords a far larger scope for expression, and it must necessarily be far more perfect than the Hebrew, which followed the same system but could apply it only in a very limited way. If either of these two languages were taught to humanity by the Gods, surely it would more likely be the Sanskrit, the perfect form of the most perfect language on earth, than the Hebrew, the roughest and the poorest. For once anyone believes in a language of divine origin, he can hardly believe at the same time that Angels or Gods or any divine Messengers have had to develop it from a rough monosyllabic form into a perfect one, as we see in terrestrial linguistic evolution.

the events in the *Bible* should be taken literally. Philo says most explicitly:

> The verbal statements are fabulous [in the Book of the Law]: it is in the allegory that we shall find the truth.

Let us give a few instances, beginning with the latest narrative, the Hebrew, and thus if possible trace the allegories to their origin.

1. Whence the Creation in six days, the seventh day as day of rest, the seven Elohim,* and the division of space into heaven and earth, in the first chapter of *Genesis*?

The division of the vault above from the Abyss, or Chaos, below is one of the first acts of creation or rather of evolution, in every cosmogony. Hermes in *Pymander* speaks of a heaven seen in seven circles with seven Gods in them. We examine the Assyrian tiles and find the same on them—the seven creative Gods busy each in his own sphere. The cuneiform legends narrate how Bel prepared the seven mansions of the Gods; how heaven was separated from the earth. In the Brâhmanical allegory everything is septenary, from the seven zones, or envelopes, of the Mundane Egg down to the seven continents, islands, seas, etc. The six days of the week and the seventh, the Sabbath, are based primarily on the seven creations of the Hindu Brahmâ, the seventh being that of man; and secondarily on the number of generation. It is preëminently and most conspicuously phallic. In the Babylonian system the seventh day, or period, was that in which man and the animals were created.

2. The Elohim make a woman out of Adam's rib.† This process is found in the Magical Texts translated by G. Smith.

> The seven Spirits bring forth the woman from the loins of the man,

explains Mr. Sayce in his *Hibbert Lectures*.‡

---

* In the first chapter of *Genesis* the word "God" represents the Elohim—Gods in the plural, not one God. This is a cunning and dishonest translation. For the whole *Kabalah* explains sufficiently that the Alhim (Elohim) are seven; each creates one of the seven things enumerated in the first chapter, and these answer allegorically to the seven creations. To make this clear, count the verses in which it is said "And God saw that it was good," and you will find that this is said seven times—in verses 4, 10, 12, 18, 21, 25, and 31. And though the compilers cunningly represent the creation of man as occurring on the sixth day, yet, having made man "male and female in the image of God," the Seven Elohim repeat the sacramental sentence, "It was good," for the seventh time, thus making of man the seventh creation, and showing the origin of this bit of cosmogony to be in the Hindu creations. The Elohim are, of course, the seven Egyptian Khnûmû, the "assistant-architects"; the seven Amshaspends of the Zoroastrians; the Seven Spirits subordinate to Ildabaoth of the Nazareans; the seven Prajâpati of the Hindus, etc.

† Gen., ii. 21 22.

‡ *Op. cit.*, p. 395, note.

The mystery of the woman who was made from the man is repeated in every national religion, and in Scriptures far antedating the Jewish. You find it in the Avestan fragments, in the Egyptian *Book of the Dead*, and finally in Brahmâ, the male, separating from himself, as a female self, Vâch, in whom he creates Virâj.

3. The two Adams of the first and second chapters in *Genesis* originated from garbled exoteric accounts coming from the Chaldeans and the Egyptian Gnostics, revised later from the Persian traditions, most of which are old Aryan allegories. As Adam Kadmon is the seventh creation,* so the Adam of dust is the eighth; and in the Purânas one finds an eighth, the Anugraha creation, and the Egyptian Gnostics had it. Irenæus, complaining of the heretics, says of the Gnostics:

> Sometimes they will have him [man] to have been made on the sixth day, and sometimes on the eighth.†

The author of *The Hebrew and Other Creations* writes:

> These two creations of man on the sixth day and on the eighth were those of the Adamic, or fleshly man, and of the spiritual man, who were known to Paul and the Gnostics as the first and second Adam, the man of earth and the man of Heaven. Irenæus also says they insisted that Moses began with the Ogdoad of the Seven Powers and their mother, Sophia (the old Kefa of Egypt, who is the *Living Word* at Ombos).‡

Sophia is also Aditi with her seven sons.

One might go on enumerating and tracing the Jewish "revelations" *ad infinitum* to their original sources, were it not that the task is superfluous, since so much is already done in that direction by others—and done thoroughly well, as in the case of Gerald Massey, who has sifted the subject to the very bottom. Hundreds of volumes, treatises, and pamphlets are being written yearly in defence of the "divine-inspiration" claim for the *Bible*; but symbolical and archæological research is coming to the rescue of truth and fact—therefore of the Esoteric Doctrine—upsetting every argument based on f ith and breaking it as an idol with feet of clay. A curious and learned book, *The Approaching End of the Age*, by H. Grattan Guinness, professes to solve the mysteries of the *Bible* chronology and to prove thereby God's direct revelation to man. Among other things its author thinks that:

> It is impossible to deny that *a septiform chronology was divinely appointed* in the elaborate ritual of Judaism.

---

* The seventh esoterically, exoterically the sixth.

† *Contra Hæreses*, I, xviii, 2.

‡ *Op. cit.* by Gerald Massey, p. 19

This statement is innocently accepted and fervently believed in by thousands and tens of thousands, only because they are ignorant of the Bibles of other nations. Two pages from a small pamphlet, a lecture by Mr. Gerald Massey,* so upset the arguments and proofs of the enthusiastic Mr. Grattan Guinness, spread over 760 pages of small print, as to prevent them from ever raising their heads any more. Mr. Massey treats of the Fall, and says:

Here, as before, the genesis does not begin at the beginning. There was an earlier Fall than that of the Primal Pair. In this the number of those who failed and fell was seven. We meet with those seven in Egypt—eight with the Mother—where they are called the "Children of Inertness," who were cast out from Am-Smen, the Paradise of the Eight; also in a Babylonian legend of Creation, as the Seven Brethren, who were Seven Kings, like the Seven Kings in the *Book of Revelation*; and the Seven Non-Sentient Powers, who became the Seven Rebel Angels that made war in heaven. The Seven Kronidæ, described as the Seven Watchers, who in the beginning were formed in the interior of heaven. The heaven, like a vault, they extended or hollowed out; that which was not visible they raised, and that which had no *exit* they opened; their work of creation being exactly identical with that of the Elohim in the *Book of Genesis*. These are the Seven elemental Powers of space, who were continued as Seven Timekeepers. It is said of them: "In watching was their office, but among the stars of heaven their watch they kept not," and their failure was the Fall. In the *Book of Enoch* the same Seven Watchers in heaven are stars which transgressed the commandment of God before their time arrived, for they came not in their proper season, therefore was he offended with them, and bound them until the period of the consummation of their crimes, at the end of the *secret*, or great year of the World, *i.e.*, the Period of Precession, when there was to be restoration and rebeginning. The Seven deposed constellations are seen by Enoch, looking like seven great blazing mountains overthrown—the seven mountains in *Revelation*, on which the Scarlet Lady sits.†

There are seven keys to this, as to every other allegory, whether in the *Bible* or in pagan religions. While Mr. Massey has hit upon the key in the mysteries of cosmogony, John Bentley in his *Hindu Astronomy* claims that the Fall of the Angels, or *War in Heaven*, as given by the Hindus, is but a figure of the calculations of time-periods, and goes on to show that among the Western nations the same war, with like results, took the form of the war of the Titans.

In short, he makes it *astronomical*. So does the author of *The Source of Measures*:

---

* *Op cit.*, p. 178.

† *The Hebrew and other Creations; with a reply to Professor A. H. Sayce*, p. 19.

The celestial sphere with the earth, was divided into twelve compartments [astronomically], and these compartments were esteemed as wives, the husbands being respectively the planets presiding over them. This being the settled scheme, want of proper correction would bring it to pass, after a time, that error and confusion would ensue by the compartments coming under the influence of the wrong planets. Instead of lawful wedlock, there would be illegal intercourse as between the planets, "*sons of Elohim*," and these compartments, "daughters of H-Adam," or the *earth*-man; and in fact the fourth verse of sixth *Genesis* will bear *this* interpretation for the usual one, *viz.*, "In the same days, or periods, there were untimely births in the earth; and also behind that, when the sons of Elohim came to the daughters of H-Adam, they begat to them the offspring of harlotry," the Text astronomically indicating this confusion.*

Do any of these learned explanations explain anything except a possible ingenious allegory, and a personification of the celestial bodies by the ancient Mythologists and Priests? Carried to their last word they would undeniably explain much, and would thus furnish one of the right seven keys, fitting a great many of the Biblical puzzles yet opening none naturally and entirely, instead of being scientific and cunning master-keys. But they yet prove one thing—that neither the septiform chronology nor the septiform theogony and evolution of all things is of divine origin in the *Bible*. For let us see the sources at which the *Bible* sipped its divine inspiration with regard to the sacred number seven. Says Mr. Massey in the same lecture:

The *Book of Genesis* tells us nothing about the nature of these Elohim, erroneously rendered "God," who are creators of the Hebrew beginning, and who are themselves preëxtant and seated when the theatre opens and the curtain ascends. It says that in the beginning the Elohim created the heaven and the earth. In thousands of books the Elohim have been discussed, but . . . with no conclusive result. . . . The Elohim are Seven in number, whether as nature-powers, gods of constellations, or planetary gods, . . . as the Pitris and Patriarchs, Manus and Fathers of earlier times. The Gnostics, however, and the Jewish *Kabalah* preserve an account of the Elohim of *Genesis* by which we are able to identify them with other forms of the seven primordial powers. . . . Their names are Ildabaoth, Jehovah (or Jao), Sabaoth, Adonai, Eloeus, Oreus, and Astanphæus. Ildabaoth signifies the Lord God of the fathers, that is the fathers who preceded the Father; and thus the seven are identical with the seven Pitris or Fathers of India (Irenæus, B. I., xxx., 5). Moreover, the Hebrew Elohim were preëxtant by name and nature as Phœnician divinities or powers. Sanchoniathon mentions them by name, and describes them as Auxiliaries of Kronos or Time. In this phase, then, the Elohim are time-keepers in heaven! In the Phœnician mythology the Elohim are the Seven sons of Sydik [Melchizedek], identical with

* *Op. cit.*, p. 243.

the Seven Kabiri, who in Egypt are the Seven sons of Ptah, and the Seven Spirits of Ra in *The Book of the Dead;* . . . in America with the seven Hohgates, . . . in Assyria with the seven Lumazi. . . . They are always seven in number . . . . who *Kab*—that is, turn round, together, whence the "Kab-iri." . . . They are also the Ili or Gods, in Assyrian, who were seven in number! . . . . They were first born of the Mother in Space,* and then the Seven Companions passed into the sphere of time as auxiliaries of Kronus, or Sons of the Male Parent. As Damascius says in his *Primitive Principles,* the Magi consider that space and time were the source of all; and from being powers of the air the gods were promoted to become time-keepers for men. Seven constellations were assigned to them. . . . . As the seven turned round in the ark of the sphere they were designated the Seven Sailors' Companions, Rishis, or Elohim. The first "Seven Stars" are not planetary. They are the leading stars of seven constellations which turned round with the Great Bear in describing the circle of the year.† These the Assyrians called the seven Lumazi, or leaders of the flocks of stars, designated sheep. On the Hebrew line of descent or development, these Elohim are identified for us by the Kabalists and Gnostics, who retained the hidden wisdom or gnosis, the clue of which is absolutely essential to any proper understanding of mythology or theology. . . . There were two constellations with seven stars each. *We* call them the Two Bears. But the seven stars of the Lesser Bear were once considered to be the seven heads of the Polar Dragon, which we meet with—as the beast with seven heads—in the Akkadian Hymns and in *Revelation.* The mythical dragon originated in the crocodile, which *is* the dragon of Egypt. . . . Now in one particular cult, the Sut-Typhonian, the first god was Sevekh [the seven-fold], who wears the crocodile's head, as well as the Serpent, and who is the Dragon, or whose constellation was the Dragon. . . . In Egypt the Great Bear was the constellation of Typhon, or *Kepha,* the old genetrix, called the Mother of the Revolutions; and the Dragon with seven heads was assigned to her son, Sevekh-Kronus, or Saturn, called the Dragon of Life. That is, the typical dragon or serpent with seven heads was female at first, and then the type was continued, as male in her son Sevekh, the Sevenfold Serpent, in Ra the Sevenfold, . . . Iao Chnubis, and others. We find these two in *The Book of Revelation.* One is the Scarlet Lady, the mother of mystery, the great harlot, who sat on a scarlet-coloured beast with seven heads, which is the Red Dragon of the Pole. She held in her hand the unclean things of her fornication. That means the emblems of the male and female, imaged by the Egyptians at the Polar Centre, the very uterus of creation, as was indicated by the Thigh constellation, called the Khepsh of Typhon, the old Dragon, in the northern birthplace of Time in heaven. The two revolved about the *pole of heaven,* or the Tree, as it was called, which was figured at the centre of the starry motion. In *The Book of Enoch* these two constellations are identified as Leviathan and Behemoth-Bekhmut, or the Dragon and Hippopotamus = Great Bear, and they are the primal pair that were first created in the Garden of Eden. So that the Egyptian first

* When they are the Anupâdakas (Parentless) of the Secret Doctrine. See Stanzas, i, 9, Vol. i, 56.

† These originated with the Âryans, who placed therein their "bright-crested" (Chitra-Shikhandan) Seven Rishis. But all this is far more Occult than appears on the surface.

mother, Kefa [or Kepha] whose name signifies "mystery," was the original of the Hebrew Chavah, our Eve; and therefore Adam is one with Sevekh the seven-fold one, the solar dragon in whom the powers of light and darkness were combined, and the sevenfold nature was shown in the seven rays worn by the Gnostic Iao-Chnubis, god of the number seven, who is Sevekh by name and a form of the father as head of the Seven.*

All this gives the key to the astronomical prototype of the allegory in *Genesis*, but it furnishes no other key to the mystery involved in the sevenfold glyph. The able Egyptologist shows also that Adam himself, according to Rabbinical and Gnostic tradition, was the chief of the Seven who fell from Heaven, and he connects these with the Patriarchs, thus agreeing with the Esoteric Teaching. For by mystic permutation and the mystery of primeval rebirths and adjustment, the Seven Kings are in reality identical with the seven Prajâpatis, the fathers and creators of mankind, and also with the Kumâras, the first sons of Brahmâ, who refused to procreate and multiply. This apparent contradiction tradition is explained by the seven-fold nature—make it four-fold as metaphysical principles and it will come to the same thing—of the celestial men, the Dhyân Chohans. This nature is made to divide and separate; and while the higher principles (Âtmâ-Buddhi) of the "Creators of Men" are said to be the Spirits of the seven constellations, their middle and lower principles are connected with the earth and are shown

> Without desire or passion, inspired with holy wisdom, estranged from the Universe and undesirous of progeny,†

remaining Kaumâric (virgin and undefiled); therefore it is said they refused to create. For this they are cursed and sentenced to be born and reborn "Adams," as the Semites would say.

Meanwhile let me quote a few lines more from Mr. G. Massey's lecture, the fruit of his long researches in Egyptology and other ancient lore, as it shows that the septenary division was at one time a universal doctrine:

> Adam as the father among the Seven is identical with the Egyptian Atum, whose other name of Adon is identical with the Hebrew Adonai. In this way the second Creation in *Genesis* reflects and continues the later creation in the mythos which explains it. The Fall of Adam to the lower world led to his being humanised on earth, by which process the celestial was turned into the mortal, and this, which

---

* *Op. cit.*, pp. 19-22.

† *Vishnu Purâna*, Wilson's Trans., i, 101. The period of these Kumâras is Pre-Adamic, *i.e.*, before the separation of sexes, and before humanity had received the creative, or sacred, fire of Prometheus.

belongs to the astronomical allegory, got literalised as the Fall of Man, or descent of the soul into matter, and the conversion of the angelic into an earthly being. . . . It is found in the [Babylonian] texts, when Ea, the first father, is said to "grant forgiveness to the conspiring gods," for whose "redemption did he create mankind." (Sayce; *Hib. Lect.*, p. 140) . . . The Elohim, then, are the Egyptian, Akkadian, Hebrew, and Phœnician form of the Universal Seven Powers, who are Seven in Egypt, Seven in Akkad, Babylon, Persia, India, Britain, and Seven among the Gnostics and Kabalists. They were the Seven fathers who preceded the Father in Heaven, because they were earlier than the individualised fatherhood on earth. . . . When the Elohim said: "Let us make man in our image, after our likeness," there were seven of them who represented the seven elements, powers, or souls that went to the making of the human being who came into existence before the Creator was represented anthropomorphically, or could have conferred the human likeness on the Adamic man. It was in the sevenfold image of the Elohim that man was first created, with his seven elements, principles or souls,* and therefore he could not have been formed in the image of the one God. The seven Gnostic Elohim tried to make a man in their own image, but could not for lack of virile power.† Thus their creation in earth and heaven was a failure . . . because they themselves were lacking in the soul of the fatherhood! When the Gnostic Ialdabaoth,‡ chief of the Seven, cried: "I am the father and God," his mother Sophia [Achamoth] replied: "Do not tell lies, Ildabaoth, for the first man (Anthropos, son of Anthropos)§ is above thee." That is, man who had now been created in the image of the fatherhood was superior to the gods who were derived from the Mother-Parent alone! ‖ For, as it had been first on earth, so was it afterwards in heaven [the Secret Doctrine teaches the reverse]; and thus the primary gods were held to be soulless like the earliest races of men. . . . The Gnostics taught that the Spirits of Wickedness, the inferior Seven, derived their origin from the great Mother alone, who produced without the fatherhood! It was in the image, then, of the sevenfold Elohim that the seven races were formed which we sometimes hear of as the Pre-Adamite races of men, because they were earlier than the fatherhood, which was individualised only in the second Hebrew Creation.¶

This shows sufficiently how the echo of the Secret Doctrine—of the Third and Fourth Races of men, made complete by the incarnation in humanity of the Mânasa Putra, Sons of Intelligence or Wisdom—reached every corner of the globe. The Jews, however, although they borrowed of the older nations the groundwork on which to build their

---

* The Secret Doctrine says that this was the second creation, not the first, and that it took place during the Third Race, when men separated, *i.e.*, began to be born as distinct men and women. See Vol. ii. of this work, Stanzas and Commentaries.

† This is a Western mangling of the Indian doctrine of the Kumâras.

‡ He was regarded by several Gnostic sects as one with Jehovah. See *Isis Unveiled*, vol. ii. p. 184.

§ Or "man, son of man." The Church found in this a *prophecy* and a confession of Christ, the "Son of Man!"

‖ See Stanza ii. 5, Secret Doctrine, ii. 16.

¶ *Op. cit.*, pp. 23, 24.

revelation, never had more than three keys out of the seven in their mind, while composing their national allegories—the astronomical, the numerical (metrology), and above all the purely anthropological, or rather physiological key. This resulted in the most phallic religion of all, and has now passed, part and parcel, into Christian theology, as is proved by the lengthy quotations made from a lecture of an able Egyptologist, who can make naught of it save astronomical myths and phallicism, as is implied by his explanations of "fatherhood" in the allegories.

SECTION XXII.

THE "ZOHAR" ON CREATION AND THE ELOHIM.

THE opening sentence in *Genesis*, as every Hebrew scholar knows, is:

בראשית ברא אלהים את השמים ואת הארץ

Now there are two well-known ways of rendering this line, as any other Hebrew writing: one exoteric, as read by the orthodox *Bible* interpreters (Christian), and the other Kabalistic, the latter, moreover, being divided into the Rabbinical and the purely Kabalistic or Occult method. As in Sanskrit writing, the words are not separated in the Hebrew, but are made to run together—especially in the old systems. For instance, the above, divided, would read: "*B'rashith bara Elohim eth hashamayim v'eth h'areths*;" and it can be made to read thus: "*B'rash ithbara Elohim ethhashamayim v'eth'arets*," thus changing the meaning entirely. The latter means, "In the beginning *God made the heavens* and the earth," whereas the former, precluding the idea of any beginning, would simply read that "out of the ever-existing Essence [divine] [or out of the *womb*—also head—thereof] the dual [or androgyne] Force [Gods] shaped the double heaven;" the upper and the lower heaven being generally explained as heaven and earth. The latter word means Esoterically the "Vehicle," as it gives the idea of an empty globe, within which the manifestation of the world takes place. Now, according to the rules of Occult symbolical reading as established in the old *Sepher Jetzirah* (in the Chaldæan *Book of Numbers**) the initial fourteen letters (or "B'rasitb' raalaim") are in themselves quite sufficient to explain the theory of "creation" without any further ex-

---

* The *Sepher Jetzirah* now known is but a portion of the original one incorporated in the Chaldæan *Book of Numbers*. The fragment now in possession of the Western Kabalists is one greatly tampered with by the Rabbis of the Middle Ages, as its masoretic points show. The "Masorah" scheme is a modern blind, dating after our era and perfected in Tiberias. (See *Isis Unveiled*, vol. ii, pp. 430-431.)

planation or qualification. Every letter of them is a sentence; and, placed side by side with the hieroglyphic or pictorial initial version of "creation" in the *Book of Dzyan*, the origin of the Phœnician and Jewish letters would soon be found out. A whole volume of explanations would give no more to the student of primitive Occult Symbology than this: the head of a bull within a circle, a straight horizontal line, a circle or sphere, then another one with three dots in it, a triangle, then the Svastika (or Jaina cross); after these come an equilateral triangle within a circle, seven small bulls' heads standing in three rows, one over the other; a black round dot (an opening), and then seven lines, meaning Chaos or Water (feminine).

Anyone acquainted with the symbolical and numerical value of the Hebrew letters will see at a glance that this glyph and the letters of "B'rasitb' raalaim" are identical in meaning. "Beth" is "abode" or "region;" "Resh," a "circle" or "head;" "Aleph," "bull" (the symbol of generative or creative power*); "Shin," a "tooth" (the exoterically—a trident or *three in one* in its Occult meaning); "Jodh," the perfect unity or "one" †; "Tau," the "root" or "foundation" (the same as the cross with the Egyptians and Âryans): again, "Beth," "Resh," and "Aleph." Then "Aleph," or seven bulls for the seven Alaim; an ox-goad, "Lamedh," active procreation; "He," the "opening" or "matrix;" "Yodh," the organ of procreation; and "Mem," "water" or "chaos," the female Power near the male that precedes it.

The most satisfactory and scientific exoteric rendering of the opening sentence of *Genesis*—on which was hung in blind faith the whole Christian religion, synthesized by its fundamental dogmas—is undeniably the one given in the Appendix to *The Source of Measures* by Mr. Ralston Skinner. He gives, and we must admit in the ablest, clearest, and most scientific way, the numerical reading of this first

* In the oldest symbolism—that used in the Egyptian hieroglyphics—when the bull's head only is found it means the Deity, the Perfect Circle, with the procreative power latent in it. When the whole bull is represented, a solar God, a *personal* deity is meant, for it is then the symbol of the active generative power.

† It took three Root-Races to degrade the symbol of the One Abstract Unity manifested in Nature as a Ray emanating from infinity (the Circle) into a phallic symbol of generation, as it was even in the *Kabalah*. This degradation began with the Fourth Race, and had its *raison d'être* in Polytheism, as the latter was invented to screen the One Universal Deity from profanation. The Christians may plead ignorance of its meaning as an excuse for its acceptance. But why sing never-ceasing laudations to the Mosaic Jews who repudiated all the other Gods, preserved the most phallic, and then most impudently proclaimed themselves Monotheists? Jesus ever steadily ignored Jehovah. He went against the Mosaic commandments. He recognized his Heavenly Father alone, and prohibited public worship.

sentence and chapter in *Genesis*. By the means of number 31, or the word "El" (1 for "Aleph" and 30 for "Lamedh"), and other numerical *Bible* symbols, compared with the measures used in the great pyramid of Egypt, he shows the perfect identity between its measurements—inches, cubits, and plan—and the numerical values of the Garden of Eden, Adam and Eve, and the Patriarchs. In short, the author shows that the pyramid contains in itself architecturally the whole of *Genesis*, and discloses the astronomical, and even the physiological, secrets in its symbols and glyphs; yet he will not admit, it would seem, the psycho-cosmical and spiritual mysteries involved in these. Nor does the author apparently see that the root of all this has to be sought in the archaic legends and the Pantheon of India.* Failing this, whither does his great and admirable labour lead him? Not further than to find out that Adam, the earth, and Moses or Jehovah "are the same"—or to the a-b-c of comparative Occult Symbology—and that the days in *Genesis* being "circles" "displayed by the Hebrews as squares," the result of the sixth-day's labour culminates in the fructifying principle. Thus the *Bible* is made to yield Phallicism, and that alone.

Nor—read in this light, and as its Hebrew texts are interpreted by Western scholars—can it ever yield anything higher or more sublime than such phallic elements, the root and the corner-stone of its dead-letter meaning. Anthropomorphism and Revelation dig the impassable chasm between the material world and the ultimate spiritual truths. That creation is not thus described in the Esoteric Doctrine is easily shown. The Roman Catholics give a reading far more approaching the true Esoteric meaning than that of the Protestant. For several of their saints and doctors admit that the formation of heaven and earth, of the celestial bodies, etc., belongs to the work of the "Seven Angels of the Presence." St. Denys calls the "Builders" "the coöperators of God," and St. Augustine goes even farther, and credits the Angels with the possession of the divine thought, the prototype, as he says, of everything created.† And, finally, St. Thomas Aquinas has a long

* Is it everything to have found out that the celestial circle of 360° is determined by "the full word-form of Elohim," and that this yields, when the word is placed in a circle, "3·1415, or the relation of circumference to a diameter of *one*." This is only its astronomical or mathematical aspect. To know the full *septenary* significance of the "Primordial Circle," the pyramid and the Kabalistic *Bible* must be read in the light of the figure on which the temples of India are built. The mathematical squaring of the circle is only the terrestrial *résumé* of the problem. The Jews were content with the six days of activity and the seventh of rest. The progenitors of mankind solved the greatest problems of the Universe with their seven Rays or Rishis.

† *Genesis* begins with the *third* stage of "creation," skipping the preliminary two.

dissertation upon this topic, calling God the primary, and the Angels the secondary, cause of all visible effects. In this, with some dogmatic differences of form, the "Angelic Doctor" approaches very nearly the Gnostic ideas. Basilides speaks of the lowest order of Angels as the Builders of our material world, and Saturnilus held, as did the Sabæans, that the Seven Angels who preside over the planets are the true creators of the world; the Kabalist-monk, Trithemius, in his *De Septem Secundis Deis*, taught the same.

The eternal *Kosmos*, the Macrocosm, is divided in the Secret Doctrine, like man, the Microcosm, into three Principles and four Vehicles,* which in their collectivity are the seven Principles. In the Chaldean or Jewish *Kabalah*, the Kosmos is divided into seven worlds: the Original, the Intelligible, the Celestial, the Elementary, the Lunar (Astral), the Infernal (Kâma-loka or Hades), and the Temporal (of man). In the Chaldæan system it is in the Intelligible World, the second, that appear the "Seven Angels of the Presence," or the Sephiroth (the three higher ones being, in fact, one, and also the sum total of all). They are also the "Builders" of the Eastern Doctrine: and it is only in the third, the celestial world, that the seven planets and our solar system are built by the seven Planetary Angels, the planets becoming their visible bodies. Hence—as correctly stated —if the universe as a whole is formed out of the Eternal *One* Substance or Essence, it is not that everlasting Essence, the Absolute Deity, that builds it into shape; this is done by the first Rays, the Angels or Dhyân Chohans, that emanate from the One Element, which becoming periodically Light and Darkness, remains eternally, in its own Principle, the one unknown yet existing Reality.

A learned Western Kabalist, Mr. S. L. MacGregor Mathers, whose reasoning and conclusions will be the more above suspicion since he is untrained in Eastern Philosophy and unacquainted with the Secret Teachings, writes on the first verse of *Genesis* in an unpublished essay:

* The three *root*-principles are, exoterically: Man, Soul, and Spirit (meaning by "man" the intelligent personality), and esoterically: Life, Soul, and Spirit; the four vehicles are Body, Astral double, Animal (or human) Soul, and Divine Soul (Sthûla-Sharîra, Linga-Sharîra, Kâma-rûpa, and Buddhi, the vehicle of Âtma or Spirit). Or, to make it still clearer: (1) the *Seventh Principle* has for its vehicle the Sixth (Buddhi); (2) the vehicle of Manas is Kâma-rûpa; (3) that of [illegible] is the Linga-Sharîra (the "double" of man; the Linga-Sharîra proper can never leave the body till death; that which appears is an astral body, reflecting the physical body and serving as a vehicle for the human soul, or intelligence); and (4) the Body, the physical vehicle of all the above collectively. The Occultist recognises the same order as existing for the cosmical totality, the psycho-cosmical Universe.

"*Berasheth Bara* Elohim—"In the beginning the Elohim created!" Who are these Elohim of *Genesis?*

"*Va-Yivra Elohim Ath Ha-Adam Be-Tzalmo, Be-Tzelem Elohim Bara Otho, Zakhar Vnqebah Bara Otham*—"And the Elohim created the Adam in Their own Image, in the Image of the Elohim created They them, Male and Female created They them!" Who are they, the Elohim? The ordinary English translation of the *Bible* renders the word Elohim by "God:" it translates a *plural* noun by a *singular* one. The only excuse brought forward for this is the somewhat lame one that the word is certainly plural, but is not to be used in a plural sense: that it is "a plural denoting excellence." But this is only an assumption whose value may be justly gauged by *Genesis* i. 26, translated in the orthodox Biblical version thus: "And God [Elohim] said, 'Let us make man in our own image, after our likeness.'" Here is a distinct admission of the fact that "Elohim" is *not* a "plural of excellence," but a plural noun denoting more than one being.*

What, then, is the proper translation of "Elohim," and to whom is it referable? "Elohim" is not only a plural, but a *feminine plural!* And yet the translators of the *Bible* have rendered it by a *masculine singular!* Elohim is the plural of the feminine noun El-h, for the final letter, -h, marks the gender. It, however, instead of forming the plural in -oth, takes the usual termination of the masculine plural, which is -im.

Although in the great majority of cases the nouns of both genders take the terminations appropriated to them respectively, there are yet many masculines which form the plural in -oth, as well as feminine which form it in -im while some nouns of each gender take alternately both. It must be observed, however, that the termination of the plural does not affect its gender, which remains the same as in the singular. . . . .

To find the real meaning of the symbolism involved in this word Elohim we must go to that key of Jewish Esoteric Doctrine, the little-known and less-understood *Kabalah*. There we shall find that this word represents two united masculine and feminine Potencies, co-equal and co-eternal, conjoined in everlasting union for the maintenance of the Universe—the great Father and Mother of Nature, into whom the Eternal One conforms himself before the Universe can subsist. For the teaching of the *Kabalah* is that before the Deity conformed himself thus—*i.e.* as

---

* St. Denys, the Areopagite, the supposed contemporary of St. Paul, his co-disciple, and first Bishop of St. Denis, near Paris, teaches that the bulk of the "work of creation" was performed by the "*Seven* Spirits of the Presence"—God's *co-operators*, owing to a participation of the divinity in them. (*Hierarch.*, p. 196.) And Saint Augustine also thinks that "things were rather created in the angelic minds than in Nature, that is to say, that the angels perceived and knew them (all things) in their thoughts before they could spring forth into actual existence." (*Vid. De Genesis ad Litteram* p., II.) (Summarised from De Mirville, Vol. II., pp. 337-338.) Thus the early Christian Fathers, even a non-initiate like St. Augustine, ascribed the creation of the visible world to Angels, or Secondary Powers, while St. Denys not only specifies these as the "*Seven* Spirits of the Presence," but shows them owing their power to the informing divine energy—Fohat in the Secret Doctrine. But the theological darkness which caused the Western races to cling so desperately to the *Geo*-centric System, made them also neglect and despise all those fragments of the true Religion which would have deprived them and the little globe they took for the centre of the Universe of the signal honour of having been expressly "created" by the One, Secondless, Infinite God!

male and female—the Worlds of the Universe could not subsist, or, in the words of *Genesis*, that "the earth was formless and void." Thus, then, is the conformation of the Elohim, the end of the Formless and the Void and the Darkness, for only after that conformation can the *Ruach Elohim*—the "Spirit of the Elohim"—vibrate upon the countenance of the Waters. But this is a very small part of the information which the Initiate can derive from the *Kabalah* concerning the dual *Elohim*.

Attention must here be called to the confusion—if not worse—which reigns in the Western interpretations of the *Kabalah*. *The Eternal One* is said to conform himself into two: the Great Father and Mother of Nature. To begin with, it is a horribly anthropomorphic conception to apply terms implying sexual distinction to the earliest and first differentiations of the One. And it is even more erroneous to identify these first differentiations—the Purusha and Prakriti of Indian Philosophy—with the Elohim, the creative powers here spoken of, and to ascribe to these (to our intellects) unimaginable abstractions the formation and construction of this visible world, full of pain, sin and sorrow. In truth, the "creation by the Elohim" spoken of herein is but a much later "creation," and the Elohim far from being supreme, or even exalted powers in Nature, are only lower Angels. This was the teaching of the Gnostics, the most philosophical of all the early Christian Churches. They taught that the imperfections of the world were due to the imperfection of its Architects or Builders—the imperfect, and therefore inferior, Angels. The Hebrew Elohim correspond to the Prajâpati of the Hindus, and it is shown elsewhere from the Esoteric interpretation of the Purânas that the Prajâpati were the fashioners of man's material and astral form only; that they could not give him intelligence or reason, and therefore in symbolical language they "failed to create man." But, not to repeat what the reader can find elsewhere in this work, his attention needs only to be called to the fact that "creation" in this passage is not the Primary Creation, and that the Elohim are not "*God*," nor even the higher Planetary Spirits, but the Architects of this visible physical planet and of man's material body, or encasement.

A fundamental doctrine of the *Kabalah* is that the gradual development of the Deity from negative to positive Existence is symbolized by the gradual development of the Ten Numbers of the denary scale of numeration, from the Zero, through the Unity, into the Plurality. This is the doctrine of the Sephiroth, or Emanations.

For the inward and concealed Negative Form concentrates a centre which is the primal Unity. But the Unity is one and indivisible: it can neither be increased by multiplication nor decreased by division, for $1 \times 1 = 1$, and no more; and $1 \div 1 = 1$, and no less. And it is this changelessness of the Unity, or Monad, which makes it a fitting type of the One and Changeless Deity. It answers thus to the Christian idea of God the Father, for as the Unity is the parent of the other numbers, so is the Deity the Father of All.

The philosophical Eastern mind would never fall into the error which the *connotation* of these words implies. With them the "One and Changeless"—Parabrahman—the Absolute All and One, cannot be conceived as standing in any *relation* to things finite and conditioned, and hence they would never use such terms as these, which in their very essence imply such a relation. Do they, then, absolutely sever man from God? On the contrary. They feel a closer union than the Western mind has done in calling God the "Father of All," for they know that in his immortal essence man *is* himself the Changeless, Secondless One.

But we have just said that the Unity is one and changeless by either multiplication or division; how then is two, the Duad, formed? By reflection. For, unlike Zero, the Unity is partly definable—that is, in its positive aspect; and the definition creates an Eikon or Eidolon of itself which, together with itself, forms a Duad; and thus the number two is to a certain extent analogous to the Christian idea of the Son as the Second Person. And as the Monad vibrates, and recoils into the Darkness of the Primary Thought, so is the Duad left as its vice-gerent and representative, and thus co-equal with the Positive Duad is the Triune Idea, the number three, co-equal and co-eternal with the Duad in the bosom of the Unity, yet, as it were, proceeding therefrom in the numerical conception of its sequence.

This explanation would seem to imply that Mr. Mathers is aware that this "creation" is not the truly divine or primary one, since the Monad—the first manifestation on *our* plane of objectivity—"recoils into the Darkness of the Primal Thought," *i.e.*, into the subjectivity of the first divine Creation.

And this, again, also partly answers to the Christian idea of the Holy Ghost, and of the whole three forming a Trinity in unity. This also explains the fact in geometry of the three right lines being the smallest number which will make a plane rectilineal figure, while two can never enclose a space, being powerless and without effect till completed by the number Three. These three first numbers of the decimal scale the Qabalists call by the names of Kether, the Crown, Chokmah, Wisdom, and Binah, Understanding; and they furthermore associate with them these divine names: with the Unity, Eheich, "I exist;" with the Duad, Yah; and with the Triad, Elohim; they especially also call the Duad, Abba—the Father, and the Triad, Aima—the Mother, whose eternal conjunction is symbolized in the word Elohim.

But what especially strikes the student of the *Kabalah* is the malicious persistency with which the translators of the *Bible* have jealously crowded out of sight and suppressed every reference to the feminine form of the Deity. They have, as we have just seen, translated the feminine plural "Elohim," by the masculine singular "God." But they have done more than this; they have carefully hidden the fact that the word Ruach—the "Spirit"—is feminine, and that consequently the Holy Ghost of the *New Testament* is a feminine Potency. How many Christians are cognizant of the fact that in the account of the Incarnation in *Luke* i. 35, two divine Potencies are mentioned?

"The Holy Ghost shall come upon thee, and the Power of the Highest shall overshadow thee." The Holy Ghost (the feminine Potency) descends, and the Power of the Highest (the masculine Potency) is united therewith. "Therefore also that holy thing which shall be born of thee shall be called the Son of God"—of the Elohim namely, seeing that these two Potencies descend.

In the *Sepher Yetzirah*, or *Book of Formation*, we read:

"One is She the Ruach Elohim Chiim—(Spirit of the Living Elohim) ... Voice, Spirit, and Word; and this is She, the Spirit of the Holy One." Here again we see the intimate connection which exists between the Holy Spirit and the Elohim. Furthermore, farther on in this same *Book of Formation*—which, be it remembered, one of the oldest of the Kabalistical Books, and whose authorship is ascribed to Abraham the Patriarch—we shall find the idea of a Feminine Trinity in the first place, from whom a masculine Trinity proceeds; or, as it is said in the text: "Three Mothers whence proceed three Fathers." And yet this double Trinity forms, as it were, but one complete Trinity. Again it is worthy of note that the Second and Third Sephiroth (Wisdom and Understanding) are both distinguished by feminine names, Chokmah and Binah, notwithstanding that to the former more particularly the masculine idea, and to the latter the feminine, are attributed under the titles of Abba and Aima (or Father and Mother). This Aima (the Great Mother) is magnificently symbolized in the twelfth chapter of the *Apocalypse*, which is undoubtedly one of the most Kabalistical books in the *Bible*. In fact, without the Kabalistical keys its meaning is utterly unintelligible.

Now, in the Hebrew, as in the Greek, alphabet, there are no distinct numeral characters, and consequently each letter has a certain numerical value attached to it. From this circumstance results the important fact that every Hebrew word constitutes a number, and every number a word. This is referred to in the *Revelations* (xiii. 18) in mentioning the "number of the beast"! In the *Kabalah* words of equal numerical values are supposed to have a certain explanatory connection with each other. This forms the science of Gematria, which is the first division of the Literal *Kabalah*. Furthermore, each letter of the Hebrew alphabet had for the Initiates of the *Kabalah* a certain hieroglyphical value and meaning which, rightly applied, gave to each word the value of a mystical sentence; and this again was variable according to the relative positions of the letters with regard to each other. From these various Kabalistical points of view let us now examine this word Elohim.

First then we can divide the word into the two words, which signify "The Feminine Divinity of the Waters;" compare with the Greek Aphrodite, "sprung from the foam of the sea." Again it is divisible into the "Mighty One, Star of the Sea," or "the Mighty One breathing forth the Spirit upon the Waters." Also by combination of the letters we get "the Silent Power of Iah." And again, "My God, the Former of the Universe," for *Mah* is a secret Kabalistical name applied to the idea of Formation. Also we obtain "Who is my God." Furthermore "the Mother in Iah."

The total number is 1 + 30 + 5 + 10 + 40 = 86 = "Violent heat," or "the Power of Fire." If we add together the three middle letters we obtain 45, and the first and last letters yield 41, making thus "the Mother of Formation." Lastly, we shall find the two divine names "El" and "Yah," together with the letter *m*, which signifies "Water," for Mem, the name of this letter, means "water."

If we divide it into its component letters and take them as hieroglyphical signs we shall have:

"Will perfected through Sacrifice progressing through successive Transformation by Inspiration."

The last few paragraphs of the above, in which the word "Elohim" is Kabalistically analyzed, show conclusively enough that the Elohim are not one, nor two, nor even a trinity, but a Host—the army of the creative powers.

The Christian Church, in making of Jehovah—one of these very Elohim—the one Supreme God, has introduced hopeless confusion into the celestial hierarchy, in spite of the volumes written by Thomas Aquinas and his school on the subject. The only explanation to be found in all their treatises on the nature and essence of the numberless classes of celestial beings mentioned in the *Bible*—Archangels, Thrones, Seraphim, Cherubim, Messengers, etc.—is that "The angelic host is God's militia." They are "Gods *the creatures*," while he is "God *the Creator*;" but of their true functions—of their actual place in the economy of Nature—not one word is said. They are

More brilliant than the flames, more rapid than the wind, and they live in love and harmony, mutually enlightening each other, feeding on bread and a mystic beverage—the communion wine and water?—surrounding as with *a river of fire* the throne of the Lamb, and veiling their faces with their wings. This throne of love and glory they leave only to carry to the stars, the earth, the kingdoms and all the sons of God, their brothers and pupils, in short, to all creatures *like themselves* the divine influence. . . . . As to their number, it is that of the great army of Heaven (Sabaoth), more numerous than the stars. . . . . Theology shows us these rational luminaries, each constituting a species, and containing in their natures such or another position of Nature: covering immense space, though of a determined area; residing—incorporeal though they are—within circumscribed limits; . . . more rapid than light or thunderbolt, disposing of all the elements of Nature, providing at will inexplicable mirages [illusions?], objective and subjec-

and sole Deity, so that the attributes of that God become their property. These great Gods proclaim themselves uncreate. . . . Neith is "that which is," as Jehovah;* Thoth is self-created† without having been begotten, etc. Judaism annihilating these potencies before the grandeur of its God, they cease to be simply Powers, like Philo's Archangels, like the Sephiroth of the *Kabalah*, like the Ogdoades of the Gnostics—they merge together and become transformed into God himself.‡

Jehovah is thus, as the *Kabalah* teaches, at best but the "Heavenly Man," Adam Kadmon, used by the self-created Spirit, the Logos, as a chariot, a vehicle in His descent towards manifestation in the phenomenal world.

Such are the teachings of the Archaic Wisdom, nor can they be repudiated even by the orthodox Christian, if he be sincere and open-minded in the study of his own Scripture. For if he reads St. Paul's *Epistles* carefully he will find that the Secret Doctrine and the *Kabalah* are fully admitted by the "Apostle of the Gentiles." The Gnosis which he appears to condemn is no less for him than for Plato, "the supreme knowledge of the truth and of the One Being;"§ for what St. Paul condemns is not the true, but only the false, Gnosis and its abuses: otherwise how could he use the language of a Platonist *pur sang?* The Ideas, types (Archai), of the Greek Philosophers; the Intelligences of Pythagoras; the Æons or Emanations of the Pantheists; the Logos or Word, Chief of these Intelligences; the Sophia or Wisdom; the Demiurgos, the Builder of the world under the direction of the Father, the Unmanifested Logos, from which He emanates; Ain-Suph, the Unknown of the Infinite; the angelic Periods; the Seven Spirits who are the representatives of the *Seven* of all the older cosmogonies—are all to be found in his writings, recognized by the Church as canonical and divinely inspired. Therein, too, may be recognized the Depths of Ahriman, Rector of this our World, the "God of this World;" the Pleroma of the Intelligences; the Archontes of the air; the Principalities, the Kabalistic Metatron; and they can easily be identified again in the Roman Catholic writers when read in the original Greek and Latin texts, English translations giving but a very poor idea of the real contents of these.

* Neith is Aditi, evidently.

† The Self-created Logos, Nârâyana, Purushottama, and others.

‡ *Moïse et Apis*, pp. 32-35. Quoted by De Mirville.

§ See *Republic*, I. vi.

SECTION XXIII.

WHAT THE OCCULTISTS AND KABALISTS HAVE TO SAY.

THE *Zohar*, an unfathomable store of hidden wisdom and mystery, is very often appealed to by Roman Catholic writers. A very learned Rabbi, now the Chevalier Drach, having been converted to Roman Catholicism, and being a great Hebraist, thought fit to step into the shoes of Picus de Mirandola and John Reuchlin, and to assure his new co-religionists that the *Zohar* contained in it pretty nearly all the dogmas of Catholicism. It is not our province to show here how far he has succeeded or failed; only to bring one instance of his explanations and preface it with the following:

The *Zohar*, as already shown, is not a genuine production of the Hebrew mind. It is the repository and compendium of the oldest doctrines of the East, transmitted orally at first, and then written down in independent treatises during the Captivity at Babylon, and finally brought together by Rabbi Simeon Ben Iochai, toward the beginning of the Christian era. As Mosaic cosmogony was born under a new form in Mesopotamian countries, so the *Zohar* was a vehicle in which were focussed rays from the light of Universal Wisdom. Whatever likenesses are found between it and the Christian teachings, the compilers of the *Zohar* never had Christ in their minds. Were it otherwise there would not be one single Jew of the Mosaic law left in the world by this time. Again, if one is to accept literally what the *Zohar* says, then any religion under the sun may find corroboration in its symbols and allegorical sayings; and this, simply because this work is the echo of the primitive truths, and every creed is founded on some of these; the *Zohar* being but a veil of the Secret Doctrine. This is so evident that we have only to point to the said ex-Rabbi, the Chevalier Drach, to prove the fact.

In Part III, fol. 87 (col. 346th) the *Zohar* treats of the Spirit guiding the Sun, its Rector, explaining that it is not the Sun itself that is meant thereby, but the Spirit "on, or *under*" the Sun. Drach is anxious to show that it was Christ who was meant by that "Sun," or the Solar Spirit therein. In his comment upon that passage which refers to the Solar Spirit as "that stone which the builders rejected," he asserts most positively that this

> Sun-stone (*pierre soleil*) is identical with Christ, who was that stone,

and that therefore

> The sun is undeniably (*sans contredit*) the second hypostasis of the Deity,* or Christ.

If this be true, then the Vaidic or pre-Vaidic Âryans, Chaldeans and Egyptians, like all Occultists past, present, and future, Jews included, have been Christians from all eternity. If this be not so, then modern Church Christianity is Paganism pure and simple exoterically, and transcendental and practical Magic, or Occultism, Esoterically. For this "stone" has a manifold significance, a dual existence, with gradations, a regular progression and retrogression. It is a "mystery" indeed.

The Occultists are quite ready to agree with St. Chrysostom, that the infidels—the *profane*, rather—

> Being blinded by sun-light, thus lose sight of the true Sun in the contemplation of the false one.

But if that Saint, and along with him now the Hebraist Drach, chose to see in the *Zohar* and the Kabalistic Sun "the *second* hypostasis," this is no reason why all others should be blinded by them. The mystery of the Sun is the grandest perhaps, of all the innumerable mysteries of Occultism. A Gordian knot, truly, but one that cannot be severed with the double-edged sword of scholastic casuistry. It is a true *deo dignus vindice nodus*, and can be untied only by the Gods. The meaning of this is plain, and every Kabalist will understand it.

Contra solem ne loquaris was not said by Pythagoras with regard to the visible Sun. It was the "Sun of Initiation" that was meant, in its triple form—two of which are the "Day-Sun" and the "Night-Sun."

If behind the physical luminary there were no mystery that people sensed instinctively, why should every nation, from the primitive

* *Harmonie entre l'Église et la Synagogue*, t. II., p. 427, by the Chevalier Drach. See De Mirville iv. 38, 39.

peoples down to the Parsis of to-day, have turned towards the Sun during prayers? The Solar Trinity is not Mazdean, but is universal, and is as old as man. All the temples in Antiquity were invariably made to face the Sun, their portals to open to the East. See the old temples of Memphis and Baalbec, the Pyramids of the Old and of the New (?) Worlds, the Round Towers of Ireland, and the Serapeum of Egypt. The Initiates alone could give a philosophical explanation of this, and a reason for it—its mysticism notwithstanding—were only the world ready to receive it, which alas! it is not. The last of the Solar Priests in Europe was the Imperial Initiate, Julian, now called the Apostate.* He tried to benefit the world by revealing at least a portion of the great mystery of the τριπλάσιος and—*he died*. "There are three in one," he said of the Sun—the central Sun† being a precaution of Nature: the first is the universal cause of all, Sovereign Good and perfection; the Second Power is paramount Intelligence, having dominion over all reasonable beings, νοεροῖς; the third is the visible Sun. The pure energy of solar intelligence proceeds from the luminous seat occupied by our Sun in the centre of heaven, that pure energy being the Logos of our system; the "Mysterious Word Spirit produces all through the Sun, and never operates through any other medium," says Hermes Trismegistus. For it is *in* the Sun, more than in any other heavenly body that the [unknown] Power placed the

---

* Julian died for the same crime as Socrates. Both divulged a portion of the solar mystery, the heliocentric system being only a part of what was given during Initiation—one consciously, the other unconsciously, the Greek Sage never having been initiated. It was not the real solar system that was preserved in such secrecy, but the mysteries connected with the Sun's constitution. Socrates was sentenced to death by earthly and worldly judges; Julian died a violent death because the hitherto protecting hand was withdrawn from him, and, no longer shielded by it, he was simply left to his destiny or Karma. For the student of Occultism there is a suggestive difference between the two kinds of death. Another memorable instance of the unconscious divulging of secrets pertaining to mysteries is that of the poet, P. Ovidius Naso, who, like Socrates, had not been initiated. In his case, the Emperor Augustus, who was an Initiate, mercifully changed the penalty of death into banishment to Tomos on the Euxine. This sudden change from unbounded royal favour to banishment has been a fruitful scheme of speculation to classical scholars not initiated into the Mysteries. They have quoted Ovid's own lines to show that it was some great and heinous immorality of the Emperor of which Ovid had become unwillingly cognizant. The inexorable law of the death penalty, always following upon the revelation of any portion of the Mysteries to the profane, was unknown to them. Instead of seeing the amiable and merciful act of the Emperor in its true light, they have made it an occasion for traducing his moral character. The poet's own words can be no evidence, because as he was not an Initiate, it could not be explained to him in what his offence consisted. There have been comparatively modern instances of poets unconsciously revealing in their verses so much of the hidden knowledge as to make even Initiates suppose them to be fellow-Initiates, and come to talk to them on the subject. This only shows that the sensitive poetic temperament is sometimes so far transported beyond the bounds of ordinary sense as to get glimpses into what has been impressed on the Astral Light. In the *Light of Asia* there are two passages that might make an Initiate of the first degree think that Mr. Edwin Arnold had been initiated himself in the Himâlyan *Ashrams*, but this is not so.

† A proof that Julian was acquainted with the heliocentric system.

seat of its habitation. Only neither Hermes Trismegistus nor Julian (an initiated Occultist), nor any other, meant by this Unknown Deity Jehovah, or Jupiter. They referred to the cause that produced all the manifested "great Gods" or Demiurgi (the Hebrew God included) of our system. Nor was our visible, *material* Sun meant, for the latter was only the manifested symbol. Philolaus the Pythagorean, explains and completes Trismegistus by saying:

> The Sun is a mirror of fire, the splendour of whose flames by their reflection in that mirror [the Sun] is poured upon us, and that splendour we call image.

It is evident that Philolaus referred to the central spiritual Sun, whose beams and effulgence are only mirrored by our central Star, the Sun. This is as clear to the Occultists as it was to the Pythagoreans. As for the profane of pagan antiquity, it was, of course, the physical Sun that was the "highest God" for them, as it seems—if Chevalier Drach's view be accepted—to have now virtually become for the modern Roman Catholics. If words mean anything, the statement made by the Chevalier Drach that "this sun is, undeniably, the second hypostasis of the Deity," imply what we say; as "this Sun" refers to the Kabalistic Sun, and "hypostasis" means substance or subsistence of the Godhead or Trinity—distinctly personal. As the author, being an ex-Rabbi, thoroughly versed in Hebrew, and in the mysteries of the *Zohar*, ought to know the value of words; and as, moreover, in writing this, he was bent upon reconciling "the seeming contradictions," as he puts it, between Judaism and Christianity—the fact becomes quite evident.

But all this pertains to questions and problems which will be solved naturally and in the course of the development of the doctrine. The Roman Catholic Church stands accused, not of worshipping under other names the Divine Beings worshipped by all nations in antiquity, but of declaring idolatrous, not only the Pagans ancient and modern, but every Christian nation that has freed itself from the Roman yoke. The accusation brought against herself by more than one man of Science, of worshipping the stars like true Sabæans of old, stands to this day uncontradicted, yet no star-worshipper has ever addressed his adoration to the material stars and planets, as will be shown before the last page of this work is written; none the less is it true that those Philosophers alone who studied Astrology and Magic knew that the last word of those sciences was to be sought in, and expected from, the Occult forces emanating from those constellations.

SECTION XXIV.

Modern Kabalists in Science and Occult Astronomy.

There is a physical, an astral, and a super-astral Universe in the three chief divisions of the *Kabalah*; as there are terrestrial, super-terrestrial, and spiritual Beings. The "Seven Planetary Spirits" may be ridiculed by Scientists to their hearts' content, yet the need of intelligent ruling and guiding Forces is so much felt to this day that scientific men and specialists, who will not hear of Occultism or of ancient systems, find themselves obliged to generate in their inner consciousness some kind of semi-mystical system. Metcalf's "sun-force" theory, and that of Zaliwsky, a learned Pole, which made Electricity the Universal Force and placed its storehouse in the Sun,* were revivals of the Kabalistic teachings. Zaliwsky tried to prove that Electricity, producing "the most powerful, attractive, calorific, and luminous effects," was present in the physical constitution of the Sun and explained its peculiarities. This is very near the Occult teaching. It is only by admitting the gaseous nature of the Sun-reflector, and the powerful Magnetism and Electricity of the solar attraction and repulsion, that one can explain (*a*) the evident absence of any waste of power and luminosity in the Sun—inexplicable by the ordinary laws of combustion; and (*b*) the behaviour of the planets, so often contradicting every accepted rule of weight and gravity. And Zaliwsky makes this "solar electricity" "*differ from anything known on earth.*"

Father Secchi may be suspected of having sought to introduce

> *Forces of quite a new order* and quite foreign to gravitation, which he had discovered in Space,†

---

* *La Gravitation par l'Electricité*, p. 7, quoted by De Mirville, iv. 156.

† De Mirville, iv. 157.

in order to reconcile Astronomy with theological Astronomy. But Nagy, a member of the Hungarian Academy of Sciences, was no clerical, and yet he develops a theory on the necessity of intelligent Forces whose complacency "would lend itself to all the whims of the comets." He suspects that:

> Notwithstanding all the actual researches on the rapidity of light—that amusing *product of an unknown force* . . . which we see too frequently to understand—that light is motionless in reality.*

C. E. Love, the well-known railway builder and engineer in France, tired of blind forces, made all the (then) "imponderable agents"—now called "forces"—subordinates of Electricity, and declares the latter to be an

> Intelligence—albeit molecular in nature and material.†

In the author's opinion these Forces are atomistic agents, endowed with intelligence, spontaneous will, and motion,‡ and he thus, like the Kabalists, makes the causal Forces substantial, while the Forces that act on this plane are only the effects of the former, as with him matter is eternal, and the Gods also;§ so is the Soul likewise, though it has inherent in itself a still higher Soul [Spirit], preëxistent, endowed with memory, and superior to Electric Force; the latter is subservient to the higher Souls, those superior Souls forcing it to act according to the eternal laws. The concept is rather hazy, but is evidently on the Occult lines. Moreover, the system proposed is entirely pantheistic, and is worked out in a purely scientific volume. Monotheists and Roman Catholics fall foul of it, of course; but one who believes in the Planetary Spirits and who endows Nature with living Intelligences, must always expect this.

In this connection, however, it is curious that after the moderns have so laughed at the ignorance of the ancients,

> Who, knowing only of seven planets [yet having an ogdoad which *did not* include the earth!], invented therefore seven Spirits to fit in with the number,

Babinet should have vindicated the "superstition" unconsciously to himself. In the *Revue des Deux Mondes* this eminent French Astronomer writes:

---

* *Memoir on the Solar System*, p. 7, De Mirville, iv. 157.

† *Essai sur l'Identité des Agents Producteurs du Son, de la Lumière*, etc., p. 15, *Ibid.*

‡ *Ibid.*, p. 218.

§ Summarised from *Ibid.*, p. 223. De Mirville, iv. 158.

The ogdoad of the Ancients included the earth [which is an error], *i.e.*, eight, or seven according to whether or not the earth was comprised in the number.*

De Mirville assures his readers that:

M. Babinet was telling me but a few days ago that we had in reality only eight big planets, including the earth, and so many small ones between Mars and Jupiter . . . . Herschel offering to call all those beyond the seven primary planets asteroids! †

There is a problem to be solved in this connection. How do Astronomers know that Neptune is a planet, or even that it is a body belonging to our system? Being found on the very confines of our Planetary World, so called, the latter was arbitrarily expanded to receive it; but what really mathematical and infallible proof have Astronomers that it is (*a*) a planet, and (*b*) one of *our* planets? None at all! It is at such an immeasurable distance from us, the

Apparent diameter of the sun being to Neptune but one-fortieth of the sun's apparent diameter to us,

and it is so dim and hazy when seen through the best telescope that it looks like an astronomical romance to call it one of our planets. Neptune's heat and light are reduced to $\frac{1}{900}$ part of the heat and light received by the earth. His motion and that of his satellites have always looked suspicious. They do not agree—in appearance, at least—with those of the other planets. His system is retrograde, etc. But even the latter abnormal fact resulted only in the creation of new hypotheses by our Astronomers, who forthwith suggested a probable overturn of Neptune, his collision with another body, etc Was Adams' and Leverrier's discovery so welcomed because Neptune was as necessary as was Ether to throw a new glory upon astronomical prevision, upon the certitude of modern scientific data, and principally upon the power of mathematical analysis? It would so appear. A new planet that widens our planetary domain by more than four hundred million leagues is worthy of annexation. Yet, as in the case of terrestrial annexation, scientific authority may be proved "right" only because it has "might." Neptune's motion happens to be dimly perceived: Eureka! it is a planet! A mere motion, however, proves very little. It is now an ascertained fact in Astronomy that there are no absolutely fixed stars in Nature,‡ even though such stars should

* May, 1855. *Ibid.*, p. 139.

† *La Terre et notre Système solaire.* De Mirville, iv. 139.

‡ If, as Sir W. Herschel thought, the so-called fixed stars have resulted from, and owe their origin to nebular combustion, they cannot be fixed any more than is our sun, which was believed to be

continue to exist in astronomical parlance, while they have [illegible] from the scientific imagination. Occultism, however, has a [illegible] theory of its own with regard to Neptune.

Occultism says that if several hypotheses resting on [illegible] tion—which have been accepted only because they have been [illegible] by eminent men of learning—are taken away from the Science [illegible] Modern Astronomy, to which they serve as props, then even the [illegible] sumably universal law of gravitation will be found to be contrary [illegible] most ordinary truths of mechanics. And really one can hardly [illegible] Christians—foremost of all the Roman Catholics—however [illegible] some of these may themselves be, for refusing to quarrel with [illegible] Church for the sake of scientific beliefs. Nor can we even blame [illegible] for accepting in the secresy of their hearts—as some of them [illegible] theological "Virtues" and "Archons" of Darkness, instead of [illegible] blind forces offered them by Science.

> Never can there be intervention of any sort in the marshalling and the [illegible] precession of the celestial bodies! The law of gravitation is the law of [illegible] ever witnessed a stone rising in the air against gravitation? The permanence [illegible] the universal law is shown in the behaviour of the sidereal worlds and globes [illegible] nally faithful to their primitive orbits; never wandering beyond their respective paths. Nor is there any intervention needed, as it could only be [illegible] Whether the first sidereal incipient rotation took place owing to an inter[illegible] chance, or to the spontaneous development of latent primordial forces; or [illegible] whether that impulse was given once for all by God or Gods—it does not make the slightest difference. At this stage of cosmic evolution no intervention, [illegible] inferior, is admissible. Were any to take place, the universal clock-work [illegible] stop, and Kosmos would fall into pieces.

Such are stray sentences, pearls of wisdom, fallen from time to time, from scientific lips, and now chosen at random to illustrate a [illegible] We lift our diminished heads and look heavenward. Such seems to [illegible] the fact: worlds, suns, and stars, the shining myriads of the heavenly hosts, remind the Poet of an infinite, shoreless ocean, whereon [illegible] swiftly numberless squadrons of ships, millions upon millions of cruisers, large and small, crossing each other, whirling and gyrating [illegible]

---

motionless and is now found to rotate around its axis every twenty-five days. As the [illegible] nearest to the sun, however, is eight-thousand times farther away from him than is Neptune, the illusions furnished by the telescopes must be also eight-thousand times as great. We will therefore leave the question at rest, repeating only what A. Maury said in his work (*La Terre et l'Homme*, published in 1858): "It is utterly impossible, so far, to decide anything concerning Neptune's constitution, analogy alone authorising us to ascribe to him a rotary motion like that of other planets" (De Mirville, iv. 140).

every direction; and Science teaches us, that though they be without rudder or compass or any beacon to guide them, they are nevertheless secure from collision—almost secure, at any rate, save in chance accidents—as the whole celestial machine is built upon and guided by an immutable, albeit blind, law, and by constant and accelerating force or forces. "Built upon" by whom? "By self-evolution," is the answer. Moreover, as dynamics teach that

> A body in motion tends to continue in the same state of relative rest or motion unless acted upon by some external force,

this force has to be regarded as self-generated—even if not eternal, since this would amount to the recognition of perpetual motion—and so well self-calculated and self-adjusted as to last from the beginning to the end of Kosmos. But "self-generation" has still to generate from something, generation *ex-nihilo* being as contrary to reason as it is to Science. Thus we are placed once more between the horns of a dilemma: are we to believe in perpetual motion or in self-generation *ex-nihilo*? And if in neither, who or what is that something, which first produced that force or those forces?

There are such things in mechanics as superior levers, which give the impulse and act upon secondary or inferior levers. The former, however, need an impulse and occasional renovation, otherwise they would themselves very soon stop and fall back into their original status. What is the external force which puts and retains them in motion? Another dilemma!

As to the law of cosmical *non-intervention*, it could be justified only in one case, namely, if the celestial mechanism were perfect; but it is not. The so-called unalterable motions of celestial bodies alter and change incessantly; they are very often disturbed, and the wheels of even the sidereal locomotive itself occasionally jump off their invisible rails, as may be easily proved. Otherwise why should Laplace speak of the probable occurrence at some future time of an out-and-out reform in the arrangement of the planets;* or Lagrange maintain the gradual narrowing of the orbits; or our modern Astronomers, again, declare that the fuel in the sun is slowly disappearing? If the laws and forces which govern the behaviour of the celestial bodies are immutable, such modifications and wearing-out of substance or fuel, of force and fluids, would be impossible; yet they are not denied. There-

* *Exposition du vrai System du Monde*, p. 282.

fore one has to suppose that such modifications will have to rely upon the laws of forces, which will have to self-regenerate themselves the more on such occasions, thus producing an astral antinomy, and a kind of physical palinomy, since, as Laplace says, one would then see them disobeying themselves and reacting in a way contrary to all their attributes and properties.

Newton felt very uncomfortable about the moon. Her behaviour in progressively narrowing the circumference of her orbit around the earth made him nervous, lest it should end one day in our satellite falling upon the earth. The world, he confessed, needed repairing, and that very often.* In this he was corroborated by Herschel.† He speaks of real and quite considerable deviations, besides those which are only apparent, but gets some consolation from his conviction that somebody or something will probably see to things.

We may be answered that the personal beliefs of some pious Astronomers, however great they may be as scientific characters, are no proofs of the actual existence and presence in space of intelligent supramundane Beings, of either Gods or Angels. It is the behaviour of the stars and planets themselves that has to be analysed and inferences must be drawn therefrom. Renan asserts that nothing that we know of the sidereal bodies warrants the idea of the presence of any Intelligence, whether internal or external to them.

Let us see, says Reynaud, if this is a fact, or only one more empty scientific assumption.

> The orbits traversed by the planets are far from being immutable. They are, on the contrary, subject to perpetual mutation in position, as in form. Elongations, contractions, and orbital widenings, oscillations from right to left, slackening and quickening of speed . . . . and all this on a plane which seems to vacillate.‡

As is very pertinently observed by des Mousseux:

> Here is a path having little of the mathematical and mechanical precision claimed for it; for we know of no clock which, having gone slow for several minutes should catch up the right time *of itself* and *without a turn of the key*.

So much for blind law and force. As for the physical impossibility—a miracle indeed in the sight of Science—of a stone raised in the air against the law of gravitation, this is what Babinet—the deadliest

---

* See the passage quoted by Herschel in *Natural Philosophy*, p. 105. De Mirville, iv. 165.

† *Loc. cit.*

‡ *Terre et Ciel*, p. 28. *Ibid.*

enemy and opponent of the phenomena of levitation—(cited by Arago) says:

Everyone knows the theory of *bolides* [meteors] and aerolithes. . . . In Connecticut an immense aerolith was seen [a mass of eighteen hundred feet in diameter], bombarding a whole American zone and returning to the spot [in mid-air] from which it had started.*

Thus we find in both of the cases above cited—that of self-correcting planets and of meteors of gigantic size flying back into the air—a "blind force" regulating and resisting the natural tendencies of "blind matter," and even occasionally repairing its mistakes and correcting its failures. This is far more miraculous and even "extravagant," one would say, than any "Angel-guided" Element.

Bold is he who laughs at the idea of Von Haller, who declares that:

The stars are perhaps an abode of glorious Spirits; as here Vice reigns, there is Virtue master.†

* *Œuvres d'Arago*, vol. i., p. 219; quoted by De Mirville, iii. 462.

† "*Die Sterne sind vielleicht ein Sitz verklarter Geister;*
Wie hier das Laster herrscht, ist dort die Tugend Meister."

SECTION XXV.

Eastern and Western Occultism.

In *The Theosophist* for March, 1886,* in an answer to the "Solar Sphinx," a member of the London Lodge of the Theosophical Society wrote as follows:

> We hold and believe that the revival of Occult Knowledge now in progress will some day demonstrate that the Western system represents ranges of perceptions which the Eastern—at least as expounded in the pages of *The Theosophist*—has yet to attain.†

The writer is not the only person labouring under this erroneous impression. Greater Kabalists than he had said the same in the United States. This only proves that the knowledge possessed by Western Occultists of the true Philosophy, and the "ranges of perceptions" and thought of the Eastern doctrines, is very superficial. This assertion will be easily demonstrated by giving a few instances, instituting comparisons between the two interpretations of one and the same doctrine—the Hermetic Universal Doctrine. It is the more needed since, were

---

* *Op. cit.*, p. 411.

† Whenever Occult doctrines were expounded in the pages of *The Theosophist*, care was taken each time to declare a subject incomplete when the whole could not be given in its fulness, and no writer has ever tried to mislead the reader. As to the Western "ranges of perception" concerning doctrines really Occult, the Eastern Occultists have been made acquainted with them for some time past. Thus they are enabled to assert with confidence that the West may be in possession of Hermetic philosophy as a speculative system of dialectics, the latter being used in the West admirably well, but it lacks entirely the knowledge of Occultism. The genuine Eastern Occultist keeps silent and unknown, never publishes what he knows, and rarely even speaks of it, as he knows too well the penalty of indiscretion.

we to neglect bringing forward such comparisons, our work would be left incomplete.

We may take the late Éliphas Lévi, rightly referred to by another Western Mystic, Mr. Kenneth Mackenzie, as "one of the greatest representatives of modern Occult Philosophy,"* as presumably the best and most learned expounder of the Chaldæan *Kabalah*, and compare his teaching with that of Eastern Occultists. In his unpublished manuscripts and letters, lent to us by a Theosophist, who was for fifteen years his pupil, we had hoped to find that which he was unwilling to publish. What we do find, however, disappoints us greatly. We will take these teachings, then, as containing the essence of Western or Kabalistic Occultism, analyzing and comparing them with the Eastern interpretation as we go on.

Éliphas Lévi teaches correctly, though in language rather too rhapsodically rhetorical to be sufficiently clear to the beginner, that

> Eternal life is Motion equilibrated by the alternate manifestations of force.

But why does he not add that this perpetual motion is independent of the manifested Forces at work? He says:

> Chaos is the Tohu-vah-bohu of perpetual motion and the sum total of primordial matter;

and he fails to add that Matter is "primordial" only at the beginning of every new reconstruction of the Universe matter *in abscondito*, as it is called by the Alchemists, is eternal, indestructible, without beginning or end. It is regarded by Eastern Occultists as the eternal Root of all, the Mûlaprakriti of the Vedântin, and the Svabhâvat of the Buddhist, the Divine Essence, in short, or Substance; the radiations from This are periodically aggregated into graduated forms, from pure Spirit to gross Matter; the Root, or Space, is in its abstract presence the Deity Itself, the Ineffable and Unknown One Cause.

Ain-Suph with him also is the Boundless, the infinite and One Unity, secondless and causeless as Parabrahman. Ain-Suph is the indivisible point, and therefore, as "being everywhere and nowhere," is the absolute All. It is also "Darkness" because it is absolute Light, and the Root of the seven fundamental Cosmic Principles. Yet Éliphas Lévi, by simply stating that "Darkness was upon the face of the Earth," fails to show (*a*) that "Darkness" in this sense is Deity Itself, and he is

* See *The Royal Masonic Cyclopædia*, art. "Sepher Jetzirah."

therefore withholding the only philosophical solution of this problem for the human mind; and (*b*) he allows the unwary student to believe that by "Earth" our own little globe—an atom in the Universe—is meant. In short, this teaching does not embrace the Occult Cosmogony, but deals simply with Occult Geology and the formation of our own tiny speck. This is further shown by his making a *résumé* of the Sephirothal Tree in this wise:

God is harmony, the astronomy of Powers and Unity outside of the World.

This seems to suggest (*a*) that he teaches the existence of an extra-cosmic God, thus limiting and conditioning both the Kosmos and its divine Infinity and Omnipresence, which cannot be extraneous to or outside of one single atom; and (*b*) that by skipping the whole of the pre-cosmic period—the manifested Kosmos here being meant—the very root of Occult teaching, he explains only the Kabalistic meaning of the dead-letter of the *Bible* and *Genesis*, leaving its spirit and essence untouched. Surely the "ranges of perception" of the Western mind will not be greatly enlarged by such a limited teaching.

Having said a few words on Tohu-vah-bohu—the meaning of which Wordsworth rendered graphically as "higgledy-piggledy"—and having explained that this term denoted Cosmos, he teaches that:

Above the dark abyss [Chaos] were the Waters; . . . the earth [*is here?*] was Tohu-vah-bohu, *i.e.*, in confusion, and darkness covered the face of the Deep, and vehement Breath moved on the Waters when the Spirit exclaimed [?], "Let there be light," and there was light. Thus the earth [our globe, of course] was in a state of cataclysm; *thick* vapours veiled the immensity of the sky, the earth was covered with waters and a violent wind was agitating this dark ocean, when at a given moment the equilibrium revealed itself and light reäppeared; the letters that compose the Hebrew word "Bereshith" (the first word of *Genesis*) are "Beth," the binary, the verb manifested by the act, a *feminine* letter; then "Resh," the Verbum and Life, number 20, the disc multiplied by 2; and "Aleph," the spiritual principle, the Unit, a masculine letter.

Place these letters in a triangle and you have the absolute Unity, that without being included into numbers creates the number, the first manifestation, which is 2, and these two united by harmony resulting from the analogy of contraries [opposites], make 1, only. This is why God is called Elohim (plural).

All this is very ingenious, but is very puzzling, besides being incorrect. For owing to the first sentence, "Above the dark abyss were the Waters," the French Kabalist leads the student away from the right track. This an Eastern Chela will see at a glance, and even one of the profane may see it. For if the Tohu-vah-bohu is "under" and the Waters are is "above," then these two are quite distinct from each other, and this is not the case. This statement is a very important one, inasmuch as it entirely changes the spirit and nature of Cosmogony, and brings it down to a level with exoteric *Genesis*—perhaps it was so stated with an eye to this result. The Tohu-vah-bohu is the "Great Deep" and is identical with "the Waters of Chaos," or the primordial Darkness. By stating the fact otherwise it makes both "the Great Deep" and the "Waters"—which cannot be separated except in the phenomenal world—limited as to space and conditioned as to their nature. Thus Éliphas in his desire to conceal the last word of Esoteric Philosophy, fails—whether intentionally or otherwise does not matter—to point out the fundamental principle of the one true Occult Philosophy, namely, the unity and absolute homogeneity of the One Eternal Divine Element, and he makes of the Deity a male God. Then he says:

> Above the Waters was the powerful Breath of the Elohim [the creative Dhyân Chohans]. Above the Breath appeared the Light, and above the Light the Word . . . . . that created it.

Now the fact is quite the reverse of this: it is the Primeval Light that creates the Word or Logos, Who in His turn creates physical light. To prove and illustrate what he says he gives the following figure:

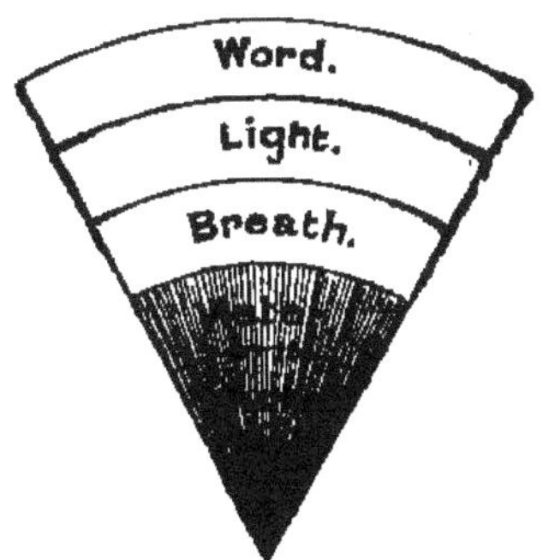

Now any Eastern Occultist upon seeing this would not hesitate to pronounce it a "left-hand" magic figure. It is entirely reversed, and it represents the third stage of religious thought, that current in Dvapara Yuga, when the one principle is already separated into male and female, and humanity is approaching the fall into materiality which brings the Kali Yuga. A student of Eastern Occultism would draw it thus:

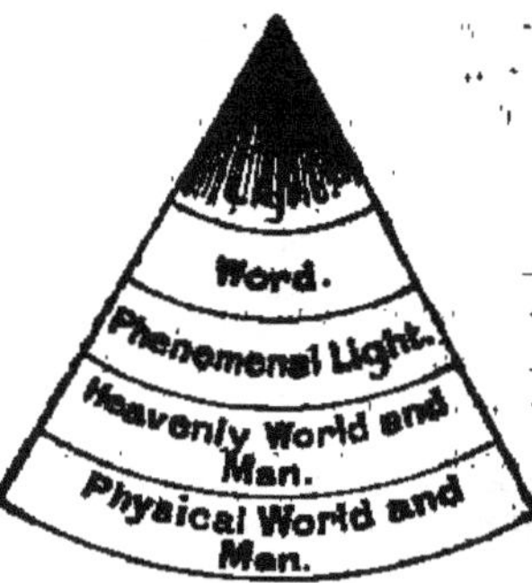

For the Secret Doctrine teaches us that the reconstruction of the Universe takes place in this wise: At the periods of new generation, perpetual Motion becomes Breath; from the Breath comes forth primordial Light, through whose radiance manifests the Eternal Thought concealed in darkness, and this becomes the Word (Mantra).* It is *That* (the Mantra or Word) from which all This (the Universe) sprang into being.

Further on Éliphas Lévi says:

> This [the concealed Deity] radiated a ray into the Eternal Essence [Waters of Space] and, fructifying thereby the primordial germ, the Essence expanded,† giving birth to the Heavenly Man from whose mind were born all forms.

The *Kabalah* states very nearly the same. To learn what it really teaches one has to reverse the order in which Éliphas Lévi gives it, replacing the word "above" by that of "in," as there cannot surely be any "above" or "under" in the Absolute. This is what he says:

> Above the waters the powerful breath of the Elohim; above the Breath the Light; above Light the Word, or the Speech that created it. We see here the spheres of evolution: the souls [?] driven from the dark centre (Darkness) toward the luminous circumference. At the bottom of the lowest circle is the Tohu-vah-bohu, or the chaos which precedes all manifestation [*Naissances*—generation]; then the region of Water; then Breath; then Light; and, lastly, the Word.

* In the exoteric sense, the Mantra (or that psychic faculty or power that conveys perception of thought) is the older portion of the *Vedas*, the second part of which is composed of the *Brâhmanas*. In Esoteric phraseology Mantra is the Word made flesh, or rendered objective, through divine magic.

† The secret meaning of the word "Brahmâ" is 'expansion," "increase,' or "growth."

The construction of the above sentences shows that the learned Abbé had a decided tendency to anthropomorphize creation, even though the latter has to be shaped out of preëxisting material, as the *Zohar* shows plainly enough.

This is how the "great" Western Kabalist gets out of the difficulty: he keeps silent on the first stage of evolution and imagines a second Chaos. Thus he says:

> The Tohu-vah-bohu is the Latin Limbus, or twilight of the morning and evening of life.* It is in perpetual motion,† it decomposes continually,‡ and the work of putrefaction accelerates, because the world is advancing towards regeneration.§ The Tohu-vah-bohu of the Hebrews is not exactly the confusion of things called Chaos by the Greeks, and which is found described in the commencement of the Metamorphosis of Ovid; it is something greater and more profound; it is the foundation of religion, it is the philosophical affirmation of the immateriality of God.

Rather an affirmation of the materiality of a personal God. If a man has to seek his Deity in the Hades of the ancients—for the Tohu-vah-bohu, or the Limbus of the Greeks, is the Hall of Hades—then one can wonder no longer at the accusations brought forward by the Church against the "witches" and sorcerers versed in Western Kabalism, that they adored the goat Mendes, or the devil personified by certain spooks and Elementals. But in face of the task Éliphas Lévi had set before himself—that of reconciling Jewish Magic with Roman ecclesiasticism—he could say nothing else.

Then he explains the first sentence in *Genesis:*

> Let us put on one side the vulgar translation of the sacred texts and see what is hidden in the first chapter of *Genesis.*

He then gives the Hebrew text quite correctly, but transliterates it:

> Bereschith Bara Eloim uth aschamam ouatti aares ouares ayete Tohu-vah-bohu. . . . Ouimas Eloim rai avur ouisi aour.

And he then explains:

> The first word, "Bereschith," signifies "genesis," a word equivalent to "nature."

---

* Why not give at once its theological meaning, as we find it in Webster? With the Roman Catholics it means simply "purgatory," the borderland between heaven and hell (*Limbus patrum* and *Limbus infantum*), the one for all men, whether good, bad or indifferent; the other for the souls of unbaptised children! With the ancients it meant simply that which in *Esoteric Buddhism* is called the Kâma Loka, between Devachan and Avitchi.

† As Chaos, the eternal Element, not as the Kâma Loka surely?

‡ A proof that by this word Éliphas Lévi means the lowest region of the terrestrial Âkâsha.

§ Evidently he is concerned only with our periodical world, or the terrestrial globe.

"The act of generation or production," we [illegible]

He then continues:

> The phrase, then, is incorrectly translated in the *Bible*. It is not "In the beginning," for it should be at the stage of the *generating force*,* [illegible] exclude every idea of the *ex-nihilo* . . . as *nothing* cannot produce [illegible]. The word "Eloim" or "Elohim" signifies the generating Powers, and [illegible] Occult sense of the first verse. . . . "Bereschith" ("[illegible]" [illegible] "Bara" ("created") "Eloim" ("the forces") "Athat-ashamaim" ("[illegible]" "ouath" and "oaris" ("the earth"); that is to say, "The generative [illegible] created indefinitely (eternally†) those forces that are the equilibrated [illegible] that we call heaven and earth, meaning the space and the bodies, the [illegible] the fixed, the movement and the weight.

Now this, if it be correct, is too vague to be understood by [illegible] ignorant of the Kabalistic teaching. Not only are his explanations [illegible] satisfactory and misleading—in his published works they are [illegible] worse—but his Hebrew transliteration is entirely wrong: it [illegible] the student, who would compare it for himself with the [illegible] symbols and numerals of the words and letters of the Hebrew [illegible] from finding anything of that he might have found were the words [illegible]rectly spelt in the French transliteration.

Compared even with exoteric Hindu Cosmogony, the philosophy which Éliphas Lévi gives out as Kabalistic is simply mystical [illegible] Catholicism adapted to the Christian *Kabalah*. His *Histoire de la Magie* shows it plainly, and reveals also his object, which he does not even [illegible] to conceal. For, while stating with his Church, that

> The Christian religion has imposed silence on the lying oracles of the Gentiles and put an end to the prestige of the false gods,‡

he promises to prove in his work that the real Sanctum Regnum, the great Magic Art, is in that Star of Bethlehem which led the three Magi to adore the Saviour of the World. He says:

> We will prove that the study of the sacred Pentagram had to lead all the Magi to know the new name which should be raised above all names, and before which every being capable of worship has to bend his knee.§

---

* In the "reawakening" of the Forces would be more correct.

† An action which is incessant in eternity cannot be called "creation;" it is evolution, and the eternally or ever-becoming of the Greek Philosopher and the Hindu Vedântin; it is the Sat and the one Beingness of Parmenides, or the Being identical with Thought. Now how can the Potencies be said to "create movement," once it is seen movement never had any beginning, but existed in the Eternity? Why not say that the reawakened Potencies transferred motion from the eternal to the temporal plane of being? Surely this is not Creation.

‡ *Histoire de la Magie*. Int., p. 1.

§ *Histoire de la Magie*. Int., p. 2.

This shows that Lévi's *Kabalah* is mystic Christianity, and not Occultism; for Occultism is universal and knows no difference between the "Saviours" (or great Avatâras) of the several old nations. Éliphas Lévi was not an exception in preaching Christianity under a disguise of Kabalism. He was undeniably "the greatest representative of modern Occult Philosophy," as it is studied in Roman Catholic countries generally, where it is fitted to the preconceptions of Christian students. But he never taught the real universal *Kabalah*, and least of all did he teach Eastern Occultism. Let the student compare the Eastern and Western teaching, and see whether the philosophy of the *Upanishads* "has yet to attain the ranges of perception" of this Western system. Everyone has the right to defend the system he prefers, but in doing this, there is no need to throw slurs upon the system of one's brother.

In view of the great resemblance between many of the fundamental "truths" of Christianity and the "myths" of Brâhmanism, there have been serious attempts made lately to prove that the *Bhagavad Gitâ* and most of the *Brâhmanas* and the *Purânas* are of a far later date than the Mosaic Books and even than the *Gospels*. But were it possible that an enforced success should be obtained in this direction, such argument cannot achieve its object, since the *Rig Veda* remains. Brought down to the most modern limits of the age assigned to it, its date cannot be made to overlap that of the *Pentateuch*, which is admittedly later.

The Orientalists know well that they cannot make away with the landmarks, followed by all subsequent religions, set up in that "Bible of Humanity" called the *Rig Veda*. It is there that at the very dawn of intellectual humanity were laid the foundation-stones of all the faiths and creeds, of every fane and church built from first to last; and they are still there. Universal "myths," personifications of Powers divine and cosmic, primary and secondary, and historical personages of all the now-existing as well as of extinct religions are to be found in the seven chief Deities and their 330,000,000 correlations of the *Rig Veda*, and those Seven, with the odd millions, are the Rays of the one boundless Unity.

But to THIS can never be offered profane worship. It can only be the "object of the most abstract meditation, which Hindus practise in order to obtain absorption in it." At the beginning of every "dawn" of "Creation," eternal Light—which is darkness—assumes the aspect of so-called Chaos: chaos to the human intellect; the eternal Root to the superhuman or spiritual sense.

"Osiris is a black God." These were the words pronounced at "low breath" at Initiation in Egypt, because Osiris Noumenon is darkness to the mortal. In this Chaos are formed the "Waters," Mother Isis, Aditi, etc. They are the "Waters of Life," in which primordial germs are created—or rather reäwakened—by the primordial Light. It is Purushottama, or the Divine Spirit, which in its capacity of Nârâyana, the Mover on the Waters of Space, fructifies and infuses the Breath of life into that germ which becomes the "Golden Mundane Egg," in which the male Brahmâ is created;* and from this the first Prajâpati, the Lord of Beings, emerges, and becomes the progenitor of mankind. And though it is not he, but the Absolute, that is said to contain the Universe in Itself, yet it is the duty of the male Brahmâ to manifest it in a visible form. Hence he has to be connected with the procreation of species, and assumes, like Jehovah and other male Gods in subsequent anthropomorphism, a phallic symbol. At best every such male God, the "Father" of all, becomes the "Archetypal Man." Between him and the Infinite Deity stretches an abyss. In the theistic religions of personal Gods the latter are degraded from abstract Forces into physical potencies. The Water of Life—the "Deep" of Mother Nature—is viewed in its terrestrial aspect in anthropomorphic religions. Behold, how holy it has become by theological magic! It is held sacred and is deified now as of old in almost every religion. But if Christians use it as a means of spiritual purification in baptism and prayer; if Hindus pay reverence to their sacred streams, tanks, and rivers; if Parsî, Mahommedan and Christian alike believe in its efficacy, surely that element must have some great and Occult significance. In Occultism it stands for the Fifth Principle of Kosmos, in the lower septenary: for the whole visible Universe was built by Water, say the Kabalists who know the difference between the two waters—the "Waters of Life" and those of Salvation—so confused together in dogmatic religions. The "King-Preacher" says of himself:

> I, the Preacher, was king over Israel in Jerusalem, and I gave my heart to seek and search out by wisdom concerning all *things* that are done under heaven.†

Speaking of the great work and glory of the Elohim‡—unified into the

* The Vaishnavas, who regard Vishnu as the Supreme God and the fashioner of the Universe, claim that Brahmâ sprang from the navel of Vishnu, the "imperishable," or rather from the lotus that grew from it. But the "navel" here means the Central Point, the mathematical symbol of Infinitude, or Parabrahman, the One and the Secondless.

† *Ecclesiastes*, i. 12, 13.

‡ It is probably needless to say here what everyone knows. The translation of the Protestant *Bible* is not a word for word rendering of the earlier Greek and Latin *Bibles*: the sense is very often disfigured, and "God" is put where "Jahve" and "Elohim" stand.

"Lord God" in the English *Bible*, whose garment, he tells us, is light and heaven the curtain—he refers to the builder

Who layeth the beams of his chambers in the waters,*

that is, the divine Host of the Sephiroth, who have constructed the Universe out of the Deep, the Waters of Chaos. Moses and Thales were right in saying that only earth and water can bring forth a living Soul, water being on this plane the principle of all things. Moses was an Initiate, Thales a Philosopher—*i.e.*, a Scientist, for the words were synonymous in his day.

The secret meaning of this is that water and earth stand in the Mosaic Books for the prima materia and the creative (feminine) Principle on our plane. In Egypt Osiris was Fire, and Isis was the Earth or its synonym Water; the two opposing elements—just because of their opposite properties—being necessary to each other for a common object: that of procreation. The earth needs solar heat and rain to make her throw out her germs. But these procreative properties of Fire and Water, or Spirit and Matter, are symbols but of physical generation. While the Jewish Kabalists symbolized these elements only in their application to manifested things, and reverenced them as the emblems for the production of terrestrial life, the Eastern Philosophy noticed them only as an illusive emanation from their spiritual prototypes, and no unclean or unholy thought marred its Esoteric religious symbology.

Chaos, as shown elsewhere, is Theos, which becomes Kosmos: it is Space, the container of everything in the Universe. As Occult Teachings assert, it is called by the Chaldæans, Egyptians, and every other nation Tohu-vah-bohu, or Chaos, Confusion, because Space is the great storehouse of Creation, whence proceed not forms alone, but also ideas, which could receive their expression only through the Logos, the Word, Verbum, or Sound.

The numbers 1, 2, 3, 4 *are the successive emanations from Mother* [*Space*] *as she forms running downward her garment, spreading it upon the seven steps of Creation.*† *The roller returns upon itself, as one end joins the other*

---

* *Psalms*, civ. 2, 3.

† To avoid misunderstanding of the word "creation" so often used by us, the remarks of the author of *Through the Gates of Gold* may be quoted owing to their clearness and simplicity. "The words 'to create' are often understood by the ordinary mind to convey the idea of evolving something out of nothing. This is clearly not its meaning. We are mentally obliged to provide our Creator with chaos from which to produce the worlds. The tiller of the soil, who is the typical producer of social life, must have his material: his earth, his sky, rain and sun, and the seeds to place

in infinitude, and the numbers 4, 3, and 2 are disclosed, as it is only the side of the veil that we can perceive, the first number being lost in its inaccessible solitude.

. . . *Father, which is Boundless Time, generates Mother, which is infinite Space, in Eternity; and Mother generates Father in Manvantaras, which are divisions of durations, that Day when that world becomes one ocean. Then the Mother becomes Nârâ [Waters—the Great Deep] for Nara [the Supreme Spirit] to rest—or move—upon, when, it is said, that 1, 2, 3, 4 descend and abide in the world of the unseen, while the 4, 3, 2, become the limits in the visible world to deal with the manifestations of Father [Time].**

This relates to the Mahâyugas which in figures become 432, and with the addition of noughts, 4,320,000.

Now it is surpassingly strange, if it be a mere coincidence, that the numerical value of Tohu-vah-bohu, or "Chaos," in the *Bible*—which Chaos, of course, is the "Mother" Deep, or the Waters of Space—should yield the same figures. For this is what is found in a Kabalist manuscript:

It is said of the Heavens and the Earth in the second verse of *Genesis* that they were "Chaos and Confusion"—that is, they were "Tohu-vah-bohu;" "and darkness was upon the face of the deep," *i.e.*, "the perfect material out of which construction was to be made lacked organization." The order of the digits of these words as they stand—*i.e.*,† the letters rendered by their numerical value—is 6,526,654 and 2,386. By art speech these are key-working numbers loosely shuffled together, the germs and keys of construction, but to be recognised, one by one, as need and required. They follow symmetrically in the work as immediately following the first sentence of grand enunciation: "In Rash developed itself Gods, the heavens and the earth."

Multiply the numbers of the letters of "Tohu-vah-bohu" together continuously from right to left, placing the consecutive single products as we go, and we will have the following series of values, *viz.*, (*a*) 30, 60, 360, 2,160, 10,800, 43,200, or as by the characterizing digits; 3, 6, 36, 216, 108, and 432; (*b*) 20, 120, 720, 1,440, 7,200, or 2, 12, 72, 144, 72, 432, the series closing in 432, one of the most famous numbers of antiquity, and which, though obscured, crops out in the chronology up to the Flood.‡ . . .

---

within the earth. Out of nothing he can produce nothing. Out of a void nature cannot arise; there is that material beyond, behind, or within, from which she is shaped by our desire for a Universe." (P. 72.)

* Commentary on Stanza ix. on Cycles.

† Or, read from right to left, the letters and their corresponding numerals stand thus: "t," 9; "h," 5; "bh," 2; "v," 6; "v," 6; "h," 5; "v" or "w," 6; which yields "thuvbhu," or "Tohu-vah-bohu."

‡ Mr. Ralston Skinner's MSS.

This shows that the Hebrew usage of play upon the numbers must have come to the Jews from India. As we have seen, the final series yields, besides many another combination, the figures 108 and 1008—the number of the names of Vishnu, whence the 108 grains of the Yogî's rosary—and close with 432, the truly "famous" number in Indian and Chaldæan antiquity, appearing in the cycle of 4,320,000 years in the former, and in the 432,000 years, the duration of the Chaldæan divine dynasties.

SECTION XXVI.

THE IDOLS AND THE TERAPHIM.

THE meaning of the "fairy-tale" told by the Chaldæan Qû-tâmy is easily understood. His *modus operandi* with the "idol of the moon" was that of all the Semites, before Terah, Abraham's father, made images—the Teraphim, called after him—or the "chosen people" of Israel ceased divining by them. These teraphim were just as much "idols" as is any pagan image or statue.* The injunction "Thou shalt not bow to a graven image," or teraphim, must have either come at a later date, or have been disregarded, since the bowing-down to and the divining by the teraphim seem to have been so orthodox and general that the "Lord" actually threatens the Israelites, through Hosea, to deprive them of their teraphim.

> For the children of Israel shall abide many days without a king, . . . without a sacrifice, and without an image.

Matzebah, or statue, or pillar, is explained in the *Bible* to mean "without an ephod and without teraphim."†

Father Kircher supports very strongly the idea that the statue of the Egyptian Serapis was identical in every way with those of the seraphim, or teraphim, in the temple of Solomon. Says Louis de Dieu:

> They were, perhaps, images of angels, or statues dedicated to the angels, the presence of one of these spirits being thus attracted into a teraphim and answering the inquirers [consultans]; and even in this hypothesis the word "teraphim" would

---

* That the teraphim was a statue, and no small article either, is shown in *Samuel* xix., where Michal takes a teraphim ("image," as it is translated) and puts it in bed to represent David, her husband, who ran away from Saul (see verse 13, *et seq.*). It was thus of the size and shape of a human figure—a statue or real *idol*.

† *Op. cit.*, iii. 4

become the equivalent of "seraphim" by changing the "t" into "s" in the manner of Syrians.*

What says the *Septuagint?* The teraphim are translated successively by εἴδωλα—forms in someone's likeness; eidolon, an "astral body;" γλυπτὰ—the sculptured; κενοτάφια—sculptures in the sense of containing something hidden, or receptacles; δήλους—manifestations; ἀληθείας—truths or realities; μορφώματα or φωτισμοὺς—luminous, shining likenesses. The latter expression shows plainly what the teraphim were. The *Vulgate* translates the term by "annuntientes," the "messengers who announce," and it thus becomes certain that the teraphim were the oracles. They were the animated statues, the Gods who revealed themselves to the masses through the Initiated Priests and Adepts in the Egyptian, Chaldæan, Greek, and other temples.

As to the way of divining, or learning one's fate, and of being instructed by the teraphim,† it is explained quite plainly by Maimonides and Seldenus. The former says:

> The worshippers of the teraphim claimed that the light of the principal stars [planets], penetrating into and filling the carved statue through and through, the angelic virtue [of the regents, or animating principle in the planets] conversed with them, teaching them many most useful arts and sciences.‡

In his turn Seldenus explains the same, adding that the teraphim§ were built and fashioned in accordance with the position of their respective planets, each of the teraphim being consecrated to a special "star-angel," those that the Greeks called stoichæ, as also according to figures located in the sky and called the "tutelary Gods":

> Those who traced out the στοιχεῖα were called στοιχειωματικοί [or the diviners by the planets] and the στοιχεῖα.‖

Ammianus Marcellinus states that the ancient divinations were always

---

* Louis de Dieu, *Genesis*, xxxi. 19. See De Mirville, iii. 257.

† "The teraphim of Abram's father, Terah, the 'maker of images,' were the Kabeiri Gods, and we see them worshipped by Micah, by the Danites, and others. (*Judges*, xvii.-xviii., etc.) Teraphim were identical with seraphim, and these were serpent images, the origin of which is in the Sanskrit 'Sarpa' (the 'serpent') a symbol sacred to all the deities as a symbol of immortality. Kiyun, or the God Kivan, worshipped by the Hebrews in the wilderness, is Shiva, the Hindu Saturn. (The Zendic 'h' is 's' in India; thus, 'Hapta' is 'Sapta;' 'Hindu' is 'Sindhaya.' (A. Wilder.) 'The "s" continually softens to "h" from Greece to Calcutta, from the Caucasus to Egypt,' says Dunlap. Therefore the letters 'k,' 'h,' and 's' are interchangeable. The Greek story shows that Dardanus, the Arcadian, having received them as a dowry, carried them to Samothrace, and thence to Troy; and they were worshipped long before the days of glory of Tyre or Sidon, though the former had been built 2760 B.C. From where did Dardanus derive them?" *Isis Unveiled*, i. 570.

‡ Maimon. *More Nevochim*, III. xxx.

§ Those dedicated to the sun were made in gold, and those to the moon in silver.

‖ *De Diis Syriis, Teraph.* II. Synt. p. 31.

accomplished with the help of the "spirits" of the elements (spiritus elementorum), or as they are called in Greek πνεύματα τῶν στοιχείων. But the latter are not the "spirits" of the stars (planets), nor are they divine Beings; they are simply the creatures inhabiting their respective elements, called by the Kabalists, elementary spirits, and by the Theosophists elementals.* Father Kircher, the Jesuit, tells the reader: —

> Every god had such instruments of divination to speak through. Each had its speciality.

Serapis gave instruction on agriculture; Anubis taught science; Horus advised upon psychic and spiritual matters; Isis was consulted on the rising of the Nile, and so on.†

This historical fact, furnished by one of the ablest and most erudite among the Jesuits, is unfortunate for the prestige of the "Lord God of Israel" with regard to his claims to priority and to his being the one living God. Jehovah, on the admission of the *Old Testament* itself, conversed with his elect in no other way, and this places him on a par with every other Pagan God, even of the inferior classes. In *Judges*, xvii., we read of Micah having an ephod and a teraphim fabricated, and consecrating them to Jehovah (see the *Septuagint* and the *Vulgate*); these objects were made by a founder from the two hundred shekels of silver given to him by his mother. True, King James' "Holy Bible" explains this little bit of idolatry by saying:

> In those days there was no king in Israel, but every man did that which was right in his own eyes.

Yet the act must have been orthodox, since Micah, after hiring a priest, a diviner, for his ephod and teraphim, declares: "Now know I that the Lord will do me good." And if Micah's act—who

> Had an house of Gods, and made an ephod and teraphim and consecrated one of his sons

to their service, as also to that of the "graven image" dedicated "unto the Lord" by his mother—now seems prejudicial, it was not so in those days of one religion and one lip. How can the Latin Church blame the act, since Kircher, one of her best writers, calls the teraphim "the holy instruments of primitive revelations;" since *Genesis* shows us Rebecca going "to enquire of the Lord,"‡ and the Lord answering her (certainly

* Those that the Kabalists call *elementary* spirits are sylphs, gnomes, undines and salamanders, nature-spirits, in short. The spirits of the angels formed a distinct class.

† *Œdipus*, ii. 444.

‡ *Op. cit.*, xxv. 22 *et seq.*

through his teraphim), and delivering to her several prophecies? And if this be not sufficient, there is Saul, who deplores the silence of the ephod,* and David who consults the thummim, and receives oral advice from the Lord as to the best way of killing his enemies.

The thummim and urim, however—the object in our days of so much conjecture and speculation—was not an invention of the Jews, nor had it originated with them, despite the minute instruction given about it by Jehovah to Moses. For the priest-hierophant of the Egyptian temples wore a breastplate of precious stones, in every way similar to that of the high priest of the Israelites.

> The high-priests of Egypt wore suspended on their necks an image of sapphire, called *Truth*, the manifestation of truth becoming evident in it.

Seldenus is not the only Christian writer who assimilates the Jewish to the Pagan teraphim, and expressed a conviction that the former had borrowed them from the Egyptians. Moreover, we are told by Döllinger, a preëminently Roman Catholic writer:

> The teraphim were used and remained in many Jewish families to the days of Josiah.†

As to the personal opinion of Döllinger, a Papist, and of Seldenus, a Protestant—both of whom trace Jehovah in the teraphim of the Jews and "evil spirits" in those of the Pagans—it is the usual one-sided judgment of *odium theologicum* and sectarianism. Seldenus is right, however, in arguing that in the days of old, all such modes of communication had been primarily established for purposes of divine and angelic communications only. But

> The holy Spirit (spirits, rather) spake [not] to the children of Israel [alone] by urim and thummim, while the tabernacle remained,

as Dr. A. Cruden would have people believe. Nor had the Jews alone need of a "tabernacle" for such a kind of theophanic, or divine communication; for no Bath-Kol (or "Daughter of the divine Voice"), called thummim, could be heard whether by Jew, Pagan, or Christian, were there not a fit tabernacle for it. The "tabernacle" was simply the archaic telephone of those days of Magic when Occult powers were acquired by Initiation, just as they are now. The nineteenth century

* The ephod was a linen garment worn by the high priest, but as the thummim was attached to it, the entire paraphernalia of divination was often comprised in that single word, ephod. See I. *Sam.*, xxviii. 6, and xxx. 7, 8.

† *Paganism and Judaism*, iv. 197.

has replaced with an electric telephone the "tabernacle" of special metals, wood, and special arrangements, and has natural mediums instead of high priests and hierophants. Why should people wonder, then, that instead of reaching Planetary Spirits and Gods, believers should now communicate with no greater beings than elementals and animated shells—the demons of Porphyry? Who these were, he tells us candidly in his work *On the Good and Bad Demons*:

> They whose ambition is to be taken for Gods, and whose leader demands to be recognized as the Supreme God.

Most decidedly—and it is not the Theosophists who will ever deny the fact—there are good as well as bad spirits, beneficent and malevolent "Gods" in all ages. The whole trouble was, and still is, to know which is which. And this, we maintain, the Christian Church knows no more than her profane flock. If anything proves this, it is, most decidedly, the numberless theological blunders made in this direction. It is idle to call the Gods of the heathen "devils," and then to copy their symbols in such a servile manner, enforcing the distinction between the good and the bad with no weightier proof than that they are respectively Christian and Pagan. The planets—the elements of the Zodiac—have not figured only at Heliopolis as the twelve stones called the "mysteries of the elements" (elementorum arcana). On the authority of many an orthodox Christian writer they were found also in Solomon's temple, and may be seen to this day in several old Italian churches, and even in Notre Dame of Paris.

One would really say that the warning in Clement's *Stromateis* has been given in vain, though he is supposed to quote words pronounced by St. Peter. He says:

> Do not adore God as the Jews do, who think they are the only ones to know Deity and fail to perceive that, instead of God, they are worshipping angels, the lunar months, and the moon.*

Who after reading the above can fail to feel surprise that, notwithstanding such understanding of the Jewish mistake, the Christians are still worshipping the Jewish Jehovah, the Spirit who spoke through his teraphim! That this is so, and that Jehovah was simply the "tutelary genius," or spirit, of the people of Israel—only one of the pneumata tōn stoicheiōn (or "great spirits of the elements"), not even a high "Planetary"—is demonstrated on the authority of St. Paul and of

* *Op. cit.*, I. vi. 5.

Clemens Alexandrinus, if the words they use have any meaning. With the latter, the word στοιχεῖα signifies not only elements, but also

> Generative cosmological principles, and notably the signs [or constellations] of the Zodiac, of the months, days, the sun and the moon.*

The expression is used by Aristotle in the same sense. He says, τῶν ἀστρῶν στοιχεῖα,† while Diogenes Laertius calls δώδεκα στοιχεῖα, the twelve signs of the Zodiac.‡ Now having the positive evidence of Ammianus Marcellinus to the effect that

> Ancient divination was always accomplished with the help of the spirits of the elements,

or the same πνεύματα τῶν στοιχείων, and seeing in the *Bible* numerous passages that (*a*) the Israelites, including Saul and David, resorted to the same divination, and used the same means; and (*b*) that it was their "Lord"—namely, Jehovah—who answered them, what else can we believe Jehovah to be than a "spiritus elementorum"?

Hence one sees no great difference between the "idol of the moon"—the Chaldæan teraphim through which spoke Saturn—and the idol of urim and thummim, the organ of Jehovah. Occult rites, scientific at the beginning—and forming the most solemn and sacred of sciences—have fallen through the degeneration of mankind into Sorcery, now called "superstition." As Diogenes explains in his *History*:

> The Kaldhi, having made long observations on the planets and knowing better than anyone else the meaning of their motions and their influences, predict to people their futurity. They regard their doctrine of the *five* great orbs—which they call interpreters, and we, planets—as the most important. And though they allege that it is the *sun* that furnishes them with most of the predictions for great forthcoming events, yet they worship more particularly Saturn. Such predictions made to a number of kings, especially to Alexander, Antigonus, Seleucus, Nicanor, etc., . . . have been so marvellously realised that people were struck with admiration.§

It follows from the above that the declaration made by Qû-tâmy, the Chaldæan Adept—to the effect that all that he means to impart in his work to the profane had been told by Saturn to the moon, by the latter to her idol, and by that idol, or teraphim, to himself, the scribe—no more implied idolatry than did the practice of the same method by King

* *Discourse to the Gentiles*, p. 146.

† *De Gener.*, I. II. iv.

‡ See *Cosmos*, by Ménage, I., vi., § 101.

§ *Op. cit.*, I. ii.

David. One fails to perceive in it, therefore, either an apocrypha or a "fairy-tale." The above-named Chaldæan Initiate lived at a period far anterior to that ascribed to Moses, in whose day the Sacred Science of the sanctuary was still in a flourishing condition. It began to decline only when such scoffers as Lucian had been admitted, and the pearls of the Occult Science had been too often thrown to the hungry dogs of criticism and ignorance.

SECTION XXVII.

EGYPTIAN MAGIC.

FEW of our students of Occultism have had the opportunity of examining Egyptian papyri—those living, or rather re-arisen witnesses that Magic, good and bad, was practised many thousands of years back into the night of time. The use of the papyrus prevailed up to the eighth century of our era, when it was given up, and its fabrication fell into disuse. The most curious of the exhumed documents were immediately purchased and taken away from the country. Yet there are a number of beautifully-preserved papyri at Bulak, Cairo, though the greater number have never been yet properly read.*

Others—those that have been carried away and may be found in the museums and public libraries of Europe—have fared no better. In the days of the Vicomte de Rougé, some twenty-five years ago, only a few of them "were two-thirds deciphered;" and among those some most interesting legends, inserted parenthetically and for purposes of explaining royal expenses, are in the Register of the Sacred Accounts.

This may be verified in the so-called "Harris" and Anastasi collections, and in some papyri recently exhumed; one of these gives an account of a whole series of magic feats performed before the Pharaohs Ramses II. and III. A curious document, the first-mentioned, truly. It is a papyrus of the fifteenth century B.C., written during the reign of Ramses V., the last king of the eighteenth dynasty, and is the work of the scribe Thoutmes, who notes down some of the events with

* "The characters employed on those parchments," writes De Mirville, "are sometimes hieroglyphies, placed perpendicularly, a kind of lineary tachygraphy (abridged characters), where the image is often reduced to a simple stroke; at other times placed in horizontal lines; then the hieratic or sacred writing, going from right to left as in all Semitic languages; lastly, the characters of the country, used for official documents, mostly contracts, etc., but which since the Ptolemies has been also adopted for the monuments," v. 81, 82. A copy of the Harris papyrus, translated by Chabas—*Papyrus magique*—may be studied at the British Museum.

regard to defaulters occurring on the twelfth and thirteenth days of the month of Paophs. The document shows that in those days of "miracles" in Egypt the taxpayers were not found among the living alone, but every mummy was included. All and everything was taxed; and the Khou of the mummy, in default, was punished "by the priest-exorciser, who deprived it of the liberty of action." Now what was the Khou? Simply the astral body, or the aerial simulacrum of the corpse or the mummy—that which in China is called the Hauen, and in India the Bhût.

Upon reading this papyrus to-day, an Orientalist is pretty sure to fling it aside in disgust, attributing the whole affair to the crass superstition of the ancients. Truly phenomenal and inexplicable must have been the dullness and credulity of that otherwise highly philosophical and civilized nation if it could carry on for so many consecutive ages for thousands of years, such a system of mutual deception! A system whereby the people were deceived by the priests, the priests by their King-Hierophants, and the latter themselves were cheated by the ghosts, which were, in their turn, but "the fruits of hallucination." The whole of antiquity, from Menes to Cleopatra, from Manu to Vikramaditya, from Orpheus down to the last Roman augur, was hysterical, we are told. This must have been so, if the whole was not a system of fraud. Life and death were guided by, and were under the sway of, sacred "conjuring." For there is hardly a papyrus, though it be a simple document of purchase and sale, a deed belonging to daily transactions of the most ordinary kind, that has not Magic, white or black, mixed up in it. It looks as though the sacred scribes of the Nile had purposely, and in a prophetic spirit of race-hatred, carried out the (to them) most unprofitable task of deceiving and puzzling the generations of a future white race of unbelievers yet unborn! Anyhow, the papyri are full of Magic, as are likewise the stelæ. We learn, moreover, that the papyrus was not merely a smooth-surfaced parchment, a fabric made of

> Ligneous matter from a shrub, the pellicles of which superposed one over the other formed a kind of writing-paper;

but that the shrub itself, the implements and tools for fabricating the parchment, etc., were all previously subjected to a process of magical preparation—according to the ordinance of the Gods, who had taught that art, as they had all others, to their Priest-Hierophants.

There are, however, some modern Orientalists who seem to have an inkling of the true nature of such things, and especially of the analogy and the relations that exist between the Magic of old and our modern-day phenomena. Chabas is one of these, for he indulges, in his translation of the "Harris" papyrus, in the following reflections:

Without having recourse to the imposing ceremonies of the wand of Hermes, or to the obscure formulæ of an unfathomable mysticism, a mesmerizer in our own day will, by means of a few passes, disturb the organic faculties of a subject, inculcate the knowledge of foreign languages, transport him to a far-distant country, or into secret places, make him guess the thoughts of those absent, read in closed letters, etc. . . . The antre of the modern sybil is a modest-looking room, the tripod has made room for a small round table, a hat, a plate, a piece of furniture of the most vulgar kind; only the latter is even superior to the oracle of antiquity [how does M. Chabas know?], inasmuch as the latter only spoke,* while the oracle of our day writes its answers. At the command of the medium the spirits of the dead descend to make the furniture creak, and the authors of bygone centuries deliver to us works written by them beyond the grave. Human credulity has no narrower limits to-day than it had at the dawn of historical times. . . . As teratology is an essential part of general physiology now, so the *pretended* Occult Sciences occupy in the annals of humanity a place which is not without its importance, and deserve for more than one reason the attention of the philosopher and the historian.†

Selecting the two Champollions, Lenormand, Bunsen, Vicomte de Rougé, and several other Egyptologists to serve as our witnesses, let us see what they say of Egyptian Magic and Sorcery. They may get out of the difficulty by accounting for each "superstitious belief" and practice by attributing them to a chronic psychological and physiological derangement, and to collective hysteria, if they like; still facts are there, staring us in the face, from the hundreds of these mysterious papyri, exhumed after a rest of four, five, and more thousands of years, with their magical containments and evidence of antediluvian Magic.

A small library, found at Thebes, has furnished fragments of every kind of ancient literature, many of which are dated, and several of which have thus been assigned to the accepted age of Moses. Books or manuscripts on ethics, history, religion and medicine, calendars and

* And what of the "Mene, mene, tekel, upharsin," the words that "the fingers of a man's hand," whose body and arm remained invisible, wrote on the walls of Belshazzar's palace? (*Daniel*, v.) What of the writings of Simon the Magician, and the magic characters on the walls and in the air of the crypts of Initiation, without mentioning the tables of stone on which the finger of God wrote the commandments? Between the writing of one God and other Gods the difference, if any, lies only in their respective natures; and if the tree is to be known by its fruits, then preference would have to be given always to the Pagan Gods. It is the immortal "To be or not to be." Either all of them are—or at any rate, may be—true, or all are surely pious frauds and the result of credulity.

† *Papyrus Magique*, p. 186.

registers, poems and novels—everything—may be had in that peculiar collection; and old legends—traditions of long forgotten ages (please to remark this: legends recorded during the Mosaic period)—are found referred to therein as belonging to an immense antiquity, to the period of the dynasties of Gods and Giants. Their chief contents, however, are formulæ of exorcisms against black Magic, and funeral rituals: true breviaries, or the *vade mecum* of every pilgrim-traveller to eternity. These funeral texts are generally written in hieratic characters. At the head of the papyrus is invariably placed a series of scenes, showing the defunct appearing before a host of Deities successively, who have to examine him. Then comes the judgment of the Soul, while the third act begins with the launching of that Soul into the divine light. Such papyri are often forty feet long.*

The following is extracted from general descriptions. It will show how the moderns understand and interpret Egyptian (and other) Symbology.

The papyrus of the priest Nevo-loo (or Nevolen), at the Louvre, may be selected for one case. First of all there is the bark carrying the coffin, a black chest containing the defunct's mummy. His mother, Ammenbem-Heb, and his sister, Hooissanoob, are near; at the head and feet of the corpse stand Nephtys and Isis clothed in red, and near them a priest of Osiris clad in his panther's skin, his censer in his right hand, and four assistants carrying the mummy's intestines. The coffin is received by the God Anubis (of the jackal's head), from the hands of female weepers. Then the Soul rises from its mummy and the Khou (astral body) of the defunct. The former begins its worship of the four genii of the East, of the sacred birds, and of Ammon as a ram; Brought into the "Palace of Truth," the defunct is before his judges. While the Soul, a scarabæus, stands in the presence of Osiris, his astral Khou is at the door. Much laughter is provoked in the West by the invocations to various Deities, presiding over each of the limbs of the mummy, and of the living human body. Only judge: in the papyrus of the mummy Petamenoph "the anatomy becomes theographical," "astrology is applied to physiology," or rather "to the anatomy of the human body, the heart and the soul." The defunct's "hair belongs to the Nile, his eyes to Venus (Isis), his ears to Macedo, the guardian of the tropics; his nose to Anubis, his left temple to the Spirit dwelling

* See Maspero's *Guide to the Bulak Museum*, among others.

in the sun. . . . What a series of intolerable absurdities and ignoble prayers . . . to Osiris, imploring him to give the defunct in the other world, geese, eggs, pork, etc." *

It might have been prudent, perhaps, to have waited to ascertain whether all these terms of "geese, eggs, and pork" had not some other Occult meaning. The Indian Yogi who, in an *exoteric* work, is invited to drink a certain intoxicating liquor till he loses his senses, was also regarded as a drunkard representing his sect and class, until it was found that the Esoteric sense of that "spirit" was quite different: that it meant divine light, and stood for the ambrosia of Secret Wisdom. The symbols of the dove and the lamb which abound now in Eastern and Western Christian Churches may also be exhumed long ages hence, and speculated upon as objects of present-day worship. And then some "Occidentalist," in the forthcoming ages of high Asiatic civilization and learning, may write karmically upon the same as follows: "The ignorant and superstitious Gnostics and Agnostics of the sects of 'Pope' and 'Calvin' (the two monster Gods of the Dynamite-Christian period) adored a pigeon and a sheep!" There will be portable hand-fetishes in all and every age for the satisfaction and reverence of the rabble, and the Gods of one race will always be degraded into devils by the next one. The cycles revolve within the depths of Lethe, and Karma shall reach Europe as it has Asia and her religions.

Nevertheless,

> This grand and dignified language [in the *Book of the Dead*], these pictures full of majesty, this orthodoxy of the whole evidently proving a very precise doctrine concerning the immortality of the soul and its personal survival, . . .

as shown by De Rougé and the Abbé Van Drival, have charmed some Orientalists. The psychostasy (or judgment of the Soul) is certainly a whole poem to him who can read it correctly and interpret the images therein. In that picture we see Osiris, the horned, with his sceptre hooked at the end—the original of the pastoral bishop's crook or crosier—the Soul hovering above, encouraged by Tmei, daughter of the Sun of Righteousness and Goddess of Mercy and Justice; Horus and Anubis, weighing the deeds of the soul. One of these papyri shows the Soul found guilty of gluttony sentenced to be re-born on earth as a hog; forthwith comes the learned conclusion of an Orientalist,

* De Mirville (from whom much of the preceding is taken), v. 81, 85.

"This is an indisputable proof of belief in *metempsychosis*, of transmigration *into animals*," etc.

Perchance the Occult law of Karma might explain the sentence otherwise. It may, for all our Orientalists know, refer to the physiological vice in store for the Soul when re-incarnated—a vice that will lead that personality into a thousand and one scrapes and misadventures.

"Tortures to begin with, then metempsychosis *during* 3,000 *years* as a hawk, an eagle, a lotus-flower, a heron, a stork, a swallow, a serpent, and a crocodile: one admits that the consolation of such a progress was far from being satisfactory,"

argues De Mirville, in his work on the Satanic character of the Gods of Egypt.* Again, a simple suggestion may throw on this a great light. Are the Orientalists quite sure they have read correctly the "metempsychosis during 3,000 years"? The Occult Doctrine teaches that Karma waits at the threshold of Devachan (the Amenti of the Egyptians) for 3,000 years; that then the eternal *Ego* is reincarnated *de novo*, to be punished in its new temporary personality for sins committed in the preceding birth, and the suffering for which, in one shape or another, will atone for past misdeeds. And the hawk, the lotus-flower, the heron, serpent, or bird—every object in Nature, in short—had its symbolical and manifold meaning in ancient religious emblems. The man who all his life acted hypocritically and passed for a good man, but had been in sober reality watching like a bird of prey his chance to pounce upon his fellow-creatures, and had deprived them of their property, will be sentenced by Karma to bear the punishment for hypocrisy and covetousness in a future life. What will it be? Since every human unit has ultimately to progress in his evolution, and since that "man" will be reborn at some future time as a good, sincere, well-meaning man, his sentence to be re-incarnated as a hawk may simply mean that he will then be regarded metaphorically as such. That, notwithstanding his real, good, intrinsic qualities, he will, perhaps during a long life, be unjustly and falsely charged with and suspected of greed and hypocrisy and of secret exactions, all of which will make him suffer more than he can bear. The law of retribution can never err, and yet how many such innocent victims of false appearance and human malice do we not meet in this world of incessant illusion, of mistake and deliberate wickedness. We see them

* See De Mirville, v. 84, 85.

every day, and they may be found within the personal experience of each of us. What Orientalist can say with any degree of assurance that he has understood the religions of old? The metaphorical language of the priests has never been more than superficially revealed, and the hieroglyphics have been very poorly mastered to this day.*

What says *Isis Unveiled* on this question of Egyptian rebirth and transmigration, and does it clash with anything that we say now?

It will be observed that this philosophy of cycles, which was allegorized by the Egyptian Hierophants in the "cycle of necessity," explains at the same time the allegory of the "Fall of Man." According to the Arabian descriptions, each of the seven chambers of the pyramids—those grandest of all cosmic symbols—was known by the name of a planet. The peculiar architecture of the pyramids shows in itself the drift of the metaphysical thought of their builders. The apex is lost in the clear blue sky of the land of the Pharaohs, and typifies the primordial point lost in the unseen Universe from whence started the first race of the spiritual prototypes of man. Each mummy from the moment that it was embalmed lost its physical individuality in one sense: it symbolised the human race. Placed in such a way as was best calculated to aid the exit of the "Soul," the latter had to pass through the seven planetary chambers before it made its exit through the symbolical apex. Each chamber typified, at the same time, one of the seven spheres [of our Chain] and one of the seven higher types of physico-spiritual humanity alleged to be above our own. Every 3000 years the soul, representative of its race, had to return to its primal point of departure before it underwent another evolution into a more perfected spiritual and physical transformation. We must go deep indeed into the abstruse metaphysics of Oriental mysticism before we can realise fully the infinitude of the subjects that were embraced at one sweep by the majestic thought of its exponents.†

This is all Magic when once the details are given; and it relates at the same time to the evolution of our seven Root-Races, each with the characteristics of its special guardian or "God," and his Planet. The astral body of each Initiate, after death, had to reënact in its funeral mystery the drama of the birth and death of each Race—the past and the future—and pass through the seven "planetary chambers," which, as said above, typified also the seven spheres of our Chain.

The mystic doctrine of Eastern Occultism teaches that

"*The Spiritual Ego* [*not the astral Khou*] *has to revisit, before it incarnates into a new body, the scenes it left at its last disincarnation. It*

* One sees this difficulty arise even with a perfectly known language like Sanskrit, the meaning of which is far easier to comprehend than the hieratic writings of Egypt. Everyone knows how hopelessly the Sanskritists are often puzzled over the real meaning and how they fail in rendering the meaning correctly in their respective translations, in which one Orientalist contradicts the other.

† *Op. cit.*, i. 297.

*has to see for itself and take cognizance of all the effects produced by the causes [the Nidânas] generated by its actions in a previous life, that, seeing, it should recognize the justice of the decree, and help the law of Retribution [Karma] instead of impeding it."**

The translations by Vicomte de Rougé of several Egyptian papyri, imperfect as they may be, give us one advantage: they show undeniably the presence in them of white, divine Magic, as well as of Sorcery, and the practice of both throughout all the dynasties. The *Book of the Dead*, far older than *Genesis*† or any other book of the Old Testament, shows it in every line. It is full of incessant prayers and exorcisms against the Black Art. Therein Osiris is the conqueror of the "aerial demons." The worshipper implores his help against Matat, "from whose eye proceeds the invisible arrow." This "invisible arrow" that proceeds from the eye of the Sorcerer (whether living or dead) and that "circulates throughout the world," is the evil eye, cosmic in its origin, terrestrial in its effects on the microcosmical plane. It is not the Latin Christians whom it behoves to view this as a superstition. Their Church indulges in the same belief, and has even a prayer against the "arrow circulating in darkness."

The most interesting of all those documents, however, is the "Harris" papyrus, called in France "*le papyrus magique* de Chabas," as it was first translated by the latter. It is a manuscript written in hieratic characters, translated, commented upon, and published in 1860 by M. Chabas, but purchased at Thebes in 1855 by Mr. Harris. Its age is given at between twenty-eight and thirty centuries. We quote a few extracts from these translations:

> Calendar of lucky and unlucky days: . . . He who makes a bull work on the 20th of the month of Pharmuths will surely die; he who on the 24th day of the same month pronounces the name of Seth aloud will see trouble reigning in his house from that day; . . . he who on the 5th day of Patchous leaves his house falls sick and dies.

Exclaims the translator, whose cultured instincts are revolted:

> If one had not these words under our eyes, one could never believe in such servitude at the epoch of the Ramessides.‡

---

* Book II., Commentary.

† Bunsen and Champollion so declare, and Dr. Carpenter says that the *Book of the Dead*, sculptured on the oldest monuments, with "the very phrases we find in the *New Testament* in connection with the Day of Judgment . . . was engraved probably 2,000 years before the time of Christ." (See *Isis Unveiled*, i., 518.)

‡ De Mirville, v. 88. Just such a calendar and horoscope interdictions exist in India to our day, as well as in China and all the Buddhist countries.

We belong to the nineteenth century of the Christian era, and are therefore at the height of civilization, and under the benign sway and enlightening influence of the Christian Church, instead of being subject to the Pagan Gods of old. Nevertheless we personally know dozens, and have heard of hundreds, of educated, highly-intellectual persons who would as soon think of committing suicide as of starting on any business on a Friday, of dining at a table where thirteen sit down, or of beginning a long journey on a Monday. Napoleon the Great became pale when he saw three candles lit on a table. Moreover, we may gladly concur with De Mirville in this, at any rate, that such "superstitions" are "the outcome of observation and experience." If the former had never agreed with facts, the authority of the *Calendar*, he thinks, would not have lasted for a week. But to resume:

> *Genethliacal influences*: The child born on the 5th day of Paophi will be killed by a bull; on the 27th by a serpent. Born on the 4th of the month of Athyr, he will succumb to blows.

This is a question of horoscopic predictions; judiciary astrology is firmly believed in in our own age, and has been proven to be scientifically possible by Kepler.

Of the Khous two kinds were distinguished: first, the justified Khous, *i.e.*, those who had been absolved from sin by Osiris when they were brought before his tribunal; these lived a second life. Secondly, there were the guilty Khous, "the Khous dead a second time;" these were the damned. Second death did not annihilate them, but they were doomed to wander about and to torture people. Their existence had phases analogous to those of the living man, a bond so intimate between the dead and the living that one sees how the observation of religious funeral rites and exorcisms and prayers (or rather magic incantations) should have become necessary.* Says one prayer:

> Do not permit that the venom should master his limbs [of the defunct], . . . that he should be penetrated by any male dead, or any female dead; or that the shadow of any spirit should haunt him (or her).†

M. Chabas adds:

> These Khous were beings of that kind to which human beings belong after their death; they were exorcised in the name of the god Chons. . . . The Manes then could enter the bodies of the living, haunt and obsess them. Formulæ and talismans, and especially statues or *divine figures*, were used against such *formidable* invasions.‡ . . . They were combated by the help of the divine power, the god

* See De Mirville, iii. 65.

† *Pap. Mag.*, p. 163.

‡ *Ibid.*, p. 168.

Chons being famed for such deliverances. The Khou, in obeying the orders of the god, none the less preserved the precious faculty inherent in him of incorporating himself in any other body at will.

The most frequent formula of exorcism is as follows. It is very suggestive:

> Men, gods, elect, dead spirits, amous, negroes, menti-u, do not look at this soul to show cruelty toward it.

This is addressed to all who were acquainted *with Magic.*

"Amulets and mystic names." This chapter is called "very mysterious," and contains invocations to Penhakahakaherher and Uranakarsankrobite, and other such easy names. Says Chabas:

> We have proofs that mystic names similar to these were in common use during the stay of the Israelites in Egypt.

And we may add that, whether got from the Egyptians or the Hebrews, these are sorcery names. The student can consult the works of Éliphas Lévi, such as his *Grimoire des Sorciers.* In these exorcisms Osiris is called Mamuram-Kahab, and is implored to prevent the twice-dead Khou from attacking the justified Khou and his next of kin, since the accursed (astral spook)

> Can take any form he likes and penetrate at will into any locality or body.

In studying Egyptian papyri, one begins to find that the subjects of the Pharaohs were not very much inclined to the Spiritism or Spiritualism of their day. They dreaded the "blessed spirit" of the dead more than a Roman Catholic dreads the devil!

But how uncalled-for and unjust is the charge against the Gods of Egypt that they are these "devils," and against the priests of exercising their magic powers with the help of "the fallen angels," may be seen in more than one papyrus. For one often finds in them records of Sorcerers sentenced to the death penalty, as though they had been living under the protection of the holy Christian Inquisition. Here is one case during the reign of Ramses III, quoted by De Mirville from Chabas.

> The first page begins with these words: "From the place where I am to the people of my country." There is reason to suppose, as one will see, that the person who wrote this, in the first personal pronoun, is a magistrate making a report, and attesting it before men, after an accustomed formula, for here is the main part of this accusation: "This Hai, a bad man, was an overseer [or perhaps keeper] of sheep: he said: 'Can I have a book that will give me great power?' . . . And a book was given him with the formulæ of Ramses-Meri-Amen, the great God, his

royal master; and he succeeded in getting a divine power enabling him to fascinate men. He also succeeded in building a place and in finding a very *deep place*, and produced men of Menh [magical homunculi?] and . . . love-writings . . stealing them from the Khen [the occult library of the palace] by the hand of the stonemason Atirma, . . . by forcing one of the supervisors to go aside, and acting magically on the others. Then he sought to read futurity by them and succeeded. All the horrors and abominations he had conceived in his heart, he did them really, he practised them all, and other great crimes as well, such as *the horror* [?] of all the Gods and Goddesses. Likewise let the prescriptions *great* [*severe?*] *unto death* be done unto him, such as the divine words order to be done to him." The accusation does not stop there, it specifies the crimes. The first line speaks of a hand paralysed by means of the *men of Menh*, to whom it is simply said, "*Let such an effect be produced*," and it is produced. Then come the *great abominations*, such as deserve death. . . . The judges who had examined him (the culprit) reported saying, "Let him die according to the order of Pharaoh, and according to what is written in the lines of the divine language."

M. Chabas remarks:

Documents of this kind abound, but the task of analysing them all cannot be attempted with the limited means we possess.*

Then there is an inscription taken in the temple of Khons, the God who had power over the elementaries, at Thebes. It was presented by M. Prisse d'Avenne to the Imperial—now National—Library of Paris, and was translated first by Mr. S. Birch. There is in it a whole romance of Magic. It dates from the day of Ramses XII.† of the twentieth dynasty; it is from the rendering of M. de Rougé as quoted by De Mirville, that we now translate it.

This monument tells us that one of the Ramses of the twentieth dynasty, while collecting at Naharain the tributes paid to Egypt by the Asiatic nations, fell in love with a daughter of the chief of Bakhten, one of his tributaries, married her and, bringing her to Egypt with him, raised her to the dignity of Queen, under the royal name of Ranefrou. Soon afterwards the chief of Bakhten dispatched a messenger to Ramses, praying the assistance of Egyptian science for Bent-Rosh, a young sister of the queen, attacked with illness in all her limbs.

The messenger asked expressly that a "wise-man" [an Initiate—Reh-Het] should be sent. The king gave orders that all the hierogrammatists of the palace and the guardians of the secret books of the Khen should be sent for, and choosing from among them the royal scribe Thoth-em-Hebi, an intelligent man, well versed in writing, charged him to examine the sickness.

* Maimonides in his *Treatise on Idolatry* says, speaking of the Jewish teraphim: "They talked with men." To this day Christian Sorcerers in Italy, and negro Voodoos at New Orleans fabricate small wax figures in the likeness of their victims, and transpierce them with needles, the *wound*, as on the teraphim or Menh, being repercussed on the living, often killing them. Mysterious deaths are still many, and not all are traced to the guilty hand.

† The Ramses of Lepsius, who reigned some 1300 years before our era.

> Arrived at Bakhten, Thoth-em-Hebi found that Bent-Reshi was possessed by a Khou (Em-seh-'eru ker h'ou), but declared himself too weak to engage in a struggle with him.*
>
> Eleven years elapsed, and the young girl's state did not improve. The Chief of Bakhten again sent his messenger, and on his formal demand Khons-peiri-Seklerem-Zam, one of the divine forms of Chons—God the Son in the Theban Trinity—was dispatched to Bakhten. . . .
>
> The God [incarnate] having saluted (*besa*) the patient, she felt immediately relieved, and the Khou who was in her manifested forthwith his intention of obeying the orders of the God. "O great God, who forcest the phantom to vanish," said the Khou, "I am thy slave and I will return whence I came!"†

Evidently Khons-peiri-Seklerem-Zam was a real Hierophant of the class named the "Sons of God," since he is said to be one of the forms of the God Khons; which means either that he was considered as an incarnation of that God—an Avatâra—or that he was a full Initiate. The same text shows that the temple to which he belonged was one of those to which a School of Magic was attached. There was a Khem in it, or that portion of the temple which was inaccessible to all but the highest priest, the library or depository of secret works, to the study and care of which special priests were appointed (those whom all the Pharaohs consulted in cases of great importance), and wherein they communicated with the Gods and obtained advice from them. Does not Lucian tell his readers in his description of the temple of Hierapolis, of "Gods who manifest their presence independently?"‡ And further on that he once travelled with a priest from Memphis, who told him he had passed twenty-three years in the subterranean crypts of his temple, receiving instructions on Magic from the Goddess Isis herself. Again we read that it was by Mercury himself that the great Sesostris (Ramses II.) was instructed in the Sacred Sciences. On which Jablonsky remarks that we have here the reason why Amun (Ammon)—whence he thinks our "Amen" is derived—was a real evocation to the light.§

In the Papyrus Anastasi, which teems with various formulæ for the

---

* One may judge how trustworthy are the translations of such Egyptian documents when the sentence is rendered in three different ways by three Egyptologists. Rougé says: "He found her in a state *to fall under the power of spirits*," or, "with her limbs quite stiff," (?) another version; and Chabas translates: "And the Scribe found the Khou too wicked." Between her being in possession of an evil Khou and "with her limbs quite stiff," there is a difference.

† De Mirville, v. 247, 248.

‡ Some translators would have Lucian speak of the inhabitants of the city, but they fail to show that this view is maintainable.

§ De Mirville, v. 256, 257.

evocation of Gods, and with exorcisms against Khous and the elementary demons, the seventh paragraph shows plainly the difference made between the real Gods, the Planetary Angels, and those shells of mortals which are left behind in Kâma-loka, as though to tempt mankind and to puzzle it the more hopelessly in its vain search after the truth, outside the Occult Sciences and the veil of Initiation. This seventh verse says with regard to such divine evocations or theomantic consultations:

> One must invoke that divine and great name * only in cases of absolute necessity, and when one feels absolutely pure and irreproachable.

Not so in the formula of black Magic. Reuvens, speaking of the two rituals of Magic of the Anastasi collection, remarks that they

> Undeniably form the most instructive commentary upon the *Egyptian mysteries* attributed to Jamblichus, and the best pendant to that classical work, for understanding the thaumaturgy of the philosophical sects, thaumaturgy based on ancient Egyptian religion. According to Jamblichus, thaumaturgy was exercised by the ministry of secondary genii.†

Reuvens closes with a remark which is very suggestive and is very important to the Occultists who defend the antiquity and genuineness of their documents, for he says:

> All that he [Jamblichus] gives out as theology we find as history in our papyri.

But then how deny the authenticity, the credibility, and, beyond all, the trustworthiness of those classical writers, who all wrote about Magic and its Mysteries in a most worshipful spirit of admiration and reverence? Listen to Pindarus, who exclaims:

> Happy he who descends into the grave thus initiated, for he knows the end of his life and the kingdom‡ given by Jupiter.§

---

* How can de Mirville see Satan in the Egyptian God of the great divine Name, when he himself admits that nothing was greater than the name of the oracle of Dodona, as it was that of the God of the Jews, IAO, or Jehovah? That oracle had been brought by the Pelasgians to Dodona more than fourteen centuries B.C. and left with the forefathers of the Hellenes, and its history is well-known and may be read in Herodotus. Jupiter, who loved the fair nymph of the ocean, Dodona, had ordered Pelasgus to carry his cult to Thessaly. The name of the God of that oracle at the temple of Dodona was Zeus Pelasgicos, the Zeuspater (God the Father), or as De Mirville explains: "It was the name *par excellence*, the name that the Jews held as the ineffable, the unpronounceable Name—in short, *Jaoh-pater*, *i.e.*, 'he who was, who is, and who will be,' otherwise the Eternal." And the author admits that Maury is right "in discovering in the name of the Vaidic Indra the Biblical Jehovah," and does not even attempt to deny the etymological connection between the two names—"the *great* and the *lost* name with the sun and the thunder-bolts." Strange confessions, and still stranger contradictions.

† Reuvens' *Letter to Letronne on the 75th number of the Papyri Anastasi.*" See De Mirville, v. 258.

‡ The Eleusinian Fields.

§ *Fragments*, ix.

Or to Cicero:

> Initiation not only teaches us to feel happy in this life, but also to die with better hope.*

Plato, Pausanias, Strabo, Diodorus and dozens of others bring their evidence as to the great boon of Initiation; all the great as well as partially-initiated Adepts, share the enthusiasm of Cicero.

> Does not Plutarch, thinking of what he had learned in his initiation, console himself for the loss of his wife? Had he not obtained the certitude at the Mysteries of Bacchus that "the soul [spirit] remains incorruptible, and that there is a hereafter"? . . . Aristophanes went even farther: "All those who participated in the Mysteries," he says, "led an innocent, calm, and holy life; they died looking for the light of the Eleusinian Fields [Devachan], while the rest could never expect anything but eternal darkness [ignorance?].
>
> . . . And when one thinks about the importance attached by the States to the principle and the correct celebration of the Mysteries, to the stipulations made in their treaties for the security of their celebration, one sees to what degree those Mysteries had so long occupied their first and their last thought.
>
> It was the greatest among public as well as private preoccupations, and this is only natural, since according to Döllinger, "the Eleusinian Mysteries were viewed as the efflorescence of all the Greek religion, as the purest essence of all its conceptions."†
>
> Not only conspirators were refused admittance therein, but those who had not denounced them; traitors, perjurers, debauchees,‡ . . . so that Porphyry could say that: "Our soul has to be at the moment of death as it was during the Mysteries, *i.e.*, exempt from any blemishes, passion, envy, hatred, or anger."§

Truly,

> Magic was considered a Divine Science which led to a participation in the attributes of the Divinity itself.‖

Herodotus, Thales, Parmenides, Empedocles, Orpheus, Pythagoras, all went, each in his day, in search of the wisdom of Egypt's great Hierophants, in the hope of solving the problems of the universe.

Says Philo:

> The Mysteries were known to unveil the secret operations of Nature.¶
>
> The prodigies accomplished by the priests of theurgic magic are so well authenticated and the evidence—if human testimony is worth anything at all—is so overwhelming that, rather than confess that the pagan theurgists far outrivalled the

---

* *De Legibus*, II. iv.

† *Judaism and Paganism*, i. 184.

‡ *Frag. of Styg.*, *ap. Stob.*

§ *De Special. Legi.*

‖ De Mirville, v. 278, 279.

¶ *Isis Unveiled*, i. 25.

Christians in miracles, Sir David Brewster conceded to the former the greatest proficiency in physics and everything that pertains to natural philosophy. Science finds herself in a very disagreeable dilemma. . . .

"Magic," says Psellus, "formed the last part of the sacerdotal science. It investigated the nature, power, and quality of everything sublunary; of the elements and their parts, of animals, of various plants and their fruits, of stones and herbs. In short, it explored the essence and power of everything. From hence, therefore, it produced its effects. And it formed *statues* [magnetized] which procure health, and made all various figures and things [talismans], which could equally become the instruments of disease as well as of health. Often, too, celestial fire is made to appear through magic, and then statues laugh and lamps are spontaneously enkindled."*

This assertion of Psellus that Magic "made statues which procure health," is now proven to the world to be no dream, no vain boast of a hallucinated Theurgist. As Reuvens says, it becomes "history." For it is found in the *Papyrus Magique* of Harris and on the votive stele just mentioned. Both Chabas and De Rougé state that:

On the eighteenth line of this very mutilated monument is found the formula with regard to the acquiescence of the God (Chons) who made his consent known by a motion he imparted to his statue.†

There was even a dispute over it between the two Orientalists. While M. de Rougé wanted to translate the word "Han" by "favour" or "grace," M. Chabas insisted that "Han" meant a "movement" or "*a sign*" made by the statue.

Excesses of power, abuse of knowledge and personal ambition very often led selfish and unscrupulous Initiates to black Magic, just as the same causes led to precisely the same thing among Christian popes and cardinals; and it was black Magic that led finally to the abolition of the Mysteries, and not Christianity, as is often erroneously thought. Read Mommsen's *Roman History*, vol. i., and you will find that it was the Pagans themselves who put an end to the desecration of the Divine Science. As early as 560 B.C. the Romans had discovered an Occult association, a school of black Magic of the most revolting kind; it celebrated mysteries brought from Etruria, and very soon the moral pestilence had spread all over Italy

More than seven thousand Initiates were prosecuted, and most of them were sentenced to death. . . .

Later on, Titus-Livius shows us another three thousand Initiates sentenced during a single year for the crime of poisoning.‡

* *Isis Unveiled*, i. 282, 283. † De Mirville, v. 248. ‡ De Mirville, v. 282.

And yet black Magic is derided and denied!

Pauthier may or may not be too enthusiastic in saying that [illegible] appears to him as

> "The grand and primitive hearth of human thought, that has ended by [illegible] the whole ancient world,"

but he was right in his idea. That primitive thought led to Occult knowledge, which in our Fifth Race is reflected from the [illegible] days of the Egyptian Pharaohs down to our modern times. Hardly a hieratic papyrus is exhumed with the tightly swathed-up mummies of kings and high priests that does not contain some interesting information for the modern students of Occultism.

All that is, of course, derided Magic, the outcome of primitive knowledge and of revelation, though it was practised in such ungodly ways by the Atlantean Sorcerers that it has since become necessary for the subsequent Race to draw a thick veil over the practices which were used to obtain so-called magical effects on the psychic and on the physical planes. In the letter no one in our century will believe the statements, with the exception of the Roman Catholics, and these will give the acts a satanic origin. Nevertheless, Magic is so mixed up with the history of the world, that if the latter is ever to be written it has to rely upon the discoveries of Archæology, Egyptology, and hieratic writings and inscriptions; if it insists that they must be free from that "superstition of the ages" it will never see the light. One can well imagine the embarrassing position in which serious Egyptologists, Assyriologists, savants and academicians find themselves. Forced to translate and interpret the old papyri and the archaic inscriptions on stelæ and Babylonian cylinders, they find themselves compelled from first to last to face the distasteful, and to them repulsive, subject of Magic, with its incantations and paraphernalia. Here they find sober and grave narratives from the pens of learned scribes, made up under the direct supervision of Chaldæan or Egyptian Hierophants, the most learned among the Philosophers of antiquity. These statements were written at the solemn hour of the death and burial of Pharaohs, High Priests, and other mighty ones of the land of Chemi; their purpose was the introduction of the newly-born, Osirified Soul before the awful tribunal of the "Great Judge" in the region of Amenti—there where a *lie* was said to outweigh the greatest crimes. Were the Scribes and Hierophants, Pharaohs, and King-Priests all fools or frauds to have either believed in, or tried to make others believe in, such "cock-and bull stories" as are found in the most respectable papyri? Yet there is no help for it. Corroborated by Plato and Herodotus, by Manetho and Syncellus, as by all the greatest and most trustworthy authors and philosophers who wrote upon the subject, those papyri note down—as seriously as they note any history, or any fact so well known and accepted as to need no commentary—whole royal dynasties of Manes, to wit, of shadows and phantoms (astral bodies), and such feats of magic skill, and such Occult phenomena, that the most credulous Occultist of our own times would hesitate to believe them to be true.

The Orientalists have found a plank of salvation, while yet publishing and delivering the papyri to the criticism of literary Sadducees: they generally call them "romances of the days of Pharaoh So-and-So." The idea is ingenious, if not absolutely fair.

SECTION XXVIII.

THE ORIGIN OF THE MYSTERIES.

ALL that is explained in the preceding Sections and a hundredfold more was taught in the Mysteries from time immemorial. If the first appearance of those institutions is a matter of historical tradition with regard to some of the later nations, their origin must certainly be assigned to the time of the Fourth Root Race. The Mysteries were imparted to the elect of that Race when the average Atlantean had begun to fall too deeply into sin to be trusted with the secrets of Nature. Their establishment is attributed in the Secret Works to the King-Initiates of the divine dynasties, when the "Sons of God" had gradually allowed their country to become Kookarma-des (the land of vice).

The antiquity of the Mysteries may be inferred from the history of the worship of Hercules in Egypt. This Hercules, according to what the priests told Herodotus, was not Grecian, for he says:

> Of the Grecian Hercules I could in no part of Egypt procure any knowledge: . . . the name was never borrowed by Egypt from Greece. . . . Hercules, ... as they [the priests] affirm, is one of the twelve (great Gods), who were reproduced from the earlier eight Gods 17,000 years before the year of Amasis.

Hercules is of Indian origin, and—his Biblical chronology put aside—Colonel Tod was quite right in his suggestion that he was Balarâma or Baladeva. Now one must read the *Purânas* with the Esoteric key in one's hand in order to find out how on almost every page they corroborate the Secret Doctrine. The ancient classical writers so well understood this truth that they unanimously attributed to Asia the origin of Hercules.

> A section of the *Mahâbhârata* is devoted to the history of the Herculâ, of which race was Vyasa. . . . Diodorus has the same legend with some variety. He

says: "Hercules was born amongst the Indians and, like the Greeks, they furnish him with a club and lion's hide." Both [Krishna and Baladeva] are (lords) of the race (cûla) of Heri (Heri-cul-es) of which the Greeks might have made the compound Hercules.*

The Occult Doctrine explains that Hercules was the last incarnation of one of the seven "Lords of the Flame," as Krishna's brother, Baladeva. That his incarnations occurred during the Third, Fourth, and Fifth Root-Races, and that his worship was brought into Egypt from Lanka and India by the later immigrants. That he was borrowed by the Greeks from the Egyptians is certain, the more so as the Greeks place his birth at Thebes, and only his twelve labours at Argos. Now we find in the *Vishnu Purâna* a complete corroboration of the statement made in the Secret Teachings, of which Purânic allegory the following is a short summary:

Raivata, a grandson of Sharyâti, Manu's fourth son, finding no man worthy of his lovely daughter, repaired with her to Brahmâ's region to consult the God in this emergency. Upon his arrival, Hâhâ, Hûhû, and other Gandharvas were singing before the throne, and Raivata, waiting till they had done, imagined that but one Muhûrta (instant) had passed, whereas long ages had elapsed. When they had finished Raivata prostrated himself and explained his perplexity. Then Brahmâ asked him whom he wished for a son-in-law, and upon hearing a few personages named, the Father of the World smiled and said: "Of those whom you have named the third and fourth generation [Root-Races] no longer survive, for many successions of ages [Chatur-Yuga, or the four Yuga cycles] have passed away while you were listening to our songsters. Now on earth the twenty-eighth great age of the present Manu is nearly finished and the Kali period is at hand. You must therefore bestow this virgin-gem upon some other husband. For you are now alone."

Then the Râja Raivata is told to proceed to Kushasthali, his ancient capital, which was now called Dvârakâ, and where reigned in his stead a portion of the divine being (Vishnu) in the person of Baladeva, the brother of Krishna, regarded as the seventh incarnation of Vishnu whenever Krishna is taken as a full divinity.

"Being thus instructed by the Lotus-born [Brahmâ], Raivata returned with his daughter to earth, where he found the race of men dwindled in stature [see what is said in the Stanzas and Commentaries of the races of mankind gradually decreasing in stature]; . . .

* Tod's *Rajasthan*, i. 36.

reduced in vigour, and enfeebled in intellect. Repairing to the city of Kushasthali, he found it much altered," because, according to the allegorical explanation of the commentator, "Krishna had reclaimed from the sea a portion of the country," which means in plain language that the continents had all been changed meanwhile—and "had renovated the city"—or rather built a new one, Dvârakâ; for one reads in the *Bhagavad Purâna** that Kushasthali was founded and built by Raivata within the sea; and subsequent discoveries showed that it was the same, or on the same spot, as Dvârakâ. Therefore it was on an island before. The allegory in *Vishnu Purâna* shows King Raivata giving his daughter to "the wielder of the ploughshare"—or rather "the plough-bannered"—Baladeva, who "beholding the damsel of excessively lofty height. . . . shortened her with the end of his ploughshare, and she became his wife."†

This is a plain allusion to the Third and Fourth Races—to the Atlantean giants and the successive incarnations of the "Sons of the Flame" and other orders of Dhyân Chohans in the heroes and kings of mankind, down to the Kali Yuga, or Black Age, the beginning of which is within historical times. Another *coincidence*: Thebes is the city of a hundred gates, and Dvârakâ is so called from its many gateways or doors, from the word "Dvâra," "gateway." Both Hercules and Baladeva are of a passionate, hot temper, and both are renowned for the fairness of their white skins. There is not the slightest doubt that Hercules is Baladeva in Greek dress. Arrian notices the great similarity between the Theban and the Hindu Hercules, the latter being worshipped by the Suraseni who built Methorea, or Mathurâ, Krishna's birthplace. The same writer places Sandracottus (Chandragupta, the grandfather of King Asoka, of the clan of Morya) in the direct line of the descendants of Baladeva.

There were no Mysteries in the beginning, we are taught. Knowledge (Vidyâ) was common property, and it reigned universally throughout the Golden Age (Satya Yuga). As says the Commentary:

Men had not created evil yet in those days of bliss and purity, for they were of God-like more than of human nature.

But when mankind, rapidly increasing in numbers, increased also in variety of idiosyncrasies of body and mind, then incarnated Spirit showed its weakness. Natural exaggerations, and along with these

---

* *Op. cit.*, ix. iii. 28.

† *Vishnu Purâna*, iv. i. Wilson's translation, III. 248-254.

superstitions, arose in the less cultured and healthy minds. Selfishness was born out of desires and passions hitherto unknown, and but too often knowledge and power were abused, until finally it became necessary to limit the number of those *who knew*. Thus arose Initiation.

Every separate nation now arranged for itself a religious system, according to its enlightenment and spiritual wants. Worship of mere form being discarded by the wise men, these confined true knowledge to the very few. The need of veiling truth to protect it from desecration becoming more apparent with every generation, a thin veil was used at first, which had to be gradually thickened according to the spread of personality and selfishness, and this led to the Mysteries. They came to be established in every country and among every people, while to avoid strife and misunderstanding exoteric beliefs were allowed to grow up in the minds of the profane masses. Inoffensive and innocent in their incipient stage—like a historical event arranged in the form of a fairy tale, adapted for and comprehensible to the child's mind—in those distant ages such beliefs could be allowed to grow and make the popular faith without any danger to the more philosophical and abstruse truths taught in the sanctuaries. Logical and scientific observation of the phenomena in Nature, which alone leads man to the knowledge of eternal truths—provided he approaches the threshold of observation unbiassed by preconception and sees with his spiritual eye before he looks at things from their physical aspect—does not lie within the province of the masses. The marvels of the One Spirit of Truth, the ever-concealed and inaccessible Deity, can be unravelled and assimilated only through Its manifestations by the secondary "Gods,' Its acting powers. While the One and Universal Cause has to remain for ever *in abscondito*, Its manifold action may be traced through the effects in Nature. The latter alone being comprehensible and manifest to average mankind, the Powers causing those effects were allowed to grow in the imagination of the populace. Ages later in the Fifth, the Âryan, Race some unscrupulous priests began to take advantage of the too-easy beliefs of the people in every country, and finally raised those secondary Powers to the rank of God and Gods, thus succeeding in isolating them altogether from the One Universal Cause of all causes.*

* There were no Brâhmans as a hereditary caste in days of old. In those long-departed ages a man became a Brâhman through personal merit and Initiation. Gradually, however, despotism crept in, and the son of a Brâhman was created a Brâhman by right of protection first, then by that of heredity. The rights of blood replaced those of real merit, and thus arose the body of Brâhmans, which was soon changed into a powerful caste.

Henceforward the knowledge of the primeval truths remained entirely in the hands of the Initiates.

The Mysteries had their weak points and their defects, as every institution wedded with the human element must necessarily have. Voltaire has characterised their benefits in a few words:

> In the chaos of popular superstitions there existed an institution which has ever prevented man from falling into absolute brutality: it was that of the Mysteries.

Verily, as Ragon puts it of Masonry:

> Its temple has Time for duration, the Universe for space. . . . "Let us divide that we may rule," have said the crafty; "Let us unite to resist," have said the first Masons.*

Or rather, the Initiates whom the Masons have never ceased to claim as their primitive and direct Masters. The first and fundamental principle of moral strength and power is association and solidarity of thought and purpose. "The Sons of Will and Yoga" united in the beginning to resist the terrible and ever-growing iniquities of the left-hand Adepts, the Atlanteans. This led to the foundation of still more Secret Schools, temples of learning, and of Mysteries inaccessible to all except after the most terrible trials and probations.

Anything that might be said of the earliest Adepts and their divine Masters would be regarded as fiction. It is necessary, therefore, if we would know something of the primitive Initiates to judge of the tree by its fruits; to examine the bearing and the work of their successors in the Fifth Race as reflected in the works of the classic writers and the great Philosophers. How were Initiation and the Initiates regarded during some 2,000 years by the Greek and Roman writers? Cicero informs his readers in very clear terms. He says:

> An Initiate must practise all the virtues in his power: justice, fidelity, liberality, modesty, temperance; these virtues cause men to forget the talents that he may lack.†

Ragon says:

> When the Egyptian priests said: "All for the people, nothing through the people," they were right: in an ignorant nation truth must be revealed only to

---

* *Des Initiations Anciennes and Modernes.* "The mysteries," says Ragon, "were the gift of India." In this he is mistaken, for the Āryan race had brought the mysteries of Initiation from Atlantis. Nevertheless he is right in saying that the mysteries preceded all civilisations, and that by polishing the mind and morals of the peoples they served as a base for all the laws—civil, political, and religious.

† *De Off.*, i. 33.

trustworthy persons. . . . . We have seen in our days, "all through the people, nothing for the people," a false and dangerous system. The real axiom ought to be: "All for the people and *with* the people." *

But in order to achieve this reform the masses have to pass through a dual transformation: (*a*) to become divorced from every element of exoteric superstition and priestcraft, and (*b*) to become educated men, free from every danger of being enslaved whether by a man or an idea.

This, in view of the preceding, may seem paradoxical. The Initiates were "priests," we may be told—at any rate, all the Hindu, Egyptian, Chaldæan, Greek, Phœnician, and other Hierophants and Adepts were priests in the temples, and it was they who invented their respective exoteric creeds. To this the answer is possible: "The cowl does not make the friar." If one may believe tradition and the unanimous opinion of ancient writers, added to the examples we have in the "priests" of India, the most conservative nation in the world, it becomes quite certain that the Egyptian priests were no more priests in the sense we give to the word than are the temple Brâhmans. They could never be regarded as such if we take as our standard the European clergy. Laurens observes very correctly that:

> The priests of Egypt were not, strictly speaking, ministers of religion. The word "priest," which translation has been badly interpreted, had an acceptation very different from the one that is applied to it among us. In the language of antiquity, and especially in the sense of the initiation of the priests of ancient Egypt, the word "priest" is synonymous with that of "philosopher." . . . The institution of the Egyptian priests seems to have been really a confederation of sages gathered to study the art of ruling men, to centre the domain of truth, modulate its propagation, and arrest its too dangerous dispersion.†

The Egyptian Priests, like the Brâhmans of old, held the reins of the governing powers, a system that descended to them by direct inheritance from the Initiates of the great Atlantis. The pure cult of Nature in the earliest patriarchal days—the word "patriarch" applying in its first original sense to the Progenitors of the human race,‡ the Fathers, Chiefs, and Instructors of primitive men—became the heirloom of those

---

* *Des Initiations*, p. 22.

† *Essais Historiques sur la Franc-Maçonnerie*, pp. 142, 143.

‡ The word "patriarch" is composed of the Greek word "Patria" ("family," "tribe," or "nation" and "Archos" (a "chief"), the paternal principle. The Jewish Patriarchs who were pastors, passed their name to the Christian Patriarchs; yet they were no priests, but were simply the heads of their tribes, like the Indian Rishis.

alone who could discern the noumenon beneath the phenomenon. Later, the Initiates transmitted their knowledge to the human Kings, as their divine Masters had passed it to their forefathers. It was their prerogative and duty to reveal the secrets of Nature that were useful to mankind—the hidden virtues of plants, the art of healing the sick, and of bringing about brotherly love and mutual help among mankind. No Initiate was one if he could not heal—aye, recall to life from apparent death (coma) those who, too long neglected, would have indeed died during their lethargy.* Those who showed such powers were forthwith set above the crowds, and were regarded as Kings and Initiates. Gautama Buddha was a King-Initiate, a healer, and recalled to life those who were in the hands of death. Jesus and Apollonius were healers, and were both addressed as Kings by their followers. Had they failed to raise those who were to all intents and purposes the dead, few of their names would have passed down to posterity; for this was the first and crucial test, the certain sign that the Adept had upon Him the invisible hand of a primordial divine Master, or was an incarnation of one of the "Gods."

The later royal privilege descended to our Fifth Race kings through the kings of Egypt. The latter were all initiated into the mysteries of medicine, and they healed the sick, even when, owing to the terrible trials and labours of final Initiation, they were unable to become full Hierophants. They were healers by privilege and by tradition, and were assisted in the healing art by the Hierophants of the temples, when they themselves were ignorant of Occult curative Science. So also in far later historical times we find Pyrrhus curing the sick by simply touching them with his foot; Vespasian and Hadrian needed only to pronounce a few words taught to them by their Hierophants, in order to restore sight to the blind and health to the cripple. From that time onward history has recorded cases of the same privilege conferred on the emperors and kings of almost every nation.†

That which is known of the Priests of Egypt and of the ancient

* There is no need to observe here that the resurrection of a really dead body is an impossibility in Nature.

† The kings of Hungary claimed that they could cure the jaundice; the Dukes of Burgundy were credited with preserving people from the plague; the kings of Spain delivered those possessed by the devil. The prerogative of curing the king's evil was given to the kings of France, in reward for the virtues of good King Robert. Francis the First, during a short stay at Marseilles for his son's wedding, touched and cured of that disease upwards of 500 persons. The kings of England had the same privilege.

Brâhmans, corroborated as it is by all the ancient classics and historical writers, gives us the right to believe in that which is only traditional in the opinion of sceptics. Whence the wonderful knowledge of the Egyptian Priests in every department of Science, unless they had it from a still more ancient source? The famous "Four," the seats of learning in old Egypt, are more historically certain than the beginnings of modern England. It was in the great Theban sanctuary that Pythagoras upon his arrival from India studied the Science of Occult numbers. It was in Memphis that Orpheus popularized his too-abtruse Indian metaphysics for the use of Magna Grecia; and thence Thales, and ages later Democritus, obtained all they knew. It is to Saïs that all the honour must be given of the wonderful legislation and the art of ruling people, imparted by its Priests to Lycurgus and Solon, who will both remain objects of admiration for generations to come. And had Plato and Eudoxus never gone to worship at the shrine of Heliopolis, most probably the one would have never astonished future generations with his ethics, nor the other with his wonderful knowledge of mathematics.*

The great modern writer on the Mysteries of Egyptian Initiation—one, however, who knew nothing of those in India—the late Ragon, has not exaggerated in maintaining that:

> All the notions possessed by Hindustan, Persia, Syria, Arabia, Chaldæa, Sydonia, and the priests of Babylonia, [on the secrets of Nature], was known to the Egyptian priests. It is thus Indian philosophy, without mysteries, which, having penetrated into Chaldæa and ancient Persia, gave rise to the doctrine of Egyptian Mysteries.†

The Mysteries preceded the hieroglyphics.‡ They gave birth to the latter, as permanent records were needed to preserve and commemorate their secrets. It is primitive Philosophy§ that has served as the

---

* See Laurens' *Essais Historiques* for further information as to the world-wide, universal knowledge of the Egyptian Priests.

† *Des Initiations*, p. 24.

‡ The word comes from the Greek "hieros" ("sacred") and "glupho" ("I grave"). The Egyptian characters were sacred to the Gods, as the Indian Devanâgarî is the language of the Gods.

§ The same author had (as Occultists have) a very reasonable objection to the modern etymology of the word "philosophy," which is interpreted "love of wisdom," and is nothing of the kind. The philosophers were scientists, and philosophy was a real science—not simply verbiage, as it is in our day. The term is composed of two Greek words whose meaning is intended to convey its secret sense, and ought to be interpreted as "wisdom of love." Now it is in the last word, "love," that lies hidden the esoteric significance: for "love" does not stand here as a noun, nor does it mean "affection" or "fondness," but is the term used for Eros, that primordial principle in divine creation, synonymous with πόθος, the abstract desire in Nature for procreation, resulting in an everlasting series of

foundation-stone for modern Philosophy; only the progeny, while perpetuating the features of the external body, has lost on its way the Soul and Spirit of its parent.

Initiation, though it contained neither rules and principles, nor any special teaching of Science—as now understood—was veritable Science, and the Science of sciences. And though devoid of dogma, of physical discipline, and of exclusive ritual, it was yet the one true Religion—that of eternal truth. Outwardly it was a school, a college, wherein were taught sciences, arts, ethics, legislation, philanthropy, the cult of the true and real nature of cosmic phenomena; secretly, during the Mysteries, practical proofs of the latter were given. Those who could learn truth on all things—*i.e.*, those who could look the great Isis in her unveiled face and bear the awful majesty of the Goddess—became Initiates. But the children of the Fifth Race had fallen too deeply into matter always to do so with impunity. Those who failed disappeared from the world, without leaving a trace behind. Which of the highest kings would have dared to claim any individual, however high his social standing, from the stern priests, once that the victim had crossed the threshold of their sacred Adytum?

The noble precepts taught by the Initiates of the early races passed to India, Egypt, and Greece, to China and Chaldæa, and thus spread all over the world. All that is good, noble, and grand in human nature, every divine faculty and aspiration, were cultured by the Priest-Philosophers who sought to develop them in their Initiates. Their code of ethics, based on altruism, has become universal. It is found in Confucius, the "atheist," who taught that "he who loves not his brother has no virtue in him," and in the *Old Testament* precept, "Thou shalt love thy neighbour as thyself."* The greater Initiates became like unto Gods, and Socrates, in Plato's *Phædo*, is represented as saying:

The Initiates are sure to come into the company of the Gods.

In the same work the great Athenian Sage is made to say:—

phenomena. It means "divine love," that universal element of divine omnipresence spread throughout Nature and which is at once the chief cause and effect. The "wisdom of love" (or "philosophy") meant attraction to and love of everything hidden beneath objective phenomena and the knowledge thereof. Philosophy meant the highest Adeptship—love of and assimilation with Deity. In his modesty Pythagoras even refused to be called a Philosopher (or one who knows every hidden thing in things visible; cause and effect, or absolute truth), and called himself simply a Sage, an aspirant to philosophy, or to Wisdom of Love—love in its exoteric meaning being as degraded by men then as it is now by its purely terrestrial application.

* *Lev.*, xix. 18.

It is quite apparent that those who have established the Mysteries, or the secret assemblies of the Initiates, were no mean persons, but powerful genii, who from the first ages had endeavoured to make us understand under those enigmas that he who will reach the invisible regions unpurified will be hurled into the abyss [the Eighth Sphere of the Occult Doctrine; that is, he will lose his personality for ever], while he who will attain them purged of the maculations of this world, and accomplished in virtues, will be received in the abode of the Gods.

Said Clemens Alexandrinus, referring to the Mysteries:

Here ends all teaching. One sees Nature and all things.

A Christian Father of the Church speaks then as did the Pagan Pretextatus, the pro-consul of Achaia (fourth century A.D.), "a man of eminent virtues," who remarked that to deprive the Greeks of "the sacred Mysteries which bind in one the whole of mankind," was to render their very lives worthless to them. Would the Mysteries have ever obtained the highest praise from the noblest men of antiquity had they not been of more than human origin? Read all that is said of this unparalleled institution, as much by those who had never been initiated, as by the Initiates themselves. Consult Plato, Euripides, Socrates, Aristophanes, Pindar, Plutarch, Isocrates, Diodorus, Cicero, Epictetus, Marcus Aurelius, not to name dozens of other famous Sages and writers. That which the Gods and Angels had *revealed*, exoteric religions, beginning with that of Moses, *reveiled* and hid for ages from the sight of the world. Joseph, the son of Jacob, was an Initiate, otherwise he would not have married Aseneth, the daughter of Petephre ("Potiphar"—"he who belongs to Phre," the Sun-God), priest of Heliopolis and governor of On.* Every truth *revealed* by Jesus, and which even the Jews and early Christians understood, was *reveiled* by the Church that pretends to serve Him. Read what Seneca says, as quoted by Dr. Kenealy:

"The world being melted and having reëntered the bosom of Jupiter [or Parabrahman], this God continues for some time totally concentred in himself and remains concealed, as it were, wholly immersed in the contemplation of his own ideas. Afterwards we see a new world spring from him. . . . An innocent race of men is formed." And again, speaking of a mundane dissolution as involving the destruction or death of all, he [Seneca] teaches us that when the laws of Nature shall be buried in ruin and the last day of the world shall come, the Southern Pole shall crush, as it falls, all the regions of Africa; and the North Pole shall overwhelm all the countries beneath its axis. *The affrighted sun shall be deprived of its light;*

* "On," "the "Sun," the Egyptian name of Heliopolis (the "City of the Sun").

the palace of heaven, falling to decay, shall produce at once both life and death; but some kind of dissolution shall equally seize upon all the deities, who will thus return to their original chaos.*

One might fancy oneself reading the Purânic account by Parâshara of the great Pralaya. It is nearly the same thing, idea for idea. Has Christianity nothing of the kind? Let the reader open any English *Bible* and read chapter iii. of the *Second Epistle of Peter*, and he will find there the same ideas.

> There shall come in the last days scoffers, ... saying, Where is the promise of his coming? for since the fathers fell asleep all things continue as they were from the beginning of the creation. For this they willingly are ignorant of, that by the word of God the heavens were of old, and the earth standing out of the water and in the water: whereby the world that then was, being overflowed with water, perished. But the heavens and the earth, which are now, by the same word are . . . . reserved unto fire, ... in the which the heavens shall pass away with a great noise, and the elements shall melt with fervent heat. . . . Nevertheless we . . . . look for new heavens and a new earth.

If the interpreters chose to see in this a reference to a creation, a deluge, and a promised coming of Christ, when they will live in a New Jerusalem in heaven, that is no fault of Peter. What he meant was the destruction of the Fifth Race and the appearance of a new continent for the Sixth Race.

The Druids understood the meaning of the Sun in Taurus, therefore when all the fires were extinguished on the 1st of November their sacred and inextinguishable fire remained alone to illumine the horizon like those of the Magi and the modern Zoroastrian. And like the early Fifth Race and the later Chaldæans and Greeks, and again like the Christians (who do it to this day without suspecting the real meaning), they greeted the "Morning-Star," the beautiful Venus-Lucifer.† Strabo speaks of an island near Britannia where Ceres and Persephone were worshipped with the same rites as in Samothrace, and this was the sacred Ierna, where a perpetual fire was lit. The Druids believed in the rebirth of man, not, as Lucian explains,

> That the same *Spirit* shall animate a new body, not here, but in a different world,

but in a series of reïncarnations in this same world; for as Diodorus

---

* *Book of God*, p. 160.

† Mr. Kenealy quotes, in his *Book of God*, Vallancey, who says: "I had not been a week landed in Ireland from Gibraltar, where I had studied Hebrew and Chaldaic under Jews of various countries, when I heard a peasant girl say to a boor standing by her '*Feuch an Maddin Nag*' ('Behold the morning star'), pointing to the planet Venus, the Maddena Nag of the Chaldeans."

says, they declared that the souls of men after a determinate period would pass into other bodies.*

These tenets came to the Fifth Race Aryans from their ancestors of the Fourth Race, the Atlanteans. They piously preserved the teachings, while their parent Root-Race, becoming with every generation more arrogant, owing to the acquisition of superhuman powers, were gradually approaching their end.

* There was a time when the whole world, the totality of mankind, had one religion, as they were of "one lip." "All the religions of the earth were at first one, and emanated from one centre," says Faber.

SECTION XXIX.

THE TRIAL OF THE SUN INITIATE.

WE will begin with the ancient Mysteries—those received from the Atlanteans by the primitive Aryans—whose mental and intellectual state Professor Max Müller has described with such a masterly hand, yet left so incomplete withal.

He says: We have in it [in the *Rig Veda*] a period of the intellectual life of man to which there is no parallel in any other part of the world. In the hymns of the Veda we see man left to himself to solve the riddle of this world. . . . He invokes the gods around him, he praises, he worships them. But still with all these gods . . . beneath him, and above him, the early poet seems ill at rest within himself. There, too, in his own breast, he has discovered a power that is never mute when he prays, never absent when he fears and trembles. It seems to inspire his prayers and yet to listen to them; it seems to live in him, and yet to support him and all around him. The only name he can find for this mysterious power is "Brahman;" for brahman meant originally force, will, wish, and the propulsive power of creation. But this impersonal brahman too, as soon as it is named, grows into something strange and divine. It ends by being one of many gods, one of the great triad, worshipped to the present day. And still the thought within him has no real name; that power which is nothing but itself, which supports the gods, the heavens, and every living being, floats before his mind, conceived but not expressed. At last he calls it "Âtman," for âtman, originally breath or spirit, comes to mean Self and Self alone, Self, whether divine or human; Self, whether creating or suffering; Self, whether One or All; but always Self, independent and free. "Who has seen the first-born?" says the poet, "when he who had no bones (*i.e.*, form) bore him that had bones? Where was the life, the blood, the Self of the world? Who went to ask this from any one who knew it?" (*Rig Veda*, I, 164, 4.) This idea of a divine Self once expressed, everything else must acknowledge its supremacy; *Self* is the Lord of all things; it is the King of all things; as all the spokes of a wheel are contained in the nave and circumference, all things are contained in this Self; all selves are contained in this *Self*." (Brihadâranyaka, IV. v. 15).*

* *Chips from a German Workshop*, i. 69, 70.

This Self, the highest, the one, and the universal, was symbolised on the plane of mortals by the Sun, its life-giving effulgence being in its turn the emblem of the Soul—killing the terrestrial passions which have ever been an impediment to the re-union of the Unit Self (the Spirit) with the All-Self. Hence the allegorical mystery, only the broad features of which may be given here. It was enacted by the "Sons of the Fire-Mist" and of "Light." The second Sun (the "second hypostasis" of Rabbi Drach) appeared as put on his trial, Vishvakarma, the Hierophant, cutting off seven of his beams, and replacing them with a crown of brambles, when the "Sun" became Vikarttana, shorn of his beams or rays. After that, the Sun—enacted by a neophyte ready to be initiated—was made to descend into Pâtâla, the nether regions, on a trial of Tantalus. Coming out of it triumphant, he emerged from this region of lust and iniquity, to re-become Karmasâkshin, witness of the Karma of men,* and arose once more triumphant in all the glory of his regeneration, as the Graha-Râjah, King of the Constellations, and was addressed as Gabhastiman, "re-possessed of his rays."

The "fable" in the popular Pantheon of India, founded upon, and born out of the poetical mysticism of the *Rig-Veda*—the sayings of which were mostly all dramatised during the religious Mysteries—grew in the course of its exoteric evolution into the following allegory. It may be found now in several of the *Purânas* and in other Scriptures. In the *Rig-Veda* and its Hymns, Vishvakarma, a Mystery-God, is the Logos, the Demiurgos, one of the greatest Gods, and spoken of in two of the hymns as the highest. He is the Omnificent (Vishvakarma), called the "Great Architect of the Universe," the

> All-seeing God, ... the father, the generator, the disposer, who gives the gods their names, and is beyond the comprehension of mortals,

as is every Mystery-God. Esoterically, He is the personification of the creative manifested Power; and mystically He is the seventh principle in man, in its collectivity. For He is the son of Bhuvana, the self-created, luminous Essence, and of the virtuous, chaste and lovely Yoga-Siddhâ, the virgin Goddess, whose name speaks for itself, since it personified Yoga-power, the "chaste mother" that creates the Adepts. In the Rig-Vaidic Hymns, Vishvakarma performs the "great sacrifice," *i.e.*, sacrifices himself for the world; or, as the *Nirukta* is made to say, translated by the Orientalists:

* Sûrya, the Sun, is one of the nine divinities that witness all human actions.

Vishvakarma first of all offers up all the world in a sacrifice, and finishes by sacrificing himself.

In the mystical representations of his character, Vishvakarma is often called Vittoba, and is pictured as the "Victim," the "Man-God" or the Avatâra crucified in space.

[Of the true Mysteries, the real Initiations, nothing of course can be said in public; they can be known only to those who are able to experience them. But a few hints can be given of the great ceremonial Mysteries of Antiquity, which stood to the public as the real Mysteries, and into which candidates were initiated with much ceremony and display of Occult Arts. Behind these, in silence and darkness, were the true Mysteries, as they have always existed and continue to exist. In Egypt, as in Chaldæa and later in Greece, the Mysteries were celebrated at stated times, and the first day was a public holiday, on which, with much pomp, the candidates were escorted to the Great Pyramid and passed thereinto out of sight. The second day was devoted to ceremonies of purification, at the close of which the candidate was presented with a white robe; on the third day]* he was tried and examined as to his proficiency in Occult learning. On the fourth day, after another ceremony symbolical of purification, he was sent alone to pass through various trials, finally becoming entranced in a subterranean crypt, in utter darkness, for two days and two nights. In Egypt, the entranced neophyte was placed in an empty sarcophagus in the Pyramid, where the initiatory rites took place. In India and Central Asia, he was bound on a lathe, and when his body had become like that of one dead (entranced), he was carried into the crypt. Then the Hierophant kept watch over him "guiding the apparitional soul (astral body) from this world of Samsâra (or delusion) to the *nether* kingdoms, from which, if successful, he had the right of releasing *seven suffering souls*" (Elementaries). Clothed with his Anandamayakosha, the body of bliss—the Srotâpanna remained there where we have no right to follow him, and upon returning—received the *Word*, with or without the "heart's blood" of the Hierophant.†

* [There is a gap in H. P. B.'s MS., and the paragraph in brackets supplies what was wanting.—A. B.]

† In *Isis Unveiled*, Vol. II., pp. 41, 42, a portion of this rite is referred to. Speaking of the dogma of Atonement, it is traced to ancient "heathendom" again. We say: "This cornerstone of a church which had believed herself built on a firm rock for long centuries, is now excavated by science and proved to come from the Gnostics. Professor Draper shows it as hardly known in the days of Tertullian, and as having 'originated among the Gnostic heretics' (see *Conflict Between Re-*

Only in truth the Hierophant was never killed—neither in India nor elsewhere, the murder being simply feigned—unless the Initiator had chosen the Initiate for his successor and had decided to pass to him the last and supreme WORD, after which he had to die—only one man in a nation having the right to know that word. Many are those grand Initiates who have thus passed out of the world's sight, disappearing

> As mysteriously from the sight of men as Moses from the top of Mount Pisgah (*Nebo*, oracular Wisdom), after he had laid his hands upon Joshua, who thus became "full of the spirit of wisdom," *i.e.*, initiated.

But he died, he was not killed. For killing, if really done, would belong to black, not to divine Magic. It is the transmission of light, rather than a transfer of life, of life spiritual and divine, and it is the shedding of Wisdom, not of blood. But the uninitiated inventors of theological Christianity took the allegorical language *à la lettre*; and instituted a dogma, the crude, misunderstood expression of which horrifies and repels the spiritual "heathen."

All these Hierophants and Initiates were types of the Sun and of the Creative Principle (spiritual potency) as were Vishvakarma and

---

ligion and Science, p. 224). . . . But there are sufficient proofs to show that it *originated* among them no more than did their anointed Christos and Sophia. The former they modelled on the original of the King Messiah, the male principle of wisdom, and the latter on the third Sephiroth, from the Chaldæan *Kabalah*, and even from the Hindu Brahmâ and Sarasvati, and the Pagan Dionysius and Demeter. And here we are on firm ground, if it were only because it is now proved that the *New Testament* never appeared in its complete form, such as we find it now, till 300 years after the period of the apostles, and the *Zohar* and other Kabalistic books are found to belong to the first century before our era, if not to be far older still.

"The Gnostics entertained many of the Essenean ideas; and the Essenes had their greater and minor Mysteries at least two centuries before our era. They were the *Isarim* or *Initiates*, the descendants of the Egyptian hierophants, in whose country they had been settled for several centuries before they were converted to Buddhistic monasticism by the missionaries of King Asoka, and amalgamated later with the earliest Christians; and they existed, probably, before the old Egyptian temples were desecrated and ruined in the incessant invasions of Persians, Greeks, and other conquering hordes. The hierophants had their atonement enacted in the Mystery of Initiation ages before the Gnostics, or even the Essenes, had appeared. It was known among hierophants as the Baptism of Blood, and was considered not as an atonement for the 'fall of man' in Eden, but simply as an expiation for the past, present, and future sins of ignorant, but nevertheless polluted mankind. The hierophant had the option of either offering his pure and sinless life as a sacrifice for his race to the gods whom he hoped to rejoin, or an animal victim. The former depended entirely on their own will. At the last moment of the solemn 'new birth,' the Initiator passed 'the word' to the initiated, and immediately after the latter had a weapon placed in his right hand, and was ordered *to strike*. This is the true origin of the Christian dogma of atonement."

As Ballanche says, quoted by Ragon: "Destruction is the great God of the World," justifying therefore the philosophical conception of the Hindu Shiva. According to this immutable and sacred law, the Initiate was compelled to kill the Initiator; otherwise initiation remained incomplete. . . . It is death that generates life." *Orthodoxie maçonnique*, p. 104. All that, however, was emblematic and exoteric. Weapon and killing must be understood in their allegorical sense.

Vikarttana, from the origin of the Mysteries. Ragon, the learned Mason, gives curious details and explanations with regard to these rites. He shows that the biblical Hiram, the great hero of Masonry (the "widow's son") a type taken from Osiris, is the Sun-God, the inventor of arts, and the "architect," the name Hiram meaning the *elevated*, a title belonging to the Sun. Every Occultist knows how closely related to Osiris and the Pyramids are the narratives in *Kings* concerning Solomon, his Temple and its construction; he knows also that the whole of the Masonic rite of Initiation is based upon the Biblical allegory of the construction of that Temple, Masons conveniently forgetting, or perhaps ignoring, the fact that the latter narrative is modelled upon Egyptian and still earlier symbolisms. Ragon explains it by showing that the three companions of Hiram, the "three murderers," typify the three last months of the year; and that Hiram stands for the Sun—from its summer solstice downwards, when it begins decreasing—the whole rite being an astronomical allegory. . . . .

During the summer solstice, the Sun provokes songs of gratitude from all that breathes; hence Hiram, who represents it, can give to whomsoever has the right to it, the sacred Word, that is to say life. When the Sun descends to the inferior signs all Nature becomes mute, and Hiram can no longer give the sacred Word to the companions, who represent the three inert months of the year. The first companion strikes Hiram feebly with a rule twenty-four inches long, symbol of the twenty-four hours which make up each diurnal revolution; it is the first distribution of time, which after the exaltation of the mighty star, feebly assails his existence, giving him the first blow. The second companion strikes him with an *iron square*, symbol of the last season, figured by the intersections of two right lines, which would divide into four equal parts the Zodiacal circle, whose centre symbolises Hiram's heart, where it touches the point of the four squares representing the four seasons: second distribution of time, which at that period strikes a heavier blow at the solar existence. The third companion strikes him mortally on his forehead with a heavy blow of his mallet, whose cylindrical form symbolises the year, the ring or circle: third distribution of time, the accomplishment of which deals the last blow to the existence of the *expiring* Sun. From this interpretation it has been inferred that *Hiram*, a *founder* of metals, the hero of the new legend with the title of *architect*, is Osiris (the Sun) of modern initiation; that *Isis*, his widow, is the *Lodge*, the emblem of the Earth (*loka* in Sanskrit, the world) and that *Horus*, son of Osiris (or of light) and the widow's son, is the *free Mason*, that is to say, the *Initiate* who inhabits the terrestrial lodge (*the child of the Widow, and of Light*.)*

And here again, our friends the Jesuits have to be mentioned, for the above rite is of their making. To give one instance of their success in

* *Orthodoxie maçonnique*, pp. 102-104.

throwing dust into the eyes of ordinary individuals to prevent their seeing the truths of Occultism, we will point out what they did in what is now called Freemasonry.

This Brotherhood does possess a considerable portion of the symbolism, formulæ, and ritual of Occultism, handed down from time immemorial from the primeval Initiations. To render this Brotherhood a mere harmless negation, the Jesuits sent some of their most able emissaries into the Order, who first made the simple brethren believe that the true secret was lost with Hiram Abiff; and then induced them to put this belief into their formularies. They then invented specious but spurious higher degress, pretending to give further light upon this lost secret, to lead the candidate on and amuse him with forms borrowed from the real thing but containing no substance, and all artfully contrived to lead the aspiring Neophyte to nowhere. And yet men of good sense and abilities, in other respects, will meet at intervals, and with solemn face, zeal and earnestness, go through the mockery of revealing "substituted secrets" instead of the real thing.

If the reader turns to a very remarkable and very useful work called *The Royal Masonic Cyclopædia*, Art. "Rosicrucianism," he will find its author, a high and learned Mason, showing what the Jesuits have done to destroy Masonry. Speaking of the period when the existence of this mysterious Brotherhood (of which many pretend to know "something" if not a good deal, and know in fact nothing) was first made known, he says:

> There was a dread among the great masses of society in byegone days of the unseen—a dread, as recent events and phenomena show very clearly, not yet overcome in its entirety. Hence students of Nature and mind were forced into an obscurity not altogether unwelcome. . . . The Kabalistic reveries of a Johann Reuchlin led to the fiery action of a Luther, and the patient labours of Trittenheim produced the modern system of diplomatic cipher writing. . . . It is very worthy of remark, that one particular century, and that in which the Rosicrucians first showed themselves, is distinguished in history as the era in which most of these efforts at throwing off the trammels of the past [Popery and Ecclesiasticism] occurred. Hence the opposition of the losing party, and their virulence against anything mysterious or unknown. They freely organised pseudo-Rosicrucian and Masonic societies in return; and these societies were instructed to irregularly entrap the weaker brethren of the True and Invisible Order, and then triumphantly betray anything they might be so inconsiderate as to communicate to the superiors of these transitory and unmeaning associations. Every wile was adopted by the authorities, fighting in self-defence against the progress of truth, to engage, by persuasion, interest or terror, such as might be cajoled into receiving the Pope as Master—

when gained, as many converts to that faith know, but dare not own, they are treated with neglect, and left to fight the battle of life as best they may, not even being admitted to the knowledge of such miserable aporrheta as the Romish faith considers itself entitled to withhold.

But if Masonry has been spoiled, none is able to crush the real, invisible Rosicrucian and the Eastern Initiate. The symbolism of Vishvakarma and Sûrya Vikarttana has survived, where Hiram Abiff was indeed murdered, and we will now return to it. It is not simply an astronomical, but is the most solemn rite, an inheritance from the Archaic Mysteries that has crossed the ages and is used to this day. It typifies a whole drama of the Cycle of Life, of progressive incarnations, and of psychic as well as of physiological secrets, of which neither the Church nor Science knows anything, though it is this rite that has led the former to the greatest of its Christian Mysteries.

SECTION XXX.

THE MYSTERY "SUN OF INITIATION."

THE antiquity of the Secret Doctrine may be better realised when it is shown at what point of history its Mysteries had already been desecrated, by being made subservient to the personal ambition of despot-ruler and crafty priest. These profoundly philosophical and scientifically composed religious dramas, in which were enacted the grandest truths of the Occult or Spiritual Universe and the hidden lore of learning, had become subject to persecution long before the days when Plato and even Pythagoras flourished. Withal, primal revelations given to Mankind have not died with the Mysteries; they are still preserved as heirlooms for future and more spiritual generations.

It has been already stated in *Isis Unveiled*,* that so far back as in the days of Aristotle, the great Mysteries had already lost their primitive grandeur and solemnity. Their rites had fallen into desuetude, and they had to a great degree degenerated into mere priestly speculations and had become religious shams. It is useless to state when they first appeared in Europe and Greece, since recognised history may almost be said to begin with Aristotle, everything before him appearing to be in an inextricable chronological confusion. Suffice it to say, that in Egypt the Mysteries had been known since the days of Menes, and that the Greeks received them only when Orpheus introduced them from India. In an article "Was writing known before Pânini?"† it is stated that the Pândus had acquired universal dominion and had taught the "sacrificial" Mysteries to other races as far back as 3,300 B.C. Indeed, when Orpheus, the son of Apollo or Helios, received from his father the phorminx—the seven-stringed lyre, symbolical of the sevenfold mystery

---

* *Op. cit.*, i. 15.

† *Five Years of Theosophy*, p. 258. A curious question to start and to deny, when it is well-known even to the Orientalists that, to take but one case, there is Yaska, who was a predecessor of Pânini, and his work still exists; there are seventeen writers of Nirukta (glossary) known to have preceded Yaska.

of Initiation—these Mysteries were already hoary with age in Central Asia and India. According to Herodotus it was Orpheus who brought them from India, and Orpheus is far anterior to Homer and Hesiod. Thus even in the days of Aristotle few were the true Adepts left in Europe and even in Egypt. The heirs of those who had been dispersed by the conquering swords of various invaders of old Egypt had been dispersed in their turn. As 8,000 or 9,000 years earlier the stream of knowledge had been slowly running down from the tablelands of Central Asia into India and towards Europe and Northern Africa, so about 500 years B.C. it had begun to flow backward to its old home and birthplace. During the two thousand subsequent years the knowledge of the existence of great Adepts nearly died out in Europe. Nevertheless, in some secret places the Mysteries were still enacted in all their primitive purity. The "Sun of Righteousness" still blazed high on *the midnight sky*; and, while darkness was upon the face of the profane world, there was the eternal light in the Adyta on the nights of Initiation. The *true* Mysteries were never made public. Eleusinia and Agræ for the multitudes; the God Εὐβουλῆ "of the good counsel," the great Orphic Deity, for the neophyte.

This mystery God—mistaken by our Symbologists for the Sun—who was He? Everyone who has any idea of the ancient Egyptian exoteric faith is quite aware that for the multitudes Osiris was the Sun in Heaven, "the Heavenly King," Ro-Imphab; that by the Greeks the Sun was called the "Eye of Jupiter," as for the modern orthodox Parsi he is "the Eye of Ormuzd:" that the Sun, moreover, was addressed as the "All-seeing God" (πολυόφθαλμος) as the "God Saviour," and the "saving God" (Αἴτιον τῆς σωτηρίας). Read the papyrus of Papheronmes at Berlin, and the stela as rendered by Mariette Bey,* and see what they say:

> Glory to thee, O Sun, divine child! . . . thy rays carry life to the pure and to those ready. . . . The Gods [the "Sons of God"] who approach thee tremble with delight and awe. . . . Thou art the first born, the Son of God, the Word.†

The Church has now seized upon these terms and sees presentiments of the coming Christ in these expressions in the initiatory rites and

---

* *La Mère d'Apis*, p. 47.

† One just initiated is called the "first-born," and in India he becomes dwija, "twice born," only after his final and supreme Initiation. Every Adept is a "Son of God" and a "Son of Light," after receiving the "Word," when he becomes the "Word" himself, after receiving the seven divine attributes or the "lyre of Apollo."

prophetic utterances of the Pagan Oracles. They are nothing of the kind, for they were applied to every worthy Initiate. If the expressions that were used in hieratic writings and glyphs thousands of years before our era are now found in the laudatory hymns and prayers of Christian Churches, it is simply because they have been unblushingly appropriated by the Latin Christians, in the full hope of never being detected by posterity. Everything that could be done had been done to destroy the original Pagan manuscripts and the Church felt secure. Christianity has undeniably had her great Seers and Prophets, like every other religion; but their claims are not strengthened by denying their predecessors.

Listen to Plato:

> Know then, Glaucus, that when I speak of the production of good, it is the Sun I mean. The Son has a perfect analogy with his Father.

Iamblichus calls the Sun "the image of divine intelligence or Wisdom." Eusebius, repeating the words of Philo, calls the rising Sun (ἀνατολή) the chief Angel, the most ancient, adding that the Archangel who is *polyonymous* (of many names) is the Verbum or Christ. The word Sol (Sun) being derived from *solus*, the One, or the "He alone," and its Greek name Helios meaning the "Most High," the emblem becomes comprehensible. Nevertheless, the Ancients made a difference between the Sun and its prototype.

Socrates saluted the rising Sun as does a true Pârsî or Zoroastrian in our own day; and Homer and Euripides, as Plato did after them several times, mention the Jupiter-Logos, the "Word" or the Sun. Nevertheless, the Christians maintain that since the oracle consulted on the God Iao answered: "It is the Sun," therefore

> The Jehovah of the Jews was well known to the Pagans and Greeks;*

and "Iao is our Jehovah." The first part of the proposition has nothing, it seems, to do with the second part, and least of all can the conclusion be regarded as correct. But if the Christians are so anxious to prove the identity, Occultists have nothing against it. Only, in such case, Jehovah is also Bacchus. It is very strange that the people of civilised Christendom should until now hold on so desperately to the skirts of the idolatrous Jews—Sabæans and Sun worshippers as they were,† like the rabble of Chaldæa—and that they should fail to see that the later Jehovah is but a Jewish development of the Ja-va, or the

* See De Mirville, iv. 15.

† II. Kings, xxiii. 4-11.

Iao, of the Phoenicians; that this name, in short, was the secret name of a Mystery-God, one of the many Kabiri. "Highest God" as He was for one little nation, he never was so regarded by the Initiates who conducted the Mysteries; for them he was but a Planetary Spirit attached to the visible Sun; and the visible Sun is only the central Star, not the central spiritual Sun.

> And the Angel of the Lord said unto him [Manoah] "Why askest thou thus after my name, seeing it is secret."*

However this may be, the identity of the Jehovah of Mount Sinai with the God Bacchus is hardly disputable, and he is surely—as already shown in *Isis Unveiled*—Dionysos.† Wherever Bacchus was worshipped there was a tradition of Nyssa,‡ and a cave where he was reared. Outside Greece, Bacchus was the all-powerful "Zagreus, the highest of Gods," in whose service was Orpheus, the founder of the Mysteries. Now, unless it be conceded that Moses was an initiated Priest, an Adept, whose actions are all narrated allegorically, then it must be admitted that he personally, together with his hosts of Israelites, worshipped Bacchus.

> And Moses built an altar, and called the name of it *Jehovah Nissi* [or, Iao-nisi, or again Dionisi].§

To strengthen the statement we have further to remember that the place where Osiris, the Egyptian Zagreus or Bacchus, was born, was Mount Sinai, which is called by the Egyptians Mount Nissa. The brazen serpent was a nis, נחש, and the month of the Jewish Passover is Nisan.

---

* *Judges*, xiii. 18. Samson, Manoah's son, was an Initiate of that "Mystery" Lord, Ja-va; he was consecrated before his birth to become a "Nazarite" (a chela) an Adept. His sin with Dalilah, and the cropping of his long hair that "no razor was to touch" shows how well he kept his sacred vow. The allegory of Samson proves the Esotericism of the *Bible*, as also the character of the "Mystery Gods" of the Jews. True, Movers gives a definition of the Phoenician idea of the ideal sunlight as a spiritual influence issuing from the highest God, Iao, "the light conceivable only by intellect—the physical and spiritual Principle of all things; out of which the soul emanates." It was the male Essence, or Wisdom, while the primitive matter or *Chaos* was the female. Thus the first two principles, co-eternal and infinite, were already with the primitive Phoenicians, spirit and matter. But this is the echo of Jewish thought, not the opinion of Pagan Philosophers.

† See *Isis Unveiled*, ii. 526.

‡ Beth-San or Scythopolis in Palestine had that designation: so had a spot on Mount Parnassus. But Diodorus declares that Nyssa was between Phoenicia and Egypt; Euripides states that Dionysos came to Greece from India; and Diodorus adds his testimony: "Osiris was brought up in Nyssa, in Arabia the Happy; he was the son of Zeus, and was named from his father (nominative Zeus, genitive *Dios*) and the place Dio-Nysos"—the Zeus or Jove of Nyssa. This identity of name or title is very significant. In Greece Dionysos was second only to Zeus, and Pindar says: "So Father Zeus governs all things, and Bacchus he governs also."

§ *Ex.*, xvii. 15

SECTION XXXI.

The Objects of the Mysteries.

The earliest Mysteries recorded in history are those of Samothrace. After the distribution of pure Fire, a new life began. This was the new birth of the Initiate, after which, like the Brâhmans of old in India, he became a dwija—a "twice born,"

> Initiated into that which may be rightly called the most blessed of all Mysteries . . . being ourselves pure,*

says Plato. Diodorus Siculus, Herodotus, and Sanchoniathon the Phœnician—the oldest of Historians—say that these Mysteries originated in the night of time, thousands of years probably before the historical period. Iamblichus informs us that Pythagoras

> Was initiated in all the Mysteries of Byblus and Tyre, in the sacred operations of the Syrians, and in the Mysteries of the Phœnicians.†

As was said in *Isis Unveiled:*

> When men like Pythagoras, Plato and Iamblichus, renowned for their severe morality, took part in the Mysteries and spoke of them with veneration, it ill behoves our modern critics to judge them [and their Initiates] upon their merely external aspect.

Yet this is what has been done until now, especially by the Christian Fathers. Clement Alexandrinus stigmatises the Mysteries as "indecent and diabolical" though his words, showing that the Eleusinian Mysteries were identical with, and even, as he would allege, borrowed from, those of the Jews, are quoted elsewhere in this work. The Mysteries were composed of two parts, of which the Lesser were performed

---

* *Phædrus*, Cary's translation, p. 326.

† *Life of Pythagoras*, p. 297. "Since Pythagoras," he adds, "also spent two and twenty years in the adyta of the temples in Egypt, associated with the Magians in Babylon, and was instructed by them in their venerable knowledge, it is not at all wonderful that he was skilled in Magic or Theurgy, and was therefore able to perform things which surpass merely human power, and which appear to be perfectly incredible to the vulgar" (p. 298).

at Agræ, and the Greater at Eleusis, and Clement had been himself initiated. But the Katharsis, or trials of purification, have ever been misunderstood. Iamblichus explains the worst; and his explanation ought to be perfectly satisfactory, at any rate for every unprejudiced mind.

He says:—

Exhibitions of this kind in the Mysteries were designed to free us from licentious passions, by gratifying the sight, and at the same time vanquishing all evil thought, through the awful sanctity with which these rites were accompanied.

Dr. Warburton remarks:

The wisest and best men in the Pagan world are unanimous in this, that the Mysteries were instituted pure, and proposed the noblest ends by the worthiest means.

Although persons of both sexes and all classes were allowed to take part in the Mysteries, and a participation in them was even obligatory, very few indeed attained the higher and final Initiation in these celebrated rites. The gradation of the Mysteries is given us by Proclus in the fourth book of his *Theology of Plato.*

The perfective rite, precedes in order the initiation Telete, *Muesis*, and the initiation, *Epopteia*, or the final apocalypse [revelation].

Theon of Smyrna, in *Mathematica*, also divides the mystic rites into five parts:

The first of which is the previous purification; for neither are the Mysteries communicated to all who are willing to receive them; but there are certain persons who are prevented by the voice of the crier . . . . . . since it is necessary that such as are not expelled from the Mysteries should first be refined by certain purifications: but after purification the reception of the sacred rites succeeds. The third part is denominated *epopteia* or reception. And the fourth, which is the end and design of the revelation, is (the investiture) the binding of the head and fixing of the crowns* . . . whether after this he [the initiated person] becomes a torchbearer, or an hierophant of the Mysteries, or sustains some other part of the sacerdotal office. But the fifth, which is produced from all these, *is friendship and interior communion with God.* And this was the last and most awful of all the Mysteries.†

The chief objects of the Mysteries, represented as diabolical by the

---

* This expression must not be understood simply literally; for, as in the initiation of certain Brotherhoods, it has a secret meaning that we have just explained; it was hinted at by Pythagoras, when he describes his feelings after the Initiation, and says that he was crowned by the Gods in whose presence he had drunk "the waters of life"—in the Hindu Mysteries there was the fount of life, and *soma*, the sacred drink.

† *Eleusinian and Bacchic Mysteries*, T. Taylor, p. 46, 47.

Christian Fathers and ridiculed by modern writers, were instituted with the highest and the most moral purpose in view. There is no need to repeat here that which has been already described in *Isis Unveiled** that whether through temple Initiation or the private study of Theurgy, every student obtained the proof of the immortality of his Spirit, and the survival of his Soul. What the last *epopteia* was is alluded to by Plato in *Phædrus*:

Being *initiated* in those *Mysteries*, which it is lawful to call the most blessed of all mysteries . . . we were freed from the molestations of evils, which otherwise await us in a future period of time. Likewise in consequence of this divine *initiation*, we became spectators of entire, simple, immoveable, and blessed visions, resident in a pure light.†

This veiled confession shows that the Initiates enjoyed Theophany—saw visions of Gods and of real immortal Spirits. As Taylor correctly infers:

The most sublime part of the *epopteia* or final revealing, consisted in beholding the Gods [the high Planetary Spirits] themselves, invested with a resplendent light.‡

The statement of Proclus upon the subject is unequivocal:

In all the Initiations and Mysteries, the Gods exhibit many forms of themselves, and appear in a variety of shapes; and sometimes indeed a formless light of themselves is held forth to the view; sometimes this light is according *to a human form* and sometimes it proceeds into a different shape.§

Again we have

Whatever is on earth is the resemblance and shadow of something that is in the sphere, while that resplendent thing [the prototype of the Soul-Spirit] remaineth in *unchangeable* condition, it is well also with its shadow. When that resplendent one removeth far from its shadow life removeth [from the latter] to a distance. Again that light is the shadow of something more resplendent than itself.‖

Thus speaks the *Desatir*, in the *Book of Shet* (the prophet Zirtusht), thereby showing the identity of its Esoteric doctrines with those of the Greek Philosophers.

The second statement of Plato confirms the view that the Mysteries of the Ancients were identical with the Initiations practised even now among the Buddhist and the Hindu Adepts. The higher

* ii. 111, 113.

† *Eleusinian and Bacchic Mysteries*, p. 63.

‡ *Op. cit.*, p. 65.

§ Quoted by Taylor, p. 66.

‖ Verses 35-38.

visions, the most truthful, were produced through a regular discipline of gradual Initiations, and the development of psychical powers. In Europe and Egypt the Mystæ were brought into close union with those whom Proclus calls "mystical natures," "resplendent Gods" because, as Plato says:

> [We] were ourselves pure and immaculate, being liberated from this surrounding vestment, which we denominate body, and to which we are now bound like an oyster to its shell.*

As to the East,

> The doctrine of planetary and terrestrial Pitris was revealed *entirely* in ancient India, as well as now, only at the last moment of initiation, and to the adepts of superior degrees.†

The word *Pitris* may now be explained and something else added. In India the chela of the third degree of Initiation has two Gurus: One, the living Adept; the other the disembodied and glorified Mahâtmâ, Who remains the adviser or instructor of even the high Adepts. Few are the accepted chelas who even see their living Master, their Guru, till the day and hour of their final and for ever binding vow. It is this that was meant in *Isis Unveiled*, when it was stated that few of the *fakirs* (the word *chela* being unknown to Europe and America in those days) however

> Pure, and honest, and self-devoted, have yet ever seen the astral form of a purely *human pitar* (an ancestor or father), otherwise than at the solemn moment of their first and last initiation. It is in the presence of his instructor, the Guru, and just before the *vatou*-fakir [the just initiated chela] is despatched into the world of the living, with his seven-knotted bamboo wand for all protection, that he is suddenly placed face to face with the unknown PRESENCE [of his Pitar or Father, the glorified invisible Master, or disembodied Mahâtmâ]. He sees it, and falls prostrate at the feet of the evanescent form, but is not entrusted with the great secret of its evocation, for it is the supreme mystery of the holy syllable.

The Initiate, says Éliphas Lévi, *knows*; therefore, "he dares all and keeps silent." Says the great French Kabalist:

> You may see him often sad, never discouraged or desperate; often poor, never humbled or wretched; often persecuted, never cowed down or vanquished. For he remembers the widowhood and the murder of Orpheus, the exile and solitary death of Moses, the martyrdom of the prophets, the tortures of Apollonius, the Cross of the Saviour. He knows in what forlorn state died Agrippa, whose memory is slandered to this day; he knows the trials that broke down the great Paracelsus, and

* *Phædrus*, 64, quoted by Taylor, p. 64. † *Isis Unveiled*, ii. 114.

all that Raymond Lully had to suffer before he arrived at a bloody death. He remembers Swedenborg having to feign insanity, and losing even his reason before his knowledge was forgiven to him; St. Martin, who had to hide himself all his life; Cagliostro, who died forsaken in the cells of the Inquisition *; Cazotte, who perished on the guillotine. Successor of so many victims, he dares, nevertheless, but understands the more the necessity to keep silent.†

Masonry—not the political institution known as the Scotch Lodge, but real Masonry, some rites of which are still preserved in the Grand Orient of France, and that Elias Ashmole, a celebrated English Occult Philosopher of the XVIIth century, tried in vain to remodel, after the manner of the Indian and Egyptian Mysteries—Masonry rests, according to Ragon, the great authority upon the subject, upon three fundamental degrees: the triple duty of a Mason is to study *whence he comes, what he is*, and *whither he goes;* the study that is, of God, of himself, and of the future transformation.‡ Masonic Initiation was modelled on that in the lesser Mysteries. The third degree was one used in both Egypt and India from time immemorial, and the remembrance of it lingers to this day in every Lodge, under the name of the death and resurrection of Hiram Abiff, the "Widow's Son." In Egypt the latter was called "Osiris;" in India "Loka-chakshu" (Eye of the World), and "Dinakara" (day-maker) or the Sun—and the rite itself was everywhere named the "gate of death." The coffin, or sarcophagus, of Osiris, killed by Typhon, was brought in and placed in the middle of the Hall of the Dead, with the Initiates all around it and the candidate near by. The latter was asked whether he had participated in the murder, and notwithstanding his denial, and after sundry and very hard trials, the Initiator feigned to strike him on the head with a hatchet; he was thrown down, swathed in bandages like a mummy, and wept over. Then came lightning and thunder, the supposed corpse was surrounded with fire, and was finally raised.

Ragon speaks of a rumour that charged the Emperor Commodus—when he was at one time enacting the part of the Initiator—with having played this part in the initiatory drama so seriously that he actually killed the postulant when dealing him the blow with the hatchet. This shows that the *lesser* Mysteries had not quite died out in the second century A.D.

---

* This is false, and the Abbé Constant (Éliphas Lévi) *knew* it was so. Why did he promulgate the untruth?

† *Dogme de la Haute Magie*, i. 219, 220.

‡ *Orthodoxie Maçonnique*, p. 99.

The Mysteries were carried into South and Central America, Northern Mexico and Peru by the Atlanteans in those days when

A pedestrian from the North [of what was once upon a time also India] might have reached—hardly wetting his feet—the Alaskan Peninsula, through Manchooria, across the *future* Gulf of Tartary, the Kurile and Aleutian Islands; while another traveller, furnished with a canoe and starting from the South, could have walked over from Siam, crossed the Polynesian Islands and trudged into any part of the continent of South America.*

They continued to exist down to the day of the Spanish invaders. These destroyed the Mexican and Peruvian records, but were prevented from laying their desecrating hands upon the many Pyramids—the lodges of an ancient Initiation—whose ruins are scattered over Puente Nacional, Cholula, and Teotihuacan. The ruins of Palenque, of Ococimgo in Chiapas, and others in Central America are known to all. If the pyramids and temples of Guiengola and Mitla ever betray their secrets, the present Doctrine will then be shown to have been the forerunner of the grandest truths in Nature. Meanwhile they have a claim to be called Mitla, "the place of sadness" and "the abode of the (desecrated) dead."

* *Five Years of Theosophy*, p. 214.

SECTION XXXII.

TRACES OF THE MYSTERIES.

SAYS the *Royal Masonic Cyclopædia*, art. "Sun:"

> In all times, the Sun has necessarily played an important part as a symbol, and especially in Freemasonry. The W.M. represents the rising sun, the J.W. the sun at the meridian, and the S.W. the setting sun. In the Druidical rites, the Arch-Druid represented the sun, and was aided by two other officers, one representing the Moon in the West, and the other the Sun at the South in its meridian. It is quite unnecessary to enter into any lengthened discussion on this symbol.

It is the more "unnecessary" since J. M. Ragon has discussed it very fully, as one may find at the end of Section XXIX., where part of his explanations have been quoted. Freemasonry derived her rites from the East, as we have said. And if it be true to say of the modern Rosicrucians that "they are invested with a knowledge of chaos, not perhaps a very desirable acquisition," the remark is still more true when applied to all the other branches of Masonry, since the knowledge of their members about the full signification of their symbols is *nil*. Dozens of hypotheses are resorted to, one more unlikely than the other, as to the "Round Towers" of Ireland; one fact is enough to show the ignorance of the Masons, namely, that, according to the *Royal Masonic Cyclopædia*, the idea that they are connected with Masonic Initiation may be at once dismissed as unworthy of notice. The "Towers," which are found throughout the East in Asia, were connected with the Mystery-Initiations, namely, with the Vishvakarma and the Vikarttana rites. The candidates for Initiation were placed in them for three days and three nights, wherever there was no temple with a subterranean crypt close at hand. These round towers were built for no other purposes. Discredited as are all such monuments of Pagan origin by the Christian clergy, who thus "soil their own nest," they are still the living and indestructible relics of the Wisdom of old.

Nothing exists in this objective and illusive world of ours that cannot be made to serve two purposes—a good and a bad one. Thus in later ages, the Initiates of the *Left* Path and the anthropomorphists took in hand most of those venerable ruins, then silent and deserted by their first wise inmates, and turned them indeed into phallic monuments. But this was a deliberate, wilful, and vicious misinterpretation of their real meaning, a deflection from their first use. The Sun—though it was, even for the multitudes, μόνος οὐρανοῦ θεός, "the only and one King and God in Heaven," and the Εὐβουλῆ, "the God of Good Counsel" of Orpheus—had in every exoteric popular religion a dual aspect which was anthropomorphised by the profane. Thus the Sun was Osiris-*Typhon*, Ormuzd-*Ahriman*, Bel-Jupiter and *Baal*, the life-giving and the *death*-giving luminary. And thus one and the same monolith, pillar, pyramid, tower or temple, originally built to glorify the first principle or aspect, might become in time an idol-fane, or worse, a phallic emblem in its crude and brutal form. The Lingam of the Hindus has a spiritual and highly philosophical meaning; while the missionaries see in it but an "indecent emblem;" it has just the meaning which is to be found in all those baalim, chammanim, and the bamoth with the pillars of unhewn stone of the Bible, set up for the glorification of the male Jehovah. But this does not alter the fact that the pureia of the Greeks, the nur-hags of Sardinia, the teocalli of Mexico, etc., were all in the beginning of the same character as the "Round Towers" of Ireland. They were sacred places of Initiation.

In 1877, the writer, quoting the authority and opinions of some most eminent scholars, ventured to assert that there was a great difference between the terms *Chrestos* and *Christos*, a difference having a profound and Esoteric meaning. Also that while *Christos* means "to live" and "to be born into a new life," *Chrestos*, in "Initiation" phraseology, signified the death of the inner, lower, or personal nature in man; thus is given the key to the Brâhmanical title, the twice-born; and finally,

> There were *Chrestians* long before the era of Christianity, and the Essenes belonged to them.* . . .

For this epithets sufficiently opprobrious to characterise the writer could hardly be found. And yet then as well as now, the author never

* In I. *Peter*, ii 3 Jesus is called "the Lord Chrestos."

attempted a statement of such a serious nature without showing as many learned authorities for it as could be mustered. Thus on the next page it was said:

Lepsius shows that the word *Nofre* means Chrestos, "good," and that one of the titles of Osiris, "Onnofre," must be translated "the goodness of God made manifest." "The worship of Christ was not universal at this early date," explains Mackenzie, "by which I mean that Christolatry had not been introduced; but the worship of *Chrestos*—the Good Principle—had preceded it by many centuries, and even survived the general adoption of Christianity, as shown on monuments still in existence. . . . Again, we have an inscription which is pre-Christian on an epitaphial tablet (Spon. *Misc. Erud.*, Ant., x. xviii. 2). Υαχινθε Λαρισσαιων Δημοσιε Ηρως Χρηστε Χαιρε, and de Rossi (*Roma Sotterranea*, tome i., tav. xxi.) gives us another example from the catacombs—"Ælia Chreste, in Pace."*

To-day the writer is able to add to all those testimonies the corroboration of an erudite author, who proves whatever he undertakes to show on the authority of geometrical demonstration. There is a most curious passage with remarks and explanations in the *Source of Measures*, whose author has probably never heard of the "Mystery-God" Visvakarma of the early Âryans. Treating on the difference between the terms Chrest and Christ, he ends by saying that:

There were two Messiahs: one who went down into the pit for the salvation of this world; this was the Sun shorn of his golden rays, and crowned with blackened ones (symbolising this loss), as the thorns: the other was the triumphant Messiah mounting up to the summit of the arch of heaven, and *personified as the Lion of the Tribe of Judah*. In both instances he had the cross; once in humiliation and once holding it in his control as the law of creation, He being Jehovah.

And then the author proceeds to give "the fact" that "there were two Messiahs," etc., as quoted above. And this—leaving the divine and mystic character and claim for Jesus entirely independent of this event of His mortal life—shows Him, beyond any doubt, as an Initiate of the Egyptian Mysteries, where the same rite of Death and of spiritual Resurrection for the neophyte, or the suffering Chrestos on his trial and new birth by Regeneration, was enacted—for this was a universally adopted rite.

The "pit" into which the Eastern Initiate was made to descend was, as shown before, Pâtâla, one of the seven regions of the nether world, over which ruled Vâsuki, the great "snake God." This pit, Pâtâla, has

* *Isis Unveiled*, ii. 323

in the Eastern Symbolism precisely the same manifold meaning as is found by Mr. Ralston Skinner in the Hebrew word *shiac*, in its application to the case in hand. For it was the synonym of Scorpio. Pâtâla's depths being "impregnated with the brightness of the generative Sun"—represented by the "newly born" into the glory; and Pâtâla was and is in a sense, "a pit, a grave, the place of death, and the door of Hades or Sheol"—as, in the partially exoteric Initiations in India, the candidate had to pass through the matrix of the heifer before proceeding to Pâtâla. In its non-mystic sense it is the Antipodes, America being referred to in India as Pâtâla. But in its symbolism it meant all that, and much more. The fact alone that Vâsuki, the ruling Deity of Pâtâla, is represented in the Hindu Pantheon as the great Nâga (Serpent)—who was used by the Gods and Asuras as a rope round the mountain Mandara, at the churning of the ocean for Amrita, the water of immortality—connects him directly with Initiation.

For he is Shesha Nâga also, serving as a couch for Vishnu, and upholding the seven worlds; and he is also Ananta, "the endless," and the symbol of eternity—hence the "God of Secret Wisdom," degraded by the Church to the *rôle* of the tempting Serpent, of Satan. That what is now said is correct may be verified by the evidence of even the exoteric rendering of the attributes of various Gods and Sages both in the Hindu and the Buddhist Pantheons. Two instances will suffice to show how little our best and most erudite Orientalists are capable of dealing correctly and fairly with the symbolism of Eastern nations, while remaining ignorant of the corresponding points to be found only in Occultism and the Secret Doctrine.

(1) The learned Orientalist and Tibetan traveller, Professor Emil Schlagintweit, mentions in one of his works on Tibet, a national legend to the effect that

> Nâgârjuna [a "mythological" personage "without any real existence," the learned German scholar thinks] received the book Paramârtha, or according to others, the book *Avatamsaka*, from the Nâgas, fabulous creatures of the nature of serpents, who occupy a place among the beings superior to man, and are regarded as protectors of the law of Buddha. To these spiritual beings Shâkyamuni is said to have taught a more philosophical religious system than to men, who were not sufficiently advanced to understand it at the time of his appearance.*

Nor are men sufficiently advanced for it now; for "the more philo-

* *Buddhism in Tibet*, p. 31.

sophical religious system" is the Secret Doctrine, the Occult Eastern Philosophy, which is the corner-stone of all sciences rejected by the unwise builders even at this day, and more to-day perhaps than ever before, in the great conceit of our age. The allegory means simply that Nâgârjuna having been initiated by the "Serpents"—the Adepts, "the wise ones"—and driven out from India by the Brâhmans, who dreaded to have their Mysteries and sacerdotal Science divulged (the real cause of their hatred of Buddhism), went away to China and Tibet, where he initiated many into the truths of the hidden Mysteries taught by Gautama Buddha.

(a) The hidden symbolism of Nârada—the great Rishi and the author of some of the Rig-Vaidic hymns, who incarnated again later on during Krishna's time—has never been understood. Yet, in connection with the Occult Sciences, Nârada, the son of Brahmâ, is one of the most prominent characters; he is directly connected in his first incarnation with the "Builders"—hence with the seven "Rectors" of the Christian Church, who "helped God in the work of creation." This grand personification is hardly noticed by our Orientalists, who refer only to that which he is alleged to have said of Pâtâla, namely, "that it is a place of sexual and sensual gratifications." This is thought to be amusing, and the reflection is suggested that Nârada, no doubt, "found the place delightful." Yet this sentence simply shows him to have been an Initiate, connected directly with the Mysteries, and walking, as all the other neophytes, before and after him, had to walk, in "the pit among the thorns" in the "sacrificial *Chrest* condition," as the suffering victim made to descend thereinto—a mystery, truly!

Nârada is one of the seven Rishis, the "mind-born sons" of Brahmâ. The fact of his having been during his incarnation a high Initiate—he, like Orpheus, being the founder of the Mysteries—is corroborated, and made evident by his history. The *Mahâbhârata* states that Nârada, having frustrated the scheme formed for peopling the universe, in order to remain true to his vow of chastity, was cursed by Daksha, and sentenced to be born once more. Again, when born during Krishna's time, he is accused of calling his father Brahmâ "a false teacher," because the latter advised him to get married, and he refused to do so. This shows him to have been an Initiate, going against the orthodox worship and religion. It is curious to find this Rishi and leader among the "Builders" and the "Heavenly Host" as the prototype of the Christian "leader" of the same "Host"—the Archangel Mikael. Both are the male "Virgins," and both are the only ones among their respective "Hosts" who refuse to create. Nârada is said to have dissuaded the Hari-ashvas, the five thousand sons of Daksha, begotten by him for the purpose of peopling the Earth, from producing offspring. Since then the Hari-ashvas have "dispersed themselves through the regions, and have never returned." The Initiates are, perhaps, the incarnations of these Hari-ashvas?

It was on the seventh day, the third of his ultimate trial, that the neophyte arose, a regenerated man, who, having passed through his second spiritual birth, returned to earth a glorified and triumphant conqueror of Death, a Hierophant.

An Eastern neophyte in his Chrest condition may be seen in a curious engraving in Moor's *Hindu Pantheon*, whose author mistook another form of the crucified Sun or Vishnu, Vittoba, for Krishna, and calls it "Krishna crucified in Space." The engraving is also given in Dr. Lundy's *Monumental Christianity*, in which work the reverend author has collected as many proofs as his ponderous volume could hold of "Christian symbols *before* Christianity," as he expresses it. Thus he shows us Krishna and Apollo as good shepherds, Krishna holding the cruciform Conch and the Chakra, and Krishna "crucified in Space," as he calls it. Of this figure it may be truly said, as the author says of it himself:

> This representation I believe to be anterior to Christianity. . . . It looks like a Christian crucifix in many respects. . . . The drawing, the attitude, the nail-marks in hands and feet, indicate a Christian origin, while the Parthian coronet of seven points, the absence of the wood, and of the usual inscription, and the rays of glory above, would seem to point to some other than a Christian origin. Can it be the victim-man, or the priest and victim both in one, of the Hindu Mythology, who offered himself a sacrifice before the worlds were?

It is surely so.

> Can it be Plato's Second God who impressed himself on the universe in the form of the cross? Or is it his divine man, who would be scourged, tormented, fettered, have his eyes burnt out; and lastly . . . *would be crucified?*

It is all that and much more; archaic religious Philosophy was universal, and its Mysteries are as old as man. It is the eternal symbol of the personified Sun—astronomically purified—in its mystic meaning regenerated, and symbolised by all the Initiates in memory of a sinless Humanity when all were "Sons of God." Now, mankind has become the "Son of Evil" truly. Does all this take anything away from the dignity of Christ as an ideal, or of Jesus, as a divine man? Not at all. On the contrary, made to stand alone, glorified above all other "Sons of God," He can only foment evil feelings in all those many millioned nations who do not believe in the Christian system, provoking their hatred and leading to iniquitous wars and strifes. If, on the other hand, we place Him among a long series of "Sons of God" and Sons of divine Light, every man may then be left to choose for himself, among those many ideals, which he will choose as a God to call to his help, and worship on earth as in Heaven.

Many among those called "Saviours" were "good shepherds," as was Krishna for one, and all of them are said to have "crushed the serpent's head"—in other words to have conquered their sensual nature and to have mastered divine and Occult Wisdom. Apollo killed Python, a fact which exonerates him from the charge of being himself the great Dragon, Satan: Krishna slew the snake Kalinâga, the Black Serpent; and the Scandinavian Thor bruised the head of the symbolical reptile with his crucifixion mace.

In Egypt every city of importance was separated from its burial-place by a sacred lake. The same ceremony of judgment, as is described in *The Book of the Dead*—"that precious and mysterious book" (Bunsen)—as taking place in the world of Spirit, took place on earth during the burial of the mummy. Forty-two judges or assessors assembled on the shore and judged the departed "Soul" according to its actions when in the body. After that the priests returned within the sacred precincts and instructed the neophytes upon the probable fate of the Soul, and the solemn drama that was then taking place in the invisible realm whither the Soul had fled. The immortality of the Spirit was strongly inculcated on the neophytes by the *Al-om-jah*—the name of the highest Egyptian Hierophant. In the Crata Nepoa—the priestly Mysteries in Egypt—the following are described as four out of the seven degrees of Initiation.

After a preliminary trial at Thebes, where the neophyte had to pass through many probations, called the "Twelve Tortures," he was commanded, in order that he might come out triumphant, to govern his passions and never lose for a moment the idea of his inner God or seventh Principle. Then, as a symbol of the wanderings of the unpurified Soul, he had to ascend several ladders and wander in darkness in a cave with many doors, all of which were locked. Having overcome all, he received the degree of Pastophoris, after which he became, in the second and third degrees, the Neocoris and Melanephoris. Brought into a vast subterranean chamber, thickly furnished with mummies lying in state, he was placed in presence of the coffin which contained the mutilated body of Osiris. This was the hall called the "Gates of Death," whence the verse in Job:

> Have the gates of Death been opened to thee,
> Hast thou seen the doors of the shadow of death?

Thus asks the "Lord," the Hierophant, the Al-om-jah, the Initiator of Job, alluding to this third degree of Initiation. For the Book of *Job* is the poem of Initiation *par excellence*.

When the neophyte had conquered the terrors of this trial, he was conducted to the "Hall of Spirits," to be judged by them. Among the rules in which he was instructed, he was commanded:

> Never to either desire or seek revenge; to be always ready to help a brother in danger, even unto the risk of his own life; to bury every dead body; to honour his parents above all; to respect old age, and protect those weaker than himself; and finally, to ever bear in mind the hour of death, and that of resurrection in a new and imperishable body.

Purity and chastity were highly recommended, and adultery was threatened with death. Thus the Egyptian neophyte was made a Kristophoros. In this degree the mystery-name of IAO was communicated to him.

Let the reader compare the above sublime precepts with the precepts of Buddha, and the noble commandments in the "Rule of Life" for the ascetics of India, and he will understand the unity of the Secret Doctrine everywhere.

It is impossible to deny the presence of a sexual element in many religious symbols, but this fact is not in the least open to censure, once it becomes generally known that—in the religious traditions of every country—man was not born in the first "human" race from father and mother. From the bright "mind-born Sons of Brahmâ," the Rishis, and from Adam Kadmon with his Emanations, the Sephiroth, down to the "parentless," the Anupâdaka, or the Dhyani-Buddhas, from whom sprang the Bodhisattvas and Manushi-Buddhas, the earthly Initiates—men—the first race of men was with every nation held as being born without father or mother. Man, the "Manushi-Buddha," the Manu, the "Enosh," son of Seth, or the "Son of Man," as he is called—is born in the present way only as the consequence the unavoidable fatality, of the law of natural evolution. Mankind—having reached the last limit, and that turning point where its spiritual nature had to make room for mere physical organisation—had to "fall into matter" and generation. But man's evolution and involution are cyclic. He will end as he began. Of course to our grossly material minds even the sublime symbolism of Kosmos conceived in the matrix of Space after the divine Unit had entered into and fructified it with Its holy fiat, will no doubt suggest materiality. Not so with primitive mankind. The initiatory rite in the Mysteries of the self-sacrificing Victim that dies a spiritual death to save the world from destruction—really from depopulation—was established during the Fourth Race, to commemorate an event, which, physiologically, has now become the Mystery of Mysteries among the world-problems. In the Jewish script it is Cain and the female Abel who are the sacrificed and sacrificing couple—both immolating themselves (as permutations of Adam and Eve, or the dual Jehovah) and shedding their blood "of separation and union," for the sake of and to save mankind by inaugurating a new physiological race. Later still, when the neophyte, as already mentioned, in order to be re-born once more into his lost spiritual state, had to pass through the entrails (the womb) of a *virgin* heifer * killed at the moment of the rite, it involved again a mystery and one as great, for it referred to the process of birth, or rather the first entrance of man on to this earth, through Vâch—"the melodious cow who milks forth sustenance and water"—and who is the female Logos. It had also reference to the same self-sacrifice of the "divine Hermaphrodite"—of the third Root-Race—the transformation of Humanity into truly physical men, after the loss of spiritual potency. When, the fruit of evil having been tasted along with the fruit of good, there was as a result the gradual atrophy of spirituality and a strengthening of the materiality in man, then he was doomed to be born thenceforth through the present process. This is the Mystery of the Hermaphrodite, which the Ancients kept so secret and veiled. It was neither the absence of moral feeling, nor the presence of gross sensuality in them that made them imagine their Deities under a dual aspect ; but rather their knowledge of the mysteries and processes of primitive Nature. The Science of Physiology was better known to them than it is to us now. It is in this

* The Âryans replaced the living cow by one made of gold, silver or any other metal, and the rite is preserved to this day, when one desires to become a Brâhman, a twice-born, in India.

that lies buried the key to the Symbolism of old, the true focus of national thought, and the strange dual-sexed images of nearly every God and Goddess in both pagan and monotheistic Pantheons.

Says Sir William Drummond in *Œdipus Judaicus*:

The truths of science were the arcana of the priests because these truths were the foundations of religion.

But why should the missionaries so cruelly twit the Vaishnavas and Krishna worshippers for the supposed grossly indecent meaning of their symbols, since it is made clear beyond the slightest doubt, and by the most unprejudiced writers, that Chrestos in the pit—whether the pit be taken as meaning the grave or hell—had likewise a sexual element in it, from the very origin of the symbol.

This fact is no longer denied to-day. The "Brothers of the Rosy Cross" of the Middle Ages were as good Christians as any to be found in Europe, nevertheless, all their rites were based on symbols whose meaning was pre-eminently phallic and sexual. Their biographer, Hargrave Jennings, the best modern authority on Rosicrucianism, speaking of this mystic Brotherhood, describes how

The tortures and the sacrifice of Calvary, the Passion of the Cross, were, in their [the Rose-Croix's] glorious blessed magic and triumph, the protest and appeal.

Protest—by whom? The answer is, the protest of the crucified Rose, the greatest and the most unveiled of all sexual symbols—the Yoni and Lingam, the "victim" and the "murderer," the female and male principles in Nature. Open the last work of that author, *Phallicism*, and see in what glowing terms he describes the sexual symbolism in that which is most sacred to the Christian:

The flowing blood streamed from the crown, or the piercing circlet of the thorns of Hell. The Rose is feminine. Its lustrous carmine petals are guarded with thorns. The Rose is the most beautiful of flowers. The Rose is the Queen of God's Garden (Mary, the Virgin). It is not the Rose alone which is the magical idea, or truth. But it is the "crucified rose," or the "martyred rose" (by the grand mystic apocalyptic figure) which is the talisman, the standard, the object of adoration of all the "Sons of Wisdom" or the true Rosicrucians.*

Not of *all* the "Sons of Wisdom," by any means, not even of the *true* Rosicrucian. For the latter would never put in such sickening relievo, in such a purely sensual and terrestrial, not to say animal light, the grandest, the noblest of Nature's symbols. To the Rosi-

* *Op. cit.*, p. 241.

crucian, the "Rose" was the symbol of Nature, of the ever prolific and virgin Earth, or Isis, the mother and nourisher of man, considered as feminine and represented as a virgin woman by the Egyptian Initiates. Like every other personification of Nature and the Earth she is the sister and wife of Osiris, as the two characters answer to the personified symbol of the Earth, both she and the Sun being the progeny of the same mysterious Father, because the Earth is fecundated by the Sun—according to the earliest Mysticism—by divine insufflation. It was the pure ideal of mystic Nature that was personified in the "World Virgins," the "Celestial Maidens," and later on by the human Virgin, Mary, the Mother of the Saviour, the *Salvator Mundi* now chosen by the Christian World. And it was the character of the Jewish maiden that was adapted by Theology to archaic Symbolism,* and not the Pagan symbol that was modelled for the new occasion.

We know through Herodotus that the Mysteries were brought from India by Orpheus—a hero far anterior to both Homer and Hesiod. Very little is really known of him, and till very lately Orphic literature, and even the Argonauts, were attributed to Onamacritus, a contemporary of Pisistratus, Solon and Pythagoras—who was credited with their compilation in the present form toward the close of the sixth century B.C., or 800 years after the time of Orpheus. But we are told that in the days of Pausanias there was a sacerdotal family, who, like the Brâhmans with the *Vedas*, had committed to memory all the Orphic Hymns, and that they were usually thus transmitted from one generation to another. By placing Orpheus so far back as 1200 B.C., official Science—so careful in her chronology to choose in each case as late a period as possible—admits that the Mysteries, or in other words Occultism dramatised, belong to a still earlier epoch than the Chaldæans and Egyptians.

The downfall of the Mysteries in Europe may now be mentioned.

---

* In Ragon's *Orthodoxie Maçonnique*, p. 105, *note*, we find the following statement—borrowed from Albumazar the Arabian, probably: "*The Virgin of the Magi and Chaldæans.* The Chaldæan sphere [globe] showed in its heavens a newly-born babe, called *Christ and Jesus*; it was placed in the arms of the Celestial Virgin. It was to this Virgin that Eratosthenes, the Alexandrian Librarian, born 276 years before our era, gave the name of Isis, mother of Horus." This is only what Kircher gives (in *Œdipus Ægypticus*, iii. 5), quoting Albumazar: "In the first decan of the Virgin rises a maid, called Aderenosa, that is pure, immaculate virgin . . . sitting upon an embroidered throne nursing a boy . . .; a boy, named Jessus . . . which signifies Issa, whom they also call Christ in Greek." (See *Isis Unveiled*, ii. 491.)

SECTION XXXIII.

THE LAST OF THE MYSTERIES IN EUROPE.

As was predicted by the great Hermes in his dialogue with Æsculapius, the time had indeed come when impious foreigners accused Egypt of adoring monsters, and naught but the letters engraved in stone upon her monuments survived—enigmas unintelligible to posterity. Her sacred Scribes and Hierophants became wanderers upon the face of the earth. Those who had remained in Egypt found themselves obliged for fear of a profanation of the sacred Mysteries to seek refuge in deserts and mountains, to form and establish secret societies and brotherhoods—such as the Essenes; those who had crossed the oceans to India and even to the (now-called) New World, bound themselves by solemn oaths to keep silent, and to preserve secret their Sacred Knowledge and Science; thus these were buried deeper than ever out of human sight. In Central Asia and on the northern borderlands of India, the triumphant sword of Aristotle's pupil swept away from his path of conquest every vestige of a once pure Religion: and its Adepts receded further and further from that path into the most hidden spots of the globe. The cycle of * * * * being at its close, the first hour for the disappearance of the Mysteries struck on the clock of the Races, with the Macedonian conqueror. The first strokes of its last hour sounded in the year 47 B.C. Alesia* the famous city in Gaul, the Thebes of the Kelts, so renowned for its ancient rites of Initiation and Mysteries, was, as J. M. Ragon well describes it:

> The ancient metropolis and the tomb of Initiation, of the religion of the Druids and of the freedom of Gaul.†

---

* Now called *St. Reine* (Côte d'Or) on the two streams, the Ose and the Oserain. Its fall is a historical fact in Keltic Gaulish History.

† *Orthodoxie Maçonnique*, p. 22.

It was during the first century before our era, that the last and supreme hour of the great Mysteries had struck. History shows the populations of Central Gaul revolting against the Roman yoke. The country was subject to Cæsar, and the revolt was crushed; the result was the slaughter of the garrison at Alesia (or Alisa), and of all its inhabitants, including the Druids, the college-priests and the neophytes; after this the whole city was plundered and razed to the ground.

Bibractis, a city as large and as famous, not far from Alesia, perished a few years later. J. M. Ragon describes her end as follows:

> Bibractis, the mother of sciences, the soul of the early nations [in Europe], a town equally famous for its sacred college of Druids, its civilisation, its schools, in which 40,000 students were taught philosophy, literature, grammar, jurisprudence, medicine, astrology, occult sciences, architecture, etc. Rival of Thebes, of Memphis, of Athens and of Rome, it possessed an amphitheatre, surrounded with colossal statues, and accommodating 100,000 spectators, gladiators, a capitol, temples of Janus, Pluto, Proserpine, Jupiter, Apollo, Minerva, Cybele, Venus and Anubis; and in the midst of those sumptuous edifices the Naumachy, with its vast basin, an incredible construction, a gigantic work wherein floated boats and galleys devoted to naval games; then a *Champ de Mars*, an aqueduct, fountains, public baths; finally fortifications and walls, the construction of which dated from the heroic ages.*

Such was the last city in Gaul wherein died for Europe the secrets of the Initiations of the Great Mysteries, the Mysteries of Nature, and of her forgotten Occult truths. The rolls and manuscripts of the famous Alexandrian Library were burned and destroyed by the same Cæsar,† but while History deprecates the action of the Arab general, Amrus, who gave the final touch to this act of vandalism perpetrated by the great conqueror, it has not a word to say to the latter for his destruction of nearly the same amount of precious rolls in Alesia, nor to the destroyer of Bibractis. While Sacrovir—chief of the Gauls, who revolted against Roman despotism under Tiberius, and was defeated by Silius in the year 21 of our era—was burning himself alive with his fellow conspirators on a funeral pyre before the gates of the city, as Ragon tells us, the latter was sacked and plundered, and all her treasures of literature on the Occult Sciences perished by fire. The once majestic city, Bibractis, has now become Autun, Ragon explains.

---

* *Op. cit.* p. 22.

† The Christian mob in 389 of our era completed the work of destruction upon what remained; most of the priceless works were saved for students of Occultism, but lost to the world.

A few monuments of glorious antiquity are still there, such as the temples of Janus and of Cybele.

Ragon goes on:

Arles, founded two thousand years before Christ, was sacked in 270. This metropolis of Gaul, restored 40 years later by Constantine, has preserved to this day a few remains of its ancient splendour; amphitheatre, capitol, an obelisk, a block of granite 17 metres high, a triumphal arch, catacombs, etc. Thus ended Kelto-Gaulic civilisation. Cæsar, as a barbarian worthy of Rome, had already accomplished the destruction of the ancient Mysteries by the sack of the temples and their initiatory colleges, and by the massacre of the Initiates and the Druids. Remained Rome; but she never had but the lesser Mysteries, shadows of the Secret Sciences. The Great Initiation was extinct.*

A few further extracts may be given from his *Occult Masonry*, as they bear directly upon our subject. However learned and erudite, some of the chronological mistakes of that author are very great. He says:—

After deified man (Hermes) came the King-Priest [the Hierophant] Menes was the first legislator and the founder of Thebes of the hundred palaces. He filled that city with magnificent splendour; it is from his day that the sacerdotal epoch of Egypt dates. The priests reigned, for it is they who made the laws. It is said that there have been three hundred and twenty-nine [Hierophants] since his time—all of whom have remained unknown.

After that, genuine Adepts having become scarce, the author shows the Priests choosing false ones from the midst of slaves, whom they exhibited, having crowned and deified them, for the adoration of the ignorant masses.

Tired of reigning in such a servile way, the kings rebelled and freed themselves. Then came Sesostris, the founder of Memphis (1613, they say, before our era). To the sacerdotal election to the throne succeeded that of the warriors. . . Cheops who reigned from 1178 to 1122 built the great Pyramid which bears his name. He is accused of having persecuted theocracy and closed the temples.

This is utterly incorrect, though Ragon repeats "History." The Pyramid called by the name of Cheops is the Great Pyramid, the building of which even Baron Bunsen assigned to 5,000 B.C. He says in *Egypt's Place in Universal History*:

* *Op. cit.* p. 23. J. M. Ragon, a Belgian by birth, and a Mason, knew more about Occultism than any other non-initiated writer. For fifty years he studied the ancient Mysteries wherever he could find accounts of them. In 1805, he founded at Paris the Brotherhood of *Les Trinosophes*, in which Lodge he delivered for years lectures on Ancient and Modern Initiation (in 1818 and again in 1841), which were published, and now are lost. Then he became the writer in chief of *Hermes*, a masonic paper. His best works were *La Maçonnerie Occulte* and the *Fastes Initiatiques*. After his death, in 1866, a number of his MSS. remained in the possession of the Grand Orient of France. A high Mason told the writer that Ragon had corresponded for years with two Orientalists in Syria and Egypt, one of whom is a Kopt gentleman.

The Origines of Egypt go back to the sixth millennium before Christ.*

And as the Mysteries were performed and the Initiations took place in that Pyramid—for indeed it was built for that purpose—it looks strange and an utter contradiction with known facts in the history of the Mysteries, to suppose that Cheops, if the builder of that Pyramid, ever turned against the initiated Priests and their temples. Moreover, as far as the Secret Doctrine teaches, it was not Cheops who built the Pyramid of that name, whatever else he might have done.

Yet, it is quite true that

Owing to an Ethiopian invasion and the federated government of twelve chiefs, royalty fell into the hands of Amasis, a man of low birth.

This was in 570 B.C., and it is Amasis who destroyed priestly power. And

Thus perished that ancient theocracy which showed its crowned priests for so many centuries to Egypt and the whole world.

Egypt had gathered the students of all countries around her Priests and Hierophants before Alexandria was founded. Ennemoser asks:

How comes it that so little has become known of the Mysteries and of their particular contents, through so many ages, and amongst so many different times and people? The answer is that it is again owing to the universally strict silence of the initiated. Another cause may be found in the destruction and total loss of all the written memorials of the secret knowledge of the remotest antiquity.

Numa's books, described by Livy, consisting of natural philosophy, were found in his tomb; but they were not allowed to be made known, lest they should reveal the most secret mysteries of the state religion. . . . The senate and the tribunes of the people determined . . . that the books themselves should be burned, which was done.†

Cassain mentions a treatise, well-known in the fourth and fifth centuries, which was accredited to Ham, the son of Noah, who in his turn was reputed to have received it from Jared, the fourth generation from Seth, the son of Adam.

Alchemy also was first taught in Egypt by her learned Priests, though the first appearance of this system is as old as man. Many writers have declared that Adam was the first Adept; but that was a blind and a pun upon the name, which is "red earth" in one of its meanings. The correct information—under its allegorical veil—is found in the sixth chapter of Genesis, which speaks of the "Sons of God" who took wives of the daughters of men, after which they communicated

* *Op. cit.*, iv. 462.

† *History of Magic*, ii. 11.

to these wives many a mystery and secret of the phenomenal world. The cradle of Alchemy, says Olaus Borrichius, is to be sought in the most distant times. Democritus of Abdera was an Alchemist, and a Hermetic Philosopher. Clement of Alexandria wrote considerably upon the Science, and Moses and Solomon are called proficients in it. We are told by W. Godwin:

> The first authentic record on this subject is an edict of Diocletian about 300 years A.D., ordering a diligent search to be made in Egypt for all the ancient books which treated of the art of making gold and silver, that they might, without distinction, be consigned to the flames.

The Alchemy of the Chaldæans and the old Chinamen is not even the parent of that Alchemy which revived among the Arabians many centuries later. There is a spiritual Alchemy and a physical transmutation. The knowledge of both was imparted at the Initiations.

SECTION XXXIV.

THE POST-CHRISTIAN SUCCESSORS TO THE MYSTERIES.

THE Eleusinian Mysteries were no more. Yet it was these which gave their principal features to the Neo-platonic school of Ammonius Saccas, for the Eclectic System was chiefly characterised by its Theurgy and ecstasis. It was Iamblichus who added to it the Egyptian doctrine of Theurgy with its practices, and Porphyry, the Jew, who opposed this new element. The school, however, with but few exceptions, practised asceticism and contemplation, its mystics passing through a discipline as rigorous as that of the Hindu devotee. Their efforts never tended so much to develop the successful practice of thaumaturgy, necromancy or sorcery—such as they are now accused of—as to evolve the higher faculties of the inner man, the Spiritual Ego. The school held that a number of spiritual beings, denizens of spheres quite independent of the earth and of the human cycle, were mediators between the "Gods" and men, and even between man and the Supreme Soul. To put it in plainer language, the soul of man became, owing to the help of the Planetary Spirits, "recipient of the soul of the world" as Emerson puts it. Apollonius of Tyana asserted his possession of such a power in these words (quoted by Professor Wilder in his *Neo-Platonism*):

> I can see the present and the future in a clear mirror. The sage [Adept] need not wait for the vapours of the earth and the corruption of the air to foresee plagues and fevers; he must know them later than God, but earlier than the people. The *theoi* or gods see the future; common men, the present; sages, that which is about to take place. My peculiar abstemious mode of living produces such an acuteness of the senses, or creates some other faculty, so that the greatest and most remarkable things may be performed.*

---

* *Neo-Platonism and Alchemy*, p. 15.

Professor A. Wilder's comment thereupon is remarkable:

This is what may be termed *spiritual photography*. The soul is the camera in which facts and events, future, past, and present, are alike fixed; and the mind becomes conscious of them. Beyond our everyday world of limits, all is as one day or state—the past and future comprised in the present. Probably this is the "great day," the "last day," the "day of the Lord," of the Bible writers—the day into which everyone passes by death or *ecstasis*. Then the soul is freed from the constraint of the body, and its nobler part is united to higher nature and becomes partaker in the wisdom and foreknowledge of the higher beings.*

How far the system practised by the Neo-Platonists was identical with that of the old and the modern Vedântins may be inferred from what Dr. A. Wilder says of the Alexandrian Theosophists.

The anterior idea of the New Platonists was that of a single Supreme Essence. . . All the old philosophies contained the doctrine that *θεοί*, *theoi*, gods or disposers, angels, demons, and other spiritual agencies, emanated from the Supreme Being. Ammonius accepted the doctrine of the Books of Hermes, that from the divine All proceeded the Divine Wisdom or Amun; that from Wisdom proceeded the Demiurge or Creator; and from the Creator, the subordinate spiritual beings; the world and its peoples being the last. The first is contained in the second, the first and second in the third, and so on through the entire series.†

This is a perfect echo of the belief of the Vedântins, and it proceeds directly from the secret teachings of the East. The same author says:

Akin to this is the doctrine of the Jewish Kabala which was taught by the Perushim or Pharisees, who probably borrowed it, as their sectarian designation would seem to indicate, from the Magians of Persia. It is substantially embodied in the following synopsis.

The Divine Being is the All, the source of all existence, the Infinite; and He cannot be known. The Universe reveals Him, and subsists by Him. At the beginning His effulgence went forth everywhere.‡ Eventually He retired within Himself and so formed around Him a vacant space. Into this He transmitted His first Emanation, a Ray, containing in it the generative and conceptive power, and hence the name IE, or Jah. This in its turn produced the *tikkun*, the pattern or idea of form; and in this emanation, which also contained the male and female, or generative and conceptive potencies, were the three primitive forces of Light, Spirit and Life. This Tikkun is united to the Ray, or first emanation, and pervaded by it: and by that union is also in perpetual communication with the infinite source. It is the pattern, the primitive man, the Adam Kadmon, the *macrocosm* of

* *Loc. cit.*

† *Op. cit.*, pp. 9, 10.

‡ This Divine Effulgence and Essence is the light of the Logos; only the Vedântin would not use the pronoun "He," but would say "It."

Pythagoras and other philosophers. From it proceeded the *Sephiroth*. . . . From the Sephiroth in turn emanated the four worlds, each proceeding out of the one immediately above it, and the lower one enveloping its superior. These worlds became less pure as they descended in the scale, the lowest of all being the material world.*

This veiled enunciation of the Secret Teaching will be clear to our readers by this time. These worlds are:

Aziluth is peopled with the purest emanations [the First, almost spiritual, Race of the human beings that were to inhabit] the Fourth; the second, *Beriah*, by a lower order, the servants of the former [the second Race]; the third, *Jesirah*, by the cherubim and seraphim, the Elohim and B'ni Elohim ["Sons of Gods" or *Elohim*, our Third Race]. The fourth world, *Asiah*, is inhabited by the Klipputh, of whom Belial is chief [the Atlantean Sorcerers].†

These worlds are all the earthly duplicates of their heavenly prototypes, the mortal and temporary reflections and shadows of the more durable, if not eternal, races dwelling in other, to us, invisible worlds. The souls of the men of our Fifth Race derive their elements from these four worlds—Root Races—that preceded ours: namely, our intellect, Manas, the fifth principle, our passions and mental and corporeal appetites. A conflict having arisen, called "war in heaven," among our prototypical worlds, war came to pass, æons later, between the Atlanteans‡ of Asiah, and those of the third Root Race, the B'ni Elohim or the "Sons of God,"§ and then evil and wickedness were intensified. Mankind (in the last sub-race of the third Root Race) having

Sinned in their first parent [a physiological allegory, truly!] from whose soul every human soul is an emanation,

says the *Zohar*, men were "exiled" into more material bodies to

Expiate that sin and become proficient in goodness.

To accomplish the cycle of necessity, rather, explains the doctrine; to progress on their task of evolution, from which task none of us can be freed, neither by death nor suicide, for each of us have to pass through the "Valley of Thorns" before he emerges into the plains of divine light and rest. And thus men will continue to be born in new bodies

Till they have become sufficiently pure to enter a higher form of existence.

---

* *Loc. cit.*, *note*, p. 10.

† *Loc. cit.*, *note*.

‡ See *Esoteric Buddhism*, by A. P. Sinnett, Fifth Edition.

§ See *Isis Unveiled*, Vol. I., pp. 589-595. The "Sons of God" and their war with the giants and magicians.

This means only that Mankind, from the First down to the latter Seventh Race, is composed of one and the same company of actors, who have descended from higher spheres to perform their artistic tour on this our planet, Earth. Starting as pure spirits on our downward journey around the world (verily!) with the knowledge of truth—now feebly echoed in the Occult Doctrines—inherent in us, cyclic law brings us down to the reversed apex of matter, which is lost down here on earth and the bottom of which we have already struck; and then the same law of spiritual gravity will make us slowly ascend to still higher, still purer spheres than those we started from.

Foresight, prophecy, oracular powers! Illusive fancies of man's dwarfed perceptions, which see actual images in reflections and shadows, and mistake past actualities for prophetic images of a future that has no room in Eternity. Our macrocosm and its smallest micro-cosm, man, are both repeating the same play of universal and individual events at each station, as on every stage on which Karma leads them to enact their respective dramas of life. False prophets could have no existence had there been no true prophets. And so there were, and many of both classes, and in all ages. Only, none of these ever saw anything but that which had already come to pass, and had been, before, prototypically enacted in higher spheres—if the event foretold related to national or public weal or woe—or in some preceding life, if it concerned only an individual, for every such event is stamped as an indelible record of the Past and Future, which are only, after all, the ever Present in Eternity. The "worlds" and the purifications spoken of in the *Zohar* and other Kabalistic books, relate to our globe and races no more and no less than they relate to other globes and other races that have preceded our own in the great cycle. It was such fundamental truths as these that were performed in allegorical plays and images during the Mysteries, the last Act of which, the Epilogue for the Mystæ, was the *anastasis* or "continued existence," as also the "Soul transformation."

Hence, the author of *Neo-platonism and Alchemy* shows us that all such Eclectic doctrines were strongly reflected in the *Epistles of Paul*; and were

Inculcated more or less among the Churches. Hence, such passages as these "Ye were dead in errors and sins; ye walked according to the *æon* of this world, according to the *archon* that has the domination of the air." "We wrestle not against flesh and blood, but against the dominations, against potencies, against the lords of darkness, and against the mischievousness of spirits in the empyrean regions." But Paul was evidently hostile to the effort to blend his gospel with the gnostic ideas of the Hebrew-Egyptian school, as seems to have been attempted at Ephesus; and accordingly, wrote to Timothy, his favourite disciple, "Keep safe the precious charge entrusted to thee; and reject the new doctrines and the antagonistic principles of the gnosis, falsely so-called, of which some have made profession and gone astray from the faith."*

But as the Gnosis is the Science pertaining to our Higher Self, as blind faith is a matter of temperament and emotionalism, and as Paul's doctrine was still newer and his interpretations far more thickly veiled, to keep the inner truths hidden far away from the Gnostic, preference has been given to the former by every earnest seeker after truth.

Besides this, the great Teachers who professed the so-called "false Gnosis" were very numerous in the days of the Apostles, and were as great as any converted Rabbi could be. If Porphyry, the Jew Malek, went against Theurgy on account of old traditional recollections, there were other teachers who practised it. Plotinus, Iamblichus, Proclus were all thaumaturgists, and the latter

Elaborated the entire theosophy and theurgy of his predecessors into a complete system.†

As to Ammonius,

Countenanced by Clemens and Athenagoras, in the Church, and by learned men of the Synagogue, the Academy, and the Grove, he fulfilled his labour by teaching a common doctrine for all.‡

Thus it is not Judaism and Christianity that re-modelled the ancient Pagan Wisdom, but rather the latter that put its heathen curb, quietly and insensibly, on the new faith; and this, moreover, was still further influenced by the Eclectic Theosophical system, the direct emanation of the Wisdom Religion. All that is grand and noble in Christian theology comes from Neo-Platonism. It is too well-known to now need much repetition that Ammonius Saccas, the God-taught *(theodidaktos)* and the lover of the truth *(philalethes)*, in establishing his school, made a direct attempt to benefit the world by teaching those portions of the Secret Science that were permitted by its direct guardians to be revealed in those days.§ The modern movement of our own Theo-

* *Loc. cit.*, note.

† *Op. cit.*, p. 18.

‡ *Op. cit.*, p. 8.

§ No orthodox Christian has ever equalled, far less surpassed, in the practice of true Christ-like virtues and ethics, or in the beauty of his moral nature, Ammonius, the Alexandrian pervert from Christianity (he was born from Christian parents).

sophical Society was begun on the same principles; for the Neo-Platonic school of Ammonius aimed, as we do, at the reconcilement of all sects and peoples, under the once common faith of the Golden Age, trying to induce the nations to lay aside their contentions—in religious matters at any rate—by proving to them that their various beliefs are all the more or less legitimate children of one common parent, the Wisdom Religion.

Nor was the Eclectic Theosophical system—as some writers inspired by Rome would make the world believe—developed only during the third century of our era; but it belongs to a much earlier age, as has been shown by Diogenes Laertius. He traces it to the beginning of the dynasty of the Ptolemies; to the great seer and prophet, the Egyptian Priest Pot-Amun, of the temple of the God of that name—for Amun is the God of Wisdom. Unto that day the communication between the Adepts of Upper India and Bactria and the Philosophers of the West had never ceased.

Under Philadelphus . . . the Hellenic teachers became rivals of the College of Rabbis of Babylon. The Buddhistic, Vedântic and Magian systems were expounded along with the philosophies of Greece. . . . Aristobulus, the Jew, declared that the ethics of Aristotle were derived from the law of Moses (!); and Philo, after him, attempted to interpret the Pentateuch in accordance with the doctrines of Pythagoras and the Academy. In Josephus it is said that, in the Book of the Genesis, Moses wrote philosophically—that is, in the figurative style; and the Essenes of Carmel were reproduced in the Therapeutæ of Egypt, who, in turn, were declared by Eusebius to be identical with the Christians, though they actually existed long before the Christian era. Indeed, in its turn, Christianity also was taught at Alexandria, and underwent an analogous metamorphosis. Pantænus, Athenagoras and Clement were thoroughly instructed in the Platonic philosophy, and comprehended its essential unity with the oriental systems.*

Ammonius, though the son of Christian parents, was a *lover of the* truth, a true Philaletheian foremost of all. He set his heart upon the work of reconciling the different systems into a harmonious whole, for he had already perceived the tendency of Christianity to raise itself on the hecatomb which it had constructed out of all other creeds and faiths. What says history?

The ecclesiastical historian, Mosheim, declares that

Ammonius, conceiving that not only the philosophers of Greece, but also all those of the different barbarous nations, were perfectly in unison with each other with regard to every essential point, made it his business so to temper and expound the tenets of all these various sects, as to make it appear they had all of them originated from one and the same source, and all tended to one and the same end. Again, Mosheim says that Ammonius taught that the religion of the multitude went hand in hand with philosophy, and with her had shared the fate of being by degrees corrupted and obscured with mere human conceits, superstition, and lies; that it ought, therefore, to be brought back to its original purity by purging it of this dross and expounding it upon philosophical principles; and that the whole which Christ had in view was to reinstate and restore to its primitive integrity the Wisdom of the Ancients.*

Now what was that "Wisdom of the Ancients" that the Founder of Christianity "had in view"? The system taught by Ammonius in his Eclectic Theosophical School was made of the crumbs permitted to be gathered from the antediluvian lore; those Neo-Platonic teachings are described in the *Edinburgh Encyclopædia* as follows:

He [Ammonius] adopted the doctrines which were received in Egypt concerning the Universe and the Deity, considered as constituting one great whole; concerning the eternity of the world, the nature of souls, the empire of Providence [Karma] and the government of the world by demons [*daimons* or spirits, archangels]. He also established a system of moral discipline which allowed the people in general to live according to the laws of their country and the dictates of nature; but required the wise to exalt their minds by contemplation, and to mortify the body,† so that they might be capable of enjoying the presence and assistance of the demons [including their own *daimon* or Seventh Principle] . . . and ascending after death to the presence of the Supreme [Soul] Parent. In order to reconcile the popular religions, and particularly the Christian, with this new system, he made the whole history of the heathen gods an allegory, maintaining that they were only celestial ministers‡ entitled to an inferior kind of worship; and he acknowledged that Jesus Christ was an excellent man and the friend of God, but alleged that it was not his design entirely to abolish the worship of demons,§ and that his only intention was to purify the ancient religion.

No more could be declared except for those Philaletheians who were initiated, "persons duly instructed and disciplined" to whom Ammonius communicated his more important doctrines,

Imposing on them the obligations of secrecy, as was done before him by Zoroaster and Pythagoras, and in the Mysteries [where an oath was required from the

* Quoted by Dr. Wilder, p. 5.

† "Mortification" is here meant in the moral, not the physical sense; to restrain every lust and passion, and live on the simplest diet possible.

‡ This is the Neo-Platonic teaching adopted as a doctrine in the Roman Catholic Church, with its worship of the Seven Spirits.

§ The Church has made of it the worship of devils, "Daimon" is Spirit, and relates to our divine Spirit, the seventh Principle and to the Dhyân Chohans. Jesus prohibited going to the temple or church "as Pharisees do" but commanded that man should retire for prayer (communion with his God) into a private closet. Is it Jesus who would have countenanced in the face of the starving millions, the building of the most gorgeous churches?

neophytes or catechumens not to divulge what they had learned). The great Pythagoras divided his teachings into exoteric and esoteric.*

Has not Jesus done the same, since He declared to His disciples that to them it was given to know the mysteries of the kingdom of heaven, whereas to the multitudes it was not given, and therefore He spoke in parables which had a two-fold meaning?

Dr. A. Wilder proceeds:

> Thus Ammonius found his work ready to his hand. His deep spiritual intuition, his extensive learning, and his familiarity with the Christian fathers, Pantænus, Clement and Athenagoras, and with the most erudite philosophers of the time, all fitted him for the labour he performed so thoroughly. . . . The results of his ministration are perceptible at the present day in every country of the Christian world; every prominent system of doctrine now bearing the marks of his plastic hand. Every ancient philosophy has had its votaries among the moderns; and even Judaism, oldest of them all, has taken upon itself changes which were suggested by the "God-taught" Alexandrian.†

The Neo-Platonic School of Alexandria founded by Ammonius—the prototype proposed for the Theosophical Society—taught Theurgy and Magic, as much as they were taught in the days of Pythagoras, and by others far earlier than his period. For Proclus says that the doctrines of Orpheus, who was an Indian and came from India, were the origin of the systems afterwards promulgated.

> What Orpheus delivered in hidden allegories, Pythagoras learned when he was initiated into the Orphic Mysteries; and Plato next received a perfect knowledge of them from Orphic and Pythagorean writings.‡

The Philaletheians had their division into neophytes (*chelas*) and Initiates, or Masters; and the eclectic system was characterised by three distinct features, which are purely Vedântic; a Supreme Essence, One and Universal; the eternity and indivisibility of the human spirit; and Theurgy, which is Mantricism. So also, as we have seen, they had their secret or Esoteric teachings like any other mystic school. Nor were they allowed to reveal anything of their secret tenets, any more than were the Initiates of the Mysteries. Only the penalties incurred by the revealers of the secrets of the latter were far more terrible, and this prohibition has survived to this day, not only in India, but even among the Jewish Kabalists in Asia.§

* *Op. cit.*, p. 7.

† *Op. cit.*, p. 7.

‡ *Op. cit.*, p. 18.

§ The *Talmud* gives the story of the four Tanaim, who are made, in allegorical terms, to enter into the *garden of delights*, *i.e.*, to be initiated into the occult and final science.

One of the reasons for such secrecy may be the undoubtedly serious difficulties and hardships of chelaship, and the dangers attending Initiation. The modern candidate has, like his predecessor of old, to either conquer or die; when, which is still worse, he does not lose his reason. There is no danger to him who is true and sincere, and, especially, unselfish. For he is thus prepared beforehand to meet any temptation.

> He, who fully recognised the power of his immortal spirit, and never doubted for one moment its omnipotent protection, had naught to fear. But woe to the candidate in whom the slightest physical fear—sickly child of matter—made him lose sight and faith in his own invulnerability. He who was not wholly confident of his moral fitness to accept the burden of these tremendous secrets was doomed.*

There were no such dangers in Neo-Platonic Initiations. The selfish and the unworthy failed in their object, and in the failure was the punishment. The chief aim was "reunion of the part with the *all*." This All was One, with numberless names. Whether called *Dui*, the "bright Lord of Heaven" by the Aryan; *Iao*, by the Chaldæan and Kabalist; *Iabe* by the Samaritan; the *Tiu* or *Tuisco* by the Northman; *Duw*, by the Briton; *Zeus*, by the Thracian or *Jupiter* by the Roman—it was *the* Being, the *Facit*, One and Supreme,† the unborn and the inexhaustible source of every emanation, the fountain of life and light eternal, a Ray of which every one of us carries in him on this earth. The knowledge of this Mystery had reached the Neo-Platonists from India through Pythagoras, and still later through Apollonius of Tyana and the rules and methods for producing ecstasy had come from the same lore of the divine Vidyâ, the Gnosis. For Âryavarta, the bright focus into which had been poured in the beginning of time the flames

"According to the teaching of our holy masters the names of the four who entered the garden of delight, are: Ben Asai, Ben Zoma, Acher, and Rabbi Akiba. . . .

"Ben Asai looked and—lost his sight.

"Ben Zoma looked and—lost his reason.

"Acher made depredations in the plantation" (mixed up the whole and failed). "But Akiba, who had entered in peace came out of it in peace; for the saint, whose name he blessed, had said, 'This old man is worthy of serving us with glory.'"

"The learned commentators of the *Talmud*, the Rabbis of the synagogue, explain that the *garden of delight*, in which those four personages are made to enter, is but that mysterious science, the most terrible of sciences for weak intellects, which it leads directly to insanity," says A. Franck, in his *Kabbalah*. It is not the pure at heart and he who studies but with a view to perfecting himself and so more easily acquiring the promised immortality, who need have any fear; but rather he who makes of the science of sciences a sinful pretext for worldly motives, who should tremble. The latter will never understand the kabalistic evocations of the supreme initiation.—*Isis Unveiled*, ii. 119.

* *Isis Unveiled*, ii. 119.

† See *Neo-Platonism*, p. 9.

of Divine Wisdom, had become the centre from which radiated the "tongues of fire" into every portion of the globe. What was Samâdhi but that

> Sublime ecstasy, in which state things divine and the mysteries of [illegible] revealed to us.

of which Porphyry speaks?

> The efflux from the divine soul is imparted to the human spirit in [illegible] abundance, accomplishing for the soul a union with the divine, and enabling it while in the body to be partaker of the life which is not in the body,

he explains elsewhere.

Thus under the title of Magic was taught every Science, physical and metaphysical, natural or deemed supernatural by those who are ignorant of the omnipresence and universality of Nature.

> Divine Magic makes of man a God; human magic creates a new fiend.

We wrote in *Isis Unveiled*:

> In the oldest documents now in the possession of the World—the *Vedas* and the older laws of Manu—we find many magical rites practised and permitted by the Brâhmans.* Tibet, Japan, and China, teach in the present age that which was taught by the oldest Chaldæans. The clergy of these respective countries [illegible] moreover what they teach—namely, that the practice of moral and physical [illegible] and of certain austerities, developes the vital soul-power of self-illumination. Affording to man the control over his own immortal spirit, it gives him truly magical powers over the elementary spirits inferior to himself. In the West we find magic of as high an antiquity as in the East. The Druids of Great Britain practised it in the silent crypts of their deep caves; and Pliny devotes many a chapter to the "wisdom" † of the leaders of the Celts. The Semothees—the Druids of the Gauls—expounded the physical as well as the spiritual sciences. They taught the secrets of the universe, the harmonious progress of the heavenly bodies, the formation of the earth, and above all—the immortality of the Soul.‡ In their sacred groves—natural academies built by the hand of the Invisible Architect—the initiates assembled at the still hour of midnight, to learn about what [illegible] once was, and what he will be.§ They needed no artificial illumination, nor life-drawing gas, to light up their temples, for the chaste goddess of night beamed her most silvery rays on their oak-crowned heads; and their white-robed sacred bards knew how to converse with the solitary queen of the starry vault.‖

During the palmy days of Neo-Platonism these Bards were no more,

---

* See the Code published by Sir William Jones, Chapter ix. p. 11.

† Pliny: *Hist. Nat.*, xxx. 1; *Ib.*, xvi. 14; xxv. 9, etc.

‡ Pomponius ascribes to them the knowledge of the highest sciences.

§ Cæsar, iii. 14.

‖ Pliny, xxx. *Isis Unveiled*, i. 18.

for their cycle had run its course, and the last of the Druids had perished at Bibractis and Alesia. But the Neo-Platonic school was for a long time successful, powerful and prosperous. Still, while adopting Âryan Wisdom in its doctrines, the school failed to follow the wisdom of the Brâhmans in practice. It showed its moral and intellectual superiority too openly, caring too much for the great and powerful of this earth. While the Brâhmans and their great Yogis—experts in matters of philosophy, metaphysics, astronomy, morals and religion—preserved their dignity under the sway of the most powerful princes, remained aloof from the world and would not condescend to visit them or ask for the slightest favour,* the Emperors Alexander, Severus, and Julian, and the greatest among the aristocracy of the land, embraced the tenets of the Neo-Platonists, who mixed freely with the world. The system flourished for several centuries and comprised within the ranks of its followers the ablest and most learned among the men of the time; Hypatia, the teacher of the Bishop Synesius, was one of the ornaments of the School until the fatal and shameful day when she was murdered by the Christian mob at the instigation of Bishop Cyril of Alexandria. The school was finally removed to Athens, and closed by order of the Emperor Justinian.

How accurate is Dr. Wilder's remark that

> Modern writers have commented upon the peculiar views of the Neo-Platonists upon these [metaphysical] subjects, seldom representing them correctly, even if this was desired or intended.†

The few speculations on the sublunary, material, and spiritual universes that they did put into writing—Ammonius never having himself written a line, after the wont of reformers—could not enable posterity to judge them rightly, even had not the early Christian Vandals, the later crusaders, and the fanatics of the Middle Ages, destroyed three parts of that which remained of the Alexandrian Library and its later schools.

Professor Draper shows that Cardinal Ximenes alone

* "The care which they took in educating youth, in familiarising it with generous and virtuous sentiments, did them peculiar honour, and their maxims and discourses, as recorded by historians, prove that they were expert in matters of philosophy, metaphysics, astronomy, morality and religion," says a modern writer. "If kings or princes desired the advice or the blessings of the holy men, they were either obliged to go themselves, or to send messengers. To these men no secret power of either plant or mineral was unknown. They had fathomed nature to its depths, while psychology and physiology were to them open books, and the result was that science that is now termed, so superciliously, *magic*."

† *Op. cit.*, p. 9.

Delivered to the flames in the squares of Granada eighty thousand Arabic manuscripts, many of them translations of classical authors.

In the Vatican Library, whole passages in the most rare and precious treatises of the Ancients were found erased and blotted out, "for the sake of interlining them with absurd psalmodies!" Moreover it is well known that over thirty-six volumes written by Porphyry were burnt and otherwise destroyed by the "Fathers." Most of the little that is known of the doctrines of the Eclectics is found in the writings of Plotinus and of those same Church Fathers.

Says the author of *Neo-Platonism:*

What Plato was to Socrates, and the Apostle John to the head of the Christian faith, Plotinus became to the God-taught Ammonius. To Plotinus, Origenes and Longinus we are indebted for what is known of the Philalethean system. They were duly instructed, initiated and entrusted with the interior doctrines.*

This accounts marvellously for Origen's calling people "idiots" who believe in the Garden of Eden and Adam and Eve fables; as also for the fact that so few of the writings of that Church Father have passed to posterity. Between the secrecy imposed, the vows of silence, and that which was maliciously destroyed by every foul means, it is indeed miraculous that even so much of the Philaletheian tenets has reached the world.

* *Op. cit.*, p. 11.

SECTION XXXV.

Symbolism of Sun and Stars.

And the Heaven was visible in Seven Circles and the planets appeared with all their signs, in star-form, and the stars were divided and numbered with the rulers that were in them, and their revolving course, through the agency of the divine Spirit.*

Here Spirit denotes Pneuma, collective Deity, manifested in its "Builders," or, as the Church has it, "the seven Spirits of the Presence," the *mediantibus angelis* of whom Thomas Aquinas says that "God never works but through them."

These seven "rulers" or mediating Angels were the Kabiri Gods of the Ancients. This was so evident, that it forced from the Church, together with the admission of the fact, an explanation and a theory, whose clumsiness and evident sophistry are such that it must fail to impress. The world is asked to believe, that while the Planetary Angels of the Church are divine Beings, the genuine "Seraphim,"† these very same angels, under identical names and planets, were and are "false"—as Gods of the ancients. They are no better than pretenders; the cunning copies of the real Angels, produced beforehand through the craft and power of Lucifer and of the fallen Angels, Now, what are the Kabiri?

Kabiri, as a name, is derived from Habir חבר, great, and also from Venus, this Goddess being called to the present day Kabar, as is also her star. The Kabiri were worshipped at Hebron, the city of the Anakim, or anakas (kings, princes). They are the highest Planetary Spirits, the "greatest Gods" and "the powerful." Varro, following Orpheus,

---

* *Hermes*, iv. 6.

† From *Saraph* שרף "fiery, burning," plural (see *Isaiah*, vi. 2-6). They are regarded as the personal attendants of the Almighty, "his messengers," angels or metratons. In *Revelation* they are the "seven burning lamps" in attendance before the throne.

calls these Gods δυνατοί, "divine Powers." The word Kabiri when applied to men, and the words Heber, Gheber (with reference to Nimrod, or the "giants" of *Genesis*, vi.) and Kabir, are all derived from the "mysterious Word"—the Ineffable and the "Unpronounceable." Thus it is they who represent *tsaba*, the "host of heaven." The Church, however, bowing before the angel Anael (the regent of Venus),* connects the planet Venus with Lucifer, the chief of the rebels under Satan—so poetically apostrophized by the prophet Isaiah as "O Lucifer, son of the morning."† All the Mystery Gods were Kabiri. As these "seven lictors" relate directly to the Secret Doctrine their real status is of the greatest importance.

Suidas defines the Kabiri as the Gods who command all the other dæmons (Spirits), καβείρους δαίμονας. Macrobius introduces them as

> Those Penates and tutelary deities, through whom we live and learn and know (*Saturn*, I. iii. ch. iv.).

The teraphim through which the Hebrews consulted the oracles of the Urim and the Thummim, were the symbolical hieroglyphics of the Kabiri. Nevertheless, the good Fathers have made of Kibir the synonym, of devil and of daimon (spirit) a demon.

The Mysteries of the Kabiri at Hebron (Pagan and Jewish) were presided over by the seven Planetary Gods, among the rest by Jupiter and Saturn under their mystery names, and they are referred to as ἀξιόχερσος and ἀξιόχερσα, and by Euripides as ἀξιόχρεως ὁ θεός. Creuzer, moreover, shows that whether in Phœnicia or in Egypt, the Kabiri were always the seven planets as known in antiquity, who, together with their Father the Sun—referred to elsewhere as their "elder brother"—composed a powerful ogdoad;‡ the eight superior powers, as πάρεδροι, or solar assessors, danced around him the sacred circular dance, the symbol of the rotation of the planets around the Sun. Jehovah and Saturn, moreover, are one.

It is quite natural, therefore, to find a French writer, D'Anselme,

* Venus with the Chaldæans and Egyptians was the wife of *Proteus*, and is regarded as the mother of the Kabiri, the sons of Phta or Emepth—the divine light or the Sun. The angels answer to the stars in the following order: The Sun, the Moon, Mars, Venus, Mercury, Jupiter, and Saturn; Michael, Gabriel, Samael, Anael, Raphael, Zachariel, and Orifiel; this is in religion and Christian Kabalism; astrologically and esoterically the places of the "regents" stand otherwise, as also in the Jewish, or rather the real Chaldæan *Kabalah*.

† *Loc. cit.*, xiv. 12.

‡ This is one more proof that the Ancients knew of seven planets besides the Sun; for otherwise which is the eighth in such a case? The seventh, with two others, as stated, were "mystery" planets, whether Uranus or any other.

applying the same terms of ἀξιόχερσος and ἀξιόχερσα to Jehovah and his word, and they are correctly so applied. For if the "circle dance" prescribed by the Amazons for the Mysteries—being the "circle dance" of the planets, and characterised as "the motion of the divine Spirit carried on the waves of the great Deep"—can now be called "infernal" and "lascivious" when performed by the Pagans, then the same epithets ought to be applied to David's dance;* and to the dance of the daughters of Shiloh,† and to the leaping of the prophets of Baal:‡ they were all identical and all belonged to Sabæan worship. King David's dance, during which he uncovered himself before his maid-servants in a public thoroughfare, saying:

> I will *play* (act wantonly) before יהוה (Jehovah), and I will yet be more vile than this,

was certainly more reprehensible than any "circle dance" during the Mysteries, or even than the modern Râsa Mandala in India,§ which is the same thing. It was David who introduced Jehovistic worship into Judea, after sojourning so long among the Tyrians and Philistines, where these rites were common.

> David knew nothing of Moses; and if he introduced the Jehovah-worship, it was not in its monotheistic character, but simply as that of one of the many (*Kabirean*) gods of the neighbouring nations, a tutelary deity of his own, יהוה, to whom he had given the preference—whom he had chosen among "all other (Kabeiri) gods."‖

and who was one of the "associates," Chabir, of the Sun. The Shakers dance the "circle dance" to this day when turning round for the Holy Ghost to move them. In India it is Nârâ-yana who is "the mover on the waters;" and Nârâyana is Vishnu in his secondary form, and Vishnu has Krishna for an Avatâra, in whose honour the "circle dance" is still enacted by the Nautch-girls of the temples, he being the Sun-God and they the planets as symbolised by the gopis.

Let the reader turn to the works of De Mirville, a Roman Catholic writer, or to *Monumental Christianity*, by Dr. Lundy, a Protestant

---

* II. *Sam.*, vi. 20-22.

† *Judges*, xxi. 21, *et seq.*

‡ I. *Kings*, xviii. 26.

§ This dance—the Râsa Mandala, enacted by the Gopis or shepherdesses of Krishna, the Sun-God, is enacted to this day in Râjputâna in India, and is undeniably the same theo-astronomical and symbolical dance of the planets and the Zodiacal signs, that was danced thousands of years before our era.

‖ *Isis Unveiled*, ii. 45.

divine, if he wants to appreciate to any degree the subtlety and [illegible] of their reasonings. No one ignorant of the occult versions can [illegible] be impressed with the proofs brought forward to show how [illegible] and perseveringly "Satan has worked for long millenniums to [illegible] humanity" unblessed with an infallible Church, in order to [illegible] himself recognised as the "One living God," and his fiends [illegible] Angels. The reader must be patient, and study with attention [illegible] the author says on behalf of his Church. To compare it, the [illegible] with the version of the Occultists, a few points may be quoted [illegible] verbatim.

St. Peter tells us: "May the divine Lucifer arise in your hearts"* [Now this [illegible] is Christ]. . . . "I will send my Son from the Sun," said the Eternal, [illegible] the voice of prophetic traditions; and prophecy having become history the [illegible] lists repeated in their turn: The *Sun rising* from on high visited us.†

Now God says, through Malachi, that the Sun shall arise for [illegible] who fear his name. What Malachi meant by "the Sun of Righteousness" the Kabalists alone can tell; but what the Greek, and even [illegible] Protestant, theologians understood by the term is of course Christ, referred to metaphorically. Only, as the sentence, "I will send [illegible] Son from the Sun," is borrowed verbatim from a Sibylline Book, it becomes very hard to understand how it can be attributed to, or [illegible] with any prophecy relating to the Christian Saviour, unless, [illegible] the latter is to be identified with Apollo. Virgil, again, says, "[illegible] comes the Virgin's and Apollo's reign," and Apollo, or Apollyon, [illegible] this day viewed as a form of Satan, and is taken to mean the Antichrist. If the Sibylline promise, "He will send his Son from the Sun" applies to Christ, then either Christ and Apollo are one—and [illegible] why call the latter a demon?—or the prophecy had nothing to do with the Christian Saviour, and, in such a case, why appropriate it at all?

But De Mirville goes further. He shows us St. Denys, the Areopagite, affirming that

The Sun is the special signification, and the statue of God.‡ . . . It is by the

---

* II. *Epistle*, i. 19. The English text says: "Until the day-star arise in your heart," [illegible] alteration which does not really matter—as *Lucifer* is the day as well as the "morning" star—[illegible] is less shocking to pious ears. There are a number of such alterations in the Protestant bibles.

† Again the English translation changes the word "Sun" into "day-spring." The [illegible] Catholics are decidedly braver and more sincere than the Protestant theologians. De Mirville, iv. 34, 38.

‡ Thus said the Egyptians and the Sabæans in days of old, the symbol of whose manifested [illegible] Osiris and Bel, was the sun. But they had a higher deity.

Eastern door that the glory of the Lord penetrated into the temples [of the Jews and Christians, that divine glory being Sun-light.] . . . "We build our churches towards the east," says in his turn St. Ambrose, "for during the Mysteries we begin by renouncing him who is in the west."

"He who is in the west" is Typhon, the Egyptian god of darkness—the west having been held by them as the "Typhonic Gate of Death." Thus, having borrowed Osiris from the Egyptians, the Church Fathers thought little of helping themselves to his brother Typhon. Then again:

The prophet Baruch* speaks of the stars that rejoice in their *vessels* and *citadels* (Chap. iii.); and *Ecclesiastes* applies the same terms to the sun, which is said to be "the admirable vessel of the most High," and the "citadel of the Lord" φυλαχη.†

In every case there is no doubt about the thing, for the sacred writer says, It is a *Spirit* who rules the sun's course. Hear what he says (in *Eccles.*, i. 6), "The sun also ariseth—and its spirit lighting all in its circular path (gyrat gyrans) returneth according to his circuits."‡

De Mirville seems to quote from texts either rejected by or unknown to Protestants, in whose bible there is no forty-third chapter of *Ecclesiastes;* nor is the sun made to go "in circuits" in the latter, but the wind. This is a question to be settled between the Roman and the Protestant Churches. Our point is the strong element of Sabæanism or Heliolatry present in Christianity.

An Œcumenical Council having authoritatively put a stop to Christian Astrolatry by declaring that there were no sidereal Souls in sun, moon, or planets, St. Thomas took upon himself to settle the point in dispute. The "angelic doctor" announced that such expressions did not mean a "soul," but only an Intelligence, not resident in the sun or stars, but one that assisted them, "a guiding and directing intelligence."§

---

* Exiled from the Protestant bible but left in the *Apocrypha* which, according to Article VI. of the Church of England, "she doth read for example of life and instruction of manners" (?), but not to establish any doctrine.

† *Cornelius a Lapide*, v. 248.

‡ *Ecclesiastes*, xliii. The above quotations are taken from De Mirville's chapter "On Christian and Jewish Solar Theology," iv. 35-38.

§ Nevertheless the Church has preserved in her most sacred rites the "star-rites" of the Pagan Initiates. In the pre-Christian Mithraic Mysteries, the candidate who overcame successfully the "twelve Tortures" which preceded the final Initiation, received a small round cake or wafer of unleavened bread, symbolising in one of its meanings, the solar disc, and known as the manna (heavenly bread). . . . A lamb, or a bull even, was killed, and with the blood the candidate had to be sprinkled, as in the case of the Emperor Julian's initiation. The seven rules or mysteries that are represented in the *Revelation* as the seven seals which are opened in order were then delivered to the newly born.

Thereupon the author, comforted by the explanation, quotes Clement the Alexandrian, and reminds the reader of the opinion of that philosopher, the inter-relation that exists "between the seven branches of the candlestick—the seven stars of the Revelation," and the sun:

> The six branches (says Clement) fixed to the central candlestick have lamps, but the sun placed in the midst of the wandering ones (πλανητῶν) pours his light on them all; this golden candlestick hides one more mystery: it is the sign of Christ, not only in shape, but because he sheds his light through the ministry of the seven spirits primarily created, and who are the Seven Eyes of the Lord. Therefore the principal planets are to the seven primeval spirits, according to St. Clement, that which the candlestick-sun is to Christ Himself, namely their vessels, their φυλακαί.

Plain enough, to be sure; though one fails to see that this explanation even helps the situation. The seven-branched chandelier of the Israelites, as well as the "wanderers" of the Greeks, had a far more natural meaning, a purely astrological one to begin with. In fact, from Magi and Chaldæans down to the much-laughed-at Zadkiel, every astrological work will tell its reader that the Sun placed in the midst of the planets, with Saturn, Jupiter and Mars on one side, and Venus, Mercury and the Moon on the other, the planets' line crossing through the whole Earth, has always meant what Hermes tells us, namely, the thread of destiny, or that whose action (influence) is called destiny.* But symbol for symbol we prefer the sun to a candlestick. One can understand how the latter came to represent the sun and planets, but no one can admire the chosen symbol. There is poetry and grandeur in the sun when it is made to symbolize the "Eye of Ormuzd," or of Osiris, and is regarded as the Vâhan (vehicle) of the highest Deity. But one must for ever fail to perceive that any particular glory is rendered to Christ by assigning to him the trunk of a candlestick,† in a Jewish synagogue, as a mystical seat of honour.

There are then positively two suns, a sun adored and a sun adoring. The *Apocalypse* proves it.

> The Word is found in Chap. vii., in the angel who ascends with the rising of the sun, having the seal of the living God. . . . While commentators differ on the personality of this angel, St. Ambrose and many other theologians see in him

---

* Truly says S. T. Coleridge: "Instinctively the reason has always pointed out to men the ultimate end of various sciences. . . . There is no doubt but that astrology of some sort or other will be the last achievement of astronomy; there must be chemical relations between the planets . . . the difference of their magnitude compared with that of their distances is not explicable otherwise." Between planets and our earth with its mankind, we may add.

† "Christ then," the author says (p. 40), "is represented by the trunk of the candlestick."

Christ himself. . . . He is the *Sun adored.* But in Chap. xix. we find an angel standing *in* the sun, inviting all the nations to gather to the great supper of the Lamb. This time it is literally and simply the angel of the sun—who cannot be mistaken for the "Word," since the prophet distinguishes him from the Word, the King of Kings and the Lord of Lords. . . . The angel *in* the sun seems to be an adoring sun. Who may be the latter? And who else can he be but the Morning Star, the guardian angel of the Word, his *ferouer*, or *angel of the face*, as the Word is the angel of the Face (presence) of his Father, his principal attribute and strength, as his name itself implies (Mikael), the powerful rector glorified by the Church, the *Rector potens* who will fell the Antichrist, the Vice-Word, in short, who represents his master, and seems to be *one with him.**

Yes, Mikael is the alleged conqueror of Ormuzd, Osiris, Apollo, Krishna, Mithra, etc., of all the Solar Gods, in short, known and unknown, now treated as demons and as "Satan." Nevertheless, the "Conqueror" has not disdained to don the war-spoils of the vanquished foes—their personalities, attributes, even their names—to become the *alter ego* of these demons.

Thus the Sun-God here is *Honover* or the Eternal. The prince is Ormuzd, since he is the first of the seven Amshaspends [the demon copies of the seven original angels] (*caput angelorum*); the lamb (*hamal*), the Shepherd of the Zodiac and the antagonist of the snake. But the Sun (the Eye of Ormuzd) has also his rector, Korshid or the *Mitraton*, who is the *Ferouer* of the face of Ormuzd, his Ized, or the morning star. The Mazdeans had a triple Sun. . . . For us this *Korshid-Mitraton* is the first of the *psychopompian* genii, and the guide of the sun, the immolator of the terrestrial Bull [or lamb] whose wounds are licked by the serpent [on the famous Mithraic monument].†

St. Paul, in speaking of the rulers of this world, the Cosmocratores, only said what was said by all the primitive Philosophers of the ten centuries before the Christian era, only he was scarcely understood, and was often wilfully misinterpreted. Damascius repeats the teachings of the Pagan writers when he explains that

There are seven series of cosmocratores or cosmic forces, which are double: the higher ones commissioned to support and guide the superior world; the lower ones, the inferior world [our own].

And he is but saying what the ancients taught. Iamblichus gives this dogma of the duality of all the planets and celestial bodies, of gods and daimons (spirits). He also divides the Archontes into two classes—the more and the less spiritual; the latter more connected with and clothed with matter, as having a *form*, while the former are bodiless

* De Mirville, iv. 41, 42. † De Mirville, iv. 42.

(*arûpa*). But what have Satan and his angels to do with all this? Perhaps only that the identity of the Zoroastrian dogma with the Christian, and of Mithra, Ormuzd, and Ahriman with the Christian Father, Son, and Devil, might be accounted for. And when we say "Zoroastrian dogmas" we mean the exoteric teaching. How explain the same relations between Mithra and Ormuzd as those between the Archangel Mikael and Christ?

Ahura Mazda says to holy Zaratushta: "When I *created* [emanated] Mithra . . . I created him that he should be invoked and adored equally with myself."

For the sake of necessary reforms, the Zoroastrian Âryans transformed the Devas, the bright Gods of India, into devs or devils. It was their Karma that in their turn the Christians should vindicate on this point the Hindus. Now Ormuzd and Mithra have become the devs of Christ and Mikael, the dark lining and aspect of the Saviour and Angel. The day of the Karma of Christian theology will come in its turn. Already the Protestants have begun the first chapter of the religion that will seek to transform the "Seven Spirits" and the host of the Roman Catholics into demons and idols. Every religion has its Karma, as has every individual. That which is due to human conception and is built on the abasement of our brothers who disagree with us, must have its day. "There is no religion higher than truth."

The Zoroastrians, Mazdeans, and Persians borrowed their conceptions from India; the Jews borrowed their theory of angels from Persia; the Christians borrowed from the Jews.

Hence the latest interpretation by Christian theology—to the great disgust of the synagogue, forced to share the symbolical candlestick with the hereditary enemy—that the seven-branched candlestick represents the seven Churches of Asia and the seven planets which are the angels of those Churches. Hence also, the conviction that the Mosaic Jews, the inventors of that symbol for their tabernacle, were a kind of Sabæans, who blended their planets and the spirits thereof into one, and called them—only far later—Jehovah. For this we have the testimony of Clemens Alexandrinus, St. Hieronymus and others.

And Clement, as an Initiate of the Mysteries—at which the secret of the heliocentric system was taught several thousands of years before Galileo and Copernicus—proves it by explaining that

By these various symbols connected with (sidereal) phenomena the totality of all the creatures which bind heaven with earth, are figured. . . . The chandelier represented the motion of the seven luminaries, describing their astral revolution. To the right and the left of that candelabrum projected the six branches, each of which had its lamp, because the Sun placed as a candelabrum in the middle of other planets distributes light to them.* . . . As to the cherubs having twelve wings between the two, they represent to us the sensuous world in the twelve zodiacal signs.†

And yet, in the face of all this evidence, sun, moon, planets, all are shown as being demoniacal before, and divine only after, the appearance of Christ. All know the Orphic verse: "It is Zeus, it is Adas, it is the Sun, it is Bacchus," these names having been all synonymous for classic poets and writers. Thus for Democritus "Deity is but a soul in an orbicular fire," and that fire is the Sun. For Iamblichus the sun was "the image of divine intelligence"; for Plato "an immortal living Being." Hence the oracle of Claros when asked to say who was the Jehovah of the Jews, answered, "It is the Sun." We may add the words in *Psalm* xix. 4

In the sun hath he placed a tabernacle for himself‡ . . . his going forth is from the end of the heaven, and his circuit unto the ends of it: and there is nothing hid from the heat thereof.

Jehovah then is the sun, and thence also the Christ of the Roman Church. And now the criticism of Dupuis on that verse becomes comprehensible, as also the despair of the Abbé Foucher. "Nothing is more favourable to Sabæism than this text of the Vulgate!" he exclaims. And, however disfigured may be the words and sense in the English authorised bible, the Vulgate and the Septuagint both give the correct text of the original, and translate the latter: "In the sun he established his abode"; while the Vulgate regards the "heat" as coming direct from God and not from the sun alone, since it is God who issues forth from, and dwells in the sun and performs the circuit: *in sole posuit . . . . et ipse exultavit.* From these facts it will be seen that the Protestants were right in charging St. Justin with saying that

God has permitted us to worship the sun.

---

* Notwithstanding the above, written in the earliest Christian period by the renegade Neo-Platonist, the Church persists to this day in her wilful error. Helpless against Galileo, she now tries to throw a doubt even on the heliocentric system!

† *Stromateis*, V., vi.

‡ The English bible has: "In them (the Heavens) hath he set a tabernacle for the sun," which is incorrect and has no sense in view of the verse that follows, for there *are* things "hid from the heat thereof" if the latter word is to be applied to the sun.

And this, notwithstanding the lame excuses that what was really meant was that

> God permitted himself to be worshipped in, or within, the sun,

which is all the same.

It will be seen from the above, that while the Pagans located in the sun and planets only the inferior powers of Nature, the representative Spirits, so to say, of Apollo, Bacchus, Osiris, and other solar gods, the Christians, in their hatred of Philosophy, appropriated the sidereal localities, and now limit them to the use of their anthropomorphic deity and his angels—new transformations of the old, old gods. Something had to be done in order to dispose of the ancient tenants, so they were disgraced into "demons," wicked devils.

SECTION XXXVI.

PAGAN SIDEREAL WORSHIP, OR ASTROLOGY.

THE Teraphim of Abram's father *Terah*, the "maker of images," and the Kabiri Gods are directly connected with ancient Sabæan worship or Astrolatry. Kiyun, or the God Kivan, worshipped by the Jews in the wilderness, is Saturn and Shiva, later on called Jehovah. Astrology existed before astronomy, and *Astronomus* was the title of the highest hierophant in Egypt.* One of the names of the Jewish Jehovah, "Sabaoth," or the "Lord of Hosts" (*tsabaoth*), belongs to the Chaldæan Sabæans (or *Tsabæans*), and has for its root the word *tsab*, meaning a "car," a "ship," and "an army"; sabaoth thus meaning literally the *army of the ship*, the *crew*, or a *naval host*, the sky being metaphorically referred to as the "upper ocean" in the doctrine.

In his interesting volumes, *The God of Moses*, Lacour explains that all such words as

> The celestial armies or the hosts of heaven, signify not only the totality of the heavenly constellations, but also the Aleim on whom they are dependent; the *aleitzbaout* are the forces or *souls* of the constellations, the potencies that maintain and guide the planets in this order and procession; . . . the Jao-va-Tzbaout signifies Him, the supreme chief of those celestial bodies.

In his collectivity, as the chief "Order of Spirits," not a chief Spirit.

The Sabæans having worshipped in the *graven* images only the celestial hosts — angels and gods whose habitations were the planets, never in truth worshipped the stars. For on Plato's authority, we know that among the stars and constellations, the

* When the hierophant took his last degree, he emerged from the sacred recess called *Manneras* and was given the golden *Tau*, the Egyptian Cross, which was subsequently placed on his breast, and buried with him.

planets alone had a right to the title of *theoi* (Gods), as that name was derived from the verb θεῖν, to run or to circulate. Seldenus also tells us that they were likewise called

> θεοὶ βουλαῖοι (God-Councillors) and ῥαβδοφόροι (*lictors*) as they (the planets) were present at the sun's consistory, *solis consistoris adstantes*.

Says the learned Kircher:

> The sceptres the seven presiding angels were armed with, explain these names of Rhabdophores and lictors given to them.

Reduced to its simplest expression and popular meaning, this is of course fetish worship. Yet esoteric astrolatry was not at all the worship of idols, since under the names of "Councillors" and "Lictors" present at the "Sun's consistory," it was not the planets in their material bodies that were meant, but their Regents or "Souls" (Spirits). If the prayer "Our Father in heaven," or "Saint" so-and-so in "Heaven" is not an idolatrous invocation, then "Our Father in Mercury," or "Our Lady in Venus," "Queen of Heaven," etc., is no more so; for it is precisely the same thing, the name making no difference in the act. The word used in the Christian prayer, "in heaven" cannot mean anything abstract. A dwelling—whether of Gods, angels or Saints (every one of these being anthropomorphic individualities and beings)—must necessarily mean a locality, some defined spot in that "heaven"; hence it is quite immaterial for purposes of worship whether that spot be considered as "heaven" in general, meaning nowhere in particular, or in the Sun, Moon or Jupiter.

The argument is futile that there were

> Two deities, and two distinct hierarchies or *tsabas* in heaven, in the ancient world as in our modern times . . . the one, the living God and his host, and the other, *Satan*, Lucifer with his councillors and lictors, or the *fallen* angels.

Our opponents say that it is the latter which Plato with the whole of antiquity worshipped, and which two-thirds of humanity worship to this day. "The whole question is to know how to discern between the two."

Protestant Christians fail to find any mention of angels in the Pentateuch, we may therefore leave them aside. The Roman Catholics and the Kabalists find such mention; the former, because they have accepted Jewish angelology, without suspecting that the "tsabæan Hosts" were colonists and settlers on Judæan territory from the lands of the Gentiles; the latter, because they accepted the bulk of the

Secret Doctrine, keeping the kernel for themselves and leaving the husks to the unwary.

Cornelius a Lapide points out and proves the meaning of the word *tsaba* in the first verse of Chapter ii. of *Genesis*; and he does so correctly, guided, as he probably was, by learned Kabalists. The Protestants are certainly wrong in their contention, for angels *are* mentioned in the Pentateuch under the word *tsaba*, which means "hosts" of angels. In the Vulgate the word is translated *ornatus*, meaning the "sidereal army," the *ornament* also of the sky—kabalistically. The biblical scholars of the Protestant Church, and the *savants* among the materialists, who failed to find "angels" mentioned by Moses, have thus committed a serious error. For the verse reads:

> Thus the heaven and the earth were finished and all the host of them,

the "host" meaning "the army of stars and angels": the last two words being, it seems, convertible terms in Church phraseology. A Lapide is cited as an authority for this; he says that

> *Tsaba* does not mean *either one* or the other but "*the one and the other*," or both, *siderum ac angelorum*.

If the Roman Catholics are right on this point, so are the Occultists when they claim that the angels worshipped in the Church of Rome are none else than their "Seven Planets," the Dhyân Chohans of Buddhistic Esoteric Philosophy, or the Kumâras, "the mind-born sons of Brahmâ," known under the patronymic of Vaidhâtra. The identity between the Kumâras, the Builders or cosmic Dhyân Chohans, and the Seven Angels of the Stars, will be found without one single flaw if their respective biographies are studied, and especially the characteristics of their chiefs, Sanat-Kumâra (Sanat Sujâta), and Michael the Archangel. Together with the Kabirim (Planets), the name of the above in Chaldæa, they were all "*divine* Powers" (Forces). Fuerot says that the name Kabiri was used to denote the *seven* sons of צדיק, meaning Pater Sadic, Cain, or Jupiter, or again of Jehovah. There are seven Kumâras—four exoteric and three secret—the names of the latter being found in the *Sânkhya Bhâshya*, by Gaudapâdâchârya.* They are all "Virgin Gods," who remain eternally pure and innocent and decline to create progeny. In their primitive aspect, these Âryan seven "mind-born sons" of God are not the regents of

* The three secret names are "Sana, Sanat Sujâta, and Kapila;" while the four exoteric Gods are called, Sanat Kumâra, Sananda, Sanaka and Sanâtana.

the planets, but dwell far beyond the planetary region. But the same mysterious transference from one character or dignity to another is found in the Christian Angel-scheme. The "Seven Spirits of the Presence" attend perpetually on God, and yet we find them under the same names of Mikael, Gabriel, Raphael, etc., as "Star-regents," or the informing deities of the seven planets. Suffice it to say that the Archangel Michael is called "the invincible virgin combatant" as he "refused to create,"* which would connect him with both Sanat-Sujâta and the Kumâra who is the God of War.

The above has to be demonstrated by a few quotations. Commenting upon St. John's "Seven Golden Candlesticks," Cornelius a Lapide says:

> These seven lights relate to the seven branches of the candlestick by which were represented the seven [principal] planets in the temples of Moses and Solomon . . . or, better still, to the seven principal Spirits, commissioned to watch over the salvation of men and churches.

St. Jerome says:

> In truth the candlestick with the seven branches was the type of the world and its planets.

St. Thomas Aquinas, the great Roman Catholic doctor writes:

> I do not remember having ever met in the works of saints or philosophers a denial that the planets are guided by spiritual beings. . . . It seems to me that it may be proved to demonstration that the celestial bodies are guided by some intelligence, either directly by God, or by the mediation of angels. But the latter opinion seems to be far more consonant with the order of things asserted by St. Denys to be without exception, that everything on earth is, as a rule, governed by God through intermediary agencies.†

And now let the reader recall what the Pagans say of this. All the classical authors and philosophers who have treated the subject, repeat with Hermes Trismegistus, that the seven Rectors—the planets including the sun—were the associates, or the co-workers, of the Unknown All represented by the Demiurgos—commissioned to contain

* Another Kumâra, the "God of War" is called in the Hindu system the "eternal celibate"—, "the virgin warrior." He is the Âryan St. Michael.

† We give the original: "Coelestia corpora moveri a spirituali creatura, a nemine Sanctorum vel philosophorum, negatum, legisse me memini. (*Opusc.* X. art. iii.). . . . Mihi autem videtur, quod *Demonstrative* probari posset, quod ab aliquo intellectu corpora coelestia moveantur, vel a Deo immediate, vel a mediantibus angelis. Sed quod mediantibus angelis ea moveat, congruit rerum ordine, quem Dionysius infallibilem asserit, ut inferiora a Deo per *Media* secundum cursum communem administrentur" (*Opusc.* II. art. ii.), and if so, and God *never* meddles with the once for ever established laws of Nature, leaving it to his administrators, why should their being called Gods by the "heathen" be deemed idolatrous?

the Cosmos—our planetary world—within seven circles. Plutarch shows them representing "the circle of the celestial worlds." Again, Denys of Thracia and the learned Clemens of Alexandria both describe the Rectors as being shown in the Egyptian temples in the shape of mysterious wheels or spheres always in motion, which made the Initiates affirm that the problem of perpetual motion had been solved by the celestial wheels in the Initiation Adyta.* This doctrine of Hermes was that of Pythagoras and of Orpheus before him. It is called by Proclus "the God-given" doctrine. Iamblichus speaks of it with the greatest reverence. Philostratus tells his readers that the whole sidereal court of the Babylonian heaven was represented in the temples

> In globes made of sapphires and supporting the golden images of their respective gods.

The temples of Persia were especially famous for these representations. If Cedrenus can be credited

> The Emperor Heraclius on his entry into the city of Bazaeum was struck with admiration and wonder before the immense machine fabricated for King Chosroes, which represented the night-sky with the planets and all their revolutions, with the angels presiding over them.†

It was on such "spheres" that Pythagoras studied Astronomy in the *adyta arcana* of the temples to which he had access. And it was there on his Initiation, that the eternal rotation of those spheres—"the mysterious wheels" as they are called by Clemens and Denys, and which Plutarch calls "world-wheels"—demonstrated to him the verity

---

* In one of Des Mousseaux's volumes on Demonology (*Œuvres des Demons* if we do not mistake the statement of the Abbé Huc is found, and the author testifies to having heard the following story repeatedly from the Abbé himself. In a lamasery of Tibet, the missionary found the following:

It is a simple canvas without the slightest mechanical apparatus attached, as the visitor may prove by examining it at his leisure. It represents a moonlit landscape, but the moon is not at all motionless and dead; quite the reverse, for, according to the Abbé, one would say that our moon herself, or at least her living double, lighted the picture. Each phase, each aspect, each movement of our satellite, is repeated in her facsimile, in the movement and progress of the moon in the sacred picture. "You see this planet in the painting ride as a crescent, or full, shine brightly, pass behind the clouds, peep out or set, in a manner corresponding in the most extraordinary way with the real luminary. It is, in a word, a most perfect and resplendent reproduction of the pale queen of the night, which received the adoration of so many people in the days of old." We know from the most reliable sources and numerous eye-witnesses, that such "machines"—not canvas paintings—do exist in certain temples of Tibet; as also the "sidereal wheels" representing the planets, and kept for the same purposes—astrological and magical. Huc's statement was translated in *Isis Unveiled* from Des Mousseaux's volume.

† Cedrenus, p. 338. Whether produced by *clockwork or magic* power, such machines—whole celestial spheres with planets rotating—were found in the Sanctuaries, and some exist to this day in Japan, in a secret subterranean temple of the old Mikados, as well as in two other places.

of what had been divulged to him, namely, the heliocentric system, the great secret of the Adyta. All the discoveries of modern astronomy, like all the secrets that can be revealed to it in future ages, were contained in the secret observatories and Initiation Halls of the temples of old India and Egypt. It is in them that the Chaldean made his calculations, revealing to the world of the profane no more than it was fit to receive.

We may, and shall be told, no doubt, that Uranus was unknown to the ancients, and that they were forced to reckon the sun amongst the planets and as their chief. How does anyone know? Uranus is a modern *name*; but one thing is certain: the ancients had a planet, "the mystery planet," that they never named and that the highest Astronomus, the Hierophant, alone could "confabulate with." But this seventh planet was not the sun, but the hidden Divine Hierophant, who was said to have a crown, and to embrace within its wheel "seventy-seven smaller wheels." In the archaic secret system of the Hindus, the sun is the visible Logos "Sûrya"; over him there is another, the divine or heavenly Man—who, after having established the system of the world of matter on the archetype of the Unseen Universe, or Macrocosm, conducted during the Mysteries the heavenly Râsa Mandala; when he was said:

> To give with his right foot the impulse to *Tyam* or Bhûmi [Earth] that makes her rotate in a double revolution.

What says Hermes again? When explaining Egyptian Cosmology he exclaims:

> Listen, O my son . . . the Power has also formed seven agents, who contain within their circles the material world, and whose action is called destiny. . . . When all became subject to man, the Seven, willing to favour human intelligence, communicated to him their powers. But as soon as man knew their true essence and his own nature, he desired to penetrate within and beyond the circles and thus break their circumference by usurping the power of him who has dominion over the Fire [Sun] itself; after which, having robbed one of the Wheels of the Sun of the sacred fire, he fell into slavery.*

It is *not* Prometheus who is meant here. Prometheus is a symbol and a personification of the whole of mankind in relation to an event which occurred during its childhood, so to say—the "Baptism by Fire"—which is a mystery within the great Promethean Mystery, one that

* Champollion's *Ægypte Moderne*, p. 42.

may be at present mentioned only in its broad general features. By reason of the extraordinary growth of human intellect and the development in our age of the fifth principle (Manas) in man, its rapid progress has paralysed spiritual perceptions. It is at the expense of wisdom that intellect generally lives, and mankind is quite unprepared in its present condition to comprehend the awful drama of human disobedience to the laws of Nature and the subsequent Fall, as a result. It can only be hinted at, in its place.

SECTION XXXVII.

THE SOULS OF THE STARS—UNIVERSAL HELIOLATRY.

IN order to show that the Ancients have never "mistaken stars for Gods," or Angels and the sun for the highest Gods and God, but have worshipped only the Spirit of all, and have reverenced the minor Gods supposed to reside in the sun and planets—the difference between these two worships has to be pointed out. Saturn, "the Father of Gods" must not be confused with his namesake—the planet of the same name with its eight moons and three rings. The two—though in one sense identical, as are, for instance, physical man and his soul—must be separated in the question of worship. This has to be done the more carefully in the case of the seven planets and their Spirits, as the whole formation of the universe is attributed to them in the Secret Teachings. The same difference has to be shown again between the stars of the Great Bear, the Riksha and the Chitra Shikhandina, "the bright-crested," and the Rishis—the mortal Sages who appeared on earth during the Satya Yuga. If all of these have been so far closely united in the visions of the seers of every age—the bible seers included—there must have been a reason for it. Nor need one go back so far as into the periods of "superstition" and "unscientific fancies" to find great men in our epoch sharing in them. It is well known that Kepler, the eminent astronomer, in common with many other great men who believed that the heavenly bodies ruled favourably or adversely the fates of men and nations—fully credited besides this the fact that all heavenly bodies, even our own earth, are endowed with living and thinking souls.

Le Couturier's opinion is worthy of notice in this relation:

We are too inclined to criticise unsparingly everything concerning astrology and its ideas; nevertheless our criticism, to be one, ought at least to know, lest it should be proved aimless, what those ideas in truth are. And when among the men we thus criticize, we find such names as those of Regiomontanus, Tycho Brahe, Kepler, etc., there is reason why we should be careful. Kepler was an astrologer by profession, and became an astronomer in consequence. He was earning his livelihood by genethliac figures, which, indicating the state of the heavens at the moment of the birth of individuals, were a means to which everyone resorted for horoscopes. That great man was a believer in the principles of astrology, without accepting all its foolish results.*

But astrology is nevertheless proclaimed as a sinful science, and together with Occultism is tabooed by the Churches. It is very doubtful, however, whether mystic "star worship" can be so easily laughed down as people imagine—at any rate by Christians. The hosts of Angels, Cherubs and Planetary Archangels are identical with the minor Gods of the Pagans. As to their "great Gods," if Mars has been shown—on the admission of even the enemies of the Pagan astrologers—to have been regarded by the latter simply as the personified strength of the one highest impersonal Deity, Mercury being personified as its omniscience, Jupiter as its omnipotency, and so on, then the "superstition" of the Pagan has indeed become the "religion" of the masses of the civilized nations. For with the latter, Jehovah is the synthesis of the seven Elohim, the eternal centre of all those attributes and forces, the Alei of the Aleim, and the Adonai of the Adonim. And if with them Mars is now called St. Michael, the "*strength* of God," Mercury Gabriel, the "omniscience and fortitude of the Lord," and Raphael "the blessing or healing power of God," this is simply a change of names, the characters behind the masks remaining the same.

The Dalai-lama's mitre has seven ridges in honour of the seven chief Dhyâni Buddhas. In the funeral ritual of the Egyptians the defunct is made to exclaim:

Salutation to you, O Princes, who stand in the presence of Osiris. . . . Send me the grace to have my sins destroyed, as you have done for the seven spirits who follow their Lord!†

Brahmâ's head is ornamented with seven rays, and he is followed by the seven Rishis, in the seven Svargas. China has her seven Pagodas;

---

* *Musée des Sciences*, p. 230.

† Translated by the Vicomte de Rougemont. See *Les Annales de Philosophie Chrétienne*, 7th year, 1861.

the Greeks had their seven Cyclopes, seven Demiurgi, and the Mystery Gods, the seven Kabiri, whose chief was Jupiter-Saturn; and with the Jews, Jehovah. Now the latter Deity has become chief of all, the highest and the one God, and his old place is taken by "Mikael" (Michael). He is the "Chief of the Host" (*tsaba*); the "Archistrategus of the Lord's army"; the "Conqueror of the Devil"—Victor diaboli—and the "Archisatrap of the Sacred Militia," he who slew the "Great Dragon." Unfortunately astrology and symbology, having no inducement to veil old things with new masks, have preserved the real name of Mikael—"that was Jehovah"—Mikael being the Angel of the face of the Lord,* "the guardian of the planets," and the living image of God. He represents the Deity in his visits to earth, for as it is well expressed in Hebrew, he is one מיכאל, who is as God, or who is like unto God. It is he who cast out the serpent.†

Mikael, being the regent of the planet Saturn, is—*Saturn*.‡ His mystery-name is Sabbathiel, because he presides over the Jewish Sabbath, as also over the astrological Saturday. Once identified, the reputation of the Christian conqueror of the devil is in still greater danger from further identifications. Biblical angels are called Malachim, the messengers between God (or rather *the gods*) and men. In Hebrew מלאך Malach, is also "a King," and Malech or Melech was likewise Moloch, or again Saturn, the Seb of Egypt, to whom *Dies Saturni*, or the Sabbath, was dedicated. The Sabeans separated and distinguished the planet Saturn from its God far more than the Roman Catholics do their angels from their stars; and the Kabalists make of the Archangel Mikael the patron of the seventh work of magic.

> In theological symbolism . . . Jupiter [the Sun] is the risen and glorious Saviour, and Saturn, God the Father, or the Jehovah of Moses,§

says Éliphas Lévi, who *ought* to know. Jehovah and the Saviour, Saturn and Jupiter, being thus one, and Mikael being called the living image of God, it does seem dangerous for the Church to call Saturn, Satan—*le dieu mauvais*. However, Rome is strong in casuistry and will get out of this as she got out of every other identification, with glory to herself and to her own full satisfaction. Nevertheless all her

---

* Isaiah, lxiii. 9.

† Chapter xii. of *Revelation*: "There was war in heaven, Mikael and his angels fought against the Dragon," (verse 7) and the great dragon was cast out (9).

‡ He is also the informing Spirit of the Sun and Jupiter, and even of Venus.

§ *Dogme et Rituel*, ii. 116.

dogmas and rituals seem like so many pages torn out from the history of Occultism, and then distorted. The extremely thin partition that separates the Kabalistic and Chaldæan Theogony from the Roman Catholic Angelology and Theodicy is now confessed by at least one Roman Catholic writer. One can hardly believe one's eyes in finding the following (the passages italicized by us should be carefully noticed):

> One of the most characteristic features of our Holy Scriptures is *the calculated discretion used in the enunciation of the mysteries less directly useful to salvation*. . . . Thus, beyond those "myriads of myriads" of angelic creatures just noticed* and all these prudently elementary divisions, there are certainly many others, whose very names have not yet reached us.† "For," excellently says St. John Chrysostom, "there are doubtless, (*sine dubio*,) many other *Virtues* [celestial beings] whose denominations we are yet far from knowing. . . . The nine orders are not by any means the only populations in heaven, where, on the contrary, *are to be found numberless tribes* of inhabitants infinitely varied, and of which it would be impossible *to give the slightest idea* through human tongue. . . . Paul, who *had learned their names*, reveals to us their existence." (*De Incomprehensibili Natura Dei*, Bk. IV.) . . . .
>
> It would thus amount *to a gross mistake to see merely errors* in the Angelology of the Kabalists and Gnostics, so severely treated by the Apostle of the Gentiles, for his imposing censure reached *only their exaggerations and vicious interpretations*, and still more, *the application of those noble* titles *to the miserable personalities of demoniacal usurpers*.‡ Often nothing so resemble each other as *the language of the judges and that of the convicts* [of saints and Occultists]. One has to penetrate deeply into this *dual* study [of creed and profession] and what is still better, *to trust blindly to the authority of the tribunal* [the Church of Rome, of course] to enable oneself to seize precisely the point of the error. The *Gnosis* condemned by St. Paul remains, nevertheless, for him as for Plato the supreme knowledge of all truths, and of the *Being par excellence*, ὁ ὄντως ὤν (*Republ.* Bk. VI). The Ideas, *types*, ἀρχαὶ of the Greek philosopher, the *Intelligences* of Pythagoras, the *aeons* or *emanations*, the occasion of so much reproach to the first heretics, the Logos or Word, Chief of these Intelligences, the *Demiurgos*, the architect of the world under his father's direction [of the Pagans], the unknown God, the *En-soph*, or the *It of the Infinite* [of the Kabalists], the angelical *periods*,§ the *seven* spirits, the Depths of *Ahriman*, the World's *Rectors*, the *Archontes* of the air, the *God of this world*, the *pleroma* of the

---

* If enumerated, they will be found to be the Hindu "divisions" and choirs of Devas, and the Dhyân Chohans of Esoteric Buddhism.

† But this fact has not prevented the Roman Church rom adopting them all the same, accepting them from ignorant, though perchance sincere Church Fathers, who had borrowed them from Kabalists—Jews and Pagans.

‡ To call "usurpers" those who preceded the Christian Beings for whose benefit these same titles were borrowed, is carrying paradoxical anachronism a little too far!

§ Or the *divine ages*, the "days and years of Brahmâ."

intelligences, down to *Metatron* the angel of the Jews, *all this is found word for word, as so many truths, in the works of our greatest doctors, and in St. Paul*.*

If an Occultist, eager to charge the Church with a numberless series of plagiarisms were to write the above, could he have written more strongly? And have we, or have we not, the right, after such a complete confession, to reverse the tables and to say of Roman Catholics and others what is said of the Gnostics and Occultists. "They used our expressions and rejected our doctrines." For it is not the "promoters of the false Gnosis"—who had all those expressions from their archaic ancestors—who helped themselves to Christian expressions, but verily the Christian Fathers and Theologians, who helped themselves to our nest, and have tried ever since to soil it.

The words above quoted will explain much to those who are searching for truth and for truth only. They will show the origin of certain rites in the Church inexplicable hitherto to the simple-minded, and will give the reason why such words as "Our Lord the Sun" were used in prayer by Christians up to the fifth and even sixth century of our era, and embodied in the Liturgy, until altered into "Our Lord, the God." Let us remember that the early Christians painted Christ on the walls of their subterranean necropolis, as a shepherd in the guise of, and invested with all the attributes of Apollo, driving away the wolf, Fenris, who seeks to devour the Sun and his Satellites.

* De Mirville, ii. 325, 326. So we say too. And this shows that it is to the Kabalists and Magicians that the Church is indebted for her dogmas and names. Paul never condemned *real Gnosis*, but the *false* one, now accepted by the Church.

SECTION XXXVIII.

ASTROLOGY AND ASTROLATRY.

THE books of Hermes Trismegistus contain the exoteric meaning, still veiled for all but the Occultist, of the Astrology and Astrolatry of the Khaldi. The two subjects are closely connected. Astrolatry, or the adoration of the heavenly host, is the natural result of only half-revealed Astrology, whose Adepts carefully concealed from the non-initiated masses its Occult principles and the wisdom imparted to them by the Regents of the Planets—the "Angels." Hence, divine Astrology for the Initiates; superstitious Astrolatry for the profane. St. Justin asserts it:

> From the first invention of the hieroglyphics it was not the vulgar, but the distinguished and select men who became initiated in the secrecy of the temples into the science of every kind of Astrology—even into its most abject kind: that Astrology which later on found itself prostituted in the public thoroughfares.

There was a vast difference between the Sacred Science taught by Petosiris and Necepso—the first Astrologers mentioned in the Egyptian manuscripts, believed to have lived during the reign of Ramses II. (Sesostris) *—and the miserable charlatanry of the quacks called Chaldæans, who degraded the Divine Knowledge under the last Emperors of Rome. Indeed, one may fairly describe the two as the "high ceremonial Astrology" and "astrological Astrolatry." The first depended on the knowledge by the Initiates of those (to us) immaterial Forces or Spiritual Entities that affect matter and guide it. Called by the ancient Philosophers the Archontes and the Cosmocratores, they were the types or paradigms on the higher planes of the lower and more material beings on the scale of evolution, whom we call Elementals and Nature-Spirits, to whom the Sabæans bowed and whom they worshipped, without suspecting the essential difference. Hence

* Sesostris, or Pharaoh Ramses II., whose mummy was unswathed in 1886 by Maspero of the Bulak Museum, and recognised as that of the greatest king of Egypt, whose grandson, Ramses III. was the last king of an ancient kingdom.

the latter kind when not a mere pretence, degenerated but too often into Black Magic. It was the favourite form of popular or exoteric Astrology, entirely ignorant of the apotelesmatic principles of the primitive Science, the doctrines of which were imparted only in Initiation. Thus, while the real Hierophants soared like Demi-Gods to the very summit of spiritual knowledge, the *hoi polloi* among the Sabæans crouched, steeped in superstition—ten millenniums back, as they do now—in the cold and lethal shadow of the valleys of matter. Sidereal influence is dual. There is the physical and physiological influence, that of exotericism; and the high spiritual, intellectual and moral influence, imparted by the knowledge of the planetary Gods. Bailly, speaking with only an imperfect knowledge of the former, called Astrology, so far back as the eighteenth century, "The very foolish mother of a very wise daughter"—Astronomy. On the other hand, Arago, a luminary of the nineteenth century, supports the reality of the sidereal influence of the Sun, Moon and Planets. He asks:

> Where do we find lunar influences refuted by arguments that science would dare to avow?

But even Bailly, having, as he thought, put down Astrology as publicly practised, dares not do the same with the real Astrology. He says:

> Judiciary Astrology was at its origin the result of a profound system, the work of an enlightened nation that would wander too far into the mysteries of God and Nature.

A Scientist of a more recent date, a member of the Institute of France, and a professor of History, Ph. Lebas, discovers (unconsciously to himself) the very root of Astrology in his able article on the subject in the *Dictionnaire Encyclopédique de France*. He well understands, he tells his readers, that the adhesion to that Science of such a number of highly intellectual men should be in itself a sufficient motive for believing that all Astrology is not folly:

> While proclaiming in politics the sovereignty of the people and of public opinion, can we admit, as heretofore, that mankind allowed itself to be radically deceived in this only: that an absolute and gross absurdity reigned in the minds of whole nations for so many centuries without being based on anything save—on one hand human imbecility, and on the other charlatanry? How for fifty centuries and more can most men have been either dupes or knaves? . . . Even though we may find it impossible to decide between and separate the realities of Astrology from the elements of invention and empty dreaming in it, . . . let us, nevertheless, repeat with Bossuet and all modern philosophers, that "nothing that has been dominant could be absolutely false." Is it not true, at all events, that there is a

physical reaction on one another among the planets? Is it not again true, that the planets have an influence on the atmosphere, and consequently at any rate a mediate action on vegetation and animals? Has not modern science demonstrated now these two points beyond any doubt? . . . Is it any less true that human liberty of action is not absolute: that all is bound, that all weighs, planets as the rest, on each individual will; that Providence [*or Karma*] acts on us and directs men through those relations that it has established between them and the visible objects and the whole universe? . . . Astrolatry, in its essence, is nothing but that; we are bound to recognise that an instinct superior to the age they lived in guided the efforts of the ancient Magi. As to the materialism and annihilation of human moral freedom with which Bailly charges their theory (Astrology), the reprobate has no sense whatever. All the great astrologers admitted, without one single exception, that man could reäct against the influence of the stars. This principle is established in the Ptolemæian *Tetrabiblos*, the true astrological Scriptures, in chapters ii. and iii. of book i.*

Thomas Aquinas had corroborated Lebas in anticipation; he says:

The celestial bodies are *the cause of all that happens in this sublunary world*, they act indirectly on human actions; but not all the effects produced by them are unavoidable.†

The Occultists and Theosophists are the first to confess that there is white and black Astrology. Nevertheless, Astrology has to be studied in both aspects by those who wish to become proficient in it; and the good or bad results obtained do not depend upon the principles, which are the same in both kinds, but in the Astrologer himself. Thus Pythagoras, who established the whole Copernican system by the Books of Hermes 2,000 years before Galileo's predecessor was born, found and studied in them the whole Science of divine Theogony, of the communication with, and the evocation of, the world's Rectors—the Princes of the "Principalities" of St. Paul—the nativity of each Planet and of the Universe itself, the formulæ of incantations and the consecration of each portion of the human body to the respective Zodiacal sign corresponding to it. All this cannot be regarded as childish and absurd—still less "devilish"—save by those who are, and wish to remain, tyros in the Philosophy of the Occult Sciences. No true thinker—no one who recognises the presence of a common bond between man and visible, as well as invisible, Nature—would see in the old relics of Archaic Wisdom—such as the *Petemenoph Papyrus*, for instance—"childish nonsense and absurdity," as many Academicians

* *Op. cit.*, p. 422.

† *Summa*, Quest. xv. Art. v., upon Astrologers, and Vol. III. pp. 2-29.

and Scientists have done. But upon finding in such ancient documents the application of the Hermetic rules and laws, such as:—

> The consecration of one's hair to the celestial Nile; of the left temple to the living Spirit in the sun, and in the right one to the spirit of Ammon,

he will endeavour to study and comprehend better the "law of correspondences." Nor will he disbelieve in the antiquity of the Zodiac on the plea that some Orientalists have thought fit to declare that the Zodiac was not very ancient, being only the invention of the Greeks of the Macedonian period. For this statement, besides having been shown to be entirely erroneous by a number of other reasons, can be entirely disproved by facts relating to the latest discoveries in Egypt, and by the more accurate readings of hieroglyphical and inscriptions of the earliest dynasties. The published polemics on the contents of the so-called "Magic" Papyri of the Anastasi collection indicate the antiquity of the Zodiac. As the *Lettres à Letronne* say:—

The papyri discourse at length upon the four *bases* or

> Foundations of the world, the identity of which it is impossible, according to Champollion, to mistake, as one is forced to recognise in them the Pillars of the World of St. Paul. It is they who are invoked with the gods of all the celestial zones, quite analogous, once more, to the *Spiritualia nequitiæ in cœlestibus* of the same Apostle.*
>
> That invocation was made in the proper terms . . . of the formula, reproduced far too faithfully by Jamblichus for it to be possible to refuse him any longer the merit of having transmitted to posterity the ancient and primitive spirit of the Egyptian Astrologers.†

As Letronne had tried to prove that all the genuine Egyptian Zodiacs had been manufactured during the Roman period, the Sensaos mummy is brought forward to show that:

> All the Zodiacal monuments in Egypt were chiefly astronomical. Royal tombs and funereal rituals are so many tables of constellations and of their influences for all the hours of every month.
>
> Thus the genethliac tables themselves prove that they are far older than the period assigned to their origin; all the Zodiacs of the sarcophagi of later epochs

---

* "The principalities and powers [born] in heavenly places" (*Ephes.*, iii. 10). The verse, "For though there be that are called Gods, whether in heaven or on earth, as there be Gods many and lords many" (I. *Corinth.*, viii. 5), shows, at any rate, the recognition by Paul of a plurality of "Gods" whom he calls "daemons" ("spirits"—never *devils*). Principalities, Thrones, Dominions, Rectors, etc. are all Jewish and Christian names for the Gods of the ancients—the Archangels and Angels of the former being in every case the Devas and the Dhyân Chohans of the more ancient religions.

† Answer by Reuvens to Letronne with regard to his mistaken notions about the Zodiac of Dendera.

being simple reminiscences of the Zodiacs belonging to the mythological [archaic] period.

Primitive Astrology was as far above modern judiciary Astrology, so-called, as the guides (the Planets and Zodiacal signs) are above the lamp-posts. Berosus shows the sidereal sovereignty of Bel and Mylitta (Sun and Moon), and only "the twelve lords of the Zodiacal Gods," the "thirty-six Gods Counsellors" and the "twenty-four Stars, judges of this world," which support and guide the Universe (our solar system), watch over mortals and reveal to mankind its fate and their own decrees. Judiciary Astrology as it is now known, is correctly denominated by the Latin Church the

> Materialistic and pantheistic prophesying by the objective planet itself, independently of its Rector [the Mlac of the Jews, the ministers of the Eternal commissioned by him to announce his will to mortals]; the ascension or conjunction of the planet at the moment of the birth of an individual deciding his fortune and the moment and mode of his death.*

Every student of Occultism knows that the heavenly bodies are closely related during each Manvantara with the mankind of that special cycle; and there are some who believe that each great character born during that period has—as every other mortal has, only in a far stronger degree—his destiny outlined within his proper constellation or star, traced as a self-prophecy, an anticipated autobiography, by the indwelling Spirit of that particular star. The human Monad in its first beginning is that Spirit, or the Soul of that star (Planet) itself. As our Sun radiates its light and beams on every body in space within the boundaries of its system, so the Regent of every Planet-star, the Parent-monad, shoots out from itself the Monad of every "pilgrim" Soul born under its house within its own group. The Regents are esoterically seven, whether in the Sephiroth, the "Angels of the Presence," the Rishis, or the Amshaspends. "The One is no number" is said in all the esoteric works.

* St. Augustine (*De Gen.*, I. iii.) and Delrio (*Disquisit.*, Vol. IV., chap. iii.) are quoted by De Mirville, to show that "the more astrologers speak the truth and the better they prophesy it, the more one has to feel diffident, seeing that their agreement with the devil becomes thereby the more apparent." The famous statement made by Juvenal (*Satires*, vi.) to the effect that "not one single astrologer could be found who did not pay dearly for the help he received from his genius"—no more proves the latter to be a devil than the death of Socrates proves his daimon to have been a native from the nether world—if such there be. Such argument only demonstrates human stupidity and wickedness, once reason is made subservient to prejudice and fanaticism of every sort. "Most of the great writers of antiquity, Cicero and Tacitus among them, believed in Astrology and the realization of its prophecies;" and "the penalty of death decreed nearly everywhere against those mathematicians [astrologers] who happened to predict falsely diminished neither their number nor their tranquillity of mind."

From the Kasdim and Gazzim (Astrologers) the noble, primitive science passed to the Khartumim Asaphim (or Theologians) and the Hakamim (or scientists, the Magicians of the lower class), and from these to the Jews during their captivity. The Books of Moses had been buried in oblivion for centuries, and when re-discovered by Hilkiah had lost their true sense for the people of Israel. Primitive Occult Astrology was on the decline when Daniel, the last of the Jewish Initiates of the old school, became the chief of the Magi and Astrologers of Chaldea. In those days even Egypt, who had her wisdom from the same source as Babylon, had degenerated from her former grandeur, and her glory had begun to fade out. Still, the science of old had left her eternal imprint on the world, and the seven great Primitive Gods reigned for ever in the Astrology and in the division of time of every nation upon the face of the earth. The names of the days of our (Christian) week are those of the Gods of the Chaldæans, who translated them from those of the Âryans; the uniformity of these antediluvian names in every nation, from the Goths back to the Indians, would remain inexplicable, as Sir W. Jones thought, had not the riddle been explained to us by the invitation made by the Chaldæan oracles, recorded by Porphyry and quoted by Eusebius:

> To carry those names first to the Egyptian and Phœnician colonies, then to the Greeks, with the express recommendation that each God should be invoked only on that day that had been called by his name. . . .
>
> Thus Apollo says in those oracles: "I must be invoked on the day of the Sun, Mercury after his directions, then Chronos [Saturn], then Venus, and do not fail to call seven times each of those gods." *

This is slightly erroneous. Greece did not get her astrological instruction from Egypt or from Chaldæa, but direct from Orpheus, as Lucian tells us.† It was Orpheus, as he says, who imparted the Indian Sciences to nearly all the great monarchs of antiquity; and it was they, the ancient kings favoured by the Planetary Gods, who recorded the principles of Astrology—as did Ptolemus, for instance. Thus Lucian writes:

> The Bœotian Tiresias acquired the greatest reputation in the art of predicting futurity. . . . In those days divination was not as slightly treated as it is now; and nothing was ever undertaken without previous consultation with diviners, whose oracles were all directed by astrology. . . . At Delphos the virgin charged

* *Præparatio Evangelica*, I. xiv.

† *Ast.*, iv. 60.

missioned to announce futurity was the symbol of the Heavenly Virgin, . . . and Our Lady.

On the sarcophagus of an Egyptian Pharaoh, Neith, mother of Ra, the heifer that brings forth the Sun, her body spangled with stars, and wearing the solar and lunar discs, is equally referred to as the "Heavenly Virgin" and "Our Lady of the Starry Vault."

Modern judiciary Astrology in its present form began only during the time of Diodorus, as he apprises the world.* But Chaldæan Astrology was believed in by most of the great men in History, such as Cæsar, Pliny, Cicero—whose best friends, Nigidius Figulus and Lucius Tarrutius, were themselves Astrologers, the former being famous as a prophet. Marcus Antonius never travelled without an Astrologer recommended to him by Cleopatra. Augustus, when ascending the throne, had his horoscope drawn by Theagenes. Tiberius discovered pretenders to his throne by means of Astrology and divination. Vitellius dared not exile the Chaldæans, as they had announced the day of their banishment as that of his death. Vespasian consulted them daily; Domitian would not move without being advised by the prophets; Adrian was a learned Astrologer himself; and all of them, ending with Julian (called the *Apostate* because he would not become one), believed in, and addressed their prayers to, the Planetary "Gods." The Emperor Adrian, moreover, "predicted from the January calends up to December 31st, every event that happened to him daily." Under the wisest emperors Rome had a School of Astrology, wherein were secretly taught the occult influences of the Sun, Moon, and Saturn.† Judiciary Astrology is used to this day by the Kabalists; and Éliphas Lévi, the modern French Magus, teaches its rudiments in his *Dogme et Rituel de la Haute Magie.* But the key to ceremonial or ritualistic Astrology, with the teraphim and the urim and thummim of Magic, is lost to Europe. Hence our century of Materialism shrugs its shoulders and sees in Astrology—a pretender.

Not all scientists scoff at it, however, and one may rejoice in reading in the *Musée des Sciences*‡ the suggestive and fair remarks made by Le Couturier, a man of science of no mean reputation. He thinks it curious

---

* *Hist.*, I. ii.

† All these particulars may be found more fully and far more completely in Champollion Figeac's *Égypte*.

‡ *Op. cit.*, p. 230.

to notice that while the bold speculations of Democritus are found vindicated by Dalton,

The reveries of the alchemists are also on their way to a certain rehabilitation. They receive renewed life from the minute investigations of their successors, the chemists; a very remarkable thing indeed is to see how much modern discoveries have served to vindicate, of late, the theories of the Middle Ages from the charge of absurdity laid at their door. Thus, if, as demonstrated by Col. Sabine, the direction of a piece of steel, hung a few feet above the soil, may be influenced by the position of the moon, whose body is at a distance of 240,000 miles from our planet, who then could accuse of extravagance the belief of the ancient astrologers [or the modern, either] in the influence of the stars on human destiny.*

* *Op. cit.*, p. 230.

SECTION XXXIX.

Cycles and Avatâras.

We have already drawn attention to the facts that the record of the life of a World-Saviour is emblematical, and must be read by its mystic meaning, and that the figures 432 have a cosmic evolutionary significance. We find these two facts throwing light on the origin of the exoteric Christian religion, and clearing away much of the obscurity surrounding its beginnings. For is it not clear that the names and characters in the Synoptical Gospels and in that of St. John are not historical? Is it not evident that the compilers of the life of Christ, desirous to show that the birth of their Master was a cosmic, astronomical, and divinely-preördained event, attempted to coördinate the same with the end of the secret cycle, 4,320? When facts are collated this answers to them as little as does the other cycle of "thirty-three solar years, seven months, and seven days," which has also been brought forward as supporting the same claim, the soli-lunar cycle in which the Sun gains on the Moon one solar year. The combination of the three figures, 4, 3, 2, with cyphers according to the cycle and Manvantara concerned, was, and is, preëminently Hindu. It will remain a secret even though several of its significant features are revealed. It relates, for instance, to the Pralaya of the races in their periodical dissolution, before which events a special Avatâra has always to descend and incarnate on earth. These figures were adopted by all the older nations, such as those of Egypt and Chaldæa, and before them were current among the Atlanteans. Evidently some of the more learned among the early Church Fathers who had dabbled, whilst Pagans, in temple secrets, knew them to relate to the Avatâric or Messianic mystery, and tried to apply this cycle to the birth of their Messiah; they failed because the figures relate to the respective ends of the Root-Races and not to any individual. In their badly-directed efforts, moreover, an error of five years occurred. Is it possible, if their claims as to the importance and universality of the event were correct, that such a vital mistake should have been allowed to creep into a chronological computation preördained and traced in the heavens by the finger of God? Again, what were the Pagan and even Jewish Initiates doing, if this claim as to Jesus be correct? Could they, the custodians of the keys to the secret cycles and Avatâras, the heirs of all the Âryan, Egyptian, and Chaldæan wisdom, have failed to recognise their great "God Incarnate," one with Jehovah,* their Saviour of the latter days, him whom all the nations of Asia still expect as their Kalki Avatâra, Maitreya Buddha, Sosiosh, Messiah, etc.?

The simple secret is this: There are cycles within greater cycles, which are all contained in the one Kalpa of 4,320,000 years. It is at the end of this cycle that the Kalki Avatâra is expected—the Avatâra Whose name and characteristics are secret, Who will come forth from Shamballa, the "City of Gods," which is in the West for some nations, in the East for others, in the North or South for yet others. And this is the reason why, from the Indian Rishi to Virgil, and from Zoroaster down to the latest Sibyl, all have, since the beginning of the Fifth Race prophesied, sung, and promised the cyclic return of the Virgin—Virgo the constellation—and the birth of a divine child who should bring back to our earth the Golden Age.

No one, however fanatical, would have sufficient hardihood to maintain that the Christian era has ever been a return to the Golden Age —Virgo having actually entered into Libra since then. Let us trace as briefly as possible the Christian traditions to their true origin.

First of all, they discover in a few lines from Virgil a direct prophecy of the birth of Christ. Yet it is impossible to detect in this prophecy any feature of the present age. It is in the famous fourth Eclogue in which, half a century before our era, Pollio is made to ask the Muses of Sicily to sing to him about greater events.

> The last era of Cumæan song is now arrived and the grand series of ages (that series which recurs again and again in the course of our mundane revolutions) begins afresh. Now the Virgin Astræa returns, and the reign of Saturn recom-

* In the 1,326 places in the *New Testament* where the word "God" is mentioned nothing signifies that in God are included more beings than God. On the contrary in 17 places God is called the only God. The places where the Father is so-called amount to 320. In 105 places God is addressed with high-sounding titles. In 90 places all prayers and thanks are addressed to the Father; 320 times in the *New Testament* is the Son declared to be inferior to the Father; 85 times is Jesus called the "Son of Man;" 70 times is he called a man. In not one single place in the Bible is it said that God holds within him three different Beings or Persons, and yet is one Being or Person.—Dr. Karl von Bergen's *Lectures in Sweden*.

mences. Now a new progeny *descends from the celestial realms.* Do thou, chaste Lucina, smile propitious to the infant Boy who will bring to a close the present Age of Iron,* and introduce throughout the whole world the Age of Gold. . . . He shall share the life of Gods and shall see heroes mingled in society with Gods, himself be seen by them and all the peaceful world. . . . Then shall the herds no longer dread the huge lion, the serpent also shall die: and the poison's deceptive plant shall perish. Come then, dear child of the Gods, great descendant of Jupiter! . . . The time is near. See, the world is shaken with its globe saluting thee: the earth, the regions of the sea, and the heavens sublime.†

It is in these few lines, called the "Sibylline prophecy about the coming of Christ," that his followers now see a direct foretelling of the event. Now who will presume to maintain that either at the birth of Jesus or since the establishment of the so-called Christian religion, any portion of the above-quoted sentences can be shown as prophetic? Has the "last age"—the Age of Iron, or Kali Yuga—closed since then? Quite the reverse, since it is shown to be in full sway just now, not only because the Hindus use the name, but by universal personal experience. Where is that "new race that has descended from the celestial realms"? Was it the race that emerged from Paganism into Christianity? Or is it our present race, with nations ever red-hot for fight, jealous and envious, ready to pounce upon each other, showing mutual hatred that would put to blush cats and dogs, ever lying and deceiving one another? Is it this age of ours that is the promised "Golden Age"—in which neither the venom of the serpent nor of any plant is any longer lethal, and in which we are all secure under the mild sway of God-chosen sovereigns? The wildest fancy of an opium-eater could hardly suggest a more inappropriate description, if it is to be applied to our age or to any age since the year one of our era. What of the mutual slaughter of sects, of Christians by Pagans, and of Pagans and Heretics by Christians; the horrors of the Middle Ages and of the Inquisition; Napoleon, and since his day, an "armed peace" at best—at the worst, torrents of blood, shed for supremacy over acres of land, and a handful of heathen: millions of soldiers under arms, ready for battle; a diplomatic body playing at Cains and Judases; and instead of the "mild sway of a divine sovereign" the universal, though unrecognised, sway of Cæsarism, of "might" in lieu of "right," and the breeding therefrom of anarchists, socialists, pétroleuses, and destroyers of every description?

* Kali Yuga, the Black or Iron Age.

† Virgil, *Eclogue*, iv.

The Sibylline prophecy and Virgil's inspirational poetry remain unfulfilled in every point, as we see.

> The fields are yellow with soft ears of corn;

but so they were before our era:

> The blushing grapes shall hang from the rude brambles, and dewy honey shall [or may] distil from the rugged oak;

but they have not thus done, so far. We must look for another interpretation. What is it? The Sibylline Prophetess spoke, as thousands of other Prophets and Seers have spoken, though even the few such records that have survived are rejected by Christian and infidel, and their interpretations are only allowed and accepted among the Initiated. The Sibyl alluded to cycles in general and to the great cycle especially. Let us remember how the Purânas corroborate the above, among others the *Vishnu Purâna*:

> When the practices taught by the Vedas, and the Institutes of Law shall have nearly ceased, and the close of the Kali Yuga [the "Iron Age" of Virgil] shall be nigh, an aspect of that divine Being who exists of his own spiritual nature in the character of Brahmâ and even is the beginning and the end [*Alpha and Omega*], . . . shall descend upon earth: he will be born in the family of Vishnuyasha, an eminent Brâhman of Shamballah . . . endowed with the eight superhuman powers. By his irresistible might he will destroy . . . all whose minds are devoted to iniquity. He will then reëstablish righteousness upon earth; and the minds of those who live at the end of the [Kali] Age shall be awakened, and shall be as pellucid as crystal.* The men who are thus changed by virtue of that peculiar time shall be as the seeds of human beings [the Shistha, the survivors of the future cataclysm], and shall give birth to a race who shall follow the laws of the Krita [or Satya] Yuga [the age of purity, or the "Golden Age"]. For it is said: "When the sun and moon and Tishya [asterisms] and the planet Jupiter are in one mansion the Krita Age [the Golden] shall return.†

The astronomical cycles of the Hindus—those taught publicly—have been sufficiently well understood, but the esoteric meaning thereof, in its application to transcendental subjects connected with them, has ever remained a dead-letter. The number of cycles was enormous; it ranged from the Mahâ Yuga cycle of 4,320,000 years down to the small septenary and quinquennial cycles, the latter being composed of the five years called respectively the

---

* At the close of our Race, people, it is said, through suffering and discontent will become more spiritual. Clairvoyance will become a general faculty. We shall be approaching the spiritual state of the Third and Second Races.

† *Vishnu Purâna*, IV., xxiv. 228, Wilson's translation.

Samvatsara, Parivatsara, Idvatsara, Anuvatsara, and Vatsara, each having secret attributes or qualities attached to them. Vriddhagarga gives these in a treatise, now the property of a Trans-Himâlayan Matham (or temple); and describes the relation between this quinquennial and the Brihaspati cycle, based on the conjunction of the Sun and Moon every sixtieth year: a cycle as mysterious—for national events in general and those of the Âryan Hindu nation especially—as it is important.

SECTION XI.

SECRET CYCLES.

THE former five-year cycle comprehends sixty solar-sidereal months of 1800 days, sixty-one solar months (or 1830 days); sixty-two lunar months (or 1860 lunations), and sixty-seven lunar-asterismal months (or 1809 such days).

In his *Kála Sankalita*, Col. Warren very properly regards these years as cycles; this they are, for each year has its own special importance as having some bearing upon, and connection with, specified events in individual horoscopes. He writes that in the cycle of sixty there

> Are contained five cycles of twelve years, each supposed equal to one year of the planet (Brihaspati, or Jupiter) . . . I mention this cycle because I found it mentioned in some books, but I know of no nation or tribe that reckons time after that account.*

The ignorance is very natural, since Col. Warren could know nothing of the secret cycles and their meanings. He adds:

> The names of the five cycles or Yugas are: . . . (1) Samvatsara, (2) Parivatsara, (3) Idvatsara, (4) Anuvatsara, (5) Udravatsara.

The learned Colonel might, however, have assured himself that there were "other nations" which had the same secret cycle, if he had but remembered that the Romans also had their *lustrum* of five years (from the Hindus undeniably) which represented the same period if multiplied by 12.† Near Benares there are still the relics of all these cycle-records, and of astronomical instruments cut out of solid rock, the everlasting records of Archaic Initiation, called by Sir W. Jones

---

* *Op. cit.*, p. 212.

† At any rate, the temple secret meaning was the same.

(as suggested by the prudent Brâhmans who surrounded him) old "back records" or reckonings. But in Stonehenge they exist to this day. Higgins says that Waltire found the barrows of tumuli surrounding this giant-temple represented accurately the situation and magnitude of the fixed stars, forming a complete orrery or planisphere. As Colebrooke found out, it is the cycle of the *Vedas*, recorded in the *Jyotisha*, one of the Vedângas, a treatise on Astronomy, which is the basis of calculation for all other cycles, larger or smaller;* and the *Vedas* were written in characters, archaic though they be, long after those natural observations, made by the aid of their gigantic mathematical and astronomical instruments, had been recorded by the men of the Third Race, who had received their instruction from the Dhyân Chohans. Maurice speaks truly when he observes that all such

> Circular stone monuments were intended as durable symbols of astronomical cycles by a race who, not having, or for political reasons, forbidding the use of letters, had no other permanent method of instructing their disciples or handing down their knowledge to posterity.

He errs only in the last idea. It was to conceal their knowledge from profane posterity, leaving it as an heirloom only to the Initiates, that such monuments, at once rock observatories and astronomical treatises, were cut out.

It is no news that as the Hindus divided the earth into seven zones, so the more western peoples—Chaldæans, Phœnicians, and even the Jews, who got their learning either directly or indirectly from the Brâhmans—made all their secret and sacred numerations by 6 and 12, though using the number 7 whenever this would not lend itself to handling. Thus the numerical base of 6, the exoteric figure given by Ârya Bhatta, was made good use of. From the first secret cycle of 600—the Naros, transformed successively into 60,000 and 60 and 6, and, with other noughts added into other secret cycles—down to the smallest, an Archæologist and Mathematician can easily find it repeated in every country, known to every nation. Hence the globe was divided into 60 degrees, which, multiplied by 60, became 3,600 the "great year." Hence also the hour with its 60 minutes of 60 seconds each. The Asiatic people count a cycle of 60 years also, after which comes the lucky seventh decad, and the Chinese have their small cycle of 60 days, the Jews of 6 days, the Greeks of 6 centuries—the Naros again.

* *Asiat. Res.*, vol. viii. p. 470, *et seq.*

The Babylonians had a great year of 3,600, being the Naros multiplied by 6. The Tartar cycle called Van was 180 years, or three sixties; this multiplied by 12 times 12=144, makes 25,920 years, the exact period of revolution of the heavens.

India is the birthplace of arithmetic and mathematics; see "Our Figures," in *Chips from a German Workshop*, by Prof. Max Müller; [illegible] beyond a doubt. As well explained by Krishna Shâstri Godbole in the *Theosophist*:

The Jews . . . represented the units (1-9) by the first nine letters of the alphabet; the tens (10-90) by the next nine letters; the first four hundreds (100-400) by the last four letters, and the remaining ones (500-900) by the second forms of the letters "kâf" (11th), "mim" (13th), "nûn" (13th), "pe" (17th), and "sad" (18th); and they represented other numbers by combining these letters according to their value. . . . The Jews of the present period still adhere to this practice of notation in their Hebrew books. The Greeks had a numerical system similar to that used by the Jews, but they carried it a little farther by using letters of the alphabet with a dash or slant-line behind, to represent thousands (1000-9000), tens of thousands (10,000-90,000) and one hundred of thousands (100,000) the last, for instance, being represented by "rho" with a dash behind, while "rho" singly represented 100. The Romans represented all numerical values by the combination (additive when the second letter is of equal or less value) of six letters of their alphabet: i (= 1), v (= 5), x (= 10), c (for "centum" = 100), d (= 500), and m (= 1000): thus 20 = xx, 15 = xv, and 9 = ix. These are called the Roman numerals, and are adopted by all European nations when using the Roman alphabet. The Arabs first followed their neighbours, the Jews, in their method of computation, as such, so that they called it Abjad from the first four Hebrew letters—"alif," "beth," "gimel"—or rather "jimel," that is, "jim" (Arabic being wanting in "g"), and "daleth," representing the first four units. But when in the early part of the Christian era they came to India as traders, they found the country already using for computation the decimal scale of notation, which they forthwith borrowed literally; *viz.*, without altering its method of writing from left to right, at variance with their own mode of writing, which is from right to left. They introduced this system into Europe through Spain and other European countries lying along the coast of the Mediterranean and under their sway, during the dark ages of European history. It has thus become evident that the Âryas knew well mathematics or the science of computation at a time when all other nations knew but little, if anything, of it. It has also been admitted that the knowledge of arithmetic and algebra was first introduced from the Hindus by the Arabs, and then taught by them to the Western nations. This fact convincingly proves that the Âryan civilisation is older than that of any other nation in the world; and as the *Vedas* are avowedly [illegible] the oldest work of that civilisation, a presumption is raised in favour of their great antiquity.*

* *Theosophist*, August, 1881.

But while the Jewish nation, for instance—regarded so long as the first and oldest in the order of creation—knew nothing of arithmetic and remained utterly ignorant of the decimal scale of notation—the latter existed for ages in India before the actual era.

To become certain of the immense antiquity of the Âryan Asiatic nations and of their astronomical records one has to study more than the *Vedas*. The secret meaning of the latter will never be understood by the present generation of Orientalists; and the astronomical works which give openly the real dates and prove the antiquity of both the nation and its science, elude the grasp of the collectors of ollas and old manuscripts in India, the reason being too obvious to need explanation. Yet there are Astronomers and Mathematicians to this day in India, humble Shâstris and Pandits, unknown and lost in the midst of that population of phenomenal memories and metaphysical brains, who have undertaken the task and have proved to the satisfaction of many that the *Vedas* are the oldest works in the world. One of such is the Shâstri just quoted, who published in *The Theosophist* * an able treatise proving astronomically and mathematically that:

If the Post-Vaidika works alone, the Upanishads, the Brâhmanas, etc., down to the Purânas, when examined critically carry us back to 20,000 B.C., then the time of the composition of the *Vedas* themselves cannot be less than 30,000 B.C., in round numbers, a date which we may take at present as the age of that Book of books.†

And what are his proofs?

Cycles and the evidence yielded by the asterisms. Here are a few extracts from his rather lengthy treatise, selected to give an idea of his demonstrations and bearing directly on the quinquennial cycle spoken of just now. Those who feel interested in the demonstrations and are advanced mathematicians can turn to the article itself, "The Antiquity of the *Vedas*," ‡ and judge for themselves.

10. Somâkara in his commentary on the *Shesha Jyotisha* quotes a passage from the *Satapatha Brâhmana*, which contains an observation on the change of the tropics, and which is also found in the *Sâkhâyana Brâhmana*, as has been noticed by Prof. Max Müller in his preface to *Rigveda Samhitâ* (p. xx. foot-note, vol. iv.). The passage is this: . . . "The full-moon night in Phâlguna is the first night of Samvatsara, the first year of the quinquennial age." This passage clearly shows that the quinquennial age which, according to the sixth verse of the *Jyotisha*, begins on the 1st of Mâgha (January-February), once began on the 15th of Phâlguna (February-

* Aug., 1881 to Feb., 1882. † *Loc. cit.*, iv. 127. ‡ *Theosophist*, vol. iii. p. 22.

March). Now when the 15th of Phâlguna of the first year called [illegible] of the quinquennial age begins, the moon, according to the *Jyotisha*, is in

$$\frac{95}{124}\text{th} \left(= \cfrac{1}{1+\cfrac{1}{3+\cfrac{8}{29}}}\right) \text{ or } \tfrac{3}{4}\text{th of the Uttara Phâlguni, and}$$

the sun in

$$\frac{33}{124}\text{th} \left(= \cfrac{1}{3+\cfrac{1}{1+\cfrac{8}{25}}}\right) \text{ or } \tfrac{1}{4}\text{th of Pûrva Bhâdrapadâ.}$$

Hence the position of the four principal points on the ecliptic was then as follows:

The winter solstice in 3°29′ of Purva Bhâdrapadâ.

The vernal equinox in the beginning of Mrigashirsha.

The summer solstice in 10 of Purva Phâlguni.

The autumnal equinox in the middle of Jyeshtha.

The vernal equinoctial point, we have seen, coincided with the beginning of Krittikâ in 1421 B.C.; and from the beginning of Krittikâ to that of Mrigashirsha was, in consequence, 1421 + 26 2/3 × 72 = 1421 + 1920 = 3341 B.C., supposing the rate of *precession* to be 50″ a year. When we take the rate to be 3°20′ in 247 years, the time comes up to 1516 + 1960·7 = 3476·7 B.C.

When the winter solstice by its retrograde motion coincided after that with the beginning of Pûrva Bhâdrapadâ, then the commencement of the quinquennial age was changed from the 15th to the 1st of Phâlguna (February-March). This change took place 240 years after the date of the above observation, that is, in [illegible]. This date is most important, as from it an era was reckoned in after times. The commencement of the Kali or Kali Yuga (derived from "kal," "to reckon"), though said by European scholars to be an imaginary date, becomes thus an astronomical fact.

INTERCHANGE OF KRITTIKÂ AND ASHVINI.*

We thus see that the asterisms, twenty-seven in number, were counted from the Mrigashirsha when the vernal equinox was in its beginning, and that the practice of thus counting was adhered to till the vernal equinox retrograded to the beginning of Krittikâ, when it became the first of the asterisms. For then the winter solstice had changed, receding from Phâlguna (February-March) to Mâgha (January-February), one complete lunar month. And, in like manner, the place of Krittikâ

---

* The impartial study of Vaidic and Post-Vaidic works shows that the ancient Âryans knew well the precession of the equinoxes, and "that they changed their position from a certain asterism by two (occasionally three) asterisms back whenever the precession amounted to two, properly speaking to 2 11/61 asterisms or about 29°, being the motion of the sun in a lunar month, and [illegible] caused the seasons to fall back a complete lunar month. . . It appears certain that at the date of *Sûrya Siddhânta, Brahmâ Siddhânta*, and other ancient treatises on astronomy, the vernal equinoctial point had not actually reached the beginning of Ashvini, but was a few degrees east of it. . . The astronomers of Europe change westward the beginning of Aries and all other signs of the Zodiac every year by about 50″ 25, and thus make the names of the signs meaningless. But these signs are as much fixed as the asterisms themselves, and hence the Western astronomers of the present day appear to us in this respect less wary and scientific in their observations than their very ancient brethren—the Âryas."—*Theosophist*, iii. 23.

was occupied by Ashvini, that is, the latter became the first of the asterisms, heading all others, when its beginning coincided with the vernal equinoctial point, or, in other words, when the winter solstice was in Pausha (December-February). Now from the beginning of Krittikâ to that of Ashvini there are two asterisms, or 26 2/3°, and the time the equinox takes to retrograde this distance at the rate of 1 in 72 years is 1920 years; and hence the date at which the vernal equinox coincided with the commencement of Ashvini or with the end of Revati is 1920-1421 = 499 A.D.

Bentley's Opinion.

12. The next and equally-important observation we have to record here is one discussed by Mr. Bentley in his researches into the Indian antiquities. "The first lunar asterism," he says, "in the division of twenty-eight was called Mûla, that is to say, the root or origin. In the division of twenty-seven the first lunar asterism was called Jyeshtha, that is to say, the eldest or first, and consequently of the same import as the former" (*vide* his *Historical View of the Hindu Astronomy*, p. 4). From this it becomes manifest that the vernal equinox was once in the beginning of Mûla, and Mûla was reckoned the first of the asterisms when they were twenty-eight in number, including Adhijit. Now there are fourteen asterisms, or 180°, from the beginning of Mrigashirsha to that of Mûla, and hence the date at which the vernal equinox coincided with the beginning of Mûla was at least 3341 + 180 × 72 = 16,301 B.C. The position of the four principal points on the ecliptic was then as given below:

The winter solstice in the beginning of Uttara Phâlgunî in the month of Shrâvana.

The vernal equinox in the beginning of Mûla in Kârttika.

The summer solstice in the beginning of Pûrva Bhâdrapadâ in Mâgha.

The autumnal equinox in the beginning of Mrigashirsha in Vaishâkha.

A Proof from the Bhagavad Gîtâ.

13. The *Bhagavad Gîtâ*, as well as the *Bhâgavata*, makes mention of an observation which points to a still more remote antiquity than the one discovered by Mr. Bentley. The passages are given in order below:

"I am the Mârgashirsha [*viz.* the first among the months] and the spring [*viz.* the first among the seasons]."

This shows that at one time the first month of spring was Mârgashirsha. A season includes two months, and the mention of a month suggests the season.

"I am the Samvatsara among the years [which are five in number] and the spring among the seasons, and the Mârgashîrsha among the months and the Abhijit among the asterisms [which are twenty-eight in number]."

This clearly points out that at one time in the first year called Samvatsara, of the quinquennial age, the Madhu, that is, the first month of spring, was Mârgashirsha, and Abhijit was the first of the asterisms. It then coincided with the vernal equinoctial point, and thence from it the asterisms were counted. To find the date of this observation: There are three asterisms from the beginning of Mûla to the beginning of Abhijit, and hence the date in question is at least 16,301 + 3/7 × 90 ×

72 = 19,078 or about 20,000 B.C. The Samvatsara at this time began in [illegible] the winter solstitial month. . . . [illegible]

So far then 20,000 years are mathematically proved for the [illegible] of the *Vedas*. And this is simply exoteric. Any mathematician, [illegible] vided he be not blinded by preconception and prejudice, can [illegible] and an unknown but very clever amateur Astronomer, S. A. [illegible] has proved it some sixty years back.

His theory about the Hindu Yugas and their length is curious [illegible] being so very near the correct doctrine. [illegible]

It is said in volume ii. p. 131, of *Asiatic Researches* that: "The great [illegible] Yudhister reigned 27,000 years . . . at the end of the brazen age." In [illegible] ix. p. 364, we read:

"In the *beginning of the Cali Yuga*, in the reign of Yudhister. And [illegible] . . . began his reign immediately after the flood called Pralaya."

Here we find three different statements concerning Yudhister . . . [illegible] these seeming differences we must have recourse to their books of [illegible] we find the heavens and the earth divided into *five parts* of unequal [illegible] circles parallel to the equator. Attention to these divisions will be found [illegible] utmost importance . . . as it will be found that from them arose the [illegible] Maha-Yuga into its four component parts. Every astronomer knows [illegible] a point in the heavens called the pole, round which the whole seems [illegible] twenty-four hours; and that at ninety degrees from it they imagine a [illegible] the *equator*, which divides the heavens and the earth into two equal [illegible] north and the south. Between this circle and the pole there is another [illegible] circle called the circle of *perpetual apparition*: between which and the [illegible] there is a point in the heavens called the zenith, through which [illegible] imaginary circle pass, parallel to the other two; and then there wants but [illegible] circle of perpetual occultation to complete the round. . . . No astronomer [illegible] Europe besides myself has ever applied them to the development of the [illegible] mysterious numbers. We are told in the *Asiatic Researches* that Yudhister [illegible] Vicramâditya to reign in Cassimer, which is in the latitude of 36 degrees [illegible] in that latitude the circle of perpetual apparition would extend up to 72 [illegible] altitude, and from that to the zenith there are but 18 degrees, but from the [illegible] to the equator in that latitude there are 36 degrees, and from the equator [illegible] circle of perpetual occultation there are 54 degrees. Here we find the [illegible] of 180 degrees divided into four parts, in the proportion of 1, 2, 3, 4, i.e., [illegible] 54, 72. Whether the Hindu astronomers were acquainted with the motion [illegible] earth or not is of no consequence, since the appearances are the same; [illegible] will give those gentlemen of *tender consciences* any pleasure I am willing to [illegible] that they imagined the heavens rolled round the earth, but they had [illegible] stars in the path of the sun to move *forward* through the equinoctial points, [illegible] rate of fifty-four seconds of a degree in a year, which carried the whole [illegible] in 24,000 years; in which time they also observed that the angle of obliquity [illegible] so as to *extend* or *contract* the width of the tropics 4 degrees on each side, [illegible] of motion would carry the tropics from the equator to the poles in 540,000 years: in which time the Zodiac would have made twenty-two and a half revolutions, which are expressed by the parallel circles from the equator to the poles . . . or what amounts to the same thing, the north pole of the ecliptic would have moved from the north pole of the earth to the equator. . . . Thus the poles become inverted in 1,080,000 years, which is their Maha Yuga, and which they had divided into four unequal parts, in the proportions of 1, 2, 3, 4, for the reasons mentioned above; which are 108,000, 216,000, 324,000, and 432,000. Here we have the most positive proofs that the above numbers originated in *ancient astronomical observations*, and consequently are not deserving of those epithets which have been bestowed upon them by the Essayist, echoing the voice of Bentley, Wilford, Dupuis, etc.

I have now to show that the reign of Yudhister for 27,000 years is neither *absurd nor disgusting*, but perhaps the Essayist is not aware that there were several Yudhisters or Judhisters. In volume ii. p. 131, *Asiatic Researches*: "The great ancestor of Yudhister reigned 27,000 years at the end of the brazen or third age." Here I must again beg your attention to this projection. This is a plane of that machine which the second gentleman thought so very clumsy; it is that of a *prolong spheroid*, called by the ancients an atroscope. Let the longest axis represent the poles of the earth, making an angle of 28 degrees with the horizon; then will the seven divisions above the horizon to the North Pole, the temple of Buddha, and the seven from the North Pole to the circle of perpetual apparition represent the fourteen Manvantaras, or very long periods of time, each of which, according to the third volume of *Asiatic Researches*, p. 258 or 259, was the reign of a Menu. But Capt. Wilford, in volume v. p. 243, gives us the following information: "The Egyptians had fourteen dynasties, and the Hindus had fourteen dynasties, the *rulers* of which are called Menus." . . .

Who can here mistake the fourteen very long periods of time for those which constituted the Cali Yuga of Delhi, or any other place in the latitude of 28 degrees, where the blank space from the foot of Meru to the seventh circle from the equator, constitutes the part passed over by the tropic in the next age; which proportions differ considerably from those in the latitude of 36; and because the numbers in the Hindu books differ, Mr. Bentley asserts that: "This shows what little dependence is to be put in them." But, on the contrary, it shows with what accuracy the Hindus had *observed* the motions of the heavens in different latitudes.

Some of the Hindus inform us that "the earth has *two spindles* which are surrounded by *seven tiers of heavens and hells* at the distance of *one Raju* each." This needs but little explanation when it is understood that the seven divisions from the equator to their zenith are called *Rishis* or *Rashas*. But what is most to our present purpose to know is that they had given names to each of those divisions which the tropics passed over during each revolution of the Zodiac. In the latitude of 36 degrees where the Pole or Meru was nine steps high at Cassimere, they were called *Shastras*; in latitude 28 degrees at Delhi, where the Pole or Meru was seven steps high, they were called Menus; but in 24 degrees, at Cacha, where the Pole or Meru was but six steps high, they were called Sacas. But in the ninth volume (*Asiatic Researches*) Yudhister, the son of Dherma, or *Justice*, was the first of the six Sacas;

the name implies the *end*, and as everything has two ends, Yudhister is as applicable to the first as to the last. And as the division on the north of the circle of perpetual apparition is the first of the Cali Yuga, supposing the tropics to be ascending, it was called the division or reign of Yudhister. But the division which immediately precedes the circle of perpetual apparition is the last of the third or *brazen age*, and was therefore called Yudhister, and as his reign preceded the reign of the other, as the tropic ascended to the Pole or Meru, he was called *the father* of the other—"the great ancestor of Yudhister, who reigned *twenty-seven thousand years, at the end of* the brazen age." (Vol. ii. *Asiatic Researches.*)

The ancient Hindus observed that the Zodiac went forward at about the rate of fifty-four seconds a year, and to avoid greater fractions, stated it at that, which would make a complete round in 24,000 years; and observing the angle of the poles to vary nearly 4 degrees each round, stated the three numbers as such, which would have given *forty-five rounds of the Zodiac* to half a revolution of the poles; but finding that forty-five rounds would not bring the northern tropic to coincide with the circle of perpetual apparition by thirty minutes of a degree, which required the Zodiac to move one sign and a half more, which we all know it could not do in less than 3,000 years, they were, in the case before us, added to the end of the *brazen age;* which lengthen the reign of *that* Yudhister to 27,000 years instead of 24,000, but, at another time they did not alter the regular order of 24,000 years to the reign of each of these long-winded monarchs, but rounded up the time by allowing a *regency* to continue three or four thousand years. In volume ii. p. 134, *Asiatic Researches*, we are told that: "Paricshit, the great nephew and successor of Yudhister, is allowed without controversy to have reigned in the interval between the *brazen and earthen*, or Cali Ages, and to have died at the setting-in of the Cali Yug." Here we find an *interregnum* at the *end* of the *brazen* age, and *before* the setting-in of the Cali Yug: and as there can be but one brazen or Treta Yug, *i.e.*, the third age, in a Maha Yuga of 1,080,000 years: the reign of this Paricshit must have been in the second Maha Yuga, when the pole had returned to its original position, which must have taken 2,160,000 years: and this is what the Hindus call the Prajapati Yuga. Analogous to this custom is that of some nations more modern, who, fond of even numbers, have made the common year to consist of twelve months of thirty days each, and the five days and odd measure have been represented as the reign of a little serpent biting his tail, and divided into five-parts, etc.

But "Yudhister began his reign immediately *after the flood called Pralaya*," *i.e.*, at the end of the Cali Yug (or age of heat), when the tropic had passed from the pole to the other side of the circle of perpetual apparition, which coincides with the northern horizon; here the tropics or summer solstice would be again in the same parallel of north declination, at the *commencement* of their first age, as he was at the *end* of their *third age*, or Treta Yug, called the brazen age. . . . .

Enough has been said to prove that the Hindu books of science are not disgusting absurdities, originated in ignorance, vanity, and credulity; but books containing the most profound knowledge of astronomy and geography.

What, therefore, can induce those gentlemen of tender consciences to insist that Yudhister was a real mortal man I have no guess; unless it be that they fear for the fate of Jared and his grandfather, Methuselah?

THE
MYSTERY OF BUDDHA.

SECTION XLI.

THE DOCTRINE OF AVATÂRAS.

A STRANGE story—a legend rather—is persistently current among the disciples of some great Himâlayan Gurus, and even among laymen, to the effect that Gautama, the Prince of Kapilavastu, has never left the terrestrial regions, though his body died and was burnt, and its relics are preserved to this day. There is an oral tradition among the Chinese Buddhists, and a written statement among the secret books of the Lamaists of Tibet, as well as a tradition among the Âryans, that Gautama BUDDHA had two doctrines: one for the masses and His lay disciples, the other for His "elect," the Arhats. His policy and after Him that of His Arhats was, it appears, to refuse no one admission into the ranks of candidates for Arhatship, but never to divulge the final mysteries except to those who had proved themselves, during long years of probation, to be worthy of Initiation. These once accepted were consecrated and initiated without distinction of race, caste or wealth, as in the case of His western successor. It is the Arhats who have set forth and allowed this tradition to take root in the people's mind, and it is the basis, also, of the later dogma of Lamaic reincarnation or the succession of human Buddhas.

The little that can be said here upon the subject may or may not help to guide the psychic student in the right direction. It being left to the option and responsibility of the writer to tell the facts as she *personally* understood them, the blame for possible misconceptions created must fall only upon her. She has been taught the doctrine, but it was left to her sole intuition—as it is now left to the sagacity of the reader—to group the mysterious and perplexing facts together. The incomplete statements herein given are fragments of what is contained in certain secret volumes, but it is not lawful to divulge the details.

The esoteric version of the mystery given in the secret volumes may be told very briefly. The Buddhists have always stoutly denied that their BUDDHA was, as alleged by the Brâhmans, an Avatâra of Vishnu in the same sense as a man is an incarnation of his Karmic ancestor. They deny it partly, perhaps, because the esoteric meaning of the term "Mahâ Vishnu" is not known to them in its full, impersonal, and general meaning. There is a mysterious Principle in Nature called "Mahâ Vishnu," which is not the God of that name, but a principle which contains Bîja, the seed of Avatârism or, in other words, is the potency and cause of such divine incarnations. All the World-Saviours, the Bodhisattvas and the Avatâras, are the trees of salvation grown out from the one seed, the Bîja or "Mahâ Vishnu." Whether it be called Âdi-Buddha (Primeval Wisdom) or Mahâ Vishnu, it is all the same. Understood esoterically, Vishnu is both Saguna and Nirguna (with and without attributes). In the first aspect, Vishnu is the object of exoteric worship and devotion; in the second, as Nirguna, he is the culmination of the totality of spiritual wisdom in the Universe—Nirvâna,* in short—and has as worshippers all philosophical minds. In this esoteric sense the Lord BUDDHA *was* an incarnation of Mahâ Vishnu.

This is from the philosophical and purely spiritual standpoint. From the plane of illusion, however, as one would say, or from the terrestrial standpoint, those initiated *know* that He was a direct incarnation of one of the primeval "Seven Sons of Light" who are to be found in every Theogony—the Dhyân Chohans whose mission it is, from one eternity (æon) to the other, to watch over the spiritual welfare of the regions under their care. This has been already enunciated in *Esoteric Buddhism*.

One of the greatest mysteries of speculative and philosophical Mysticism—and it is one of the mysteries now to be disclosed—is the *modus operandi* in the degrees of such hypostatic transferences. As a matter of course, divine as well as human incarnations must remain a closed book to the theologian as much as to the physiologist, unless the esoteric teachings be accepted and become the religion of the world. This teaching may never be fully explained to an unprepared public; but one thing is certain and may be said now: that between the dogma

* A great deal of misconception is raised by a confusion of planes of being and misuse of expressions. For instance, certain spiritual states have been confounded with the Nirvâna of Buddha. The Nirvâna of BUDDHA is totally different from any other spiritual state of Samâdhi or even the highest Theophania enjoyed by lesser Adepts. After physical death the kinds of spiritual states reached by Adepts differ greatly.

of a newly-created soul for each new birth, and the physiological assumption of a temporary animal soul, there lies the vast region of Occult teaching * with its logical and reasonable demonstrations, the links of which may all be traced in logical and philosophical sequence in nature.

This "Mystery" is found, for him who understands its right meaning, in the dialogue between Krishna and Arjuna, in the *Bhagavad Gitâ*, chapter iv. Says the Avatâra:

> Many births of mine have passed, as also of yours, O Arjuna! All those I know, but you do not know yours, O harasser of your enemies.
>
> Although I am unborn, with exhaustless Âtmâ, and am the Lord of all that is; yet, taking up the domination of my nature I am born by the power of illusion.†
>
> Whenever, O son of Bhârata, there is decline of Dharma [the right law] and the rise of Adharma [the opposite of Dharmâ] there I manifest myself.
>
> For the salvation of the good and the destruction of wickedness, for the establishment of the law, *I am born* in every yuga.
>
> Whoever comprehends truly my divine birth and action, he, O Arjuna, having abandoned the body does not receive re-birth; he comes to me.

Thus, all the Avatâras are one and the same: the Sons of their "Father," in a direct descent and line, the "Father," or one of the seven Flames becoming, for the time being, the Son, and these two being one—in Eternity. What is the Father? Is it the absolute Cause of all?—the fathomless Eternal? No; most decidedly. It is Kâranâtmâ, the "Causal Soul" which, in its general sense, is called by the Hindus Îshvara, the Lord, and by Christians, "God," the One and Only. From the standpoint of unity it is so; but then the lowest of the Elementals could equally be viewed in such case as the "One and Only." Each human being has, moreover, his own divine Spirit or personal God. That divine Entity or Flame from which Buddhi emanates stands in the same relation to man, though on a lower plane,

---

* This region is the one possible point of conciliation between the two diametrically opposed poles of religion and science, the one with its barren fields of dogmas on faith, the other over-running with empty hypotheses, both overgrown with the weeds of error. They will never meet. The two are at feud, at an everlasting warfare with each other, but this does not prevent them from uniting against Esoteric Philosophy, which for two millenniums has had to fight against infallibility in both directions, or "mere vanity and pretence" as Antoninus defined it, and now finds the materialism of Modern Science arrayed against its truths.

† Whence some of the Gnostic Ideas? Cerinthus taught that the world and Jehovah having fallen off from virtue and primitive dignity the Supreme permitted one of his glorious Æons, whose name was the "Anointed" (Christ) to incarnate in the man Jesus. Basilides denied the reality of the body of Jesus, and calling it an "illusion" held that it was Simon of Cyrene who suffered on the Cross in his stead. All such teachings are echoes of the Eastern Doctrines.

into Nirvâna which is not eternally there; but human intellect in conceiving the Absolute must put It as the highest term in an ascending series. If this be borne in mind a great deal of misconception will be avoided. The content of this spiritual evolution is the materials of the various planes with which the Nirvânî was in contact prior to the attainment of Nirvâna. The plane on which this is true, being in the series of illusive planes, is undoubtedly not the highest. Those who search for that must go to the right source of study, the teachings of the *Upanishads*, and must go in the right spirit. Here we attempt only to indicate the direction in which the search is to be made, and in showing a few of the mysterious Occult possibilities we do not bring our readers actually to the goal. The ultimate truth can be communicated only from Guru to initiated pupil.

Having said so much, the statement still will and must appear incomprehensible, if not absurd, to many. Firstly, to all those who are unfamiliar with the doctrine of the manifold nature and various aspects of the human Monad; and secondly to those who view the septenary division of the human entity from a too materialistic standpoint. Still the intuitional Occultist, who has studied thoroughly the mysteries of Nirvâna—who knows it to be identical with Parabrahman, and hence unchangeable, eternal and no Thing but the Absolute All—will see the possibility of the fact. They know that while a Dharmakâya—or Nirvânî "without remains," as our Orientalists have translated it, being absorbed into that Nothingness, which is the one real, because Absolute, Consciousness—cannot be said to return to incarnation on Earth, the Nirvânî being no longer a he, a she, or even an it, the Nirmânakâya—or he who has obtained Nirvâna "with remains," and who is clothed in a subtle body, which makes him impervious to all outward impressions and to every mental feeling, and in whom the notion of his Ego has not entirely ceased—can do so. Again, every Eastern Occultist is aware of the fact that there are two kinds of Nirmânakâyas—the natural, and the assumed; that the former is the name or epithet given to the condition of a high ascetic, or Initiate, who has reached a stage of bliss second only to Nirvâna; while the latter means the self-sacrifice of one who voluntarily gives up the absolute Nirvâna, in order to help humanity and be still doing it good, or, in other words, to save his fellow-creatures by guiding them. It may be objected that the Dharmakâya, being a Nirvânî or Jîvanmukta, can have no "remains" left behind him after death, for having attained that state from which no further incarnations are possible, there is no need for him of a subtle body, or of the individual Ego that reincarnates from one birth to another, and that therefore the latter disappears of logical necessity; to this it is answered: it is so for all exoteric purposes and as a general law. But the case with which we are dealing is an exceptional one, and its realization lies within the Occult powers of the high Initiate, who, before entering into the state of Nirvâna, can cause his "remains" (sometimes, though not very well, called his Mâyâvi Rûpa), to remain behind,* whether he is to become a Nirvânî, or to find himself in a lower state of bliss.

Next, there are cases—rare, yet more frequent than one would be disposed to expect—which are the voluntary and conscious reincarnations of Adepts† on their trial. Every man has an Inner, a "Higher Self," and also an Astral Body. But few are those who, outside the higher degrees of Adeptship, can guide the latter, or any of the principles that animate it, when once death has closed their short terrestrial life. Yet such guidance, or their transference from the dead to a living body, is not only possible, but is of frequent occurrence, according to Occult and Kabalistic teachings. The degrees of such power of course vary greatly. To mention but three: the lowest of these degrees would allow an Adept, who has been greatly trammelled during life in his study and in the use of his powers, to choose after death another body in which he could go on with his interrupted studies, though ordinarily he would lose in it every remembrance of his previous incarnation. The next degree permits him, in addition to this, to transfer the memory of his past life to his new body; while the highest has hardly any limits in the exercise of that wonderful faculty.

As an instance of an Adept who enjoyed the first mentioned power some mediæval Kabalists cite a well-known personage of the fifteenth century—Cardinal de Cusa; Karma, due to his wonderful devotion to

* This fact of the disappearance of the vehicle of Egotism in the fully developed Yogi, who is supposed to have reached Nirvâna on earth, years before his corporeal death, has led to the law in Manu, sanctioned by millenniums of Brâhmanical authority, that such a Paramâtmâ should be held as absolutely blameless and free from sin or responsibility, do whatever he may (see last chapter of the *Laws of Manu*). Indeed, caste itself—that most despotic, uncompromising and autocratic tyrant in India—can be broken with impunity by the Yogi, who is above caste. This will give the key to our statements.

† [The word "Adept" is very loosely used by H. P. B., who often seems to have implied by it no more than the possession of special knowledge of some kind. Here it seems to mean first an uninitiated disciple and then an initiated one.—EDS.]

Esoteric study and the *Kabalah*, led the suffering Adept to seek intellectual recuperation and rest from ecclesiastical tyranny in the body of Copernicus. *Se non è vero è ben trovato*; and the perusal of the lives of the two men might easily lead a believer in such powers to a full acceptance of the alleged fact. The reader having at his command the means to do so is asked to turn to the formidable folio in Latin of the fifteenth century, called *De Docta Ignorantia*, written by the Cardinal de Cusa, in which all the theories and hypotheses—all the ideas of Copernicus are found as the key-notes to the discoveries of the great astronomer.* Who was this extraordinarily learned Cardinal? The son of a poor boatman, owing all his career, his Cardinal's hat, and the reverential awe rather than friendship of the Popes Eugenius IV., Nicholas V., and Pius II., to the extraordinary learning which seemed innate in him, since he had studied nowhere till comparatively late in life. De Cusa died in 1473; moreover, his best works were written before he was forced to enter orders—to escape persecution. Nor did the Adept escape it.

In the voluminous work of the Cardinal above-quoted is found a very suggestive sentence, the authorship of which has been variously attributed to Pascal, to Cusa himself, and to the *Zohar*, and which belongs by right to the Books of Hermes:

> The world is an infinite sphere, whose centre is everywhere and whose circumference is nowhere.

This is changed by some into: "The centre being nowhere, and the circumference everywhere," a rather heretical idea for a Cardinal, though perfectly orthodox from a Kabalistic standpoint.

---

* About fifty years before the birth of Copernicus, de Cusa wrote as follows: "Though the world may not be absolutely infinite, no one can represent it to himself as finite, since human reason is incapable of assigning to it any term. . . . For in the same way that our earth cannot be in the centre of the Universe, as thought, no more could the sphere of the fixed stars be in it. . . . Thus this world is like a vast machine, having its centre [Deity] everywhere, and its circumference nowhere [*machina mundi, quasi habens ubique centrum, et nullibi circumferentiam*]. . . . Hence, the earth not being in the centre, cannot therefore be motionless . . . . and though it is far smaller than the sun, one must not conclude for all that, that she is worse [*vilior*—more vile]. . . . One cannot see whether its inhabitants are superior to those who dwell nearer to the sun, or in other stars, as sidereal space cannot be deprived of inhabitants. . . . The earth, very likely [*forte*] one of the smallest globes, is nevertheless the cradle of intelligent beings, most noble and perfect." One cannot fail to agree with the biographer of Cardinal de Cusa, who, having no suspicion of the Occult truth, and the reason of such erudition in a writer of the fourteenth and fifteenth centuries, naively marvels at such a miraculous foreknowledge, and attributes it to God, saying of him that he was a man incomparable in every kind of philosophy, by whom many a theological mystery inaccessible to the human mind (!), veiled and neglected for centuries (*velata et neglecta*) were once more brought to light. "Pascal might have read De Cusa's works; but whence could the Cardinal have borrowed his ideas?" asks Moreri. Evidently from Hermes and the works of Pythagoras, even if the mystery of his incarnation and re-incarnation be dismissed.

The theory of rebirth must be set forth by Occultists, and then applied to special cases. The right comprehension of this psychic fact is based upon a correct view of that group of celestial Beings who are universally called the seven Primeval Gods or Angels—our Dhyân Chohans—the "Seven Primeval Rays" or Powers, adopted later on by the Christian Religion as the "Seven Angels of the Presence." Arûpa, formless, at the upper rung of the ladder of Being, materializing more and more as they descend in the scale of objectivity and form, ending in the grossest and most imperfect of the Hierarchy, man—it is the former purely spiritual group that is pointed out to us, in our Occult teaching, as the nursery and fountain-head of human beings. Therein germinates that consciousness which is the earliest manifestation from causal Consciousness—the Alpha and the Omega of divine being and life for ever. And as it proceeds downward through every phase of existence descending through man, through animal and plant, it ends its descent only in the mineral. It is represented by the double triangle—the most mysterious and the most suggestive of all mystic signs, for it is a double glyph, embracing spiritual and physical consciousness and life, the former triangle running upwards, and the lower downwards, both interlaced, and showing the various planes of the twice-seven modes of consciousness, the fourteen spheres of existence, the Lokas of the Brâhmans.

The reader may now be able to obtain a clearer comprehension of the whole thing. He will also see what is meant by the "Watchers," there being one placed as the Guardian or Regent over each of the seven divisions or regions of the earth, according to old traditions, as there is one to watch over and guide every one of the fourteen worlds or Lokas.* But it is not with any of these that we are at present concerned, but with the "Seven Breaths," so-called, that furnish man with his immortal Monad in his cyclic pilgrimage.

The Commentary on the *Book of Dzyan* says:

Descending on his region first as Lord of Glory, the Flame (or Breath), having called into conscious being the highest of the Emanations of that special region, ascends from it again to Its primeval seat, whence It watches

* This is the secret meaning of the statements about the Hierarchy of Prajâpatis or Rishis. First seven are mentioned, then ten, then twenty-one, and so on. They are "Gods" and creators of men—many of them the "Lords of Beings"; they are the "Mind-born Sons" of Brahmâ, and then they became mortal heroes, and are often shown as of a very sinful character. The Occult meaning of the Biblical Patriarchs, their genealogy, and their descendants dividing among themselves the earth, is the same. Again, Jacob's dream has the same significance.

over and guides Its countless Beams (Monads). It chooses as Its [illegible] *only those who had the Seven Virtues in them* in their previous* [illegible] *tion. As for the rest, It overshadows each with one of Its* [illegible] *. . . Yet even the "beam" is a part of the Lord of Lords.*† [illegible]

The septenary principle in man—who can be regarded as [illegible] as concerns psychic manifestation on this gross earthly plane [illegible] known to all antiquity, and may be found in every ancient [illegible] The Egyptians knew and taught it, and their division of [illegible] in every point a counterpart of the Âryan Secret Teaching. [illegible] given in *Isis Unveiled*:

> In the Egyptian notions, as in those of all other faiths founded on [illegible] man was not merely . . . . a union of soul and body; he was a trinity [illegible] Spirit was added to it. Besides, that doctrine made him consist of [illegible] Khaba (astral form or shadow), Ka (animal soul or life-principle), Ba (the [illegible] soul), and Akh (terrestrial intelligence). They had also a sixth principle, [illegible] Sah (or mummy), but the functions of this one commenced after the death of [illegible] body.‡

The seventh principle being of course the highest, uncreated [illegible] was generically called Osiris, therefore every deceased person [illegible] Osirified—or an Osiris—after death.

But in addition to reiterating the old ever-present fact of reincarna- tion and Karma—not as taught by the Spiritists, but as by the [illegible] Ancient Science in the world—Occultists must teach cyclic and evolu- tionary reincarnation: that kind of re-birth, mysterious and still incom- prehensible to many who are ignorant of the world's history, which [illegible] cautiously mentioned in *Isis Unveiled*. A general re-birth for every individual with interlude of Kâma Loka and Devachan, and a cyclic conscious reincarnation with a grand and divine object for the [illegible] Those great characters who tower like giants in the history of mankind like Siddârtha BUDDHA and Jesus in the realm of the spiritual, and Alexander the Macedonian and Napoleon the Great in the realm of physical conquests are but the reflected images of human types which had existed—not ten thousand years before, as cautiously put forward in *Isis Unveiled*, but for millions of consecutive years from the begin- ning of the Manvantara. For—with the exception of real Avatâras, as

---

* He "of the Seven Virtues" is one who, without the benefit of Initiation, becomes as pure as any Adept by the simple exertion of his own merit. Being so holy, his body at his next [illegible] becomes the Avatâra of his "Watcher" or Guardian Angel, as the Christian would put it.

† The title of the highest Dhyân Chohans.

‡ *Op. cit.*, ii. 367.

above explained—they are the same unbroken Rays (Monads), each respectively of its own special Parent-Flame—called Devas, Dhyân Chohans, or Dhyâni-Buddhas, or again, Planetary Angels, etc.—shining in æonic eternity as their prototypes. It is in their image that some men are born, and when some specific humanitarian object is in view, the latter are hypostatically animated by their divine prototypes reproduced again and again by the mysterious Powers that control and guide the destinies of our world.

No more could be said at the time when *Isis Unveiled* was written; hence the statement was limited to the single remark that

> There is no prominent character in all the annals of sacred or profane history whose prototype we cannot find in the half fictitious and half real traditions of bygone religions and mythologies. As the star, glimmering at an immeasurable distance above our heads, in the boundless immensity of the sky, reflects itself in the smooth waters of a lake, so does the imagery of men of the antediluvian ages reflect itself in the periods we can embrace in a historical retrospect.

But now that so many publications have been brought out, stating much of the doctrine, and several of them giving many an erroneous view, this vague allusion may be amplified and explained. Not only does this statement apply to prominent characters in history in general, but also to men of genius, to every remarkable man of the age, who soars beyond the common herd with some abnormally developed special capacity in him, leading to the progress and good of mankind. Each is a reincarnation of an individuality that has gone before him with capacities in the same line, bringing thus as a dowry to his new form that strong and easily re-awakened capacity or quality which had been fully developed in him in his preceding birth. Very often they are ordinary mortals, the Egos of natural men in the course of their cyclic development.

But it is with "special cases" that we are now concerned. Let us suppose that a person during his cycle of incarnations is thus selected for special purposes—the vessel being sufficiently clean—by his personal God, the Fountain-head (on the plane of the manifested) of his Monad, who thus becomes his in-dweller. That God, his own prototype or "Father in Heaven," is, in one sense, not only the image in which he, the spiritual man, is made, but in the case we are considering, it is that spiritual, individual Ego himself. This is a case of permanent, life-long Theophania. Let us bear in mind that this is neither Avatârism, as it is understood in Brâhmanical Philosophy, nor is the man thus selected a Jîvanmukta or Nirvâni, but that it is a wholly exceptional case in the realm of Mysticism. The man may or may not have been an Adept in his previous lives; he is so far, and simply, an extremely pure and spiritual individual—or one who was all that in his preceding birth, if the vessel thus selected is that of a newly-born infant. In this case, after the physical translation of such a saint or Bodhisattva, his astral principles cannot be subjected to a natural dissolution like those of any common mortal. They remain in our sphere and within human attraction and reach; and thus it is that not only a Buddha, a Shankarâchârya, or a Jesus can be said to animate several persons at one and the same time, but even the principles of a high Adept may be animating the outward tabernacles of common mortals.

A certain Ray (principle) from Sanat Kumâra spiritualized (animated) Pradyumna, the son of Krishna during the great Mahâbhârata period, while at the same time, he, Sanat Kumâra, gave spiritual instruction to King Dhritarâshtra. Moreover, it is to be remembered that Sanat Kumâra is "an eternal youth of sixteen," dwelling in Jana Loka, his own sphere or spiritual state.

Even in ordinary *mediumistic* life, so-called, it is pretty well ascertained that while the body is acting—even though only mechanically—or resting in one place, its astral double may be appearing and acting independently in another, and very often distant place. This is quite a common occurrence in mystic life and history, and if this be so with ecstatics, Seers and Mystics of every description, why cannot the same thing happen on a higher and more spiritually developed plane of existence? Admit the possibility on the lower psychic plane, then why not on a higher plane? In the cases of higher Adeptship, when the body is entirely at the command of the Inner Man, when the Spiritual Ego is completely reünited with its seventh principle even during the life-time of the personality, and the Astral Man or personal Ego has become so purified that he has gradually assimilated all the qualities and attributes of the middle nature (Buddhi and Manas in their terrestrial aspect) that personal Ego substitutes itself, so to say, for the spiritual Higher Self, and is thenceforth capable of living an independent life on earth; when corporeal death takes place the following mysterious event often happens. As a Dharmakâya, a Nirvâni "without remains," entirely free from terrestrial admixture, the Spiritual Ego cannot return to reincarnate on earth. But in such cases, it is affirmed, the personal Ego of even a Dharmakâya can remain in our sphere as a whole, and return to incarnation on earth if need be. For now it can no longer be subject, like the astral remains of any ordinary man, to gradual dissolution in the Kâma Loka (the *limbus* or purgatory of the Roman Catholic, and the "Summer-land" of the Spiritualist); it cannot die a second death, as such disintegration is called by Proclus.* It has become too holy and pure, no longer by reflected but its own natural light and spirituality, either to sleep in the unconscious slumber of a lower Nirvânic state, or to be dissolved like any ordinary astral shell and disappear in its entirety.

But in that condition known as the Nirmânakâya [the Nirvânî "with remains,"] he can still help humanity.

"Let me suffer and bear the sins of all [be reincarnated unto new misery] but let the world be saved!" was said by Gautama BUDDHA: an exclamation the real meaning of which is little understood now by his followers. "If I will that he tarry till I come, what is that to thee?"† asks the astral Jesus of Peter. "Till I come" means "till I am re-incarnated again" in a physical body. Yet the Christ of the old crucified body could truly say: "I am with my Father and one with Him," which did not prevent the astral from taking a form again nor John from tarrying indeed till his Master had come; nor hinder John from failing to recognize him when he did come, or from then opposing him. But in the Church that remark generated the absurd idea of the millennium or chiliasm, in its physical sense.

Since then the "Man of Sorrows" has returned perchance, more than once, unknown to, and undiscovered by, his blind followers. Since then also, this grand "Son of God" has been incessantly and most cruelly crucified daily and hourly by the Churches founded in his name. But the Apostles, only half-initiated, failed to tarry for their Master, and not recognizing him, spurned him every time he returned.‡

* "After death, the soul continueth in the aerial (astral) body, till it is entirely purified from all angry, sensual passions; then doth it put off by a *second death* [when arising to Devachan] the aerial body as it did the earthly one. Wherefore the ancients say that there is a celestial body always joined with the soul, which is immortal, luminous and star-like." It becomes natural then, that the "aerial body" of an Adept should have no such second dying, since it has been cleansed of all its natural impurity before its separation from the physical body. The high Initiate is a "Son of the Resurrection," "being equal unto the angels," and cannot die any more (see *Luke*, xx. 36).

† *St. John*, xxi. 21.

‡ See the extract made in the *Theosophist* from a glorious novel by Dostoievsky—a fragment entitled "The Great Inquisitor." It is a fiction, naturally, still a sublime fiction of Christ returning in Spain during the palmy days of the Inquisition, and being imprisoned and put to death by the Inquisitor, who fears lest Christ should ruin the work of Jesuit hands.

SECTION XLII.

THE SEVEN PRINCIPLES.

THE "Mystery of Buddha" is that of several other Adepts—perhaps of many. The whole trouble is to understand correctly that other mystery: that of the real fact, so abstruse and transcendental at first sight, about the "Seven Principles" in man, the reflections in man of the seven powers in Nature, physically, and of the seven Hierarchies of Being, intellectually and spiritually. Whether a man—material, ethereal, and spiritual—is for the clearer comprehension of his (broadly speaking) triple nature, divided into groups according to one or another system, the foundation and the apex of that division will be always the same. There being only three Upâdhis (bases) in man, any number of Koshas (sheaths) and their aspects may be built on these without destroying the harmony of the whole. Thus, while the Esoteric System accepts the septenary division, the Vedântic classification gives five Koshas, and the Târaka Râja Yoga simplifies them into four—the three Upâdhis synthesized by the highest principle, Âtmâ.

That which has just been stated will, of course, suggest the question: "How can a spiritual (or semi-spiritual) personality lead a triple or even a dual life, shifting respective 'Higher Selves' *ad libitum*, and be still the one eternal Monad in the infinity of a Manvantara?" The answer to this is easy for the true Occultist, while for the uninitiated profane it must appear absurd. The "Seven Principles" are, of course, the manifestation of one indivisible Spirit, but only at the end of the Manvantara, and when they come to be re-united on the plane of the One Reality does the unity appear; during the "Pilgrim's" journey the reflections of that indivisible One Flame, the aspects of the one eternal Spirit, have each the power of action on one of the manifested planes of existence—the gradual differentiations from the one unmanifested plane—on that plane namely to which it properly belongs. Our earth affording every Mâyâvic condition, it follows that the purified Egotistical Principle, the astral and personal Self of an Adept, though forming in reality one integral whole with its Highest Self (Âtmâ and Buddhi) may, nevertheless, for purposes of universal mercy and benevolence, so separate itself from its divine Monad as to lead on this plane of illusion and temporary being a distinct independent conscious life of its own under a borrowed illusive shape, thus serving at one and the same time a double purpose: the exhaustion of its own individual Karma, and the saving of millions of human beings less favoured than itself from the effects of mental blindness. If asked: "When the change described as the passage of a Buddha or a Jîvanmukta into Nirvâna takes place, where does the original consciousness which animated the body continue to reside—in the Nirvâni or in the subsequent reincarnations of the latter's 'remains' (the Nirmânakâya)?" the answer is that *imprisoned* consciousness may be a "certain knowledge from observation and experience," as Gibbon puts it, but *disembodied* consciousness is not an effect, but a cause. It is a part of the whole, or rather a Ray on the graduated scale of its manifested activity, of the one all-pervading, limitless Flame, the reflections of which alone can differentiate; and, as such, consciousness is ubiquitous, and can be neither localized nor centred on or in any particular subject, nor can it be limited. Its effects alone pertain to the region of matter, for thought is an energy that affects matter in various ways, but consciousness *per se*, as understood and explained by Occult philosophy, is the highest quality of the sentient spiritual principle in us, the Divine Soul (or Buddhi) and our Higher Ego, and does not belong to the plane of materiality. After the death of the physical man, if he be an Initiate, it becomes transformed from a human quality into the independent principle itself; the conscious Ego becoming Consciousness *per se* without any Ego, in the sense that the latter can no longer be limited or conditioned by the senses, or even by space or time. Therefore it is capable, without separating itself from or abandoning its possessor, Buddhi, of reflecting itself at the same time in its astral man that was, without being under any necessity for localizing itself. This is shown at a far lower stage in our dreams. For if consciousness can display activity during our visions, and while the body and its material brain are fast asleep—and if even during those visions it is all but ubiquitous—how much greater must be its power when entirely free from, and having no more connection with, our physical brain.

SECTION XLIII.

The Mystery of Buddha.

Now the mystery of Buddha lies in this: Gautama, an incarnation of pure Wisdom, had yet to learn in His human body and to be initiated into the world's secrets like any other mortal, until the day when He emerged from His secret recess in the Himâlayas and preached for the first time in the grove of Benares. The same with Jesus: from the age of twelve to thirty years, when He is found preaching the Sermon on the Mount, nothing is positively said or known of Him. Gautama had sworn inviolable secrecy as to the Esoteric Doctrines imparted to Him. In His immense pity for the ignorance—and as its consequence the sufferings—of mankind, desirous though He was to keep inviolate His sacred vows, He failed to keep within the prescribed limits. While constructing His Esoteric Philosophy (the "Eye-Doctrine") on the foundations of eternal Truth, He failed to conceal certain dogmas, and trespassing beyond the lawful lines, caused those dogmas to be misunderstood. In His anxiety to make away with the false Gods, He revealed in the "Seven Paths to Nirvâna" some of the mysteries of the Seven Lights of the Arûpa (formless) World. A little of the truth is often worse than no truth at all.

Truth and fiction are like oil and water: they will never mix.

His new doctrine, which represented the outward dead body of the Esoteric Teaching without its vivifying Soul, had disastrous effects: it was never correctly understood, and the doctrine itself was rejected by the Southern Buddhists. Immense philanthropy, a boundless love and charity for all creatures, were at the bottom of His unintentional mistake; but Karma little heeds intentions, whether good or bad, if they remain fruitless. If the "Good Law" as preached resulted in the most sublime code of ethics and the unparalleled philosophy of things external in the visible Kosmos, it biassed and misguided immature minds into believing there was nothing more under the outward mantle of the system, and its dead-letter only was accepted. Moreover, the new teaching unsettled many great minds which had previously followed the orthodox Brâhmanical lead.

Thus, fifty odd years after his death "the great Teacher"* having refused full Dharmakâya and Nirvâna, was pleased, for purposes of Karma and philanthropy, to be reborn. For Him death had been no death, but as expressed in the "Elixir of Life,"† He changed

A sudden plunge into darkness to a transition into a brighter light.

The shock of death was broken, and like many other Adepts, He threw off the mortal coil and left it to be burnt, and its ashes to serve as relics, and began interplanetary life, clothed in His subtle body. He was reborn as Shankara, the greatest Vedântic teacher of India, whose philosophy—based as it is entirely on the fundamental axioms of the eternal Revelation, the Shruti, or the primitive Wisdom-Religion, as Buddha from a different point of view had before based His—finds itself in the middle-ground between the too exuberantly veiled metaphysics of the orthodox Brâhmans and those of Gautama, which, stripped in their exoteric garb of every soul-vivifying hope, transcendental aspiration and symbol, appear in their cold wisdom like crystalline icicles, the skeletons of the primeval truths of Esoteric Philosophy.

Was Shankarâchârya Gautama the Buddha, then, under a new personal form? It may perhaps only puzzle the reader the more if he be told that there was the "astral" Gautama inside the outward Shankara, whose higher principle, or Âtman, was, nevertheless, his own divine prototype—the "Son of Light," indeed—the heavenly, mind-born son of Aditi.

This fact is again based on that mysterious transference of the divine ex-personality merged in the impersonal Individuality—now in its full trinitarian form of the Monad as Âtmâ-Buddhi-Manas—to a new body, whether visible or subjective. In the first case it is a Manushya-Buddha; in the second it is a Nirmânakâya. The Buddha is in Nirvâna, it is said, though this once mortal vehicle—the subtle body—of Gautama is still present among the Initiates; nor will it leave the realm of conscious Being so long as suffering mankind needs its divine help—not to the end of this Root Race, at any rate. From time to time He, the "astral" Gautama, associates Himself, in some most mysterious—

---

* When we say the "great Teacher," we do not mean His Buddhic Ego, but that principle in Him which was the vehicle of His personal or terrestrial Ego.

† *Five Years of Theosophy*, New Edition, p. 3.

to us quite incomprehensible—manner, with Avatâras and great adepts, and works through them. And several such are named.

Thus it is averred that Gautama Buddha was reincarnated in Shankarâchârya—that, as is said in *Esoteric Buddhism*:

> Shankarâchârya simply *was* Buddha in all respects in a new body.*

While the expression in its mystic sense is true, the way of putting it may be misleading until explained. Shankara was a Buddha, assuredly, but he never was a reincarnation of the Buddha, though Gautama's "Astral" Ego—or rather his Bodhisattva—may have been associated in some mysterious way with Shankarâchârya. Yes, it was perhaps the Ego, Gautama, under a new and better adapted casket—that of a Brâhman of Southern India. But the Âtman, the Higher Self that overshadowed both, was distinct from the Higher Self of the translated Buddha, which was now in Its own sphere in Kosmos.

Shankara was an Avatâra in the full sense of the term. According to Sayanâchârya, the great commentator on the *Vedas*, he is to be regarded as an Avatâra, or direct incarnation of Shiva—the Logos, the Seventh Principle in Nature—Himself. In the Secret Doctrine Shrî Shankarâchârya is regarded as the abode—for the thirty-two years of his mortal life—of a Flame, the highest of the manifested Spiritual Beings, one of the Primordial Seven Rays.

And now what is meant by a "Bodhisattva"? Buddhists of the Mahâyâna mystic system teach that each BUDDHA manifests Himself (hypostatically or otherwise) simultaneously in three worlds of Being, namely, in the world of Kâma (concupiscence or desire—the sensuous universe or our earth) in the shape of a man; in the world of Rûpa (form, yet supersensuous) as a Bodhisattva; and in the highest Spiritual World (that of purely incorporeal existences) as a Dhyâni-Buddha. The latter prevails eternally in space and time, *i.e.*, from one Mahâ-Kalpa to the other—the synthetic culmination of the three being Âdi-Buddha,† the Wisdom-Principle, which is Absolute, and therefore out of space and time. Their inter-relation is the following: The Dhyâni-Buddha, when the world needs a human Buddha,

* *Op. cit.*, p. 173, Fifth Edition.

† It would be useless to raise objections from exoteric works to statements in this, which aims to expound, however superficially, the Esoteric Teachings alone. It is because they are misled by the exoteric doctrine that Bishop Bigandet and others aver that the notion of a supreme eternal Âdi-Buddha is to be found only in writings of comparatively recent date. What is given here is taken from the secret portions of Dus Kyi Khorlo (Kâla Chakra, in Sanskrit, or the "Wheel of Time," or duration).

"creates" through the power of Dhyâna (meditation, omnipotent devotion), a mind-born son—a Bodhisattva—whose mission it is after the physical death of his human, or Manushya-Buddha, to continue his work on earth till the appearance of the subsequent Buddha. The Esoteric meaning of this teaching is clear. In the case of a simple mortal, the principles in him are only the more or less bright reflections of the seven cosmic, and the seven celestial Principles, the Hierarchy of supersensual Beings. In the case of a Buddha, they are almost the principles *in esse* themselves. The Bodhisattva replaces in him the Kârana Sharira, the Ego principle, and the rest correspondingly; and it is in this way that Esoteric Philosophy explains the meaning of the sentence that "by virtue of Dhyâna [or abstract meditation] the Dhyâni-Buddha [the Buddha's Spirit or Monad] creates a Bodhisattva," or the astrally clothed Ego within the Manushya-Buddha. Thus, while the Buddha merges back into Nirvâna whence it proceeded, the Bodhisattva remains behind to continue the Buddha's work upon earth. It is then this Bodhisattva that may have afforded the lower principles in the apparitional body of Shankarâchârya, the Avatâra.

Now to say that Buddha, after having reached Nirvâna, returned thence to reïncarnate in a new body, would be uttering a heresy from the Brâhmanical, as well as from the Buddhistic standpoint. Even in the Mahâyâna exoteric School in the teaching as to the three "Buddhic" bodies,* it is said of the Dharmakâya—the ideal formless Being—that once it is taken, the Buddha in it abandons the world of sensuous perceptions for ever, and has not, nor can he have, any more connection with it. To say, as the Esoteric or Mystic School teaches, that though Buddha is in Nirvâna he has left behind him the Nirmânakâya (the Bodhisattva) to work after him, is quite orthodox and in accordance with both the Esoteric Mahâyâna and the Prasanga Mâdhyâmika Schools, the latter an anti-esoteric and most rationalistic system. For in the *Kâla Chakra* Commentary it is shown that there is: (1) Âdi-Buddha, eternal and conditionless; then (2) come Sambhogakâya-Buddhas, or Dhyâni-Buddhas, existing from (æonic) eternity and never disappearing—the *Causal* Buddhas so to say; and (3) the Manushya-

* The three bodies are (1) the Nirmânakâya (Pru-lpai-Ku in Tibetan), in which the Bodhisattva after entering by the six Pâramitâs the Path to Nirvâna, appears to men in order to teach them; (2) Sambhogakâya (Dzog-pai-Ku), the body of bliss impervious to all physical sensations, received by one who has fulfilled the three conditions of moral perfection; and (3) Dharmakâya (in Tibetan, Chos-Ku), the Nirvânic body.

Bodhisattvas. The relation between them is determined by the definition given. Âdi-Buddha is Vajradhara, and the Dhyâni-Buddhas are Vajrasattva; yet though these two are different Beings on their respective planes, They are identical in fact, one acting through the other, as a Dhyâni through a human Buddha. One is "Endless Intelligence;" the other only "Supreme Intelligence." It is said of the Bodhisattva—who was subsequently on earth Buddha Gautama:

> Having fulfilled all the conditions for the immediate attainment of perfect Buddhaship, the Holy One preferred, from unlimited charity towards living beings, once *more* to reincarnate for the benefit of man.

The Nirvâna of the Buddhists is only the threshold of Paranirvâna, according to the Esoteric Teaching: while with the Brâhmans it is the *summum bonum*, that final state from which there is no more return—not till the next Mahâ-Kalpa, at all events. And even this last view will be opposed by some too orthodox and dogmatic Philosophers who will not accept the Esoteric Doctrine. With them Nirvâna is absolute nothingness, in which there is nothing and no one: only an unconditioned All. To understand the full characteristics of that Abstract Principle one must sense it intuitionally, and comprehend fully the "one permanent condition in the Universe," which the Hindûs define so truly as

> The state of perfect unconsciousness—bare Chidâkâsham (field of consciousness), in fact,

however paradoxical it may seem to the profane reader.*

Shankarâchârya was reputed to be an Avatâra, an assertion the writer implicitly believes in, but which other people are, of course, at liberty to reject. And as such he took the body of a southern Indian, newly-born Brâhman baby; that body, for reasons as important as they are mysterious to us, is said to have been animated by Gautama's astral personal remains. This divine Non-Ego chose as its own Upâdhi (physical basis), the ethereal, human Ego of a great Sage in this world of forms, as the fittest vehicle for Spirit to descend into.

Said Shankarâchârya:

> Parabrahman is Kartâ [Purusha], as there is no other Adhishtâthâ,† and Parabrahman is Prakriti, there being no other substance.‡

* *Five Years of Theosophy*, art. "Personal and Impersonal God," p. 129.

† Adhishtâthâ, the active or working agent in Prakriti (or matter).

‡ *Vedânta-Sûtras*, Ad. I. Pâda iv. Shl. 23. Commentary. The passage is given as follows in Thibaut's translation (Sacred Books of the East, xxxiv.), p. 286: "The Self is thus the operative cause, because there is no other ruling principle, and the material cause because there is no other substance from which the world could originate."

Now what is true of the Macrocosmical is also true of the Microcosmical plane. It is therefore nearer the truth to say—when once we accept such a possibility—that the "astral" Gautama, or the Nirmânakâya, was the Upâdhi of Shankarâchârya's spirit, rather than that the latter was a reincarnation of the former.

When a Shankarâchârya has to be born, naturally every one of the principles in the manifested mortal man must be the purest and finest that exist on earth. Consequently those principles that were once attached to Gautama, who was the direct great predecessor of Shankara, were naturally attracted to him, the economy of Nature forbidding the re-evolution of similar principles from the crude state. But it must be remembered that the higher ethereal principles are not, like the lower more material ones, visible sometimes to man (as astral bodies), and they have to be regarded in the light of separate or independent Powers or Gods, rather than as material objects. Hence the right way of representing the truth would be to say that the various principles, the Bodhisattva, of Gautama Buddha, which did not go to Nirvâna, re-united to form the middle principles of Shankarâchârya, the earthly Entity.*

It is absolutely necessary to study the doctrine of the Buddhas esoterically and understand the subtle differences between the various planes of existence to be able to comprehend correctly the above. Put more clearly, Gautama, the human Buddha, who had, exoterically, Amitâbha for his Bodhisattva and Avalokiteshvara for his Dhyâni-Buddha—the triad emanating directly from Âdi-Buddha—assimilated these by his "Dhyâna" (meditation) and thus become a Buddha ("enlightened"). In another manner this is the case with all men; every-one of us has his Bodhisattva—the middle principle, if we hold for a moment to the trinitarian division of the septenary group—and his Dhyâni-Buddha, or Chohan, the "Father of the Son." Our connecting link with the higher Hierarchy of Celestial Beings lies here in a nut-shell, only we are too sinful to assimilate them.

---

* In *Five Years of Theosophy* (art. "Shâkya Muni's Place in History," p. 234, note) it is stated that one day when our Lord sat in the Sattapanni Cave (Saptaparna) he compared man to a Saptaparna (seven leaved) plant.

"Mendicants," he said, "there are seven Buddhas in every Buddha, and there are *six* Bhikshus and but one Buddha in each mendicant. What are the *seven*? The seven branches of complete knowledge. What are the *six*? The six organs of sense. What are the five? The five elements of illusive being. And the One which is also ten? He is a true Buddha who develops in him the ten forms of holiness and subjects them all to the One." Which means that every principle in the Buddha was the highest that could be evolved on this earth; whereas in the case of other men who attain to Nirvâna this is not necessarily the case. Even as a mere human (Manushya) Buddha Gautama was a pattern for all men. But his Arhats were not necessarily so.

Six centuries after the translation of the human Buddha (Gautama), another Reformer, as noble and as loving, though less favoured by opportunity, arose in another part of the world, among another and less spiritual race. There is a great similarity between the subsequent opinions of the world about the two Saviours, the Eastern and Western. While millions became converted to the doctrines of the two Masters, the enemies of both—sectarian opponents, the most dangerous of all—tore both to shreds by insinuating maliciously distorted statements based on Occult truths, and therefore doubly dangerous. While of Buddha it is said by the Brâhmans that He was truly an Avatâra of Vishnu, but that He had come to tempt the Brâhmans from their faith, and was therefore the evil aspect of the God; of Jesus the Bardesanian Gnostics and others asserted that He was Nebu, the false Messiah, the destroyer of the old orthodox religion. "He is the founder of a new sect of Nazars," said other sectarians. In Hebrew the word "Naba" means "to speak by inspiration," (נבא and נבו is Nebo, the God of wisdom). But Nebo is also Mercury, who is Buddha in the Hindu monogram of planets. And this is shown by the fact that the Talmudists hold that Jesus was inspired by the Genius (or Regent) of Mercury confounded by Sir William Jones with Gautama Buddha. There are many other strange points of similarity between Gautama and Jesus, which cannot be noticed here.*

If both the Initiates, aware of the danger of furnishing the uncultured masses with the powers acquired by ultimate knowledge, left the innermost corner of the sanctuary in profound darkness, who, acquainted with human nature, can blame either of them for this? Yet although Gautama, actuated by prudence, left the Esoteric and most dangerous portions of the Secret Knowledge untold, and lived to the ripe old age of eighty—the Esoteric Doctrine says one hundred—years, dying with the certainty of having taught its essential truths, and of having sown the seeds for the conversion of one-third of the world, He yet perhaps revealed more than was strictly good for posterity. But Jesus, who had promised His disciples the knowledge which confers upon man the power of producing "miracles" far greater than He had ever produced Himself, died, leaving but a few faithful disciples—men only half-way to knowledge. They had therefore to struggle with a world to which they could impart only what they but half-knew themselves, and—no more. In later ages the exoteric followers of both

* See *Isis Unveiled*, ii. 132.

mangled the truths given out, often out of recognition. With regard to the adherents of the Western Master, the proof of this lies in the very fact that none of them can now produce the promised "miracles." They have to choose: either it is they who have blundered, or it is their Master who must stand arraigned for an empty promise, an uncalled-for boast.* Why such a difference in the destiny of the two? For the Occultist this enigma of the unequal favour of Karma or Providence is unriddled by the Secret Doctrine.

It is "not lawful" to speak of such things publicly, as St. Paul tells us. One more explanation only may be given in reference to this subject. It was said a few pages back that an Adept who thus sacrifices himself to live, giving up full Nirvâna, though he can never lose the knowledge acquired by him in previous existences, yet can never rise higher in such borrowed bodies. Why? Because he becomes simply the vehicle of a "Son of Light" from a still higher sphere, Who being Arûpa, has no personal astral body of His own fit for this world. Such "Sons of Light," or Dhyâni-Buddhas, are the Dharmakâyas of preceding Manvantaras, who have closed their cycles of incarnations in the ordinary sense and who, being thus Karmaless, have long ago dropped their individual Rûpas, and have become identified with the first Principle. Hence the necessity of a sacrificial Nirmânakâya, ready to suffer for the misdeeds or mistakes of the new body in its earth-pilgrimage, without any future reward on the plane of progression and rebirth, since there are no rebirths for him in the ordinary sense. The Higher Self, or Divine Monad, is not in such a case attached to the lower Ego; its connection is only temporary, and in most cases it acts through decrees of Karma. This is a real, genuine sacrifice, the explanation of which pertains to the highest Initiation of Gñâna (Occult Knowledge). It is closely linked, by a direct evolution of Spirit and involution of Matter, with the primeval and great Sacrifice at the foundation of the manifested Worlds, the gradual smothering and

---

* "Before one becomes a Buddha he must be a Bodhisattva; before evolving into a Bodhisattva he must be a Dhyâni-Buddha. . . . A Bodhisattva is the way and Path to his Father, and thence to the One Supreme Essence" (*Descent of Buddhas*, p. 17, from Âryâsanga). "I am the Way, the Truth, and the Life: no man cometh unto the Father but by me" (*St. John*, xiv. 6). The "way" is not the goal. Nowhere throughout the *New Testament* is Jesus found calling himself God, or anything higher than "a son of God," the son of a "Father" common to all, synthetically. Paul never said (I. *Tim.*, iii. 16), "God was manifest in the flesh," but "He who was manifested in the flesh" (Revised Edition). While the common herd among the Buddhists—the Burmese especially—regard Jesus as an incarnation of Devadatta, a relative who opposed the teachings of Buddha, the students of Esoteric Philosophy see in the Nazarene Sage a Bodhisattva with the spirit of Buddha Himself in Him.

death of the spiritual in the material. "The seed is not quickened except it die."* Hence in the Purusha Sûkta of the Rig Veda, the mother-fount and source of all subsequent religions, it is stated allegorically that "the thousand-headed Purusha" was slaughtered at the foundation of the World, that from his remains the Universe might arise. This is nothing more nor less than the foundation—the seed, truly—of the later many-formed symbol in various religions, including Christianity, of the sacrificial lamb. For it is a play upon the words. "Aja" (Purusha), "the unborn," or eternal Spirit, means also "lamb" in Sanskrit. Spirit disappears—dies, metaphorically—the more it gets involved in matter, and hence the sacrifice of the "unborn," or the "lamb."

Why the BUDDHA chose to make this sacrifice will be plain only to those who, to the minute knowledge of His earthly life, add that of a thorough comprehension of the laws of Karma. Such occurrences, however, belong to the most exceptional cases.

As tradition goes, the Brâhmans had committed a heavy sin by persecuting Gautama BUDDHA and His teachings instead of blending and reconciling them with the tenets of pure Vaidic Brâhmanism, as was done later by Shankarâchârya. Gautama had never gone against the *Vedas*, only against the exoteric growth of preconceived interpretations. The Shruti—divine oral revelation, the outcome of which is the *Veda*—is eternal. It reached the ear of Gautama Siddartha as it had those of the Rishis who had written it down. He accepted the revelation, while rejecting the later overgrowth of Brâhmanical thought and fancy, and built His doctrines on one and the same basis of imperishable truth. As in the case of His Western successor, Gautama, the "Merciful," the "Pure," and the "Just," was the first found in the Eastern Hierarchy of historical Adepts, if not in the world-annals of divine mortals, who was moved by that generous feeling which locks the whole of mankind within one embrace, with no petty differences of race, birth, or caste. It was He who first enunciated that grand and noble principle, and He again who first put it into practice. For the sake of the poor and the reviled, the outcast and the hapless, invited by Him to the king's festival table, He had excluded those who had hitherto sat alone in haughty seclusion and selfishness, believing that they would be defiled by the very shadow of the dis-

---

* I. *Corinth.*, xv. 36.

† *Op. cit.*, Mandala x., hymn 90.

inherited ones of the land—and these non-spiritual Brâhmans turned against Him for that preference. Since then such as these have never forgiven the prince-beggar, the son of a king, who, forgetting His rank and station, had flung widely open the doors of the forbidden sanctuary to the pariah and the man of low estate, thus giving precedence to personal merit over hereditary rank or fortune. The sin was theirs—the cause nevertheless Himself: hence the "Merciful and the Blessed One" could not go out entirely from this world of illusion and created causes without atoning for the sin of all—therefore of these Brâhmans also. If "man afflicted by man" found safe refuge with the Tathâgata, "man afflicting man" had also his share in His self-sacrificing, all-embracing and forgiving love. It is stated that He desired to atone for the sin of His enemies. Then only was He willing to become a full Dharmakâya, a Jivanmukta "without remains."

The close of Shankarâchârya's life brings us face to face with a fresh mystery. Shankarâchârya retires to a cave in the Himâlayas, permitting none of his disciples to follow him, and disappears therein for ever from the sight of the profane. Is he dead? Tradition and popular belief answer in the negative, and some of the local Gurus, if they do not emphatically corroborate, do not deny the rumour. The truth with its mysterious details as given in the Secret Doctrine is known but to them; it can be given out fully only to the direct followers of the great Dravidian Guru, and it is for them alone to reveal of it as much as they think fit. Still it is maintained that this Adept of Adepts lives to this day in his spiritual entity as a mysterious, unseen, yet overpowering presence among the Brotherhood of Shamballa, beyond, far beyond, the snowy-capped Himâlayas.

SECTION XLIV.

"REINCARNATIONS" OF BUDDHA.

EVERY section in the chapter on "Dezhin Shegpa"* (Tathâgata) of the Commentaries represents one year of that great Philosopher's life in its dual aspect of public and private teacher, the two being contrasted and commented upon. It shows the Sage reaching Buddhahood through a long course of study, meditation, and Initiations, as any other Adept would have to do, not one rung of the ladder up to the arduous "Path of Perfection" being missed. The Bodhisattva became a Buddha and a Nirvâni through personal effort and merit, after having had to undergo all the hardships of every other neophyte —not by virtue of a divine birth, as thought by some. It was only the reaching of Nirvâna while still living in the body and on this earth that was due to His having been in previous births high on the "Path of Dzyan" (knowledge, wisdom). Mental or intellectual gifts and abstract knowledge follow an Initiate in his new birth, but he has to acquire phenomenal powers anew, passing through all the successive stages. He has to acquire Rinchen-na-dun ("the seven precious gifts")† one after the other. During the period of meditation no worldly phenomena on the physical plane must be allowed to enter into his mind or cross his thoughts. Zhine-lhagthong (Sanskrit: Vipashya, religious abstract meditation) will develop in him most wonderful faculties independently of himself. The four degrees of

---

* Literally, "he who walks [or follows] in the way [or path] of his predecessors."

† Schmidt, in *Ssanang Ssetsen*, p. 471, and Schlagintweit, in *Buddhism in Tibet*, p. 53, accept these precious things *literally*, enumerating them as "the wheel, the precious stone, the royal consort, the best treasurer, the best horse, the elephant, the best leader." After this one can little wonder if "besides a Dhyâni-Buddhi and a Dhyâni-Bodhisattva" each human Buddha is furnished with "a female companion, a Shakti"—when in truth "Shakti" is simply the Soul-power, the psychic energy of the God as of the Adept. The "royal consort," the third of the "seven precious gifts," very likely led the learned Orientalist into this ludicrous error.

contemplation, or Sam-tan (Sanskrit: Dhyâna), once acquired, everything becomes easy. For, once that man has entirely got rid of the idea of individuality, merging his Self in the Universal Self, becoming, so to say, the bar of steel to which the properties inherent in the loadstone (Âdi Buddha, or Anima Mundi) are imparted, powers hitherto dormant in him are awakened, mysteries in invisible Nature are unveiled, and becoming a Thonglam-pa (a Seer) he becomes a Dhyâni-Buddha. Every Zung (Dhârani, a mystic word or mantra) of the Lokottaradharma (the highest world of causes) will be known to him.

Thus, after His outward death, twenty years later, Tathâgata in His immense love and "pitiful mercy" for erring and ignorant humanity, refused Paranirvâna * in order that He might continue to help men.

Says a Commentary:

Having reached the Path of Deliverance [Thar-lam] from transmigration, one cannot perform Tulpa † any longer, for to become a Paranirvâni is to close the circle of the Septenary Ku-Sum.‡ He has merged his borrowed Dorjesempa [Vajrasattva] into the Universal and become one with it.

Vajradhara, also Vajrasattva (Tibetan: Dorjechang and Dorjedzin, or Dorjosampa), is the regent or President of all the Dhyân Chohans or Dhyâni Buddhas, the highest, the Supreme Buddha; personal, yet never manifested objectively; the "Supreme Conqueror," the "Lord of all Mysteries," the "One without Beginning or End"—in short, the Logos of Buddhism. For, as Vajrasattva, He is simply the Tsovo (Chief) of the Dhyâni Buddhas or Dhyân Chohans, and the Supreme Intelligence in the Second World; while as Vajradhara (Dorjechang), He is all that which was enumerated above. "These two are one, and yet two," and over them is "Chang, the Supreme Unmanifested and

---

* A Bodhisattva can reach Nirvâna and live, as Buddha did, and after death he can either refuse objective reincarnation or accept and use it at his convenience for the benefit of mankind whom he can instruct in various ways while he remains in the Devachanic regions within the attraction of our earth. But having once reached Paranirvâna or "Nirvâna without remains"—the highest Dharmakâya condition, in which state he remains entirely outside of every earthly condition—he will return no more until the commencement of a new Manvantara, since he has crossed beyond the cycle of births.

† Tulpa is the voluntary incarnation of an Adept into a living body, whether of an adult, child, or new-born babe.

‡ Ku-sum is the triple form of the Nirvâna state and its respective duration in the "cycle of Non-Being." The number seven here refers to the seven Rounds of our septenary System.

Universal Wisdom that has no name." As two in one He (They) is the Power that subdued and conquered Evil from the beginning, allowing it to reign only over willing subjects on earth, and having no power over those who despise and hate it. Esoterically the allegory is easily understood; exoterically Vajradhara (Vajrasattva) is the God to whom all the evil spirits swore that they would not impede the propagation of the Good Law (Buddhism), and before whom all the demons tremble. Therefore, we say this dual personage has the same *rôle* assigned to it in canonical and dogmatic Tibetan Buddhism as have Jehovah and the Archangel Mikael, the Metatron of the Jewish Kabalists. This is easily shown. Mikael is "the angel of the face of God," or he who represents his Master. "My face shall go with thee" (in English, "presence"), before the Israelites, says God to Moses (*Exodus*, xxxiii. 14). "The angel of my presence" (Hebrew: "of my face") (*Isaiah*, lxiii. 9), etc. The Roman Catholics identify Christ with Mikael, who is also his ferouer, or "face," mystically. This is precisely the position of Vajradhara, or Vajrasattva, in Northern Buddhism. For the latter, in His Higher Self as Vajradhara (Dorjechang), is *never* manifested, except to the seven Dhyân Chohans, the primeval Builders. Esoterically, it is the Spirit of the "Seven" collectively, their seventh principle, or Âtman. Exoterically, any amount of fables may be found in *Kâla Chakra*, the most important work in the Gyut [or (D)gyu] division of the Kanjur, the division of mystic knowledge [(D)gyu]. Dorjechang (wisdom) Vajradhara, is said to live in the second Arûpa World, which connects him with Metatron, in the first world of pure Spirits, the Briatic world of the Kabalists, who call this angel El-Shaddai, the Omnipotent and Mighty One. Metatron is in Greek ἄγγελος (Messenger), or the Great Teacher. Mikael fights Satan, the Dragon, and conquers him and his Angels. Vajrasattva, who is one with Vajrapâni, the Subduer of the Evil Spirits, conquers Râhu, the Great Dragon who is always trying to devour the sun and moon (eclipses). "War in Heaven" in the Christian legend is based upon the bad angels having discovered the secrets (magical wisdom) of the good ones (Enoch), and the mystery of the "Tree of Life." Let anyone read simply the exoteric accounts in the Hindu and Buddhist Pantheons—the latter version being taken from the former—and he will find both resting on the same primeval, archaic allegory from the Secret Doctrine. In the exoteric texts (Hindu and Buddhist), the Gods churn the ocean to extract from it the Water of Life—Amrita—or the Elixir of Knowledge. In both the Dragon steals some of this, and is exiled from heaven by Vishnu, or Vajradhara, or the chief God, whatever may be his name. We find the same in the Book of *Enoch*, and it is poetized in St. John's *Revelation*. And now the allegory, with all its fanciful ornamentations, has become a dogma!

As will be found mentioned later, the Tibetan Lamaseris contain many secret and semi-secret volumes, detailing the lives of great Sages. Many of the statements in them are purposely confused, and in others the reader becomes bewildered, unless a clue be given him, by the use of one name to cover many individuals who follow the same line of teaching. Thus there is a succession of "living Buddhas'" and the name "Buddha" is given to teacher after teacher. Schlagintweit writes:

> To each human Buddha belongs a Dhyâni-Buddha, and a Dhyâni-Bodhisattva, and the unlimited number of the former also involves an equally unlimited number of the latter.*

[But if this be so—and the exoteric and semi-exoteric use of the name justify the statement—the reader must depend on his own intuition to distinguish between the Dhyâni Buddhas and the human Buddhas, and must not apply to the great BUDDHA of the Fifth Race all that is ascribed to "the Buddha" in books where, as said, blinds are constantly introduced.

In one of these books some strange and obscure statements are made which the writer gives, as before, entirely on her own responsibility, since a few may sense a meaning hidden under words misleading in their surface meaning.]† It is stated that at the age of thirty-three, Shankarâchârya, tired of his mortal body, "put it off" in the cave he had entered, and that the Bodhisattva, that served as his lower personality, was freed

> With the burden of a sin upon him which he had not committed.

At the same time it is added:

> At whatever age one puts off his outward body by free will, at that age will he be made to die a violent death against his will in his next rebirth.

* *Buddhism in Tibet*, p. 52. This same generic use of a name is found among Hindus with that of Shankarâchârya, to take but one instance. All His successors bear his name, but are not reincarnations of Him. So with the "Buddhas."

† [The words within brackets are supplied to introduce the following statements that are confused and contradictory as they stand, and which H. P. B. had probably intended to elucidate to some slight extent, as they are written two or three times with different sentences following them. The MS. is exceedingly confused, and everything H. P. B. said is here pieced together, the addition above made being marked in brackets to distinguish it from hers.—A. B.]

Now, Karma could have no hold on "Mahâ Shankara" (as Shankara is called in the secret work), as he had, as Avatâra, no Karma of his own, but a Bodhisattva—a willing sacrificial victim. Neither had the latter any responsibility for the deed, whether sinful or otherwise. Therefore we do not see the point, since Karma cannot act unjustly. There is some terrible mystery involved in all this story; one that no uninitiated intellect can ever unravel. Still, there it is, suggesting the natural query, "Who, then, was punished by Karma?" and leaving it to be answered.

A few centuries later Buddha tried one more incarnation, it is said, in * * * *, and again, fifty years subsequent to the death of this Adept, in one whose name is given as Tiani-Tsang.* No details, no further information or explanation is given. It is simply stated that the last Buddha had to work out the remains of his Karma, which none of the Gods themselves can escape, forced as he was to bury still deeper certain mysteries half revealed by him—hence misinterpreted. The words used would stand when translated :†

> Born fifty-two years too early as Shramana Gautama, the son of King Suddhodana, then retiring fifty-seven years too soon as Mahâ Shankara, who got tired of his outward form. This wilful act aroused and attracted King Karma, who killed the new form of * * * at thirty-three,‡ the age of the body that was put off. [At whatever age one puts off his outward body by free will, at that age will he be made to die in his next incarnation *against his will*.—Commentary.] He died in his next (body) at thirty-two and a little over, and again in his next at eighty—a Mâyâ, and at one hundred, in reality. The Bodhisattva chose Tiani-Tsang,§ then again the Sugata became Tsong-Kha-pa, who became thus Dezhin-Shegpa [Tathâgata—"one who follows in the way and manner of his predecessors"]. The Blessed One could do good to his generation as * * * but none to posterity, and so as Tiani-Tsang he became incarnated only for the "*remains*" [of his precedent Karma, as we understand it]. The Seven Ways and the Four Truths were once more hidden out of sight. The Merciful One confined since then his attention and fatherly care to the heart of Bodyul, the nursery-grounds of the seeds of truth. The blessed "remains" since then have overshadowed and rested in many a holy body of human Bodhisattvas.

No further information is given, least of all are there any details or

---

* King Suddhodana.

† There are several names marked simply by asterisks.

‡ Shankarâchârya died also at thirty-two years of age, or rather disappeared from the sight of his disciples, as the legend goes.

§ Does "Tiani-Tsang" stand for Apollonius of Tyana? This is a simple surmise. Some things in the life of that Adept would seem to tally with the hypothesis—others to go against it.

explanations to be found in the secret volume. All is darkness and mystery in it, for it is evidently written but for those who are already instructed. Several flaming red asterisks are placed instead of names, and the few facts given are abruptly broken off. The key of the riddle is left to the intuition of the disciple, unless the "direct followers" of Gautama the Buddha—"those who are to be denied by His Church for the next cycle"—and of Shankarâchârya, are pleased to add more.

The final section gives a kind of summary of the seventy sections —covering seventy-three years of Buddha's life *—from which the last paragraph is summarized as follows:

> Emerging from ——, the most excellent seat of the three secrets [Sang-Sum], the Master of incomparable mercy, after having performed on all the anchorites the rite of ——, and each of these having been cut off,† perceived through [the power of] Hlun-Chub ‡ what was his next duty. The Most-Illustrious meditated and asked himself whether this would help [the future] generations. What they needed was the sight of Mâyâ in a body of illusion. Which? . . . The great conqueror of pains and sorrows arose and proceeded back to his birthplace. There Sugata was welcomed by the few, for they did not know Shramana Gautama. "Shâkya [the Mighty] is in Nirvâna. . . . He has given the Science to the Shuddhas [Shûdra]," said they of Damze Yul [the country of Brâhmans: India]. . . . It was for that, born of pity, that the All-Glorious One had to retire to ——, and then appear [karmically] as Mahâ Shankara; and out of pity as ——, and again as ——, and again as Tsong-Kha-pa. . . . For, he who chooses in humiliation must go down, and he who *loves not* allows Karma to raise him.§

This passage is confessedly obscure and written for the few. It is not lawful to say any more, for the time has not yet come when nations are

* According to Esoteric teaching Buddha lived one hundred years in reality, though having reached Nirvâna in his eightieth year he was regarded as one dead to the world of the living. See article "Shâkyamuni's Place in History" in *Five Years of Theosophy*.

† It is a *secret* rite, pertaining to high Initiation, and has the same significance as the one to which Clement of Alexandria alludes when he speaks of "the token of recognition being in common with us, as by cutting off Christ" (Strom., 13). Schlagintweit wonders what it may be. "The typical representation of a hermit," he says, "is always that of a man with long, uncut hair and beard. . . . A rite very often selected, though I am unable to state for what reason, is that of Chod ('to cut' or 'to destroy') the meaning of which is anxiously kept a profound secret by the Lamas." (*Buddhism in Tibet*, p. 163.)

‡ Hlun-Chub is the divining spirit in man, the highest degree of seership.

§ The secret meaning of this sentence is that Karma exercises its sway over the Adept as much as over any other man; "Gods" can escape it as little as simple mortals. The Adept who, having reached the Path and won His Dharmakâya—the Nirvâna from which there is no return until the new grand Kalpa—prefers to use His right of choosing a condition inferior to that which belongs to Him, but that will leave him free to return whenever He thinks it advisable and under whatever personality He may select, must be prepared to take all the chances of failure—possibly—and a lower condition than was His lot—for a certainty—as it is an occult law. Karma alone is absolute justice and infallible in its selections. He who uses his rights with it (Karma) must bear the consequences—if any. Thus Buddha's first reincarnation was produced by Karma—and it led Him higher than ever; the two following were "out of pity" and * * *

clutches of concupiscence and other passions. The Arhat who observes the seven hidden precepts of Bas-pa may become Dang-ma and Lha.* He may hear the "holy voice" of . . . [Kwan-yin],† find himself within the quiet precincts of his Sangharama‡ transferred into Amitâbha Buddha.§ Becoming one with Anuttara Samyak Sambodhi,‖ he may pass through all the six worlds of Being (Rûpa-loka) and get into the first three worlds of Arûpa.¶ . . . He who listens to my secret law, preached to my select Arhats, will arrive with its help at the knowledge of Self, and thence at perfection.

It is due to entirely erroneous conceptions of Eastern thought and to ignorance of the existence of an Esoteric key to the outward Buddhist phrases that Burnouf and other great scholars have inferred from such propositions—held also by the Vedântins—as "my body is not body" and "myself is no self of mine," that Eastern psychology was all based upon non-permanency. Cousin, for instance, lecturing upon the subject, brings the two following propositions to prove, on Burnouf's authority, that, unlike Brâhmanism, Buddhism rejects the perpetuity of the thinking principle. These are:

1. Thought or Spirit**—for the faculty is not distinguished from the subject—appears only with sensation and does not survive it.

2. The Spirit cannot itself lay hold of itself, and in directing attention to itself it draws from it only the conviction of its powerlessness to see itself otherwise than as successive and transitory.

This all refers to Spirit embodied, not to the freed Spiritual Self on whom Mâyâ has no more hold. Spirit is no body; therefore have the

---

* Dang-ma, a purified soul, and Lha, a freed spirit within a living body; an Adept or Arhat. In the popular opinion in Tibet, a Lha is a disembodied spirit, something similar to the Burmese Nat, only higher.

† Kwan-yin is a synonym, for in the original another term is used, but the meaning is identical. It is the divine voice of Self, or the "Spirit-voice" in man, and the same as Vâchîshvara (the "Voice-deity") of the Brâhmans. In China, the Buddhist ritualists have degraded its meaning by anthropomorphizing it into a Goddess of the same name, with one thousand hands and eyes, and they call it Kwan-shai-yin-Bodhisat. It is the Buddhist "daïmon"-voice of Socrates.

‡ Sangharama is the *sanctum sanctorum* of an ascetic, a cave or any place he chooses for his meditation.

§ Amitâbha Buddha is in this connection the "boundless light" by which things of the subjective world are perceived.

‖ Esoterically, "the unsurpassingly merciful and enlightened heart," said of the "Perfect Ones," the Jîvan-muktas, collectively.

¶ These six worlds—seven with us—are the worlds of Nats or Spirits, with the Burmese Buddhists, and the seven higher worlds of the Vedântins.

** Two things entirely distinct from each other. The "faculty is not distinguished from the subject" only on this material plane, while thought generated by our physical brain, one that has never impressed itself at the same time on the spiritual counterpart, whether through the [illegible] of the latter or the intrinsic weakness of that thought, can never survive our body; this much is [illegible]

Orientalists made of it "nobody" and nothing. Hence they proclaim Buddhists to be Nihilists, and Vedântins to be the followers of a creed in which the "Impersonal [God] turns out on examination to be a myth"; their goal is described as

> The complete extinction of all spiritual, mental, and bodily powers by absorption into the Impersonal.*

---

* *Vedânta Sára*, translated by Major Jacob, p. 123.

SECTION XLVI

NIRVANA-MOKSHA.

THE few sentences given in the text from one of Gautama Buddha's secret teachings show how uncalled for is the epithet of "Materialist" when applied to One Whom two-thirds of those who are looked upon as great Adepts and Occultists in Asia recognize as their Master, whether under the name of Buddha or that of Shankarâchârya. The reader will remember the just-quoted words are what Buddha Sanggyas (or Pho) is alleged by the Tibetan Occultists to have taught: there are three eternal things in the Universe—the Law, Nirvâna, and Space. The Buddhists of the Southern Church claim, on the other hand, that Buddha held only two things as eternal—Âkâsha and Nirvâna. But Âkâsha being the same as Aditi,* and both being translated "Space," there is no discrepancy so far, since Nirvâna as well as Moksha, is a state. Then in both cases the great Kapilavastu Sage unifies the two, as well as the three, into one eternal Element, and ends by saying that even "that One is a Mâyâ" to one who is not a Dang-ma, a perfectly purified Soul.

The whole question hangs upon materialistic misconceptions and ignorance of Occult Metaphysics. To the man of Science who regards Space as simply a mental representation, a conception of something existing *pro formâ*, and having no real being outside our mind, Space *per se* is verily an illusion. He may fill the boundless interstellar space with an "imaginary" ether, nevertheless Space for him is an abstraction. Most of the Metaphysicians of Europe are so wide of the mark, from the purely Occult standpoint, of a correct comprehension of "Space," as are the Materialists, though the erroneous conceptions of both of course differ widely.

---

* Aditi is, according to the *Rig Veda*, "the Father and Mother of all the Gods"; and Âkâsha is held by Southern Buddhism as the Root of all, whence everything in the Universe came out, in obedience to a law of motion inherent in it; and this is the Tibetan "Space" (Tho-og).

If, bearing in mind the philosophical views of the Ancients upon this question, we compare them with what is now termed exact physical Science, it will be found that the two disagree only in inferences and names, and that their postulates are the same when reduced to their most simple expression. From the beginning of the human Æons, from the very dawn of Occult Wisdom, the regions that the men of Science fill with ether have been explored by the Seers of every age. That which the world regards simply as cosmic Space, an abstract representation, the Hindu Rishi, the Chaldæan Magus, the Egyptian Hierophant held, each and all, as the one eternal Root of all, the playground of all the Forces in Nature. It is the fountain-head of all terrestrial life, and the abode of those (to us) invisible swarms of existences—of real beings, as of the shadows only thereof, conscious and unconscious, intelligent and senseless—that surround us on all sides, that interpenetrate the atoms of our Kosmos, and see us not, as we do not either see or sense them through our physical organisms. For the Occultist "Space" and "Universe" are synonyms. In Space there is not Matter, Force, nor Spirit, but all that and much more. It is the One Element, and that one the Anima Mundi—Space, Âkâsha, Astral Light—the Root of Life which, in its eternal, ceaseless motion, like the out- and in-breathing of one boundless ocean, evolves but to reabsorb all that lives and feels and thinks and has its being in it. As said of the Universe in *Isis Unveiled*, it is:

> The combination of a thousand elements and yet the expression of a single Spirit —a chaos to the sense, a Kosmos to the reason.

Such were the views upon the subject of all the great ancient Philosophers, from Manu down to Pythagoras, from Plato to Paul.

> When the dissolution [Pralaya] had arrived at its term the great Being [Para-Âtmâ, or Para-Purusha], the Lord existing through himself, out of whom and through whom all things were, and are, and will be, . . . resolved to emanate from his own substance the various creatures.*
>
> The mystic Decad [of Pythagoras] (1 + 2 + 3 + 4 = 10) is a way of expressing this idea. The One is God;† the Two, matter; the Three, combining Monad and Duad and partaking of the nature of both, is the phenomenal world; the Tetrad, or form of perfection, expresses the emptiness of all; and the Decad, or sum of all, involves the entire Cosmos.‡

---

* *Mânava-Dharma-Shâstra*, i. 6, 7.

† The "God" of Pythagoras, the disciple of the Âryan Sages, is no personal God. Let it be remembered that he taught as a cardinal tenet that there exists a permanent Principle of Unity beneath all forms, changes, and other phenomena of the Universe.

‡ *Isis Unveiled*, i. xvi.

Plato's "God" is the "Universal Ideation," and Paul saying [illegible] him, and through him, and in him, all things are," had [illegible] Principle—never a Jehovah—in his profound mind. The [illegible] Pythagorean dogmas is the key to every great Philosophy. [illegible] general formula of unity in multiplicity, the One evolving [illegible] and pervading the All. It is the archaic doctrine of [illegible] few words.

Speusippus and Xenocrates held, like their great Master, [illegible]

The Anima Mundi (or "world-soul") was not the Deity, but a [illegible] Those philosophers never conceived of the One as an *animate nature*. [illegible] One did not *exist*, as we understand the term. Not till he (it) had united [illegible] many emanated existences (the Monad and Duad), was a being produced [illegible] τίμιον ("honoured"), the something manifested, dwells in the centre as [illegible] cumference, but it is only the reflection of the Deity—the World-Soul. [illegible] trine we find the spirit of Esoteric Buddhism.*

And it is that of Esoteric Brâhminism and of the Vedântin [illegible] The two modern philosophers, Schopenhauer and von [illegible] teach the same ideas. The Occultists say that:

The psychic and ectenic forces, the "ideo-motor" and "electro-biological [illegible] "latent thought," and even "unconscious cerebration" theories can be [illegible] in two words: the Kabalistic Astral Light.†

Schopenhauer only synthesized all this by calling it Will, [illegible] tradicted the men of Science in their materialistic views, [illegible] Hartmann did later on. The author of the *Philosophy of the Uncon*[illegible] calls their views "an instinctual prejudice."

Furthermore, he demonstrates that no experimenter can have anything [illegible] with matter properly so termed, but only with the forces into which he [illegible] The visible effects of matter are but the effects of force. He concludes [illegible] that which is now called matter is nothing but the aggregation of atomic [illegible] express which the word "matter" is used; outside of that, for science, [illegible] but a word void of sense.‡

As much, it is to be feared, as those other terms with which [illegible] now concerned, "Space," "Nirvâna," and so on.

The bold theories and opinions expressed in Schopenhauer's works [illegible] from those of the majority of our orthodox scientists.§ "In reality," [illegible]

* *Isis Unveiled*, i. xviii.

† *Isis Unveiled* i. 58.

‡ *Isis Unveiled*, i. 59.

§ While they are to a great extent identical with those of Esoteric Buddhism, the [illegible] of the East.

daring speculator, "there is neither *Matter* nor *Spirit*. The tendency to gravitation in a stone is as unexplainable as thought in the human brain. . . . If matter can—no one knows why—fall to the ground, then it can also—no one knows why—think. . . . As soon, even in mechanics, as we trespass beyond the purely mathematical, as soon as we reach the inscrutable adhesion, gravitation, and so on we are faced by phenomena which are to our senses as mysterious as the *will* and *thought* in man: we find ourselves facing the incomprehensible, for such is every force in nature. Where is, then, that *matter* which you all pretend to know so well, and from which—being so familiar with it—you draw all your conclusions and explanations, and attribute to it all things? . . . That which can be fully realized by our reason and senses is but the superficial; they can never reach the true inner substance of things. Such was the opinion of Kant. If you consider that there is in a human head some sort of a *spirit*, then you are obliged to concede the same to a stone. If your dead and utterly-passive matter can manifest a tendency toward gravitation or, like electricity, attract and repel and send out sparks then as well as the brain it can also think. In short, every particle of the so-called spirit we can replace with an equivalent of matter, and every particle of matter replace with spirit. . . . Thus, it is not the Christian division of all things into matter and spirit that can ever be found philosophically exact; but only if we divide them into *will* and *manifestation*, which form of division has naught to do with the former, for it spiritualizes everything: all that which is in the first instance real and objective—body and matter—it transforms into a representation, and every manifestation into will."*

The *matter* of science may be for all objective purposes a "dead and utterly-passive matter"; to the Occultist not an atom of it can be dead—"Life is ever present in it." We send the reader who would know more about it to our article, "Transmigration of Life-Atoms."† What we are now concerned with is the doctrine of Nirvâna.

A "system of atheism" it may be justly called, since it recognizes neither God nor Gods—least of all a Creator, as it entirely rejects creation. The *Fecit ex nihilo* is as incomprehensible to the Occult metaphysical Scientist as it is to the scientific Materialist. It is at this point that all agreement stops between the two. But if such be the sin of the Buddhist and Brâhman Occultist, then Pantheists and Atheists, and also theistical Jews—the Kabalists—must also plead "guilty" to it; yet no one would ever think of calling the Hebrews of the Kabalah "Atheists." Except the Talmudistic and Christian exoteric systems there never was a religious Philosophy, whether in the ancient or modern world, but rejected *a priori* the *ex nihilo* hypothesis, simply because Matter was always co-eternalized with Spirit.

---

* *Parerga*, II. iii. 112; quoted in *Isis Unveiled*, i. 58. † *Five years of Theosophy*, p. 338, *et seq.*

Nirvâna, as well as the Moksha of the Vedântins, [illegible] most of the Orientalists as a synonym of annihilation; [illegible] glaring injustice could be done, and this capital error [illegible] out and disproved. On this most important tenet of the [illegible] Buddhistic system—the Alpha and the Omega of "Being" [illegible] Being"—rests the whole edifice of Occult Metaphysics. [illegible] rectification of the great error concerning Nirvâna may be [illegible] accomplished with relation to the philosophically inclined, [illegible] who,

In the glass of things temporal see the image of things spiritual,

On the other hand, to that reader who could never soar beyond [illegible] details of tangible material form, our explanation will appear [illegible] less. He may comprehend and even accept the logical [illegible] from the reasons given—the true spirit will ever escape his [illegible] The word "nihil" having been misconceived from the first, [illegible] continually used as a sledge-hammer in the matter of [illegible] Philosophy. Nevertheless it is the duty of the Occultist to try [illegible] explain it.

Nirvâna and Moksha, then, as said before, have their being in [illegible] being, if such a paradox be permitted to illustrate the meaning [illegible] better. Nirvâna, as some illustrious Orientalists have attempted [illegible] prove, does mean the "blowing-out"* of all sentient existence. [illegible] like the flame of a candle burnt out to its last atom, and then [illegible] extinguished. Quite so. Nevertheless, as the old Arhat Nâg[illegible] affirmed before the king who taunted him: "Nirvâna *is*"—and Nir[illegible] is eternal. But the Orientalists deny this, and say it is not so. [illegible] their opinion Nirvâna is not a re-absorption in the Universal [illegible] not eternal bliss and rest, but it means literally "the blowing-out, [illegible] extinction, complete annihilation, and not absorption." The [illegible] *âvatâra* quoted in support of their arguments by some Sanskritists, [illegible] which gives the different interpretations of Nirvâna by the [illegible] Brâhmans, is no authority to one who goes to primeval sources [illegible] information, namely, to the Buddha who taught the doctrine. As well [illegible] quote the Chârvâka Materialists in their support.

* Prof. Max Müller, in a letter to *The Times* (April, 1857), maintained most [illegible] meant *annihilation* in the fullest sense of the word. (*Chips from a German Workshop*, I, [illegible].) [illegible] 1869, in a lecture before the General Meeting of the Association of German Philologists at [illegible] distinctly declares his belief that the Nihilism attributed to Buddha's teaching forms no part of his doctrine, and that it is wholly wrong to suppose that Nirvâna means annihilation." (Trübner's [illegible] *and Oriental Lit. Rec.*, Oct. 16th, 1869.)

If we bring as an argument the sacred Jaina books, wherein the dying Gautama Buddha is thus addressed: "Arise into Nirvi [Nirvâna] from this decrepit body into which thou hast been sent. . . . Ascend into thy former abode, O blessed Avatâra"; and if we add that this seems to us the very opposite of nihilism, we may be told that so far it may only prove a contradiction, one more discrepancy in the Buddhist faith. If again we remind the reader that since Gautama is believed to appear occasionally, re-descending from his "former abode" for the good of humanity and His faithful congregation, thus making it incontestable that Buddhism does not teach final annihilation, we shall be referred to authorities to whom such teaching is ascribed. And let us say at once: Men are no authority for us in questions of conscience, nor ought they to be for anyone else. If anyone holds to Buddha's Philosophy, let him do and say as Buddha did and said; if a man calls himself a Christian, let him follow the commandments of Christ—not the interpretations of His many dissenting priests and sects.

In *A Buddhist Catechism* the question is asked:

Are there any dogmas in Buddhism which we are required to accept on faith?

A. No. We are earnestly enjoined to accept nothing whatever on faith, whether it be written in books, handed down from our ancestors, or taught by sages. Our Lord Buddha has said that we must not believe in a thing said merely because it is said; nor traditions because they have been handed down from antiquity; nor rumours, as such; nor writings by sages, because sages wrote them: nor fancies that we may suspect to have been inspired in us by a Deva (that is, in presumed spiritual inspiration); nor from inferences drawn from some haphazard assumption we may have made; nor because of what seems an analogical necessity; nor on the mere authority of our teachers or masters. But we are to believe when the writing, doctrine, or saying is corroborated by our own reason and consciousness. "For this," says he in concluding, "I taught you not to believe merely because you have heard, but when you believed of your consciousness, then to act accordingly and abundantly."*

That Nirvâna, or rather, that state in which we are in Nirvâna, is quite the reverse of annihilation is suggested to us by our "reason and consciousness," and that is sufficient for us personally. At the same time, this fact being inadequate and very ill-adapted for the general reader, something more efficient may be added.

---

* See the *Kalama Sutta* of the *Anguttaranikayo*, as quoted in *A Buddhist Catechism*, by H. S. Olcott, President of the Theosophical Society, pp. 55, 56.

Without resorting to sources unsympathetic to Occultism, the [illegible] furnishes us with the most luminous and clear proofs that [illegible] "nihil" in the minds of the Ancient Philosophers had a meaning [illegible] different from that it has now received at the hands of Mat[illegible]. It means certainly "nothing"—or "no-thing." F. Kircher, in his [illegible] on the *Kabalah* and the Egyptian Mysteries,* explains the [illegible] admirably. He tells his readers that in the *Zohar* the first of [illegible] Sephiroth† has a name the significance of which is "the *Infinite*," [illegible] which was translated indifferently by the Kabalists as "[illegible]" "Non-Ens" ("Being" and "Non-Being"); a *Being*, inasmuch as it is the *root* and source of all other beings; *Non-Being* because Ain Soph, the Boundless and the Causeless, the Unconscious and the [illegible] Principle—resembles nought else in the Universe.

The author adds:

> This is the reason why St. Denys did not hesitate to call it Nihil.

"Nihil" therefore stands—even with some Christian theologians [illegible] thinkers, especially with the earlier ones who lived but a few [illegible] from the profound Philosophy of the initiated Pagans—as a synonym for the impersonal, divine Principle, the Infinite All, which is no [illegible] or thing—the En or Ain Soph, the Parabrahman of the Vedânta. [illegible] St. Denys was a pupil of St. Paul—an Initiate—and this fact [illegible] everything clear.

The "Nihil" is *in esse* the Absolute Deity itself, the hidden Pow[illegible] Omnipresence degraded by Monotheism into an anthropom[illegible] Being, with all the passions of a mortal on a grand scale. Union w[illegible] That is not annihilation in the sense understood in Europe.‡ In the East annihilation in Nirvâna refers but to matter: that of the visible as well as the invisible body, for the astral body, the personal double, is still matter, however sublimated. Buddha taught that the primitive Substance is eternal and unchangeable. Its vehicle is the [illegible] luminous ether, the boundless, infinite Space,

> Not a void resulting from the absence of forms, but on the contrary, the [illegible]

---

* *Œdipus Ægypt.*, II. i. 291.

† Sephir, or Aditi (mystic Space). The Sephiroth, be it understood, are identical with the [illegible] Prajâpatis, the Dhyân Chohans of Esoteric Buddhism, the Zoroastrian Amshaspends, and [illegible] the Elohim—the "Seven Angels of the Presence" of the Roman Catholic Church.

‡ According to the Eastern idea, the All comes out from the One, and returns to it again. [illegible] annihilation is simply unthinkable. Nor can eternal Matter be annihilated. Form may be [illegible] lated: co-relations may change. That is all. There can be no such thing as annihilation—[illegible] European sense—in the Universe.

tion of all forms . . . [This] denotes it to be the creation of Mâyâ, all the works of which are as nothing before the uncreated Form [Spirit], in whose profound and sacred depths all motion must cease for ever.*

Motion here refers only to illusive objects, to their change as opposed to perpetuity, rest—perpetual motion being the Eternal Law, the ceaseless Breath of the Absolute.

The mastery of Buddhistic dogmas can be attained only according to the Platonic method: from universals to particulars. The key to it lies in the refined and mystical tenets of spiritual influx and divine life.

Saith Buddha:

Whosoever is unacquainted with my Law,† *and dies in that state must return to earth until he becomes a perfect Samano* [*ascetic*]. *To achieve this object he must destroy within himself the trinity of Mâyâ.*‡ *He must extinguish his passions, unite and identify himself with the Law* [*the teaching of the Secret Doctrine*], *and comprehend the philosophy of annihilation.*§

No, it is not in the dead-letter of Buddhistical literature that scholars may ever hope to find the true solution of its metaphysical subtleties. Alone in all antiquity the Pythagoreans understood them perfectly, and it is on the (to the average Orientalist and the Materialist) incomprehensible abstractions of Buddhism that Pythagoras grounded the principal tenets of his Philosophy.

Annihilation means with the Buddhistical Philosophy only a dispersion of matter, in whatever form or *semblance* of form it may be, for everything that bears a shape was created, and thus must sooner or later perish, *i.e.*, change that shape; therefore, as something temporal, though seeming to be permanent, it is but an illusion, Mâyâ; for as eternity has neither beginning nor end, the more or less prolonged duration of some particular form passes, as it were, like an instantaneous flash of lightning. Before we have the time to realize that we have seen it, it is gone and passed for ever; hence even our astral bodies, pure ether, are but illusions of matter so long as they retain their terrestrial outline. The latter changes, says the Buddhist, according to the merits or demerits of the person during his lifetime, and this is

---

* *Isis Unveiled*, i. 289.

† The Secret Law, the "Doctrine of the Heart," so called in contrast to the "Doctrine of the Eye," or exoteric Buddhism.

‡ "Illusive matter in its triple manifestation in the earthly, and the astral or fontal Soul (the body), and the Platonian dual Soul—the rational and the irrational one."

§ *Isis Unveiled*, i. 289.

metempsychosis. When the spiritual Entity breaks loose for ever from every particle of matter, then only it enters upon the eternal and unchangeable Nirvâna. He exists in Spirit, in nothing; as a form, a shape, a semblance, he is completely annihilated, and thus will die no more, for Spirit alone is no Mâyâ, but the only Reality in an illusionary universe of ever-passing forms.

It is upon this Buddhist doctrine that the Pythagoreans grounded the principal tenets of their philosophy. "Can that Spirit which gives life and motion, and partakes of the nature of light, be reduced to nonentity?" they ask. "Can that sensitive Spirit in brutes which exercises memory, one of the rational faculties, die and become nothing?" And Whitelock Bulstrode in his able defence of Pythagoras expounds this doctrine by adding:

"If you say they [the brutes] breathe their Spirits into the air, and there vanish, that is all that I contend for. The air indeed is the proper place to receive them, being according to Laertius full of souls; and according to Epicurus [illegible] the principles of all things; for even this place wherein we walk and [illegible] much of a spiritual nature that it is invisible, and therefore may well be [illegible] of forms, since the forms of all bodies are so; we can only see and hear its effects, the air itself is too fine and above the capacity of the age. What then is the [illegible] in the region above, and what are the influences of forms that descend from thence? The *Spirits* of creatures, the Pythagoreans hold, who are emanations of the [illegible] sublimated portions of ether—emanations, *breaths, but not forms.* Ether is incorruptible—all philosophers agree in that;—and what is incorruptible is so far from *being annihilated* when it gets rid of the *form* that it lays a good claim to *immortality.*

"But what is that which has no body, no *form;* which is imponderable, invisible and indivisible—that which exists, and yet *is not?*" ask the Buddhists. "It is Nirvâna," is the answer. It is *nothing*—not a region, but rather a state.*

* *Isis Unveiled*, i. 290.

SECTION XLVII.

THE SECRET BOOKS OF "LAM-RIN" AND DZYAN.

THE *Book of Dzyan*—from the Sanskrit word "Dhyân" (mystic meditation)—is the first volume of the Commentaries upon the seven secret folios of Kiu-te, and a Glossary of the public works of the same name. Thirty-five volumes of Kiu-te for exoteric purposes and the use of the laymen may be found in the possession of the Tibetan Gelugpa Lamas, in the library of any monastery; and also fourteen books of Commentaries and Annotations on the same by the initiated Teachers.

Strictly speaking, those thirty-five books ought to be termed "The Popularised Version" of the Secret Doctrine, full of myths, blinds, and errors; the fourteen volumes of *Commentaries*, on the other hand—with their translations, annotations, and an ample glossary of Occult terms, worked out from one small archaic folio, the *Book of the Secret Wisdom of the World**—contain a digest of all the Occult Sciences. These, it appears, are kept secret and apart, in the charge of the Teshu Lama of Tji-gad-je. The Books of Kiu-te are comparatively modern, having been edited within the last millennium, whereas, the earliest volumes of the *Commentaries* are of untold antiquity, some fragments of the original cylinders having been preserved. With the exception that they explain and correct some of the too fabulous, and to every appearance, grossly-exaggerated accounts in the Books of Kiu-te†—properly so-called—the *Commentaries* have little to do with these. They stand in relation to

---

* It is from the texts of all these works that the Secret Doctrine has been given. The original matter would not make a small pamphlet, but the explanations and notes from the Commentaries and Glossaries might be worked into ten volumes as large as *Isis Unveiled*.

† The monk Della Penna makes considerable fun in his *Memoirs* (see Markham's *Tibet*) of certain statements in the Books of Kiu-te. He brings to the notice of the Christian public "the great mountain 160,000 leagues high" (a Tibetan league consisting of five miles) in the Himâlayan Range. "According to their law," he says, "in the west of this world is an eternal world . . . a paradise, and in it a Saint called Hopahma, which means 'Saint of Splendour and Infinite Light.' This Saint has many disciples who are all Chang-chub," which means, he adds in a footnote, "the Spirits of those who, on account of their perfection, do not care to become saints, and train and instruct the bodies of the reborn Lamas . . . so that they may help the living." Which means that the presumably "dead" Yang-Chhub (not "Chang-chub") are simply living Bodhisattvas, some of those known as Bhante ("the Brothers"). As to the "mountain 160,000 leagues high," the *Commentary* which gives the key to such statements explains that according to the code used by the writers, "to the west of the 'Snowy Mountain' 160 leagues [the cyphers being a blind] from a certain spot and by a direct road, is the Bhante Yul [the country or 'Seat of the Brothers'], the residence of Mahâ-Chohan . . ." etc. This is the real meaning. The "Hopahma" of Della Penna is—the Mahâ-Chohan, the Chief.

them as the Chaldæo-Jewish *Kabalah* stands to the Mosaic Books. In the work known as the *Avatamsaka Sûtra*, in section: "The Supreme Âtman [Soul] as manifested in the character of the Arhats and Pratyeka Buddhas," it is stated that:

Because from the beginning all sentient creatures have confused the truth and embraced the false, therefore there came into existence a hidden knowledge called Alaya Vijñâna.

"Who is in possession of the true knowledge?" is asked. "The great Teachers of the Snowy Mountain," is the response.

These "great Teachers" have been known to live in the "Snowy Range" of the Himâlayas for countless ages. To deny in the face of millions of Hindus the existence of their great Gurus, living in the Âshrams scattered all over the Trans- or the Cis-Himâlayan slopes is to make oneself ridiculous in their eyes. When the Buddhist Saviour appeared in India, their Âshrams—for it is rarely that these great Men are found in Lamaseries, unless on a short visit—were at the spots they now occupy, and that even before the Brâhmans themselves came from Central Asia to settle on the Indus. And before that more than one Âryan Dvija of fame and historical renown had sat at their feet, learning that which culminated later on in one or another of the great philosophical schools. Most of these Himâlayan Rishis were Âryan Brâhmans and ascetics.

No student, unless very advanced, would be benefited by the perusal of those exoteric volumes.* They must be read with a key to their meaning, and that key can only be found in the *Commentaries*. Moreover, there are some comparatively modern works that are positively injurious so far as a fair comprehension o. even exoteric Buddhism is concerned. Such are the *Buddhist Cosmos*, by Bonze Jin-ch'on of Pekin; the *Shing-Tau-ki* (or *The Records of the Enlightenment of Tathâgata*), by Wang-Puh—seventh century; *Hisai Sûtra* (or *Book of Creation*), and some others.

* In some MSS. notes before us, written by Gelung (priest) Thango-pa Chhe-go-mo, it is said: "The Roman Catholic missionaries who have visited our land (under protest) in the last century and have repaid our hospitality by turning our sacred literature into ridicule, have shown little discretion and still less knowledge. It is true that the Sacred Canon of the Tibetans, the Kahgyur and Bstan-hgyur, comprises 1707 distinct works—1083 public and 624 secret volumes, the former being composed of 350 and the latter of 77 volumes folio. May we humbly invite the good missionaries, however, to tell us when they ever succeeded in getting a glimpse of the last-named secret folios? Had they even by chance seen them I can assure the Western Pandits that these manuscripts and folios could never be understood even by a born Tibetan without a key (a) to their peculiar characters, and (b) to their hidden meaning. In our system every description of locality is figurative, every name and word purposely veiled; and one has first to study the mode of deciphering and then to learn the equivalent secret terms and symbols for nearly every word of the religious language. The Egyptian enchorial or hieratic system is child's play to our sacerdotal puzzles."

SECTION XLVIII.

AMITA BUDDHA KWAN-SHAI-YIN, AND KWAN-YIN.—WHAT THE "BOOK OF DZYAN" AND THE LAMASERIES OF TSONG-KHA-PA SAY.

As a supplement to the *Commentaries* there are many secret folios on the lives of the Buddhas and Bodhisattvas, and among these there is one on Prince Gautama and another on His reincarnation in Tsong-Kha-pa. This great Tibetan Reformer of the fourteenth century, said to be a direct incarnation of Amita Buddha, is the founder of the secret School near Tji-gad-je, attached to the private retreat of the Teshu Lama. It is with Him that began the regular system of Lamaic incarnations of Buddhas (Sang-gyas), or of Shâkya-Thub-pa (Shakyamuni). Amida or Amita Buddha is called by the author of *Chinese Buddhism*, a mythical being. He speaks of

> Amida Buddha (*Ami-to Fo*) a fabulous personage, worshipped assiduously—like Kwan-yin—by the Northern Buddhists, but unknown in Siam, Burmah, and Ceylon.*

Very likely. Yet Amida Buddha is not a "fabulous" personage, since (*a*) "Amida" is the Senzar form of "Âdi"; "Âdi-Buddhi" and "Âdi-Buddha,"† as already shown, existed ages ago as a Sanskrit term for "Primeval Soul" and "Wisdom"; and (*b*) the name was applied to Gautama Shâkyamuni, the last Buddha in India, from the seventh century, when Buddhism was introduced into Tibet. "Amitâbha" (in Chinese, "Wu-liang-shen") means literally "Boundless Age," a

---

* *Chinese Buddhism*, p. 171.

† "Buddhi" is a Sanskrit term for "discrimination" or intellect (the sixth principle), and "Buddha" is "wise," "wisdom," and also the planet Mercury.

synonym of "En," or "Ain-Suph," the "Ancient of Days," and is an epithet that connects Him directly with the Boundless Âdi-Buddhi (primeval and Universal Soul) of the Hindus, as well as with the Anima Mundi of all the ancient nations of Europe and the Boundless and Infinite of the Kabalists. If Amitâbha be a fiction of the Tibetans, or a new form of Wu-liang-sheu, "a fabulous personage," as the author-compiler of *Chinese Buddhism* tells his readers, then the "fable" must be a very ancient one. For on another page he says himself that the addition to the canon, of the books containing the

> Legends of Kwan-yin and of the Western heaven with its Buddha, Amitâbha, was also previous to the Council of Kashmere, a little before the beginning of our era,*

and he places

> the origin of the primitive Buddhist books which are common to the Northern and Southern Buddhists before 246 B.C.

"Since Tibetans accepted Buddhism only in the seventh century, A.D., how comes it that they are charged with inventing Amita-Buddha? Besides which, in Tibet, Amitâbha is called Odpag-med, which shows that it is not the name but the abstract idea that was first accepted of an unknown, invisible, and Impersonal Power—taken, moreover, from the Hindu "Âdi-Buddhi," and not from the Chinese "Amitâbha."† There is a great difference between the popular Odpag-med (Amitâbha) who sits enthroned in Devachan (Sukhâvati), according to the Mani *Kambum* Scriptures—the oldest *historical* work in Tibet, and the philosophical abstraction called Amida Buddha, the name being passed over to the earthly Buddha, Gantama.

---

* This curious contradiction may be found in *Chinese Buddhism*, pp. 171, 273. The reverend author assures his readers that "to the philosophic Buddhists . . . Amitâbha Foshi Fo, and the others are nothing but the signs of ideas" (p. 236). Very true. But so should be all other deities, beginning with such as Jehovah, Allah, etc., and if they are not simply "signs of ideas" this would only show that minds that receive them otherwise are not "philosophic"; it would not at all afford serious proof that these are personal, living Gods of these names in reality. H. P. B.

† The Chinese Amitâbha (Wu-liang-sheu) and the Tibetan Amitâbha (Odpag-med) have now become personal Gods, ruling over and living in the celestial region of Sukhâvati, or Tushita (Tibetan: Devachan); while Âdi-Buddhi, of the philosophic Hindu, and Amita Buddha of the philosophic Chinaman and Tibetan, are names for universal, primeval ideas.

SECTION XLIX.

TSONG-KHA-PA.—LOHANS IN CHINA.

IN an article, "Reincarnation in Tibet," everything that could be said about Tsong-Kha-pa was published.* It was stated that this reformer was not, as is alleged by Pârsî scholars, an incarnation of one of the celestial Dhyânis, or the five heavenly Buddhas, said to have been created by Shâkyamuni after he had risen to Nirvâna, but that he was an incarnation of Amita Buddha Himself. The records preserved in the Gon-pa, the chief Lamasery of Tda-shi-Hlumpo, show that Sang-gyas left the regions of the "Western Paradise" to incarnate Himself in Tsong-Kha-pa, in consequence of the great degradation into which His secret doctrines had fallen.

> Whenever made too public, the Good Law of Cheu [magical powers] fell invariably into sorcery or "black magic." The Dwijas, the Hoshang [Chinese monks] and the Lamas could alone be entrusted safely with the formulæ.

Until the Tsong-Kha-pa period there had been no Sang-gyas (Buddha) incarnations in Tibet.

Tsong-Kha-pa gave the signs whereby the presence of one of the twenty-five Bodhisattvas † or of the Celestial Buddhas (Dhyân Chohans) in a human body might be recognized, and He strictly forbade necromancy. This led to a split amongst the Lamas, and the malcontents allied themselves with the aboriginal Bhons against the reformed Lamaism. Even now they form a powerful sect, practising the most disgusting rites all over Sikkhim, Bhutan, Nepaul, and even on the borderlands of Tibet. It was worse then. With the permission of the Tda-shu or Teshu Lama,‡ some hundred Lohans (Arhats), to avert strife,

* See *Theosophist* for March, 1882.

† The intimate relation of the twenty-five Buddhas (Bodhisattvas) with the twenty-five Tattvas (the Conditioned or Limited) of the Hindus is interesting.

‡ It is curious to note the great importance given by European Orientalists to the Dalaï Lamas of Lhassa, and their utter ignorance as to the Tda-shu (or Teshu) Lamas, while it is the latter who began the hierarchical series of Buddha-incarnations, and are *de facto* the "popes" in Tibet; the Dalaï Lamas are the creations of Nabang-lob-Sang, the Tda-shu Lama, who was Himself the sixth incarnation of Amita, through Tsong Kha-pa, though very few seem to be aware of that fact.

went to settle in China in the famous monastery near Tien-t'-ai, where they soon became subjects for legendary lore, and continue to be so to this day. They had been already preceded by other Lohans.

The world-famous disciples of Tathâgata, called the "sweet-voiced" on account of their ability to chant the Mantras with magical effect.*

The first ones came from Kashmir in the year 3,000 of Kali Yuga (about a century before the Christian era),† while the last ones arrived at the end of the fourteenth century, 1,500 years later; and, finding no room for themselves at the lamasery of Yihigching, they built for their own use the largest monastery of all on the sacred island of Pu-to (Buddha, or Put, in Chinese), in the province of Chusan. There the Good Law, the "Doctrine of the Heart," flourished for several centuries. But when the island was desecrated by a mass of Western foreigners, the chief Lohans left for the mountains of———. In the Pagoda of Pi-yun-si, near Pekin, one can still see the "Hall of the Five-hundred Lohans." There the statues of the first-comers are arranged below, while one solitary Lohan is placed quite under the roof of the building, which seems to have been built in commemoration of their visit.

The works of the Orientalists are full of the direct landmarks of Arhats (Adepts), possessed of thaumaturgic powers, but these are spoken of—whenever the subject cannot be avoided—with unconcealed scorn. Whether innocently ignorant of, or purposely ignoring, the importance of the Occult element and symbology in the various Religions they undertake to explain, short work is generally made of such passages, and they are left untranslated. In simple justice, however, it should be allowed that much as all such miracles may have been exaggerated by popular reverence and fancy, they are neither less credible nor less attested in "heathen" annals than are those of the

* The chanting of a Mantra is not a prayer, but rather a magical sentence in which the [illegible] Occult causation connects itself with, and depends on, the will and acts of its singer. It is a succession of Sanskrit sounds, and when its string of words and sentences is pronounced according to the magical formulæ in the *Atharva Veda*, but understood by the few, some Mantras produce an instantaneous and very wonderful effect. In its esoteric sense it contains the Vâch (the "mystic speech"), which resides in the Mantra, or rather in its sounds, since it is according to the vibrations, one way or the other, of ether that the effect is produced. The "sweet singers" were called by that name because they were experts in Mantras. Hence the legend in China that the singing and melody of the Lohans are heard at dawn by the priests from their cells in the monastery of Fang-Kwang. (See *Biography of Chi-Kai* in Tien-tai-nan-tchi.)

† The celebrated Lohan, Mâdhyantika, who converted the king and whole country of Kashmir to Buddhism, sent a body of Lohans to preach the Good Law. He was the sculptor who raised to Buddha the famous statue one hundred feet high, which Hiuen-Tsaung saw at Darda, to the north of the Punjab. As the same Chinese traveller mentions a temple ten Li from Peshawur—150 feet wide and 670 feet high—which was at his time (A.D. 550) already 850 years old, Koeppen thinks that so far back as 400 B.C. Buddhism was the prevalent religion in the Punjab.

numerous Christian Saints in the church chronicles. Both have an equal right to a place in their respective histories.

If, after the beginning of persecution against Buddhism, the Arhats were no more heard of in India, it was because, their vows prohibiting retaliation, they had to leave the country and seek solitude and security in China, Tibet, Japan, and elsewhere. The sacerdotal powers of the Brâhmans being at that time unlimited, the Simons and Apolloniuses of Buddhism had as much chance of recognition and appreciation by the Brâhmanical Irenæuses and Tertullians as had their successors in the Judæan and Roman worlds. It was a historical rehearsal of the dramas that were enacted centuries later in Christendom. As in the case of the so-called "Heresiarchs" of Christianity, it was not for rejecting the *Vedas* or the sacred Syllable that the Buddhist Arhats were persecuted, but for understanding too well the secret meaning of both. It was simply because their knowledge was regarded as dangerous and their presence in India unwelcome, that they had to emigrate.

Nor were there a smaller number of Initiates among the Brâhmans themselves. Even to-day one meets most wonderfully-gifted Sâddhus and Yogis, obliged to keep themselves unnoticed and in the shadow, not only owing to the absolute secresy imposed upon them at their Initiation but also for fear of the Anglo-Indian tribunals and courts of law, wherein judges are determined to regard as charlatanry, imposition, and fraud, the exhibition of, or claim to, any abnormal powers, and one may judge of the past by the present. Centuries after our era the Initiates of the inner temples and the Mathams (monastic communities) chose a superior council, presided over by an all-powerful Brahm-Âtmâ, the Supreme Chief of all those Mahâtmâs. This pontificate could be exercised only by a Brâhman who had reached a certain age, and he it was who was the sole guardian of the mystic formula, and he was the Hierophant who created great Adepts. He alone could explain the meaning of the sacred word, AUM, and of all the religious symbols and rites. And whosoever among those Initiates of the Supreme Degree revealed to a profane a single one of the truths, even the smallest of the secrets entrusted to him, had to die; and he who received the confidence was put to death.

But there existed, and still exists to this day, a Word far surpassing the mysterious monosyllable, and which renders him who comes into possession of its key nearly the equal of Brahman. The Brahmâtmâs alone possess this key, and we know that to this day there are two great Initiates in Southern India who possess it. It can be passed on only at death, for it is the "Lost Word." No torture, no human power could force its disclosure by a Brâhman who knows it; and it is still guarded in Tibet.

Yet this secresy and this profound mystery are indeed disheartening since they alone—the Initiates of India and Tibet—could thoroughly dissipate the thick mists hanging over the history of Occultism, and force its claims to be recognized. The Delphic injunction, "*Know thyself*," seems for the few in this age. But the fault ought not to be laid at the door of the Adepts, who have done all that could be done and have gone as far as Their rules permitted, to open the eyes of the world. Only while the European shrinks from public obloquy and the ridicule unsparingly thrown on Occultists, the Asiatic is being discouraged by his own Pandits. These profess to labour under the gloomy impression that no Bîga Vidyâ, no Arhatship (Adeptship), is possible during the Kali Yuga (the "Black Age") we are now passing through. Even the Buddhists are taught that the Lord Buddha is alleged to have prophesied that the power would die out in "this millennium after His death." But this is an entire mistake. In the *Dîgha Nikâya* the Buddha says:

> Hear, Subhadra! The world will never be without Rahats, if the ascetics in my congregations well and truly keep my precepts.

A similar contradiction of the view brought forward by the Brâhmans is made by Krishna in the *Bhagavad Gîtâ*, and there is further the actual appearance of many Sâdhus and miracle-workers in the past, and even in the present age. The same holds good for China and Tibet. Among the commandments of Tsong-Kha-pa there is one that enjoins the Rahats (Arhats) to make an attempt to enlighten the world, including the "white barbarians," every century, at a certain specified period of the cycle. Up to the present day none of these attempts has been very successful. Failure has followed failure. Have we to explain the fact by the light of a certain prophecy? It is said that up to the time when Phan-chhen-rin-po-chhe (the Great Jewel of Wisdom)* condescends to be reborn in the land of the P'helings (Westerners), and appearing as the Spiritual Conqueror (Chom-den-da), destroys the errors and ignorance of the ages, it will be of little use to try to uproot the misconceptions

* A title of the Tda-shu-Hlum-po Lama.

of P'heling-pa (Europe) : her sons will listen to no one. Another prophecy declares that the Secret Doctrine shall remain in all its purity in Bhod-yul (Tibet), only to the day that it is kept free from foreign invasion. The very visits of Western natives, however friendly, would be baneful to the Tibetan populations. This is the true key to Tibetan exclusiveness.

SECTION L.

A FEW MORE MISCONCEPTIONS CORRECTED.

NOTWITHSTANDING widespread misconceptions and errors—often most amusing to one who has a certain knowledge of the true doctrines—about Buddhism generally, and especially about Buddhism in Tibet, all the Orientalists agree that the Buddha's foremost aim was to lead human beings to salvation by teaching them to practise the greatest purity and virtue, and by detaching them from the service of this illusionary world, and the love of one's still more illusionary—because so evanescent and unreal—body and physical self. And what is the good of a virtuous life, full of privations and suffering, if the only result of it is to be annihilation at the end? If even the attainment of that supreme perfection which leads the Initiate to remember the whole series of his past lives, and to foresee that of the future ones, by the full development of that inner, divine eye in him, and to acquire the knowledge that unfolds the causes * of the ever-recurring cycles of existence, brings him finally to non-being, and nothing more—then the whole system is idiotic, and Epicureanism is far more philosophical than such Buddhism. He who is unable to comprehend the subtle, and yet so potent, difference between existence in a material or physical state and a purely spiritual existence—Spirit or "Soul-life"—will never appreciate at their full value the grand teachings of the Buddha, even in their exoteric form. Individual or personal existence is the cause of pains and sorrows; collective and impersonal life-eternal is full of divine bliss and joy for ever, with neither causes nor effects to darken its light. And the hope for such a life-eternal is the keynote of the whole of Buddhism. If we are told that impersonal existence is no existence at all, but amounts to annihilation, as was maintained by some French reincarnationists, then we would ask: What difference can it

---

* The twelve Nidânas, called in Tibetan Tin-brel Chug-nyi, which are based upon the "Four Truths."

make in the spiritual perceptions of an Ego whether he enter Nirvâna loaded with the recollections only of his own personal lives—tens of thousands according to the modern reincarnationists—or whether, merged entirely in the Parabrâhmic state it becomes one with the All, with the absolute knowledge and the absolute feeling of representing collective humanities? Once that an Ego lives only ten distinct individual lives he must necessarily lose his one self, and become mixed up—merged, so to say—with these ten selves. It really seems that so long as this great mystery remains a dead-letter to the world of Western thinkers, and especially to the Orientalists, the less the latter undertake to explain it the better for Truth.

Of all the existing religious Philosophies, Buddhism is the least understood. The Lassens, Webers, Wassiljows, the Burnoufs and Juliens, and even such "eye-witnesses" of Tibetan Buddhism as Csoma de Körös and the Schlagintweits, have hitherto only added perplexity to confusion. None of these has ever received his information from a genuine Gelugpa source: all have judged Buddhism from the bits of knowledge picked up at Tibetan frontier lamaseries, in countries thickly populated by Bhutanese and Leptchas, Bhons, and red-capped Dugpas, along the line of the Himâlayas. Hundreds of volumes purchased from Burats, Shamans, and Chinese Buddhists, have been read and translated, glossed and misinterpreted according to invariable custom. Esoteric Schools would cease to be worthy of their name were their literature and doctrines to become the property of even their profane co-religionists—still less of the Western public. This is simple common-sense and logic. Nevertheless this is a fact which our Orientalists have ever refused to recognize: hence they have gone on, gravely discussing the relative merits and absurdities of idols, "soothsaying tables," and "magical figures of Phurbu" on the "square tortoise." None of these have anything to do with the real philosophical Buddhism of the Gelugpa, or even of the most educated among the Sakyapa and Kadampa sects. All such "plates" and sacrificial tables, Chinsreg magical circles, etc., were avowedly got from Sikkhim, Bhutan, and Eastern Tibet, from Bhons and Dugpas. Nevertheless, these are given as characteristics of Tibetan Buddhism! It would be as fair to judge the unread Philosophy of Bishop Berkeley after studying Christianity in the clown-worship of Neapolitan lazzaroni, dancing a mystic jig before the idol of St. Pip, or carrying the *ex-voto* in wax of the phallus of SS. Cosmo and Domiano, at Tsernie.

It is quite true that the primitive Shrâvakas (listeners or [illegible] the Shramanas (the "thought-restrainers" and the "pious") [illegible] degenerated, and that many Buddhist sects have fallen [illegible] dogmatism and ritualism. Like every other Esoteric, half-[illegible] teaching, the words of the Buddha convey a double meaning [illegible] every sect has gradually come to claim to be the only one [illegible] correct meaning, and thus to assume supremacy over the rest. [illegible] has crept in, and has fastened, like a hideous cancer, on the [illegible] early Buddhism. Nâgârjuna's Mahâyâna ("Great Vehicle") [illegible] was opposed by the Hînayâna (or "Little Vehicle") System, and [illegible] Yogâchârya of Âryâsanga became disfigured by the [illegible] from India to the shores of Mansarovara, of hosts of [illegible] with matted locks who play at being Yogis and Fakirs, pre[illegible] to work. An affected detestation of the world, and the tedious [illegible] useless practice of the counting of inhalations and exhalations [illegible] means to produce absolute tranquillity of mind or meditation, [illegible] brought this school within the region of Hatha Yoga, and [illegible] it heir to the Brâhmanical Tîrthikas. And though its Sro[illegible] Sakridâgâmin, Anâgâmin, and Arhats,* bear the same names [illegible] every school, yet the doctrines of each differ greatly, and none [illegible] is likely to gain real Abhijñâs (the supernatural abnormal five powers [illegible]

One of the chief mistakes of the Orientalists when judging [illegible] "internal (?) evidence," as they express it, was that they assumed [illegible] the Pratyeka Buddhas, the Bodhisattvas, and the "Perfect" [illegible] were a later development of Buddhism. For on these three [illegible] degrees are based the seven and twelve degrees of the Hierarchy of Adeptship. The first are those who have attained the Bodhi (wisdom) of the Buddhas, but do not become Teachers.† The human Bodhisattvas are candidates, so to say, for perfect Buddhaship (in Kalpas to come) and with the option of using their powers now if need be. "Perfect [illegible]

---

* The Srotâpatti is one who has attained the *first* Path of comprehension in the [illegible] unreal; the Sakridâgâmin is the candidate for one of the higher Initiations: "one who is to [illegible] birth once more;" the Anâgâmin is he who has attained the "third Path," or literally, "he [illegible] not be reborn again" *unless he so wishes it*, having the option of being reborn in any of the "[illegible] of the Gods," or of remaining in Devachan, or of choosing an earthly body with a [illegible] object. An Arhat is one who has reached the highest Path; he may merge into Nirvâna [illegible] here on earth.

† [The Pratyeka Buddha stands on the level of the Buddha, but His work for the world [illegible] ing to do with its teaching, and His office has always been surrounded with mystery. [illegible] terous view that He, at such superhuman height of power, wisdom and love could be [illegible] in the exoteric books, though it is hard to see how it can have arisen. H. P. B. [illegible] correct the mistake, as she had, in a careless moment, copied such a statement [illegible]

Buddhas are simply "perfect" Initiates. All these are men, and not disembodied Beings, as is given out in the Hînayâna exoteric books. Their correct character may be found only in the secret volumes of Lugrub or Nâgârjuna, the founder of the Mahâyâna system, who is said to have been initiated by the Nâgas (fabulous "Serpents," the veiled name for an Initiate or Mahâtmâ). The fabled report found in Chinese records that Nâgârjuna considered his doctrine to be in opposition to that of Gautama Buddha, until he discovered from the Nâgas that it was precisely the doctrine that had been secretly taught by Shâkyamuni Himself, is an allegory, and is based upon the reconciliation between the old Brâhmanical secret Schools in the Himâlayas and Gautama's Esoteric teachings, both parties having at first objected to the rival schools of the other. The former, the parent of all others, had been established beyond the Himâlayas for ages before the appearance of Shâkyamuni. Gautama was a pupil of this; and it was with them, those Indian Sages, that He had learned the truths of the Sungata, the emptiness and impermanence of every terrestrial, evanescent thing, and the mysteries of Prajñâ Pâramitâ, or "knowledge across the River," which finally lands the "Perfect One" in the regions of the One Reality. But His Arhats were not Himself. Some of them were ambitious, and they modified certain teachings after the great councils, and it is on account of these "heretics" that the Mother-School at first refused to allow them to blend their schools, when persecution began driving away the Esoteric Brotherhood from India. But when finally most of them submitted to the guidance and control of the chief Âshrams, then the Yogâchârya of Âryâsanga was merged into the oldest Lodge. For it is *there* from time immemorial that has lain concealed the final hope and light of the world, the salvation of mankind. Many are the names of that School and land, the name of the latter being now regarded by the Orientalists as the mythic name of a fabulous country. It is from this mysterious land, nevertheless, that the Hindu expects his Kalki Avatâra, the Buddhist his Maitreya, the Pârsî his Sosiosh, and the Jew his Messiah, and so would the Christian expect thence his Christ—if he only knew of it.

There, and there alone, reigns Paranishpanna (Gunggrub), the absolutely perfect comprehension of Being and Non-Being, the changeless true Existence in Spirit, even while the latter is seemingly still in the body, every inhabitant thereof being a Non-Ego because he has become the Perfect Ego. Their voidness is "self-existent and perfect"

—if there were profane eyes to sense and perceive [illegible] become absolute; the unreal being transformed into [illegible] Reality, and the realities of this, our world, having vanished [illegible] own nature into thin (non-existing) air. The "Absolute [illegible]" (Dondam-pay-den-pa; Sanskrit: Paramârthasatya), having [illegible] "relative truth" (Kunza-bchi-den-pa; Sanskrit: Samvritisatya) [illegible] inhabitants of the mysterious region are thus supposed to have [illegible] the state called in mystic phraseology Svasamvedana ("self-analysing reflection") and Paramârtha, or that absolute consciousness [illegible] personal merged into the impersonal Ego, which is above all [illegible] above illusion in every sense. Its "Perfect" Buddhas and Bodhisattvas may be on every nimble Buddhist tongue as celestial [illegible] unreachable Beings, while these names may suggest and say nothing [illegible] the dull perceptions of the European profane. What matters it to [illegible] who, being in this world, yet live outside and far beyond our [illegible] earth! Above Them there is but one class of Nirvânîs, [illegible] the Chos-ku (Dharmakâya), or the Nirvânîs "without remains" [illegible] pure Arûpa, the formless Breaths.*

Thence emerge occasionally the Bodhisattvas in their Prul-pa-ku (or Nirmânakâya) body and, assuming an ordinary appearance, [illegible] teach men. There are conscious, as well as unconscious, incarnations [illegible]

Most of the doctrines contained in the Yogâchârya, or [illegible] systems are Esoteric, like the rest. One day the profane Hindu [illegible] Buddhist may begin to pick the *Bible* to pieces, taking it [illegible] Education is fast spreading in Asia, and already there have been [illegible] some attempts in this direction, so that the tables may then be [illegible] turned on the Christians. Whatever conclusions the two may [illegible] at, they will never be half as absurd and unjust as some of the [illegible] launched by Christians against their respective Philosophies. [illegible] according to Spence Hardy, at death the Arhat enters Nirvâna, [illegible]

That is, he ceases to exist.

And, agreeably to Major Jacob, the Jîvanmukta, [illegible]

* It is an erroneous idea which makes the Orientalists take literally the teaching of the [illegible] School about the three different kinds of bodies, namely, the Prulpa-ku, the Longchod-[illegible], and the Chos-ku, as all pertaining to the Nirvânic condition. There are two kinds of [illegible] earthly, and that of the purely disembodied Spirits. These three "bodies" are the [illegible] all more or less physical—which are at the disposal of the Adept who has entered and [illegible] six Pâramitâs, or "Paths" of Buddha. Once He enters upon the seventh, He can [illegible] earth. See Csoma, *Jour. As. Soc. Beng.*, vii. 142; and Schott, *Buddhismus*, p. 9, [illegible] wise.

Absorbed into Brahma, enters upon an unconscious and stonelike existence.*

Shankarâchârya is shown as saying in his prolegomena to the *Shvetâshvatara*:

Gnosis, once arisen, requires nothing farther for the realization of its result: it needs *subsidia* only that it may arise.

The Theosophist, it has been argued, as long as he lives, may do good and evil as he chooses, and incur no stain, such is the efficacy of gnosis. And it is further alleged that the doctrine of Nirvâna lends itself to immoral inferences, and that the Quietists of all ages have been taxed with immorality.†

According to Wassilyew‡ and Csoma de Köros,§ the Prasanga School adopted a peculiar mode of

Deducing the absurdity and erroneousness of every esoteric opinion.‖

Correct interpretations of Buddhist Philosophy are crowned by that gloss on a thesis from the Prasanga School, that

Even an Arhat goes to hell in case he doubt anything,¶

thus making of the most free-thinking religion in the world a blind-faith system. The "threat" refers simply to the well-known law that even an Initiate may fail, and thus have his object utterly ruined, if he doubt for one moment the efficacy of his psychic powers—the alphabet of Occultism, as every Kabalist well knows.

The Tibetan sect of the Ngo-vo-nyid-med par Mraba ("they who deny existence," or "regard nature as Mâyâ")** can never be contrasted for one moment with some of the nihilistic or materialistic schools of India, such as the Chârvâka. They are pure Vedântins—if anything—in their views. And if the Yogâchâryas may be compared with, or called the Tibetan Vishishtadwaitis, the Prasanga School is surely the Adwaita Philosophy of the land. It was divided into two: one was originally founded by Bhavya, the Svantatra Madhyamika School, and the other by Buddhapâlita; both have their exoteric and esoteric divisions. It is necessary to belong to the latter to know anything of the

* *Vedânta Sâra*, translated by Major Jacob, p. 119.

† *Ibid.*, p. 122.

‡ *Der Buddhismus*, pp. 327, 357, *et seq.*, quoted by Schlagintweit.

§ *Buddhism in Tibet*, p. 41.

‖ *Jour. of As. Soc. Bengal*, vii. 144, quoted as above.

¶ *Buddhism in Tibet*, p. 44.

** They maintain also the existence of One Absolute pure Nature, Parabrahman; the illusion of everything outside of it; the leading of the individual Soul—a Ray of the "Universal"—into the true nature of existence and things by Yoga alone.

esoteric doctrines of that sect, the most metaphysical and [illegible] of all. Chandrakirti (Dava Dagpa) wrote his commentaries [illegible] Prasanga doctrines and taught publicly; and he expressly [illegible] there are two ways of entering the "Path" to Nirvâna. [illegible] man can reach by Naljorngonsum ("meditation by self-[illegible] the intuitive comprehension of the four Truths, without either [illegible]ing to a monastic order or having been initiated. In this [illegible] considered as a heresy to maintain that the visions which may [illegible] consequence of such meditation, or Vishnâ (internal knowled[illegible] not susceptible of errors (Namtog or false visions), for they are [illegible] alone having an absolute and eternal existence, can alone have [illegible] knowledge; and even the Initiate, in his Nirmânakâya* body, ma[illegible] mit an occasional mistake in accepting the false for the true in [illegible] plorations of the "Causeless" World. The Dharmakâya Bod[illegible] is alone infallible, when in real Samâdhi. Âlaya, or Ny[illegible] being the root and basis of all, invisible and incomprehensi[illegible] human eye and intellect, it can reflect only its reflection—not [illegible] Thus that reflection will be mirrored like the moon in tranquil [illegible] clear water only in the passionless Dharmakâya intellect, and [illegible] distorted by the flitting image of everything perceived in a mind [illegible] is itself liable to be disturbed.

In short, this doctrine is that of the Râj-Yoga in its practice of [illegible] two kinds of the Samâdhi state; one of the "Paths" leading to [illegible] sphere of bliss (Sukhâvati or Devachan), where man enjoys pe[illegible] unalloyed happiness, but is yet still connected with personal existe[illegible] and the other the Path that leads to entire emancipation from the worlds of illusion, self, and unreality. The first one is open to all [illegible] is reached by merit simply; the second—a hundredfold more [illegible] is reached through knowledge (Initiation). Thus the followers of the Prasanga School are nearer to Esoteric Buddhism than are the [illegible]châryas; for their views are those of the most secret Schools, and [illegible] the echo of these doctrines is heard in the *Yamyangshapda* and other works in public circulation and use. For instance, the unreality of two out of the three divisions of time is given in public works, namely (s) that there is neither past nor future, both of these divisions being

---

* Nirmânakâya (also Nirvânakâya, vulg.) is the body or Self "with remains," or the [illegible] terrestrial attributes, however spiritualised, clinging yet to that Self. An Initiate in [illegible] or in Nirvâna "without remains," is the Jîvanmukta, the Perfect Initiate, who separates [illegible] Self entirely from his body during Samâdhi. [It will be noticed that these two [illegible] used in a sense other than that previously given.—A. B.]

correlative to the present; and (*b*) that the reality of things can never be sensed or perceived except by him who has obtained the Dharmakâya body; here again is a difficulty, since this body "without remains" carries the Initiate to full Paranirvâna, if we accept the exoteric explanation verbally, and can therefore neither sense nor perceive. But evidently our Orientalists do not feel the *caveat* in such incongruities, and they proceed to speculate without pausing to reflect over it. Literature on Mysticism being enormous, and Russia, owing to the free intercourse with the Burats, Shamans, and Mongolians, having alone purchased whole libraries on Tibet, scholars ought to know better by this time. It suffices to read, however, what Csoma wrote on the origin of the Kâla Chakra System,* or Wassilyew on Buddhism, to make one give up every hope of seeing them go below the rind of the "forbidden fruit." When Schlagintweit is found saying that Tibetan Mysticism is not Yoga—

> That abstract devotion by which supernatural powers are acquired,†

as Yoga is defined by Wilson, but that it is closely related to Siberian Shamanism, and is "almost identical with the Tântrika ritual"; and that the Tibetan *Zung* is the "*Dhâranis*," and the *Gyut* only the *Tantras*—pre-Christian Tantra being judged by the ritual of the modern Tântrikas—one seems almost justified in suspecting our materialistic Orientalists of acting as the best friends and allies of the missionaries. Whatever is not known to our geographers seems to be a non-existent locality. Thus:

> Mysticism is reported to have originated in the fabulous country, Sambhala. . . . . Csoma, from *careful* investigations, places this [fabulous ?] country beyond the Sir Daria [Yaxartes] between 45° and 50° north latitude. It was first known in India in the year 965 A.D., and was introduced . . . into Tibet from India, *viâ* Kashmir, in the year 1025 A.D.‡

"It" meaning the "Dus-kyi Khorlo," or Tibetan Mysticism. A system as old as man, known in India and practised before Europe had become a continent, "was first known," we are told, only nine or ten centuries ago! The text of its books in its present form may have "originated" even later, for there are numerous such texts that have been tampered with by sects to suit the fancies of each. But who has read

* The "Sacred" Books of Dus-Kyi Khorlo ("Time Circle"). See *Jour. As. Soc.*, ii. 57. These works were abandoned to the Sikkhim Dugpas, from the time of Tsong-Kha-pa's reform.

† *Glossary of Judicial and Revenue Terms*, art. "Yoga," quoted in *Buddhism in Tibet*, p. 47.

‡ *Buddhism in Tibet*, pp. 47, 48.

the original book on Dus-Kyi Khorlo, re-written by Tsong-Kha-pa, with his Commentaries? Considering that this grand Reformer burnt every book on Sorcery on which he could lay his hands in 1387, and that he has left a whole library of his own works—not a tenth part of which has ever been made known—such statements as those above quoted are, to say the least, premature. The idea is also cherished by the happy hypothesis offered by Abbé Huc—that Tsong-Kha-pa derived his wisdom and acquired his extraordinary powers from his intercourse with a stranger from the West, "remarkable for a long nose." This stranger is believed by the good Abbé "to have been a European missionary"; hence the remarkable resemblance of the religious ritual of Tibet to the Roman Catholic service. The sanguine "Lama of Jehovah" does not say, however, who were the five foreigners who appeared in Tibet in the year 371 of our era, to disappear as suddenly and mysteriously as they came, after leaving with King Thothori-Nyang-tsan instructions how to use certain things in a casket that "had fallen from heaven" in his presence precisely fifty years before, or in the year A.D. 331.*

There is generally a hopeless confusion about Eastern dates among European scholars, but nowhere is this so great as in the case of Tibetan Buddhism. Thus, while some, correctly enough, accept the seventh century as the date of the introduction of Buddhism, there are others—such as Lassen and Koeppung, for instance—who show as good authority, the one, the construction of a Buddhist monastery on the slopes of the Kailas Range so far back as the year 137 B.C.,† and the other, Buddhism established in and north of the Punjab, as early as the year 292 B.C. The difference though trifling—only just one thousand years—is nevertheless puzzling. But even this is easily explained on Esoteric grounds. Buddhism—the veiled Esotericism of Buddha—was established and took root in the seventh century of the Christian era; while true Esoteric Buddhism, or the kernel, the very spirit of Tathâgata's doctrines, was brought to the place of its birth, the cradle of humanity, by the chosen Arhats of Buddha, who were sent to find for it a secure refuge, as

* *Buddhism in Tibet*, pp. 63, 64. The objects found in the casket, as enumerated in the mystic legend, are of course symbolical. They may be found mentioned in the *Kanjur*. They were said to be: (1) two hands joined; (2) a miniature Choten (Stûpa, or reliquary); (3) a talisman with "Om mani padme hum" inscribed on it; (4) a religious book, *Zamatog* ("a constructed vehicle") . . .

† *Alterthumskunde*, ii. 1072.

The Sage had perceived the dangers ever since he had entered upon Thonglam ("the Path of seeing," or clairvoyance).

Amidst populations deeply steeped in Sorcery the attempt proved a failure; and it was not until the School of the "Doctrine of the Heart" had merged with its predecessor, established ages earlier on the slope facing Western Tibet, that Buddhism was finally engrafted, with its two distinct Schools—the Esoteric and the exoteric divisions—in the land of the Bhon-pa.

SECTION II.

THE "DOCTRINE OF THE EYE" & THE "DOCTRINE OF THE HEART," OR THE "HEART'S SEAL."

PROFESSOR ALBRECHT WEBER was right when he declared that the Northern Buddhists

> Alone possess these [Buddhist] Scriptures complete.

For, while the Southern Buddhists have no idea of the existence of an Esoteric Doctrine—enshrined like a pearl within the shell of every religion—the Chinese and the Tibetans have preserved numerous records of the fact. Degenerate, fallen as is now the Doctrine publicly preached by Gautama, it is yet preserved in those monasteries in China that are placed beyond the reach of visitors. And though for over two millennia every new "reformer," taking something out of the original, has replaced it by some speculation of his own, still truth lingers even now among the masses. But it is only in the Trans-Himalayan fastnesses—loosely called Tibet—in the most inaccessible spots of desert and mountain, that the Esoteric "Good Law"—the "Heart's Seal"—lives to the present day in all its pristine purity.

Was Emanuel Swedenborg wrong when he remarked of the forgotten long-lost Word:

> Seek for it in China; peradventure you may find it in Great Tartary.

He had obtained this information, he tells his readers, from certain "Spirits," who told him that they performed their worship according to this (lost) ancient Word. On this it was remarked in *Isis Unveiled* that

> Other students of Occult Sciences had more than the word of "spirits" to rely upon in this special case: they have seen the books

that contain the "Word."* Perchance the names of those "Spirits" who visited the great Swedish Theosophist were Eastern. The word of a man of such undeniable and recognised integrity, of one whose learning in Mathematics, Astronomy, the natural Sciences and Philosophy was far in advance of his age, cannot be trifled with or rejected as unceremoniously as if it were the statement of a modern Theosophist; further, he claimed to pass at will into that state when the Inner Self frees itself entirely from every physical sense, and lives and breathes in a world where every secret of Nature is an open book to the Soul-eye.† Unfortunately two-thirds of his public writings are also allegorical in one sense; and, as they have been accepted literally, criticism has not spared the great Swedish Seer any more than other Seers.

Having taken a panoramic view of the hidden Sciences and Magic with their Adepts in Europe, Eastern Initiates must now be mentioned. If the presence of Esotericism in the Sacred Scriptures of the West only now begins to be suspected, after nearly two thousand years of blind faith in their *verbatim* wisdom, the same may well be granted as to the Sacred Books of the East. Therefore neither the Indian nor the Buddhist system can be understood without a key, nor can the study of comparative Religion become a "Science" until the symbols of every Religion yield their final secrets. At the best such a study will remain a loss of time, a playing at hide-and-seek.

On the authority of a Japanese *Encyclopædia*, Remusat shows the Buddha, before His death, committing the secrets of His system to His disciple, Kâsyapa, to whom alone was entrusted the sacred keeping of the Esoteric interpretation. It is called in China *Ching-fa-yin-Tsang* ("the Mystery of the Eye of the Good Doctrine"). To any student of Buddhist Esotericism the term, "the Mystery of the Eye," would show the absence of any Esotericism. Had the word "Heart" stood in its place, then it would have meant what it now only professes to convey. The "Eye Doctrine" means dogma and dead-letter form, church ritualism intended for those who are content with exoteric formulæ. The "Heart Doctrine," or the "Heart's Seal" (the Sin Yin), is the only real one. This may be found corroborated by Hiuen Tsang.

* *Op. cit.*, ii. 470.

† Unless one obtains exact information and the right method, one's visions, however correct and true in Soul-life, will ever fail to get photographed in our human memory, and certain cells of the brain are sure to play havoc with our remembrances.

In his translation of *Mahâ-Prajnâ-Pâramitâ* ([illegible] hundred and twenty volumes, it is stated that it was Buddha's [illegible] disciple Ânanda," who, after his great Master had gone into [illegible] was commissioned by Kâsyapa to promulgate "the Eye of the [illegible] trine," the "Heart" of the Law having been left with [illegible] alone.

The essential difference that exists between the two—the "Eye," [illegible] the "Heart," or the outward form and the hidden meaning [illegible] metaphysics and the Divine Wisdom—is clearly demonstrated [illegible] several volumes on "Chinese Buddhism," written by [illegible] sionaries. Having lived for years in China, they still know [illegible] than they have learned from pretentious schools calling themselves esoteric, yet freely supplying the open enemies of their faith with [illegible] fessedly ancient manuscripts and esoteric works! This [illegible] tradiction between profession and practice has never, as it [illegible] struck any of the western and reverend historians of other [illegible] secret tenets. Thus many esoteric schools are mentioned in *Chinese Buddhism* by the Rev. Joseph Edkins, who believes quite sincerely [illegible] he has made "a minute examination" of the secret tenets of [illegible] whose works "were until lately inaccessible in their original [illegible]" It really will not be saying too much to state at once that the genuine Esoteric literature is "inaccessible" to this day, and that the [illegible] able gentleman who was inspired to state that

> It does not appear that there was any secret doctrine which those who [illegible] would not divulge,

made a great mistake if he ever believed in what he says on page [illegible] of his work. Let him know at once that all those Yü-luh ("[illegible] of the Sayings") of celebrated teachers are simply blinds, as [illegible] —if not more so—than those in the Purânas of the Brâhmans. [illegible] useless to enumerate an endless string of the finest Oriental [illegible] or to bring forward the researches of Remusat, Burnouf, Koeppen, [illegible] Hilaire, and St. Julian, who are credited with having exposed, to view, the ancient Hindu world, by revealing the sacred and secret books of Buddhism: the world that they reveal has never been veiled. The mistakes of all the Orientalists may be judged by the mistake of one of the most popular, if not the greatest among them all—Prof. Max Müller. It is made with reference to what he laughingly translates as the "god Who" (Ka).

The authors of the Brâhmanas had so completely broken with the past, that, forgetful of the poetical character of the hymns and the yearning of the poets after the Unknown God, they exalted the interrogative pronoun itself into a deity, and acknowledged a god Ka (or Who?) . . . Wherever interrogative verses occur the author states that Ka is Prajâpati, or the Lord of Creatures. Nor did they stop here. Some of the hymns in which the interrogative pronoun occurred were called Kadvat, *i.e.*, having Kad or Quid. But soon a new adjective was formed, and not only the hymns but the sacrifice also offered to the god were called Kaya, or "Who"-ish. . . . At the time of Pânini this word acquired such legitimacy as to call for a separate rule explaining its formation. The Commentator here explains Ka by Brahman.

Had the commentator explained It even by Parabrahman he would have been still more in the right than he was by rendering It as "Brahman." One fails to see why the secret and sacred Mystery-Name of the highest, sexless, formless Spirit, the Absolute,—Whom no one would have dared to classify with the rest of the manifested Deities, or even to name during the primitive nomenclature of the symbolical Panthenon, should not be expressed by an interrogative pronoun. Is it those who belong to the most anthropomorphic Religion in the world who have a right to take ancient Philosophers to task for even an exaggerated religious awe and veneration?

But we are now concerned with Buddhism. Its Esotericism and oral instruction, which is written down and preserved in single copies by the highest chiefs in genuine Esoteric Schools, is shown by the author San-Kian-yi-su. Contrasting Bodhidharma with Buddha, he exclaims:

"Julai" (Tathâgata) taught great truths and the causes of things. He became the instructor of men and Devas. He saved multitudes, and spoke the contents of more than five hundred works. Hence arose the Kiau-men, or exoteric branch of the system, and it was believed to be the tradition of the *words* of Buddha. Bodhidharma brought from the Western Heaven [Shamballa] the "Seal of Truth" (true seal) and opened the fountain of contemplation in the East. He pointed directly to Buddha's heart and nature, swept away the parasitic and alien growth of book-instruction, and thus established the Tsung-men, or Esoteric branch of the system containing the tradition of the heart of Buddha.*

A few remarks made by the author of *Chinese Buddhism* throw a flood of light on the universal misconceptions of Orientalists in general, and

* *Chinese Buddhism*, p. 158. The Rev. Joseph Edkins either ignores, or—which is more probable—is utterly ignorant of the real existence of such Schools, and judges by the Chinese travesties of these, calling such Esotericism "heterodox Buddhism." And so it is, in one sense.

of the missionaries in the "lands of the Gentiles," in particular, they appeal very forcibly to the intuition of Theosophists—more particularly of those in India. The sentences to be noticed are italicised.

The common [Chinese] word for the esoteric Schools is *tsung*, the Sanskrit [illegible] . . . Orthodox Buddhism has in China slowly but steadily [illegible] The Buddhism of books and ancient traditions *has become the Buddhism of* [illegible] *contemplation*. . . . The history of ancient schools springing up long ago [illegible] Buddhist communities of India *can now be only very partially recovered*. [illegible] some light may be thrown back by China upon the religious history of the [illegible] from which Buddhism came.* In no part of the story is aid to the recovery of [illegible] lost knowledge more likely to be found than in the accounts of the patriarchs, [illegible] line of whom was completed by Bodhidharma. In seeking the best explanation [illegible] the Chinese and Japanese narrative of the patriarchs, and the [illegible] terminating in Gautama, or Shâkyamuni, it is important to know the [illegible] tions as they were early in the sixth century of our era, when the Patriarch Bodhi-dharma removed to China. . . .

In tracing the rise of the various schools of esoteric Buddhism it must be [illegible] mind that a principle somewhat similar to the dogma of apostolical succession belongs to them all. They all profess *to derive their doctrines through a* [illegible] *of teachers, each instructed personally by his predecessor, till the time of* [illegible] *dharma, and so further up in the series to Shâkyamuni himself and the* [illegible] *Buddhas.*†

It is complained further on, and is mentioned as a falling away from strict orthodox Buddhism, that *the Lamas of Tibet are received in* [illegible] *with the utmost respect* by the Emperor.

The following passages, taken from different parts of the book, summarise Mr. Edkins' views:

Hermits are not uncommonly met with in the vicinity of large Buddhist temples . . . their hair being allowed to grow unshorn. . . . The doctrine of metem-psychosis is rejected. Buddhism is one form of Pantheism on the ground that the doctrine of metempsychosis makes all nature instinct with life, and that [illegible] the Deity assuming different forms of personality, that Deity not being a self-conscious, free-acting Self-Cause, but an all-pervading Spirit. The esoteric Buddhists of China, keeping rigidly to their one doctrine,‡ say nothing of the metempsychosis, [illegible] or any other of the more material parts of the Buddhist system. . . . The Western paradise promised to the worshippers of Amida Buddha is . . . [illegible]

---

* That country—India—has lost the records of such Schools and their teachings only so far as the general public, and especially the inappreciative Western Orientalists, are concerned. It has preserved them in full in some Mathams (refuges for mystic contemplation). But it may perhaps be better to seek them with, and from, their rightful owners, the so-called "mythical" Adepts, or Mahâtmas.

† *Chinese Buddhism*, pp. 155-159.

‡ They certainly reject most emphatically the popular theory of the transmigration of human entities or Souls *into* animals, but not the evolution of men *from* animals—so far, at least, as their lower principles are concerned.

sistent with the doctrine of Nirvana [?].* . . . *It promises immortality* instead of annihilation. The great antiquity of this School is evident from the early date of the translation of the *Amida Sûtra*, which came from the hands of Kumârajiva, and the *Ku-liang-shou-King*, dating from the Han dynasty. Its extent of influence is seen in the attachment of the Tibetans and Moguls to the worship of this Buddha, and in the fact that the name of this fictitious personage [?] is more commonly heard in China than that of the historical Shâkyamuni.

We fear the learned writer is on a false track as to Nirvâna and Amita Buddha. However, here we have the evidence of a missionary to show that there are several schools of Esoteric Buddhism in the Celestial Empire. When the misuse of dogmatical orthodox Buddhist Scriptures had reached its climax, and the true spirit of the Buddha's Philosophy was nearly lost, several reformers appeared from India, who established an oral teaching. Such were Bodhidharma and Nâgârjuna, the authors of the most important works of the contemplative School in China during the first centuries of our era. It is known, moreover, as is said in *Chinese Buddhism*, that Bodhidharma became the chief founder of the Esoteric Schools, which were divided into five principal branches. The data given are correct enough, but every conclusion, without one single exception, is wrong. It was said in *Isis Unveiled* that—

Buddha teaches the doctrine of a new birth as plainly as Jesus does. Desiring to break with the ancient Mysteries, to which it was impossible to admit the ignorant masses, the Hindu reformer, though generally silent upon more than one secret dogma, clearly states his thought in several passages. Thus, he says: "*Some people are born again*; evil-doers go to hell [Avitchi]; righteous people go to heaven [Devachan]; those who are free from all worldly desires enter Nirvâna." (*Precepts of the Dhammapada*, v. 126). Elsewhere Buddha states that "it is better to believe in a future life, in which happiness or misery can be felt: for if the heart believes therein it will abandon sin and act virtuously; and even if there is no resurrection [rebirth], such a life will bring a good name and the reward of men. But those who believe in extinction at death will not fail to commit any sin that they may choose, because of their disbelief in a future." (See *Wheel of the Law*.)

How is immortality, then, "inconsistent with the doctrine of

---

* It is quite consistent, on the contrary, when explained in the light of the Esoteric Doctrine. The "Western paradise," or Western heaven, is no fiction located in transcendental space. It is a *bonâ-fide* locality in the mountains, or, to be more correct, one encircled in a desert within mountains. Hence it is assigned for the residence of those students of Esoteric Wisdom—disciples of Buddha—who have attained the rank of Lohans and Anâgâmins (Adepts). It is called "Western" simply from geographical considerations; and "the great iron mountain girdle" that surrounds the Avitchi, and the seven Lokas that encircle the "Western paradise" are a very exact representation of well-known localities and things to the Eastern student of Occultism.

Nirvâna?" The above are only a few of Buddha's openly [illegible] thoughts to his chosen Arhats; the great Saint said much [illegible] comment upon the mistaken views held in our century by the [illegible] ists, "who vainly try to fathom Tathâgata's thoughts," and [illegible] Brâhmans, "who repudiate the great Teacher to this day." [illegible] some original thoughts expressed in relation to the Buddha [illegible] study of the Secret Sciences. They are from a work written in [illegible] by a Tibetan, and published in the monastery of Tientai for [illegible] among the Buddhists

Who live in foreign lands, and are in danger of being spoiled by [illegible]

as the author truly says, every convert being not only "spoiled" [illegible] his own creed, but being also a sorry acquisition for Christianity [illegible] translation of a few passages, kindly made from that work for the [illegible] sent volumes is now given.

No profane ears having heard the mighty Chan-yan [secret and [illegible] *precepts*] of Vu-vei-Tchen-jen [Buddha *within* Buddha],* of our beloved [illegible] Bodhisattva, how can one tell what his thoughts really were? The holy [illegible] Panchhen† never offered an insight into the *One Reality* to the unreformed [illegible] tiated] Bhikkus. Few are those even among the Tu-fon [Tibetans] who [illegible] as for the Tsung-men‡ Schools, they are going with every day more [illegible] . . . . . Not even the Fa-siong-Tsung§ can give one the wisdom taught [illegible] Naljor-chod-pa [Sanskrit:‖ Yogâchârya]: . . . . it is all "Eye" Doctrine [illegible] more. The loss of a restraining guidance is felt, since the Tch'-an-si [teachers] [illegible] inward meditation [self-contemplation or Tchang-kwan] have become rare, and the Good Law is replaced by idol-worship [Siang-kyan]. It is of this [idol- or [illegible] worship] that the Barbarians [Western people] have heard, and know nothing of Bas-pa-Dharma [the secret Dharma or doctrine]. Why has truth to hide, [illegible] tortoise within its shell? Because it is now found to have become like the [illegible] tonsure knife,¶ a weapon too dangerous to use even for the Lanoo. Therefore [illegible] one can be entrusted with the knowledge [Secret Science] before his time. [illegible]

---

* The word is translated by the Orientalists as "true man without a position," (?) which [illegible] misleading. It simply means the true inner man, or Ego, "Buddha *within* Buddha" meaning [illegible] there was a Gautama *inwardly* as well as *outwardly*.

† One of the titles of Gautama Buddha in Tibet.

‡ The "Esoteric" Schools, or sects, of which there are many in China.

§ A school of contemplation founded by Hiuen-Tsang, the traveller, nearly extinct. [illegible] Tsung means "the School that unveils the inner nature of things."

‖ Esoteric, or hidden, teaching of Yoga (Chinese: Yogi-mi-keau).

¶ The "tonsure knife" is made of *meteoric* iron, and is used for the purpose of cutting [illegible] "vow-lock," or hair from the novice's head during his first ordination. It has a [illegible] blade, is sharp as a razor, and lies concealed within a hollow handle of horn. By touching [illegible] the blade jerks out like a flash of lightning, and recedes back with the same rapidity. [illegible] dexterity is required in using it without wounding the head of the young Gelung and [illegible] (candidates to become priests and nuns) during the preliminary rites, which are public.

Chagpa-Thog-mad have become rare, and the best have retired to Tushita the Blessed.*

Further on, a man seeking to master the mysteries of Esotericism before he had been declared by the initiated Tch'-an-si (teachers) to be ready to receive them, is likened to

One who would, without a lantern and on a dark night, proceed to a place full of scorpions, determined to feel on the ground for a needle his neighbour has dropped.

Again:

He who would acquire the Sacred Knowledge should, before he goes any farther "*trim his lamp* of inner understanding," and then "with the help of such good light" use his meritorious actions as a dust-cloth to remove every impurity from his mystic mirror,† so that he should be enabled to see in its lustre the faithful reflection of Self. . . . . First, this; then Tong-pa-nya,‡ lastly: Samma Sambuddha.§

In *Chinese Buddhism* a corroboration of these statements is to be found in the aphorisms of Lin-tsi:

Within the body which admits sensations, acquires knowledge, thinks, and acts, there is the "true man without a position" Wu-wei-chen-jen. He makes himself clearly visible; not the thinnest separating film hides him. Why do you not recognise nim? . . . If the mind does not come to conscious existence, there is deliverance everywhere. . . . . What is Buddha? *Ans.* A mind clear and at rest. What is the Law? *Ans.* A mind clear and enlightened. What is *Tau?* *Ans.* In every place absence of impediments and pure enlightenment. These three are one.

---

* Chagpa-Thog-mad is the Tibetan name of Âryâsanga, the founder of the Yogâchârya or Naljorchodpa School. This Sage and Initiate is said to have been taught "Wisdom" by Maitreya Buddha Himself, the Buddha of the Sixth Race, at Tushita (a celestial region presided over by Him), and as having received from Him the five books of *Champaitshos-nga*. The Secret Doctrine teaches, however, that he came from Dejung, or Shambhalla, called the "source of happiness" ("wisdom-acquired") and declared by some Orientalists to be a "fabulous" place.

† It may not be, perhaps, amiss to remind the reader of the fact that the "mirror" was a part of the symbolism of the Thesmophoria, a portion of the Eleusinian Mysteries; and that it was used in the search for Atmu, the "Hidden One," or "Self." In his excellent paper on the above-named mysteries, Dr. Alexander Wilder of New York says: "Despite the assertion of Herodotus and others that the Bacchic Mysteries were Egyptian, there exists strong probability that they came originally from India, and were Shaivitic or Buddhistical. Kore-Persep-honeia was but the goddess Parasu-pani, or Bhavani, and Zagreus is from Chakra, a country extending from ocean to ocean. If this is a Turanian story we can easily recognise the 'horns' as the crescent worn by Lama-priests, and assume the whole legend [the fable of Dionysus-Zagreus] to be based on Lama-succession and transmigration. . . . The whole story of Orpheus . . . has a Hindu ring all through." The tale of "Lama-succession and transmigration" did not originate with the Lamas, who date themselves only so far back as the seventh century, but with the Chaldæans and the Brâhmans, still earlier.

‡ The state of absolute freedom from any sin or desire.

The state during which an Adept sees the long series of his past births, and lives through all his previous incarnations in this and the other worlds. (See the admirable description in the *Light of Asia*, p. 166, 1884 ed.)

NOTE.

Papers I. II. III. of the following were written by H. P. B. and were circulated privately during her lifetime, but they were written with the idea that they would be published after a time. They are papers intended for students rather than for the ordinary reader, and will repay careful study and thought. The "Notes of some Oral Teaching" were written down by some of her pupils and were partially corrected by her, but no attempt has been made to relieve them of their fragmentary character. She had intended to make them the basis for written papers similar to the first three, but her failing health rendered this impossible, and they are published with her consent, the time for restricting them to a limited circle having expired.

ANNIE BESANT.

PAPER I.

A WARNING.

THERE is a strange law in Occultism which has been ascertained and proven by thousands of years of experience; nor has it failed to demonstrate itself, almost in every case, during the years that the Theosophical Society has been in existence. As soon as anyone pledges himself as a "Probationer," certain Occult effects ensue. Of these the first is the *throwing outward* of everything latent in the nature of the man: his faults, habits, qualities or subdued desires, whether good, bad or indifferent.

For instance, if a man be vain or a sensualist, or ambitious, whether by atavism or by karmic heirloom, those vices are sure to break out, even if he has hitherto successfully concealed and repressed them. They will come to the front irrepressibly, and he will have to fight a hundred times harder than before, until he kills all such tendencies in himself.

On the other hand, if he be good, generous, chaste and abstemious, or has any virtue hitherto latent and concealed in him, it will work its way out as irrepressibly as the rest. Thus a civilized man who hates to be considered a saint, and therefore assumes a mask, will not be able to conceal his true nature, whether base or noble.

THIS IS AN IMMUTABLE LAW IN THE DOMAIN OF THE OCCULT.

Its action is the more marked, the more earnest and sincere the desire of the candidate, and the more deeply he has felt the reality and importance of his pledge.

The ancient occult axiom, "Know Thyself," must be familiar to every student; but few if any have apprehended the real meaning of this wise exhortation of the Delphic Oracle. You all know your earthly pedigree, but who of you has ever traced all the links of heredity, astral, psychic and spiritual, which go to make you what you are. Many have written and expressed their desire to unite themselves with their Higher Ego, yet none seem to know the indissoluble link connecting their "Higher Egos" with the One Universal SELF.

For all purposes of Occultism, whether practical or purely metaphysical, such knowledge is absolutely requisite. It is proposed, therefore, to begin these papers by showing this connection in all directions with the worlds: Absolute, Archetypal, Spiritual, Mânasic, Psychic, Astral, and Elemental. Before, however, we can touch upon the higher worlds—Archetypal, Spiritual and Mânasic—we must master the relations of the seventh, the terrestrial world, the lower Prakriti, or Malkuth as in the Kabalah, to the worlds of planes which immediately follow it.

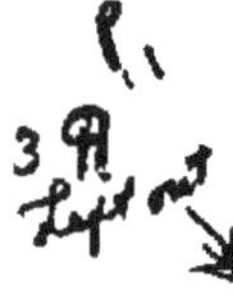

OM.

"OM," says the Âryan Adept, the son of the Fifth Race, who with this syllable begins and ends his salutation to the human being, his conjuration of, or appeal to, non-human PRESENCES.

"OM-MANI," murmurs the Turanian Adept, the descendant of the Fourth Race; and after pausing he adds, "PADME-HUM."

This famous invocation is very erroneously translated by the Orientalists as meaning, "Oh the Jewel in the Lotus." For although, literally, OM is a syllable sacred to the Deity, PADMA means "in the Lotus," and MANI is any precious stone, still neither the words themselves, nor their symbolical meaning, are thus really correctly rendered.

In this, the most sacred of all Eastern formulas, not only has every syllable a secret potency producing a definite result, but the whole invocation has seven different meanings and can produce seven distinct results, each of which may differ from the others.

The seven meanings and the seven results depend upon the intonation which is given to the whole formula and to each of its syllables; and even the numerical value of the letters is added to or diminished according as such or another rhythm is made use of. Let the student remember that number underlies form, and number guides sound. Number lies at the root of the manifested Universe: numbers and harmonious proportions guide the first differentiations of homogeneous substance into heterogeneous elements; and number and numbers set limits to the formative hand of Nature.

Know the corresponding numbers of the fundamental principle of every element and its sub-elements, learn their interaction and behaviour on the occult side of manifesting Nature, and the law of correspondences will lead you to the discovery of the greatest mysteries of macrocosmical life.

But to arrive at the macrocosmical, you must begin by the microcosmical, *i.e.*, you must study MAN, the microcosm—in this case as physical science does—inductively, proceeding from particulars to universals. At the same time, however, since a key-note is required to analyze and comprehend any combination of differentiations of sound, we must never lose sight of the Platonic method, which starts with one general view of all, and descends from the universal to the individual. This is the method adopted in Mathematics—the only *exact* science that exists in our day.

Let us study Man, therefore; but if we separate him for one moment from the Universal Whole, or view him in isolation, from a single aspect, apart from the "Heavenly Man"—the Universe symbolized by Adam Kadmon or his equivalents in every Philosophy—we shall either land in Black Magic or fail most ingloriously in our attempt.

Thus the mystic sentence, "*Om Mani Padme Hum*," when rightly understood, instead of being composed of the almost meaningless words, "Oh the Jewel in the Lotus," contains a reference to this indissoluble union between Man and the Universe, rendered in seven different ways, and having the capability of seven different applications to as many planes of thought and action.

From whatever aspect we examine it, it means: "I am that I am"; "I am in thee and thou art in me." In this conjunction and close union the good and pure man becomes a God. Whether consciously or unconsciously, he will bring about, or innocently cause to happen, unavoidable results. In the first case, if an Initiate (of course an Adept of the Right-hand Path alone is meant), he can guide a beneficent or a protecting current, and thus benefit and protect individuals and even whole nations. In the second case, although quite unaware of what he is doing, the good man becomes a shield to whomsoever he is with.

Such is the fact; but its how and why have to be explained, and this can be done only when the actual presence and potency of numbers in sounds, and hence in words and letters, have been rendered clear. The formula, "*Om Mani Padme Hum*," has been chosen as an illustration on account of its almost infinite potency in the mouth of an Adept, and of its potentiality when pronounced by any man. Be careful, all you who read this: do not use these words in vain, or when in anger, lest you become yourself the first sacrificial victim, or, what is worse, endanger those whom you love.

The profane Orientalist, who all his life skims mere externals, will tell you flippantly, and laughing at the superstition, that in Tibet this sentence is the most powerful six-syllabled incantation and is said to have been delivered to the nations of Central Asia by Padmapâni, the Tibetan Chenresi.*

But who is Padmapâni, in reality? Each of us must recognize him for himself, whenever he is ready. Each of us has within himself the "Jewel in the Lotus," call it Padmapâni, Krishna, Buddha, Christ, or whatever name we may give to our Divine Self. The exoteric story runs thus:

The supreme Buddha, or Amitâbha, they say, at the hour of the creation of man, caused a rosy ray of light to issue from his right eye. The ray emitted a sound and became Padmapâni Bodhisattva. Then the Deity allowed to stream forth from his left eye a blue ray of light, which, becoming incarnate in the two virgins Dolma, acquired the power to enlighten the minds of living beings. Amitâbha then called the combination, which forthwith took up its abode in man, "*Om Mani Padme Hum*," "I am the Jewel in the Lotus and in it I will remain." Then Padmapâni, "the One in the Lotus" vowed never to cease working until he had made Humanity feel his presence in itself and had thus saved it from the misery of rebirth. He vowed to perform the feat before the end of the Kalpa, adding that, in case of failure, he wished that his head should split into numberless fragments. The Kalpa closed; but Humanity felt him not within its cold, evil heart. Then Padmapâni's head split and was shattered into a thousand fragments. Moved with compassion, the Deity re-formed the pieces into *ten* heads, three white, and seven of various colours. And since that day man has become a perfect number, or TEN.

In this allegory the potency of SOUND, COLOUR, and NUMBER is so ingeniously introduced as to veil the real Esoteric meaning. To the outsider it reads like one of the many meaningless fairy-tales of creation; but it is pregnant with spiritual and divine, physical and magical meaning. From Amitâbha—*no colour*, or the *white glory*—are

* See *supra*, ii. 188, 189.

born the seven differentiated colours of the prism. These each emit a corresponding sound, forming the seven of the *musical scale*. As Geometry, among the Mathematical Sciences, is specially related to Architecture, and also (proceeding to Universals) to Cosmogony, so the ten Jods of the Pythagorean Tetrad, or Tetraktys, being made to symbolize the Macrocosm, the Microcosm, or man, its image, had also to be divided into ten points. For this Nature herself has provided, as will be seen.

But before this statement can be proved and the perfect correspondences between the Macrocosm and the Microcosm demonstrated, a few words of explanation are necessary.

To the learner who would study the Esoteric Sciences with their double object: (*a*) of proving Man to be identical in spiritual and physical essence with both the Absolute Principle and with God in Nature; and (*b*) of demonstrating the presence in him of the same potential powers as exist in the creative forces in Nature—to such a one a perfect knowledge of the correspondences between Colours, Sounds, and Numbers is the first requisite. As already said, the sacred formula of the far East, "*Om Mani Padme Hum*," is the one best calculated to make these correspondential qualities and functions clear to the learner.

In the allegory of Padmapâni, the Jewel (or Spiritual Ego) in the Lotus, or the symbol of androgynous man, the numbers 3, 4, 7, 10, as synthesizing the *Unit*, Man, are prominent, as I have already said. It is on the thorough knowledge and comprehension of the meaning and potency of these numbers, in their various and multiform combinations, and in their mutual correspondence with sounds or words, and colours or rates of motion (represented in physical science by vibrations), that the progress of a student in Occultism depends. Therefore we must begin with the first, initial word, OM, or AUM. OM is a "blind." The sentence "*Om Mani Padme Hum*" is not a six- but a seven-syllabled phrase, as the first syllable is double in its right pronunciation, and triple in its essence, A-UM. It represents the for ever concealed primeval triune differentiation, not *from* but *in* the ONE Absolute, and is therefore symbolized by the 4, or the Tetraktys, in the metaphysical world. It is the Unit-ray, or Âtman.

It is the Âtman, this highest Spirit in man, which, in conjunction with Buddhi and Manas, is called the upper Triad, or Trinity. This

Triad with its four lower human principles, is surrounded, enveloped as in an auric atmosphere, like the yolk of an egg (the future embryo) by the albumen and shell. This, to the perceptions of higher Beings from other planes, makes of each individuality an oval sphere of more or less radiancy.

To show the student the perfect correspondence between the birth of a Kosmos, a World, a Planetary Being, or a Child of Sin and Earth, a more definite and clear description must be given. Those acquainted with Physiology will understand it better than others.

Who, having read any the *Vishnu* or other *Purânas*, is not familiar with the exoteric allegory of the birth of Brahmâ (male-female) in the Egg of the World, Hiranyagarbha, surrounded by its seven zones, or rather planes, which in the world of form and matter become seven and fourteen Lokas; the numbers seven and fourteen reappearing as occasion requires.

Without giving out the secret analysis, the Hindus have from time immemorial compared the matrix of the Universe, and also the solar matrix, to the female uterus. It is written of the former: "Its womb is vast as the Meru," and

> The future mighty oceans lay asleep in the waters that filled its cavities, the continents, seas and mountains, the stars, planets, the gods, demons and mankind had

The whole resembled, in its inner and outer coverings, the cocoa-nut, filled interiorly with pulp, and covered externally with husk and shell. "Vast as Meru," say the texts.

> Meru was its Amnion, and the other mountains were its Chorion,

adds a verse in *Vishnu Purâna*.*

In the same way is man born in his mother's womb. As Brahmâ is surrounded, in exoteric traditions, by seven layers within and seven without the Mundane Egg, so is the embryo (the first or the seventh layer, according to the end from which we begin to count). Thus, just as Esotericism in its Cosmogony enumerates seven inner and seven outer layers, so Physiology notes the contents of the uterus as seven also, although it is completely ignorant of this being a copy of what takes place in the Universal Matrix. These contents are:

1. *Embryo*. 2. *Amniotic Fluid*, immediately surrounding the Embryo. 3. *Amnion*, a membrane derived from the Fœtus, which contains the fluid. 4. *Umbilical Vesicle*, which serves to convey nourishment orig-

* Wilson's translation, as amended by Fitzedward Hall, i. 40.

nally to the Embryo and to nourish it. 5. *Allantois*, a protrusion from the Embryo in the form of a closed bag, which spreads itself between 3 and 7, in the midst of 6, and which, after being specialized into the Placenta, serves to conduct nourishment to the Embryo. 6. *Interspace* between 3 and 7 (the Amnion and Chorion), filled with an albuminous fluid. 7. *Chorion*, or outer layer.

Now, each of these seven contents severally corresponds with, and is formed after, an antetype, one on each of the seven planes of being, with which in their turn correspond the seven states of Matter and all other forces, sensational or functional, in Nature.

The following is a bird's-eye view of the seven correspondential contents of the wombs of Nature and of Woman. We may contrast them thus:

COSMIC PROCESS. (UPPER POLE.)	HUMAN PROCESS. (LOWER POLE.)
(1) The mathematical Point, called the "Cosmic Seed," the Monad of Leibnitz; which contains the whole Universe, as the acorn the oak. This is the first bubble on the surface of boundless homogeneous Substance, or Space, the bubble of differentiation in its incipient stage. It is the beginning of the Orphic or Brahmâ's Egg. It corresponds in Astrology and Astronomy to the Sun.	(1) The terrestrial Embryo, which contains in it the future man with all his potentialities. In the series of principles of the human system it is the Âtman, or the super-spiritual principle, just as in the physical Solar System it is the Sun.
(2) The *vis vitæ* of our solar system exudes from the Sun.	(2) The Amniotic Fluid exudes from the Embryo.
(*a*) It is called, when referred to the higher planes, Âkâsha.	(*a*) It is called, on the plane of matter, Prâna.*
(*b*) It proceeds from the ten "divinities," the ten numbers of the Sun, which is itself the "Perfect Number." These are called Dis—in reality Space—the forces	(*b*) It proceeds, taking its source in the universal One Life, from the heart of man and Buddhi, over which the Seven Solar Rays (Gods) preside.

* Prâna is in reality the universal Life Principle.

spread in Space, three of which are contained in the Sun's Âtman, or seventh principle, and seven are the rays shot out by the Sun.

(3) The Ether of Space, which, in its external aspect, is the plastic crust which is supposed to envelope the Sun. On the higher plane it is the whole Universe, as the third differentiation of evolving Substance, Mûlaprakriti becoming Prakriti.

(3) The Amnion, the [illegible] containing the Amniotic [illegible] enveloping the Embryo. [illegible] the birth of man it becomes [illegible] third layer, so to say, of his [illegible] neto-vital aura.

(*a*) It corresponds mystically to the manifested Mahat, or the Intellect or Soul of the World.

(*a*) Manas, the third principle (counting from above), or the Human Soul in Man.

(4) The sidereal contents of Ether, the substantial parts of it, unknown to Modern Science, represented:

(4) Umbilical Vesicle, [illegible] as Science teaches, to nourish [illegible] Embryo originally, but, as [illegible] Science avers, to carry to the [illegible] by osmosis the cosmic [illegible] extraneous to the mother.

(*a*) In Occult and Kabalistic Mysteries, by Elementals.

(*a*) In the grown man [illegible] become the feeders of Kâma, [illegible] which they preside.

(*b*) In physical Astronomy, by meteors, comets, and all kinds of casual and phenomenal cosmic bodies.

(*b*) In the physical man, [illegible] sions and emotions, the [illegible] teors and comets of human [illegible].

(5) Life currents in Ether, having their origin in the Sun: the canals through which the vital principle of that Ether (the blood of the Cosmic Body) passes to nourish everything on the Earth and on the other Planets: from the minerals, which are thus made to grow

(5) The Allantois, a [illegible] from the Embryo, which [illegible] itself between the Amnion [illegible] Chorion; it is supposed to [illegible] the nourishment from the [illegible] to the Embryo. It [illegible] the life-principle, Prâna or Jîva.

and become specialized, from the plants, which are thus fed, to animal and man, to whom life is thus imparted.

(6) The double radiation, psychic and physical, which radiates from the Cosmic Seed and expands around the whole Kosmos, as well as around the Solar System and every Planet. In Occultism it is called the upper divine, and the lower material, Astral Light.

(6) The Allantois is divided into two layers. The interspace between the Amnion and the Chorion contains the Allantois and also an albuminous fluid.*

(7) The outer crust of every sidereal body, the Shell of the Mundane Egg, or the sphere (of our Solar System), of our Earth, and of every man and animal. In sidereal space, Ether proper; on the terrestrial plane, Air, which again is built in seven layers.

(7) The Chorion, or the *Zona Pellucida*, the globular object called Blastodermic Vesicle, the outer and the inner layers of the membrane of which go to form the physical man. The outer, or ectoderm, forms his epidermis; the inner, or endoderm, his muscles, bones, etc. Man's skin, again, is composed of seven layers.

(*a*) The primordial potential world-stuff becomes (for the Manvantaric period) the permanent globe or globes.

(*a*) The "primitive" becomes the "permanent" Chorion.

Even in the evolution of the Races we see the same order as in Nature and Man.† Placental animal-man became such only after the separation of sexes in the Third Root-Race. In the physiological evolution, the placenta is fully formed and functional only after the third month of uterine life.

---

* All the uterine contents, having a direct spiritual connection with their cosmic antetypes, are, on the physical plane, potent objects in Black Magic, and are therefore considered unclean.

† See *supra*, ii. Part I.

Let us put aside such human conceptions as a personal God, and hold to the purely divine, to that which underlies all and everything in boundless Nature. It is called by its Sanskrit Esoteric name in the *Vedas*, TAT (or THAT), a term for the unknowable Rootless Root. If we do so, we may answer these seven questions of the *Esoteric Catechism* thus:

(1) Q.—What is the Eternal Absolute?
A.—THAT.

(2) Q.—How came Kosmos into being?
A.—Through THAT.

(3) Q.—How, or what will it be when it falls back into Pralaya?
A.—In THAT.

(4) Q.—Whence all the animate, and suppositionally, the "inanimate" nature?
A.—From THAT.

(5) Q.—What is the Substance and Essence of which the Universe is formed?
A.—THAT.

(6) Q.—Into what has it been and will be again and again resolved?
A.—Into THAT.

(7) Q.—Is THAT then both the instrumental and material cause of the Universe?
A.—What else is it or can it be than THAT?

As the Universe, the Macrocosm and the Microcosm,* are *ten*, why should we divide Man into *seven* "principles"? This is the reason why the perfect number ten is divided into two; in their completeness, i.e., super-spiritually and physically, the forces are TEN: to wit, three on the subjective and inconceivable, and seven on the objective plane. Bear in mind that I am now giving you the description of the two opposite poles: (*a*) the primordial Triangle, which, as soon as it has reflected itself in the "Heavenly Man," the highest of the lower seven —disappears, returning into "Silence and Darkness"; and (*b*) the astral paradigmatic man, whose Monad (Âtmâ) is also represented by a triangle, as it has to become a ternary in conscious Devachanic interludes. The purely terrestrial man being reflected in the universe of Matter, so to say, upside down, the upper Triangle, wherein the creative ideation and the subjective potentiality of the formative faculty resides,

* The Solar System or the Earth, as the case may be.

a reason which cannot be given [illegible]

[illegible]

N, its contact with Na-
Man being the Fourth,
it a Quaternary, or Te-
the Higher Self.

5. 6. These six princi-
ting on four different
nd having their AURIC
PE on the seventh (*vide*
re those used by the
of the Right-Hand, or
Magicians.

sical Body is no princi-
s entirely ignored, being
ly in Black Magic.

entres of Action.

s) Left Eye.

RÛPA) Left Ear.

VEHICLE) Left Nostril.

radigm of the 10th (cre-
rifice in the Lower Triad.

ysical Organs are used
Dugpas in Black Magic.

is shifted in the man of clay below the seven. Thus three of the ten, containing in the archetypal world only ideative and paradigmatical potentiality, *i.e.*, existing in possibility, not in action, are in fact one. The potency of formative creation resides in the Logos, the synthesis of the seven Forces or Rays, which becomes forthwith the Quaternary, the sacred Tetraktys. This process is repeated in man, in whom the lower physical triangle becomes, in conjunction with the female One, the male-female creator, or generator. The same on a still lower plane in the animal world. A mystery above, a mystery below, truly.

This is how the upper and highest, and the lower and most animal, stand in mutual relation.

DIAGRAM I.

In this diagram, we see that physical man (or his body) does not share in the *direct*, pure waves of the divine Essence which flows from the *One in Three*, the Unmanifested, through the Manifested Logos (the upper face in the diagram). Purusha, the primeval Spirit, touches the human head and stops there. But the Spiritual Man (the synthesis of the seven principles) is directly connected with it. And here a few words ought to be said about the usual exoteric enumeration of the principles. At first an approximate division only was made and given out. *Esoteric Buddhism* begins with Âtmâ, the seventh, and ends with the Physical Body, the first. Now neither Âtmâ, which is no individual "principle," but a radiation *from* and *one with* the Unmanifested Logos; nor the Body, which is the material rind, or shell, of the Spiritual Man, can be, in strict truth, referred to as "principles." Moreover, the chief "principle" of all, one not even mentioned heretofore, is the "Luminous Egg" (Hiranyagarbha), or the invisible magnetic sphere in which every man is enveloped.* It is the direct emanation: (*a*) from the Âtmic Ray in its triple aspect of Creator, Preserver and Destroyer (Regenerator); and (*b*) from Buddhi-Manas. The *seventh* aspect of this individual Aura is the faculty of assuming the form of its body and becoming the "Radiant," the Luminous Augoeides. It is this, strictly speaking, which at times becomes the form called Mâyâvi Rûpa. Therefore, as explained in the second face of the diagram (the astral man), the Spiritual Man consists of only five

* So are the animals, the plants, and even the minerals. Reichenbach never understood what he learned through his sensitives and clairvoyants. It is the odic, or rather the auric or magnetic fluid which emanates from man, but it is also something more.

principles, as taught by the Vedântins,* who substitute for the physical this sixth, or Auric, Body, and merge the dual Manas (the dual mind, or consciousness) into one. Thus they speak of five Koshas (sheaths or principles), and call Âtmâ the sixth, yet no "principle." This is the secret of the late Subba Row's criticism of the division in *Esoteric Buddhism*. But let the student now learn the true Esoteric enumeration.

The reason why public mention of the Auric Body was not permitted was on account of its being so sacred. It is this Body which, at death, assimilates the essence of Buddhi and Manas and becomes the vehicle of these spiritual principles, *which are not objective*, and then, with the full radiation of Âtmâ upon it ascends as Manas-Taijasi into the Devachanic state. Therefore is it called by many names. It is the Sûtrâtmâ, the silver "thread" which "incarnates" from the beginning of Manvantara to the end, stringing upon itself the pearls of human existence, in other words, the spiritual aroma of every personality it *follows* through the pilgrimage of life.† It is also the material from which the Adept forms his Astral Bodies, from the Augoeides and the Mâyâvi Rûpa downwards. After the death of man, when its more ethereal particles have drawn into themselves the spiritual principles of Buddhi and the Upper Manas, and are illuminated with the radiance of Âtmâ, the Auric Body remains either in the Devachanic state of consciousness, or, in the case of a full Adept, prefers the state of Nirmânakâya, that is, one who has so purified his whole system that he is above even the divine illusion of a Devachanî. Such an Adept remains in the astral (invisible) plane connected with our earth, and henceforth moves and lives in the possession of all his principles except the Kâma Rûpa and Physical Body. In the case of the Devachanî, the Linga Sharîra—the *alter ego* of the body, which during life is within the physical envelope while the radiant aura is without—strengthened by the material particles which this aura leaves behind, remains close to the dead body and outside it, and soon fades away. In the case of the full Adept, the body alone becomes subject to dissolution, while the centre of that force which was the seat of desires and passions, disappears with its cause—the animal body.‡ But during the life of the latter, these centres are more or less active and in constant correspondence

* See *supra*, i. 181, for the Vedântic exoteric enumeration.

† See *Lucifer*, January, 1889 "Dialogue upon the Mysteries of After-Life."

with their prototypes, the cosmic centres, and their microcosms, the principles. It is only through these cosmic and spiritual centres that the physical centres (the upper seven orifices and the lower triad) can benefit by their Occult interaction, for these orifices, or openings, are channels conducting into the body the influences that *the will of man* attracts and uses, *viz.*, the cosmic forces.

This will has, of course, to act primarily through the spiritual principles. To make this clearer, let us take an example. In order to stop pain, let us say in the right eye, you have to attract to it the potent magnetism from that cosmic principle which corresponds to this eye and also to Buddhi. Create, by a powerful will effort, an imaginary line of communication between the right eye and Buddhi, locating the latter as a *centre* in the same part of the head. This line, though you may call it "imaginary," is, once you succeed in seeing it with your mental eye and give it a shape and colour, in truth as good as real. A rope in a dream *is not* and yet *is*. Moreover, according to the prismatic colour with which you endow your line, so will the influence act. Now Buddhi and Mercury correspond with each other, and both are yellow, or radiant and golden coloured. In the human system, the right eye corresponds with Buddhi and Mercury; and the left with Manas and Venus or Lucifer. Thus, if your line is golden or silvery, it will stop the pain; if red, it will increase it, for red is the colour of Kâma and corresponds with Mars. Mental or Christian Scientists have stumbled upon the *effects* without understanding the *causes*. Having found by chance the secret of producing such results owing to mental abstraction, they attribute them to their union with God (whether a personal or impersonal God they know best), whereas it is simply the effect of one or another principle. However it may be, they are on the path of discovery, although they must remain wandering for a long time to come.

Let not Esoteric students commit the same mistake. It has often been explained that neither the cosmic planes of substance nor even the human principles—with the exception of the lowest material plane or world and the physical body, which, as has been said, are no "principles,"—can be located or thought of as being in Space and Time. As the former are seven in ONE, so are we seven in ONE—that same absolute Soul of the World, which is both Matter and non-Matter, Spirit and non-Spirit, Being and non-Being. Impress yourselves well with this idea, all those of you who would study the mysteries of SELF.

Remember that with our physical senses alone at our command, none of us can hope to reach beyond gross Matter. We can [illegible] through one or another of our seven *spiritual* senses, either [illegible] or if one is a born Seer. Yet even a clairvoyant, possessed [illegible] faculties, if not an Adept, no matter how honest and sincere he [illegible] will, through his ignorance of the truths of Occult Science, [illegible] the visions he sees in the Astral Light only to mistake for [illegible] Angels the denizens of those spheres of which he [illegible] catch a glimpse, as witness Swedenborg and others.

These seven senses of ours correspond with every other [illegible] nature and in ourselves. Physically, though invisibly, [illegible] Auric Envelope (the amnion of the physical man in [illegible] has seven layers, just as Cosmic Space and our physical [illegible] have. It is this Aura which, according to our mental and [illegible] of purity or impurity, either opens for us vistas into [illegible] shuts us out altogether from anything but this three-dimension[illegible] of Matter.

Each of our seven physical senses (two of which are [illegible] to profane Science), and also of our seven states of conscio[illegible] (1) waking; (2) waking-dreaming; (3) natural sleeping; [illegible] or trance-sleep; (5) psychic; (6) super-psychic; and (7) pur[illegible] —corresponds with one of the seven Cosmic Planes, develops [illegible] one of the seven super-senses, and is connected directly, [illegible] the terrestro-spiritual plane, with the cosmic and divine centre [illegible] that gave it birth, and which is its direct creator. Each [illegible] nected with, and under the direct influence of, one of the [illegible] Planets.* These belonged to the Lesser Mysteries, whose [illegible] were called Mystai (the veiled), seeing that they were allo[illegible] perceive things only through a mist, as it were "with the eyes [illegible] while the Initiates or "Seers" of the Greater Mysteries [illegible] Epoptai (those who see things unveiled). It was the latter [illegible] were taught the true mysteries of the Zodiac and the relation[illegible] respondences between its twelve signs (two secret) and the [illegible] orifices. The latter are now of course ten in the female, and [illegible] in the male; but this is merely an external difference. In [illegible] volume of this work it is stated that till the end of the [illegible] Root-Race (when androgynous man separated into male [illegible] the ten orifices existed in the hermaphrodite, first potenti[illegible]

* See *supra*, i. 646-649.

functionally. The evolution of the human embryo shows this. For instance, the only opening formed at first is the buccal cavity, "a *cloaca* communicating with the anterior extremity of the intestine." These become later the mouth and the posterior orifice: the Logos differentiating and emanating gross matter on the lower plane, in Occult parlance. The difficulty which some students will experience in reconciling the correspondences between the Zodiac and the orifices can be easily explained. Magic is coëval with the Third Root-Race, which began by creating through Kriyâshakti and ended by generating its species in the present way.* Woman, being left with the full or perfect cosmic number 10 (the divine number of Jehovah), was deemed higher and more spiritual than man. In Egypt, in days of old, the marriage service contained an article that the woman should be the "lady of the lord," and real lord over him, the husband pledging himself to be "obedient to his wife" for the production of alchemical results such as the Elixir of Life and the Philosopher's Stone, for the *spiritual* help of the woman was needed by the male Alchemist. But woe to the Alchemist who should take this in the dead-letter sense of *physical* union. Such sacrilege would become Black Magic and be followed by certain failure. The true Alchemist of old took *aged* women to help him, carefully avoiding the young ones; and if any of them happened to be married they treated their wives for months both before and during their operations as sisters.

The error of crediting the Ancients with knowing only ten of the zodiacal signs is explained in *Isis Unveiled*.† The Ancients did know of twelve, but viewed these signs differently from ourselves. They took neither Virgo nor Scorpio singly into consideration, but regarded them as two in one, since they were made to refer directly and symbolically to the primeval dual man and his separation into sexes. During the reformation of the Zodiac, Libra was added as the twelfth sign, though it is simply an equilibrating sign, at the turning point—the mystery of separated man.

Let the student learn all this well. Meanwhile we have to recapitulate what has been said.

(1) Each human being is an incarnation of his God, in other words, one with his "Father in Heaven," just as Jesus, an Initiate, is made to say. As many men on earth, so many Gods in Heaven; and yet these

* See *supra*, i. 228, *et seq.*, and ii. *passim*.

† *Op. cit.*, ii. 456, 461, 465 *et seq.*

Gods are in reality ONE, for at the end of every period [illegible] are withdrawn, like the rays of the setting sun, into [illegible] Luminary, the Non-Manifested Logos, which in its turn is [illegible] the One Absolute. Shall we call these "Fathers" of ours [illegible] individually or collectively, and under any circumstances, [illegible]*sonal God?* Occultism answers, *Never*. All that an average [illegible] know of his "Father" is what he knows of himself, [illegible] within himself. The Soul of his "Heavenly Father" is [illegible] in him. This Soul is himself, if he be successful in [illegible]ing the Divine Individuality while in his physical, animal [illegible] to the Spirit thereof, as well expect to be heard by the Absolute [illegible] prayers and supplications are vain, unless to potential words [illegible] potent acts, and make the Aura which surrounds each one of [illegible] pure and divine that the God within us may act outwardly, [illegible] other words, become as it were an extraneous Potency. [illegible] Initiates, Saints, and very holy and pure men been enabled [illegible] others as well as themselves in the hour of need, and produce [illegible] foolishly called "miracles," each by the help and with the aid [illegible] God within himself, which he alone has enabled to act on the [illegible] plane.

(2) The word AUM or OM, which corresponds to the upper [illegible] if pronounced by a very holy and pure man, will draw out, [illegible] not only the less exalted Potencies residing in the planetary [illegible] elements, but even his Higher Self, or the "Father" within him. [illegible]nounced by an averagely good man, in the correct way, it will [illegible] strengthen him morally, especially if between two "AUMS" [illegible]tates intently upon the AUM within him, concentrating all his [illegible] upon the ineffable glory. But woe to the man who pronounces [illegible] the commission of some far-reaching sin: he will only thereby [illegible] to his own impure photosphere invisible Presences and [illegible] could not otherwise break through the Divine Envelope. [illegible]

AUM is the original of Amen. Now, Amen is not a [illegible] but, like the word Halleluiah, was borrowed by the Jews and [illegible] from the Chaldees. The latter word is often found repeated [illegible] magical inscriptions upon cups and urns among the Babylonian [illegible] Nineveh relics. Amen does not mean "so be it," or [illegible] signified in hoary antiquity almost the same as AUM. [illegible] Tanaïm (Initiates) used it for the same reason as the Âryan Adepts [illegible] AUM, and with a like success, the numerical value of *AMeN* [illegible] letters being 91, the same as the full value of *YHVH*,* 26, and *ADoNaY*, 65, or 91. Both words mean the affirmation of the being, or existence, of the sexless "Lord" within us.

(3) Esoteric Science teaches that every sound in the visible world awakens its corresponding sound in the invisible realms, and arouses to action some force or other on the Occult side of Nature. Moreover, every sound corresponds to a colour and a number (a potency spiritual, psychic or physical) and to a sensation on some plane. All these find an echo in every one of the so-far developed elements, and even on the terrestrial plane, in the Lives that swarm in the terrene atmosphere, thus prompting them to action.

Thus a prayer, unless pronounced *mentally* and addressed to one's "Father" in the silence and solitude of one's "closet," must have more frequently disastrous than beneficial results, seeing that the masses are entirely ignorant of the potent effects which they thus produce. To produce good effects, the prayer must be uttered by "one who knows how to make himself heard in silence," when it is no longer a prayer, but becomes a command. Why is Jesus shown to have forbidden his hearers to go to the public synagogues? Surely every praying man was not a hypocrite and a liar, nor a Pharisee who loved to be seen praying by people! He had a motive, we must suppose: the same motive which prompts the experienced Occultist to prevent his pupils from going into crowded places now as then, from entering churches, séance rooms, etc., unless they are in sympathy with the crowd.

There is one piece of advice to be given to beginners, who cannot help going into crowds—one which may appear superstitious, but which in the absence of Occult knowledge will be found efficacious. As well known to good Astrologers, the days of the week are not in the order of those planets whose names they bear. The fact is that the ancient Hindus and Egyptians divided the day into four parts, each day being under the protection (as ascertained by practical magic) of a planet; and every day, as correctly asserted by Dion Cassius, received the name of the planet which ruled and protected its first portion. Let the student protect himself from the "Powers of the Air" (Elementals) which throng public places, by wearing either a ring containing some jewel of the colour of the presiding planet, or else of the metal sacred to it. But the best protection is a clear conscience and a firm desire to benefit Humanity.

* *Jod-Hevah*, or male-female on the terrestrial plane, as invented by the Jews, and now made out to mean Jehovah; but signifying in reality and literally, "giving being" and "receiving life."

THE PLANETS, THE DAYS OF THE WEEK AND THEIR CORRESPONDING COLOURS AND METALS.

In the accompanying diagram the days of the week do not stand in their usual order, though they are placed in their correct sequence as determined by the order of the colours in the solar spectrum and the corresponding colours of their ruling planets. The fault of the confusion in the order of the days revealed by this comparison lies at the door of the early Christians. Adopting from the Jews their lunar months, they tried to blend them with the solar planets, and so made a mess of it; for the order of the days of the week as it now stands does not follow the order of the planets.

Now, the Ancients arranged the planets in the following order: Moon, Mercury, Venus, Sun, Mars, Jupiter, Saturn, counting the Sun as a planet for exoteric purposes. Again, the Egyptians and Indians, the two oldest nations, divided their day into four parts, each of which was under the protection and rule of a planet. In course of time each day came to be called by the name of that planet which ruled its first portion—the morning. Now, when they arranged their week, the Christians proceeded as follows: they wanted to make the day of the Sun, or Sunday, the seventh, so they named the days of the week by taking every fourth planet in turn; *e.g.*, beginning with the Moon (Monday), they counted thus: Moon, Mercury, Venus, Sun, Mars; thus Tuesday, the day whose first portion was ruled by Mars, became the second day of the week; and so on. It should be remembered also that the Moon, like the Sun, is a substitute for a secret planet.

The present division of the solar year was made several centuries later than the beginning of our era; and our week is not that of the Ancients and the Occultists. The septenary division of the four parts of the lunar phases is as old as the world, and originated with the people who reckoned time by the lunar months. The Hebrews never used it, for they counted only the seventh day, the Sabbath, though the second chapter of *Genesis* seems to speak of it. Till the days of the Cæsars there is no trace of a week of seven days among any nation save the Hindus. From India it passed to the Arabs, and reached Europe with Christianity. The Roman week consisted of eight days, and the Athenian of ten.* Thus one of the numberless contra-

* See *Notice sur le Calendrier*, J. H. Ragon.

any re-
Sound,
e rest,
s them

As the Human Principles have no Numbers *per se*, but only *correspond* to Numbers, Sounds, Colours, etc., they are not enumerated here in the order used for exoteric purposes.

DAYS OF THE WEEK.	COLOURS	SOUND. MUSICAL SCALE.	
		Sanskrit Gamut	*Italian Gamut.*
TUESDAY. *Dies Martis*, or ...iw.	1. RED.	SA.	DO.
SUNDAY. *Dies Solis*, or ...un.	2. ORANGE.	RI.	RE.
WEDNESDAY. *Dies Mercurii*, or Voden. Day of Buddha in the South, and of Voden in the North—Gods of Wisdom	3. YELLOW	GA.	MI.
SATURDAY. *Dies Saturni*, or ...aturn	4. GREEN.	MA.	FA.
THURSDAY. *Dies Jovis*, or ...hor	5. BLUE.	PA.	SOL.
FRIDAY *Dies Veneris*, or ...rige	6 INDIGO OR DARK BLUE	DA	LA.
MONDAY. *Dies Lunae*, or ...loon.	7 VIOLET	NI.	SI

dictions and fallacies of Christendom is the adoption of the Indian septenary week of the lunar reckoning, and the preservation at the same time of the mythological names of the planets.

Nor do modern Astrologers give the correspondences of the days and planets and their colours correctly; and while Occultists can give good reason for every detail of their own tables of colours, etc., it is doubtful whether the Astrologers can do the same.

To close this first Paper, let me say that the readers must in all necessity be separated into two broad divisions: those who have not quite rid themselves of the usual sceptical doubts, but who long to ascertain how much truth there may be in the claims of the Occultists; and those others who, having freed themselves from the trammels of Materialism and Relativity, feel that true and real bliss must be sought only in the knowledge and personal experience of that which the Hindu Philosopher calls the Brahmavidyâ, and the Buddhist Arhat the realization of Âdibuddha, the primeval Wisdom. Let the former pick out and study from these Papers only those explanations of the phenomena of life which profane Science is unable to give them. Even with such limitations, they will find by the end of a year or two that they will have learned more than all their Universities and Colleges can teach them. As to the sincere believers, they will be rewarded by seeing their faith transformed into knowledge. True knowledge is of Spirit and in Spirit alone, and cannot be acquired in any other way except through the region of the higher mind, the only plane from which we can penetrate the depths of the all-pervading Absoluteness. He who carries out only those laws established by human minds, who lives that life which is prescribed by the code of mortals and their fallible legislation, chooses as his guiding star a beacon which shines on the ocean of Mâyâ, or of temporary delusions, and lasts for but one incarnation. These laws are necessary for the life and welfare of physical man alone. He has chosen a pilot who directs him through the shoals of one existence, a master who parts with him, however, on the threshold of death. How much happier that man who, while strictly performing on the temporary objective plane the duties of daily life, carrying out each and every law of his country, and rendering, in short, to Cæsar what is Cæsar's, leads in reality a spiritual and permanent existence, a life with no breaks of continuity, no gaps, no interludes, not even during those periods which are the halting-places of the long pilgrimage of purely spiritual life. All the phenomena of the lower human mind disappear like the curtain of a proscenium, allowing him to live in the region beyond it, the plane of the noumenal, the one reality. If man by suppressing, if not destroying, his selfishness and personality, only succeeds in knowing himself as he is behind the veil of physical Mâyâ, he will soon stand beyond all pain, all misery, and beyond all the wear and tear of change, which is the chief originator of pain. Such a man will be physically of Matter, he will move surrounded by Matter, and yet he will live beyond and outside it. His body will be subject to change, but he himself will be entirely without it, and will experience everlasting life even while in temporary bodies of short duration. All this may be achieved by the development of unselfish universal love of Humanity, and the suppression of personality, or *selfishness*, which is the cause of all sin, and consequently of all human sorrow.

AUM

PAPER II.

AN EXPLANATION.

In view of the abstruse nature of the subjects dealt with, the present Paper will begin with an explanation of some points which remained obscure in the preceding one, as well as of some statements in which there was an appearance of contradiction.

Astrologers, of whom there are many among the Esotericists, are likely to be puzzled by some statements distinctly contradicting their teachings; whilst those who know nothing of the subject may perhaps find themselves opposed at the outset by those who have studied the exoteric systems of the Kabalah and Astrology. For let it be distinctly known, nothing of that which is printed broadcast, and available to every student in public libraries or museums, is really Esoteric, but is either mixed with deliberate "blinds," or cannot be understood and studied with profit without a complete glossary of Occult terms.

The following teachings and explanations, therefore, may be useful to the student in assisting him to formulate the teaching given in the preceding Paper.

In Diagram I. it will be observed that the 3, 7, and 10 centres are respectively as follows:

(*a*) The 3 pertain to the spiritual world of the Absolute, and therefore to the three higher principles in Man.

(*b*) The 7 belong to the spiritual, psychic, and physical worlds and to the body of man. Physics, metaphysics and hyper-physics are the triad that symbolizes man on this plane.

(*c*) The 10, or the sum total of these, is the Universe as a whole, in all its aspects, and also its Microcosm—Man, with his ten orifices.

Laying aside, for the moment, the Higher Decad (Kosmos) and the

Lower Decad (Man), the first three numbers of the separate sevens have a direct reference to the Spirit, Soul and Auric Envelope of the human being, as well as to the higher supersensual world. The lower four, or the four aspects, belong to Man also, as well as to the Universal Kosmos, the whole being synthesized by the Absolute.

If these three discrete or distributive degrees of Being be conceived, according to the Symbology of all the Eastern Religions, as contained in one Ovum, or EGG, the name of that EGG will be Svabhâvat, or the ALL-BEING on the manifested plane. This Universe has, in truth, neither centre nor periphery; but in the individual and finite mind of man it has such a definition, the natural consequence of the limitations of human thought.

In Diagram II., as already stated therein, no notice need be taken of the numbers used in the left-hand column, as these refer only to the Hierarchies of the Colours and Sounds on the metaphysical plane, and are not the characteristic numbers of the human principles or of the planets. The human principles elude enumeration, because each man differs from every other, just as no two blades of grass on the whole earth are absolutely alike. Numbering is here a question of spiritual progress and the natural predominance of one principle over another. With one man it may be Buddhi that stands as number one; with another, if he be a bestial sensualist, the Lower Manas. With one the physical body, or perhaps Prâna, the life principle, will be on the first and highest plane, as would be the case in an extremely healthy man, full of vitality; with another it may come as the sixth or even seventh downward. Again, the colours and metals corresponding to the planets and human principles, as will be observed, are not those known exoterically to modern Astrologers and Western Occultists.

Let us see whence the modern Astrologer got his notions about the correspondence of planets, metals and colours. And here we are reminded of the modern Orientalist, who, judging by appearances credits the ancient Akkadians (and also the Chaldæans, Hindus and Egyptians) with the crude notion that the Universe, and in like manner the earth, was like an inverted, bell-shaped bowl! This he demonstrates by pointing to the symbolical representations of some Akkadian inscriptions and to the Assyrian carvings. It is, however, no place here to explain how mistaken is the Assyriologist, for all such representations are simply symbolical of the *Khargakkurra*, the World-Mountain, or Meru, and relate only to the North Pole, the Land of the

Gods. Now, the Assyrians arranged their *exoteric* teaching about the planets and their correspondences as follows:

Numbers.	*Planets*	*Metals.*	*Colours.*	*Solar Days of Week.*
1.	Saturn.	Lead.	Black.	Saturday. (Whence Sabbath, in honour of Jehovah.)
2.	Jupiter.	Tin.	White, but as often Purple or Orange.	Thursday.
3.	Mars.	Iron.	Red.	Tuesday.
4.	Sun.	Gold.	Yellow-golden.	Sunday.
5.	Venus.	Copper.	Green or Yellow.	Friday.
6.	Mercury.	Quicksilver.	Blue.	Wednesday.
7.	Moon.	Silver.	Silver-white.	Monday.

This is the arrangement now adopted by Christian Astrologers, with the exception of the order of the days of the week, of which, by associating the solar planetary names with the lunar weeks, they have made a sore mess, as has been already shown in Paper I. This is the Ptolemaic geocentric system, which represents the Universe as in the following diagram, showing our Earth in the centre of the Universe, and the Sun a Planet, the fourth in number:

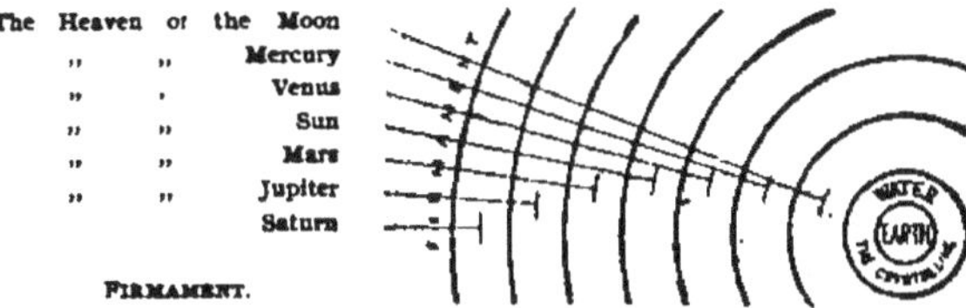

And if the Christian chronology and order of the days of the week are being daily denounced as being based on an entirely wrong astronomical foundation, it is high time to begin a reform also in Astrology built on such lines, and coming to us entirely from the Chaldæan and Assyrian exoteric mob.

But the correspondences given in these Papers are purely Esoteric.

* See *supra*, ii. 373; and . 152, *et seq.*

For this reason it follows that when the Planets of the Solar System are named or symbolized (as in Diagram II.) it must not be supposed that the planetary bodies themselves are referred to, except as types on a purely physical plane of the septenary nature of the psychic and spiritual worlds. A material planet can correspond only to a material something. Thus when Mercury is said to correspond to the right eye, it does not mean that the objective planet has any influence on the right optic organ, but that both stand rather as corresponding mystically through Buddhi. Man derives his Spiritual Soul (Buddhi) from the essence of the Mânasa Putra, the Sons of Wisdom, who are the Divine Beings (or Angels) ruling and presiding over the planet Mercury.

In the same way Venus, Manas and the left eye are set down as correspondences. Exoterically, there is, in reality, no such association of physical eyes and physical planets; but Esoterically there is; the right eye is the "Eye of Wisdom," *i.e.*, it corresponds magnetically with that Occult centre in the brain which we call the "Third Eye";* while the left corresponds with the intellectual brain, or those cells which are the organ on the physical plane of the thinking Being. The kabalistic triangle of Kether, Chokmah and Binah shows this. Chokmah and Binah, or Wisdom and Intelligence, the Father and Mother, or, again, the Father and Son, are on the same plane and reäct mutually on one another.

When the individual consciousness is turned inward, a conjunction of Manas and Buddhi takes place. In the spiritually regenerated man, this conjunction is permanent, the Higher Manas clinging to Buddhi beyond the threshold of Devachan, and the Soul, or rather the Spirit, which should not be confounded with Âtmâ, the Super-Spirit, is then said to have the "Single Eye." Esoterically, in other words, the "Third Eye" is active. Now Mercury is called Hermes, and Venus Aphrodite, and thus their conjunction in man on the psycho-physical plane gives him the name of the Hermaphrodite, or Androgyne. The absolutely Spiritual Man is, however, entirely disconnected from this. The Spiritual Man corresponds directly with the higher "coloured circles," the Divine Prism which emanates from the One Infinite White Circle; while physical man emanates from the Sephiroth, which are the Voices or Sounds of Eastern Philosophy. And these "Voices"

* See *supra*, ii. 304, *et seq.*

are lower than the "Colours," for they are the seven lower Sephiroth, or the objective Sounds, seen, not heard, as the *Zohar* shows,* and even the Old Testament also. For, when properly translated, verse 18 of chapter xx. *Exodus* would read: "And the people saw the Voices" (or Sounds, not the "thunderings" as now translated); and these Voices, or Sounds, are the Sephiroth.†

In the same way the right and left nostrils, into which is breathed the "Breath of Lives"‡ are here said to correspond with Sun and Moon, as Brahmâ-Prajâpati and Vâch, or Osiris and Isis, are the parents of the natural life. This Quaternary, *viz.:* the two eyes and two nostrils, Mercury and Venus, Sun and Moon, constitutes the Kabalistic Guardian-Angels of the Four Corners of the Earth. It is the same in the Eastern Esoteric Philosophy, which, however, adds that the Sun is not a planet, but the central star of our system, and the Moon a dead planet, from which all the principles are gone, both being substitutes, the one for an invisible inter-Mercurial planet, and the other for a planet which seems to have now altogether disappeared from view. These are the Four Mahârâjahs,§ the "Four Holy Ones" connected with Karma and Humanity, Kosmos and Man, in all their aspects. They are: the Sun, or its substitute Michael; Moon, or substitute Gabriel; Mercury, Raphael; and Venus, Uriel. It need hardly be said here again that the planetary bodies themselves, being only physical symbols, are not often referred to in the Esoteric System, but, as a rule, their cosmic, psychic, physical and spiritual forces are symbolized under these names. In short, it is the seven physical planets which are the lower Sephiroth of the *Kabalah*, and our triple physical Sun whose reflection only we see, which is symbolized, or rather personified, by the Upper Triad, or Sephirothal Crown.‖

Then, again, it will be well to point out that the numbers attached to the psychic principles in Diagram I. appear the reverse of those in exoteric writings. This is because numbers in this connection are purely arbitrary, changing with every school. Some schools count

---

* *Op. cit.*, ii. 81, 6.

† See Frank's *Die Kabbala*, p. 314, *et seq.*

‡ *Genesis*, ii. 7.

§ *Supra*, i. 147.

‖ We may refer for confirmation to Origen's works, who says that "the seven ruling daimons" (genii or planetary rulers) are Michael, the Sun (the lion-like); the second in order, the Bull, Jupiter or Suriel, etc.; and all these, the "Seven of the Presence," are the Sephiroth. The Sephirothal Tree is the Tree of the Divine Planets as given by Porphyry, or Porphyry's Tree, as it is usually called.

three, some four, some six, and others seven, as do all Esotericists. As said before,* the Esoteric School has been divided into two departments since the fourteenth century, one for the inner Lanoos, or higher Chelâs, the other for the outer circle, or lay Chelâs. Mr. Sinnett was distinctly told in the letters he received from one of the Gurus that he could not be taught the real Esoteric Doctrine, given out only to the pledged disciples of the Inner Circle. The numbers and principles do not go in regular sequence, like the skins of an onion, but the student must work out for himself the number appropriate to each of his principles, when the time comes for him to enter upon practical study. The above will suggest to the student the necessity of knowing the principles by their names and their appropriate faculties apart from any system of enumeration, or by association with their corresponding centres of actions, colours, sounds, etc., until these become inseparable.

The old and familiar mode of reckoning the principles, given in the *Theosophist* and *Esoteric Buddhism*, leads to another apparently perplexing contradiction, though it is really none at all. The principles numbered 3 and 2, *viz.*: Linga Sharira and Prâna, or Jiva, stand in the reverse order to that given in Diagram I. A moment's consideration will suffice to explain the apparent discrepancy between the exoteric enumeration, and the Esoteric order given in Diagram I. For in Diagram I. the Linga Sharira is defined as the vehicle of Prâna, or Jiva, the life principle, and as such must of necessity be inferior to Prâna, not superior as the exoteric enumeration would suggest. The principles do not stand one above the other, and thus cannot be taken in numerical sequence; their order depends upon the superiority and predominance of one or another principle, and therefore differs in every man.

The Linga Sharira is the double, or protoplasmic antetype of the body, which is its image. It is in this sense that it is called in Diagram II. the parent of the physical body, *i.e.*, the mother by conception of Prâna, the father. This idea is conveyed in the Egyptian mythology by the birth of Horus, the child of Osiris and Isis, although, like all sacred Mythoi, this has both a threefold spiritual, and a sevenfold psycho-physical application. To close the subject, Prâna, the life principle, can, in sober truth, have no number, as it pervades

* *Supra*, i, 147.

every other principle, or the human total. Each number of the seven would thus be naturally applicable to Prâna-Jiva exoterically as it is to the Auric Body Esoterically. As Pythagoras showed, Kosmos was produced not *through* or *by* number, but geometrically, *i.e.*, following the proportions of numbers.

To those who are unacquainted with the exoteric astrological natures ascribed in practice to the planetary bodies, it may be useful if we set them down here after the manner of Diagram II., in relation to their dominion over the human body, colours, metals, etc., and explain at the same time why genuine Esoteric Philosophy differs from the astrological claims.

Planets.	*Days.*	*Metals.*	*Parts of the Body.*	*Colours.*
Saturn.	Saturday.	Lead.	Right Ear, Knees and Bony System.	Black.*
Jupiter.	Thursday.	Tin.	Left Ear, Thighs, Feet and Arterial System.	Purple.†
Mars.	Tuesday.	Iron.	Forehead and Nose, the Skull, Sex-function and Muscular System.	Red.
Sun.	Sunday.	Gold.	Right Eye, Heart and Vital Centres.	Orange.‡
Venus.	Friday.	Copper.	Chin and Cheeks, Neck and Reins and the Venous System.	Yellow.§
Mercury.	Wednesday.	Quicksilver.	Mouth, Hands, Abdominal Viscera and Nervous System.	Dove or Cream.‖
Moon.	Monday.	Silver.	Breasts, Left Eye, the Fluidic System, Saliva, Lymph, etc.	White.¶

* Esoterically, green, there being no black in the prismatic ray.

† Esoterically, light blue. As a pigment, purple is a compound of red and blue, and in Eastern Occultism blue is the spiritual essence of the colour purple, while red is its material basis. In reality, Occultism makes Jupiter blue because he is the son of Saturn, which is green, and light blue as a prismatic colour contains a great deal of green. Again, the Auric Body will contain much of the colour of the Lower Manas if the man is a material sensualist, just as it will contain much of the darker hue if the Higher Manas has preponderance over the Lower.

‡ Esoterically, the Sun cannot correspond with the eye, nose, or any other organ, since, as explained, it is no planet, but a central star. It was adopted as a planet by the post-Christian Astrologers, who had never been initiated. Moreover, the true colour of the Sun is blue, and it appears yellow only owing to the effect of the absorption of vapours (chiefly metallic) by its atmosphere. All is Mâyâ on our Earth.

§ Esoterically, indigo, or dark blue, which is the compliment of yellow in the prism. Yellow is a simple or primitive colour. Manas being dual in its nature—as is its sidereal symbol, the planet

Thus it will be seen that the influence of the solar [illegible] exoteric kabalistic Astrology is by this method distributed [illegible] entire human body, the primary metals, and the gradations [illegible] from black to white; but that Esotericism recognises neither [illegible] white as colours, because it holds religiously to the seven [illegible] natural colours of the prism. Black and white are artificial tints [illegible] belong to the Earth, and are only perceived by virtue of the [illegible] construction of our physical organs. White is the absence [illegible] colours, and therefore no colour; black is simply the absence [illegible] and therefore the negative aspect of white. The seven [illegible] colours are direct emanations from the Seven Hierarchies [illegible] each of which has a direct bearing upon and relation to one [illegible] human principles, since each of these Hierarchies is, in fact, the [illegible] and source of the corresponding human principle. Each [illegible] colour is called in Occultism the "Father of the Sound" which [illegible] sponds to it; Sound being the Word, or the Logos, of its [illegible] Thought. This is the reason why sensitives connect every [illegible] with a definite sound, a fact well recognized in Modern [illegible] (*e.g.*, Francis Galton's *Human Faculty*). But black and white [illegible]

Venus, which is both the morning and evening star—the difference between the higher and [illegible] principles of Manas, whose essence is derived from the Hierarchy ruling Venus, is denoted [illegible] dark blue and green. Green, the Lower Manas, resembles the colour of the solar spectrum [illegible] appears between the yellow and the dark blue, the Higher Spiritual Manas. Indigo is the [illegible] colour of the heaven or sky, to denote the upward tendency of Manas toward [illegible] heavenly Spiritual Soul. This colour is obtained from the *indigofera tinctoria*, a plant of [illegible] highest occult properties in India, much used in White Magic, and occultly connected [illegible] This is shown by the indigo assuming a copper lustre, especially when rubbed on any hard [illegible] Another property of the dye is that it is insoluble in water and even in ether, being lighter [illegible] than any known liquid. No symbol has ever been adopted in the East without being [illegible] a logical and demonstrable reason. Therefore Eastern Symbologists, from the earliest [illegible] connected the spiritual and the animal minds of man, the one with dark blue (Newton's [illegible] true blue, free from green; and the other with pure green.

‖ Esoterically, yellow, because the colour of the Sun is orange, and Mercury now stands [illegible] the Sun in distance, as it does in colour. The planet for which the Sun is a substitute [illegible] nearer the Sun than Mercury now is, and was one of the most secret and highest planets [illegible] to have become invisible at the close of the Third Race.

¶ Esoterically, violet, because, perhaps, violet is the colour assumed by a ray of [illegible] transmitted through a very thin plate of silver, and also because the Moon shines [illegible] with light borrowed from the Sun, as the human body shines with qualifications borrowed [illegible] double—the aërial man. As the astral shadow starts the series of principles in man, [illegible] trial plane, up to the lower, animal Manas, so the violet ray starts the series of prismatic [illegible] its end up to green, both being, the one as a principle and the other as a colour, the [illegible] of all the principles and colours. Besides which, there is the same great Occult mystery [illegible] all these correspondences, both celestial and terrestrial bodies, colours and sounds... [illegible] there exists the same law of relation between the Moon and the Earth, the astral and [illegible] of man, as between the violet end of the prismatic spectrum and the indigo and the blue, [illegible] more anon.

entirely negative colours, and have no representatives in the world of subjective being.

Kabalistic Astrology says that the dominion of the planetary bodies in the human brain also is defined thus: there are seven primary groups of faculties, six of which function through the cerebrum, and the seventh through the cerebellum. This is perfectly correct Esoterically. But when it is further said that: Saturn governs the devotional faculties; Mercury, the intellectual; Jupiter, the sympathetic; the Sun, the governing faculties; Mars, the selfish; Venus, the tenacious; and the Moon, the instincts;—we say that the explanation is incomplete and even misleading. For, in the first place, the physical planets can rule only the physical body and the purely physical functions. All the mental, emotional, psychic and spiritual faculties, are influenced by the Occult properties of the scale of causes which emanate from the Hierarchies of the Spiritual Rulers of the planets, and not by the planets themselves. This scale, as given in Diagram II., leads the student to perceive in the following order: (1) colour; (2) sound; (3) the sound materializes into the spirit of the metals, *i.e.*, the metallic Elementals; (4) these materialize again into the physical metals; (5) then the harmonial and vibratory radiant essence passes into the plants, giving them colour and smell, both of which "properties" depend upon the rate of vibration of this energy per unit of time; (6) from plants it passes into the animals; (7) and finally culminates in the "principles" of man.

Thus we see the Divine Essence of our Progenitors in Heaven circling through seven stages; Spirit becoming Matter, and Matter returning to Spirit. As there is sound in Nature which is inaudible, so there is colour which is invisible, but which can be heard. The creative force, at work in its incessant task of transformation, produces colour, sound and numbers, in the shape of rates of vibration which compound and dissociate the atoms and molecules. Though invisible and inaudible to us in detail, yet the synthesis of the whole becomes audible to us on the material plane. It is that which the Chinese call the "Great Tone," or *Kung*. It is, even by scientific confession, the actual tonic of Nature, held by musicians to be the middle Fa on the keyboard of a piano. We hear it distinctly in the voice of Nature, in the roaring of the ocean, in the sound of the foliage of a great forest, in the distant roar of a great city, in the wind, the tempest and the storm; in short, in everything in Nature which has a voice or produces sound. To the

2 0

hearing of all who hearken, it culminates in a single [illegible] an unappreciable pitch, which, as said, is the F, or Fa [illegible] scale. From these particulars, that wherein lies the [illegible] the exoteric and the Esoteric nomenclature and symbolism [illegible] evident to the student of Occultism. In short, kabalistic [illegible] practised in Europe, is the semi-esoteric Secret Science, [illegible] outer and not for the inner circle. It is, furthermore, [illegible] plete and not infrequently distorted to conceal the real [illegible] it symbolizes and adapts its correspondences on the mere [illegible] of things, Esoteric Philosophy, which concerns itself [illegible] with the essence of things, accepts only such symbols as [illegible] whole ground, *i.e.*, such symbols as yield a spiritual as well as a [illegible] and physical meaning. Yet even Western Astrology has [illegible] lent work, for it has helped to carry the knowledge of the [illegible] a Secret Wisdom throughout the dangers of the Mediaeval [illegible] and their dark bigotry up to the present day, when all danger [illegible] appeared.

The order of the planets in exoteric practice is that [illegible] geocentric radii, or the distance of their several orbits from the [illegible] as a centre, *viz.*, Saturn, Jupiter, Mars, Sun, Venus, Mercury and [illegible] In the first three of these we find symbolised the celestial [illegible] supreme power in the physical, manifested universe, or Brahma, [illegible] and Shiva; while in the last four we recognize the symbols of the [illegible] restrial quaternary ruling over all natural and physical [illegible] the seasons, quarters of the day, points of the compass, and [illegible] Thus:

Spring.	Summer.	Autumn.	Winter.
Morning.	Noon.	Evening.	Night.
Youth.	Adolescence.	Manhood.	Age.
Fire.	Air.	Water.	Earth.
East.	South.	West.	North.

But Esoteric Science is not content with analogies on the [illegible] objective plane of the physical senses, and therefore it is [illegible] necessary to preface further teachings in this direction with a [illegible] explanation of the real meaning of the word Magic.

WHAT MAGIC IS, IN REALITY.

Esoteric Science is, above all, the knowledge of our relations with and, in Divine Magic,* inseparableness from our divine *Selves*—the latter meaning something else besides our own higher Spirit. Thus, before proceeding to exemplify and explain these relations, it may perhaps be useful to give the student a correct idea of the full meaning of this most misunderstood word "Magic." Many are those willing and eager to study Occultism, but very few have even an approximate idea of the Science itself. Now, very few of our American and European students can derive benefit from Sanskrit works or even their translations, as these translations are, for the most part, merely blinds to the uninitiated. I therefore propose to offer to their attention demonstrations of the aforesaid drawn from Neo-Platonic works. These are accessible in translation; and in order to throw light on that which has hitherto been full of darkness, it will suffice to point to a certain key in them. Thus the Gnosis, both pre-Christian and post-Christian, will serve our purpose admirably.

There are millions of Christians who know the name of Simon Magus, and the little that is told about him in the *Acts*; but very few who have even heard of the many motley, fantastic and contradictory details which tradition records about his life. The story of his claims and his death is to be found only in the prejudiced, half-fantastic records about him in the works of the Church Fathers, such as Irenæus, Epiphanius and St. Justin, and especially in the anonymous *Philosophumena*. Yet he is a historical character, and the appellation of "Magus" was given to him and was accepted by all his contemporaries, including the heads of the Christian Church, as a qualification indicating the miraculous powers he possessed, and irrespective of whether he was regarded as a white (divine) or a black (infernal) Magician. In this respect, opinion has always been made subservient to the Gentile or Christian proclivities of his chronicler.

It is in his system and in that of Menander, his pupil and successor, that we find what the term "Magic" meant for Initiates in those days.

Simon, as all the other Gnostics, taught that our world was created by the *lower* angels, whom he called Æons. He mentions only three

---

* Magic, *Magia*, means, in its spiritual, secret sense, the "Great Life," or divine life *in spirit*. The root is *magh*, as seen in the Sanskrit *mahat*, Zend *maz*, Greek *megas*, and Latin *magnus*, all signifying "great."

degrees of such, because it was and is useless, as we have before explained, to teach anything about the four higher ones, and he therefore begins at the plane of globes A and G. His system is as near to Occult Truth as any, so that we may examine it, as well as his pupil Menander's claims about "Magic," to find out what they meant by the term. Now, for Simon, the summit of all manifested creation was Fire. It was, with him as with us, the Universal Principle, the Infinite Potency, born from the concealed Potentiality. This Fire was the primeval cause of the manifested world of being, and was dual, having a manifested and a concealed, or secret, side.

> The secret side of the Fire is concealed in its evident [or objective] side, and the objective is produced from the secret side,*

he writes, which amounts to saying that the visible is ever present in the invisible, and the invisible in the visible. This was but a new form of stating Plato's idea of the Intelligible *(Noêton)* and the Sensible *(Aisthêton)*, and Aristotle's teaching on the Potency *(Dunamis)* and the Act *(Energeia)*. For Simon, all that can be thought of, all that can be acted upon, was perfect intelligence. Fire contained *all*. And thus all the parts of that Fire, being endowed with intelligence and reason, were susceptible of development by extension and emanation. This is our teaching of the Manifested Logos, and these parts in their primordial emanation are our Dhyân Chohans, the "Sons of Flame and Fire," or higher Æons. This "Fire" is the symbol of the active and living side of Divine Nature. Behind it lay "infinite Potentiality in Potentiality," which Simon named "that which has stood, stands and will stand," or permanent stability and personified immutability.

From the Potency of Thought, Divine Ideation thus passed to Action. Hence the series of primordial emanations through Thought begetting the Act, the objective side of Fire being the Mother, the sacred side of it being the Father. Simon called these emanations Syzygies (a united pair, or couple), for they emanated two-by-two, one as an active and the other as a passive Æon. Three couples thus emanated (or six in all, the Fire being the seventh), to which Simon gave the following names: "Mind and Thought; Voice and Name; Reason and Reflection,"† the first in each pair being male, the last female. From these primordial six emanated the six Æons of the Middle World. Let us see what Simon himself says:

---

* *Philosophumena*, vi. 9.

† *Nous, Epinoia; Phônê, Onoma; Logismos, Enthumêsis*.

Each of these six primitive beings contained the entire Infinite Potency [of its parent]; but it was there only in Potency, and not in Act. That Potency had to be called forth [or conformed] through an *image* in order that it should manifest in all its essence, virtue, grandeur and effects; for only then could the emanated Potency become similar to its parent, the eternal and infinite Potency. If, on the contrary, it remained simply potentially in the six Potencies and failed to be conformed through an image, then the Potency would not pass into action, but would get lost,*

in clearer terms, it would become atrophied, as the modern expression goes.

Now, what do these words mean if not that to be equal in all things to the Infinite Potency the Æons had to imitate it in its action, and become themselves, in their turn, emanative Principles, as was their Parent, giving life to new beings, and becoming Potencies *in actu* themselves? To produce emanations, or to have acquired the gift of Kriyâshakti,† is the direct result of that power, an effect which depends on our own action. That power, then, is inherent in man, as it is in the primordial Æons and even in the secondary Emanations, by the very fact of their and our descent from the One Primordial Principle, the Infinite Power, or Potency. Thus we find in the system of Simon Magus that the first six Æons, synthesized by the seventh, the Parent Potency, passed into Act, and emanated, in their turn, six secondary Æons, which were each synthesized by their respective Parents. In the *Philosophumena* we read that Simon compared the Æons to the "Tree of Life.' Said Simon in the *Revelation*:‡

It is written that there are two ramifications of the universal Æons, having neither beginning nor end, issued both from the same Root, the invisible and incomprehensible Potentiality, Sigê [Silence]. One of these [series of Æons] appears from above. This is the Great Potency, Universal Mind [or Divine Ideation, the Mahat of the Hindus]; it orders all things and is male. The other is from below, for it is the Great [manifested] Thought, the female Æon, generating all things. These [two kinds of Æons] corresponding§ with each other, have conjunction and manifest the middle distance [the intermediate sphere, or plane], the incomprehensible Air which has neither beginning nor end.||

This female "Air" is our Ether, or the kabalistic Astral Light. It

* *Philosophumena*, vi. 12.

† See *supra*, *sub voce*.

‡ *The Great Revelation* (*Hê Megalê Apophasis*), of which Simon himself is supposed to have been the author.

§ Literally, standing opposite each other in rows or pairs.

|| *Philosophumena*, vi. 18.

All that is eternal, pure and incorruptible is concealed in everything that is,

if only potentially, not actually. And

Everything is that image, provided the lower image (man) ascends to that highest Source and Root in Spirit and Thought.

Matter as Substance is eternal and has never been created. Therefore Simon Magus, with all the great Gnostic Teachers and Eastern Philosophers, never speaks of its beginning. "Eternal Matter" receives its various forms in the lower Æon from the Creative Angels, or Builders, as we call them. Why, then, should not Man, the direct heir of the highest Æon, do the same, by the potency of his thought, which is born from Spirit? This is Kriyâshakti, the power of producing forms on the objective plane through the potency of Ideation and Will, from invisible, indestructible Matter.

Truly says Jeremiah,* quoting the "Word of the Lord":

Before I formed thee in the belly I knew thee; and before thou camest forth out of the womb I sanctified thee,

for Jeremiah stands here for Man when he was yet an Æon, or Divine Man, both with Simon Magus and Eastern Philosophy. The first three chapters of *Genesis* are as Occult as that which is given in Paper I. For the terrestrial Paradise is the Womb, says Simon,† Eden the region surrounding it. The river which went out of Eden to water the garden is the Umbilical Cord; this cord is divided into four Heads, the streams that flowed out of it, the four canals which serve to carry nutrition to the Fœtus, *i.e.*, the two arteries and the two veins which are the channels for the blood and convey the breathing air, the unborn child, according to Simon, being entirely enveloped by the Amnion, fed through the Umbilical Cord and given vital air through the Aorta.‡

* *Op. cit.*, i. 5.

† *Philosophumena*, vi. 14.

‡ At first there are the omphalo-mesenteric vessels, two arteries and two veins, but these afterwards totally disappear, as does the "vascular area" on the Umbilical Vesicle, from which they proceed. As regards the "Umbilical Vessels" proper, the Umbilical Cord ultimately has entwined around it from right to left the one Umbilical Vein which takes the oxygenated blood from the mother to the Fœtus, and two Hypogastric or Umbilical Arteries which take the used-up blood from the Fœtus to the Placenta, the contents of the vessels being the reverse of that which prevails after birth. Thus Science corroborates the wisdom and knowledge of ancient Occultism, for in the days of Simon Magus no man, unless an Initiate, knew anything about the circulation of the blood or about Physiology. While this Paper was being printed, I received two small pamphlets from Dr. Jerome A. Anderson, which were printed in 1884 and 1888, and in which is to be found the scientific demonstration of the fœtal nutrition as advanced in Paper I. Briefly, the Fœtus is nourished by osmosis from the Amniotic Fluid and respires by means of the Placenta. Science knows little or nothing about the Amniotic Fluid and its uses. If any one cares to follow up this question, I would recommend Dr. Anderson's *Remarks on the Nutrition of the Fœtus*. (Wood & Co., New York.)

The above is given for the elucidation of that which is to follow. The disciples of Simon Magus were numerous, and were instructed by him in Magic. They made use of so-called "exorcisms" (as in the *New Testament*), incantations, philtres; believed in dreams and visions, and produced them at will; and finally forced the lower orders of spirits to obey them. Simon Magus was called "the Great Power of God," literally "the Potency of the Deity which is called Great." That which was then termed Magic we now call Theosophia, or Divine Wisdom, Power and Knowledge.

His direct disciple, Menander, was also a great Magician. Says Irenæus, among other writers:

> The successor of Simon was Menander, a Samaritan by birth, who reached the highest summits in the Science of Magic.

Thus both master and pupil are shown as having attained the highest powers in the art of enchantments, powers which can be obtained only through "the help of the Devil," as Christians claim; and yet their "works" were identical with those spoken of in the *New Testament*, wherein such phenomenal results are called divine miracles, and are, therefore, believed in and accepted as coming from and through God. But the question is, have these so-called "miracles" of the "Christ" and the Apostles ever been explained any more than the magical achievements of so-called Sorcerers and Magicians? I say, never. We Occultists do not believe in supernatural phenomena, and the Masters laugh at the word "miracle." Let us see, then, what is really the sense of the word Magic.

The source and basis of it lie in Spirit and Thought, whether on the purely divine or the terrestrial plane. Those who know the history of Simon have the two versions before them, that of White and of Black Magic, at their option, in the much talked of union of Simon with Helena, whom he called his Epinoia (Thought). Those who, like the Christians, had to discredit a dangerous rival, talk of Helena as being a beautiful and actual woman, whom Simon had met in a house of ill-fame at Tyre, and who was, according to those who wrote his life, the reincarnation of Helen of Troy. How, then, was she "Divine Thought"? The lower angels, Simon is made to say in *Philosophumena*, or the third Æons, being so material, had more badness in them than all the others. Poor man, created or emanated from them, had the vice of his origin. What was it? Only this: when the third Æons possessed themselves, in their turn, of the Divine Thought through the transmission into them of Fire, instead of making of man a complete being, according to the universal plan, they at first detained from him that Divine Spark (Thought, on Earth Manas); and that was the cause and origin of senseless man's committing the original sin as the angels had committed it æons before by refusing to create.* Finally, after detaining Epinoia prisoner amongst them and having subjected the Divine Thought to every kind of insult and desecration, they ended by shutting it into the already defiled body of man. After this, as interpreted by the enemies of Simon, she passed from one female body into another through ages and races, until Simon found and recognized her in the form of Helena, the "prostitute," the "lost sheep" of the parable. Simon is made to represent himself as the Saviour descended on Earth to rescue this "lamb" and those men in whom Epinoia is still under the dominion of the lower angels. The greatest magical feats are thus attributed to Simon through his sexual union with Helena, hence Black Magic. Indeed, the chief rites of this kind of Magic are based on such disgusting literal interpretation of noble myths, one of the noblest of which was thus invented by Simon as a symbolical mark of his own teaching. Those who understood it correctly knew what was meant by "Helena." It was the marriage of Nous (Âtmâ-Buddhi) with Manas, the union through which Will and Thought become one and are endowed with divine powers. For Âtman in man, being of an unalloyed essence, the primordial Divine Fire (or the eternal and universal "that which has stood, stands and will stand"), is of all the planes; and Buddhi is its vehicle or Thought, generated by and generating the "Father" in her turn, and also Will. She is "that which has stood, stands and will stand," thus becoming, in conjunction with Manas, male-female, in this sphere only. Hence, when Simon spoke of himself as the Father and the Son and the Holy Ghost, and of Helena as his Epinoia, Divine Thought, he meant the marriage of his Buddhi with Manas. Helena was the Shakti of the inner man, the female potency.

Now, what says Menander? The lower angels, he taught, were the emanations of Ennoia (Designing Thought). It was Ennoia who taught the Science of Magic and imparted it to him, together with the art of conquering the creative angels of the lower world. The latter stand for the passions of our lower nature. His pupils, after receiving

* *Supra*, vol. ii.

baptism from him (*i.e.*, after Initiation), were said to "resurrect from the dead" and, "growing no older," became "immortal."* This "resurrection" promised by Menander meant, of course, simply the passage from the darkness of ignorance into the light of truth, the awakening of man's immortal Spirit to inner and eternal life. This is the Science of the Râja Yogîs—Magic.

Every person who has read Neo-Platonic Philosophy knows how its chief Adepts, such as Plotinus, and especially Porphyry, fought against phenomenal Theurgy. But, beyond all of them, Jamblichus, the author of the *De Mysteriis*, lifts high the veil from the real term Theurgy, and shows us therein the true Divine Science of Râja Yoga.

Magic, he says, is a lofty and sublime Science, Divine, and exalted above all others.

> It is the great remedy for all. . . . It neither takes its source in, nor is it limited to, the body or its passions, to the human compound or its constitution; but all is derived by it from our upper Gods,

our divine Egos, which run like a silver thread from the Spark in us up to the primeval divine Fire.†

Jamblichus execrates physical phenomena, produced, as he says, by the bad demons who deceive men (the spooks of the séance room), as vehemently as he exalts Divine Theurgy. But to exercise the latter, he teaches, the Theurgist must imperatively be "a man of high morality and a chaste Soul." The other kind of Magic is used only by impure, selfish men, and has nothing of the Divine in it. No real Vates would ever consent to find in its communications anything coming from our higher Gods. Thus one (Theurgy) is the knowledge of our Father (the Higher Self); the other, subjection to our lower nature. One requires holiness of the Soul, a holiness which rejects and excludes everything corporeal; the other, the desecration of it (the Soul). One is the union with the Gods (with one's God), the source of all Good; the other intercourse with demons (Elementals), which, unless we subject them, will subject us, and lead us step by step to moral ruin (mediumship). In short:

> Theurgy unites us most strongly to divine nature. This nature begets itself through itself, moves through its own powers, supports all, and is intelligent. Being the ornament of the Universe, it invites us to intelligible truth, to perfection

* See Eusebius, *Hist. Eccles.*, lib. iii. cap. 26.

† *De Mysteriis*, p. 100, lines 10 to 19; p. 109, fol. 1.

and imparting perfection to others. It unites us so intimately to all the magic actions of the Gods, according to the capacity of each of us, that the soul having accomplished the sacred rites is consolidated in their [the Gods'] actions and intelligences, until it launches itself into and is absorbed by the primordial divine essence. This is the object of the sacred Initiations of the Egyptians.*

Now, Jamblichus shows us how this union of our Higher Soul with the Universal Soul, with the Gods, is to be effected. He speaks of Manteia, which is Samâdhi, the highest trance.† He speaks also of dream which is divine vision, when man re-becomes again a God. By Theurgy, or Râja Yoga, a man arrives at: (1) Prophetic Discernment through our God (the respective Higher Ego of each of us) revealing to us the truths of the plane on which we happen to be acting; (2) Ecstacy and Illumination; (3) Action in Spirit (in Astral Body or through Will); (4) and Domination over the minor, senseless demons (Elementals) by the very nature of our purified Egos. But this demands the complete purification of the latter. And this is called by him, Magic, through initiation into Theurgy.

But Theurgy has to be preceded by a training of our senses and the knowledge of the human Self in relation to the Divine Self. So long as man has not thoroughly mastered this preliminary study, it is idle to anthropomorphize the formless. By "formless" I mean the higher and the lower Gods, the supermundane as well as mundane Spirits, or Beings, which to beginners can be revealed only in Colours and Sounds. For none but a high Adept can perceive a "God" in its true transcendental form, which to the untrained intellect, to the Chelâ, will be visible only by its Aura. The visions of full figures casually perceived by sensitives and mediums belong to one or another of the only three categories they can see: *(a)* Astrals of living men; *(b)* Nirmânakâyas (Adepts, good or bad, whose bodies are dead, but who have learned to live in the invisible space in their ethereal personalities); and *(c)* Spooks, Elementaries and Elementals masquerading in shapes borrowed from the Astral Light in general, or from figures in the "mind's eye" of the audience, or of the medium, which are immediately reflected in their respective Auras.

Having read the foregoing, students will now better comprehend the necessity of first studying the correspondences between our "principles" —which are but the various aspects of the triune (spiritual and physical) man—and our Paradigm, the direct roots of these in the Universe.

* *De Mysteriis*, p. 290, lines 15 to 18, *et seq.*, caps. v. and vii.

† *Ibid.*, p. 100, sec. iii, cap. iii.

In view of this, we must resume our teaching about the Hierarchies directly connected and for ever linked with man.

Enough has been said to show that while for the Orientalists and profane masses the sentence, "*Om Mani Padme Hum*," means simply "Oh the Jewel in the Lotus," Esoterically it signifies "Oh my God within me." Yes; there is a God in each human being, for man was, and will re-become, God. The sentence points to the indissoluble union between Man and the Universe. For the Lotus is the universal symbol of Kosmos as the absolute totality, and the Jewel is Spiritual Man, or God.

In the preceding Paper, the correspondences between Colours, Sounds, and "Principles" were given; and those who have read our second volume will remember that these seven principles are derived from the seven great Hierarchies of Angels, or Dhyân Chohans, which are, in their turn, associated with Colours and Sounds, and form collectively the Manifested Logos.

In the eternal music of the spheres we find the perfect scale corresponding to the colours, and in the number, determined by the vibrations of colour and sound, which "underlies every form and guides every sound," we find the summing-up of the Manifested Universe.

We may illustrate these correspondences by showing the relation of colour and sound to the geometrical figures which* express the progressive stages in the manifestation of Kosmos.

But the student will certainly be liable to confusion if, in studying the Diagrams, he does not remember two things: (1) That, our plane being a plane of reflection, and therefore illusionary, *the various notations are reversed and must be counted from below upwards*. The musical scale begins from below upwards, commencing with the deep Do and ending with the far more acute Si. (2) That Kâma Rûpa (corresponding to Do in the musical scale), containing as it does all potentialities of Matter, is necessarily the starting-point on our plane. Further, it commences the notation on every plane, as corresponding to the "matter" of that plane. Again, the student must also remember that these notes have to be arranged in a circle, thus showing how Fa is the middle note of Nature. In short, musical notes, or Sounds, Colours

---

* See *supra*, i. 34; i. 4, *et seq.*; ii. 39, *et seq.*, and 605, *et seq.*

and Numbers proceed from one to seven, and not from seven to one, as erroneously shown in the spectrum of the prismatic colours, in which Red is counted first: a fact which necessitated my putting the principles and the days of the week at random in Diagram II. The musical scale and colours, according to the number of vibrations, proceed from the world of gross Matter to that of Spirit thus:

Principles.	*Colours.*	*Notes.*	*Numbers.*	*States of Matter.*
Chhâyâ, Shadow or Double.	Violet.	Si.	7.	Ether.
Higher Manas, Spiritual Intelligence.	Indigo.	La.	6.	Critical State, called Air in Occultism.
Auric Envelope.	Blue.	Sol.	5.	Steam or Vapour.
Lower Manas, or Animal Soul.	Green.	Fa.	4.	Critical State.
Buddhi, or Spiritual Soul.	Yellow.	Mi.	3.	Water.
Prâna, or Life Principle.	Orange.	Re.	2.	Critical State.
Kâma Rûpa, the Seat of Animal Life.	Red.	Do.	1.	Ice.

Here again the student is asked to dismiss from his mind any correspondence between "principles" and numbers, for reasons already given. The Esoteric enumeration cannot be made to correspond with the conventional exoteric. The one is the reality, the other is classified according to illusive appearances. The human principles, as given in *Esoteric Buddhism*, were tabulated for beginners, so as not to confuse their minds. It was half a blind.

———

COLOURS, SOUNDS AND FORMS.

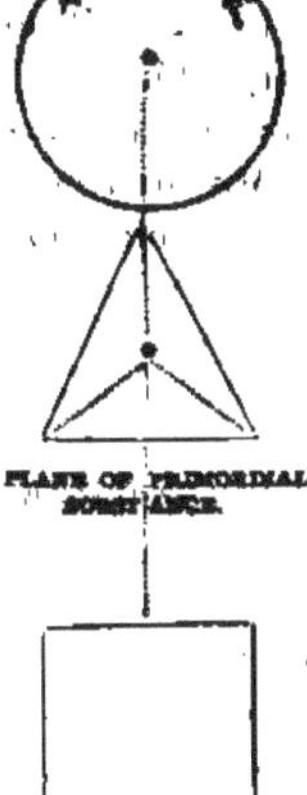

To proceed:

The Point in the Circle is the Unmanifested Logos, corresponding to Absolute Life and Absolute Sound.

The first geometrical figure after the Circle or the Spheroid is the Triangle. It corresponds to Motion, Colour and Sound. Thus the Point in the Triangle represents the Second Logos, "Father-Mother," or the White Ray which is no colour, since it contains potentially all colours. It is shown radiating from the Unmanifested Logos, or the Unspoken Word. Around the first Triangle is formed on the plane of Primordial Substance in this order (*reversed* as to our plane):

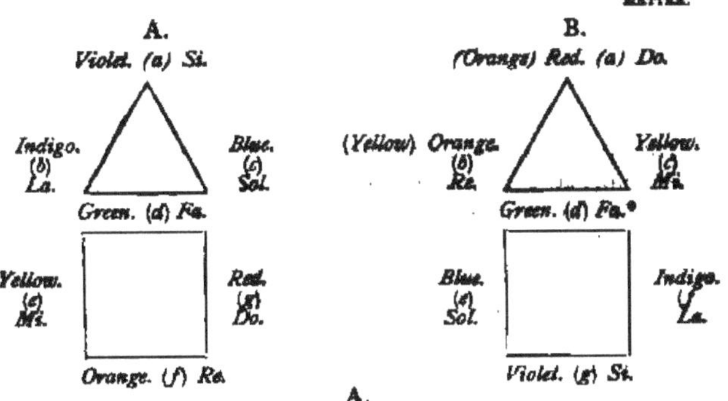

A.

(*a*) The Astral Double of Nature, or the Paradigm of all Forms.

(*b*) Divine Ideation, or Universal Mind.

(*c*) The Synthesis of Occult Nature, the Egg of Brahmâ, containing all and radiating all.

(*d*) Animal or Material Soul of Nature, source of animal and vegetable intelligence and instinct.

---

* The Master-Key or Tonic of Manifested Nature.

(*e*) The aggregate of Dhyân Chohanic Intelligences, Fohat.

(*f*) Life Principle in Nature.

(*g*) The Life Procreating Principle in Nature. That which, on the spiritual plane, corresponds to sexual affinity on the lower.

Mirrored on the plane of Gross Nature, the World of Reality is reversed and becomes on Earth and our plane:

B.

(*a*) Red is the colour of manifested dual, or male and female, sex; in man it is shown in its lowest animal form.

(*b*) Orange is the colour of the robes of the Yogis and Buddhist Priests, the colour of the Sun and Spiritual Vitality, also of the Vital Principle.

(*c*) Yellow or radiant Golden is the colour of the Spiritual, Divine Ray in every atom; in man of Buddhi.

(*d*) Green and Red are, so to speak, interchangeable colours, for Green absorbs the Red, as being threefold stronger in its vibrations than the latter; and Green is the complementary colour of extreme Red. This is why the Lower Manas and Kâma Rûpa are respectively shown as Green and Red.

(*e*) The Astral Plane, or Auric Envelope in Nature and Man.

(*f*) The Mind or rational element in Man and Nature.

(*g*) The most ethereal counterpart of the Body of man, the opposite pole, standing in point of vibration and sensitiveness as the Violet stands to the Red.

The above is on the manifested plane; after which we get the astral and the Manifested Prism, or Man on Earth. With the latter the Black Magician alone is concerned.

In Kosmos, the gradations and correlations of Colours and Sounds, and therefore of Numbers are infinite. This is suspected even in Physics, for it is ascertained that there exist slower vibrations than those of the Red, the slowest perceptible to us, and far more rapid vibrations than those of the Violet, the most rapid that our senses can perceive. But on Earth, in our physical world, the range of perceptible vibrations is limited. Our physical senses cannot take cognizance of vibrations above and below the septenary and limited gradations of the prismatic colours, for such vibrations are incapable of causing in us the

sensation of colour or sound. It will always be the graduated septenary and no more, unless we learn to paralyze our Quaternary and discern both the superior and inferior vibrations with our spiritual senses seated in the upper Triangle.

Now, on this plane of illusion, there are three fundamental colours, as demonstrated by Physical Science, Red, Blue and Yellow (or rather Orange-Yellow). Expressed in terms of the human principles they are: (1) Kâma Rûpa, the seat of the animal sensations, welded to, and serving as a vehicle for the Animal Soul or Lower Manas (Red and Green, as said, being interchangeable); (2) Auric Envelope, or the essence of man; and (3) Prâna, or Life Principle. But if from the realm of illusion, or the living man as he is on our Earth, subject to his sensuous perceptions only, we pass to that of semi-illusion, and observe the natural colours themselves, or those of the principles, that is, if we try to find out which are those that in the perfect man absorb all others, we shall find that the colours correspond and become complementary in the following way:

Violet.

(1) Red - - - - - - - - - Green.
(2) Orange - - - - - - - - - Blue.
(3) Yellow - - - - - - - - Indigo.

Violet.

A faint violet, mist-like form represents the Astral Man within an oviform bluish circle, over which radiate in ceaseless vibrations the prismatic colours. That colour is predominant, of which the corresponding principle is the most active generally, or at the particular moment when the clairvoyant perceives it. Such man appears during his waking states; and it is by the predominance of this or that colour, and by the intensity of its vibrations, that a clairvoyant, *if* he be acquainted with correspondences, can judge of the inner state or character of a person, for the latter is an open book to every practical Occultist.

In the trance state the Aura changes entirely, the seven prismatic colours being no longer discernible. In sleep also they are not all "at home." For those which belong to the spiritual elements in the man, *viz.*, Yellow, Buddhi; Indigo, Higher Manas; and the Blue of the Auric Envelope will be either hardly discernible, or altogether missing. The Spiritual Man is free during sleep, and though his physical memory may not become aware of it, lives, robed in his highest essence, in realms on other planes, in realms which are the land of reality, called dreams on our plane of illusion.

A good clairvoyant, moreover, if he had an opportunity of seeing a Yogî in the trance state and a mesmerized subject, side by side, would learn an important lesson in Occultism. He would learn to feel the difference between self-induced trance and a hypnotic state resulting from extraneous influence. In the Yogî, the "principles" of the lower Quaternary disappear entirely. Neither Red, Green, Red-Violet, nor the Auric Blue of the Body are to be seen; nothing but hardly perceptible vibrations of the golden-hued Prâna principle and a violet flame streaked with gold rushing upwards from the head, in the region where the Third Eye rests, and culminating in a point. If the student remembers that the true Violet, or the extreme end of the spectrum, is no compound colour of Red and Blue, but a homogeneous colour with vibrations seven times more rapid than those of the Red,* and that the golden hue is the essence of the three yellow hues from Orange-Red to Yellow-Orange and Yellow, he will understand the reason why: he lives in his own Auric Body, now become the vehicle of Buddhi-Manas. On the other hand, in a subject in an artificially produced hypnotic or mesmeric trance, an effect of unconscious when not of conscious Black Magic, unless produced by a high Adept, the whole set of the principles will be present, with the Higher Manas paralyzed, Buddhi severed from it through that paralysis, and the red-violet Astral Body entirely subjected to the Lower Manas and Kâma Rûpa (the green and red animal monsters in us).

One who comprehends well the above explanations will readily see how important it is for every student, whether he is striving for practical Occult powers or only for the purely psychic and spiritual gifts of clairvoyance and metaphysical knowledge, to master thoroughly the right

* Colours.	Wave-Lengths in Millimetres.	Number of Vibrations in Trillions.
Violet extreme	406	[illegible]
Violet	423	709
Violet-Indigo	439	683
Indigo	449	668
Indigo-Blue	459	654
Blue	479	631
Blue-Green	492	610
Green	512	586
Green-Yellow	532	564
Yellow	551	544
Yellow-Orange	571	525
Orange	583	514
Orange-Red	596	503
Red	620	[illegible]
Red-extreme	645	[illegible]

correspondences between the human, or nature principles, and those of Kosmos. It is ignorance which leads materialistic Science to deny the inner man and his Divine powers; knowledge and personal experience that allow the Occultist to affirm that such powers are as natural to man as swimming to fishes. It is like a Laplander, in all sincerity, denying the possibility of the catgut, strung loosely on the sounding-board of a violin producing comprehensive sounds or melody. Our principles are the Seven-Stringed Lyre of Apollo, truly. In this our age, when oblivion has shrouded ancient knowledge, men's faculties are no better than the loose strings of the violin to the Laplander. But the Occultist who knows how to tighten them and tune his violin in harmony with the vibrations of colour and sound, will extract divine harmony from them. The combination of these powers and the attuning of the Microcosm and the Macrocosm will give the geometrical equivalent of the invocation "*Om Mani Padme Hum.*"

This was why the previous knowledge of music and geometry was obligatory in the School of Pythagoras.

THE ROOTS OF COLOUR AND SOUND.

Further, each of the Primordial Seven, the first Seven Rays forming the Manifested Logos, is again sevenfold. Thus, as the seven colours of the solar spectrum correspond to the seven Rays, or Hierarchies, so each of these latter has again its seven divisions corresponding to the same series of colours. But in this case one colour, *viz.*, that which characterizes the particular Hierarchy as a whole, is predominant and more intense than the others.

These Hierarchies can only be symbolized as concentric circles of prismatic colours; each Hierarchy being represented by a series of seven concentric circles, each circle representing one of the prismatic colours in their natural order. But in each of these "wheels" one circle will be brighter and more vivid in colour than the rest, and the wheel will have a surrounding Aura (a fringe, as the physicists call it) of that colour. This colour will be the characteristic colour of that Hierarchy as a whole. Each of these Hierarchies furnishes the essence (the Soul) and is the "Builder" of one of the seven kingdoms of Nature which are the three elemental kingdoms, the mineral, the vegetable, the animal, and the kingdom of spiritual man.* Moreover, each [illegible] furnishes the Aura of one of the seven principles in man with its [illegible] colour. Further, as each of these Hierarchies is the Ruler of [illegible] Sacred Planets, it will easily be understood how Astrology [illegible] existence, and that real Astrology has a strictly scientific basis.

The symbol adopted in the Eastern School to represent the [illegible] Hierarchies of creative Powers is a wheel of seven concentric [illegible] each circle being coloured with one of the seven colours; call [illegible] Angels, if you will, or Planetary Spirits, or, again, the Seven [illegible] the Seven Sacred Planets of our system, as in our present case. [illegible] events, the concentric circles stand as symbols for Ezekiel's [illegible] with some Western Occultists and Kabalists, and for the "Builders" or Prajâpati with us.

DIAGRAM III.

The student should carefully examine the following Diagram.

Thus the Linga Sharîra is derived from the Violet sub-ray of the Violet Hierarchy; the Higher Manas is similarly derived from the Indigo sub-ray of the Indigo Hierarchy, and so on. Every man [illegible] born under a certain planet, there will always be a predominance of that planet's colour in him, because that "principle" will rule in [illegible] which has its origin in the Hierarchy in question. There will [illegible] a certain amount of the colour derived from the other planets [illegible] his Aura, but that of the ruling planet will be strongest. Now a [illegible] in whom, say, the Mercury principle is predominant, will, by [illegible] upon the Mercury principle in another person born under a [illegible] planet, be able to get him entirely under his control. For the [illegible] Mercury principle in him will overpower the weaker Mercurial [illegible] in the other. But he will have little power over persons born under the same planet as himself. This is the key to the Occult Sciences of Magnetism and Hypnotism.

The student will understand that the Orders and Hierarchies [illegible] here named after their corresponding colours, so as to avoid [illegible] numerals, which would be confusing in connection with the [illegible] principles, as the latter have no proper numbers of their own. [illegible] real Occult names of these Hierarchies cannot now be given.

* See *Five Years of Theosophy*, pp. 273 to 278.

The student must, however remember that the colours which we see with our physical eyes are not the true colours of Occult Nature, but are merely the effects produced on the mechanism of our physical organs by certain rates of vibration. For instance, Clerk Maxwell has demonstrated that the retinal effects of any colour may be imitated by properly combining three other colours. It follows, therefore, that our retina has only three distinct colour sensations, and we therefore do not perceive the seven colours which really exist, but only their "imitations," so to speak, in our physical organism.

Thus, for instance, the Orange-Red of the first "Triangle" is not a combination of Orange and Red, but the true "spiritual" Red, if the term may be allowed, while the Red (blood-red) of the spectrum is the colour of Kâma, animal desire, and is inseparable from the material plane.

DIAGRAM III.

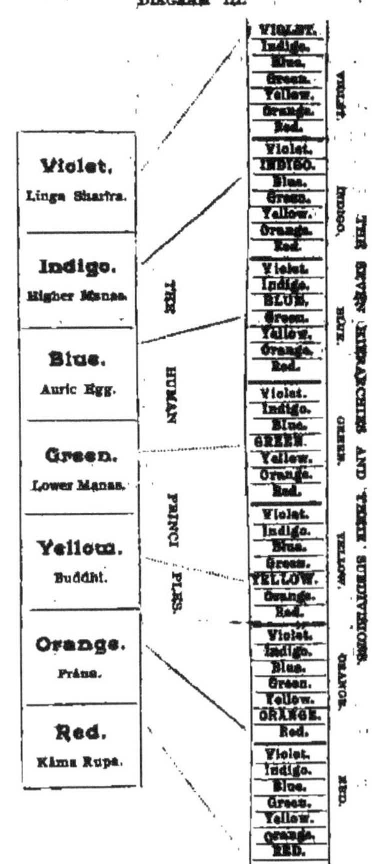

THE UNITY OF DEITY.

Esotericism, pure and simple, speaks of no personal God; therefore are we considered as Atheists. But, in reality, Occult Philosophy, as a whole, is based absolutely on the ubiquitous presence of God, the

Absolute Deity; and if IT Itself is not speculated upon, as being too sacred and yet incomprehensible as a Unit to the finite intellect, all the entire Philosophy is based upon Its Divine Powers, as being the Source of all that breathes and lives and has existence. In every ancient Religion the One was demonstrated by the many. In Egypt and India, in Chaldæa and Phœnicia, and finally in Greece, the ideas about Deity were expressed by multiples of three, five and seven; and also by eight, nine and twelve great Gods, which symbolized the powers and properties of the One and Only Deity. This was related to that infinite subdivision by irregular and odd numbers to which the metaphysics of these nations subjected their ONE DIVINITY. Thus constituted, the cycle of the Gods had all the qualities and attributes of the ONE SUPREME AND UNKNOWABLE; for in this collection of divine Personalities, or rather of Symbols personified, dwells the ONE GOD, the GOD ONE, that God which, in India, is said to have no Second.

O God Ani (the Spiritual Sun), thou residest in the agglomeration of thy divine personages.*

These words show the belief of the ancients that all manifestation proceeds from one and the same Source, all emanating from the one identical Principle which can never be completely developed except in and through the collective and entire aggregate of Its emanations.

The Pleroma of Valentinus is absolutely the Space of Occult Philosophy; for Pleroma means the "Fullness," the superior regions. It is the sum total of all the Divine manifestations and emanations expressing the *plenum* or totality of the rays proceeding from the One, differentiating on all the planes, and transforming themselves into Divine Powers, called Angels and Planetary Spirits in the Philosophy of every nation. The Gnostic Æons and Powers of the Pleroma are made to speak as the Devas and Siddhas of the *Purânas*. The Epinoia, the first female manifestation of God, the "Principle" of Simon Magus and Saturninus, holds the same language as the Logos of Basilides; and each of these is traced to the purely esoteric Alêtheia, the TRUTH of the Mysteries. All of them, we are taught, repeat at different times and in different languages the magnificent hymn of the Egyptian papyrus, thousands of years old:

The Gods adore thee, they greet thee, O the One Dark Truth.

And addressing Ra, they add:

* *Apud Grébaut Papyrus Orbiney*, p. 101.

The Gods bow before thy Majesty, by exalting the Souls of that which produces them . . . and say to thee, Peace to all emanations from the Unconscious Father of the Conscious Fathers of the Gods. . . . Thou producer of beings, we adore the souls which emanate from thee. Thou begettest us, O thou Unknown, and we greet thee in worshipping each God-Soul which descendeth from thee and liveth in us.

This is the source of the assertion:

Know ye not that ye are Gods and the temple of God.

This is shown in the "Roots of Ritualism in Church and Masonry," in *Lucifer* for March, 1889. Truly then, as said seventeen centuries ago, "Man cannot possess Truth (Alêtheia) except he participate in the Gnosis." So we may say now: No man can know the Truth unless he studies the secrets of the Pleroma of Occultism; and these secrets are all in the Theogony of the ancient Wisdom-Religion, which is the Alêtheia of Occult Science.

PAPER III.

A Word Concerning the Earlier Papers.

As many have written and almost complained to me that they could find no practical clear application of certain diagrams appended to the first two Papers, and others have spoken of their abstruseness, a short explanation is necessary.

The reason of this difficulty in most cases has been that the point of view taken was erroneous; the purely abstract and metaphysical was mistaken for, and confused with, the concrete and the physical. Let us take for example the diagrams on page 477 (Paper II.,) and say that these are entirely macrocosmic and ideal. It must be remembered that the study of Occultism proceeds from Universals to Particulars and not the reverse way, as accepted by Science. As Plato was an Initiate, he very naturally used the former method, while Aristotle, never having been initiated, scoffed at his master, and, elaborating a system of his own, left it as an heirloom to be adopted and improved by Bacon. Of a truth the aphorism of Hermetic Wisdom, "As above, so below," applies to all Esoteric instruction; but we must begin with the above; we must learn the formula before we can sum the series.

The two figures, therefore, are not meant to represent any two particular planes, but are the abstraction of a pair of planes, explanatory of the law of reflection, just as the Lower Manas is a reflection of the Higher. They must therefore be taken in the highest metaphysical sense.

The diagrams are only intended to familiarize students with the leading ideas of Occult correspondences, the very genius of metaphysical, or macrocosmic and spiritual Occultism forbidding the use of figures or even symbols further than as temporary aids. Once define an idea in words, and it loses its reality; once figure a metaphysical idea, and you materialize its spirit. Figures must be used only as ladders to scale the battlements, ladders to be disregarded when once the foot is set upon the rampart.

Let students, therefore, be very careful to spiritualize the Papers and avoid materializing them; let them always try to find the highest meaning possible, confident that in proportion as they approach the material and visible in their speculations on the Papers, so far are they from the right understanding of them. This is especially the case with these first Papers and Diagrams, for as in all true arts, so in Occultism, we must first learn the theory before we are taught the practice.

CONCERNING SECRECY.

Students ask: Why such secrecy about the details of a doctrine the body of which has been publicly revealed, as in *Esoteric Buddhism* and the *Secret Doctrine?*

To this Occultism would reply: for two reasons:—

(*a*) The whole truth is too sacred to be given out promiscuously.

(*b*) The knowledge of all the details and missing links in the exoteric teachings is too dangerous in profane hands.

The truths revealed to man by the "Planetary Spirits"—the highest Kumâras, those who incarnate no longer in the Universe during this Mahâmanvantara—who will appear on earth as Avatâras only at the beginning of every new human Race, and at the junctions or close of the two ends of the small and great cycles in time, as man became more animalized, were made to fade away from his memory. Yet, though these Teachers remain with man no longer than the time required to impress upon the plastic minds of child-humanity the eternal verities they teach, Their Spirit remains vivid though latent in mankind. And the full knowledge of the primitive revelation has remained always with a few elect, and has been transmitted from that time up to the present, from one generation of Adepts to another. As the Teachers say in the Occult Primer:

This is done so as to ensure them [the eternal truths] *from being utterly lost or forgotten in ages hereafter by the forthcoming generations.*

The mission of the Planetary Spirit is but to strike the key-note of Truth. When once He has directed the vibration of the latter to run its course uninterruptedly along the concatenation of the race to the end of the cycle, He disappears from our earth until the following Planetary Manvantara. The mission of any teacher of Esoteric truths, whether he stands at the top or the foot of the ladder of [illegible] precisely the same; as above, so below. I have only orders to [illegible] the key-note of the various Esoteric truths among the [illegible] body. These units among you who will have raised [illegible] the "Path" over their fellow-students, in their Esoteric [illegible] the "Elect," spoken of did and do in the Parent Brotherhoods, [illegible] the last explanatory details and the ultimate key to what [illegible]. No one, however, can hope to gain this privilege before the [illegible] not my humble self—find him or her worthy.

If you wish to know the real *raison d'être* for this policy, I [illegible] it to you. No use my repeating and explaining what all of you [illegible] as well as myself; at the very beginning, events have shown that [illegible] caution can be dispensed with. Of our body of several [illegible] and women, many did not seem to realise either the awful [illegible] of the pledge (which some took at the end of their pen), or the [illegible] their *personality* has to be entirely disregarded, when brought [illegible] face with their HIGHER SELF; or that all their words and [illegible] went for naught unless corroborated by actions. This was [illegible] nature, and no more; therefore it was passed leniently by, and [illegible] lease accorded by the MASTER. But apart from this there is a [illegible] lurking in the nature of the present cycle itself. Civilised [illegible] however carefully guarded by its invisible Watchers, the [illegible] kâyas, who watch over our respective races and nations, is yet, [illegible] its collective Karma, terribly under the sway of the traditional [illegible] of the Nirmânakâyas—the "Brothers of the Shadow," [illegible] disembodied; and this, as has already been told you, will [illegible] end of the first Kali Yuga cycle (1897), and a few years beyond, [illegible] smaller dark cycle happens to overlap the great one. Thus, [illegible] standing all precautions, terrible secrets are often revealed to [illegible] unworthy persons by the efforts of the "Dark Brothers" [illegible] working on human brains. This is entirely owing to the [illegible] that in certain privileged organisms, vibrations of the [illegible] put in motion by the Planetary Beings are set up, in what [illegible] philosophy would term innate ideas, and Occultism "flashes of [illegible] Some such idea based on eternal truth is awakened, and all [illegible] watchful Powers can do is to prevent its entire revelation.

Everything in this Universe of differentiated matter has [illegible] aspects, the light and the dark side, and these two [illegible]

* See "Genius," *Lucifer*, Nov., 1889, p. 227.

practically, lead the one to use, the other to abuse. Every man may become a Botanist without apparent danger to his fellow-creatures; and many a Chemist who has mastered the science of essences knows that every one of them can both heal and kill. Not an ingredient, not a poison, but can be used for both purposes—aye, from harmless wax to deadly prussic acid, from the saliva of an infant to that of the cobra di capella. This every tyro in medicine knows—theoretically, at any rate. But where is the learned Chemist in our day who has been permitted to discover the "night side" of an attribute of any substance in the three kingdoms of Science, let alone in the seven of the Occultists? Who of them has penetrated into its Arcana, into the innermost Essence of things and its primary correlations? Yet it is this knowledge alone which makes of an Occultist a genuine practical Initiate, whether he turn out a Brother of Light or a Brother of Darkness. The essence of that subtle, traceless poison, the most potent in nature, which entered into the composition of the so-called Medici and Borgia poisons, if used with discrimination by one well versed in the septenary degrees of its potentiality on each of the planes accessible to man on earth—could heal or kill every man in the world; the result depending, of course, on whether the operator was a Brother of the Light or a Brother of the Shadow. The former is prevented from doing the good he might, by racial, national, and individual Karma; the second is impeded in his fiendish work by the joint efforts of the human "Stones" of the "Guardian Wall."*

It is incorrect to think that there exists any special "powder of projection" or "philosopher's stone," or "elixir of life." The latter lurks in every flower, in every stone and mineral throughout the globe. It is the ultimate essence of *everything on its way to higher and higher evolution*. As there is no good or evil *per se*, so there is neither "elixir of life" nor "elixir of death," nor poison, *per se*, but all this is contained in one and the same universal Essence, this or the other effect, or result, depending on the degree of its differentiation and its various correlations. The *light side* of it produces life, health, bliss, divine peace, etc.; the *dark side* brings death, disease, sorrow and strife. This is proven by the knowledge of the nature of the most violent poisons; of some of them even a large quantity will produce no evil effect on the organism, whereas a grain of the same poison kills with

* See *Voice of the Silence*, pp. 68 and 94, art. 28, Glossary.

the rapidity of lightning; while the same grain, again, altered by [illegible] combination, though its quantity remains almost identical, [illegible] The number of the degrees of its differentiation is septenary, [illegible] planes of its action, each degree being either beneficent or [illegible] in its effects, according to the system into which it is introduced [illegible] who is skilled in these degrees is on the high road to [illegible] ship; he who acts at hap-hazard—as do the enormous majority [illegible] "Mind Curers," whether "Mental" or "Christian Scientists," [illegible] likely to rue the effects on himself as well as on others. [illegible] track by the example of the Indian Yogis, and of their [illegible] incorrectly outlined practices, which they have only read about [illegible] have had no opportunity to study—these new sects have rushed [illegible] long and guideless into the practice of *denying* and *affirming*. [illegible] have done more harm than good. Those who are successful owe it to their innate magnetic and healing powers, which very often counteract that which would otherwise be conducive to much evil. Beware! [illegible] Satan and the Archangel are more than twins; they are one body [illegible] one mind—*Deus est Demon inversus.*

IS THE PRACTICE OF CONCENTRATION BENEFICENT?

Such is another question often asked. I answer: Genuine concentration and meditation, *conscious and cautious*, upon one's lower self [illegible] the light of the inner divine man and the Pâramitâs, is an excellent thing. But to "sit for Yoga," with only a superficial and often distorted knowledge of the real practice, is almost invariably fatal; for ten to one the student will either develop mediumistic powers in himself or lose time and get disgusted both with practice and theory. Before one rushes into such a dangerous experiment and seeks to go beyond a minute examination of one's lower self and *its* walk in life, or that which is called in our phraseology, "The Chelâ's Daily Life Ledger," he would do well to learn at least the difference between the two aspects of "Magic," the White or Divine, and the Black or Devilish, and assure himself that by "sitting for Yoga," with no experience, as well as with no guide to show him the dangers, he does not daily and hourly cross the boundaries of the Divine to fall into the Satanic. Nevertheless, the way to learn the difference is very easy; one has only to remember that *no Esoteric truths entirely unveiled can ever be given in public print*, in book or magazine.

I ask students to turn to the *Theosophist* of November, [illegible] page 98 they will find the beginning of an excellent article by Mr. Râma Prasâd on "Nature's Finer Forces."* The value of this work is not so much in its literary merit, though it gained its author the gold medal of the *Theosophist*, as in its exposition of tenets hitherto concealed in a rare and ancient Sanskrit work on Occultism. But Mr. Râma Prasâd is not an Occultist, only an excellent Sanskrit scholar, a university graduate and a man of remarkable intelligence. His essays are almost entirely based on Tântra works, which, if read indiscriminately by a tyro in Occultism, will lead to the practice of most unmitigated Black Magic. Now, since the difference of primary importance between Black and White Magic is the object with which it is practised, and that of secondary importance the nature of the agents used for the production of phenomenal results, the line of demarcation between the two is very—*very* thin. The danger is lessened only by the fact that every *Occult* book, so-called, is Occult only in a certain sense; that is, the text is Occult merely by reason of its blinds. The symbolism has to be thoroughly understood before the reader can get at the correct sense of the teaching. Moreover, it is never complete, its several portions each being under a different title, and each containing a portion of some other work; so that without a key to these no such work divulges the whole truth. Even the famous *Shivâgama*, on which *Nature's Finer Forces* is based, "is nowhere to be found in complete form," as the author tells us. Thus, like all others, it treats of only five Tattvas instead of the seven as in Esoteric teachings.

Now, the Tattvas being simply the substratum of the seven forces of Nature, how can this be? There are seven forms of Prakriti, as Kapila's Sânkhya, the *Vishnu Purâna*, and other works teach. Prakriti is Nature, Matter (primordial and elemental); therefore logic demands that the Tattvas also should be seven. For whether Tattvas mean, as Occultism teaches, "forces of Nature," or, as the learned Râma Prâsad explains, "the substance out of which the universe is formed" and "the power by which it is sustained," it is all one; they

* The references to "Nature's Finer Forces" which follow, have respect to the eight articles which appeared in the pages of the *Theosophist* and not to the fifteen essays and the translation of a chapter of the *Shivâgama* which are contained in the book called *Nature's Finer Forces*. The *Shivâgama* in its details is purely Tântric, and nothing but harm can result from any practical following of its precepts. I would most strongly dissuade any student from attempting any of these Hatha Yoga practices, for he will either ruin himself entirely, or throw himself so far back that it will be almost impossible to regain the lost ground in this incarnation. The translation referred to has been considerably expurgated, and even now is hardly fit for publication. It recommends Black Magic of the worst kind, and is the very antipodes of spiritual Râja Yoga. Beware, I say.

3. *Buddhi*; for Buddhi is a ray of the Universal Spiritual Soul (ALAYA).

4. *Manas* (the Higher Ego); for it proceeds from Mahat, the first product or emanation of Pradhâna, which contains *potentially* all the Gunas (attributes). Mahat is Cosmic Intelligence, called the "Great Principle."*

3. *Lower Manas*, the Animal Soul, the reflection or shadow of Buddhi-Manas, having the potentialities of both, but conquered generally by its association with the Kâma elements.

As the lower man is the combined product of two aspects—physically, of his Astral Form, and psycho-physiologically of Kâma-Manas—he is not looked upon even as an aspect, but as an illusion.

The Auric Egg, on account of its nature and manifold functions, has to be well studied. As Hiranyagarbha, the Golden Womb or Egg, contains Brahmâ, the collective symbol of the Seven Universal Forces, so the Auric Egg contains, and is directly related to, both the divine and the physical man. In its essence, as said, it is eternal; in its constant correlations and transformations, during the reincarnating progress of the Ego on this earth, it is a kind of perpetual motion machine.

As given out in our second volume, the Egos or Kumâras, incarnating in man, at the end of the Third Root-Race, are not human Egos of this earth or plane, but become such only from the moment they ensoul the Animal Man, thus endowing him with his Higher Mind. Each is a "Breath" or Principle, called the Human Soul, or Manas, the Mind. As the teachings say:

"*Each is a pillar of light. Having chosen its vehicle, it expanded, surrounding with an Âkâshic Aura the human animal, while the Divine (Mânasic) Principle settled within that human form.*"

Ancient Wisdom teaches us, moreover, that from this first incarnation, the Lunar Pitris, who had made men out of their Chhâyâs, or Shadows, are absorbed by this Auric Essence, and a distinct Astral Form is now produced for each forthcoming personality of the reincarnating series of each Ego.

---

* Prâna, on earth at any rate, is thus but a mode of life, a constant cyclic motion from within outwardly and back again, an out-breathing and in-breathing of the ONE LIFE, or Jîva, the synonym of the Absolute and Unknowable Deity. Prâna is not absolute life, or Jîva, but its aspect in a world of delusion. In the *Theosophist*, May, 1888, p. 478, Prâna is said to be "one stage finer than the gross matter of the earth."

note here for chart

(abstract)

Thus the Auric Egg, reflecting all the thoughts, words and deeds of man, is:

(*a*) The preserver of every Karmic record.

(*b*) The storehouse of all the good and evil powers of man, receiving and giving out at his will—nay, at his very thought—every potentiality, which becomes, then and there, an acting potency: this Aura is the mirror in which sensitives and clairvoyants sense and perceive the real man, and see him *as he is*, not as he appears.

(*c*) As it furnishes man with his Astral Form, around which the physical entity models itself, first as a fœtus, then as a child and man, the astral growing apace with the human being, so it furnishes him during life, if an Adept, with his Mâyâvi Rûpa, or Illusion Body, which is not his *Vital*-Astral Body; and after death, with his Devachanic Entity and Kâma Rûpa, or Body of Desire (the Spook).*

In the case of the Devachanic Entity, the Ego, in order to be able to go into a state of bliss, as the "I" of its immediately preceding incarnation, has to be clothed (metaphorically speaking) with the spiritual elements of the ideas, aspirations and thoughts of the now disembodied personality; otherwise what is it that enjoys bliss and reward? Surely not the impersonal Ego, the Divine Individuality. Therefore it must be the good Karmic records of the deceased, impressed upon the Auric Substance, which furnish the Human Soul with just enough of the spiritual elements of the ex-personality, to enable it to still believe itself that body from which it has just been severed, and to receive its fruition, during a more or less prolonged period of "spiritual gestation." For Devachan is a "spiritual gestation" within an ideal matrix state, a birth of the Ego into the world of effects, which ideal, subjective birth precedes its next terrestrial birth, the latter being determined by its bad Karma, into the world of causes.†

In the case of the Spook, the Kâma Rûpa is furnished from the animal dregs of the Auric Envelope, with its daily Karmic record of animal life, so full of animal desires and selfish aspirations.‡

* It is erroneous to call the fourth human principle "Kâma Rûpa." It is no Rûpa or form at all until after death, but stands for the Kâmic elements in man, his animal desires and passions, such as anger, lust, envy, revenge, etc., the progeny of selfishness and matter.

† Here the world of effects is the Devachanic state, and the world of causes, earth life.

‡ It is this Kâma Rûpa alone that can *materialise* in mediumistic séances, which occasionally happens when it is not the Astral Double or Linga Sharîra, of the medium himself which appears. How, then, can this vile bundle of passions and terrestrial lusts, resurrected by, and gaining consciousness only through the organism of the medium, be accepted as a "departed angel" or the Spirit of a once human body? As well say of the microbic pest which fastens on a person, that "is a sweet departed angel.

"Now the Linga Sharîra remains with the Physical Body and fades out along with it. An astral entity then has to be created, a new Linga Sharîra provided, to become the bearer of all the past Tanhic and future Karma. How is this accomplished? The mediumistic 'spook,' the "departed angel," fades out and vanishes also in its turn* as an entity or full image of the personality that was, and leaves in the Kâmalokic world of effects only the record of its misdeeds and sinful thoughts and acts, known in the phraseology of Occultists as Tanhic or human Elementals. Entering into the composition of the Astral Form of the new body, into which the Ego, upon its quitting the Devachanic state, is to enter according to Karmic decree, the Elementals form that new astral entity which is born within the Auric Envelope, and of which it is often said:

> Bad Karma waits at the threshold of Devachan, with its army of Skandhas.†

"For no sooner is the Devachanic state of reward ended, than the Ego is indissolubly united with (or rather follows in the track of) the new Astral Form. Both are Karmically propelled towards the family or woman from whom is to be born the child chosen by Karma to become the vehicle of the Ego which has just awakened from the Devachanic state. Then the new Astral Form, composed partly of the pure Akâshic Essence of the Auric Egg, and partly of the terrestrial elements of the punishable sins and misdeeds of the last personality, is drawn into the woman. Once there, Nature models the fœtus of flesh around the Astral, out of the growing materials of the male seed in the female soil. Thus grows out of the essence of a decayed seed the fruit or eidolon of the dead seed, the physical fruit producing in its turn within itself another, and other seeds for future plants.

And now we may return to the Tattvas, and see what they mean in nature and man, showing thereby the great danger of indulging in fancy, amateur Yoga, without knowing what we are about."

---

* This is accomplished in more or less time, according to the degree in which the personality (whose dregs it now is) was spiritual or material. If spirituality prevailed, then the Larva, or "spook," will fade out very soon; but if the personality was very materialistic, the Kâma Rûpa may last for centuries and—in some, though very exceptional cases—even survive with the help of some of its scattered Skandhas, which are all transformed in time into Elementals. See the *Key to Theosophy*, pp. 141 *et seq.*, in which work it was impossible to go into details, but where the Skandhas are spoken of as the germs of Karmic effect.

† *Key to Theosophy*, p. 141

THE TÂTTVIC CORRELATIONS AND MEANING.

In Nature, then, we find seven Forces, or seven Centres of Force, and everything seems to respond to that number, as for instance, the septenary scale in music, or Sounds, and the septenary spectrum in Colours. I have not exhausted its nomenclature and proofs in the earlier volumes, yet enough is given to show every thinker that the facts adduced are no coincidences, but very weighty testimony.

There are several reasons why only five Tattvas are given in the Hindu systems. One of these I have already mentioned; another is that owing to our having reached only the Fifth Race, and being (so far as Science is able to ascertain) endowed with only fives enses, the two remaining senses that are still latent in man can have their existence proven only on phenomenal evidence which to the Materialist is no evidence at all. The five physical senses are made to correspond with the five lower Tattvas, the two yet undeveloped senses in man; and the two forces, or Tattvas, forgotten by Brâhmans and still unrecognized by Science, being so subjective and the highest of them so sacred, that they can only be recognized by, and known through, the highest Occult Sciences. It is easy to see that these two Tattvas and the two senses (the sixth and the seventh) correspond to the two highest human principles, Buddhi and the Auric Envelope, impregnated with the light of Âtmâ. Unless we open in ourselves, by Occult training, the sixth and seventh senses, we can never comprehend correctly their corresponding types. Thus the statement in *Nature's Finer Forces* that, in the Tâttvic scale, the highest Tattva of all is Âkâsha* (followed by [only] four, each of which becomes grosser than its predecessor), if made from the Esoteric standpoint, is erroneous. For once Âkâsha, an almost homogeneous and certainly universal Principle, is translated Ether, then Âkâsha is dwarfed and limited to our visible Universe, for assuredly it is not the Ether of Space. Ether, whatever Modern Science makes of it, is differentiated Substance; Âkâsha, having no attributes save one—SOUND, *of which it is the substratum*—is no substance even exoterically and in the minds of some Orientalists,† but rather Chaos, or the Great Spatial Void.‡

* Following *Shivâgama*, the said author enumerates the correspondences in this wise; Âkâsha, Ether, is followed by Vâyu, Gas; Tejas, Heat; Âpas, Liquid; and Prithivî, Solid.

† See Fitz-Edward Hall's notes on the *Vishnu Purâna*.

‡ The pair which we refer to as the One Life, the Root of All, and Âkâsha in its pre-differentiating period answers to the Brahma (neuter) and Aditi of some Hindus, and stands in the same relation as the Parabrahman and Mûlaprakriti of the Vedântins.

Esoterically, Âkâsha alone is *Divine* Space, and becomes Ether only on the lowest and last plane, or our visible Universe and Earth. In this case the blind is in the word "attribute," which is said to be Sound. But Sound is no attribute of Âkâsha, but its primary correlation, its primordial manifestation, the LOGOS, or Divine Ideation made Word, and that "WORD" made "Flesh." Sound may be considered as an "attribute" of Âkâsha only on the condition of anthropomorphizing the latter. It is not a characteristic of it, though it is certainly as innate in it as the idea "I am *I*" is innate in our thoughts.

Occultism teaches that Akâsha contains and includes the seven Centres of Force, therefore the six Tattvas, of which it is the seventh, or rather their synthesis. But if Âkâsha be taken, as we believe it is in this case, to represent only the exoteric idea, then the author is right; because, seeing that Âkâsha is universally omnipresent, following the Purânic limitation, *for the better comprehension of our finite intellects*, he places its commencement only beyond the four planes of our Earth-Chain,* the two higher Tattvas being as concealed to the average mortal as the sixth and seventh senses are to the materialistic mind.

Therefore, while Sanskrit and Hindu Philosophy generally speak of five Tattvas only, Occultists name seven, thus making them correspond with every septenary in Nature. The Tattvas stand in the same order as the seven macro- and micro-cosmic Forces; and as taught in Esotericism, are as follows:

(1) ÂDI TATTVA, the primordial universal Force, issuing at the beginning of manifestation, or of the "creative" period, from the eternal immutable SAT, the substratum of ALL. It corresponds to the Auric Envelope or Brahmâ's Egg, which surrounds every globe as well as every man, animal and thing. It is the vehicle containing potentially everything—Spirit and Substance, Force and Matter. Âdi Tattva, in Esoteric Cosmogony, is the Force which we refer to as proceeding from the First or Unmanifested LOGOS.

(2) ANUPÂDAKA TATTVA,† the first differentiation on the plane of being—the first being an ideal one—or that which is born by transformation from something higher than itself. With the Occultist, this Force proceeds from the Second LOGOS.

* See above, I. diagram, p. 221.

† Anupâdaka, Opapatika in Pâli, means the "parentless," born without father or mother, of *itself*, as a transformation, *e.g.*, the God Brahmâ sprung from the Lotus (the symbol of the Universe) that grows from Vishnu's navel, Vishnu typifying eternal and limitless Space, and Brahmâ the Universe and LOGOS; the mythical Buddha is also born from a Lotus.

(3) ÂKÂSHA TATTVA, this is the point from which all *exoteric* Philosophies and Religions start. Âkâsha Tattva is explained in them as Etheric Force, Ether. Hence Jupiter, the "highest" God, was named after Pater Æther; Indra, once the highest God in India, is the etheric or heavenly expanse, and so with Uranus, etc. The Christian biblical God, also, is spoken of as the Holy Ghost, Pneuma, rarefied wind or air. This the Occultists call the Force of the Third LOGOS, the Creative Force in the already Manifested Universe.

(4) VÂYU TATTVA, the aërial plane where substance is gaseous.

(5) TAIJAS TATTVA, the plane of our atmosphere, from *tejas*, luminous.

(6) ÂPAS TATTVA, watery or liquid substance or force.

(7) PRITHIVÎ TATTVA, solid earthly substance, the terrestrial spirit or force, the lowest of all.

All these correspond to our Principles, and to the seven senses and forces in man. According to the Tattva or Force generated or induced in us, so will our bodies act.

Now, what I have to say here is addressed especially to those members who are anxious to develop powers by "sitting for Yoga." You have seen, from what has been already said, that in the development of Râja Yoga, no extant works made public are of the least good; they can at best give inklings of Hatha Yoga, something that may develop mediumship at best, and in the worst case—consumption. If those who practice "meditation," and try to learn "the Science of Breath," will read attentively *Nature's Finer Forces*, they will find that it is by utilizing the five Tattvas only that this dangerous science is acquired. For in the exoteric Yoga Philosophy, and the Hatha Yoga practice, Âkâsha Tattva is placed in the head (or physical brain) of man; Tejas Tattva in the shoulders; Vâyu Tattva in the navel (the seat of all the phallic Gods, "creators" of the universe and man); Âpas Tattva in the knees; and Prithivî Tattva in the feet. Hence the two higher Tattvas and their correspondences are ignored and excluded; and, as these are the chief factors in Râja Yoga, no spiritual or intellectual phenomena of a high nature can take place. The best results obtainable will be physical phenomena and no more. As the "Five Breaths," or rather the five states of the human breath, in Hatha Yoga correspond to the above *terrestrial* planes and colours, what spiritual results can be obtained? On the contrary, they are the very reverse of the plane of Spirit, or the higher macrocosmic plane, reflected

as they are upside down, in the Astral Light. This is proved by the Tântra work, *Shivâgama*, itself. Let us compare.

First of all, remember that the Septenary of visible and invisible Nature is said in Occultism to consist of the three (and four) Fires, which grow into the forty-nine Fires. This shows that as the Macrocosm is divided into seven great planes of various differentiations of Substance—from the spiritual or subjective, to the fully objective or material, from Akâsha down to the sin-laden atmosphere of our earth—so, in its turn, each of these great planes has three aspects, based on four Principles, as already shown above. This seems to be quite natural, as even modern Science has her three states of matter and what are generally called the "critical" or intermediate states between the solid, the fluidic, and the gaseous.

Now, the Astral Light is not a universally diffused stuff, but pertains only to our earth and all other bodies of the system on the same plane of matter with it. Our Astral Light is, so to speak, the Linga Sharîra of our earth; only instead of being its primordial prototype, as in the case of our Chhâyâ, or Double, it is the reverse. Human and animal bodies grow and develop on the model of their antetypal Doubles; whereas the Astral Light is born from the terrene emanations, grows and develops after its prototypal parent, and in its treacherous waves everything from the upper planes and from the lower solid plane, the earth, both ways, is reflected *reversed*. Hence the confusion of the colours and sounds in the clairvoyance and clairaudience of the sensitive who trusts to its records, be that sensitive a Hatha Yogi or a medium. The following parallel between the Esoteric and the Tântric Tables of the Tattvas in relation to Sounds and Colours shows this very clearly:

ESOTERIC AND TÂNTRA TABLES OF THE TATTVAS.

Esoteric Principles, Tattvas or Forces, and their Correspondences with the Human Body, States of Matter and Colour. | *Tântra Tattvas and their Correspondences with the Human Body, States of Matter and Colour.*

TATTVAS.	PRINCIPLES.	STATES OF MATTER.	PARTS OF BODY.	COLOUR.	TATTVAS.	STATES OF MATTER.	PARTS OF BODY.	COLOUR.
(a) Âdi	Auric Egg	Primordial, Spiritual Substance; Âkâsha; Substratum of the Spirit of Ether	Envelopes the whole body and penetrates it. Reciprocal emanation, endosmotic and exosmotic	Synthesis of all Colours. Blue	(a) Ignored	Ignored	Ignored	Ignored
(b) Anupâdaka	Buddhi	Spiritual Essence, or Spirit; "Primordial Waters of the Deep"	Third Eye, or Pineal Gland	Yellow	(b) Ignored	Ignored	Ignored	Ignored
(c) Alaya or Âkâsha	Manas Ego	Ether of Space, or Âkâsha in its third differentiation. Critical State of Vapour	Head	Indigo	(c) Âkâsha	Ether	Head	Black or colourless
(d) Vâyu	Kâma Manas	Critical State of Matter	Throat to Navel	Green	(d) Vâyu	Gas	Navel	Blue
(e) Tejas	Kâma (Rûpa)	Essence of gross Matter; corresponds to *Ice*	Shoulders and Arms to Thighs	Red	(e) Tejas	Heat (?)	Shoulders	Red
(f) Âpas	Linga Sharira	Gross Ether or *Liquid* Air	Thighs to Knees	Violet	(f) Âpas	Liquid	Knees	White
(g) Prithivî	Living Body in Prâna or animal life	Solid and Critical State	Knees to Feet	Orange-Red†	(g) Prithivî	Solid	Feet	Yellow*

* One may see at a glance how reversed are the colours of the Tattvas, reflected in the Astral Light, when we find the Indigo called black; the green blue; the violet, white; and the orange, yellow.

† The colours, I repeat, do not here follow the prismatic scale—red, orange, yellow, green, blue, indigo and violet—because this scale is a false reflection, a true Mâyâ; whereas our esoteric scale is that of the spiritual spheres, the seven planes of the Macrocosm.

Such, then, is the Occult Science on which the modern [illegible] Yogis of India base their Soul development and powers. [illegible] known as the Hatha Yogis. Now, the science of Hatha [illegible] upon the "suppression of breath," or Prânâyâma, to which [illegible] our Masters are unanimously opposed. For what is [illegible] Literally translated, it means the "death of (vital) breath." [illegible] said, is not Jîva, the eternal fount of life immortal; nor is it [illegible] in any way with Pranava, as some think, for Pranava is a [illegible] Aum in a mystic sense. As much as has ever been taught [illegible] clearly about it is to be found in *Nature's Finer Forces*. If [illegible] tions, however, are followed, they can only lead to Black [illegible] mediumship. Several impatient Chelâs, whom we knew [illegible] India, went in for the practice of Hatha Yoga, notwithstanding [illegible] warnings. Of these, two developed consumption, of which [illegible] others became almost idiotic; another committed suicide; [illegible] developed into a regular Tântrika, a Black Magician, but his [illegible] fortunately for himself, was cut short by death.

The science of the Five Breaths, the moist, the fiery, the [illegible] has a twofold significance and two applications. The Tântrikas [illegible] literally, as relating to the regulation of the vital, lung breath, [illegible] the ancient Râja Yogis understood it as referring to the [illegible] "will" breath, which alone leads to the highest clairvoyant powers [illegible] the function of the Third Eye, and the acquisition of the true [illegible] Yoga Occult powers. The difference between the two is [illegible] The former, as shown, use the five lower Tattvas; the latter [illegible] using the three higher alone, for mental and will development, [illegible] rest only when they have completely mastered the three; hence [illegible] use only one (Âkâsha Tattva) out of the Tântric five. As well [illegible] the above stated work, "Tattvas are the modifications of Svara." Now, the Svara is the root of all sound, the substratum of the Pytha-gorean music of the spheres, Svara being that which is *beyond* Spirit in the modern acceptation of the word, the Spirit within Spirit, or [illegible] very properly translated, the "current of the life-wave," the [illegible] tion of the One Life. The Great Breath spoken of in our first volume is Âtmâ, the etymology of which is "*eternal motion*." Now while the ascetic Chelâ of our school, for his mental develop-ment, follows carefully the process of the evolution of the Uni-verse, that is, proceeds from universals to particulars, the Hatha Yogî reverses the conditions and begins by sitting for the suppression [illegible] of his (vital) breath. And if, as Hindu philosophy teaches, at the beginning of kosmic evolution, "Svara threw itself into the form of Âkâsha," and thence successively into the forms of Vâyu (air), Agni (fire), Âpas (water), and Prithivi (solid matter),* then it stands to reason that we have to begin by the higher *supersensuous* Tattvas. The Râja Yogî does not descend on the planes of substance beyond Sûkshma (subtle matter), while the Hatha Yogî develops and uses his powers only on the material plane. Some Tântrikas locate the three Nadîs, Sushumnâ, Îdâ and Pingalâ, in the medulla oblongata, the central line of which they call Sushumnâ, and the right and left divisions, Pingalâ and Îdâ, and also in the heart, to the divisions of which they apply the same names. The Trans-Himâlayan school of the ancient Indian Râja Yogîs, with which the modern Yogîs of India have little to do, locates Sushumnâ, the chief seat of these three Nadîs, in the central tube of the spinal cord, and Îdâ and Pingalâ on its left and right sides. Sushumnâ is the Brahmadanda. It is that canal (of the spinal cord), of the use of which Physiology knows no more than it does of the spleen and the pineal gland. Îdâ and Pingalâ are simply the sharps and flats of that *Fa* of human nature, the keynote and the middle key in the scale of the septenary harmony of the Principles, which, when struck in a proper way, awakens the sentries on either side, the spiritual Manas and the physical Kâma, and subdues the lower through the higher. But this effect has to be produced by the exercise of will-power, not through the scientific or trained suppression of the breath. Take a transverse section of the spinal region, and you will find sections across three columns, one of which columns transmits the volitional orders, and a second a life current of Jîva—not of Prâna, which animates the body of man—during what is called Samâdhi and like states.

He who has studied both systems, the Hatha and the Râja Yoga, finds an enormous difference between the two: one is purely psycho-physiological, the other purely psycho-spiritual. The Tântrists do not seem to go higher than the six visible and known plexuses, with each of which they connect the Tattvas; and the great stress they lay on the chief of these, the Mûladhâra Chakra (the sacral plexus), shows the material and selfish bent of their efforts towards the acquisition of powers. Their five Breaths and five Tattvas are chiefly concerned

* See *Theosophist*, February, 1888, p. 276.

with the prostatic, epigastric, cardiac, and laryngeal plex[illegible] ignoring the Âjñâ, they are positively ignorant of [illegible] laryngeal plexus. But with the followers of the old [illegible] different. We begin with the mastery of that organ which [illegible] at the base of the brain, in the pharynx, and called by W[illegible] mists the Pituitary Body. In the series of the objective cranial [illegible] corresponding to the subjective Tâttvic principles, it stand[illegible] Third Eye (Pineal Gland) as Manas stands to Buddhi; the [illegible] and awakening of the Third Eye must be performed by that [illegible] organ, that insignificant little body, of which, once again, [illegible] knows nothing at all. The one is the Energiser of Will, the o[illegible] of Clairvoyant Perception.

Those, who are Physicians, Physiologists, Anatomists, [illegible] understand me better than the rest in the following explanation.

Now, as to the functions of the Pineal Gland, or Conarium, [illegible] the Pituitary Body, we find no explanations vouchsafed by the [illegible] authorities. Indeed, on looking through the works of the [illegible] specialists, it is curious to observe how much confused ig[illegible] the human vital economy, physiological as well as psycholo[illegible] openly confessed. The following is all that can be gleaned [illegible] authorities upon these two important organs.

(1) The Pineal Gland, or Conarium, is a rounded, oblong bod[illegible] three to four lines long, of a deep reddish grey, connected with [illegible] terior part of the third ventricle of the brain. It is attached at its [illegible] two thin medullary cords, which diverge forward to the Optic T[illegible] Remember that the latter are found by the best Physiologists to [illegible] organs of reception and condensation of the most sensitive a[illegible] sorial incitations from the periphery of the body (according to [illegible] ism, from the periphery of the Auric Egg, which is our [illegible] communication with the higher, universal planes). We are [illegible] told that the two bands of the Optic Thalami, which are in[illegible] meet each other, unite on the median line, where they become the [illegible] peduncles of the Pineal Gland.

(2) The Pituitary Body, or Hypophysis Cerebri, is a small and [illegible] organ, about six lines broad, three long and three high. It is [illegible] of an anterior bean-shaped, and of a posterior and more rounded [illegible] which are uniformly united. Its component parts, we are to[illegible] almost identical with those of the Pineal Gland; yet not the slight[illegible] connection can be traced between the two centres. To this, however,

Occultists take exception; they *know* that there is a connection, and this even anatomically and physically. Dissectors, on the other hand, have to deal with corpses; and, as they themselves admit, brain-matter, of all tissues and organs, collapses and changes form the soonest—in fact, a few minutes after death. When, then, the pulsating life which expanded the mass of the brain, filled all its cavities and energized all its organs, vanishes, the cerebral mass shrinks into a sort of pasty condition, and once open passages become closed. But the contraction and even interblending of parts in this process of shrinking, and the subsequent pasty state of the brain, do not imply that there is no connection between these two organs before death. In point of fact, as Professor Owen has shown, a connection as objective as a groove and tube exists in the crania of the human fœtus and of certain fishes. When a man is in his normal condition, an Adept can see the golden Aura pulsating in both the centres, like the pulsation of the heart, which never ceases throughout life. This motion, however, under the abnormal condition of effort to develop clairvoyant faculties, becomes intensified, and the Aura takes on a stronger vibratory or swinging action. The arc of the pulsation of the Pituitary Body mounts upward, more and more, until, just as when the electric current strikes some solid object, the current finally strikes the Pineal Gland, and the dormant organ is awakened and set all glowing with the pure Âkâshic Fire. This is the psycho-physiological illustration of two organs on the physical plane, which are, respectively, the concrete symbols of the metaphysical concepts called Manas and Buddhi. The latter, in order to become conscious on this plane, needs the more differentiated fire of Manas; *but once the sixth sense has awakened the seventh,* the light which radiates from this seventh sense illumines the fields of infinitude. For a brief space of time man becomes omniscient; the Past and the Future, Space and Time, disappear and become for him the Present. If an Adept, he will store the knowledge he thus gains in his physical memory, and nothing, save the crime of indulging in Black Magic, can obliterate the remembrance of it. If only a Chelâ, portions alone of the whole truth will impress themselves on his memory, and he will have to repeat the process for years, never allowing one speck of impurity to stain him mentally or physically, before he becomes a fully initiated Adept.

It may seem strange, almost incomprehensible, that the chief success of Gupta Vidyâ, or Occult Knowledge, should depend upon such flashes of clairvoyance, and that the latter should depend [illegible] insignificant excrescences in his cranial cavity, [illegible] covered with grey sand (acervulus cerebri)," as expressed [illegible] his *Anatomic Descriptive*; yet so it is. But this sand is not [illegible] pised; nay, in truth, it is only this landmark of the internal [illegible] dent activity of the Conarium that prevents Physiologists [illegible] ing it with the absolutely useless atrophied organs, the [illegible] previous and now utterly changed anatomy of man during [illegible] of his unknown evolution. This "sand" is very mysterious [illegible] the inquiry of every Materialist. In the cavity on the anterior [illegible] of this gland, in young persons, and in its substance, in [illegible] advanced years, is found

A yellowish substance, semi-transparent, brilliant and hard, the diameter [illegible] does not exceed half a line.*

Such is the acervulus cerebri.

This brilliant "sand" is the concretion of the gland itself, [illegible] Physiologists. Perhaps not, we answer. The Pineal Gland [illegible] which the Eastern Occultist calls Devâksha, the "Divine [illegible] this day, it is the chief organ of spirituality in the human [illegible] seat of genius, the magical Sesame uttered by the purified will [illegible] Mystic, which opens all the avenues of truth for him who [illegible] to use it. The Esoteric Science teaches that Manas, the [illegible] does not accomplish its full union with the child before he [illegible] seven years of age, before which period, even according to the [illegible] of the Church and Law, no child is deemed responsible.† [illegible] comes a prisoner, one with the body, only at that age. Now [illegible] thing was observed in several thousand cases by the famous [illegible] anatomist, Wengel. With a few extremely rare exceptions, this [illegible] or golden-coloured concretion, is found only in subjects [illegible] completion of their seventh year. [illegible] the case of fools these [illegible] are very few; in congenital idiots they are completely absent. [illegible] gagni,‡ Grading,§ and Gum‖ were wise men in their generation, [illegible] are wise men to-day, since they are the only Physiologists [illegible]

---

* Sœmmerring, *De Acervulo Cerebri*, vol. ii. p. 322.

† In the Greek Eastern Church no child is allowed to go to confession before the age of [illegible] which he is considered to have reached the age of reason.

‡ *De Caus. Ep.*, vol xii.

§ *Advers. Med.*, ii. 322.

‖ *De Lapillis Glandulæ Pinealis in Quinque Ment Alien*, 1758.

who connect the calculi with mind. For, sum up the facts, that they are absent in young children, in very old people, and in idiots, and the unavoidable conclusion will be that they must be connected with mind.

Now since every mineral, vegetable and other atom is only a concretion of crystallized Spirit, or Âkâsha, the Universal Soul, why, asks Occultism, should the fact that these concretions of the Pineal Gland, are, upon analysis, found to be composed of animal matter, phosphate of lime and carbonate, serve as an objection to the statement that they are the result of the work of mental electricity upon surrounding matter?

Our seven Chakras are all situated in the head, and it is these Master Chakras which govern and rule the seven (for there are seven) principal plexuses in the body, besides the forty-two minor ones to which Physiology refuses that name. The fact that no microscope can detect such centres on the objective plane goes for nothing; no microscope has ever yet detected, nor ever will, the difference between the motor and sensory nerve-tubes, the conductors of all our bodily and psychic sensations; and yet logic alone would show that such difference exists. And if the term plexus, in this application, does not represent to the Western mind the idea conveyed by the term of the Anatomist, then call them Chakras or Padmas, or the Wheels, the Lotus Heart and Petals. Remember that Physiology, imperfect as it is, shows septenary groups all over the exterior and interior of the body; the seven head orifices, the seven "organs" at the base of the brain, the seven plexuses, the pharyngeal, laryngeal, cavernous, cardiac, epigastric, prostatic, and sacral, etc.

When the time comes, advanced students will be given the minute details about the Master Chakras and taught the use of them: till then, less difficult subjects have to be learned. If asked whether the seven plexuses, or Tâttvic centres of action, are the centres where the seven Rays of the Logos vibrate, I answer in the affirmative, simply remarking that the rays of the Logos vibrate in every atom, for the matter of that.

In these volumes it is almost revealed that the "Sons of Fohat" are the personified Forces known in a general way as Motion, Sound, Heat, Light, Cohesion, Electricity or Electric Fluid, and Nerve-Force or Magnetism. This truth, however, cannot teach the student to attune and moderate the Kundalinî of the cosmic plane with the *vital* Kundalini, the Electric Fluid with the Nerve-Force, and makes [illegible] is sure to kill himself; for the one travels at the rate of [illegible] and the other at the rate of 115,000 leagues a second. [illegible] Shaktis respectively called Para Shakti, Jñâna Shakti, etc., [illegible] mous with the "Sons of Fohat," for they are their female [illegible] the present stage, however, as their names would only be [illegible] the Western student, it is better to remember the English [illegible] as translated above. As each Force is septenary, their [illegible] course, forty-nine.

The question now mooted in Science, whether a sound is [illegible] calling forth impressions of light and colour in addition to its [illegible] sound impressions, has been answered by Occult Science ages [illegible] Every impulse or vibration of a physical object producing a [illegible] vibration of the air, that is, causing the collision of physical [illegible] the sound of which is capable of affecting the ear, produces at the [illegible] time a corresponding flash of light, which will assume some [illegible] colour. For, in the realm of hidden Forces, an *audible* sound [illegible] subjective colour; and a perceptible colour, but an *inaudible* [illegible] both proceed from the same potential substance, which Physicists [illegible] to call ether, and now refer to under various other names; but [illegible] we call plastic, through invisible SPACE. This may appear a [illegible] cal hypothesis, but facts are there to prove it. Complete deafness [illegible] instance, does not preclude the possibility of discerning [illegible] medical science has several cases on record which prove that [illegible] sounds are received by, and conveyed to, the patient's organ of [illegible] through the mind, under the form of chromatic impressions. The [illegible] fact that the intermediate tones of the chromatic musical scale [illegible] formerly written in colours shows an unconscious reminiscence of [illegible] ancient Occult teaching that colour and sound are two out of the [illegible] correlative aspects, *on our plane*, of one and the same thing, [illegible] Nature's first differentiated Substance.

Here is an example of the relation of colour to vibration well [illegible] of the attention of Occultists. Not only Adepts and advanced Chelas, but also the lower order of Psychics, such as clairvoyants and [illegible] metrists, can perceive a psychic Aura of various colours around every individual, corresponding to the temperament of the person within [illegible] In other words, the mysterious records within the Auric Egg are [illegible] the heirloom of trained Adepts alone, but sometimes also of [illegible] Psychics. Every human passion, every thought and quality, is [illegible] cated in this Aura by corresponding colours and shades of colour, and certain of these are sensed and felt rather than perceived. The best of such Psychics, as shown by Galton, can also perceive colours produced by the vibrations of musical instruments, every note suggesting a different colour. As a string vibrates and gives forth an audible note, so the nerves of the human body vibrate and thrill in correspondence with various emotions under the general impulse of the circulating vitality of Prâna, thus producing undulations in the psychic Aura of the person which result in chromatic effects.

The human nervous system as a whole, then, may be regarded as an Æolian Harp, responding to the impact of the vital force, which is no abstraction, but a dynamic reality, and manifests the subtlest shades of the individual character in colour phenomena. If these nerve vibrations are made intense enough and brought into vibratory relation with an astral element, the result is—sound. How, then, can anyone doubt the relation between the microcosmic and macrocosmic forces?

And now that I have shown that the Tântric works as explained by Râma Prâsad, and other Yoga treatises of the same character which have appeared from time to time in Theosophical journals—for note well that those of true Râja Yoga are never published—tend to Black Magic and are most dangerous to take for guides in self-training, I hope that students will be on their guard.

For, considering that no two authorities up to the present day agree as to the real location of the Chakras and Padmas in the body, and, seeing that the colours of the Tattvas as given are reversed, *e.g.*:

(*a*) Âkâsha is made black or colourless, whereas corresponding to Manas, it is indigo;

(*b*) Vâyu is made blue, whereas, corresponding to the Lower Manas, it is green;

(*c*) Âpas is made white, whereas, corresponding to the Astral Body, it is violet, with a silver, moonlike white substratum;

Tejas, red, is the only colour given correctly—from such considerations, I say, it is easy to see that these disagreements are dangerous blinds.

Further, the practice of the Five Breaths results in deadly injury, both physiologically and psychically, as already shown. It is indeed that which it is called, Prânâyâma, or the death of the breath, for it results, for the practiser, in death—in moral death always, and in physical death very frequently.

ON ESOTERIC "BLINDS" AND "THE DEATH [illegible]

As a corollary to this, and before going into still [illegible] teachings, I must redeem the promise already given. I [illegible] trate by tenets you already know, the awful doctrine of [illegible] lation. Banish from your minds all that you have [illegible] such works as *Esoteric Buddhism*, and thought you [illegible] such hypotheses as the eighth sphere and the moon, and [illegible] shares a common ancestor with the ape. Even the details [illegible] given out by myself in the *Theosophist* and *Lucifer* were [illegible] the whole truth, but only broad general ideas, hardly touched [illegible] their details. Certain passages, however, give out hints, especi[illegible] foot-notes on articles translated from Éliphas Lévi's *Letters* [illegible]

Nevertheless, personal immortality is conditional, for there [illegible] things as "soulless men," a teaching barely mentioned, althou[illegible] spoken of even in *Isis Unveiled*;† and there is an Avîtchi, righ[illegible] Hell, though it has no connection with, or similitude to, [illegible] Christian's Hell, either geographically or psychically. The truth [illegible] to Occultists and Adepts in every age could not be given [illegible] promiscuous public; hence, though almost every mystery of [illegible] Philosophy lies half concealed in *Isis* and the two earlier [illegible] the present work, I had no right to amplify or correct the [illegible] others. Readers may now compare those four volumes and [illegible] as *Esoteric Buddhism* with the diagrams and explanations [illegible] Papers, and see for themselves.

Paramâtmâ, the Spiritual Sun, may be thought of as [illegible] human Auric Egg, as it is also outside the Macrocosmic or [illegible] Egg. Why? Because, though every particle and atom are, so to [illegible] cemented with and soaked through by this Paramâtmic essence, [illegible] wrong to call it a "human" or even a "universal" Principle, [illegible] term is very likely to give rise to naught but an erroneous [illegible] philosophical and purely metaphysical concept; it is not a [illegible] but the cause of every Principle, the latter term being applied by [illegible] tists only to its shadow—the Universal Spirit that ensouls the [illegible] Kosmos whether within or beyond Space and Time.

Buddhi serves as a vehicle for that Paramâtmic shadow. [illegible]

---

* See "Stray Thoughts on Death and Satan" in the *Theosophist*, vol. iii. No. [illegible] also [illegible] Occult Truth," vols. iii. and iv.

† *Op. cit.* ii. 368, *et seq.*

is universal, and so also is the human Âtmâ. Within the Auric Egg is the macracosmic pentacle of LIFE, Prâna, containing within itself the pentagram which represents man. The universal pentacle must be pictured with its point soaring upwards, the sign of White Magic—in the human pentacle it is the lower limbs which are upward, forming the "Horns of Satan," as the Christian Kabbalists call them. This is the symbol of Matter, that of the personal man, and the recognized pentacle of the Black Magician. For this reversed pentacle does not stand only for Kâma, the fourth Principle exoterically, but it also represents physical man, the animal of flesh with its desires and passions.

Now, mark well, in order to understand that which follows, that Manas may be pictured as an upper triangle connected with the lower Manas by a thin line which binds the two together. This is the Antahkarana, that path or bridge of communication which serves as a link between the personal being whose physical brain is under the sway of the lower animal mind, and the reincarnating Individuality, the spiritual Ego, Manas, Manu, the "Divine Man." This thinking Manu alone is that which reincarnates. In truth and in nature, the two Minds, the spiritual and the physical or animal, are one, but separate into two at reincarnation. For while that portion of the Divine which goes to animate the personality, consciously separating itself, like a dense but pure shadow, from the Divine Ego,* wedges itself into the brain and senses † of the fœtus, at the completion of its seventh month, the Higher Manas does not unite itself with the child before the completion of the first seven years of its life. This detached essence, or rather the reflection or shadow of the Higher Manas, becomes, as the

* The essence of the Divine Ego is "pure flame," an entity to which nothing can be added and from which nothing can be taken; it cannot, therefore, be diminished even by countless numbers of lower minds, detached from it like flames from a flame. This is in answer to an objection by an Esotericist who asked whence was that inexhaustible essence of one and the same Individuality which was called upon to furnish a human intellect for every new personality in which it is incarnated.

† The brain, or thinking machinery, is not only in the head, but, as every physiologist who is not quite a materialist will tell you, every organ in man, heart, liver, lungs, etc., down to every nerve and muscle, has, so to speak, its own distinct brain or thinking apparatus. As our brain has naught to do in the guidance of the collective and individual work of every organ in us, what is that which guides each so unerringly in its incessant functions; that make these struggle, and that too with disease, throws it off and acts, each of them, even to the smallest, not in a clock-work manner, as alleged by some materialists (for, at the slightest disturbance or breakage the clock stops), but as an entity endowed with instinct? To say it is Nature is to say nothing, if it is not the enunciation of a fallacy; for Nature after all is but a name for these very same functions, the sum of the qualities and attributes, physical, mental, etc., in the universe and man, the total of agencies and forces guided by intelligent laws.

child grows, a distinct thinking Principle in man, to claim kinship with the physical brain. No wonder the Materialists, who perceive only this "rational soul," or mind, will not dissociate it from the brain and matter. But Occult Philosophy has ages ago solved the problem of mind, and discovered the duality of Manas. The Divine Ego strains with its point upwards towards Buddhi, and the human Ego gravitates downwards, immersed in Matter, connected with its higher, subjective half only by the Antahkarana. As its derivation suggests, this is the only connecting link during life between the two minds—the higher consciousness of the Ego and the human intelligence of the lower mind.

To understand this abstruse metaphysical doctrine fully and correctly, one has to be thoroughly impressed with an idea, which I have in vain endeavoured to impart to Theosophists at large, namely, the great axiomatic truth that the only eternal and living Reality is that which the Hindus call Paramâtmâ and Parabrahman. This is the one ever-existing Root Essence, immutable and unknowable to our physical senses, but manifest and clearly perceptible to our spiritual natures. Once imbued with that basic idea and the further conception that if It is omnipresent, universal and eternal, like abstract Space itself, we must have emanated from It and we must, some day, return into It, and all the rest becomes easy.

If so, then it stands to reason that life and death, good and evil, past and future, are all empty words, or at best, figures of speech. If the objective Universe itself is but a passing illusion on account of its beginning and finitude, then both life and death must also be aspects and illusions. They are changes of state, in fact, and no more. Real life is in the spiritual consciousness of that life, *in a conscious existence in Spirit, not Matter;* and real death is the limited perception of life, the impossibility of sensing conscious or even individual existence outside of form, or at least, of some form of Matter. Those who sincerely reject the possibility of conscious life divorced from Matter and brain-substance, are *dead units.* The words of Paul, an Initiate, become comprehensible. "Ye are dead, and your *life* is hid with Christ in God:" which is to say: Ye are personally dead matter, unconscious of your own spiritual essence, and your real life is hid with your Divine Ego (Christos) in, or merged with, God (Âtmâ); now has it departed from you, ye soulless people.* Speaking on Esoteric lines, every irreclaimably

* See *Coloss.*, [illegible]

materialistic person is a *dead Man*, a living automaton, in spite of his being endowed with great brain-power. Listen to what Aryasangha says, stating the same fact:

That which is neither Spirit nor Matter, neither Light nor Darkness, but is verily the container and root of these, that thou art. The Root projects at every Dawn its shadow on ITSELF, and that shadow thou callest Light and Life, O poor dead Form. (This) Life-Light streameth downward through the stairway of the seven worlds, the stairs of which each step become denser and darker. It is of this seven-times-seven scale that thou art the faithful climber and mirror, O little man! Thou art this, but thou knowest it not.

This is the first lesson to learn. The second is to study well the Principles of both the Kosmos and ourselves, dividing the group into the permanent and the impermanent, the higher and immortal and the lower and mortal, for thus only can we master and guide, first the lower cosmic and personal, then the higher cosmic and impersonal.

Once we can do that we have secured our immortality. But some may say: "How few are those who can do so. All such are great Adepts, and none can reach such Adeptship in one short life." Agreed; but there is an alternative. "If the Sun thou canst not be, then be the humble Planet," says the *Book of the Golden Precepts*. And if even that is beyond our reach, then let us at least endeavour to keep within the ray of some lesser star, so that its silvery light may penetrate the murky darkness, through which the stony path of life trends onward; for without this divine radiance we risk losing more than we imagine.

With regard, then, to "soulless" men, and the "second death" of the "Soul," mentioned in the second volume of *Isis Unveiled*, you will there find that I have spoken of such soulless people, and even of Avîtchi, though I leave the latter unnamed. Read from the last paragraph on page 367 to the end of the first paragraph on page 370, and then collate what is there said with what I have now to say.

The higher triad, Âtmâ-Buddhi-Manas, may be recognized from the first lines of the quotation from the Egyptian papyrus. In the *Ritual*, now the *Book of the Dead*, the purified Soul, the dual Manas, appears as "the victim of the dark influence of the Dragon Apophis," the physical personality of Kâmarûpic man, with his passions. "If it has attained the final knowledge of the heavenly and infernal Mysteries, the Gnosis"—the divine and the terrestrial Mysteries, of White and Black Magic—then the defunct personality "will triumph over its enemy"—death. This alludes to the case of a complete re-union, at the end of earth life, of the lower Manas, full of "the harvest of life" (the Ego.) But if Apophis conquers the Soul, then it is condemned to a *second* death."

These few lines from a papyrus, many thousands of years old, contain a whole revelation, known, in those days, only to the Hierophants and the Initiates. The "harvest of life" consists of the finest spiritual thoughts, of the memory of the noblest and most unselfish deeds of the personality, and the constant presence during its bliss after death of those it loved with divine, spiritual devotion.* Remember the teaching: The Human Soul, lower Manas, is the *only* and direct mediator between the personality and the Divine Ego. That which goes to make up on this earth the *personality* miscalled *individuality* by the majority, is the sum of all its mental, physical, and spiritual characteristics, which being impressed on the Human Soul, produces the *man*. Now, of all these characteristics it is the purified thoughts alone which can be impressed on the higher, immortal Ego. This is done by the Human Soul merging again, in its essence, into its parent source, commingling with its Divine Ego during life, and re-uniting itself entirely with it after the death of the physical man. Therefore, unless Kâma-Manas transmits to Buddhi-Manas such personal ideations, and such consciousness of its "I" as can be assimilated by the Divine Ego, nothing of that "I" or personality can survive in the Eternal. Only that which is worthy of the immortal God within us, and identical in its nature with the divine quintessence, can survive; for in this case it is its own, the Divine Ego's, "shadows" or emanations which ascend to it and are indrawn by it into itself again, to become once more part of its own Essence. No noble thought, no grand aspiration, desire, or divine immortal love, can come into the brain of the man of clay and settle there, except as a direct emanation from the Higher to, and through, the lower Ego; all the rest, intellectual as it may seem, proceeds from the "shadow," the *lower mind*, in its association and commingling with Kâma, and passes away and disappears for ever. But the mental and spiritual ideations of the personal "I" return to it, as parts of the Ego's Essence, and can never fade out. Thus of the personality that was, only its spiritual experiences, the memory of all that is good and noble, with the consciousness of its "I" blended with that of all the other personal "I's" that preceded it, survive and become immortal.

* See *Key to Theosophy*, pp. 147, 148, *et seq.*

There is no distinct or separate immortality for the men of earth outside of the Ego which informed them. That Higher Ego is the sole bearer of all its *alter egos* on earth and their sole representative in the mental state called Devachan. As the last embodied personality, however, has a right to its own special state of bliss, unalloyed and free from the memories of all others, it is the *last life only which is fully and realistically vivid.* Devachan is often compared to the happiest day in a series of many thousands of other "days" in the life of a person. The intensity of its happiness makes the man entirely forget all others, his past becoming obliterated.

This is what we call the Devachanic state, the reward of the personality, and it is on this old teaching that the hazy Christian notion of Paradise was built, borrowed with many other things from the Egyptian Mysteries, wherein the doctrine was enacted. And this is the meaning of the passage quoted in *Isis*. The Soul has triumphed over Apophis, the Dragon of Flesh. Henceforth, the personality will live in eternity, in its highest and noblest elements, the memory of its past deeds, while the "characteristics" of the "Dragon" will be fading out in Kâma Loka. If the question be asked, "How live in eternity, when Devachan lasts but from 1,000 to 2,000 years," the answer is: "In the same way as the recollection of each day which is worth remembering lives in the memory of each one of us." For the sake of an example, the days passed in one personal life may be taken as an illustration of each personal life, and this or that person may stand for the Divine Ego.

To obtain the key which will open the door of many a psychological mystery it is sufficient to understand and remember that which precedes and that which follows. Many a Spiritualist has felt terribly indignant on being told that personal immortality was *conditional*; and yet such is the philosophical and logical fact. Much has been said already on the subject, but no one to this day seems to have fully understood the doctrine. Moreover, it is not enough to know that such a fact is said to exist. An Occultist, or he who would become one, must know *why* it is so; for having learned and comprehended the *raison d'être*, it becomes easier to set others right in their erroneous speculations, and, most important of all, it affords one an opportunity, without saying too much, to teach other people to avoid a calamity which, sad to say, occurs in our age almost daily. This calamity will now be explained at length.

One must know little indeed of the Eastern modes of expression to fail to see in the passage quoted from the *Book of the Dead*, and in the pages of *Isis*, (*a*) an allegory for the uninitiated, containing an Esoteric teaching; and (*b*) that the two terms "second death" and "Soul" are, in one sense, blinds. "Soul" refers both to Buddhi-Manas and Kâma-Manas. As to the term "second death," the qualification "second" applies to several deaths which have to be undergone by the "Principles" during their incarnation; Occultists alone understanding fully the sense in which such a statement is made. For we have (1) the death of the Body; (2) the death of the Animal Soul in Kâma Loka; (3) the death of the Astral Linga Sharîra, following that of the Body; (4) the metaphysical death of the Higher Ego, the *immortal*, every time it "falls into matter," or incarnates in a new personality. The Animal Soul, or lower Manas, that shadow of the Divine Ego which separates from it to inform the personality, cannot by any possible means *escape death* in Kâma Loka, at any rate that portion of this reflection which remains as a terrestrial residue and cannot be impressed on the Ego. Thus the chief and most important secret with regard to that "second death," in the Esoteric teaching, was and is to this day the terrible possibility of the *death* of the Soul, that is, its severance from the Ego on earth during a person's lifetime. This is a *real* death (though with chances of resurrection), which shows no traces in a person and yet leaves him morally a living corpse. It is difficult to see why this teaching should have been preserved until now with such secrecy, when, by spreading it among people, at any rate among those who believe in reincarnation, so much good might be done. But so it was, and I had no right to question the wisdom of the prohibition, but have given it hitherto, as it was given to myself, under *pledge* not to reveal it to the world at large. But now I have permission to give it to all, revealing its tenets first to the Esotericists, and then when they have assimilated them thoroughly it will be their duty to teach others this special tenet of the "second death," and to warn all the Theosophists of its dangers.

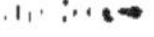

To make the teaching clearer, I shall seemingly have to go over old ground; in reality, however, it is given out with new light and new details. I have tried to hint at it in the *Theosophist* as I have done in *Isis*, but have failed to make myself understood. I will now explain it point by point.

THE PHILOSOPHICAL RATIONALE OF THE TENET.

(1) Imagine, for illustration's sake, the one homogeneous, absolute and omnipresent Essence, above the upper step of the "Stair of the seven planes of worlds," ready to start on its evolutionary journey. As its correlating reflection gradually descends, it differentiates and transforms into subjective, and finally into objective matter. Let us call it at its north pole Absolute Light; at its south pole, which to us would be the fourth or middle step, or plane, counting either way, we know it Esoterically as the One and Universal Life. Now mark the difference. Above, LIGHT; below, *Life*. The former is ever immutable, the latter manifests under the aspects of countless differentiations. According to the Occult law, all potentialities included in the higher become differentiated reflections in the lower; and according to the same law, nothing which is differentiated can be blended with the homogeneous.

Again, nothing can endure of that which lives and breathes and has its being in the seething waves of the world, or plane of differentiation. Thus Buddhi and Manas being both primordial rays of the One Flame, the former the vehicle, the upâdhi or vâhana, of the one eternal Essence, the latter the vehicle of Mahat or Divine Ideation (Mahâ-Buddhi in the *Purânas*), the Universal Intelligent Soul—neither of them, as such, can become extinct or be annihilated, either in essence or consciousness. But the physical personality with its Linga Sharira, and the animal soul, with its Kâma,* can and do become so. They are born in the realm of illusion, and must vanish like a fleecy cloud from the blue and eternal sky.

He who has read these volumes with any degree of attention, must know the origin of the human Egos, called Monads, generically, and what they were before they were forced to incarnate in the human animal. The divine beings whom Karma led to act in the drama of Manvantaric life, are entities from higher and earlier worlds and planets, whose Karma had not been exhausted when their world went into Pralaya. Such is the teaching; but whether it is so or not, the Higher Egos are—as compared to such forms of transitory, terrestrial mud as ourselves—Divine Beings, Gods, immortal throughout the Mahâmanvantara, or the 311,040,000,000,000 years during which the Age of Brahmâ lasts. And as the Divine Egos, in

* Kâma Rûpa, the vehicle of the Lower Manas, is said to dwell in the physical brain, in the five physical senses and in all the sense-organs of the physical body.

order to re-become the One Essence, or be indrawn [illegible] have to purify themselves in the fire of suffering and individual experience, so also have the terrestrial Egos, the personalities, [illegible] likewise, if they would partake of the immortality of the Higher [illegible] This they can achieve by crushing in themselves all that [illegible] the lower personal nature of their "selves" and by aspiring [illegible] fuse their thinking Kâmic Principle into that of the Higher Ego [illegible] (*i.e.*, our personalities) become immortal by the mere fact of [illegible] ing moral nature being grafted on our Divine Triune Monad, [illegible] Buddhi-Manas, the three in one and one in three (aspects). [illegible] Monad manifested on earth by the incarnating Ego is that [illegible] called the Tree of Life Eternal, that can only be approached by [illegible] the fruit of knowledge, the Knowledge of Good and Evil, or of [illegible] Divine Wisdom.

In the Esoteric teachings, this Ego is the fifth Principle [illegible] But the student who has read and understood the first two [illegible] knows something more. He is aware that the seventh [illegible] human, but a universal Principle in which man participates [illegible] does equally every physical and subjective atom, and also every [illegible] of grass and everything that lives or is in Space, whether it be [illegible] of it or not. He knows, moreover, that if man is more closely connected with it, and assimilates it with a hundredfold more power, [illegible] simply because he is endowed with the highest consciousness on [illegible] earth; that man, in short, may become a Spirit, a Deva, or a God [illegible] his next transformation, whereas neither a stone nor a vegetable, [illegible] an animal, can do so before they become men in their proper turn.

(2) Now what are the functions of Buddhi? On this plane it [illegible] none, unless it is united with Manas, the conscious Ego. [illegible] stands to the divine Root Essence in the same relation as Mûlaprakriti to Parabrahman, in the Vedânta School; or as Alaya the Universal [illegible] to the One Eternal Spirit, or that which is beyond Spirit. It is its [illegible] vehicle, one remove from that Absolute, which can have no relation whatever to the finite and the conditioned.

(3) What, again, is Manas and its functions? In its purely [illegible] physical aspect, Manas, though one remove on the downward plane from Buddhi, is still so immeasurably higher than the physical [illegible] that it cannot enter into direct relation with the personality, [illegible] through its reflection, the lower mind. Manas is *Spiritual Self-Consciousness* in itself, and Divine Consciousness when united with [illegible]

which is the true "producer" of that "production" (vikâra), or Self-Consciousness, through Mahat. Buddhi-Manas, therefore, is entirely unfit to manifest during its periodical incarnations, except through the human mind or lower Manas. Both are linked together and are inseparable, and can have as little to do with the lower Tanmâtras,* or rudimentary atoms, as the homogeneous with the heterogeneous. It is, therefore, the task of the lower Manas, or thinking personality, if it would blend itself with its God, the Divine Ego, to dissipate and paralyze the Tanmâtras, or properties of the material form. Therefore, Manas is shown double, as the Ego and Mind of Man. It is Kâma-Manas, or the lower Ego, which, deluded into a notion of independent existence, as the "producer" in its turn and the sovereign of the five Tanmâtras, becomes *Ego-ism*, the selfish Self, in which case it has to be considered as Mahâbhûtic and finite, in the sense of its being connected with Ahankâra, the personal "I-creating" faculty. Hence

> Manas has to be regarded as eternal and non-eternal; eternal in its atomic nature (paramanu rûpa), as eternal substance (dravya), finite (kârya rûpa) when linked as a duad with Kâma (animal desire or human *egoistic* volition), a lower production, in short.†

While, therefore, the INDIVIDUAL EGO, owing o its essence and nature, is immortal throughout eternity, with a form (rûpa), which prevails during the whole life cycles of the Fourth Round, its *Sosie*, or resemblance, the personal Ego, has to win its immortality.

(4) Antahkarana is the name of that imaginary bridge, the *path* which lies between the Divine and the human Egos, for they are *Egos*, during human life, to rebecome *one* Ego in Devachan or Nirvâna. This may seem difficult to understand, but in reality, with the help of a familiar, though fanciful illustration, it becomes quite simple. Let us figure to ourselves a bright lamp in the middle of a room, casting its light upon the wall. Let the lamp represent the Divine Ego, and the light thrown on the wall the lower Manas, and let the wall stand for the body. That portion of the atmosphere which transmits the ray from the lamp to the wall, will then represent the Antahkarana. We must further suppose that the light thus cast is endowed with reason and intelligence, and

---

* Tanmâtra means subtle and rudimentary form, the gross type of the finer elements. The five Tanmâtras are really the characteristic properties or qualities of matter and of all the elements; the real spirit of the word is "something" or "merely transcendental," in the sense of properties or qualities.

† See *Theosophist*, August, 1883, "The Real and the Unreal."

possesses, moreover, the faculty of dissipating all the evil shadows which pass across the wall, and of attracting all brightnesses to itself, receiving their indelible impressions. Now, it is in the power of the human Ego to chase away the shadows, or sins, and multiply the brightnesses, or good deeds, which make these impressions, and thus through Antahkarana, ensure its own permanent connection, and its final re-union, with the Divine Ego. Remember that the latter cannot take place while there remains a single taint of the terrestrial, or of matter, in the purity of that light. On the other hand, the connection cannot be entirely ruptured, and final re-union prevented, so long as there remains one spiritual deed, or potentiality to serve as a thread of union; but the moment this last spark is extinguished, and the last potentiality exhausted, then comes the severance. In an Eastern parable, the Divine Ego is likened to the Master who sends out his labourers to till the ground and to gather in the harvest, and who is content to keep the field so long as it can yield even the smallest return. But when the ground becomes absolutely sterile, not only is it abandoned, but the labourer also (the lower Manas) perishes.

On the other hand, however, still using our simile, when the light thrown on the wall, or the rational human Ego, reaches the point of actual spiritual exhaustion, the Antahkarana disappears, no more light is transmitted, and the lamp becomes non-existent to the ray. The light which has been absorbed gradually disappears and "Soul eclipse" occurs; the being lives on earth and then passes into Kâma Loka as a mere surviving congeries of material qualities; it can never pass onwards towards Devachan, but is reborn immediately, a human animal and scourge.

This simile, however fantastic, will help us to seize the correct idea. Save through the blending of the moral nature with the Divine Ego, there is no immortality for the personal Ego. It is only the most spiritual emanations of the personal Human Soul which survive. Having, during a lifetime, been imbued with the notion and feeling of the "I am I" of its personality, the Human Soul, the bearer of the very essence of the Karmic deeds of the physical man, becomes, after the death of the latter, part and parcel of the Divine Flame, the Ego. It becomes immortal through the mere fact that it is now strongly grafted on the Monad, which is the "Tree of Life Eternal."

And now we must speak of the tenet of the "second death." What happens to the Kâmic Human Soul, which is always that of a debased and wicked man or of a soulless person? This mystery will now be explained.

The personal Soul in this case, *viz.*, in that of one who has never had a thought not concerned with the animal self, having nothing to transmit to the Higher, or to add to the sum of the experiences gleaned from past incarnations which its memory is to preserve throughout eternity—this personal Soul becomes separated from the Ego. It can graft nothing of self on that eternal trunk whose sap throws out millions of personalities, like leaves from its branches, leaves which wither, die and fall at the end of their season. These personalities bud, blossom forth and expire, some without leaving a trace behind, others after commingling their own life with that of the parent stem. It is the Souls of the former class that are doomed to annihilation, or Avîtchi, a state so badly understood, and still worse described by some Theosophical writers, but which is not only located on our earth, but is in fact this very earth itself.

Thus we see that Antahkarana has been destroyed before the lower man has had an opportunity of assimilating the Higher and becoming at one with it; and therefore the Kâmic "Soul" becomes a separate entity, to live henceforth, for a short or long period according to its Karma, as a "soulless" creature.

But before I elaborate this question, I must explain more clearly the meaning and functions of the Antahkarana. As already said, it may be represented as a narrow bridge connecting the Higher and the lower Manas. If you look at the Glossary of the *Voice of the Silence*, pp. 88 and 89, you will find that it is a projection of the lower Manas, or, rather, the link between the latter and the Higher Ego, or, between the Human and the Divine or Spiritual Soul.*

At death it is destroyed as a path, or medium of communication, and its remains survive as Kâma Rûpa,

the "shell." It is this which the Spiritualists see sometimes appearing in the séance rooms as materialized "forms," which they foolishly mistake for the "Spirits of the Departed."† So far is this from being

* As the author of *Esoteric Buddhism* and the *Occult World* called Manas the Human Soul, and Buddhi the Spiritual Soul, I have left these terms unchanged in the *Voice*, seeing that it was a book intended for the public.

† In the exoteric teachings of Râja Yoga, Antahkarana is called the inner organ of perception and is divided into four parts: the (lower) Manas, Buddhi (reason), Ahankâra (personality), and Chitta (thinking faculty). It also, together with several other organs, forms a part of Jîva, Soul called also Lingadeh Esotericists, however, must not be misled by this popular version.

SELFISHNESS

the case, that in dreams, though Antahkarana is there, the [illegible] is only half awake; therefore, Antahkarana is said to be [illegible] *insane* during our normal sleeping state. If such is the case during [illegible] periodical death, or sleep, of the living body, one may judge what [illegible] consciousness of Antahkarana is like when it has been [illegible] after the "eternal sleep" into Kâma Rûpa.

But to return. In order not to confuse the mind of the [illegible] student with the abstruse difficulties of Indian metaphysics, let [illegible] view the lower Manas, or Mind, as the personal Ego during the [illegible] state, and as Antahkarana only during those moments when it [illegible] towards its Higher Ego, and thus becomes the medium of communica-tion between the two. It is for this reason that it is called the " [illegible] Now, when a limb or organ belonging to the physical organism is [illegible] in disuse, it becomes weak and finally atrophies. So also is it [illegible] mental faculties; and hence the atrophy of the lower mind-function called Antahkarana, becomes comprehensible in both [illegible] materialistic and depraved natures.

According to Esoteric Philosophy, however, the teaching is [illegible] follows: Seeing that the faculty and function of Antahkarana is [illegible] necessary as the medium of the ear for hearing, or that of the [illegible] seeing; then so long as the feeling of Ahankâra, that is, of [illegible] personal "I" or selfishness, is not entirely crushed out in a man, [illegible] the lower mind not entirely merged into and become one with the Higher Buddhi-Manas, it stands to reason that to destroy Antahkarana is like destroying a bridge over an impassable chasm; *the traveller* [illegible] *never reach the goal on the other shore.* And here lies the [illegible] between the exoteric and Esoteric teaching. The former [illegible] Vedânta state that so long as Mind (the lower) clings through Antah-karana to Spirit (Buddhi-Manas) it is impossible for it to acquire [illegible] Spiritual Wisdom, Gnyâna, and that this can only be attained by [illegible]-ing to come *en rapport* with the Universal Soul (Âtmâ); that, in [illegible] is by ignoring the Higher Mind altogether that one reaches Râja [illegible] We say it is not so. No single rung of the ladder leading to know[illegible] can be skipped. No personality can ever reach or bring itself [illegible] communication with Âtmâ, except through Buddhi-Manas; to try [illegible] become a Jîvanmukta or a Mahâtmâ, before one has become an [illegible] or even a Narjol (a sinless man) is like trying to reach Ceylon [illegible] India without crossing the sea. Therefore we are told [illegible] destroy Antahkarana before the personal is absolutely under [illegible]

trol of the impersonal Ego, we risk to lose the latter and be severed for ever from it, unless indeed we hasten to re-establish the communication by a supreme and final effort.

It is only when we are indissolubly linked with the essence of the Divine Mind, that we have to destroy Antahkarana.

Like as a solitary warrior pursued by an army, seeks refuge in a stronghold; to cut himself off from the enemy, he first destroys the drawbridge, and then only commences to destroy the pursuer; so must the Srotâpatti act before he slays Antahkarana.

Or as an Occult axiom has it:

The Unit becomes Three, and Three generate Four. It is for the latter [the Quaternary] to rebecome Three, and for the Divine Three to expand into the Absolute One.

Monads, which become Duads on the differentiated plane, to develop into Triads during the cycle of incarnations, even when incarnated know neither space nor time, but are diffused through the lower Principles of the Quaternary, being omnipresent and omniscient in their nature. But this omniscience is innate, and can manifest its reflected light only through that which is at least semi-terrestrial or material; even as the physical brain which, in its turn, is the vehicle of the lower Manas enthroned in Kâma Rûpa. And it is this which is gradually annihilated in cases of "second death."

But such annihilation—which is in reality the absence of the slightest trace of the doomed Soul from the eternal MEMORY, and therefore signifies annihilation in eternity—does not mean simply discontinuation of human life on earth, for earth is Avîtchi, and the worst Avîtchi possible. Expelled for ever from the consciousness of the Individuality, the reincarnating Ego, the physical atoms and psychic vibrations of the now separate personality are immediately reincarnated on the same earth, only in a lower and still more abject creature, a human being only in form, doomed to Karmic torments during the whole of its new life. Moreover, if it persists in its criminal or debauched course, it will suffer a long series of immediate reincarnations.

Here two questions present themselves: (1) What becomes of the Higher Ego in such cases? (2) What kind of an animal is a human creature born soulless?

Before answering these two very natural queries, I have to draw the attention of all of you who are born in Christian countries to the fact that the romance of the vicarious atonement and the mission of Jesus, as it now stands, was drawn or borrowed by some unknown Gnostic Initiate from the mysterious and weird tenet of the earthly experience of the reincarnating Ego. The latter is indeed the sacrificial victim of, and through, its own Karma in previous Manvantaras which takes upon itself voluntarily the duty of saving what would be otherwise failures, men or personalities. Eastern truth is thus more philosophical and logical than Western fiction. The Christos, or Buddhi-Manas of each man is not quite an innocent and sinless God, though he, one aspect of it, is the "Father," being of the same essence with the Universal Spirit, and at the same time the "Son," for Manas is the second remove from the "Father." By incarnation the Divine Son makes itself responsible

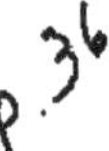

for the sins of all the personalities which it will inform. This it can do only through its proxy or reflection, the lower Manas. The only case in which the Divine Ego can escape individual penalty and responsibility as a guiding Principle, is when it has to break off from the personality, because matter, with its psychic and astral vibrations, is then, by the very intensity of its combinations, placed beyond the control of the Ego. Apophis, the Dragon, having become the conqueror, the reincarnating Manas, separating itself gradually from its tabernable, breaks finally asunder from the psycho-animal Soul.

Thus, in answer to the first question, I say:

(1) The Divine Ego does one of two things; either (*a*) it recommences immediately under its own Karmic impulses a fresh series of incarnations; or (*b*) it seeks and finds refuge in the bosom of the Mother, Alaya, the Universal Soul, of which the Manvantaric aspect is Mahat. Freed from the life-impressions of the personality, it merges into a kind of Nirvânic interlude, wherein there can be nothing but the eternal Present, which absorbs the Past and Future. Bereft of the "labourer," both field and harvest now being lost, the Master, in the infinitude of his thought, naturally preserves no recollection of the finite and evanescent illusion which had been his last personality. And then, indeed, is the latter annihilated.

(2) The future of the lower Manas is more terrible, and still more terrible to humanity than to the now animal man. It sometimes happens that after the separation the exhausted Soul, now become supremely animal, fades out in Kâma Loka, as do all other animal souls. But seeing that the more material is the human mind, the longer it lasts, even in the intermediate stage, it frequently happens that after the present life of the soulless man is ended, he is again and again

reincarnated into new personalities, each one more abject than the other. The impulse of *animal life* is too strong; it cannot wear itself out in one or two lives only. In rarer cases, however, when the lower Manas is doomed to exhaust itself by *starvation;* when there is no longer hope that even a remnant of a lower light will, owing to favourable conditions—say, even a short period of spiritual aspiration and repentance—attract back to itself its Parent Ego, and Karma leads the Higher Ego back to new incarnations, [then something far more dreadful may happen.] The Kâma-Mânasic spook may become that which is called in Occultism the "Dweller on the Threshold." This Dweller is not like that which is described so graphically in *Zanoni*, but an actual fact in Nature and not a fiction in romance, however beautiful the latter may be. Bulwer, however, must have got the idea from some Eastern Initiate. This Dweller, led by affinity and attraction, forces itself into the astral current, and through the Auric Envelope, of the new tabernacle inhabited by the Parent Ego, and declares war to the lower light which has replaced it. This, of course, can only happen in the case of the moral weakness of the personality so obsessed. No one strong in virtue, and righteous in his walk of life, can risk or dread any such thing; but only those depraved in heart. Robert Louis Stevenson had a glimpse of a true vision indeed when he wrote his *Strange Case of Dr. Jekyll and Mr. Hyde*. His story is a true allegory. Every Chelâ will recognise in it a substratum of truth, and in Mr. Hyde a Dweller, an obsessor of the personality, the tabernacle of the Parent Spirit.

"This is a nightmare tale!" I was often told by one, now no more in our ranks, who had a most pronounced "Dweller," a "Mr. Hyde," as an almost constant companion. "How can such a process take place without one's knowledge?" It can and does so happen, and I have almost described it once before in the *Theosophist*.

> The Soul, the lower Mind, becomes as a half animal principle almost paralyzed with daily vice, and grows gradually unconscious of its subjective half, the Lord, one of the mighty Host; [and] in proportion to the rapid sensuous development of the brain and nerves, sooner or later, it (the personal Soul) finally loses sight of its divine mission on earth.

Truly,

> Like the vampire, the brain feeds and lives and grows in strength at the expense of its spiritual parent . . . and the personal half-unconscious Soul becomes senseless, beyond hope of redemption. It is powerless to discern the voice of its

God. It aims but at the development and fuller comprehension of [illegible] life; and thus can discover but the mysteries of physical nature. [illegible] by becoming virtually dead, during the life of the body; and ends [illegible] pletely—that is, by being *annihilated as a complete immortal Soul.* [illegible] trophe may often happen long years before one's physical death: "We [illegible] less men and women at every step in life." And when death arrives [illegible] is no more a Soul (the reincarnating Spiritual Ego) to liberate [illegible] *fled years before.*

Result: Bereft of its guiding Principles, but strengthened [illegible] material elements, Kâma-Manas, from being a "derived light" [illegible] becomes an independent Entity. After thus suffering itself [illegible] lower and lower on the animal plane, when the hour strikes [illegible] earthly body to die, one of two things happens: either Kâma-[illegible] immediately reborn in Myalba, the state of Avîtchi on earth,* [illegible] become too strong in evil—"immortal in Satan" is the Occult [illegible] sion—it is sometimes allowed, for Karmic purposes, to remain [illegible] active state of Avîtchi in the terrestrial Aura. Then through [illegible] and loss of all hope it becomes like the mythical "devil" in its [illegible] wickedness; it continues in its elements, which are imbued [illegible] and through with the essence of Matter; for evil is coeval with [illegible] rent asunder from Spirit. And when its Higher Ego has once [illegible] reincarnated, evolving a new reflection, or Kâma-Manas, the [illegible] lower Ego, like a Frankenstein's monster, will ever feel attracted [illegible] Father, who repudiates his son, and will become a regular "Dweller [illegible] the Threshold" of terrestrial life. I gave the outlines of the [illegible] doctrine in the *Theosophist* of October, 1881, and November, 188[illegible] could not go into details, and therefore got very much embarr[illegible] when called upon to explain. Yet I have written there plainly [illegible] about "useless drones," those who refuse to become co-workers [illegible] Nature and who perish by millions during the Manvantaric life-[illegible] those, as in the case in hand, who prefer to be ever suffering in [illegible] under Karmic law rather than give up their lives "in evil," and [illegible] those who are co-workers with Nature for destruction. These [illegible] thoroughly wicked and depraved men, but yet as highly intell[illegible] and acutely *spiritual* for evil, as those who are spiritual for good.

The (lower) Egos of these may escape the law of final destruction or annihilation for ages to come.

* The Earth, or earth-life rather, is the only Avîtchi (Hell) that exists for the men of our [illegible] on this globe. Avîtchi is a state, not a locality, a counterpart of Devachan. Such a state [illegible] Soul wherever it goes, whether into Kâma Loka, as a semi-conscious Spook, or into a [illegible] when reborn to suffer Avîtchi. Our Philosophy recognizes no other Hell.

Thus we find two kinds of soulless beings on earth: those who have lost their Higher Ego in the present incarnation, and those who are born soulless, having been severed from their Spiritual Soul in the preceding birth. The former are candidates for Avitchi; the latter are "Mr. Hydes," whether *in* or *out* of human bodies, whether incarnated or hanging about as invisible though potent ghouls. In such men, cunning develops to an enormous degree, and no one except those who are familiar with the doctrine would suspect them of being soulless, for neither Religion nor Science has the least suspicion that such facts actually exist in Nature.

There is, however, still hope for a person who has lost his Higher Soul through his vices, while he is yet in the body. He may be still redeemed and made to turn on his material nature. For either an intense feeling of repentance, or one single earnest appeal to the Ego that has fled, or best of all, an active effort to amend one's ways, may bring the Higher Ego back again. The thread of connection is not altogether broken, though the Ego is now beyond forcible reach, for "Antahkarana is destroyed," and the personal Entity has one foot already in Myalba;* yet it is not entirely beyond hearing a strong spiritual appeal. There is another statement made in *Isis Unveiled*† on this subject. It is said that this terrible death may be sometimes avoided by the knowledge of the mysterious NAME, the "WORD."‡ What this "WORD," which is not a "Word" but a *Sound*, is, you all know. Its potency lies in the rhythm or the accent. This means simply that even a bad person may, by the study of the Sacred Science, be redeemed and stopped on the path of destruction. But unless he is in thorough union with his Higher Ego, he may repeat it, parrot-like, ten thousand times a day, and the "Word" will not help him. On the contrary, if not entirely at one with his Higher Triad, it may produce quite the reverse of a beneficent effect, the Brothers of the Shadow using it very often for malicious objects; in which case it awakens and stirs up naught but the evil, material elements of Nature. But if one's nature is good, and sincerely strives towards the HIGHER SELF, which is that Aum, through one's Higher Ego, which is its third

* See *Voice of the Silence*, p. 97.

† *Loc. cit.*

‡ Read the last footnote on p. 368, vol. ii. of *Isis Unveiled*, and you will see that even profane Egyptologists and men who, like Bunsen, were ignorant of Initiation, were struck by their own discoveries when they found the "Word" mentioned in old papyri.

letter, and Buddhi the second, there is no attack of the [illegible] Apophis which it will not repel. From those to whom [illegible] much is expected. He who knocks at the door of the [illegible] knowledge of its sacredness, and after obtaining admission [illegible] from the threshold, or turns round and says, "Oh, there's [illegible] it!" and thus loses his chance of learning the whole truth [illegible] await his Karma.

Such are then the Esoteric explanations of that which [illegible] so many who have found what they thought contradictions in [illegible] Theosophical writings, including "Fragments of Occult Truth," vols. iii. and iv. of *The Theosophist*, etc. Before finally dismissing [illegible] subject, I must add a caution, which pray keep well in mind. [illegible] be very natural for those of you who are Esotericists to hope [illegible] of you belong so far to the soulless portion of mankind, and [illegible] can feel quite easy about Avitchi, even as the good citizen [illegible] penal laws. Though not, perhaps, exactly on the Path as yet, [illegible] skirting its border, and many of you in the right direction. [illegible] such venal faults as are inevitable under our social environment [illegible] the blasting wickedness described in the Editor's notes on [illegible] Lévi's "Satan,"* there is an abyss. If not become "immortal [illegible] by identification with (our) God," or AUM, Âtmâ-Buddhi-Manas, [illegible] have surely not made ourselves "immortal in evil" by coalescence [illegible] Satan, the lower Self. You forget, however, that everything [illegible] have a beginning; that the first step on a slippery mountain [illegible] the necessary antecedent to one's falling precipitately to the [illegible] and into the arms of death. Be it far from me the suspicion [illegible] of the Esoteric students have reached to any considerable point [illegible] the plane of spiritual descent. All the same I warn you [illegible] taking the first step. You may not reach the bottom in this life [illegible] next, but you may now generate causes which will insure your [illegible] destruction in your third, fourth, fifth, or even some subsequent [illegible] In the great Indian epic you may read how a mother whose [illegible] family of warrior sons were slaughtered in battle, complained [illegible] Krishna that though she had the spiritual vision to enable [illegible] back fifty incarnations, yet she could see no sin of hers that could have begotten so dreadful a Karma; and Krishna answered her: [illegible] thou could'st look back to thy fifty-first anterior birth, as I [illegible] would'st see thyself killing in wanton cruelty the same number of

* See *Theosophist*, vol. iii., October, 1882, p. 13.

ants as that of the sons thou hast now lost." This, of course, is only a poetical exaggeration; yet it is a striking image to show how great results come from apparently trifling causes.

Good and evil are relative, and are intensified or lessened according to the conditions by which man is surrounded. One who belongs to that which we call the "useless portion of mankind," that is to say, the lay majority, is in many cases irresponsible. Crimes committed in Avidyâ, or ignorance, involve physical but not moral responsibilities or Karma. Take, for example, the case of idiots, children, savages, and people who know no better. But the case of each who is pledged to the HIGHER SELF is quite another matter. *You cannot invoke this Divine Witness with impunity*, and once that you have put yourselves under its tutelage, you have asked the Radiant Light to shine and search through all the dark corners of your being; consciously you have invoked the Divine Justice of Karma to take note of your motive, to scrutinize your actions, and to enter up all in your account. The step is irrevocable as that of the infant taking birth. Never again can you force yourselves back into the matrix of Avidyâ and irresponsibility. Though you flee to the uttermost parts of the earth, and hide yourselves from the sight of men, or seek oblivion in the tumult of the social whirl, that Light will find you out and lighten your every thought, word and deed. All H. P. B. can do is to send to each earnest one among you a most sincerely fraternal sympathy and hope for a good outcome to your endeavours. Nevertheless, be not discouraged, but try, ever keep trying;* twenty failures are not irremediable if followed by as many undaunted struggles upward. Is it not so that mountains are climbed? And know further, that if Karma relentlessly records in the Esotericist's account, bad deeds that in the ignorant would be overlooked, yet, equally true is it that each of his good deeds is, by reason of his association with the Higher Self, a hundredfold intensified as a potentiality for good.

Finally, keep ever in mind the consciousness that though you see no Master by your bedside, nor hear one audible whisper in the silence of the still night, yet the Holy Power is about you, the Holy Light is shining into your hour of spiritual need and aspirations, and it will be no fault of the MASTERS, or of their humble mouthpiece and servant, if through perversity or moral feebleness some of you cut yourselves off from these higher potencies, and step upon the declivity that leads to Avitchi.

* Read pp. 40 and 63 in the *Voice of the Silence*.

APPENDIX.

NOTES ON PAPERS I., II., and III.

PAGE 436.

Students in the west have little or no idea of the forces [illegible] in Sound, the Âkâshic vibrations that may be set up by [illegible] understand how to pronounce certain words. The Om, or [illegible] *mani padme hum*" are in spiritual affinity with cosmic forces, [illegible] out a knowledge of the natural arrangement, or of the order [illegible] the syllables stand, very little can be achieved. "Om" [illegible] Aum, that may be pronounced as two, three or seven syllables [illegible] up different vibrations.

Now, letters, as vocal sounds, cannot fail to correspond with [illegible] notes, and therefore with numbers and colours; hence also with [illegible] and Tattvas. He who remembers that the Universe is built up [illegible] the Tattvas will readily understand something of the power that [illegible] be exercised by vocal sounds. Every letter in the alphabet, [illegible] divided into three, four, or seven septenaries, or forty-nine letters [illegible] its own colour, or shade of colour. He who has learnt the colours [illegible] the alphabetical letters, and the corresponding numbers of the [illegible] and the forty-nine colours and shades on the scale of planes [illegible] and knows their respective order in the seven planes, will easily [illegible] the art of bringing them into affinity or interplay. But here a difficulty arises. The Senzar and Sanskrit alphabets, and other Occult [illegible] besides other potencies, have a number, colour, and distinct [illegible] for every letter, and so had also the old Mosaic Hebrew. [illegible] many students know any of these tongues? When the time [illegible] therefore, it must suffice to teach the students the numbers and [illegible] attached to the Latin letters only (N.B. as pronounced in Latin [illegible] Anglo-Saxon, Scotch, or Irish). This, however, would be at [illegible] premature.

The colour and number of not only the planets but also the zodiacal constellations corresponding to every letter of the alphabet, are necessary to make any special syllable, and even letter, *operative.** Therefore if a student would make Buddhi operative, for instance, he would have to intone the first words of the Mantra on the note *mi*. But he would have still further to accentuate the *mi*, and produce mentally the yellow colour corresponding to this sound and note, on every letter M in "*Om mani padme hum*"; this, not because the note bears the same name in the vernacular, Sanskrit, or even the Senzar, for it does not—but because the letter M follows the first letter, and is in this sacred formula also the seventh and the fourth. As Buddhi it is second; as Buddhi-Manas it is the second and third combined.

contributed by students from explanations H. P. B.

PAGE 439.† given by H.P.B.

The Pythagorean Four, or Tetraktys, was the symbol of the Kosmos, as containing within itself, the point, the line, the superficies, the solid; in other words, the essentials of all forms. Its mystical representation is the point within the triangle. The Decad or perfect number is contained in the Four; thus, 1+2+3+4=10.

PAGE 453.

	SUNDAY.	MONDAY.	TUESDAY.	WED'D'Y.	THU'DAY.	FRIDAY.	SAT'DAY.
First Quarter.	☉	☽	♂	☿	♃	♀	♄
Second Quarter.	♂	☿	♃	♀	♄	☉	☽
Third Quarter.	♃	♀	♄	☉	☽	♂	☿
Fourth Quarter.	♄	☉	☽	♂	♀	♃	♀

PAGE 477. O.

The difficult passage: "Bear in mind . . . . a mystery below truly,"‡ may become a little more clear to the student if slightly ampli-

* See *Voice of the Silence*, p. viii.
† The following notes were contributed by students and approved by H. P. B.
‡ See page 444.

fied. The "primordial Triangle" is the Second Logos, which reflects itself as a Triangle in the Third Logos, or Heavenly Man, and then disappears. The Third Logos, containing the "potency of demiurgic creation," develops the Tetraktys from the Triangle, and manifests the Seven, the Creative Force, making a Decad with the primordial Triangle which originated it. When this heavenly Triangle and Tetraktys are reflected in the Universe of Matter, as the astral paradigmatic man, they are reversed, and the Triangle, or formative potency, is thrown below the Quaternary, with its apex pointing downwards: the Monad of this astral paradigmatic man is the upper Triangle, bearing to the Quaternary and Triangle the relation borne by the primordial Triangle to the Heavenly Man. Hence the phrase "the upper Triangle . . . is shifted in the man of clay below the *seven*." Here again the Point tracing the Triangle, the Monad becoming the Ternary, with the Quaternary and the lower creative triangle, make up the Decad, the perfect number. "As above, so below."

The student will do well to relate the knowledge here acquired to that given on p. 477. Here the upper Triangle is given as Violet, Indigo, Blue, associating Violet as the paradigm of all forms with Indigo as Mahat, and blue as the Âtmic Aura. In the Quaternary, Yellow, as substance, is associated with Yellow-Orange, Life, and Red-Orange, the creative potency. Green is the plane between.

The next stage is not explained. Green passes upwards to Violet, Indigo, Blue, the Triangle opening out to receive it, and so forming the square, Violet, Indigo, Blue, Green. This leaves the Red-Orange, Yellow-Orange, and Yellow, and these, having thus lost their fourth member, can only form a triangle. This triangle revolves, to point downwards for the descent into matter, and "mirrored on the plane of gross nature, it is reversed," and appears as in the diagram following these words.

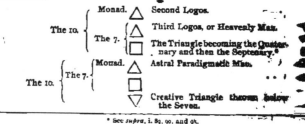

The 10.		Monad.	△	Second Logos.
	The 7.		△	Third Logos, or Heavenly Man.
			□	The Triangle becoming the Quaternary and then the Septenary.*
The 10.	The 7.	Monad.	△	Astral Paradigmatic Man.
			□	
			▽	Creative Triangle thrown below the Seven.

* See *supra*, i. 89, 90, and 95.

In the perfect man the Red will be absorbed by the Green; Yellow will become one with Indigo; Yellow-Orange will be absorbed in Blue; Violet will remain outside the True Man, though connected with him. Or, to translate the colours: Kâma will be absorbed in the Lower Manas; Buddhi will become one with Manas; Prâna will be absorbed in the Auric Egg; the physical body remains, connected but outside the real life.

A. B.

PAGE 481.

To the five senses at present the property of mankind two more on this globe are to be added. The sixth sense is the psychic sense of colour. The seventh is that of spiritual sound. In the second instruction, the corrected rates of vibration for the seven primary colours and their modulations are given. Inspecting these, it appears that each colour differs from the proceeding one by a step of 42, or 6 × 7.

462 Red	+42=504	Third Octave of psychic colour perceptions.
504 Orange	+42=546	
546 Yellow	+42=588	
588 Green	+42=630	
630 Blue	+42=672	
672 Indigo	+42=714	
714 Violet	+42=756	
756 Red		

Carrying the process backward, ana subtracting 42, we find that the first or ground colour is green, for this globe.

— Green	First semi-octave
42 Blue	
84 Indigo	
126 Violet	
168 Red	Second octave.
210 Orange	
252 Yellow	
294 Green	
336 Blue	
378 Indigo	
420 Violet	
462 Red	

The second and fourth octaves would be heat and actinic rays, and are invisible to our present perception.

The seventh sense is that of spiritual sound; and, since the vibrations of the sixth progress by steps of 6 × 7, those of the seventh progress by steps of 7 × 7. This is their table:

— Fa	...	Green Sound	First semi-octave.
49 Sol	...	Blue "	
98 La	...	Indigo "	
147 Si	...	Violet "	

196 Do	...	Red Sound	Second Octave.
245 Re	...	Orange "	
294 Mi	...	Yellow "	
343 Fa	...	Green "	
392 Sol	...	Blue "	
441 La	...	Indigo "	
490 Si	...	Violet "	
539 Do	...	Red "	
Etc., etc.			

The fifth sense is in our possession: it is possibly that of geometrical form, and its steps of progression would be 5 × 7, or 35.

The fourth sense is that of physical hearing, music, and its progressions are 28, or 4 × 7. The truth of this is demonstrated by the fact that it is in accord with the theories of Science as to the vibrations of musical notes. Our scale is as follows:

—, 28, 56, 84, 112, 140, 168, 196, 224, 252, 280, 308, 336, 364, 392, 420, 448, 476, 504, 532, 560, 588, 616, 644, 672, 700.

According to musical science, the notes C, E, G, are as 4, 5, 6, in their ratios of vibrations. The same ratio obtains between the notes of the triplet G, B, D, and F, A, C. This gives the scale, and reducing the vibrations to C as 1, the ratios of the seven notes to C are

1	9/8	5/4	4/3	3/2	5/3	15/8	2
C	D	E	F	G	A	B	C'

Reducing these to whole numbers, we get for one octave:

24	27	30	32	36	40	45	48
C	D	E	F	G	A	B	C'

By a similar calculation we can put an octave below C', and above C'. Writing these three octaves in line, and multiplying by seven we obtain a nearly exact correspondence with our table of vibration for the fourth sense.

MUSICAL TABLE.

FOURTH SENSE.				SCALE RATIO.				PRODUCT.
28	...	...	...	4	×	7	=	28 E
56	...	...	...	8	×	7	=	56 F
84	...	...	...	12	×	7	=	84 G
112	...	...	...	16	×	7	=	112 A
140	...	...	...	20	×	7	=	140 B
168	...	...	...	24	×	7	=	168 C
196	...	...	...	27	×	7	=	189 D
...	...	...	...	30	×	7	=	210 E
224	...	...	...	32	×	7	=	224 F
252	...	...	...	36	×	7	=	252 G
280	...	...	...	40	×	7	=	280 A
308	...	...	...	45	×	7	=	315 B

FOURTH SENSE.				SCALE RATIO.				PRODUCT.
336	...	...	...	48	×	7	=	336 C
364	...	...	...	54	×	7	=	378 D
392								
420	...	...	...	60	×	7	=	420 E
448	...	...	...	64	×	7	=	448 F
476								
504	...	...	...	72	×	7	=	504 G
532								
560	...	...	...	80	×	7	=	560 A
588								
616	...	...	...	90	×	7	=	630 B
644								
672	...	...	...	96	×	7	=	672 C

H. C.

tion of Akâsha, into which, as the child became a man, he might, ... Adept, weave the materials needed for special purposes, etc.]

A. Taking the question in the sense of an Adept putting ... thing into or acting on the Auric Egg of a child, then this could ... done, as the Auric Egg is Karmic, and not even an Adept ... fere with such Karmic record. If the Adept were to put ... the Auric Egg of another, for which the person is not responsible, ... which does not come from the Higher Self of that personality, ... could Karmic justice be maintained?

The Adept can draw into his own Auric Egg from his plane, ... even from that of the globe or of the universe, according to his degree. This envelope is the receptacle of all Karmic causes, and photographs all things like a sensitive plate.

The child has a very small Auric Egg which is in colour ... pure white. At birth the Auric Egg consists of almost pure A... plus the Tanhâs, which, until the seventh year, remain potential ... latency.

The Auric Egg of an idiot cannot be said to be human, ... is not tinged with Manas. It is Âkâshic vibrations rather ... Auric Egg—the material envelope, such as that of the ... mineral or other object.

The Auric Egg is the transmitter from the periodical lives ... Life eternal, *i.e.*, from Prâna to Jîva. It disappears, but remains ...

The reason why the confession of the Roman Catholic and ... Churches is so great a sin is because the confessor interferes ... Auric Egg of the penitent by means of his will power, ... artificially emanations from his own Auric Egg and casting ... germination into the Auric Egg of his subject. It is on the same ... as hypnotic suggestion.

The above remarks apply equally to Hypnotism, although ... latter is a psycho-physical force, and it is this which constitutes ... its many serious dangers. At the same time "a good thing may ... through dirty channels," as in the case of the breaking by ... of the alcohol or opium habit. Mesmerism may be used ... Occultist to remove evil habits, if the intention be perfectly pure, ... on the higher plane intention is everything, and good ... must work for good.

Q. Is the Auric Egg the expansion of the "Pillar of ... Mânasic Principle, and so not surrounding the child till its ...

A. It is the Auric Egg. The Auric Egg is quite pure at birth, but it is a question whether the higher or lower Manas will colour it at the seventh year. The Mânasic expansion is pure Âkâsha. The ray of Manas is let down into the vortex of the lower Principles, and being discoloured, and so limited by the Kâmic Tanhâs and by the defects of the bodily organism, forms the personality. Hereditary Karma can reach the child before the seventh year, but no individual Karma can come into play till the descent of the Manas.

The Auric Egg is to the Man
As „ Astral Light „ Earth
„ „ Ether „ Astral Light
„ „ Akâsha „ Ether

The critical states are left out in the enumeration. They are the Laya Centres, or missing links in our consciousness, and separate these four planes from one another.

THE DWELLER.

The "Dweller on the Threshold" is found in two cases: (*a*) In the case of the separation of the Triangle from the Quaternary; (*b*) When Kâmic desires and passions are so intense that the Kâma Rûpa persists in Kâma Loka beyond the Devachanic period of the Ego, and thus survives the reincarnation of the Devachanic Entity (*e.g.*, when reincarnation occurs within two hundred or three hundred years). The "Dweller" being drawn by affinity towards the Reincarnating Ego to whom it had belonged, and being unable to reach it, fastens on the Kâma of the new personality, and becomes the Dweller on the Threshold, strengthening the Kâmic element and thus lending it a dangerous potency. Some become mad from this cause.

INTELLECT.

The white Adept is not always at first of powerful intellect. In fact, H. P. B had known Adepts whose intellectual powers were originally below the average. It is the Adept's purity, his equal love to all, his working with Nature, with Karma, with his "Inner God," that give him his power. Intellect by itself alone will make the Black Magician. For intellect alone is accompanied with pride and selfishness: it is the intellectual *plus* the spiritual that raises man. For spirituality prevents pride and vanity.

Metaphysics are the domain of the Higher Manas; whereas

Physics are that of Kâma-Manas, which does the thinking in Physical Science and on material things. Kâma-Manas, like every other Principle, is of seven degrees. The Mathematician without metaphysics, however great he may be, will not reach Metaphysics; but the Metaphysician will master the highest conceptions of Mathematics, and will apply them, without learning the latter. To a born Metaphysician the Psychic Plane will not be of much account; he will see through it immediately he enters it, inasmuch as it is not the thing he seeks. With respect to Music and other Arts, they are the children of either the Mânasic or Kâma-Mânasic Principle, proportionately as Soul or technicality predominates.

KARMA.

After each incarnation, when the Mânasic Ray returns to its [illegible] the Ego, some of its atoms remain behind and scatter. These Manasic atoms, Tânhic and other "causes," being of the same nature as the Manas, are attracted to it by strong bonds of affinity, and on the reincarnation of the Ego are unerringly attracted to it and constitute its Karma. Until these are all gathered up, the individuality is not free from rebirth. The Higher Manas is responsible for the Ray it sends forth. If the Ray be not soiled, no bad Karma is generated.

THE TURÎYA STATE.

You should bear in mind that, in becoming Karma-less, good Karma as well as bad, has to be gotten rid of, and that Nidânas, leading towards the acquisition of good Karma, are as binding as those leading in the other direction. For both are Karma.

Yogîs cannot attain the Turîya state unless the Triangle is separated from the Quaternary.

MAHAT.

Mahat is the manifested universal Parabrâhmic Mind (for one Manvantara) on the Third Plane [of Kosmos]. It is the Law whereby the Light falls from plane to plane and differentiates. The Mânasaputras are its emanations.

Man alone is capable of conceiving the Universe on this plane of existence.

Existence *is*; but when the entity does not feel it, for that entity it is not. The pain of an operation exists, though the patient does not feel it, and for the patient it is not.

HOW TO ADVANCE.

Q. What is the correct pronunciation of AUM?

A. It should first be practised physically, always at the same pitch, which must be discovered in the same way as the particular colour of the student is found, for each has his own tone.

Aum consists of two vowels and one semi-vowel, which latter must be prolonged. Just as Nature has its Fa, so each man has his: man being differentiated from Nature. The body may be compared to an instrument and the Ego to the player. You begin by producing effects on yourself; then little by little you learn to play on the Tattvas and Principles; learn first the notes, then the chords, then the melodies. Once the student is master of every chord, he may begin to be a co-worker with Nature and for others. He may then, by the experience he has gained of his own nature, and by the knowledge of the chords, strike such as will be beneficial in another, and so will serve as a key-note for beneficial results.

Try to have a clear representation of the geometrical triangle on every plane, the conception gradually growing more metaphysical, and ending with the subjective Triangle, Âtmâ-Buddhi-Manas. It is only by the knowledge of this Triangle under all forms that you can succeed, *e.g.* in enclosing the past and the future in the present. Remember that you have to merge the Quaternary in the Triangle. The Lower Manas is drawn upwards, with the Kâma, Prâna and Linga, leaving only the physical body behind, the lower reinforcing the higher.

Advance may be made in Occultism even in Devachan, if the Mind and Soul be set thereon during life; but it is only as in a dream, and the knowledge will fade away as memory of a dream fades, unless it be kept alive by conscious study.

FEAR AND HATRED.

Fear and hatred are essentially one and the same. He who fears nothing will never hate, and he who hates nothing will never fear.

THE TRIANGLE.

Q. What is the meaning of the phrase: "Form a clear image of the Triangle on every plane;" e.g., *on the Astral Plane, what should one think of as the Triangle?*

A. [H. P. B. asked whether the question signified the meaning of the Triangle or the way to represent the Triangle on the [illegible] light." The questioner explaining that the latter [illegible] H. P. B. said that] it was only in the Turîya state, the [illegible] seven steps of Râja Yoga that the Yogî can represent to [illegible] which is abstract. Below this state, the perceptive power [illegible] ditioned, must have some form to contemplate; it cannot [illegible] itself the Arûpa. In the Turîya state the Triangle is [illegible] felt. Below the Turîya state there must be a symbol [illegible] Âtmâ-Buddhi-Manas. It is not a mere geometrical Triangle [illegible] Triad imaged, to make thought possible. Of this Triad, we [illegible] some kind of representation of Manas, however indistinct; [illegible] Âtmâ no image can be formed. We must try to represent the [illegible] to ourselves on higher and higher planes. We must figure [illegible] overshadowed by Buddhi, and immersed in Âtmâ. Only [illegible] Higher Ego, can be represented; we may think it as the [illegible] the radiant figure in *Zanoni*. A very good Psychic might see [illegible]

PSYCHIC VISION.

Psychic vision, however, is not to be desired, since Psyche is [illegible] and evil. More and more as Science advances, the psychic [illegible] reached and understood; Psychism has in it nothing that is [illegible] Science is right on its own plane, from its own standpoint. The [illegible] the Conservation of Energy implies that psychic motion is [illegible] motion. Psychic motion being only motion on the Psychic [illegible] material plane, the Psychologist is right who sees in it nothing [illegible] matter. Animals have no Spirit, but they have psychic vision, [illegible] sensitive to psychic conditions; observe how these react [illegible] health, their bodily state.

Motion is the abstract Deity; on the highest plane it is [illegible] absolute; but on the lowest it is merely mechanical. Psychic [illegible] within the sphere of physical motion. Ere psychic action [illegible] developed in the brain and nerves, there must be adequate [illegible] which generates it on the Physical Plane. The paralysed [illegible] cannot generate action in the physical body, cannot think. [illegible] merely see on a plane of different material density; the [illegible] glimpses sometimes obtained by them come from a plane beyond. [illegible] Psychic's vision is that of one coming, as it were, into a lighted [illegible] and seeing everything there by an artificial light: when the [illegible] extinguished, vision is lost. Spiritual vision sees by the light [illegible] the light hidden beneath the bushel of the body, by which we can see clearly and independently of all outside. The Psychic seeing by an external light, the vision is coloured by the nature of that light.

X. saying that she felt as though she saw on three planes, H. P. B. answered that each plane was sevenfold, the Astral as every other. She gave as an example on the Physical Plane the vision of a table with the sense of sight; seeing it still, with the eyes closed, by retinal impression; the image of it conserved in the brain; it can be recalled by memory; it can be seen in dream; or as an aggregate of atoms; or as disintegrated. All these are on the Physical Plane. Then we can begin again on the Astral Plane, and obtain another septenary. This hint should be followed and worked out.

TRIANGLE AND QUATERNARY.

Q. Why is the violet, the colour of the Linga Sharira, placed at the apex of the △, when the Macrocosm is figured as △ □, thus throwing the yellow, Buddhi, into the lower Quaternary?

A. It is wrong to speak of the "lower Quaternary" in the Macrocosm. It is the Tetraktys, the highest, the most sacred of all symbols. There comes a moment when, in the highest meditation, the Lower Manas is withdrawn into the Triad, which thus becomes the Quaternary, the Tetraktys of Pythagoras, leaving what was the Quaternary as the lower Triad, which is then reversed. The Triad is reflected in the Lower Manas. The Higher Manas cannot reflect itself, but when the Green passes upward it becomes a mirror for the Higher; it is then no more Green, having passed from its associations. The Psyche then becomes spiritual, the Ternary is reflected in the Fourth, and the Tetraktys is formed. So long as you are not dead, there must be something to reflect the Higher Triad; for there must be something to bring back to the waking consciousness the experiences passed through on the higher plane. The Lower Manas is as a tablet which retains the impressions made on it during trance.

The Turiya state is entered on the Fourth Path; it is figured in the diagram on p. 478, in the Second Paper.

Q. What is the meaning of a triangle formed of lines of light appearing in the midst of intense vibrating blue?

A. Seeing the Triangle outside is nothing; it is merely a reflection of the Triad on the Auric Envelope, and proves that the seer is outside the Triangle. It should be seen in quite another way. You must endeavour to merge yourself in it, to ... are merely seeing things in the Astral. "When ... in any one of you, you will have something ...

Q. With reference to the "Pillar of Light" ... the Auric Envelope the Higher Ego, and that it ... Pass-Not?

[This question was not answered, as going too far ... Not is at the circumference of the manifested Universe.]

NIDÂNAS.

Q. The root of the Nidânas is Avidyâ. How does this differ ... How many Nidânas are there Esoterically?

A. Again too much is asked. The Nidânas, the concatenation of causes and effects (not in the sense of the Orientalists), are not caused by ignorance. They are produced by Dhyân Chohans and ... certainly cannot be said to act in ignorance. We produce ... ignorance. Each cause started on the Physical Plane acts ... every plane to all eternity. They are eternal effects, reflected from plane to plane on to the "screen of eternity."

MANAS.

Q. What is the septenary classification of Manas? ... degrees of the Lower Manas, and presumably there are seven ... Higher. Are there then fourteen degrees of Manas, or is Manas ... whole, divided into forty-nine Mânasic fires?

A. Certainly there are fourteen, but you want to run before ... walk. First learn the three, and then go on to the forty-nine ... are three Sons of Agni; they become seven, and then evolve ... forty-nine. But you are still ignorant how to produce ... Learn first how to produce the "Sacred Fire," spoken of ... *Purânas.* The forty-nine fires are all states of Kundalini ... duced in ourselves by the friction of the Triad. First learn the ... of the body, and then that of each Principle. But first of all ... first Triad (the three vital airs)

THE SPINAL CORD.

Q. What is the sympathetic nerve and its function in Occultism ... found only after a certain stage of animal evolution, and would ... evolving in complexity towards a second spinal cord.

A. At the end of the next Round, Humanity will again ...

male-female, and then there will be two spinal cords. In the Seventh Race the two will merge into the one. The evolution corresponds to the Races, and with the evolution of the Races the sympathetic developes into a true spinal cord. We are returning up the arc only with self-consciousness added. The Sixth Race will correspond to the "pudding bags," but will have the perfection of form with the highest intelligence and spirituality.

Anatomists are beginning to find new ramifications and new modifications in the human body. They are in error on many points, *e.g.*, as to the spleen, which they call the manufactory of white blood corpuscles, but which is really the vehicle of the Linga Sharira. Occultists know each minute portion of the heart, and have a name for each. They call them by the names of the Gods, as Brahmâ's Hall, Vishnu's Hall, etc. They correspond with parts of the brain. The very atoms of the body are the thirty-three crores of Gods.

The sympathetic nerve is played on by the Tântrikas, who call it Shiva's Vînâ.

PRÂNA.

Q. What is the relation of man to Prâna—the periodical life?

A. Jiva becomes Prâna only when the child is born and begins to breathe. It is the breath of life, Nephesh. There is no Prâna on the Astral Plane.

ANTAHKARANA.

Q. The Antahkarana is the link between the Higher and the Lower Egos; does it correspond to the umbilical cord in projection?

A. No; the umbilical cord joining the astral to the physical body is a real thing. Antahkarana is imaginary, a figure of speech, and is only the bridging over from the Higher to the Lower Manas. Antahkarana only exists when you commence to "throw your thought upwards and downwards." The Mâyâvi Rûpa, or Mânasic body, has no material connection with the physical body, no umbilical cord. It is spiritual and ethereal, and passes everywhere without let or hindrance. It entirely differs from the astral body, which, if injured, acts by repercussion on the physical body. The Devachanic entity, even previous to birth, can be affected by the Skandhas, but these have nothing to do with the Antahkarana. It is affected, *e.g.*, by the desire for reincarnation.

Q. We are told in The Voice of the Silence *that we have to become*

"the path itself," and in another passage that Antahkarana ...
Does this mean anything more than that we have to bridge ...
between the consciousness of the Lower and the Higher Ego ...

A. That is all.

Q. We are told that there are seven portals on the Path ...
a sevenfold division of Antahkarana? Also, is Antahkarana ...
field?

A. It is the battlefield. There are seven divisions in the Antah-karana. As you pass from each to the next you approach the Higher Manas. When you have bridged the fourth you may consider yourself fortunate.

MISCELLANEOUS.

Q. We are told that AUM *"should be practised physically" ...*
mean that, colour being more differentiated than sound, it is ...
the colours that we shall get at the real sound of each of us? ...
can only have its Spiritual and Occult signification when ...
Âtmâ-Buddhi-Manas of each person?

A. AUM means good action, not merely lip-sound. You must say it in deeds.

Q. With reference to the △, is not the Âtmâ-Buddhi-Manas ...
for each entity, according to the plane on which he is?

A. Each Principle is on a different plane. The Chela ... to one after the other, assimilating each, until the three are one ... is the real root of the Trinity.

Q. In The Secret Doctrine *we are told that Âkâsha is ...*
Pradhâna. Âkâsha is the Auric Egg of the earth, and yet ...
Mahat. What then is the relation of Manas to the Auric Egg?

A. Mûlaprakriti is the same as Âkâsha (seven degrees) ... the positive aspect of Âkâsha, and is the Manas of the Kosmos ... Mahat is to Âkâsha as Manas is to Buddhi, and Pradhâna is but ... name for Mûlaprakriti.

The Auric Egg is Âkâsha and has seven degrees. Being ... abstract substance, it reflects abstract ideas, but also reflects ... concrete things.

The Third Logos and Mahat are one, and are the same as the Universal Mind, Alaya.

The Tetraktys is the Chatur Vidyâ, or the fourfold knowledge ... the four-faced Brahmâ.

NÂDIS.

Q. Have the Nâdis any fixed relationship to the vertebræ? can they be located opposite to or between any vertebræ? can they be regarded as occupying each a given and fixed extent in the cord? Do they correspond to the divisions of the cord known to Anatomists?

A. H. P. B. believed that the Nâdis corresponded to regions of the spinal cord known to Anatomists. There are thus six or seven Nâdis or plexuses along the spinal cord. The term, however, is not technical but general, and applies to any knot, centre, ganglion, etc. The sacred Nâdis are those which run along or above Sushumnâ. Six are known to Science, and one (near the atlas) unknown. Even the Târaka Râja Yogis speak only of six, and will not mention the sacred seventh.

Idâ and Pingalâ play along the curved wall of the cord in which is Sushumnâ. They are semi-material, positive and negative, sun and moon, and start into action the free and spiritual current of Sushumnâ. They have distinct paths of their own, otherwise they would radiate all over the body. By concentration on Idâ and Pingalâ is generated the "sacred fire."

Another name for Shiva's Vinâ (sympathetic system) is Kâlî's Vinâ.

The sympathetic cords and Idâ and Pingalâ start from a sacred spot above the medulla oblongata, called Triveni. This is one of the sacred centres, another of which is Brahmarandra, which is, if you like, the grey matter of the brain. It is also the anterior fontanelle in the new-born child.

The spinal column is called Brahmadanda, the stick of Brahmâ. This is again symbolized by the bamboo rod carried by Ascetics. The Yogis on the other sides of the Himâlayas, who assemble regularly at Lake Mânsarovara, carry a triple knotted bamboo stick, and are called Tridandins. This has the same signification as the Brâhmanical cord, which has many other meanings besides the three vital airs: *e.g.*, it symbolizes the three initiations of a Brâhman, taking place: (*a*) at birth, when he receives his mystery name from the family Astrologer, who is supposed to have received it from the Devas (he is also thus said to be initiated by the Devas); a Hindu will sooner die than reveal this name; (*b*) at seven, when he receives the cord; and (*c*) at eleven or twelve, when he is initiated into his caste.

Q. If it is right to study the body and its organs, with their [illegible] *dences, will you give the main outline of these in connection with the* [illegible] *and with the diagram of the orifices.*

A. The Spleen - corresponds to the Linga [illegible]
" Liver - - " " Kâma [illegible]
" Heart - - " " Prâna [illegible]
" Corpora-quadrigemina " " Kâma-Manas [illegible]
" Pituitary body " " Manas-Antahkarana [illegible]
" Pineal gland " " Manas, [illegible]

until it is touched by the vibrating light of Kundalinî, which [illegible] ceeds from Buddhi, when it becomes Buddhi-Manas.

The pineal gland corresponds with Divine Thought. The pituitary body is the organ of the Psychic Plane. Psychic vision is caused by the molecular motion of this body, which is directly connected with the optic nerve, and thus affects the sight and gives rise to hallucinations. Its motion may readily cause flashes of light, such as may be obtained by pressing the eyeballs. Drunkenness and fever produce illusions of sight and hearing by the action of the pituitary body. This body is sometimes so affected by drunkenness that it is paralysed. [illegible] influence on the optic nerve is thus produced and the current [illegible] reversed, the colour will probably be complementary.

SEVENS.

Q. If the physical body is no part of the real human septenary, is the physical material world one of the seven planes of the Kosmic septenary?

A. It is. The body is not a Principle in Esoteric parlance, [illegible] the body and the Linga are both on the same plane; then the [illegible] Egg makes the seventh. The body is an Upâdhi rather than a Principle. The earth and its astral light are as closely related to each other as the body and its Linga, the earth being the Upâdhi. [illegible] plane in its lowest division is the earth, in its highest the astral. [illegible] terrestrial astral light should of course not be confounded with the universal Astral Light.

Q. A physical object was spoken of as a septenary on the physical plane, inasmuch as we could (1) *directly contact it;* (2) *rationally* [illegible] *duce it;* (3) *remember it;* (4) *dream of it;* (5) *view it* [illegible] (6) *view it disintegrated;* (7)—*What is the seventh?*

These are seven ways in which we view it: the septenary is [illegible] *seeing one thing. Is it objectively septenary?*

A. The seventh bridges across from one plane to another. The last is the idea, the privation of matter, and carries you to the next plane. The highest of one plane touches the lowest of the next. Seven is a factor in nature, as in colours and sounds. There are seven degrees in the same piece of wood, each perceived by one of the seven senses. In wood the smell is the most material degree, while in other substances it may be the sixth. Substances are septenary apart from the consciousness of the viewer.

The psychometer, seeing a morsel, say of a table a thousand years hence, would see the whole; for every atom reflects the whole body to which it belongs, just as with the Monads of Leibnitz.

After the seven material subdivisions are the seven divisions of the Astral, which is its second Principle. The disintegrated matter—the highest of the material subdivisions—is the privation of the idea of it—the fourth.

The number fourteen is the first step between seven and forty-nine. Each septenary is really a fourteen, because each of the seven has its two aspects. Thus fourteen signifies the inter-relation of two planes in its turn. The septenary is to be clearly traced in the lunar months, fevers, gestations, etc. On it is based the week of the Jews and the septenary Hierarchies of the Lord of Hosts.

SOUNDS.

Q. Sound is an attribute of Âkâsha; but we cannot cognise anything on the Âkâshic plane; on what plane then do we recognise sound? On what plane is sound produced by the physical contact of bodies? Is there sound on seven planes, and is the physical plane one of them?

A. The physical plane is one of them. You cannot see Âkâsha, but you can sense it from the Fourth Path. You may not be fully conscious of it, and yet you may sense it. Âkâsha is at the root of the manifestation of all sounds. Sound is the expression and manifestation of that which is behind it, and which is the parent of many correlations. All Nature is a sounding-board; or rather Âkâsha is the sounding-board of Nature. It is the Deity, the one Life, the one Existence. (Hearing is the vibration of molecular particles; the order is seen in the sentence, "The disciple feels, hears, sees.")

Sound can have no end. H. P. B. remarked with regard to a tap made by a pencil on the table: "By this time it has affected the whole universe. The particle which has had its wear and tear destroys some-

138

thing which passes into something else. It is eternal in the effects it produces." A sound, if not previously produced on the Astral Plane, and before that on the Âkâshic, could not be produced at all. [illegible] is the bridge between nerve cells and mental powers. [illegible]

Q. *"Colours are psychic, and sounds are spiritual." What, admitting that these are vibrations, is the successive order (these corresponding to sight and hearing) of the other senses?*

A. This phrase was not to be taken out of its context, otherwise confusion would arise. All are on all planes. The First Race had touch all over like a sounding board; this touch differentiated into the other senses, which developed with the Races. The "sense" of the First Race was that of touch, meaning the power of their atoms to vibrate in unison with external atoms. The "touch" would be almost the same as sympathy.

The senses were on a different plane with each Race; *e.g.*, the Fourth Race had very much more developed senses than ourselves, but on another plane. It was also a very material Race. The sixth and seventh senses will merge into the Âkâshic Sound. "It depends on what degree of matter the sense of touch relates itself as to what we call it."

PRÂNA.

Q. Is Prâna the production of the countless "lives" of the human body, and therefore, to some extent, of the congeries of the cells or atoms of the body?

A. No; Prâna is the parent of the "lives." As an example, a sponge may be immersed in an ocean. The water in the sponge's interior may be compared to Prâna; outside is Jîva. Prâna is the motor-principle in life. The "lives" leave Prâna; Prâna does not leave them. Take out the sponge from the water, and it becomes dry, thus symbolizing death. Every principle is a differentiation of Jîva, but the life-motion in each is Prâna, the "breath of life." Kâma depends on Prâna, without which there would be no Kâma. Prâna wakes the Kâmic germs to life; it makes all desires vital and living. [illegible]

THE SECOND SPINAL CORD.

Q. With reference to the answer to the question on the second cord, what is it that will become a second spinal cord in the Sixth Race? [illegible] Idâ and Pingalâ have separate physical ducts?

A. It is the sympathetic cords which will grow together and form another spinal cord. Idâ and Pingalâ will be joined with Sushumnâ, and they will become one. Idâ is on the left side of the cord, and Pingalâ on the right.

INITIATES.

Pythagoras was an Initiate, one of the grandest of Scientists. His disciple, Archytas, was marvellously apt in applied Science. Plato and Euclid were Initiates, but not Socrates. No real Initiates were married. Euclid learned his Geometry in the Mysteries. Modern men of Science only rediscover the old truths.

KOSMIC CONSCIOUSNESS.

H. P. B. proceeded to explain Kosmic Consciousness, which is, like all else, on seven planes, of which three are inconceivable, and four are cognizable by the highest Adept. She sketched the planes as in the following diagram:

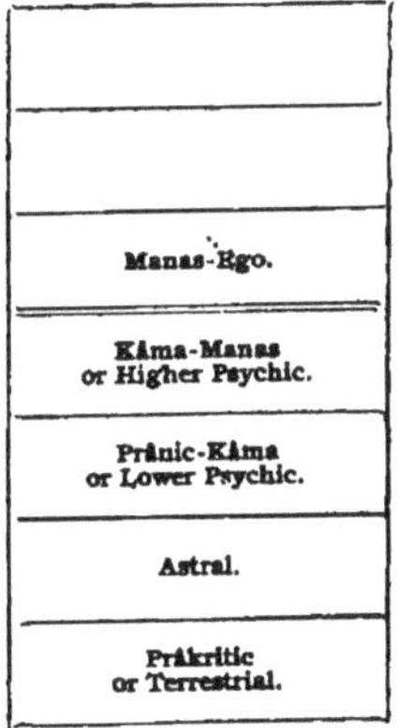

Taking the lowest only, the Terrestrial (it was afterwards decided to call this plane Prâkritic), it is divisible into seven planes, and these again into seven, making the forty-nine.

TERRESTRIAL.

She then took the lowest plane of Prakriti, or the true Terrestrial, and divided it as follows:—

True terrestrial planes, or 7th Prâkritic.

7	Para-Ego or Âtmic.
6	Inner-Ego or Buddhic.
5	Ego-Manas.
4	Kâma-Manas or Lower Manas.
3	Prânic Kâma or Psychic.
2	Astral.
1	Objective.

Its objective or sensuous plane is that which is sensed by the five physical senses.

On its second plane things are reversed.

Its third plane is psychic: here is the instinct which prevents a kitten going into the water and getting drowned.

The following table of the terrestrial, objective consciousness was given:

1. Sensuous.
2. Instinctual.
3. Physiological-emotional.
4. Passional "
5. Mental "
6. Spiritual "
7. *x*.

ASTRAL.

The three lower Prâkritic are related to the three lower of the Astral Plane immediately succeeding.

7	
6	Astral Buddhi.
5	Astral Manas.
4	Astral Kâma-Manas.
3	Astral Psychic, or Prânic.
2	Astral Astral.
1	Astral Objective.

With regard to the first division of the second plane, H. P. B. reminded her pupils that all seen on it must be reversed in translating it, *e.g*, with numbers which appeared backwards. The Astral Objective corresponds in everything to the Terrestrial Objective.

The second division corresponds to the second of the lower plane, but the objects are of extreme tenuity, an astralized Astral. This plane is the limit of the ordinary medium, beyond which he cannot go. A non-mediumistic person to reach it must be asleep or in a trance, or under the influence of laughing-gas; or in ordinary delirium people pass on to this plane.

The third, the Prânic, is of an intensely vivid nature. Extreme delirium carries the patient to this plane. In delirium tremens the sufferer passes to this and to the one above it. Lunatics are often conscious on this plane, where they see terrible visions. It runs into the—

Fourth division, the worst of the astral planes, Kâmic and terrible. Hence come the images that tempt; images of drunkards in Kâma Loka impelling others to drink; images of all vices inoculating men with the desire to commit crimes. The weak imitate these images in a kind of monkeyish fashion, so falling beneath their influence. This is also the cause of epidemics of vices, and cycles of disaster, of accidents of all kinds coming in groups. Extreme delirium tremens is on this plane.

The fifth division is that of premonitions in dreams, of [illegible] the lower mentality, glimpses into the past and future, the [illegible] things mental and not spiritual. The mesmerised clairvoyant [illegible] this plane, and even, if good, may go higher.

The sixth is the plane from which come all beautiful [illegible] art, poetry, and music; high types of dreams, flashes of genius. [illegible] we have glimpses of past incarnations, without being able to [illegible] analyze them.

We are on the seventh plane at the moment of death or in [illegible] visions. The drowning man is here when he remembers [illegible] The memory of events of this plane must be centred in the [illegible] seat of Buddha." There it will remain, but impressions from [illegible] are not made on the physical brain.

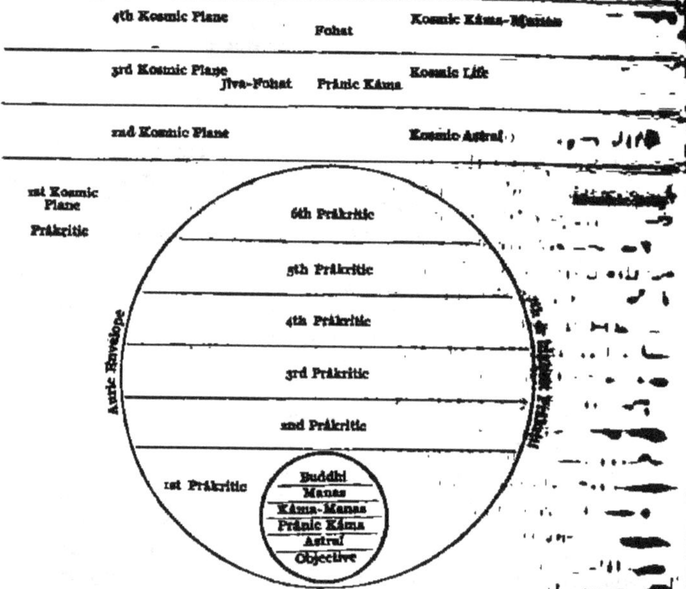

[In this diagram all the Kosmic Planes should be figured as of one [illegible] given to the lowest plane, Prakriti. Further, within the circle all [illegible] Planes should be of one size—that given to the first, or lowest. To do [illegible] make so large a diagram that the planes are compressed.—ED.]

GENERAL NOTES.

The two planes above dealt with are the only two used in the Hatha Yoga.

Prâna and the Auric Envelope are essentially the same, and again, as Jîva, it is the same as the Universal Deity. This, in its Fifth Principle, is Mahat, in its Sixth, Alaya. (The Universal Life is also seven-principled.) Mahat is the highest *Entity* in Kosmos; beyond this is no diviner Entity; it is of subtlest matter, Sûkshma. In us this is Manas, and the very Logoi are less high, not having gained experience. The Mânasic Entity will not be destroyed, even at the end of the Mahâ-manvantara, when all the Gods are absorbed, but will re-emerge from Parabrâhmic latency.

Consciousness is the Kosmic seed of superkosmic omniscience. It has the potentiality of budding into the Divine Consciousness.

Rude physical health is a drawback to seership. This was the case with Swedenborg.

Fohat is everywhere: it runs like a thread through all, and has its own seven divisions.

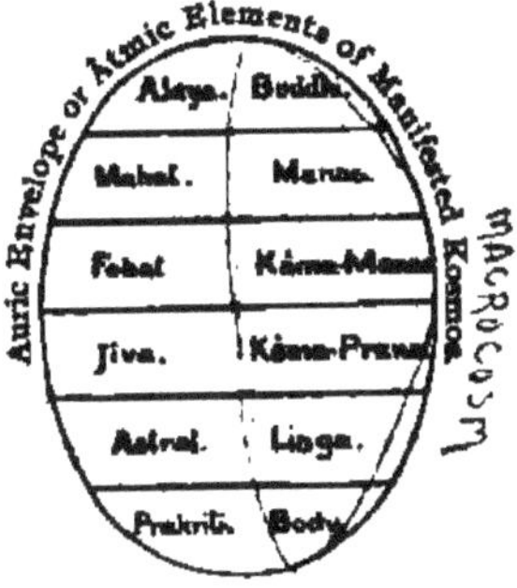

KOSMIC PLANES AS SIX WITH AURIC EGG AS SEVENTH.

In the Kosmic Auric Envelope is all the Karma of the manifesting Universe. This is the Hiranyagarbha. Jiva is everywhere, and so with the other Principles.

The above diagram represents the type of all the Solar Systems.

Mahat, single before informing the Universe, differentiates when informing it, as does Manas in man.

Mahat as Divine Ideation.

| Fohat.

Kosmic Substance.

Manas.

| Antahkarana.

Lower Manas.

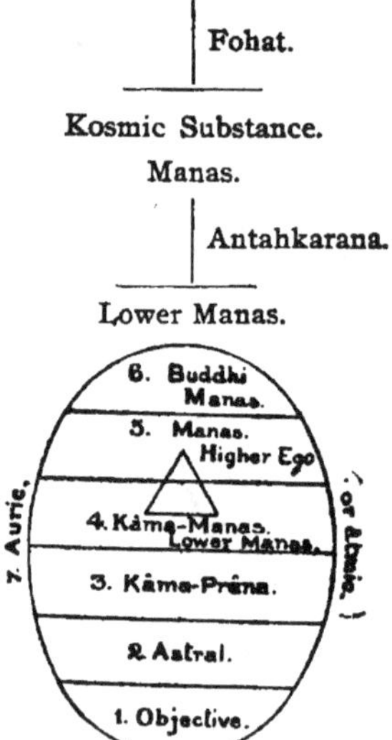

Taking this figure to represent the human Principles and planes of consciousness, then

* The Fourth Globe of every Planetary Chain.

7, 6, 5 represent respectively, Shiva, Vishnu, Brahmâ, Brahmâ being the lowest.

Shiva is the four-faced Brahmâ; the Creator, Preserver, Destroyer, and Regenerator.

Between 5 and 4 comes the Antahkarana. The △ represents the Christos, the Sacrificial Victim crucified between the thieves; this is the double-faced entity. The Vedântins make this a quaternary for a blind: Antahkarana, Chit, Buddhi, and Manas.

MANVANTARIC ASPECT OF PARABRAHMAN AND MÛLAPRAKRITI.

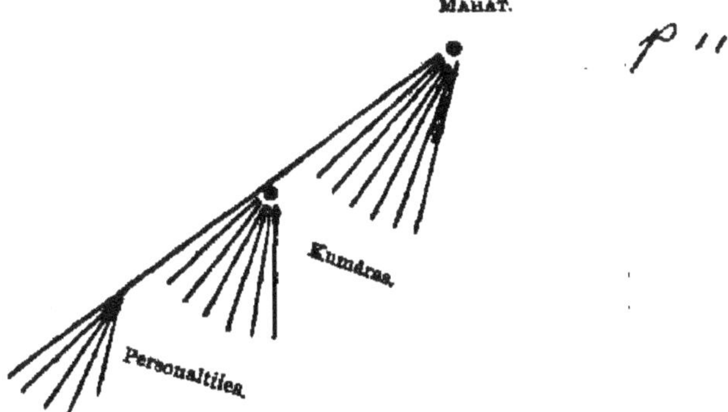

Attributes, Mâyâvi Rûpas, etc.

N.B.—The number of Rays is arbitrary and without significance.

Perceptive life begins with the Astral: it is not our physical atoms which see, etc.

Consciousness proper begins between Kâma and Manas. Âtmâ-Buddhi acts more in the atoms of the body, in the bacilli, microbes, etc., than in Man himself.

OBJECTIVE CONSCIOUSNESS.

Sensuous objective consciousness includes all that pertains to the five physical senses in man, and rules in animals, birds, fishes and some insects. Here are the "Lives"; their consciousness is in Âtmâ-Buddhi: these are entirely without Manas.

ASTRAL CONSCIOUSNESS.

That of some plants (*e.g.*, sensitive), of ants, spiders, and some light-flies (Indian), but not of bees.

The vertebrate animals in general are without this consciousness, but the placental Mammals have all the potentialities of human consciousness, though at present, of course, dormant.

Idiots are on this plane. The common expression "he has lost his mind" is an Occult truth. For when through fright or other cause the lower mind becomes paralyzed, then the consciousness is on the Astral Plane. The study of lunacy will throw much light on these points. This may be called the "nerve plane." It is cognized by our "nervous centres" of which Physiology knows nothing, *e.g.*, the clairvoyant reading with the eyes bandaged, reading with the tips of the fingers, the pit of the stomach, etc. This sense is greatly developed in the deaf and dumb.

KÂMA-PRÂNIC CONSCIOUSNESS.

The general life-consciousness which belongs to all the objective world, even to the stones; for if stones were not living they could not decay, emit a spark, etc. Affinity between chemical elements is a manifestation of this Kâmic consciousness.

KÂMA-MÂNASIC CONSCIOUSNESS.

The instinctual consciousness of animals and idiots in its lowest degrees, the planes of sensation: in man these are rationalized, *e.g.*, a dog shut in a room has the instinct to get out, but cannot because its instinct is not sufficiently rationalized to take the necessary means; whereas a man at once takes in the situation and extricates himself. The highest degree of this Kâma-Mânasic consciousness is the psychic. Thus there are seven degrees from the instinctual animal to the rationalized instinctual and psychic.

MÂNASIC CONSCIOUSNESS.

From this plane Manas stretches upwards to Mahat.

BUDDHIC CONSCIOUSNESS.

The plane of Buddhi and the Auric Envelope. From here it goes to the Father in heaven, Âtmâ, and reflects all that is in the Auric Envelope. Five and six therefore cover the planes from the psychic to the divine.

MISCELLANEOUS.

Reason is a thing that oscillates between right and wrong. But Intelligence—Intuition—is higher, it is the clear vision.

To get rid of Kâma we must crush out all our material instincts—"crush out matter." The flesh is a thing of habit; it will repeat mechanically a good impulse as well as a bad one. It is not the flesh which is always the tempter; in nine cases out of ten it is the Lower Manas, which, by its images, leads the flesh into temptation.

The highest Adept begins his Samâdhi on the Fourth Solar Plane, but cannot go outside the Solar System. When he begins Samâdhi he is on a par with some of the Dhyân Chohans, but he transcends them as he rises to the seventh plane (Nirvâna).

The Silent Watcher is on the Fourth Kosmic Plane.

The higher Mind directs the Will: the lower turns it into selfish Desire.

The head should not be covered in meditation. It is covered in Samâdhi.

The Dhyân Chohans are passionless, pure and mindless. They have no struggle, no passions to crush.

The Dhyân Chohans are made to pass through the School of Life. "God goes to School."

The best of us in the future will be Mânasaputras; the lowest will be Pitris. We are seven intellectual Hierarchies here. This earth becomes the moon of the next earth.

The "Pitris" are the Astral overshadowed by Âtmâ-Buddhi, falling into matter. The "Pudding-bags" had Life and Âtmâ-Buddhi, but no Manas. They were therefore senseless. The reason for all evolution is the gaining of experience.

In the Fifth Round all of us will play the part of Pitris. We shall have to go and shoot out our Chhâyâs into another humanity, and remain until that humanity is perfected. The Pitris have finished their office in this Round and have gone into Nirvâna; but they will return to do the same office up to the middle point of the Fifth Round. The Fourth or Kâmic Hierarchy of the Pitris becomes the "man of flesh."

The astral body is first in the womb; then comes the germ that fructifies it. It is then clothed with matter, as were the Pitris.

The Chhâyâ is really the lower Manas, the shadow of the higher Mind. This Chhâyâ makes the Mâyâvi Rûpa. The Ray clothes itself in the highest degree of the Astral Plane. The Mâyâvi Rûpa is composed of the astral body as Upâdhi, the guiding intelligence from the heart, the attributes and qualities from the Auric Envelope. [illegible]

The Auric Envelope takes up the light of Âtmâ, and [illegible] the coronal, circling round the head. [illegible]

The Auric Fluid is a combination of the Life and Will principles, the life and the will being one and the same in Kosmos. [illegible] from the eyes and hands, when directed by the will of the [illegible]

The Auric Light surrounds all bodies: it is the "aura" [illegible] from them, whether they be animal, vegetable, or mineral. [illegible] light, *e.g.*, seen round magnets.

Âtmâ-Buddhi-Manas in man corresponds to the three Logoi in Kosmos. They not only correspond, but each is the [illegible] Kosmos to Microcosmos. The third Logos, Mahat, becomes [illegible] man, Manas being only Mahat individualized, as the sun-rays [illegible] dividualized in bodies that absorb them. The sun-rays give life [illegible] fertilize what is already there, and the individual is formed. [illegible] to say, fertilizes, and Manas is the result.

Buddhi-Manas is the Kshetrajña.

There are seven planes of Mahat, as of all else.

THE HUMAN PRINCIPLES.

Here H. P. B. drew two diagrams, illustrating different [illegible] representing the human principles. In the first [illegible]

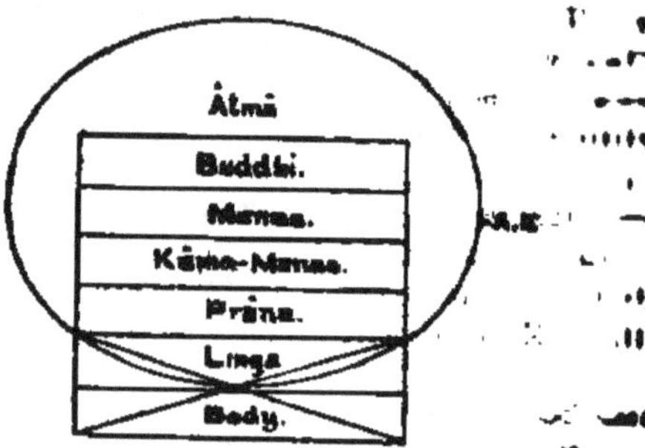

the two lower are disregarded; they go out, disintegrate [illegible] account. Remain five, under the radiation of Âtmâ. [illegible]

In the second:

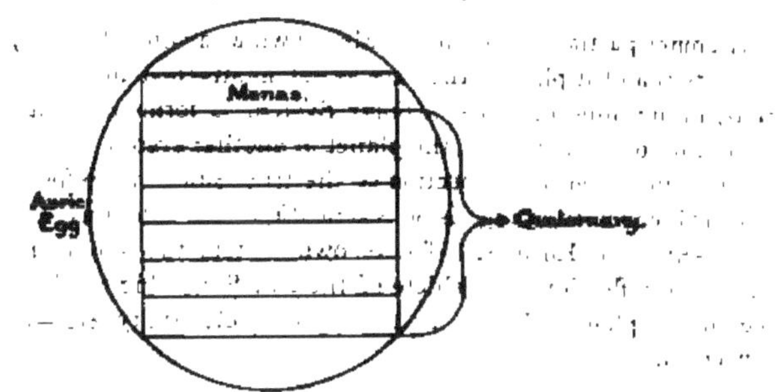

the lower Quaternary is regarded as mere matter, objective illusion, and there remain Manas and the Auric Egg, the higher Principles being reflected in the Auric Egg. In all these systems remember the main principle, the descent and re-ascent of the Spirit, in man as in Kosmos. The Spirit is drawn downwards as by spiritual gravitation.

Seeking further for the cause of this, the students were checked, H. P. B. giving only a suggestion on the three Logoi:

1. Potentiality of Mind (Absolute Thought).
2. Thought in Germ.
3. Ideation in Activity

NOTES.

Protective variation, *e.g.*, identity of colouring of insects and of that on which they feed, was explained to be the work of Nature Elementals.

Form is on different planes, and the forms of one plane may be formless to dwellers on another. The Kosmocratores build on planes in the Divine Mind, visible to them though not to us. The principle of limitation—*principium individuationis*—is Form: this principle is Divine Law manifested in Kosmic Matter, which, in its essence, is limitless. The Auric Egg is the limit of man as Hiranyagarbha of the Kosmos.

The first step towards the accomplishment of Kriyâshakti is the use of the Imagination. To imagine a thing is to firmly create a model of what you desire, perfect in all its details. The Will is then brought into action, and the form is thereby transferred to the objective world. This is creation by Kriyâshakti.

SUNS AND PLANETS.

A comet partially cools and settles down as a sun. It then gradually attracts round it planets that are as yet unattached to any centre, and thus, in millions of years, a Solar System is formed. The worn-out planet becomes a moon to the planet of another system.

The sun we see is a reflection of the true Sun: this reflection, as an outward concrete thing, is a Kâma-Rûpa, all the suns forming the Kâma-Rûpa of Kosmos. To its own system the sun is Buddhi, as being the reflection and vehicle of the true Sun, which is Âtmâ, invisible on this plane. All the Fohatic forces—electricity, etc.—are in this reflection.

THE MOON.

At the beginning of the evolution of our globe, the moon was much nearer to the earth, and larger than it is now. It has retreated from us, and shrunk much in size. (The moon gave all her Principles to the earth, while the Pitris gave only their Chhâyâs to man.)

The influences of the moon are wholly psycho-physiological. It is dead, sending out injurious emanations like a corpse. It vampirizes the earth and its inhabitants, so that any one sleeping in its rays suffers, losing some of his life-force. A white cloth is a protection, the rays not passing through it, and the head especially should be thus guarded. It has most power when it is full. It throws off particles which we absorb, and is gradually disintegrating. Where there is snow the moon looks like a corpse, being unable, through the white snow, to vampirize effectually. Hence snow-covered mountains are free from its bad influences. The moon is phosphorescent.

The Râkshakas of Lanka and the Atlanteans are said to have subjected the moon. The Thessalians learned from them their Magic.

Esoterically, the moon is the symbol of the Lower Manas; it is also the symbol of the Astral.

Plants which under the sun's rays are beneficent are maleficent under those of the moon. Herbs containing poisons are most active when gathered under the moon's rays.

A new moon will appear during the Seventh Round, and our moon will finally disintegrate and disappear. There is now a planet, the "Mystery Planet," behind the moon, and it is gradually dying. Finally the time will come for it to send its Principles to a new Laya Centre, and there a new planet will form, to belong to another Solar System, the present Mystery Planet then functioning as moon to that new globe. This moon will have nothing to do with our earth, though it will come within our range of vision.

THE SOLAR SYSTEM.

All the visible planets placed in our Solar System by Astronomers belong to it, except Neptune. There are also some others not known to Science, belonging to it, and "all moons which are not yet visible for next things."

The planets only move in our consciousness. The Rulers of the seven Secret Planets have no influence on this earth, as this earth has on other planets. It is the sun and moon which really have not only a mental, but also a physical effect. The effect of the sun on humanity is connected with Kâma-Prâna, with the most physical Kâmic elements in us; it is the vital principle which helps growth. The effect of the moon is chiefly Kâma-Mânasic or psycho-physiological; it acts on the psychological brain, on the brain-mind.

PRECIOUS STONES.

In answer to a question, H. P. B. said that the diamond and the ruby were under the sun, the sapphire under the moon—"but what does it matter to you?"

TIME.

When once out of the body, and not subject to the habit of consciousness formed by others, time does not exist.

Cycles and epochs depend on consciousness: we are not here for the first time; the cycles return because we come back into conscious existence. Cycles are measured by the consciousness of humanity and not by Nature. It is because we are the same people as in past epochs that these events occur to us.

DEATH.

The Hindus look upon death as impure, owing to the disintegration of the body and the passing from one plane to another. "I believe in transformation, not in death."

ATOMS.

The Atom is the Soul of the molecule. It is the six Principles, and the molecule is the body thereof. The Atom is the Âtman of the objective Kosmos, *i.e.*, it is on the seventh plane of the lowest Prakriti.

TERMS.

H. P. B. began by saying that students ought to know the correct meaning of the Sanskrit terms used in Occultism, and should learn the Occult Symbology. To begin with one had better learn the correct Esoteric classification and names of the fourteen (7 × 2) and seven (Septa) Lokas found in the exoteric texts. These are given there in a very confused manner, and are full of "blinds." To illustrate this three classifications are given below.

LOKAS.

1. The general exoteric, orthodox and tântric category:
   - Bhûr-loka.
   - Bhuvar-loka.
   - Swar-loka.
   - Mahar-loka.
   - Janar-loka.
   - Tapar-loka.
   - Satya-loka.

The second seven are as follows.

2. The Sânkhya category, and that of some Vedântins,
   - Brahmâ-loka.
   - Pitri-loka.
   - Soma-loka.
   - Indra-loka.
   - Gandharva-loka.
   - Râkshasa-loka
   - Yaksha-loka.

And an eighth.

3. The Vedântic, the nearest approach to the Esoteric:
   - Atala.
   - Vitala.
   - Sutala.
   - Talâtala (or Karatala).
   - Rasâtala.
   - Mahâtala.
   - Pâtâla.

Each and all correspond Esoterically to the Kosmic or Dhyân Chohanic Hierarchies, and to the human States of Consciousness and their divisions (forty-nine). To appreciate this the meanings of the terms used in the Vedântic classification must be first understood.

Tala means *place*.
Atala means no place.
Vitala means some change for the better: *i.e.*, better for matter, in that more matter enters into it, or, in other words, it becomes more differentiated. This is an ancient Occult term.
Sutala means good, excellent, place.
Karatala means something that can be grasped or touched (from kara, a hand): *i.e.*, the state in which matter becomes tangible.
Rasâtala means place of taste; a place you can sense with one of the organs of sense.
Mahâtala means exoterically "great place"; but, Esoterically, a place including all others subjectively, and potentially including all that precedes it.
Pâtâla means something under the feet (from pada, foot), the upâdhi, or basis, of anything, the antipodes, America, etc.

Each of the Lokas, places, worlds, states, etc., corresponds with and is transformed into five (exoterically) and seven (Esoterically) states or Tattvas, for which there are no definite names. These in the main divisions cited below make up the forty-nine Fires:

5 and 7 Tanmâtras, outer and inner senses.
5 and 7 Bhûtas, or elements.
5 and 7 Gnyânendryas, or organs of sensation.
5 and 7 Karmendryas, or organs of action.

These correspond in general to States of Consciousness, to the Hierarchies of Dhyân Chohans, to the Tattvas, etc. These Tattvas transform themselves into the whole Universe. The fourteen Lokas are made of seven with seven reflections: above, below; within, without; subjective, objective; pure, impure; positive, negative; etc.

EXPLANATION OF THE STATES OF CONSCIOUSNESS CORRESPONDING TO THE VEDÂNTIC CLASSIFICATION OF LOKAS

7. Atala. The Âtmic or Auric state or locality: it emanates directly from ABSOLUTENESS, and is the first something in the Universe. Its correspondence is the Hierarchy of non-substantial primordial Beings, in a place which is no place (for us), a state which is no state. This

Hierarchy contains the primordial plane, all that was, is and will be, from the beginning to the end of the Mahâmanvantara; all is there. This statement should not, however, be taken to imply Kismet; the latter is contrary to all the teachings of Occultism.

Here are the Hierarchies of the Dhyâni Buddhas. Their state is that of Parasamâdhi, of the Dharmakâya; a state where no progress is possible. The entities there may be said to be crystallized in purity, in homogeneity.

6. *Vitala.* Here are the Hierarchies of the celestial Buddhas, or Bodhisattvas, who are said to emanate from the seven Dhyâni Buddhas. It is related on earth to Samâdhi, to the Buddhic consciousness in man. No Adept, save one, can be higher than this and live; if he passes into the Âtmic or Dharmakâya state (Alaya) he can return to earth no more. These two states are purely hyper-metaphysical.

5. *Sutala.* A differential state corresponding on earth with the Higher Manas, and therefore with Shabda (Sound), the Logos, our Higher Ego; and also to the Manushi Buddha state, like that of Gautama, on earth. This is the third stage of Samâdhi (which is septenary). Here belong the Hierarchies of the Kumâras—the Agnishvattas, etc.

4. *Karatala* corresponds with Sparsha (touch) and to the Hierarchies of ethereal, semi-objective Dhyân Chohans of the astral matter of the Mânasa-Manas, or the pure ray of Manas, that is the Lower Manas before it is mixed with Kâma (as in the young child). They are called Sparsha Devas, the Devas endowed with touch. These Hierarchies of Devas are progressive: the first have one sense; the second two; and so on to seven: each containing all the senses potentially, but not yet developed. Sparsha would be rendered better by affinity, contact.

3. *Rasâtala,* or Rûpatala: corresponds to the Hierarchies of Rûpa or Sight Devas, possessed of three senses, sight, hearing, and touch. These are the Kâma-Mânasic entities, and the higher Elementals. With the Rosicrucians they were the Sylphs and Undines. It corresponds on earth with an artificial state of consciousness, such as that produced by hypnotism and drugs (morphia, etc.).

2. *Mahâtala.* Corresponds to the Hierarchies of Rasa or Taste Devas, and includes a state of consciousness embracing the lower five senses and emanations of life and being. It corresponds to Kâma and Prâna in man, and to Salamanders and Gnomes in nature.

1. *Pâtâla.* Corresponds to the Hierarchies of Gandha or Smell

Devâs, the underworld or antipodes: Myalba. The sphere of irrational animals, having no feeling save that of self-preservation and gratification of the senses: also of intensely selfish human beings, waking or sleeping. This is why Nârada is said to have visited Pâtâla when he was cursed to be reborn. He reported that life there was very pleasant for those "who had never left their birth-place"; they were very happy. It is the earthly state, and corresponds with the sense of smell. Here are also animal Dugpas, Elementals of animals, and Nature Spirits.

FURTHER EXPLANATIONS OF THE SAME CLASSIFICATIONS.

7. Auric, Âtmic, Alayic, sense or state. One of full potentiality, but not of activity.

6. Buddhic; the sense of being one with the universe; the impossibility of imagining oneself apart from it.

(It was asked why the term Alayic was here given to the Âtmic and not to the Buddhic state. *Ans.* These classifications are not hard and fast divisions. A term may change places according as the classification is exoteric, Esoteric or practical. For students the effort should be to bring all things down to states of consciousness. Buddhi is really one and indivisible. It is a feeling within, absolutely inexpressible in words. All cataloguing is useless to explain it.)

5. Shâbdic, sense of hearing.

4. Spârshic, sense of touch.

3. Rûpic, the state of feeling oneself a body and perceiving it (rûpa = form).

2. Râsic, sense of taste.

1. Gândhic, sense of smell.

All the Kosmic and anthropic states and senses correspond with our organs of sensation, Gnyânendryas, rudimentary organs for receiving knowledge through direct contact, sight, etc. These are the faculties of Sharîra, through Netra (eyes), nose, speech, etc., and also with the organs of action, Karmendryas, hands, feet, etc.

Exoterically, there are five sets of five, giving twenty-five. Of these twenty are facultative and five Buddhic. Exoterically Buddhi is said to perceive; Esoterically it reaches perception only through the Higher Manas. Each of these twenty is both positive and negative, thus making forty in all. There are two subjective states answering to each of the four sets of five, hence eight in all. These being subjective cannot be doubled. Thus we have 40 + 8 = 48 cognitions of Buddhi. These with Mâyâ, which includes them all, make 49. (Once that you have reached the cognition of Mâyâ, you are an Adept.)

TABLE.

5 + 5	Tanmâtras	2	subjective.
5 + 5	Bhûtas	2	"
5 + 5	Gnyânendryas	2	"
5 + 5	Karmendryas	2	"
20 + 20		8	

20 + 20 + 8 + Mâyâ = 49.

THE LOKAS.

In their exoteric blinds the Brâhmans count fourteen Lokas (earth included), of which seven are objective, though not apparent, and seven subjective, yet fully demonstrable to the Inner Man. There are seven Divine Lokas and seven infernal (terrestrial) Lokas.

Seven Divine Lokas.	Seven Infernal (Terrestrial) Lokas.
1. Bhûrloka (the earth).	1. Pâtâla (our earth).
2. Bhuvarloka (between the earth and the sun [Munis]).	2. Mahâtala.
3. Svarloka (between the sun and the Pole Star [Yogîs]).	3. Rasâtala.
4. Maharloka (between the earth and the utmost limit of the Solar System).*	4. Talâtala (or Karatala).
5. Janarloka (beyond the Solar System, the abode of the Kumâras who do not belong to this plane).	5. Sutala.
6. Taparloka (still beyond the Mahâtmic region, the dwelling of the Vairâja deities).	6. Vitala.
7. Satyaloka (the abode of the Nirvanîs).	7. Atala.

* All these "spaces" denote the special magnetic currents, the planes of substance, and the degrees of approach that the consciousness of the Yogî, or Chelâ, performs towards assimilation with the inhabitants of the Lokas.

SPIRIT

ELEMENTS.	DIVINE LOKAS, OR STATES.	INFERNAL (TERRESTRIAL) TALAS, OR STATES.	PLANES OF … HIE…
Bhûtas.		Rûpa.	
1. *Earth.* Bhûmi. Prithivî.	1. *Bhûrloka.* The habitat of thinking and good men. Psychic State.	1. *Pâtâla.* Man's animal gross body and the personality dwell here.	1. Abode … state of infa… innocence … instinctual
2. *Water.* Âpas.	2. *Bhuvarloka.* State in which the man thinks more of his inner condition than of his personality. His Astral passes into this sphere, and so does its substance. Higher Psychic State.	2. *Mahâtala.* Abode of man's astral, shadow of the gross body, which shadow takes up the characteristics of this sphere.	2. Region … Light and … Abode of c… spirits, el… the other … Devas, the … animal w… instinct
3. *Air.* Vâyu.	3. *Svarloka.* State when the Yogî has lost all tastes and started towards Reunion. Holy State.	3. *Rasâtala.* Where the Kâma longs for the taste (Rasa) of everything.	3. Devach… or plane o… reasoned h… aspiration … of Kâma-M… elementals.
4. *Fire.* Agni. Tejas.	4. *Maharloka.* Where the Lower Manas has lost all Kâmic affinity. Superholy State.	4. *Talâtala.* Where the Lower Manas clings to the sentient and objective life; is Kâmic.	4. Plane … giving wa… weak. Ab… among the … sphere of … one end, an… selfishness
Bhûtas.		Rûpa.	
Elementary Substances. 5. *Ether.*	5. *Janarloka.* Manas is entirely freed from Kâma, and becomes one with the Ego. Kumâra State.	5. *Sutala.* Manas becomes in it entirely the slave of Kâma, and at one with the animal man.	5. Abode … the Sons of … má. Omni… ing all tha… realm of M… its sway
6. *Divine Flame.*	6. *Taparloka.* Even if it is again re-born, it has now become (invulnerable, inconsumable. Innate Christos) State. ONE WITH EGO KUMARA	6. *Vitala.* When this is reached, the Higher breaks off entirely from the Lower. (The chord is snapped.)	6. Plane … inconsumal … divine fire … Vairâjas, t… the Sun.
7. *Âkâsha.* Elementary Substances.	7. *Satyaloka.* In this state the Yogî reaches the highest Samâdhi. He is at the threshold of the great choice.	7. *Atala.* Man dies but to be directly reborn. No place means no Devachan. Spiritual death, annihilation.	7. Plane of … *tum est* in … universe: t…

These the Brâhmans read from the bottom.

Now all these fourteen are planes from without within, and (the seven Divine) States of Consciousness through which man can pass—and *must* pass, once he is determined to go through the seven paths and portals of Dhyâni; one need not be disembodied for this, and all this is reached on earth, and in one or many of the incarnations.

See the order: the four lower ones (1, 2, 3, 4), are *rûpa*; *i.e.*, they are performed by the Inner Man with the full concurrence of the diviner portions, or elements, of the Lower Manas, and consciously by the personal man. The three higher states cannot be reached and remembered by the latter, unless he is a fully initiated Adept. A Hatha Yogî will never pass beyond the Maharloka, psychically, and the Talâtala (double or dual place), physico-mentally. To become a Râja Yogî, one has to ascend up to the seventh portal, the Satyaloka. For such, the Master Yogis tell us, is the fruition of Yajna, or sacrifice. When the Bhûr, Bhuvar and Svarga (states) are once passed, and the Yogî's consciousness centred in Maharloka, it is in the last plane and state between entire identification of the Personal and the Higher Manas.

One thing to remember: while the infernal (or terrestrial) states are also the seven divisions of the earth, for planes and states, as much as they are Kosmic divisions, the divine Saptaloka are purely subjective, and begin with the psychic Astral Light plane, ending with the Satya or Jîvanmukta state. These fourteen Lokas, or spheres, form the extent of the whole Brahmânda (world). The four lower are transitory, with all their dwellers, and the three higher eternal; *i.e.*, the former states, planes and subjects, to these, last only a Day of Brahmâ, changing with every Kalpa: the latter endure for an Age of Brahmâ.

In Diagram V. only Body, Astral, Kâma, Lower Manas, Higher Manas, Buddhi and Auric Âtmâ are given. Life is a Universal Kosmic principle, and no more than Âtman does it belong to individuals.

In answer to questions on the diagram, H. P. B. said that Touch and Taste have no order. Elements have a regular order, but Fire pervades them all. Every sense pervades every other. There is no universal order, that being first in each which is most developed.

Students must learn the correspondences: then concentrate on the organs and so reach their corresponding states of consciousness. Take them in order beginning with the lowest, and working steadily upwards. A medium might irregularly catch glimpses of higher, but would not thus gain orderly development.

The greatest phenomena are produced by touching and centring the attention upon the little finger.

The Lokas and Talas are reflections the one of the other; and so are the Hierarchies in each, in pairs of opposites, at the two poles of the sphere. Everywhere are such opposites: good and evil, light and darkness, male and female.

H. P. B. could not say why blue was the colour of the earth. Blue is a colour by itself, a primary. Indigo is a colour, not a shade of blue, so is violet.

The Vairâjas belong to, are the fiery Egos of, other Manvantaras. They have already been purified in the fire of passions. It is they who refused to create. They have reached the Seventh Portal, and have refused Nirvâna, remaining for succeeding Manvantaras.

The seven steps of Antahkarana correspond with the Lokas.

Samâdhi is the highest state on earth that can be reached in the body. Beyond that the Initiate must have become a Nirmânakâya.

Purity of mind is of greater importance than purity of body. If the Upâdhi be not perfectly pure, it cannot preserve recollections coming from a higher state. An act may be performed to which little or no attention is paid, and it is of comparatively small importance. But if thought of, dwelt on in the mind, the effect is a thousand times greater. The thoughts must be kept pure.

Remember that Kâma, while having bad passions and emotions, helps you to evolve by giving also the desire and impulse necessary for rising.

The flesh, the body, the human being in his material part, is, on this plane, the most difficult thing to subject. The highest Adept, put into a new body, has to struggle against it and subdue it, and finds its subjugation difficult.

The Liver is the General, the Spleen is the Aide-de-Camp. All that the Liver does not accomplish is taken up and completed by the Spleen.

H. P. B. was asked whether each person must pass through the fourteen states, and answered that the Lokas and Talas represented planes on this earth, through some of which all must pass, and through all of which the disciple must pass, on his way to Adeptship. Everyone passes through the lower Lokas, but not necessarily through the corresponding Talas. There are two poles in everything: seven states in every state.

Vitala represents a sublime as well as an infernal state. That state which for the mortal is a complete separation of the Ego from the personality is for a Buddha a mere temporary separation. For the Buddha it is a Kosmic state.

The Brâhmans and Buddhists regard the Talas as hells, but in reality the term is figurative. We are in hell whenever we are in misery, suffer misfortune and so on.

FORMS IN THE ASTRAL LIGHT.

The Elementals in the Astral light are reflections. Everything on earth is reflected there. It is from these that photographs are sometimes obtained through mediums. The mediums unconsciously produce them as forms. The Adepts produce them consciously through Kriyâshakti, bringing them down by a process that may be compared to the focussing of rays of light by a burning glass.

STATES OF CONSCIOUSNESS.

Bhûrloka is the waking state in which we normally live; it is the state in which animals also are, when they sense food, a danger, etc. To be in Svarloka is to be completely abstracted on this plane, leaving only instinct to work, so that on the material plane you would behave as an animal. Yogîs are known who have become crystallized in this state, and then they must be nourished by others. A Yogî near Allahabad had been for fifty-three years sitting on a stone; his Chelâs plunge him into the river every night and then replace him. During the day his consciousness returns to Bhûrloka, and he talks and teaches. A Yogî was found on an island near Calcutta round whose limbs the roots of trees had grown. He was cut out, and in the endeavour to awaken him so many outrages were inflicted on him that he died.

Q. Is it possible to be in more than one state of consciousness at once?

A. The consciousness cannot be entirely on two planes at once. The higher and lower states are not wholly incompatible, but if you are on the higher you will wool-gather on the lower. In order to remember the higher state on returning to the lower, the memory must be carried upwards to the higher. An Adept may apparently enjoy a dual consciousness; when he desires not to see he can abstract himself: he may be in a higher state and yet return answers to questions addressed to him. But in this case he will ultimately go down to the material plane, shooting up again to the higher plane afterwards. [illegible] only salvation in adverse conditions.

The lower you go in the Talas the more intellectual you become and the less spiritual. You may be a mentally good man but be not spiritual. Intellect may remain very closely related to Manas. A man may be in a Loka and visit one and all the Talas, his condition depending on the Loka to which he belongs. Thus a man in Bhûrloka only may pass into the Talas and go to the devil. If he dwells in Bhuvarloka he cannot become as bad. If he has reached the Satya state he can go into any Tala without danger; buoyed up by his own purity he can never be engulfed. The Talas are brain intellect states, while the Lokas—or more accurately the three higher—are spiritual.

Manas absorbs the light of Buddhi. Buddhi is Arûpa, and can absorb nothing. When the Ego takes all the light of Buddhi, it takes that of Âtmâ, Buddhi being the vehicle, and thus the three become one. This done, the *full* Adept is one spiritually, but has a body. The fourfold Path is finished and he is one. The Masters' bodies are, as far as they are concerned, illusionary, and hence they do not grow old, become wrinkled, etc.

The student, who is not naturally psychic, should fix the thought-consciousness in a higher plane and nail it there. Let him make a bundle of the four lower and pin them to a higher state. He should centre on this higher, trying not to permit the body and intellect to draw him down and carry him away. Play ducks and drakes with the body, eating, drinking and sleeping, but living always on the [illegible]

MOTHER-LOVE.

Mother-love is an instinct, the same in the human being and in the animal, and often stronger in the latter. The continuance of this love in human beings is due to association, to blood magnetism and to psychic affinity. Families are sometimes formed of those who have lived together before, but often not. The causes at work are very complex and have to be balanced. Sometimes when a child with very bad Karma is to be born, parents of a callous type are chosen, or they may die before the Karmic results appear. Or the suffering through the child may be their own Karma. Mother-love as an instinct is between Rasâtala and Talâtala.

The Lipikas keep man's Karmic record, and impress it on the Astral Light.

Vacillating people pass from one state of consciousness to another.

Thought arises before desire. The thought acts on the brain, the brain on the organ, and then desire awakes. It is not the outer stimulus that arouses the organ. Thought therefore must be slain ere desire can be extinguished. The student must guard his thoughts. Five minutes' thought may undo the work of five years; and though the five years' work will be run through more rapidly the second time, yet time is lost.

CONSCIOUSNESS.

H. P. B. began by challenging the views of consciousness in the West, commenting on the lack of definition in the leading Philosophies. No distinction was made between consciousness and self-consciousness, and yet in this lay the difference between man and the animal. The animal was conscious only, not self-conscious; the animal does not know the Ego as Subject, as does man. There is therefore an enormous difference between the consciousness of the bird, the insect, the beast, and that of man.

But the full consciousness of man is self-consciousness—that which makes us say, "*I* do that." If there is pleasure it must be traced to some one experiencing it. Now the difference between the consciousness of man and of animals is that while there is a Self in the animal, the animal is not conscious of the Self. Spencer reasons on consciousness, but when he comes to a gap he merely jumps over it. So again Hume, when he says that on introspection he sees merely feelings and can never find any "I," forgets that without an "I" no seeing of feelings would be possible. What is it that studies the feelings? The animal is not conscious of the feeling "I am I." It has instinct, but instinct is not self-consciousness. Self-consciousness is an attribute of the mind, not of the soul, the *anima*, whence the very name *animal* is taken. Humanity had no self-consciousness until the coming of the Mânasaputras in the Third Race. Consciousness, brain-consciousness, is the field of the light of the Ego, of the Auric Egg, of the Higher Manas. The cells of the leg are conscious, but they are the slaves of the idea; they are not self-conscious, they cannot originate an idea, although when they are tired they can convey to the brain an uneasy sensation, and so give rise to the idea of fatigue. Instinct is the lower state of consciousness. Man has consciousness running through the four lower keys of his septenary consciousness; there are seven states of consciousness in his consciousness, which is none the less indivisible and pre-eminently one, a unit. There are millions and millions of states of consciousness, as there are millions and millions of leaves; but as you cannot find two leaves alike, so you cannot find two states of consciousness alike; a state is never exactly repeated.

Is memory a thing born in us that it can give birth to the ego? Knowledge, feeling, volition, are colleagues of the mind, not functions of it. Memory is an artificial thing, an adjunct of relativeness; it can be sharpened or left dull, and it depends on the condition of the brain cells which store all impressions; knowledge, feeling, volition, cannot be correlated, do what you will. They are not produced from each other, nor produced from mind, but are principles, colleagues. We cannot have knowledge without memory, for memory stores all things, garnishing and furnishing. If you teach a child nothing, it will know nothing. Brain-consciousness depends on the intensity of the light shed by the Higher Manas on the Lower, and the extent of affinity between the brain and this light. Brain-mind is conditioned by the responsiveness of the brain to this light; it is the field of consciousness of the Manas. The animal has the Monad and the Manas latent, but its brain cannot respond. All potentialities are there, but are dormant. There are certain accepted errors in the West which vitiate all their theories.

How many impressions can a man receive simultaneously into his consciousness and record? The Westerns say one: Occultists say normally seven, and abnormally fourteen, seventeen, nineteen, twenty-one, up to forty-nine, impressions can be simultaneously received. Occultism teaches that the consciousness always receives a sevenfold impression and stores it in the memory. You can prove it by striking at once the seven notes of the musical scale: the seven sounds reach the consciousness simultaneously, but the untrained ear can only recognize them one after another, and if you choose you can measure the intervals. The trained ear will hear the seven notes at once simultaneously. And experiment has shown that in two or three weeks a man may be trained to receive seventeen or eighteen impressions of colour, the intervals decreasing with practice.

Memory is acquired for this life, and can be expanded. Genius is the greatest responsiveness of the brain and brain-memory to the Higher Manas. Impressions on any sense are stored in the memory.

Before a physical sense is developed there is a mental feeling which proceeds to become a physical sense. Fishes who are blind, living in the deep sea, or subterranean waters, if they are put into a pond will in a few generations develop eyes. But in their previous state there is a sense of seeing, though no physical sight; how else should they in the darkness find their way, avoid dangers, etc.? The mind will take in and store all kinds of things mechanically and unconsciously, and will throw them into the memory as unconscious perceptions. If the attention is greatly engrossed in any way, the sense perception of any injury is not felt at the time, but later the suffering enters into consciousness. So, returning to our example of the seven notes struck simultaneously, we have one impression, but the ear is affected in succession by the notes one after another, so that they are stored in the brain-mind in order, for the untrained consciousness cannot register them simultaneously. All depends on training and on attention. Thus the transference of a sensation passing from any organ to the consciousness is almost simultaneous if your attention is fixed on it, but if any noise distracts your attention, then it will take a fraction more of a second before it reaches your consciousness. The Occultist should train himself to receive and transmit along the line of the seven scales of his consciousness every impression, or impressions, simultaneously. He who reduces the intervals of physical time the most has made the most progress.

CONSCIOUSNESS, ITS SEVEN SCALES.

There are seven scales or shades of consciousness, of the Unit; *e.g.*, in a moment of pleasure or pain; four lower and three higher.

1. Physical sense-perception:	Perception of the cell (if paralyzed, the sense is there, though *you* do not feel it).
2. Self-perception or apperception:	*I.e.*, self-perception of cell.
3. Psychic apperception:	Of astral double, döppelganger, carrying it higher to the
4. Vital perception:	Physical feeling, sensations of pleasure and pain, of quality.

These are the four lower scales, and belong to the psycho-physiological man.

5. Mânasic discernment of the Lower Manas:	Mânasic self-perception.

6. Will perception: Volitional perception, the voluntary taking in of an idea, as we can regard or disregard physical pain.

7. Spiritual, entirely conscious apperception: Because it reaches the Higher self-conscious Manas.

[Apperception means self-perception, conscious action, not, as with Leibnitz, but when attention is fixed on the perception.]

You can take these on any planes: *e.g.*, bad news passes through the four lower stages before coming to the heart.

Or take Sound:

1. It strikes the ear.
2. Self-perception of the ear.
3. On the psychic or mental, which carries it to
4. Vital (harsh, soft; strong, weak; etc.).

THE EGO.

One of the best proofs that there is an Ego, a true Field of Consciousness, is the fact already mentioned, that a state of consciousness is never exactly reproduced, though you should live a hundred years, and pass through milliards and milliards. In an active day, how many states and substates there are; it would be impossible to have cells enough for all. This will help you to understand why some mental states and abstract things follow the Ego into Devachan, and why others merely scatter in space. That which touches the Entity has an affinity for it, as a noble action, is immortal and goes with it into Devachan, forming part and parcel of the biography of the personality which is disintegrating. A lofty emotion runs through the seven stages, and touches the Ego, the mind that plays its tunes in the brain cells. We can analyze the work of consciousness and describe it, but we cannot define consciousness unless we postulate a Subject.

BHÛRLOKA.

The Bhûrloka begins with the Lower Manas. Animals do not think as do men. The dog thinks more of his master being angry than of the actual pain of the lash. The animal does not suffer in memory or in imagination, feeling past and future as well as actual present pain.

PINEAL GLAND.

The special physical organ of perception is the brain, and perception is located in the aura of the pineal gland. This aura answers in vibrations to any impressions, but it can only be sensed, not perceived, in the living man. During the process of thought manifesting in consciousness, a constant vibration occurs in the light of this aura, and a clairvoyant looking at the brain of a living man may almost count, see with the spiritual eye, the seven scales, the seven shades of light, passing from the dullest to the brightest. You touch your hand; before you touch it the vibration is already in the aura of the pineal gland, and has its own shade of colour. It is this aura which causes the wear and tear of the organ, by the vibrations it sets up. The brain, set vibrating, conveys the vibrations to the spinal cord, and so to the rest of the body. Happiness as well as sorrow sets up these strong vibrations, and so wears out the body. Powerful vibrations of joy or sorrow may thus kill.

THE HEART.

The septenary disturbance and play of light around the pineal gland are reflected in the heart, or rather the aura of the heart, which vibrates and illumines the seven brains of the heart, just as does the aura round the pineal gland. This is the exoterically four- but Esoterically seven-leaved lotus, the Saptaparna, the cave of Buddha, with its seven compartments.

ASTRAL AND EGO.

There is a difference between the nature and the essence of the Astral Body and the Ego. The Astral Body is molecular, however etherealized it may be: the Ego is atomic, spiritual. The Atoms are spiritual, and are for ever invisible on this plane; molecules form around them, they remaining as the higher invisible principles of the molecules. The eyes are the most Occult of our senses: close them and you pass to the mental plane. Stop all the senses and you are entirely on another plane.

INDIVIDUALITY.

If twelve people are smoking together, the smoke of their cigarettes may mingle, but the molecules of the smoke from each have an affinity with each other, and they remain distinct for ever and ever, no matter how the whole mass may interblend. So a drop of water, [illegible] into the ocean retains its individuality. It has become [illegible] life of its own, like a man, and cannot be annihilated. [illegible] people would appear as a group in the Astral Light, but [illegible] permanent; but a group meeting to study Occultism would [illegible] the impression would be more permanent. The higher [illegible] spiritual the affinity, the more permanent the cohesion.

LOWER MANAS.

The Lower Manas is an emanation from the Higher Manas, [illegible] the same nature as the Higher. This nature can make no i[illegible] on this plane, nor receive any: an Archangel, having no [illegible] would be senseless on this plane, and could neither give nor [illegible] impressions. So the Lower Manas clothes itself with the [illegible] the Astral Light; this astral envelope shuts it out from its [illegible] except through the Antahkarana which is its only salvation. [illegible] and you become an animal.

KÂMA.

Kâma is life, it is the essence of the blood. When this [illegible] blood the latter congeals. Prâna is universal on this plane [illegible] the vital principle, Prânic, rather than Prâna.

SELF-HOOD.

Qualities determine the properties of "Self-hood." As, for [illegible] two wolves placed in the same environment would probably [illegible] differently.

The field of the consciousness of the Higher Ego is never [illegible] in the Astral Light. The Auric Envelope receives the impr[illegible] both the Higher and the Lower Manas, and it is the latter [illegible] that are also reflected in the Astral Light. Whereas the [illegible] all things spiritual, all that which reaches, or is not rejected [illegible] Higher Ego is not reflected in the Astral Light, because it [illegible] low a plane. But during the life of a man, this essence, with [illegible] to Karmic ends, is impressed on the Auric Envelope, and after [illegible] and the separation of the Principles is united with the Uni[illegible] Mind (that is to say, those "impressions" which are superior to [illegible] the Devachanic Plane), to await there Karmically until the day [illegible] the Ego is to be reincarnated. [There are thus three sets of impr[illegible] which we may call the Kâmic, Devachanic and Mânasic.] For [illegible] no matter how high, must have their Karmic rewards and punishments on earth. These spiritual impressions are made more or less on the brain; otherwise the Lower Ego would not be responsible. There are some impressions, however, received through the brain, which are not of our previous experience. In the case of the Adept the brain is trained to retain these impressions.

The Reincarnating Ray may, for convenience, be separated into two aspects: the lower Kâmic Ego is scattered in Kâma Loka; the Mânasic part accomplishes its cycle and returns to the Higher Ego. It is, in reality, this Higher Ego which is, so to speak, punished, which suffers. This is the true crucifixion of the Christos—the most abstruse but yet the most important mystery of Occultism; all the cycle of our lives hangs on it. It is indeed the Higher Ego that is the sufferer; for remember that the abstract consciousness of the higher personal consciousness will remain impressed on the Ego, since it must be part and parcel of its eternity. All our grandest impressions are impressed on the Higher Ego, because they are of the same nature as itself.

Patriotism and great actions in national service are not altogether good, from the point of view of the highest. To benefit a portion of humanity is good; but to do so at the expense of the rest is bad. Therefore, in patriotism, etc., the venom is present with the good. For though the inner essence of the Higher Ego is unsoilable, the outer garment may be soiled. Thus both the bad and the good of such thoughts and actions are impressed on the Auric Envelope and the Karma of the bad is taken up by the Higher Ego, though it is perfectly guiltless of it. Thus both sets of impressions, after death, scatter in the Universal Mind, and at reincarnation the Ego sends out a Ray which is itself, into a new personality, and there suffers. It suffers in the Self-consciousness that it has created by its own accumulated experiences.

Every one of our Egos has the Karma of past Manvantaras behind. There are seven Hierarchies of Egos, some of which, *e.g.*, in inferior tribes, may be said to be only just beginning the present cycle. The Ego starts with Divine Consciousness; no past, no future, no separation. It is long before realizing that it is itself. Only after many births does it begin to discern, by this collectivity of experience, that it is individual. At the end of its cycle of reincarnation it is still the same Divine Consciousness, but it has now become individualized Self-consciousness.

The feeling of responsibility is inspired by the presence of the Light of the Higher Ego. As the Ego in its cycle of re-birth becomes more and more individualised, it learns more and more by suffering to recognise its own responsibility, by which it finally gains Self-consciousness, the consciousness of all the Egos of the whole Universe. Absolute Being, to have the idea or sensation of all this, must pass through all experience individually, not universally, so that when it returns it should be of the same omniscience as the Universal Mind *plus* the memory of all that it has passed through.

At the Day "Be with us" every Ego has to remember all the cycles of its past reincarnations for Manvantaras. The Ego comes in contact with this earth, all seven Principles become one, it sees all that it has done therein. It sees the stream of its past reincarnations by a certain divine light. It sees all humanity at once, but still there is ever, as it were, a stream which is always the "I."

We should therefore always endeavour to accentuate our responsibility.

The Higher Ego is, as it were, a globe of pure divine light, a Unit from a higher plane, on which is no differentiation. Descending to a plane of differentiation it emanates a Ray, which it can only manifest through the personality which is already differentiated. A portion of this Ray, the Lower Manas, during life, may so crystallize itself and become one with Kâma that it will remain assimilated with Matter. That portion which retains its purity forms Antahkarana. The whole fate of an incarnation depends on whether Antahkarana will be able to restrain the Kâma-Manas or not. After death the higher light (Antahkarana) which bears the impressions and memory of all good and noble aspirations, assimilates itself with the Higher Ego, the rest is dissociated in space, and comes back as bad Karma awaiting the personality.

The feeling of responsibility is the beginning of Wisdom, a proof that Ahankâra is beginning to fade out, the beginning of losing the sense of separateness.

KÂMA RÛPA.

The Kâma Rûpa eventually breaks up and goes into animals. All red-blooded animals come from man. The cold-blooded are from the matter of the past. The blood is the Kâma Rûpa.

The white corpuscles are the scavengers, "devourers"; they

oozed out of the Astral through the spleen, and are of the same essence as the Astral. They are the sweat-born of the Chhâyâ. Kâma is everywhere in the body. The red cells are drops of electrical fluid, the perspiration of all the organs oozed out from every cell. They are the progeny of the Fohatic Principle.

HEART.

There are seven brains in the heart, the Upâdhis and symbols of the seven Hierarchies.

THE FIRES.

The fires are always playing round the pineal gland, but when Kundalinî illuminates them for a brief instant the whole universe is seen. Even in deep sleep the Third Eye opens. This is good for Manas, who profits by it, though we ourselves do not remember

PERCEPTION.

In answer to a question on the seven stages of perception, H. P. B. said that thought should be centred on the highest, the seventh, and then an attempt to transcend this will prove that it is impossible to go beyond it on this plane. There is nothing in the brain to carry the thinker on, and if thought is to rise yet further it must be thought without a brain. Let the eyes be closed, the will set not to let the brain work, and then the point may be transcended and the student will pass to the next plane. All the seven stages of perception come before Antahkarana; if you can pass beyond them you are on the Mânasic Plane.

Try to imagine something which transcends your power of thought, say, the nature of the Dhyân Chohans. Then make the brain passive, and pass beyond; you will see a white radiant light, like silver, but opalescent as mother of pearl; then waves of colour will pass over it, beginning in the tenderest violet, and through bronze shades of green to indigo with metallic lustre, and that colour will remain. If you see this you are on another plane. You should pass through seven stages.

When a colour comes, glance at it, and if it is not good reject it. Let your attention be arrested only on the green, indigo and yellow. These are good colours. The eyes being connected with the brain, the colour you see most easily will be the colour of the personality. If you see red, it is merely physiological, and is to be disregarded. Green-bronze is the Lower Manas, yellow-bronze the Antahkarana, indigo-bronze is Manas. These are to be observed, and when the yellow-bronze merges into the indigo you are on the Mânasic Plane.

On the Mânasic Plane you see the Noumena, the essence of the phenomena. You do not see people or other consciousnesses, but have enough to do to keep your own. The trained Seer can see Noumena always. The Adept sees the Noumena on this plane, the reality of things, so cannot be deceived.

In meditation the beginner may waver backwards and forwards between two planes. You hear the ticking of a clock on this plane, then on the astral—the soul of the ticking. When clocks are stopped here the ticking goes on on higher planes, in the astral, and then in the ether, until the last bit of the clock is gone. It is the same as with a dead body, which sends out emanations until the last molecule is disintegrated.

There is no time in meditation, because there is no succession of states of consciousness on this plane.

Violet is the colour of the Astral. You begin with it, but should not stay in it; try to pass on. When you see a sheet of violet, you are beginning unconsciously to form a Mâyâvi Rûpa. Fix your attention, and if you go away keep your consciousness firmly to the Mânasic Body; do not lose sight of it, hold on like grim death.

CONSCIOUSNESS.

The consciousness which is merely the animal consciousness is made up of the consciousness of all the cells in the body except those of the heart. The heart is the king, the most important organ in the body of man. Even if the head be severed from the body, the heart will continue to beat for thirty minutes. It will beat for some hours if wrapped in cotton wool and put in a warm place. The spot in the heart which is the last of all to die is the seat of life, the centre of all, Brahmâ, the first spot that lives in the fœtus and the last that dies. When a Yogî is buried in a trance it is this spot that lives, though the rest of the body be dead, and as long as this is alive the Yogî can be resurrected. This spot contains potentially mind, life, energy, and will. During life it radiates prismatic colours, fiery and opalescent. The heart is the centre of spiritual consciousness, as the brain is the centre of intellectual. But this consciousness cannot be guided by the person, nor its energy directed by him until he is at one with Buddhi-Manas; until then it guides him—if it can. Hence the pangs of remorse, the prickings of conscience; they come from the heart, not the head. In the heart is the only manifested God, the other two are invisible, and it is this which represents the Triad, Âtmâ-Buddhi-Manas.

In reply to a question whether the consciousness might not be concentrated in the heart, and so the promptings of the Spirit caught, H. P. B. said that any one who could thus concentrate would be at one with Manas, would have united Kâma-Manas to the Higher Manas. The Higher Manas could not directly guide man, it could only act through the Lower Manas.

There are three principal centres in man, Heart, Head, and Navel: any two of which may be + or — to each other, according to the relative predominance of the centres.

The heart represents the Higher Triad; the liver and spleen represent the Quaternary. The solar plexus is the brain of the stomach.

H. P. B. was asked if the three centres above-named would represent the Christos, crucified between two thieves; she said it might serve as an analogy, but these figures must not be over-driven. It must never be forgotten that the Lower Manas is the same in its essence as the Higher, and may become one with it by rejecting Kâmic impulses. The crucifixion of the Christos represents the self-sacrifice of the Higher Manas, the Father that sends his only begotten Son into the world to take upon him our sins: the Christ-myth came from the Mysteries. So also did the life of Apollonius of Tyana; this was suppressed by the Fathers of the Church because of its striking similarity to the life of Christ.

The psycho-intellectual man is all in the head with its seven gateways; the spiritual man is in the heart. The convolutions are formed by thought.

The third ventricle in life is filled with light, and not with a liquid as after death.

There are seven cavities in the brain which are quite empty during life, and it is in these that visions must be reflected if they are to remain in the memory. These centres are, in Occultism, called the seven harmonies, the scale of the divine harmonies. They are filled with Âkâsha, each with its own colour, according to the state of consciousness in which you are. The sixth is the pineal gland, which is hollow and empty during life: the seventh is the whole; the fifth is the third ventricle: the fourth the pituitary body. When Manas is united to Âtmâ-Buddhi, or when Âtmâ-Buddhi is centred in Manas, it acts in the three higher cavities, radiating, sending forth a halo of light, and this is visible in the case of a very holy person.

The cerebellum is the centre, the storehouse, of all the forces; it is the Kâma of the head. The pineal gland corresponds to the uterus, its peduncles to the Fallopian tubes. The pituitary body is only its servant, its torch-bearer, like the servants bearing lights that used to run before the carriage of a princess. Man is thus androgyne so far as his head is concerned.

Man contains in himself every element that is found in the Universe. There is nothing in the Macrocosm that is not in the Microcosm. The pineal gland, as was said, is quite empty during life; the pituitary contains various essences. The granules in the pineal gland are precipitated after death within the cavity.

The cerebellum furnishes the materials for ideation; the frontal lobes of the cerebrum are the finishers and polishers of the materials, but they cannot create of themselves.

Clairvoyant perception is the consciousness of touch; thus reading letters, psychometrizing substances, etc., may be done at the pit of the stomach. Every sense has its consciousness, and you can have consciousness through every sense. There may be consciousness on the plane of sight, though the brain be paralyzed; the eyes of a paralyzed person will show terror. So with the sense of hearing. Those who are physically blind, deaf or dumb, are still possessed of the psychic counterparts of these senses.

WILL AND DESIRE.

Eros in man is the will of the genius to create great pictures, great music, things that will live and serve the race. It has nothing in common with the animal desire to create. Will is of the Higher Manas. It is the universal harmonious tendency acting by the Higher Manas. Desire is the outcome of separateness, aiming at the satisfaction of Self in Matter. The path opened between the Higher Ego and the Lower enables the Ego to act on the personal self.

CONVERSION.

It is not true that a man powerful in evil can suddenly be converted and become as powerful for good. His vehicle is too defiled, and he can at best but neutralize the evil, balancing up the bad Karmic causes he has set in motion, at any rate for this incarnation. You cannot take a herring barrel and use it for attar of roses: the wood is too soaked through with the drippings. When evil impulses and tendencies have become impressed on the physical nature, they cannot at once be reversed. The molecules of the body have been set in a Kâmic direction, and though they have sufficient intelligence to discern between things on their own plane, *i.e.*, to avoid things harmful to themselves, they cannot understand a change of direction, the impulse to which is from another plane. If they are forced too violently, disease, madness or death will result.

ORIGINES.

Absolute eternal motion, Parabrahman, which is nothing and everything, motion inconceivably rapid, in this motion throws off a film, which is Energy, Eros. It thus transforms itself to Mûlaprakriti, primordial Substance which is still Energy. This Energy, still transforming itself in its ceaseless and inconceivable motion, becomes the Atom, or rather the germ of the Atom, and then it is on the Third Plane.

Our Manas is a Ray from the World-Soul and is withdrawn at Pralaya; "it is perhaps the Lower Manas of Parabrahman," that is, of the Parabrahman of the manifested Universe. The first film is Energy, or motion on the manifested plane; Alaya is the Third Logos, Mahâ-Buddhi, Mahat. We always begin on the Third Plane; beyond that all is inconceivable. Âtmâ is focussed in Buddhi, but is embodied only in Manas, these being the Spirit, Soul and Body of the Universe.

DREAMS.

We may have evil experiences in dreams as well as good. We should, therefore, train ourselves so as to awaken directly we tend to do wrong.

The Lower Manas is asleep in sense-dreams, the animal consciousness being then guided towards the Astral Light by Kâma; the tendency of such sense-dreams is always towards the animal.

If we could remember our dreams in deep sleep, then we should be able to remember all our past incarnations.

NIDÂNAS.

There are twelve Nidânas, exoteric and Esoteric, the fundamental doctrine of Buddhism.

So also there are twelve exoteric Buddhist Sûttas, called Nidânas, each giving one Nidâna.

The Nidânas have a dual meaning. They are:

(1) The twelve causes of sentient existence, through the twelve links of subjective with objective Nature, or between the subjective and objective Natures.

(2) A concatenation of causes and effects.

Every cause produces an effect, and this effect becomes in its turn a cause. Each of these has as Upâdhi (basis), one of the sub-divisions of one of the Nidânas, and also an effect or consequence.

Both bases and effects belong to one or another Nidâna, each having from three to seventeen, eighteen and twenty-one sub-divisions.

The names of the twelve Nidânas are:

(1) Jarâmarana.	(7) Sparsha.
(2) Jâti.	(8) Chadayâtana.
(3) Bhava.	(9) Nâmarûpa.
(4) Upâdâna.	(10) Vignâna.
(5) Trishnâ.	(11) Samskâra.
(6) Vedanâ.	(12) Avidyâ.*

(1) JARÂMARANA, lit. death in consequence of decrepitude. Note that death and not life comes as the first of the Nidânas. This is the first fundamental in Buddhist Philosophy; every Atom, at every moment, as soon as it is born begins dying.

The five Skandhas are founded on it; they are its effects or products. Moreover, in its turn, it is based on the five Skandhas. They are mutual things, one gives to the other.

(2) JÂTI, lit. Birth.

That is to say, Birth according to one of the four modes of Chaturyoni (the four wombs), *viz.*:

(i) Through the womb, like Mammalia.

(ii) Through Eggs.

(iii) Ethereal or liquid Germs—fish spawn, pollen, insects, etc.

(iv) Anupâdaka—Nirmânakâyas, Gods, etc.

That is to say that birth takes place by one of these modes. You must be born in one of the six objective modes of existence, or in the seventh which is subjective. These four are within six modes of existence, viz.:

---

* [If the Nidânas are read the reverse way, *i.e.*, from 12 to 1, they give the evolutionary [illegible]

Exoterically:—

(i) Devas; (ii) Men; (iii) Asuras; (iv) Men in Hell; (v) Pretas, devouring demons on earth; (vi) animals.

Esoterically:—

(i) Higher Gods; (ii) Devas or Pitris (all classes); (iii) Nirmânakâyas; (iv) Bodhisattvas; (v) Men in Myalba; (vi) Kâma Rûpic existences, whether of men or animals, in Kâma Loka or the Astral Light; (vii) Elementals (Subjective Existences).

(3) BHAVA = Karmic existence, not life existence, but as a moral agent which determines *where* you will be born, *i.e.*, in which of the Triloka, Bhûr, Bhuvar or Svar (seven Lokas in reality).

The cause or Nidâna of Bhava is Upâdâna, that is, the clinging to existence, that which makes us desire life in whatever form.

Its effect is Jâti in one or another of the Triloka and under whatever conditions.

Nidânas are the detailed expression of the law of Karma under twelve aspects; or we might say the law of Karma under twelve Nidânic aspects.

SKANDHAS.

Skandhas are the germs of life on all the seven planes of Being, and make up the totality of the subjective and objective man. Every vibration we have made is a Skandha. The Skandhas are closely united to the pictures in the Astral Light, which is the medium of impressions, and the Skandhas, or vibrations, connected with subjective or objective man, are the links which attract the Reincarnating Ego, the germs left behind when it went into Devachan which have to be picked up again and exhausted by a new personality. The exoteric Skandhas have to do with the physical atoms and vibrations, or objective man; the Esoteric with the internal and subjective man.

A mental change, or a glimpse of spiritual truth, may make a man suddenly change to the truth even at his death, thus creating good Skandhas for the next life. The last acts or thoughts of a man have an enormous effect upon his future life, but he would still have to suffer for his misdeeds, and this is the basis of the idea of a death-bed repentance. But the Karmic effects of the past life must follow, for the man in his next birth must pick up the Skandhas or vibratory impressions that he left in the Astral Light, since nothing comes from nothing in Occultism, and there must be a link between the lives. New Skandhas are born from their old parents.

It is wrong to speak of Tanhâs in the plural; there is only one Tanhâ, *the desire to live*. This develops into a multitude or congeries of ideas. The Skandhas are Karmic and non-Karmic. Skandhas may produce Elementals by unconscious Kriyâshakti. Every Elemental that is thrown out by man must return to him sooner or later, since it is his own vibration. They thus become his Frankenstein. Elementals are simply effects producing effects. They are disembodied thoughts, good and bad. They remain crystallized in the Astral Light and are attracted by affinity and galvanized back into life again, when their originator returns to earth-life. You can paralyze them by reverse effects. Elementals are caught like a disease, and hence are dangerous to ourselves and to others. This is why it is dangerous to influence others. The Elementals which live after your death are those which you implant in others: the rest remain latent till you are reincarnated, when they come to life in you. "Thus," H. P. B. said, "if you are badly taught by me or incited thereby to do something wrong, you would go on after my death and sin through me, and I should have to bear the Karma. Calvin, for instance, will have to suffer for all the wrong teaching he has given, though he gave it with good intentions. The worst * * * * does is to arrest the progress of truth. Even Buddha made mistakes. He applied his teachings to people who were not ready; and this has produced Nidânas."

SUBTLE BODIES.

When a man visits another in his Astral Body, it is the Linga Sharîra which goes, but this cannot happen at any great distance. When a man *thinks* of another at a distance very intently, he sometimes appears to that person.

In this case it is the Mâyâvi Rûpa, which is created by unconscious Kriyâshakti, and the man himself is not conscious of appearing. If he were, and projected his Mâyâvi Rûpa consciously, he would be an Adept.* No two persons can be simultaneously conscious of each another's presence, unless one be an Adept. Dugpas use the Mâyâvi Rûpa and sorcerers also. Dugpas work on the Linga Sharîra of other people.

The Linga Sharîra in the spleen is the perfect picture of the man and is good or bad, according to his own nature. The Astral Body is the subjective image of the man which is to be, the first germ in the

* [*I.e.*, an Initiate, the word Adept being used by H. P. B. to cover all grades of Initiation. As above seen, she used the words Mâyâvi Rûpa in more than one sense.—Ed.]

matrix, the model of the physical body in which the child is formed and developed. The Linga Sharîra may be hurt by a sharp instrument, and would not face a sword or bayonet, although it would easily pass through a table or other piece of furniture.

Nothing however can hurt the Mâyâvi Rûpa or thought-body, since it is purely subjective. When swords are struck at shades, it is the sword itself, not its Linga Sharîra or Astral that cuts. Sharp instruments alone can penetrate Astrals, *e.g.*, under water, a blow will not affect you, but a cut will.

The projection of the Astral Body should not be attempted, but the power of Kriyâshakti should be exercised in the projection of the Mâyâvi Rûpa.

FIRE.

Fire is not an Element but a divine thing. The physical flame is the objective vehicle of the highest Spirit. The Fire Elementals are the highest. Everything in this world has its Aura and its Spirit. The flame you apply to the candle has nothing to do with the candle itself. The Aura of the object comes into conjunction with the lowest part of the other. Granite cannot burn because its Aura is Fire. Fire Elementals have no consciousness on this plane, they are too high, reflecting the divinity of their own source. Other Elementals have consciousness on this plane as they reflect man and his nature. There is a very great difference between the mineral and vegetable kingdoms. The wick of the lamp, for instance, is negative. It is made positive by fire, the oil being the medium. Æther is Fire. The lowest part of Æther is the flame which you see. Fire is Divinity in its subjective presence throughout the universe. Under other conditions, this Universal Fire manifests as water, air and earth. It is the one Element in our visible Universe which is the Kriyâshakti of all forms of life. It is that which gives light, heat, death, life, etc. It is even the blood. In all its various manifestations it is essentially *one*.

It is the "seven Cosmocratores."

Evidence of the esteem in which Fire was held are to be found in the *Old Testament*. The Pillar of Fire, the Burning Bush, the Shining Face of Moses—all Fire. Fire is like a looking-glass in its nature, and reflects the beams of the first order of subjective manifestations which are supposed to be thrown on to the screen of the first outlines of the created universe; in their lower aspect these are the creations of Fire.

Fire in the grossest aspect of its essence is the first form [illegible] the lower forms of the first subjective beings which are [illegible] The first divine chaotic thoughts are the Fire Elementals. [illegible] earth they take form and come flitting in the flame [illegible] Salamanders or lower Fire Elementals. In the air you [illegible] of living and conscious beings, besides our thoughts which [illegible] up. The Fire Elementals are related to the sense of sight [illegible] the Elementals of all the other senses. Thus through sight [illegible] have the consciousness of feeling, hearing, tasting, etc., [illegible] included in the sense of sight.

HINTS ON THE FUTURE.

As time passes on there will be more and more ether in [illegible] When ether fills the air, then will be born children without [illegible] In Virginia there is an apple tree of a special kind. It does not [illegible] but bears fruit from a kind of berry without any seeds. [illegible] gradually extend to animals and then to men. Women [illegible] children without impregnation, and in the Seventh Round [illegible] appear men who can reproduce themselves. In the Seventh [illegible] the Fourth Round, men will change their skins every year [illegible] have new toe and finger nails. People will become more psychic, [illegible] spiritual. Last of all in the Seventh Round, Buddhas will be [illegible] without sin. The Fourth Round is the longest in the Kali Yuga, [illegible] the Fifth, then the Sixth, and the Seventh Round will be very [illegible]

THE EGOS.

In explaining the relations of the Higher and Lower Ego, [illegible] and the "Death of the Soul," the following figure was drawn:

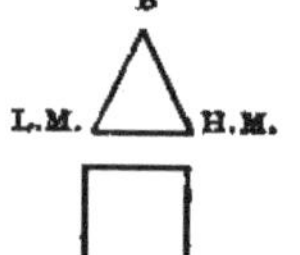

On the separation of the Principles at death the Higher Ego [illegible] said to go to Devachan by reason of the experiences of the [illegible] Higher Ego in its own plane is the Kumâra.

The Lower Quaternary dissolves; the body rots, the [illegible] fades out.

At reincarnation the Higher Ego shoots out a Ray, the Lower [illegible]

Its energies are upward and downward. The upward tendencies become its Devachanic experiences; the lower are Kâmic. The Higher Manas stands to Buddhi as the Lower Manas to the Higher.

As to the question of responsibility, it may be understood by an example. If you take the form of Jack the Ripper, you must suffer for its misdeeds, for the law will punish the murderer and hold him responsible. You are the sacrificial victim. In the same way the Higher Ego is the Christos, the sacrificial victim for the Lower Manas. The Ego takes the responsibility of every body it informs.

You borrow some money to lend it to another; the other runs away, but it is you who are responsible. The mission of the Higher Ego is to shoot out a Ray to be a Soul in a child.

Thus the Ego incarnates in a thousand bodies, taking upon itself the sins and responsibilities of each body. At every incarnation a new Ray is emitted, and yet it is the same Ray in essence, the same in you and me and every one. The dross of the incarnation disintegrates, the good goes to Devachan.

The Flame is eternal. From the Flame of the Higher Ego, the Lower is lighted, and from this a lower vehicle, and so on.

And yet the Lower Manas is such as it makes itself. It is possible for it to act differently in like conditions, for it has reason and self-conscious knowledge of right and wrong, and good and evil, given to it. It is in fact endowed with all the attributes of the Divine Soul. In this the Ray is the Higher Manas, the speck of responsibility on earth.

The part of the essence is the essence, but while it is out of itself, so to say, it can get soiled and polluted. The Ray can be manifested on this earth because it can send forth its Mâyâvi Rûpa. But the Higher cannot, so it has to send forth a Ray. We may look upon the Higher Ego as the Sun, and the personal Manases as its Rays. If we take away the surrounding air and light the Ray may be said to return to the Sun, so with the Lower Manas and Lower Quaternary.

The Higher Ego can only manifest through its attributes.

In cases of sudden death, the Lower Manas no more disappears than does the Kâma Rûpa after death. After the severance the Ray may be said to snap or be dropped. After death such a man cannot go to Devachan, nor yet remain in Kâma Loka; his fate is to reincarnate immediately. Such an entity is then an animal Soul *plus* the intelligence of the severed Ray. The manifestation of this intelligence in the next birth will depend entirely on the physical formation of the brain and on education.

Such a Soul may be re-united with its Higher Ego in the next birth, if the environment is such as to give it a chance of aspiration (this is the "grace" of the Christians); or it may go on for two or three incarnations, the Ray becoming weaker and weaker, and gradually dissipating, until it is born a congenital idiot and then finally dissipated in lower forms.

There are enormous mysteries connected with the Lower Manas.

With regard to some intellectual giants, they are in somewhat the same condition as smaller men, for their Higher Ego is paralyzed; that is to say, their spiritual nature is atrophied.

The Manas can pass its essence to several vehicles, e.g., the Mâyâvi Rûpa, etc., and even to Elementals which it can ensoul, as the Rosicrucians taught.

The Mâyâvi Rûpa may be sometimes so vitalized that it goes on to another plane and unites with the beings of that plane and ensouls them.

People who bestow great affection upon animal pets are ensouling them to a certain extent, and such animal Souls progress very rapidly; in return such persons get back the animal vitality and magnetism. It is, however, against Nature to thus accentuate animal evolution, and on the whole is bad.

MONADIC EVOLUTION.

The Kumâras do not direct the evolution of the Lunar Pitris. To understand the latter, we might take the analogy of the blood.

The blood may be compared to the universal Life Principle, the corpuscles to the Monads. The different kinds of corpuscles are the same as the various classes of Monads and various kingdoms, not, however, because of their essence being different, but because of the environment in which they are. The Chhâyâ is the permanent seed, and Weissmann in his hereditary germ theory is very near truth.

H. P. B. was asked whether there was one Ego to one permanent Chhâyâ seed, oversouling it in a series of incarnations; her answer was: "No, it is Heaven and Earth kissing each other."

The animal Souls are in temporary forms and shells in which they gain experience, and in which they prepare materials for higher evolution.

Until the age of seven the astral atavic germ forms and moulds the body; after that the body forms the Astral.

The Astral and the Mind mutually react on each other.

The meaning of the passage in the *Upanishads*, where it says that the Gods feed on men, is that the Higher Ego obtains its earth experience through the Lower.

ASTRAL BODY.

The Astral can get out unconsciously to the person and wander about.

The Chhâyâ is the same as the Astral Body.

The germ or life essence of it is in the spleen.

"The Chhâyâ is coiled up in the spleen." It is from this that the Astral is formed; it evolves in a shadowy curling or gyrating essence like smoke, gradually taking form as it grows. But it is not projected from the physical, atom for atom. This latter intermolecular form is the Kâma Rûpa. At death every cell and molecule gives out its essence, and from it is formed the Astral of the Kâma Rûpa; but this can never come out during life.

The Chhâyâ in order to become visible draws upon the surrounding atmosphere, attracting the atoms to itself; the Linga Sharîra could not form *in vacuo*. The fact of the Astral Body accounts for the Arabian and Eastern tales of Djins and bottle imps, etc.

In spiritualistic phenomena, the resemblance to deceased persons is mostly caused by the imagination. The clothing of such phantoms is formed from the living atoms of the medium, and is no real clothing, and has nothing to do with the clothing of the medium. "All the clothing of a materialization has been paid for."

The Astral supports life; it is the reservoir or sponge of life, gathering it up from all the natural kingdoms around, and is the intermediary between the kingdoms of Prânic and physical life.

Life cannot come immediately from the subjective to the objective, for Nature goes gradually through each sphere. Therefore the Linga Sharîra is the intermediary between Prâna and our physical body, and pumps in the life.

The spleen is consequently a very delicate organ, but the physical spleen is only a cover for the real spleen.

Now Life is in reality Divinity, Parabrahman. But in order to manifest on the Physical Plane it must be assimilated; and as the purely physical is too gross, it must have a medium, *viz.*, the Astral.

Astral matter is not homogeneous, and the Astral Light is nothing but the shadow of the real Divine Light; it is however not molecular.

Those (Kâmarûpic) entities which are below the Devachanic Plane are in Kâma Loka and only possess intelligence like monkeys. There are no entities in the four lower kingdoms possessing intelligence which can communicate with men, but the Elementals have instincts like animals. It is, however, possible for the Sylphs (the Air Elementals, the wickedest things in the world) to communicate, but they require to be propitiated.

Spooks (Kâmarûpic entities) can only give the information they see immediately before them. They see things in the Aura of people, although the people may not be aware of them themselves.

Earth-bound spirits are Kâmalokic entities that have been so materialistic that they cannot be dissolved for a long time. They have only a glimmering of consciousness and do not know why they are held, some sleep, some preserve a glimmering of consciousness and suffer torture.

In the case of people who have very little Devachan, the greater part of the consciousness remains in Kâma Loka, and may last far beyond the normal period of one hundred and fifty years and remain over until the next reincarnation of the Spirit. This then becomes the Dweller on the Threshold and fights with the new Astral.

The acme of Kâma is the sexual instinct, *e.g.*, idiots have such desires and also food appetites, etc., and nothing else.

Devachan is a state on a plane of spiritual consciousness; Kâma Loka is a place of physical consciousness. It is the shadow of the animal world and that of instinctual feelings. When the consciousness thinks of spiritual things, it is on a spiritual plane.

If one's thoughts are of nature, flowers, etc, then the consciousness is on the material plane.

But if thoughts are about eating, drinking, etc., and the passions, then the consciousness is in the Kâmalokic plane, which is the plane of animal instincts pure and simple.

NEWNHAM, COWELL & GRIPPER, LD
75, CHISWELL STREET,
LONDON, E.C